This is not only first-rate but de[s] [...] holistic approach to the human person is crucial for addressing the embodied habits of anxiety.

J. P. Moreland, Distinguished Professor of Philosophy,
Talbot School of Theology, Biola University;
author of *Finding Quiet*

Certain books have the ability to transform our understanding of ourselves, of life, and of ministry. For me, The Logic of the Body is one such paradigm-shaping book. This is Christian scholarship at its best—careful exegesis of biblical passages, illuminating retrieval of historical categories, thoughtful and critical engagement with modern science and secular sources, all in order to do constructive theology in service of the church. Every pastor, theologian, and counselor needs to read this book.

Joe Rigney, assistant professor of theology and
literature, Bethlehem College & Seminary

Demonstrated mastery of a highly circumscribed academic area is a hallmark of late modern scholarship. But how are we ever to gain a greater grasp of the whole, in order to approximate, analogically, more of the divine understanding, the true aim of Christian scholarship? Collaboration is essential, but also individuals willing to transcend late modern disciplinary boundaries and do their best to master multiple academic areas. LaPine has demonstrated such transdisciplinary competence in this remarkable synthesis of classic and contemporary Christian theological and philosophical reflection and secular empirical research on the role of the emotions in healthy human functioning. It also exemplifies what some would call a Christian psychology.

Eric L. Johnson, director of the Gideon Institute for
Christian Psychology & Counseling; professor of Christian
psychology at Houston Baptist University

I am grateful for LaPine's new study in theological anthropology, *The Logic of the Body*. A careful, scholarly piece of retrieval theology, it judiciously draws on the riches of the historical tradition in conversation with contemporary philosophy, neuroscience, and psychology, in order to develop a constructive theology of the emotions for today. It is not simply an academic study, however. With a sympathetic eye, LaPine uncovers a blindspot in the contemporary, Reformed tradition's under-developed anthropology, which tends to underestimate the role of the body in our emotional life. This has effects in our pastoral counsel. In its place, he puts forth a holistic model suited to both Biblical revelation and a more careful pastoral practice. And as a pastor to college students wrestling with every emotional malady spanning from anxiety to depression, addiction to self-harm, this is what I appreciate most. LaPine manages to shine new light on the way Christ redeems us in the Gospel, both body and soul, and yes, emotions too.

Derek Rishmawy, RUF Campus Minister at UC Irvine;
PhD candidate at Trinity Evangelical Divinity School;
cohost of the Mere Fidelity podcast

Matthew LaPine's *The Logic of the Body: Retrieving Theological Psychology* is both a timely and learned contribution to the ongoing academic conversation about the intersection of theology and psychology. More importantly, it is an invaluable contribution to pastoral theology. Pastors need to know what it means to be human, and they need to know what it means to be flawed moral agents. LaPine speaks to both of these perennial issues and adds to this important conversation, offering a fresh and original contribution that is imminently serviceable in the life and ministry of the local church. Highly recommended!

Todd Wilson, cofounder and president of the Center
for Pastor Theologians; author of *Real Christian* and
Mere Sexuality; coauthor of *The Pastor Theologian*

Few books are more relevant to the pastor's care of souls than Matthew LaPine's book, *The Logic of the Body*. Representing the best of evangelical scholarship, LaPine leans on church history and faithful exegesis to charter a helpful vision of the body's part in sanctification. His proposal for an eschatologically sensitive psychology produces hope, realism, and compassion for the pilgrim's progress in this life. This book is a crucial tool for the high stakes of ministry.

Jonathan Parnell, lead pastor, Cities Church, Saint Paul, Minnesota; author, *Mercy for Today* and *Never Settle for Normal*

Far too often when dealing with negative emotions we divide body and soul, not seeing individuals holistically. I'm thankful for Matt's faithful work to present a comprehensive biblical treatment of theological psychology. In this book, he humbly offers us a more responsible, sophisticated, and compelling framework for handling emotions. I believe this book will greatly benefit the church.

Laura Wifler, cofounder of Risen Motherhood; podcaster; coauthor, *Risen Motherhood: Gospel Hope for Everyday Moments*

All too often, Christian attempts to show mercy to those struggling with mental illness have caused harm because of questionable assumptions about the human body and the human person. This book is a greatly needed theological and historical exploration of those assumptions.

Alex Tuckness, professor of political science, Iowa State University; coauthor of *The Decline of Mercy in Public Life*

As a work of theology, *The Logic of the Body* is a rare blend of first-rate scholarship and first-rate pastoral insight. LaPine accomplishes what few even attempt: He writes a work that must be considered by both the academy and the church. By offering a more robust evangelical theology of how people change, the insights of *The Logic of the Body* have reshaped my approach to pastoral care and community life in the local church. If you are a pastor who wants to faithfully apply the Gospel in a way that is both true to Scripture and true to life, take the time to carefully read this book.

Mark Vance, lead pastor, Cornerstone Church, Ames, IA

Matthew LaPine pulls from history, theologians, scholars, experience, story, and ultimately scripture to lead us on a pathway of grace through the messy world of seemingly contradictory solutions surrounding mental health. This book not only helps those of us doing ministry in real-time but also gives a balm of hope to those who struggle with our own mental health battles, showing that there might be a way and a whole new type of conversation we can have around these topics. With both the gentleness of a shepherd and the fortitude of a well-studied and engaged mind, Matthew shows us a new way to minister and learn about mental health as believers.

Andrea Burke, women's ministry director at Grace Road Church, Rochester, NY; host of Good Enough podcast

Emotions and embodiment are two vital aspects of the human experience, and yet far too often Christian accounts have pitted them against one another in problematic ways. Thankfully, Matthew LaPine's volume pushes us to avoid picking between a psychological account and a theological one, but instead aims to help us see them together in a fresh way. His proposal offers much insightful reflection for all of us who care about more holistic accounts of the human person.

Kelly M. Kapic, professor of theological studies, Covenant College; author of *Embodied Hope*

Contemporary Protestantism has written therapeutic checks that its moral psychology just can't cover. One of the most pressing orders of the day is to develop an anthropology and moral psychology that does real justice to the whole counsel of God. Theologians also need to avoid ignoring or simply parroting neurophysiology. Matthew LaPine prompts such development with this argument for a holistic and tiered psychology. All future work in this area will have to engage with his arguments.

Michael Allen, John Dyer Trimble Professor of Systematic Theology, Reformed Theological Seminary

Having suffered from serious public-speaking anxiety in my 20s and 30s, I read Dr. LaPine's book with great interest. Is an anxious Christian a contradiction in terms, caused by lack of faith? In showing why the answer to this question is "no," LaPine masterfully engages Thomas Aquinas and contemporary thinkers such as J. P. Moreland in defense of a "dualistic holism." This is a most welcome book from a young doctor of the soul.

Matthew Levering, James N. and Mary D. Perry
Jr. Chair of Theology, Mundelein Seminary

A theological account of what it means to be human—that creature specially made by God and for God—cannot afford to ignore the topic of human emotions insofar as their devastation by sin is one of the chief causes of our departure from God and their sanctification by grace is one of the chief ways in which God moves us into deeper fellowship with himself. In this learned study, Matthew LaPine demonstrates the promise of a broadly Thomist approach to human emotions for theological anthropology. Learning its lessons well will benefit anyone involved in the care of souls.

Scott Swain, president and James Woodrow Hassell Professor
of Systematic Theology, Reformed Theological Seminary

The *The* **LOGIC** *of the* **BODY**

Retrieving Theological Psychology

To Andrea,

Blessings on your work!

Matt

STUDIES IN HISTORICAL & SYSTEMATIC THEOLOGY

H
S ✛ S
T

The LOGIC
of the BODY

Retrieving Theological Psychology

MATTHEW A. LAPINE

STUDIES IN HISTORICAL AND SYSTEMATIC THEOLOGY

LEXHAM PRESS

The Logic of the Body: Retrieving Theological Psychology
Studies in Historical and Systematic Theology

Copyright 2020 Matthew A. LaPine

Lexham Press, 1313 Commercial St., Bellingham, WA 98225
LexhamPress.com

Print ISBN 9781683594253
Digital ISBN 9781683594260
Library of Congress Number 2020943015

Lexham Editorial: Todd Hains, Lisa Eary, Elizabeth Vince, Abigail Stocker
Cover Design: Owen Craft
Typesetting: ProjectLuz.com

To Molly

We share everything, and this book is yours as much as mine

CONTENTS

Foreword xiii

Preface xvii

Abbreviations...xix

Introduction..1
    Problem 1
    Theological Psychology: A Path Forward..........................4
    Governing Assumption and Thesis 6
    Methodology and Approach 7
    Chapter Overview 13
    Literature Review...16
    Excursus: Passions and Affections 19

1 Emotional Voluntarism 23
    The Explanation Dilemma...24
    The Treatment Dilemma 32
    Recovery Project..39

2 The Psychology of Thomas Aquinas...............................41
    The Hylomorphic Powers of the Soul 43
    Aquinas's Physiology 51
    Acts and Passions 58
    Habit and Virtue...82
    Conclusion..90

3 Developments in Medieval and Renaissance Psychology 92
    The Nature of the Soul 94
    The Functions of the Soul: The Ascendency of the Will in
        Action Theory..105
    Conclusion..127

4 The Psychology of John Calvin 129
   Calvin's Sources 131
   The Soul, the Body, and the *Imago Dei* 137
   The Neglected Body 142
   Substance and Immortality of the Soul 151
   Faculties 159
   Calvin on the Will 169
   Affections, Passions, and Virtue 178
   Virtue and Vice 186
   Historical Postscript 192

5 Modern Reformed Psychology 197
   Reformed Theological Context 198
   Embedded Psychological Assumptions 199
   Reformed Formulations of Body and Soul 201
   Evaluation 217

6 Book of Nature: Body and Soul 220
   The State of the Soul in Review 221
   Theological and Philosophical Arguments for Dualism 224
   Theological and Philosophical Arguments for Monism 232
   Thomistic Dualism 243

7 Book of Scripture: The Body in Biblical Theology 252
   Biblical Theological Reflections on Human Agency 254

8 Book of Nature: Embodied Emotion 283
   Setting the Stage: Emotion and Cognition 284
   LeDoux's New Model 286
   A Model 314
   The Subjective Logic 319

9 Book of Scripture: Commanding Emotion 323
   Elliott's Psychological Assumptions 323
   An Alternate Reading of Matthew 6:25–34 327
   Conclusion 344

Conclusion 347
    Revisiting Mary 347
    Six Theses on Therapy and Embodiment.......................... 350

Appendix: On the Heart 357

Bibliography.. 365

Subject/Author Index.. 405

Scripture Index 410

FOREWORD

—

I have been eagerly anticipating this book. Now that I've got it, I have to figure out where it goes in my library. Does it belong with my other theology books, or should I add it to my Christian counseling shelf? If with theology: biblical, historical, or systematic? I don't have any books on psychology or counseling with "body" in their titles.

Truth be told, this book doesn't fit into a clear category. Or perhaps the problem is that my thinking is buttoned down and overly stuffy. Maybe if I just take a peek inside ... "Reformed theologians may have adopted a reductive set of categories for speaking of emotion." Gulp. I'm a Reformed theologian, and now I have two problems: how to classify this book, and how to talk about emotions. My heart is pounding, and I'm beginning to sweat. I'm only in the introduction, and already I'm feeling anxious.

Everyday life is filled with experiences (hopefully more meaningful than the one I've just recounted) that occasion one sort of emotion or another, often disruptive ones. "Do not be anxious," says Jesus (Matt 6:31). Yet there are times when, try as we might, we cannot will ourselves into a state of peace. The poet W. H. Auden was the voice of his own generation and of much of the twentieth century when he penned his Pulitzer-prize winning poem *The Age of Anxiety*. The poem attracted the attention of the composer Leonard Bernstein, who thought it poignantly expressed modern humanity's search for faith. Bernstein composed a symphony based on the poem in 1949. The music was later made into a ballet by the choreographer Jerome Robbins. Think about it, a ballet entitled *The Age of Anxiety*. This more or less sums up what Matthew LaPine's book is all about: bodies in soulful motion expressing, if not the logic, then the lyricism of negative human emotion.

Auden wrote his poem after the Second World War. It was indeed an age of anxiety. The world had just suffered the trauma of D-Day, the Holocaust, and Hiroshima. LaPine's book is not primarily about trauma but rather, as he says in the opening line, *humanness*. Trauma is part, not the whole, of the human condition. And yet, for Blaise Pascal, simply thinking about the human condition was trauma enough. His *Pensées* feature not anxiety but misery, the misery of "man without God." Pascal summarizes his thesis and his argument in short order: "That nature is corrupt. Proved by nature itself." Pascal's thoughts, like LaPine's, are about humanness. Pascal's conclusion? We are a mystery to ourselves.

In this book, LaPine does not resolve the essential mystery of the human condition, but he does make it more intelligible. He does so by bringing together things that for too long have been kept apart: mind and body, psychology and theology, Aquinas and Calvin. The connecting link in each case is *embodied emotion*. If we could sort out what embodied emotions are, specify what they do, and figure out how to tame them, we would be well on our way to bridging the aforementioned dichotomies—and making progress in humanness.

This book is a work of retrieval that looks back in order to move forward. Theologies of retrieval have had quite an impact in recent years, starting with the retrieval of patristic and medieval theology at Vatican II. The Protestant Reformers were also engaged in retrieval. Their battle cry, "*Ad fontes!*" was a call to return to Scripture in its original languages. Not every retrieval goes back to Scripture or to church tradition, but LaPine's does. He brings Reformed theology into dialogue with both the apostle Paul and Thomas Aquinas. Retrieval is an exercise in *ressourcement*, mining the past's resources for the sake of engaging present problems. In particular, LaPine wants to recover insights into embodied human agency and passivity. He therefore retrieves a psychology that existed before the modern empirical science was invented in the nineteenth century; it's a way of thinking about the nature of the soul and its function that incorporates theological notions like sin and grace.

We can't classify *The Logic of the Body* under retrieval theology only, because LaPine also engages contemporary science. Most books on theology and science are still at square one—that is, creation (and evolution). Theologians typically dialogue with the natural sciences: physics, biology, etc. Psychology is one of the human sciences, but today it encompasses more than the study of the psyche or soul. We now know that many psychological phenomena are inextricably linked to physical and chemical processes in the brain. Part of the value of LaPine's insistence on *theological* psychology is that it resists the modern, reductionist tendency to explain our emotional life exclusively in terms of brain function.

At the same time, LaPine anticipates and avoids the temptation to ignore modern science—and the body—and go directly to soul. In that way lies docetism, the ancient heresy that denied the reality of Jesus' physical body. Docetism is no less heretical when it migrates from Christology into anthropology. Theology should never back down when reality is at stake, and it is a denial of reality to pretend that human beings are not in some mysterious ways identified with their bodies. Indeed, LaPine locates our emotional life in the gray area between mind and body—a space that, for Reformed theologians, has become a theological no-man's-land.

What, then, is the "logic" of the body? We speak of "gut feeling" or "gut instinct." Recent science would add "gut intelligence," for a neurochemical highway exists between the brain in our heads and what is sometimes referred to as the body's "second brain." The logic of the body is more than causal or mechanical. Researchers in artificial intelligence have recognized that if computers are to display genuine human intelligence, they must develop the ability to understand and express emotions (i.e., they must do more than compute). Emotions affect perception, learning, and decision making, and to the extent that emotions are connected to the body, then the body, too, is involved in emotional intelligence. As has been said, the body keeps score, and not with scars only.

In this book, then, LaPine deals with neuroscience and psychology as well as theology. What is at stake is self-knowledge and human flourishing. How do we handle unpleasant emotions? My father was a pharmacist, and when I was growing up he regularly filled more prescriptions for drugs like Valium, Xanax, and Zoloft than anything else. I learned years ago that many people need medication to cope with their anxiety. But our bodies, through having experiences and learning how to handle negative emotions, also have other ways of coping. LaPine here retrieves biblical wisdom: "Let not sin therefore reign in your mortal body" (Rom 6:12). The body is not the source of sin. When the apostle Paul speaks of "flesh" he refers to our fallen existence under the regime of Adam. If it were not so, he could not go on to exhort his readers to "offer the parts of your body to [God] as instruments of righteousness" (Rom 6:13).

It is not often that we think of body parts as instruments of righteousness. It is just here that LaPine retrieves things from medieval theology for the sake of a more realistic and up-to-date Reformed theology, arguing for a dualistic, holist picture of the organic self. In this view, minds govern bodies. Yet, as we all know, tired bodies can protest this government. Sometimes they revolt. LaPine does not want us to think about the mind-body relation in terms of a master and a slave. The better—because more biblical—image is that of covenantal privilege and responsibility. As covenantal stewards, our renewed minds (Rom 12:2) exercise a kind of husbandry over our bodies, managing our physical resources so that the whole person can embody the mind of Christ. This is the tonic that distressed Christians and those who counsel them desperately need.

Where in one's library does LaPine's *The Logic of the Body* therefore belong? Classify it under "enriched Reformed theological anthropology." Heartbeat normal. Anxiety resolved.

Kevin J. Vanhoozer
Libertyville, Illinois
July 2020

PREFACE

—

When I gave an earlier version of this book to friends for input, I gave them either the full version or what I called the very short version. Specialists received the full version and the average reader the shorter one. For readers who want easier access to this book, the very short version focused on emotional voluntarism, which is our responsibility to alter our emotions by thinking true thoughts (chapter 1), my model of emotion (chapter 8), an analysis of Jesus' command "do not be anxious" (chapter 9), and the conclusion.

Specialists will want to consult specific discussions. The first half of the book (chapters 2–4) justifies historically the idea of a properly theological psychology and builds on existing categories. Chapter 5 surveys Reformed theologians on theological psychology from the beginning of the empirical discipline of psychology until now. Chapter 6 will interest those tracking the debate between non-reductive physicalists and dualists. Chapter 7 is a biblical theological sampling on how the body factors in human agency, which may have more general interest.

There are a few places where I used the term "man" to refer to humanity, particularly when discussing the Reformed doctrine of man. I preserved the language of "the man" and "the woman" from Genesis 1–3 to match the Hebrew text. I have also cited many Scripture texts as examples, which might seem irrelevant to the English reader, but throughout I am referring to the base text in Greek and Hebrew.

There are many people I would like to thank, though I cannot list them all. First, my wife, Molly, has given so much to this project that she should almost be listed as a co-author. We are writing our lives together, and it is difficult to know where she stops and I begin. Many friends have supported the two of us along the way, including Brian and Jeanne Ames, Brian and Jennifer Skanron, Adam and Annie Klinkner, Jordan and Krista Daggett, Joe and Kelly Bright, and Mark and Crystal Vance. Thanks also to both my family and my wife's family, who have sacrificially given so much to us. Thanks to Cornerstone Church and Salt School of Theology for encouraging me to give my time to writing. Thanks to the many readers who gave help, correction, and encouragement along the way, including Paul Maxwell, Joe Rigney, David Mathis, Jonathan Parnell, J. P. Moreland, Eric L. Johnson, and David Murray. A very warm thanks to Todd Hains and the Lexham editorial staff—thank you for investing in this project and making it better. Thank you to Joy Andrews and Allie Houseman for helping with proofing and indexing. Finally, thank you to my committee, Kevin Vanhoozer, David Luy, and Richard Averbeck, but especially for Kevin's patience as we whacked through the brush of uncharted territory over long lunches at Wildberry. He warned me.

ABBREVIATIONS

—

CO   Calvin, John. *Joannis Calvini opera quae supersunt omnia. Corpus reformatorum.* Edited by Edouard Cunitz, Johann-Wilhelm Baum, Eduard Wilhelm, and Eugen Reuss. 58 vols. Brunsvigae: C. A. Schwetschke, 1863–1900.

BDAG   *A Greek-English Lexicon of the New Testament and Other Early Christian Literature*, rev. and ed. Frederick William Danker, 3rd ed. Chicago: University of Chicago Press, 2000.

LSJ   *A Greek-English Lexicon.* Edited by Henry George Liddell and Robert Scott. Revised by Henry Stuart Jones and Roderick McKenzie. Oxford: Clarendon Press, 1940. Accessed online: http://perseus.uchicago.edu/Reference/LSJ.html.

NPNF   *A Select Library of Nicene and Post-Nicene Fathers of the Christian Church.* Edited by Philip Schaff and Henry Wace. 28 vols. In 2 series. 1886–1889.

OED   *Oxford English Dictionary Online (OED Online).* Oxford University Press. oed.com.

QDV   *Questiones Disputatae de Veritate*, in Thomas Aquinas. *The Disputed Questions on Truth.* Translated by Robert William Schmidt. Vol. 3. Chicago: Henry Regnery Company, 1952–1954.

SEP   *Stanford Encyclopedia of Philosophy.* Stanford University. plato.stanford.edu.

ST   Aquinas, Thomas. *Summa Theologiae.* Translated by Alfred J. Freddoso. Updated January 10, 2018. https://www3.nd.edu/~afreddos/summa-translation/TOC.htm.

INTRODUCTION

—

PROBLEM

T his is a book about humanness. I am asking questions about what we think about ourselves as flawed moral agents and what we do about it. At some point, most of us will be faced with negative emotions such as fear, anger, anxiety, or despair. Then we will ask ourselves why we feel the way we do and whether we ought to feel this way. To answer these questions, we can adopt two culturally available but very different explanatory stories about these unwanted emotions—one from contemporary psychology and the other from Christian theology. I present them here as competing stories in the hope that I can reconcile them with my proposal for retrieving theological psychology.

Often, to adopt a theological perspective is to adopt a set of moral assumptions about our emotions. These assumptions emphasize responsibility for emotions as judgments about the world. Emotions may run contrary to God's will. For example, we could be sinfully anxious about tomorrow. To adopt a psychological perspective is to adopt a very different set of assumptions that might seem to be at odds with the theological ones. For example, it may seem impossible not to be anxious about tomorrow.[1]

As a brief caricature, the theological story goes something like this.[2] Emotion is important for true religion. As Jonathan Edwards writes, "True

---

1. One might ask, how can something outside my control be moral? At this point I am appealing to a commonsense notion of "emotion," which includes appraisal (personal significance of an emotional object), bodily changes, and feelings of bodily changes. I will clarify emotion in Chapter 8.

2. I will develop the nuances of these stories more explicitly in Chapter 2.

religion, in great part, consists in holy affections."[3] These affections are produced spontaneously by the Holy Spirit, except in people who persist in unbelief. Thus, a negative emotion can betray the deep unbelief of the person who feels it.[4] Negative emotions like fear are especially suspect since they function like a language, telling us something about our distrust of God (2 Tim 1:7).[5] In this way, emotions may be a barometer of personal sinfulness.[6] The theological story tends to be cognitive, emphasizing emotions as judgments, and volitional, emphasizing personal responsibility for emotions.[7]

The psychological story, by contrast, is roughly that emotions are feelings of bodily changes. This summarizes the oft-cited definition of emotion from William James, "our feeling of the same [bodily] changes as they occur is the emotion."[8] From a neuroscientific point of view, Joseph LeDoux writes, "I view emotions as biological functions of the nervous system."[9] So,

---

3. Jonathan Edwards, *Religious Affections*, I.1, vol. 1, *The Works of Jonathan Edwards*, ed. Henry Rogers, Sereno Edwards Dwight, and Edward Hickman (Peabody, MA: Hendrickson, 2004), 236.

4. Matthew Elliott advocates the view that emotions may indicate our deep beliefs. Matthew A. Elliott, *Faithful Feelings: Rethinking Emotion in the New Testament* (Grand Rapids: Kregel, 2006), 27. Elliott talks about emotions as appraisals. He takes a cognitive approach, which he means does not promote "the separation of emotion and cognition" (31). For more examples, see Chapter 1.

5. Ed Welch writes, "Think of emotions as a language. They say something—something very important—and part of our job is to figure out what they are saying. ... Scripture consistently identifies our emotions as matters of our hearts, which is another way of saying that they are important and we should pay attention to them. They usually reveal our true selves, and we hope to know each other in that deeper way." Ed Welch, "Emotions Are a Language," *CCEF* (blog), last modified August 5, 2016, www.ccef.org/resources/blog/emotions-are-a-language.

6. So Jon Bloom writes, "God designed your emotions to be gauges, not guides. ... [Emotions like delight, affection, fear, anger, joy] reveal what your heart loves, trusts, and fears." Jon Bloom, "Your Emotions Are a Gauge, Not a Guide," *Desiring God*, August 3, 2012, www.desiringgod.org/articles/your-emotions-are-a-gauge-not-a-guide.

7. When I say that this approach is "volitional," I do not mean to imply that it is Pelagian, only that advocates of this view sometimes speak as though changing emotion is like changing behavior. Brian Borgman writes, "If God commands us to do something and we don't do it, what is our normal course of action? Confession and repentance. Why should the protocol be any different when we fail to feel the way God commands us to feel?" He writes elsewhere, "The truth rightly embraced and believed will give you an experience." Brian S. Borgman, *Feelings and Faith: Cultivating Godly Emotions in the Christian Life* (Wheaton, IL: Crossway, 2009), 80, 77.

8. William James, "What is an Emotion?" *Mind* 9 (1884): 189–90.

9. Joseph E. LeDoux, *The Emotional Brain: The Mysterious Underpinnings of Emotional Life* (New York: Simon & Schuster, 1996), 12. Again, this is a caricature to be developed later. It is

emotion has to do with how our brains and bodies respond to our experiences. As a result, emotion is more about health than morality. Emotions may evidence dysfunction, imbalance, or even unhealthy social contexts, but insofar as they are less voluntary, they are less moral. As Joseph LeDoux further writes, "emotions are things that happen to us rather than things we will to occur."[10] The psychological story approaches emotions far more passively than the theological story.[11]

These two stories are reconcilable. However, it is heartbreaking that a sufferer is often forced to choose between these stories in a desperate attempt to cope.[12] Sufferers must know why they are suffering to do something about it. Our explanations give us hope that we have identified the problem and can address it. But these two stories force a dilemma on us: Negative emotion comes from a moral problem in me or a non-moral problem with my environment or my body. Too often people who experience psychological pain can lose hope in the theological story and find it in the psychological one; thereby the psychological story eclipses the theological.

Because as a theologian I am concerned not to allow the theological story to be eclipsed, I am suggesting that we consider the ways we speak about emotion within current theological discourse. One reason why the psychological story seems to be true rather than the theological one is a lack of psychological nuance in contemporary Reformed evangelical theology.[13] Eric Johnson writes, "In contrast to Catholics and liberal Protestants, there is not much evidence that conservative Protestants thought much about psychology in the early twentieth century."[14] Reformed theologians

---

difficult to say anything simple about the emotional debate. A major issue involves what sort of cognition or mental activity is involved in emotion. Psychologists who are cognitivist tend to prefer the term "appraisal." Both Prinz and LeDoux have pointed out that the fear circuits actually bypass the neocortex. As Prinz says, "perhaps fear can occur without cognition." Jesse Prinz, *Gut Reactions: A Perceptual Theory of Emotion* (Oxford: Oxford University Press, 2006), 34. My point here is that the psychological literature has a strong behavioral vein.

10. LeDoux, *Emotional Brain*, 19.

11. This is a rough characterization. Clinical psychologists especially need to leverage personal agency in psychotherapy.

12. Thanks to Annie Klinkner for this insight.

13. I am aware that the Reformed tradition is large and diverse. I have Reformed evangelicals in mind here and will drop the adjective "evangelical" for the remainder of this work only for the sake of simplicity.

14. Eric L. Johnson, *Psychology & Christianity: Five Views* (Downers Grove, IL: IVP Academic, 2010), 28.

could have more to say about psychology that draws from the Christian tradition. It may be time to retrieve a more comprehensive Protestant theological psychology.

THEOLOGICAL PSYCHOLOGY:
A PATH FORWARD

In the next chapter I will sharpen this critique by explaining what I call "emotional voluntarism." Basically, this is the view that we are responsible for emotions as intrusive mental states that show what we truly believe. Moreover, bad thinking or false belief may be overcome by applying the gospel through voluntary mental work. The chief difficulty with emotional voluntarism is that it fails to account for how the body qualifies our emotions in two characteristic ways: the body makes them less voluntary than actions and more recalcitrant to change. I will describe two features of human psychology that account for these characteristics: (1) a tiered psychology, higher and lower psychological powers functioning somewhat independently but contributing to each other reciprocally; and (2) a holistic account of body and soul that accounts for embodied plasticity, by which I mean possessing the potential to be habituated.[15] My fear is that

---

15. The terms "plasticity" and "neuroplasticity" in contemporary psychology refer to the capacity to form new neuropathways. Following William James, I am using the term in a somewhat idiosyncratic way throughout this book. In mechanical engineering, "plasticity" refers to a solid's capacity to undergo irreversible deformation while "elasticity" refers to its capacity to hold its shape. The definition of plasticity in mechanical engineering assumes that the new form is elastic, that is, assumes that the new form is durable. I think this assumption is also present in psychological uses of the term. The new pathways that form are durable.

James is credited for introducing the word plasticity into psychology. He writes,

> the material in question opposes a certain resistance to the modifying cause, which it takes time to overcome, but the gradual yielding whereof often saves the material from being disintegrated altogether. *When the structure has yielded, the same inertia becomes a condition of its comparative permanence in the new form, and of the new habits the body then manifests. Plasticity, then, in the wide sense of the word, means the possession of a structure weak enough to yield to an influence, but strong enough not to yield at once. ... the phenomena of habit in living beings are due to the plasticity of the organic materials of which their bodies are composed.*

William James, *The Principles of Psychology* (New York: Henry Holt, 1890), 105, emphasis added.

So, James's use of plasticity involves both plasticity (the capacity to yield) and elasticity (the capacity to hold that new structure). Following James, I will use "plasticity" as the capacity for our bodies to take a new shape (malleability) and subsequently to hold that shape (durability). This is the capacity that enables habit formation.

by neglecting questions about the soul's powers—what they are (intellect, will, etc.), what their properties are, how they interact, etc.—and the place of emotions in them, Reformed theologians may have adopted a reductive set of categories for speaking of emotion that fail to account for how the body qualifies agency. It may be time to reinvigorate Reformed theological psychology.

But is it obvious that theological psychology needs to be recovered? After all, when was psychology a concern of theology? It is important to remember that psychology as the "study of the soul" has a very long history.[16] For example, psychological theorizing was a key subcategory of philosophy as a subset of ethics or natural philosophy from Plato until at least the eighteenth century.[17] Platonic and Aristotelian psychology (theories of the soul and its powers) have been foundational to philosophical and theological thought. It is easy to miss the fact that categories of virtue ethics like "virtue" or "vice" are psychological categories, having to do with the habits of the soul's powers. It was the rise of empirical methods of psychological investigation that initiated the disciplinary split between psychology and theology.

---

16. The word "psychology" only dates back to the sixteenth century (it was perhaps used by Melanchthon), but the theorizing about psychology has always been a part of philosophy and theology. It is not my aim to deny a place for psychology as a discrete discipline but merely to build bridges between theology and some very common observations psychologists make about how people change emotionally.

17. Alexander and Shelton point out that there are "two histories of Western psychology," first, "the story of great ideas about the human psyche," and second, "the story of a sparkling new profession called 'psychology' that was born in the nineteenth century to great expectations." This work is interested in the former. They helpfully add, "Scholars who approach the big issues of the human psyche cannot be divided into 'scientists' on the one hand and 'philosophers' on the other. Rather, the best of them use every means at their disposal, including science and history as well as logic, introspection, mathematics, speculative philosophy, and anecdotal observation." Bruce K. Alexander and Curtis P. Shelton, *A History of Psychology in Western Civilization* (Cambridge: Cambridge University Press, 2014), 1, 16. Alan Kim writes, "since ancient times, psychology had been a basic part of philosophical speculation." Alan Kim, "Wilhelm Maximillian Wundt," *Stanford Encyclopedia of Philosophy*, September 10, 2016, plato. stanford.edu/entries/wilhelm-wundt/.

Katharine Park and Eckhard Kessler note, "Philosophers and scientists of the Renaissance did not treat psychology, the philosophical study of the soul, as an independent discipline. Following the medieval tradition, they place it within the broader context of natural philosophy, and they approached it, like other sub-divisions of natural philosophy." Katharine Park and Eckhard Kessler, "The Concept of Psychology," in *The Cambridge History of Renaissance Philosophy*, ed. Charles B. Schmitt, Quentin Skinner, and Eckhard Kessler (Cambridge: Cambridge University Press, 1988), 455.

Recent Reformed systematic theologies have sparse psychological concerns, such as an interest in the body and soul problem, the nature of the *imago Dei*, the dichotomy vs. trichotomy debate, etc. But a host of historical psychological issues are largely ignored by Reformed evangelicals, including the powers of the soul, the priority of the powers, virtues and vices, the interaction of grace, temptation, and demonic suggestion with these powers, etc.[18] These issues and others need systemic theological treatment. Insofar as psychology is concerned with the inner dimension of what it means to be human—what it means to bear the *imago Dei*—it is a fundamental doctrinal locus that interfaces with many of the others.

GOVERNING ASSUMPTION AND THESIS

A governing assumption of this work is that any approach to psychology that does not account for how the body qualifies human emotion is inadequate.[19] The positive thesis responds to this governing assumption: Reformed psychology can gain empirical consistency and pastoral nuance by endorsing a genuinely holistic and tiered model of emotion, which is sensitive to how the body qualifies emotion.

A psychological model is genuinely holistic when it seriously accounts for how the body qualifies the range of psychological functions, even thought—or when none of its functions are abstracted from either of a subject's metaphysical constituents, body or soul. In other words, a psychological theorist must account for how thought is accomplished by and qualified by neuropathways and for how emotion is not merely instinctual but rational. A dualistic holism will be roughly empirically equivalent with materialist monism, but with mental causation. A model is tiered when it distinguishes emotional appraisal from thinking *and emotional* arousal from willing.

This is a project for constructively retrieving and reframing historical theological categories. Because Reformed theology has an underdeveloped psychology, it may actually be in a worse position to integrate the

---

18. In Chapter 5, I will survey a range Reformed systematic theologies that have very little to say about emotions.

19. Thought is qualified by the body in the same way that my driving is qualified by my 2005 Chevrolet Cobalt. I can only stop and start so fast, the wear on my engine and brakes contributing to these limited capacities.

discoveries of contemporary psychology than the theological psychology of the Middle Ages. Where Reformed psychology has not paid close attention to how human agency is qualified by embodiment, the psychology of the Middle Ages had a much more physiologically developed theory. Yet, my aim is not primarily to deconstruct contemporary theological assumptions, but to recommend a model as a basis for practical theology. My thesis positively recommends a Thomistic-like model as a way of accounting for the difficulties in overcoming negative emotion.[20] The most significant contributions of this model are its accounting both for the relationship between the psychological tiers of consciousness and the unconscious and for the constraints that embodiment places on a person, both positively as the ground for character formation and negatively on resistance to change.

METHODOLOGY AND APPROACH

METHOD

Theologians must acknowledge that reading the Bible and reflecting theologically are always midstream within an ongoing tradition. This work is just one instance of a great tradition of theological reflection on humanity within the ecclesiastical context. To acknowledge this has methodological implications. I am conscientiously contributing a cycle to a much larger hermeneutical spiral within the greater catholic tradition of understanding humankind. I am taking a fresh look at the redemptive narrative in light of human embodiment in conversation with the Bible, the Reformed and catholic tradition, and empirical research.

There is also another context for this work. I am attempting to contribute to transdisciplinary scholarship—working across disciplinary lines, which gives biblical reasoning the priority.[21] This project is just one part of a reduction of the arts and sciences into theology—rather than an

---

20. I am intentionally echoing J. P. Moreland with the use of "Thomistic-like" terminology. J. P. Moreland, "Tweaking Dallas Willard's Ontology of the Human Person," *Journal of Spiritual Formation & Soul Care* 8, no. 2 (2015): 198–202. I admit that Thomistic psychology does not *entirely* pass my test of holism because it does abstract the intellect (but not thought) from the body in some sense.

21. This term is from Eric Johnson, organizer of the The Transdisciplinary Group, which met in Houston, TX in 2017.

integration of disciplines.[22] To reduce is from the Latin *redūcere*, "to lead or bring back" or "to bring home."[23] The type of theological psychology that I am advocating practices reduction in this good sense by leading disciplinary observations back to a theological frame. Kevin Vanhoozer says, "Ironically enough, it is only when a discipline tries to be autonomous and work by its own light only, that it falls prey to reductionism in the modern sense of the term."[24] To be very clear from the outset, I am advocating for theological psychology to be theological all the way down. I come to the "book of nature" as a theologian. (This is the personal coefficient, as Polanyi calls it, of my work.[25]) As Herman Bavinck writes, "The mind of the Christian is not satisfied until every form of existence has been referred to the triune God."[26] I see this work as contributing to the third step of John Webster's theological theology, that is, treating "all other things ... relative to God, under the aspect of creatureliness."[27] Webster writes, "attention to non-divine things is a necessity for theology, whose accomplishment of its task remains incomplete unless it addresses itself also to these things."[28] As embodied creatures, human beings are an effect of God the creator; our psychological powers are received from God. This again highlights my expanded notion of psychology. In this sense, psychology is an important part of theology and must be dependent on theological notions of humanity, personhood, and moral agency.

But to what extent does modern psychology illuminate this program? Psychology in the broader sense has a relation to its narrower modern empirical discipline as pioneered by its modern father Wilhelm Wundt. Is modern psychology an independent source for theology or a Trojan horse

---

22. This way of putting it is from Kevin J. Vanhoozer, "Trinitarian Transdisciplinary Hermeneutics: A New Reduction of the Arts (and Sciences) to the Divine Economy" (paper, Transdisciplinary Conference in Houston, TX, February 23, 2017).

23. OED Online, s.v. "reduced, v.," accessed February 2, 2018, www.oed.com/.

24. This is taken from an unpublished transcript. Vanhoozer, "Trinitarian Transdisciplinary Hermeneutics," 10.

25. Michael Polanyi, *Personal Knowledge: Towards a Post-Critical Philosophy* (Chicago: University of Chicago Press, 1974), 141.

26. Herman Bavinck, *The Doctrine of God*, trans. William Hendricksen (Grand Rapids: Eerdmans, 1951), 329.

27. John Webster, "What Makes Theology Theological?" *The Journal of Analytic Theology* 3 (2015): 18.

28. Webster, "What Makes Theology Theological," 18.

for theological peril? Modern psychology has methods of uncovering and describing reality that are particularly effective but can be theologically loaded. The reason is that all scientific knowing arises from apprenticeship into a tradition. So the entire disciplinary structure of psychology is maintained by apprenticing new practitioners into a tradition involving trust and dissent. As Michael Polanyi writes, "nobody knows more than a tiny fragment of science well enough to judge its validity and value at first hand."[29] Each scientist must trust accredited members of the scientific community within a common tradition. This does not somehow invalidate the tradition, but it does alert us to the perils of working across disciplinary lines. A transdisciplinary theologian must attend to reality while acknowledging the metaphysical assumptions within the fabric of mutual trust of a tradition. To cite just one example, modern psychologists largely assume that emotions are adaptive functions, inherited from more primitive forms of life rather than created traits for communion with God.

If contemporary psychology is theoretically and theologically loaded, how does a theologian use it? As I have said, psychology is particularly adept at giving attention to certain aspects of reality. Again, this project is not aimed at integrating disciplines, but attending to reality by way of the book of Scripture and the book of nature. Both sources of revelation are divinely given, but the former explicitly frames how we are to understand the latter. Scripture is the *norma normans non normata*, the norming norm that is not normed; it is our magisterial authority. Nature is what saturates concepts, gives content to God's thoughts. Yet God's word is primary because his word brings into being all that is, nature included. Being (and epistemology) proceeds from his speech; what he says is. Humankind approaches nature within loving covenantal relationship with God through the regenerated gifts with which we have been endowed, (embodied) reason and perception, following God's unfolding guidance through his prophets and apostles, his Son, and latterly, through the Scriptures which have been passed down and interpreted through his church and by the power of the Holy Spirit. The very words of God stand, while the ministers of his word, like our capacities and tradition, clarify and saturate the concepts. So insofar as modern psychology helps us to attend to reality, it

---

29. Polanyi, *Personal Knowledge*, 165.

can only be a valuable ministerial aid to understanding human creature-liness. As Eric Johnson writes,

> Moreover, Late Modern psychology has strengths which the Christian tradition has historically lacked, for example, an emphasis on empirical research, comparative psychology, and a developmental orientation, to say nothing of the massive body of psychological knowledge discovered by the research and theory of this community's work! Indeed, a love for God leads Christians to relish and utilize the significant contributions of Late Modern psychology, since they are due ultimately to God's creation grace. As Calvin (1559/1960) opined: "If we regard the Spirit of God as the sole foundation of truth, we shall neither reject the truth itself, nor despise it wherever it shall appear, unless we wish to dishonor the Spirit of God" (p. 273).[30]

Finally, it must be admitted that psychology, even in the broader sense, is a highly idiosyncratic area of study. It is by its very nature the paradigmatic case of transdisciplinary work involving the natural sciences insofar as the empirical research is concerned; knotty philosophical problems of body and soul and mind and body; detailed psychological investigations about the functions of consciousness; and deep theological questions about the origins, capacities, and ends of humankind. The uniqueness of the topic only stresses the need for clear theological reasoning about it. As Reformed theologians have noted, the Bible itself seems not to provide a fully formed psychology, but a framework as well as some rough but essential data-background and control beliefs for more finely grained theorizing.[31] Fine-grained theological reasoning on emotion seems crucial to a host of Christian doctrines, sin and sanctification especially. This is an area where the book of nature helpfully nuances and enriches our reading of the inspired concepts of Scriptures. A thoroughly theological psychology, which leads empirical observations back to what is in Christ, as revealed in the Bible, seems especially warranted in this case.

---

30. Eric L. Johnson, *God and Soul Care: The Therapeutic Resources of the Christian Faith* (Downers Grove, IL: IVP Academic, 2017), 29.

31. These distinctions are from Nicholas Wolterstorff, *Reason within the Bounds of Religion* (Grand Rapids: Eerdmans, 1984), 63–66.

Approach

To honor the biblical, catholic, and empirical contexts of this project, my approach is first descriptive and then prescriptive. The first half of the book is a historical treatment of the psychology of Thomas Aquinas and John Calvin as well as a description of the major developments between them.[32] This historical section is aimed at three things. First, it allows introduction of the conceptual categories that will frame the constructive proposal. The categories of Thomas Aquinas are important not only because he represents what Peter King calls "the mainstream mediaeval view,"[33] but also because his view stimulated a string of controversies about theological psychology that carried through the Renaissance to modern philosophy. Second, the historical section allows me to compare and contrast the psychologies of Aquinas and Calvin on the faculties and plasticity, the metaphysical ground of habit formation. Third, it provides a partial explanation for the disappearance of the habit of virtue from Calvin's psychology.

I will analyze the psychologies with an evaluative question along the way: How do these theologians account for the ways the body qualifies agency with their psychological categories, especially the faculties? I am particularly interested in two psychological features: how the psychologies organize the powers (with or without hierarchy), and how they manage embodied plasticity with respect to emotion.[34] I will clarify a number of

---

32. The most significant omission from this project is a treatment of Jonathan Edwards. The scope of the project precludes anything like a fair treatment of him. The really fascinating problem is to what extent his psychology is consistent with the broader Reformed tradition, and what sort of influence he finally exercised on Reformed theology of emotions. This may be the focus of additional work.

33. Peter King, "The Inner Cathedral: Mental Architecture in High Scholasticism," *Vivarium* 46 (2008): 253–74. Katharine Park notes that the most influential philosophers of Medieval psychology were, "Albertus Magnus, Thomas Aquinas, Duns Scotus, and to a lesser extent Jean de Jandun, William of Ockham and Jean Buridan." Aquinas, Scotus, Ockham, and Buridan will receive treatment in the third chapter. See also Katharine Park, "The Organic Soul," in *The Cambridge History of Renaissance Philosophy*, ed. Charles B. Schmitt and Quentin Skinner (Cambridge: Cambridge University Press, 1988), 464.

34. In the first half of the book, I will not focus on the restoration of the faculties by either common (or creation) grace or special (or redemptive) grace, except as they relate to the types of virtue the theologians affirm. My analysis assumes that a certain kind of change is possible for anyone, but that this change has nothing to do with merit before God. This seems quite obvious when we consider that counselors help all types of people. The change that is accessible to everyone might be called civic virtue, or to use the phrase attributed to Augustine, "glittering vice." Real spiritual change comes through participation in union with God involving both in word and deed. This is precisely how Aquinas talked about "true

psychological categories such as intellect, will, passions, affections, sense appetite, etc. I will identify how the faculty of "sense appetite" is helpful in accounting for plasticity and how the faculty was disregarded. Since this is an analysis of the categories grounding emotional ontology, I will restrict my inquiry to how the psychological categories manage embodiment. I acknowledge that the theologians may have therapeutic methods that may not be implied by, or even consistent with, their explicit psychological categories. I take these instances to be happy accidents of pastoral or personal wisdom, but not strictly relevant to my analysis of psychological categories.

Explicitly addressing psychological categories, including faculties, is not an arbitrary decision. By doing so I am conscientiously attempting to honor the way medieval theologians conceived of their subject matter. Gary Hatfield has argued convincingly that the key thread of the development of early modern philosophy is an argument over the "powers of human cognitive faculties."[35] For example, the real explanatory power of the wax candle illustration of René Descartes is in showing that intellect can operate independently from "phantasms," intellect can grasp all the forms wax may take—contrary to the common Aristotelian view. On Hatfield's reading, the early modern turn away from Aristotelianism is a metaphysical shift over what powers "reason" possessed, culminating in Kant's transcendental logic and twelve pure concepts of understanding, ordered under quantity, quality, relation, and modality. While Aristotelians ascribed to the intellect an active power of discerning the essence of things, Kant rejected the intellect's access to the *noumena*, the thing itself, *Ding an sich*, and described its capacities only in terms of how it organized subjective experience. Kant reflects the culmination of a shift in adopting meager metaphysical principles for epistemological reasons.[36] Hatfield's observations about early modern philosophy imply *a minore ad maius* the greater importance of

---

virtue" (infused virtue and spiritual gifts). Also, with respect to redemptive grace, a governing assumption of this work is that redemptive grace is no less operative in the Spirit's application of the word in obedience than he is in the hearing of the word (1 Cor 15:10; Phil 2:13). Eric Johnson helpfully taxonomizes the orientations that psychotherapy can take in *God and Soul Care*. He suggests that the most comprehensive form of therapy works with both the resources in creation and in redemptive grace; Johnson, *God and Soul Care*, 92–98.

35. Gary Hatfield, "The Working of the Intellect: Mind and Psychology," *IRCS Technical Reports Series* 90 (1996): 1–36.

36. Even this way of putting it is not exactly satisfactory, since epistemology is not necessarily more fundamental than metaphysics. Robert Audi puts it this way:

attending to the powers of the faculties in the medievals, since it was the deductive metaphysical convictions that grounded their epistemological ones, rather than the other way around.[37] It is right to pay attention to the powers of the soul since there are metaphysical convictions, and not merely epistemological ones, that are reflected in medieval theologians' descriptions of the faculties. As Aquinas says, "action follows being" (*agere sequitur esse*; I-II.55.2 ad. 1),[38] so evaluating the actions and passions of the psyche involves investigating being as Paul Gondreau suggests: "unlocking the meaning of the passions can only begin with a grasp of the type of 'being' from which these actions come."[39]

CHAPTER OVERVIEW

Chapter 1 develops the research problem and prompt. I will discuss what emotional voluntarism is and how attending to embodiment addresses it. The next three chapters cover historical developments in theological psychology. Chapter 2 covers the psychology of Thomas Aquinas, paying special attention to his view of how the body qualifies agency within the lower faculties. I will argue that his view is holistic in the sense that body and soul produce a single intention and the possibility of internal conflict arising from higher and lower powers. Moreover, I will show how the composite lower powers are directly malleable via experience, but also governed by

---

The issue of realism is at the heart of metaphysics; that of rationality is at the heart of epistemology. Neither of these issues can be isolated from the other, nor can we separate epistemology and metaphysics. Our account of what there is constrains our theory of rational belief, and hence of rationality in general; and our theory of rational belief constrains our ontological outlook. It may be, however, that philosophers naturally tend to take one or the other of these two philosophical domains, epistemology or metaphysics, or some account developed therein, as primary. If we give priority to epistemology, we tend to produce an ontology that posits the sorts of objects about which our epistemology says we can have knowledge or justified belief; and if we give metaphysics priority, we tend to produce an account of rational belief which allows knowledge or justified belief about the sorts of things our ontology countenances as real.

Robert Audi, "Realism, Rationality, and Philosophical Method," *Proceedings and Addresses of the American Philosophical Association* 61, no. 1 (1987): 65.

37. I owe this insight to Douglas Blount.

38. Thomas Aquinas, *Summa Theologiae*, trans. Alfred J. Freddoso, updated January 10, 2018. www3.nd.edu/~afreddos/summa-translation/TOC.htm.

39. Paul Gondreau, *The Passions of Christ's Soul in the Theology of St. Thomas Aquinas* (Scranton, PA: University of Scranton Press, 2009), 105.

the top-down (political) rule of the rational powers. Chapter 3 discusses some major developments in theological psychology between Aquinas and Calvin, providing at least a partial background for understanding how certain distinctive features of the psychology of Aquinas are not represented in Calvin's. Chapter 4 discusses John Calvin's psychology, particularly how he differs from Aquinas on the crucial issue of plasticity.

In the prescriptive portion of the work, I will propose a model of the body and soul, which honors the biblical tensions of anthropological holism and dualism and the empirical insights of contemporary neuroscience. Drawing from J. P. Moreland, I will argue for a Thomistic-like view, which is both dualistic and genuinely holistic. This model can both maintain a metaphysical distinction between the soul and body while seriously integrating the insights of neuroscience. A properly holistic model seriously accounts for how the body qualifies the range of psychological functions, rather than seeing the soul and body as accounting for discrete psychological functions, like thinking and feeling. I am pushing back on an approach to emotion that looks to one or the other as the discrete source of any particular emotion. My model opens up an understanding of spirituality where God concerns himself with bodies and matter within the economy of salvation. I wish to suggest that from creation to redemption, the Bible maintains a consistent concern for the *shalom* of not only divine and human relations, but also for the material world and individual bodies. Human beings have a moral responsibility to listen to the word of God as a matter of "husbanding," in the original sense of tilling and cultivating, our bodies to flourish in communion with God in Christ and by the power of the Holy Spirit.[40] We are God's under-gardeners. This responsibility runs from Eden to the eschaton, as noted in the Romans 8:23—awaiting the "redemption of our bodies."

Chapter 5 forms a bridge between the historical work on Calvin and the current discussion about theological psychology among Reformed theologians by resuming the history after the establishment of the discipline of psychology and by providing immediate theological context for my

---

40. For the older transitive sense: "To tend as a husbandman or farmer, to cultivate; to till (the ground); to dress or prune (trees and plants)," see OED Online, s.v. "husband, v.," accessed February 2, 2018, www.oed.com/.

constructive work. It highlights a developing lineage of holistic thinking about the body-soul relation within the Reformed tradition, along with a reluctance to get into the details of what holism means. The tradition has largely underdeveloped its views on the nature of the soul or emotions since psychology became an empirical discipline. Chapter 6 represents a sort of negotiation between the book of nature and the book of Scripture on the issue of the soul. I contrast the approaches of John Cooper and Nancey Murphy on the soul, observing the explanatory advantages of each position. I propose a dualistic holism that best accounts for the strengths of both perspectives, J. P. Moreland's Thomistic-like dualism.[41] The advantage of this model for my argument is that it allows me to take embodied plasticity seriously. Chapter 7 serves two functions. First, it looks back to the previous chapter by establishing biblical-theological warrant for holism on the grounds that the plan of salvation involves materiality and embodiment. Second, it looks forward by establishing biblical warrant for an account of biblical agency that assumes the possibility of conflict between body and mind as psychological principles, rather than body and soul as metaphysical ones. This accords very well with a holistic way of seeing the human person and anticipates my model of tiered (higher and lower) psychological faculties.

In Chapter 8, I propose a Thomistic-like model of emotion in conversation with neuroscientist Joseph LeDoux. Comparing this model with the work of Aquinas will help to make sense of the relationship between the body and cognition in the experience of emotion. Finally, in Chapter 9 I will illustrate how my model reads texts where the Bible seems to command emotion with a treatment of Matthew 6:25–34 within its theological and canonical context.

---

41. John Cooper in the preface to the second printing of *Body, Soul, and Life Everlasting* endorses dualistic holism as an alternate way of framing his position. He suggests, "If 'dualistic holism' seems better to those who wish to emphasize unity instead of duality, I am pleased to endorse it." John Cooper, *Body, Soul, and Life Everlasting*, 2nd ed. (Grand Rapids: Eerdmans, 2000), xxviii.

LITERATURE REVIEW

This project is one without a clear exemplar; it is difficult to find constructive Protestant works dedicated solely to theological psychology.[42] There
are a few possible exceptions, such as Ellen Charry's two books, *By the
Renewing of Your Minds* (1997) and *God and the Art of Happiness* (2010). In *By
the Renewing of Your Minds*, Charry evaluates the artegenic (virtue forming)
aspect of key theologians throughout Christian history. *God and the Art
of Happiness* represents a sort of theology of happiness (asherism) drawing both from historical theology and biblical exegesis.[43] In this work, her
constructive engagement with historical theology and the Bible mirrors
my method. However, my work is aimed more explicitly at human nature.
Another exception is an unpublished dissertation by Paul Allen Lewis titled,
"Rethinking Emotions and the Moral Life in Light of Thomas Aquinas and
Jonathan Edwards."[44] Lewis cites Edwards and Aquinas as positive exem-
plars for correcting some contemporary deficiencies in modern theories
of emotion. However, his project is focused on mediating an ongoing philosophical debate about emotion rather than offering constructive theological reflection. Beyond this work, there are a few clusters of works that
have similar interests to mine. They can be grouped into the following
categories: (1) historical works on moral philosophy from the medieval
period to just after the Reformation; (2) Aquinas or virtue ethics studies;
and (3) works about emotion that are either theologically or philosophically motivated.

The first cluster of related works are of historical theology and philos-
ophy. There are valuable, sweeping works like Simo Knuuttila, *Emotions
in Ancient and Medieval Philosophy* (2004); Henrik Lagerlund and Mikko
Yrjönsuuri, *Emotions and Choice from Boethius to Descartes* (2002); Thomas
Dixon, *From Passions to Emotions* (2003); and Risto Saarinen, *Weakness of
Will in Renaissance and Reformation Thought* (2011), along with Ruth Harvey,

---

42. There are signs that the topic is just beginning to generate broader interest. For example, Fuller Theological Seminary hosted an integration symposium titled "Reviving Christian
Psychology" featuring Ellen Charry in 2007.

43. Ellen T. Charry, *By the Renewing of Your Minds: The Pastoral Function of Christian Doctrine*
(Oxford: Oxford University Press, 1999); *God and the Art of Happiness* (Grand Rapids: Eerdmans,
2010).

44. Paul Allen Lewis, "Rethinking Emotions and the Moral Life in Light of Thomas Aquinas
and Jonathan Edwards" (PhD diss., Duke University, 1991).

The Inward Wits (1975), which covers the physiological background of the received view.[45] Finally, there are secondary sources on the various time periods being covered.[46] Again, none of these works are aimed at making constructive use of their description and analysis.

In the second category, the most important work for my project is by Nicholas Lombardo, *The Logic of Desire* (2011). Lombardo argues that Aquinas regarded passions as essential to virtue, that these involve the contribution of the body, and that moral virtue resides primarily then in the sense appetite, not the intellect.[47] Lombardo specifically makes appli-

---

45. Simo Knuuttila, *Emotions in Ancient and Medieval Philosophy* (Oxford: Oxford University Press, 2004); Henrik Lagerlund and Mikko Yrjönsuuri, eds., *Emotions and Choice from Boethius to Descartes* (Dordrecht: Kluwer Academic, 2002); Thomas Dixon, *From Passions to Emotions: The Creation of a Secular Psychological Category* (New York: Cambridge University Press, 2003); Risto Saarinen, *Weakness of Will in Renaissance and Reformation Thought* (Oxford: Oxford University Press, 2011); E. Ruth Harvey, *The Inward Wits: Psychological Theory in the Middle Ages and the Renaissance*, ed. E.H. Gombrich and J.B. Trapp, Warburg Institute Surveys VI, (London: Trinity Press, 1975). See also Simo Knuuttila, *Modalities in Medieval Philosophy* (New York: Routledge, 1993); Jill Kraye and Risto Saarinen, eds., *Moral Philosophy on the Threshold of Modernity*, The New Synthese Historical Library, vol. 57 (Dordrecht: Springer, 2005).

46. Peter King, "Aquinas on the Emotions," in *The Oxford Handbook of Aquinas*, ed. Brian Davies and Eleonore Stump (Oxford: Oxford University Press, 2011), 209–26; Peter King, "Aquinas on the Passions," in *Aquinas's Moral Theory: Essays in Honor of Norman Kretzmann*, ed. Scott MacDonald and Eleonore Stump (Ithaca, NY: Cornell University Press, 1999), 101–32; Peter King, "The Inner Cathedral: Mental Architecture in High Scholasticism," *Vivarium* 46 (2008): 253–74; Heiko Augustinus Oberman, *The Harvest of Medieval Theology* (Grand Rapids: Baker Academic, 1983); Heiko Augustinus Oberman "Via Antiqua and Via Moderna: Late Medieval Prolegomena to Early Reformation Thought," *Journal of the History of Ideas* 48, no. 1 (January–March, 1987): 23–40; Heiko Augustinus Oberman "Fourteenth-Century Religious Thought: A Premature Profile," *Speculum* 53, no. 1 (January, 1978): 80–93; Dewey Hoitenga, *John Calvin and the Will: A Critique and Corrective* (Grand Rapids: Baker, 1997); Paul Helm, *John Calvin's Ideas* (Oxford: Oxford University Press, 2004); Anthony N. S. Lane, "Calvin's Use of the Fathers and the Medievals," *Calvin Theological Journal* 16 (1981): 149–205; Richard Muller, "*Fides* and *Cognitio* in Relation to the Problem of Intellect and Will in the Theology of John Calvin," *Calvin Theological Journal* 25 (1990): 207–24; Richard Muller, *Post-Reformation Reformed Dogmatics: The Rise and Development of Reformed Orthodoxy, ca. 1520 to ca. 1725*, 4 vols. (Grand Rapids: Baker Academic, 2003); Richard Muller, "Scholasticism, Reformation, Orthodoxy, and the Persistence of Christian Aristotelianism," *Trinity Journal* 19, no. 2 (1998): 81–96; Richard Muller, *The Unaccommodated Calvin: Studies in the Foundation of Theological Tradition*, ed. David C. Steinmetz, Oxford Studies in Historical Theology (Oxford: Oxford University Press, 2000); David S. Sytsma, "The Logic of the Heart: Analyzing the Affections in Early Reformed Orthodoxy," in *Church and School in Early Modern Protestantism: Studies in Honor of Richard A. Muller on the Maturation of a Theological Tradition*, ed. Jordan J. Ballor, David S. Sytsma, and Jason Zuidema (Boston, Brill, 2013), 471–88; see also Perry Miller, *The New England Mind: The Seventeenth Century* (Cambridge, MA: Harvard University Press, 1954).

47. Nicholas E. Lombardo, *The Logic of Desire: Aquinas on Emotion* (Washington, DC: The Catholic University of America Press, 2011), 16–17n61; cf. Sarah Coakley, ed., *Faith Rationality and the Passions* (Malden, MA: Wiley-Blackwell, 2012); Norman Kretzmann and Eleonore

cation to the nature of emotion at the end of the book. I am following his reading and application of Aquinas on emotion closely. There are also several articles that explicitly unpack the value of Aquinas's psychology for modern psychology, including Giuseppe Butera, "Thomas Aquinas and Cognitive Therapy" (2010), which anticipates the connections I will make between the medieval view of emotion and modern psychology.[48]

Third, there is the literature on the philosophy and psychology of emotion and the now familiar debate between cognitivists (e.g., Robert Solomon, Richard Lazarus, etc.) and non-cognitivists (William James, Carl Lange, Robert Zajonc, etc.). This literature forms the background of my inquiry.[49] While I will not develop the lines of controversy at length, my

Stump, *The Cambridge Companion to Thomas Aquinas* (Cambridge: Cambridge University Press, 1993); Robert Miner, *Thomas Aquinas on the Passions* (Cambridge: Cambridge University Press, 2009); Paul Gondreau, "The Passions and the Moral Life: Appreciating the Originality of Aquinas," *Thomist* 71 (2007): 419–50.

48. Giuseppe Butera, "Thomas Aquinas and Cognitive Therapy: An Exploration of the Promise of Thomistic Psychology," *Philosophy, Psychiatry, & Psychology* 17, no. 4 (December 2010): 347–66; George Mora, "Thomas Aquinas and Modern Psychology: A Reassessment," *Psychoanalytic Review* 64, no. 4 (Winter 1977): 495–530; Frank J. Moncher, "A Psychotherapy of Virtue: Reflection on St. Thomas Aquinas' Theology of Moral Virtue," *Journal of Psychology and Christianity* 20, no. 4 (2001): 320–41.

49. Joseph E. LeDoux, *Emotional Brain*; Joseph E. LeDoux, *Anxious: Using the Brain to Understand and Treat Fear and Anxiety* (New York: Penguin Books, 2015); Karim Nader, Glenn E. Schafe, and Joseph LeDoux, "Fear Memories Require Protein Synthesis in the Amygdala for Reconsolidation after Retrieval," *Nature* 406 (August 2000): 722–26; Joseph E. LeDoux and Richard Brown, "A Higher-order Theory of Emotional Consciousness," *Proceedings of the National Academy of Sciences* 114, no. 10 (January 2017): E2016–25; Robert C. Roberts, *Emotion: An Essay in Aid of Moral Psychology* (Cambridge: Cambridge University Press, 2003); Jesse Prinz, *Gut Reactions: A Perceptual Theory of Emotion* (Oxford: Oxford University Press, 2006).

See also William James, "What is an Emotion?" *Mind* 9 (1884): 188–205; Walter B. Cannon, *The Wisdom of the Body* (London: Kegan Paul, 1932); Magda B. Arnold, *Emotion and Personality* (New York: Columbia University Press, 1960); Stanley Schachter and Jerome E. Singer, "Cognitive, Social, and Physiological Determinants of the Emotional State," *Psychological Review* 69, no. 5 (September 1962): 379–99; Robert Solomon, *The Passions: The Myth and Nature of Human Emotion* (Notre Dame: University of Notre Dame Press, 1983); Amélie Oksenberg Rorty, "Aristotle on the Metaphysical Status of the *Pathe*," *The Review of Metaphysics* 27, no. 3 (March 1984): 521–46; Nico H. Frijda, *The Emotions* (Cambridge: Cambridge University Press, 1987); Ronald de Sousa, *The Rationality of Emotion* (Cambridge, MA: MIT Press, 1987); Carroll E. Izard, "Four Systems for Emotion Activation," *Psychological Review* 100, no. 1 (January 1993): 68–90; Antonio R. Damasio, *Descartes' Error: Emotion, Reason, and the Human Brain* (New York: Grosset/ Putnam, 1994); Richard S. Lazarus and Bernice N. Lazarus, *Passion and Reason: Making Sense of Our Emotions* (Oxford: Oxford University Press, 1996); Richard Lazarus, "From Psychological Stress to the Emotions: A History of Changing Outlooks," *Annual Review of Psychology* 44 (1993): 1–21; Paul E. Griffiths, *What Emotions Really Are: The Problem of Psychological Categories* (Chicago: University of Chicago Press, 1997); John F. Kihlstrom et al., "The Emotional Unconscious," in *Counterpoints: Cognition and Emotion*, ed. E. Eich et al. (New York: Oxford University

proposal conscientiously attempts to mediate the gap between those who see emotion as biological and adaptive reactions (non-cognitive) and those who see emotion as some sort of rational or quasi-rational appraisal or judgment (cognitive).[50] Finally, Matthew Elliott and Brian Borgman are important conversation partners because they engage the biblical text and are representatives of a theological perspective on emotions.[51]

EXCURSUS: PASSIONS AND AFFECTIONS

Finally, I must say a few words about a terminological problem with this work. I will use the words "passion" and "emotion" roughly interchangeably. Because Thomas Dixon has objected quite forcibly to this practice, I wish to say a few words in defense. Dixon argues that the single concept of "emotion" is a poor substitute for the richer range of terms, appetite, passions, and affections.[52] He writes,

> Thomas Brown, whom I have previously designated the "inventor of the emotions" … subsumed the "appetites," "passions," and "affections" under a single category: the "emotions." … Two decades later, McCosh (1880) enumerated over 100 discrete feeling states that fell into the category. How could anyone possibly devise a single theory, or a simple conceptual definition, that could cover such a wide range of different mental states? The answer is that no one could.[53]

Dixon especially objects to the anachronism of translating passions with emotions. Emotion has "tended to be defined in an amoral way as an autonomous physical or mental state characterised by vivid feeling and physical agitation." By contrast, passions have been defined "in more morally

---

Press, 2000), 30–86; Martha Nussbaum, *Upheavals of Thought: The Intelligence of Emotions* (Cambridge: Cambridge University Press, 2003); Jaak Panksepp, *Affective Neuroscience: The Foundations of Human and Animal Emotions* (Oxford: Oxford University Press, 2004).

50. Joseph LeDoux describes this controversy from a neuroscientific perspective in *Emotional Brain*.

51. Matthew A. Elliott, *Faithful Feelings: Rethinking Emotion in the New Testament* (Grand Rapids: Kregel, 2006); Brian S. Borgman, *Feelings and Faith: Cultivating Godly Emotions in the Christian Life* (Wheaton, IL: Crossway, 2009); cf. Karl Allen Kuhn, *The Heart of Biblical Narrative: Rediscovering Biblical Appeal to the Emotions* (Minneapolis: Fortress, 2009).

52. Thomas Dixon, "'Emotion': The History of a Keyword in Crisis," *Emotion Review* 4, no. 4 (October 2012), 340.

53. Dixon, "Emotion," 340.

and theologically engaged ways as a disobedient and morally dangerous movement of the soul."[54] Dixon also insists that it is a mistake to overlook the distinction between passions and affections. These are metaphysically freighted terms. According to Dixon, passions for Augustine and Aquinas are "unruly forces," "symptoms of the fall," and "directed toward worldly objects." Whereas affections are more proper and directed "towards goodness, truth and, ultimately God."[55] Dixon writes,

> The will was divided by Aquinas into two "appetites": the higher intellectual appetite (the will proper), whose movements were the affections; and the lower, non-rational sense appetite, whose movements were the appetites and passions. It is particularly important, then, to realize that—contrary to popular opinion—classical Christian views about reason and the passions were equivalent neither to the view that reason and the "emotions" are inevitably at war, nor to the idea that "emotions" overpower us against our will. Appetites, passions, and affections, on the classical Christian view, were all movements of different parts of the will, and the affections, at least, were potentially informed by reason.[56]

This characterization may be accurate about the area of Dixon's particular expertise, the Victorian period. However, it is a significant misrepresentation of Aquinas in two important respects. First, the passions are not movements of the will, but of the separate power of the sensitive appetite. Unlike Renaissance and early modern theologians, Aquinas possessed a tiered psychology that did not relegate the senses to the irrational body. Second, Dixon wrongly insists that sense appetite is non-rational and that the passions are irrational movements. Affections play a relatively insignificant role in the psychology of Aquinas—Peter King calls them pseudopassions—while the rationality of the passions and their role in virtue is crucial to it.[57] Dixon's reading of the non-rationality of sense appetite only applies to the timeframe where he has expertise. Nicholas Lombardo

---

54. Thomas Dixon, *From Passions to Emotions: The Creation of a Secular Psychological Category* (Cambridge: Cambridge University Press, 2006), 18.

55. Dixon, *From Passions to Emotions*, 29.

56. Dixon, *From Passions to Emotions*, 22.

57. See King, "Aquinas on the Passions," 105n7.

criticizes Dixon's reading because Aquinas "often uses the word 'affection' interchangeably with the word 'passion' and in such a way that bodily modification is implied." Calvin also does this. Moreover, Lombardo adds, "Aquinas not only discusses virtuous passions frequently, he regards passions as essential to virtue."[58]

As a result, I will anachronistically use passions roughly to map with emotions. I do this for the same reasons that Dixon is happy to use the term "psychology" to refer to works done prior to the establishment of the empirical discipline. Dixon thinks this not a methodological anomaly because there is no important difference in terminology that makes the anachronism problematic; ancient and modern psychologists are referring to the same basic real phenomena. Dixon seems to want to push against the hegemony of the empirical discipline. Likewise, I see no important difference in using emotions to refer to passions, since they cover roughly the same semantic domain in the figures I am treating and because I want to push against the hegemony of modern psychology. Indeed, an important premise of my argument is that we can learn how to think about emotions by how Aquinas talks about the passions.

Finally, I am not invested in recovering historical categories for their own sake. When historical categories correspond to and uncover some aspect of reality, as I think sense appetite does, then it is worth recovering them. With reference to the term "affections," I find it hard to trace precisely what it means. It does not seem to consistently refer to an obvious aspect of human psychology. What I want to know is this: to what set of psychological and physiological phenomena does the concept refer? There are a few possible ways of speaking of this. If "affections" means something like a moral emotion, then the concept begs the key question. If affections might be the sort of movements that are a direct result of thought, then I only point out that emotions may arise from many objects, including thought. If affections might be the sort of emotions that are not deeply physiologically involved, then I wonder how to distinguish them

---

58. Lombardo, *Logic of Desire*, 15; he also adds on additional critique: "Aquinas does not hold that the only proper objects of the passions are incorporeal ideals. Virtuous passions may well respond to abstract ideals, either by being shaped by rational considerations or by sharing by overflow in the affections of the will. Similarly, the affections of the will may rejoice or sorrow virtuously in sense objects (see *ST* I–II 31.3, 34.1, 34.4)." Lombardo, *Logic of Desire*, 16–17.

from attitudes. If affections are rational and cognitively respectable in contradistinction to passions, then I think we may have misunderstood the term "passions," at least in Aquinas. I suspect that there is real incoherence in how these terms are used by Renaissance and early modern theologians, and that this results from how they arranged psychological furniture, so to speak. This is a problem that Aquinas seems not to have shared. In my opinion, the only viable path for understanding affections is as a sort of rational and long-term inclination. If the term is used in this way, then I am happy with it. I will demonstrate how, in the late medieval period, passions and affections came to be conceived of as qualities or inclinations rather than movements. I think this was a mistake, but perhaps preserving the term "affections" as a longstanding inclination may be useful. But if this is so, then affections are something closer to psychological orientation than they are to emotion.[59] For this reason, I will continue to assume that in ancient and medieval language, "passions" and "affections" have a great deal of overlap. I see no reason to develop the discrete category of affections for the purposes of this work.

---

59. Gerald R. McDermott uses the term "preferences" to refer to "affections" in Jonathan Edwards. I take it that this is reasonably close to what I am suggesting. However, even this is difficult to map psychologically. Is an inclination a habit of the passions, i.e., virtue or vice? Is inclination a settled determination to act and feel a certain way like "decision" or Aristotle's notion of the voluntary? There are still problems with this. I am inclined to think that medieval psychology is far more reasonable than Renaissance and early modern psychology. Gerald R. McDermott, "Jonathan Edwards on the Affections of the Spirit," in *The Spirit, The Affections, and the Christian Tradition,* ed. Dale M. Coulter and Amos Young (Notre Dame, IN: University of Notre Dame Press, 2016), 280–83.

1

—

EMOTIONAL VOLUNTARISM

S uppose that a woman named Mary is suffering from rising anxiety. Mary is finding it difficult to let go of worries that she knows her husband will call ridiculous. She always has tended to be safe about things like turning off the oven or checking the doors at night. But her anxiety is making life progressively more difficult for her. As a wife and new mom, her mind is constantly occupied with worry, especially about unintentionally harming her child. She finds herself checking and rechecking safety issues like the car seat or the front door. The worries seem to come out of nowhere. She is too ashamed to communicate her anxieties to her husband, who might help steady her. She knows that her anxiety is causing strain on her marriage and fears that her husband will finally have it with her. He expresses exasperation over her worries—for example, that she will accidentally feed her child something toxic. He even sometimes uses the word "crazy." She seems to be noticing that he is getting distant. How can we know what is happening here? Is this a pattern of sinful anxiety? Or might it be a psychological disorder? Is this the gradual late onset of obsessive-compulsive disorder (OCD) as described by the DSM-V?[1]

For now, I want to draw our attention to the fact that we want to know where the anxiety is coming from. All pains leave us searching for causes because we think that identifying the cause can help us to treat the pain and to avoid future pain. Just as we might see an orthopedic surgeon to

---

1. The DSM-V criteria are all present here. Of onset it says, "Males have an earlier age at onset than females: nearly 25% of males have onset before age 10 years. The onset of symptoms is typically gradual; however, acute onset has also been reported." *Diagnostic and Statistical Manual of Mental Disorders*, 5th ed. (Washington, DC: American Psychiatric Association, 2013), 237, 239.

diagnose persistent knee pain, so also we see wise friends, pastors, counselors, doctors, and psychiatrists to diagnose psychological pain. We want
to know what has gone wrong.

Because we want to understand psychological pain, it poses an introspective dilemma for many Christians. We tend to attribute the internal
pain of anxiety either to sinful desires or beliefs, taking advice from the
church, or to aspects of our experience that are out of our control such
as inherited traits, traumatic experience, or disease, taking advice from
psychology. A key aim for this book is to collapse this dilemma by mod-
eling how our agency and experience (active and passive aspects) come
together to produce emotion; genes, thoughts, actions, and experiences
all contribute to emotional experience. In what follows, I will elaborate
on the two poles of this introspective dilemma.

THE EXPLANATION DILEMMA

Emotional Voluntarism

On one side of the introspective dilemma, we have a theological perspective
on negative emotions. From a generically Reformed evangelical perspective,[2] negative emotions have moral valence and can be right or wrong. In
fact, emotions are crucial for true religion.[3] Consequently, Reformed theologians often speak of our responsibility for emotions in terms of what I
will call emotional voluntarism.[4] We might summarize this view as follows:

---

2. I acknowledge that the Reformed tradition is quite broad. For the sake of simplicity,
I will leave out the words "evangelical" and "American" when referring to the Reformed
tradition after this point, but my focus remains this narrower group. All of my examples are
from people who could generically be called Reformed evangelicals.

3. "True religion, in great part, consists in holy affections." Jonathan Edwards, *Religious
Affections*, I.1, vol. 1, *The Works of Jonathan Edwards*, ed. Henry Rogers, Sereno Edwards Dwight,
and Edward Hickman (Peabody, MA: Hendrickson, 2004), 236.

4. When I say that this approach is voluntarist, I mean that emotion arises from the
voluntary action of the will. I do not mean to imply that it is Pelagian; only that advocates of
this view sometimes speak as though changing emotion is like choosing alternate behavior.
Matthew Elliott writes, "Secondly, emotions may be changed by changing the beliefs and
evaluations that cause them. This may occur in all kinds of ways. A person may talk himself
into another belief." Matthew Elliott, *Faithful Feelings: Rethinking Emotion in the New Testament*
(Grand Rapids: Kregel, 2006), 38. Brian Borgman writes, "If God commands us to do something
and we don't do it, what is our normal course of action? Confession and repentance. Why
should the protocol be any different when we fail to feel the way God commands us to feel?"
He writes elsewhere, "The truth rightly embraced and believed will give you an experience."

We are responsible for emotions as intrusive mental states that show what we truly believe. Moreover, the illicit desire or false belief may be overcome by applying the gospel through voluntary mental work.[5] Briefly, emotional voluntarism includes the following elements:

(1) Emotion as judgment: Emotion is strictly or first a mental state.

(2) Emotions of the heart: Since emotions are morally significant, the proper subject of emotion is the heart, though perhaps some emotions are sourced in or influenced by the body.

(3) Deep belief associationism and legitimacy: Emotion is a mental state that arises when a deep belief is elicited into consciousness; the beliefs that surface unbidden are also our truest.[6]

Brian S. Borgman, *Feelings and Faith: Cultivating Godly Emotions in the Christian Life* (Wheaton, IL: Crossway, 2009), 80, 77.

5. I am using the language of mental work quite deliberately here for two reasons. First, that mental work is work is obvious to anyone who has encountered OCD. Second, it follows that a competitive relation between human and divine agency cannot be sustained by suggesting that God is wholly responsible for producing emotions if only I do the non-work of remembering and appreciating his grace. By contrast, I am assuming a non-competitive or concurrent relation between divine and human agency in sanctification where God works as we work (1 Cor 15:10; Phil 2:13). This is how Calvin viewed divine and human agency. Calvin maintained a strong competitive framework in the context of justification and merit. On the other hand, in the context of sanctification by the indwelling Holy Spirit, Charles Raith writes, "Calvin's account of the relationship between divine and human activity is in general deeply Augustinian and noncompetitive." In this case, Calvin appeals to a "participatory relationship between God's activity and human activity." Charles Raith, *After Merit: John Calvin's Theology of Works and Rewards* (Göttingen: Vanderhoeck & Ruprecht, 2016), 111. A non-competitive framework both expands the range of available means of grace for emotional change (e.g., liturgical participation) and refuses to acknowledge exercises of intentional mental focusing as non-work.

6. I will not elaborate on associationism, but it is the view that "mental and moral phenomena may be accounted for by association of ideas" (Oxford English Dictionary, s.v. "associationism," accessed September 4, 2018, https://www.oed.com/). Associationism was popular among British empiricists and treated by Herman Bavinck in his *Beginselen der Psychologie* (1897). Explanations of associationism often rely on metaphors like ideas surfacing in water because of relations to external objects. I am primarily appealing to it for this metaphor, that external objects only bring up what is under the surface of consciousness. Philosophically, associationism posited some sorts of psychic laws that were like the laws of nature; this inclined empiricists to a mostly passive version of the psyche, unlike faculty psychology.

(4) Mental voluntarism: Emotions as mental states are changeable by shifting attention, mainly through internal speech (e.g., repenting of false beliefs) to bring about new mental states.

(5) Emotional duty: People are duty bound to address any emotional aberrance as quickly as possible, since this is within their power.

I will briefly unpack these elements with examples. First, most recent Reformed evangelicals hold a cognitivist philosophical account of emotion. Emotion is a sort of judgment or construal of my state of affairs that expresses some sort of interest or attitude. For example, Matthew Elliott cites favorably the definition of philosopher William Lyons, "The evaluation central to the concept of emotion is an evaluation of some object, event or situation in the world about me in relation to me, or according to my norms. Thus, my emotions reveal whether I see the world or some aspect of it as threatening or welcoming, pleasant or painful, regrettable or a solace, and so on."[7] Robert Roberts has a nuanced version of this, calling emotions "concerned-based construals," signifying that while emotions are cognitive (construal, judgments), they are also interested (concern-based, or valenced with respect to a judgment).[8]

---

7. Elliott, Faithful Feelings, 31; William Lyons, Emotion (Cambridge: Cambridge University Press, 1980), xi. To be fair, Matthew Elliott argues that something like the opposite assumptions were common among biblical scholars of the late twentieth century; Elliott, Faithful Feelings, 17–18.

8. That emotions are construals seems to run counter to the older Reformed view that the proper subject of emotion is the will, since the will is an appetitive faculty. John Calvin and Jonathan Edwards are two clear examples of theologians who argue that human beings have two faculties, intellect and will, locating emotions in the latter. John Calvin is helpful because he aligns the mind with the intellect and the heart with the will when talking about psychology. He does recognize that the Bible uses the terms a bit differently but continues to maintain the distinction when talking about psychology. By the nineteenth century, there developed an additional feeling faculty, which I will not address. Cf. Asa Burton, Essays on Some of the First Principles of Metaphysicks, Ethicks, and Theology (Portland: Mirror, 1824), 17; Douglas A. Sweeney and Allen C. Guelzo, The New England Theology (Eugene, OR: Wipf & Stock, 2006), 179–86; Charles Finney, Finney's Systematic Theology: The Complete and Newly Expanded 1878 Edition (Minneapolis: Bethany House, 1994), 139. Bavinck rejects the feeling faculty. Herman Bavinck, Foundations of Psychology, trans. Jack Vanden Born (Master's thesis, Calvin College, 1981), [Herman Bavinck, Beginselen der Psychologie, 2nd ed. (Kampen: J. H. Kok, 1923)].

Second, Reformed evangelicals commonly assume that emotions come from the heart, which is the soul and the center of human agency. Ed Welch is explicit about this. In *Blame It on the Brain*, he writes,

> In the Bible, "spirit" (*pneuma*) shares its field of meaning with a number of words. Included are terms such as "heart" (*kardia*), "mind" (*dianoia, phrenes,* and *nous*), "soul" (Greek: *psuche.* Hebrew: *nephesh*), "conscience" (*suneidesis*), "inner self" (1 Peter 3:4), and "inner man" (2 Cor. 4:16). Even though these words have different emphases, they can be used almost interchangeably—and I will use them that way.[9]

Elsewhere Welch writes, "The differences between body and soul can be summarized this way: the soul is the moral epicenter of the person. In our souls or hearts, we make allegiances to ourselves and our idols or to the true God. ... The body is our means of service in a physical world. It is never described in moral terms."[10] John Piper draws a similar distinction between the human heart and body. He writes, "The human heart does not replenish itself with sleep. The body does, but not the heart. The spiritual air leaks from our tires, and the gas is consumed in the day. We replenish our hearts not with sleep, but with the Word of God and prayer."[11] Piper does admit that the body in some way modulates the phenomenology of emotion,[12] but at least spiritual emotion is not ultimately dependent on the body, since "presumably redeemed people will have strong emotions of adoration and satisfaction at God's right hand after they die and before their bodies are raised from the dead (see Phil. 1:23; Rev. 6:10)."[13] The assumption that the

---

9. Edward Welch, *Blame It on the Brain* (Phillipsburg, NJ: P&R, 1998), 35; I do not agree with him about the semantic overlap of these terms.

10. Edward Welch, "Sinners Learning to Act the Miracle," in *Acting the Miracle: God's Work and Ours in the Mystery of Sanctification,* ed. John Piper and David Mathis (Wheaton, IL: Crossway, 2013), 70.

11. John Piper, *When I Don't Desire God* (Wheaton, IL: Crossway, 2013), 116.

12. He writes, "Proper eating and exercising and sleeping has a marked effect on the mind and its ability to process natural beauty and biblical truth." Piper, *When I Don't Desire God,* 178.

13. Piper, *When I Don't Desire God,* 179. Thomas Aquinas agrees about the intermediate state but qualifies his view; both earthly life and resurrection life feature embodied emotion. He argues that while beatitude essentially consists in knowing God's essence with our intellectual powers, the composite sentient powers are involved both antecedently, in the present life as the senses provide the phantasms for the intellect, and consequently, after the resurrection by "a certain overflow into the body and into the bodily senses, in order

heart is the true source of emotion is also implicit in the common phrase that our emotions reveal our true beliefs.[14] "*Our emotion reveals truth about ourselves and our beliefs.* The emotions of others or their lack of emotion often shows us what they think, value, and believe."[15] I do not have space to fully refute the claim that the heart is just the human soul in distinction to the body, metaphysically speaking. But this claim is not supported by an analysis of the biblical concepts *lēv* or *kardia*.[16]

Third, and relatedly, these accounts also involve a depth assumption about the heart where emotions are passively intruding mental states that come from the deepest source of our agency, especially implying the genuineness of deep belief versus the falseness of what we purport to believe

---

that they might be perfected in their operations" (*ST* I–II.3.3). Both imperfect beatitude in the present time and perfect human beatitude in the resurrection involves the senses, so also the body. Even the virtues that exist in the embodied organs will persist in them after the resurrection (*ST* I–II.67.1 ad. 3).

14. Cf. Jon Bloom, "Lay Aside the Weight of Moodiness," *Desiring God* (blog), August 12, 2016, www.desiringgod.org/articles/lay-aside-the-weight-of-moodiness; Jon Bloom, "Your Emotions Are a Gauge, Not a Guide," *Desiring God* (blog), August 3, 2012, www.desiringgod.org/articles/your-emotions-are-a-gauge-not-a-guide; Neil T. Anderson, *Freedom in Christ: Small-Group Bible Study* (Ventura, CA: Gospel Light, 2004), 41; Dan Allender and Tremper Longman, *The Cry of the Soul: How Our Emotions Reveal Our Deepest Problem about God* (Colorado Springs: NavPress, 1994), 14; "Lent Day 7: The Prayer," *Redeemer Churches & Ministries* (blog), https://www.redeemer.com/learn/resources_by_topic/lenten_devotionals/lent_day_7_the_prayer/; Elliott, *Faithful Feelings*, 37, 264; Edward Welch, "Emotions are a Language," *CCEF* (blog), August 5, 2016, https://www.ccef.org/resources/blog/emotions-are-a-language.

15. Matthew Elliott, *Faithful Feelings*, 37; emphasis added. This reminds me of the well-known remark from Albert Camus about his book *L'Étranger*: "In our society, any man who doesn't cry at his mother's funeral is liable to be condemned to death."

16. In Old Testament terms, according to *HALOT*, the heart (*lēv*) has a wide range of possible meanings: the physical organ (1 Sam 25:37); the "seat of vital force" (Ps 22:26); the inner self (Jer 4:18); moral inclination (Gen 6:5); determination (Gen 42:28); of the will (Num 16:28); attention, awareness or reason (Exod 9:12); the mind generally (Gen 8:21); conscience (1 Sam 25:31); generally in the middle of something (Prov 23:34); God's heart (Jer 32:39); etc. Ludwig Koehler, et al., *The Hebrew and Aramaic Lexicon of the Old Testament*, trans. M. E. J. Richardson, G. J. Jongeling-Vos, and L. J. De Regt, 5 vols. (Leiden: Brill, 2000). The term does not neatly map on any traditional categories of faculty psychology. In the New Testament, the Greek terms *kardia* (heart) and *psychē* (soul) have quite a bit of semantic overlap but not as metaphysical disjuncts to the body. According to BDAG, the heart has two primary meanings, (1) "the seat of all physical, spiritual, and mental life," and (2) the heart as the interior or center of something (e.g., the sea, Ezek 27:4). The first definition encompasses both physical life (Ps 101:5 LXX; 103:15 LXX) and a wide range of psychic dimensions, not merely willing: the entire inner life (Luke 16:15); conscious awareness (Eph 1:18); thinking (Luke 1:51); comprehending (Acts 16:14); remembering (Luke 2:19) ; the will (2 Cor 9:7); moral character (Jas 4:8); source of emotion and desires (Luke 24:32); and a dwelling place of heavenly powers (Rom 5:5). W. Bauer et al., *A Greek-English Lexicon of the New Testament and Other Early Christian Literature*, 3rd ed. (Chicago: University of Chicago Press, 2000). See Appendix A.

on the surface. When emotion surfaces, it reveals our deep drives such that the true nature of the soul is revealed. For example, Brian Borgman writes, "the emotions ... express the values and evaluations of a person and influence motives and conduct"; they "tell us what we really, really believe."[17] The implication is that we may be deeply mistaken about what drives us ultimately. Ed Welch visually represents this inside-out metaphor of agency as a heart inside a circle (Figure 1.1),[18] where the "heart represents the soul, the circle represents the body."[19] The heart represents the source of our agency, thus the source of emotion, excepting certain purely bodily feelings.[20]

Figure 1.1, Welch's Graphic of the Embodied Soul.

Fourth, if emotions are mental states, passively intruding mental states, emotional voluntarists tend to assume that by mere mental choosing, a person may alter mental judgments; I call this mental voluntarism. People may use internal speech to attack the propositional attitudes directly; or more indirectly, they may choose to channel their attention differently. For example, Brian Borgman writes, "I overcome anxiety by focusing on the consolations, the promises, you have given me in your Word."[21]

---

17. Borgman, *Feelings and Faith*, 103, 128.

18. Welch, "Sinners Learning," 70.

19. Welch, "Sinners Learning," 70.

20. Welch has a model of the mental life that is difficult to make sense of. In *Blame It on the Brain*, he suggests that certain abilities really do emerge out of brain activity such as "reason, conceptual abilities, and many other processes we consider distinctively human." However, he adds that moral behavior comes from the domain of the heart. There is a similar ambiguity about the source of emotion. "What about our emotions? Are they related more to the heart or the body? A brief response is that emotions are typically a response of the entire person, heart *and* body. But they can proceed from *either* the heart or the body. Depression, for example, when traceable to personal sin or guilt, is caused by the heart. Yet in future chapters we will see that depression can also be caused by bodily weakness." Perhaps the easiest way to explain it is that Welch seems to think feelings of depression come from the body while the emotion of depression comes from the heart, assuming emotion is a heart language. However, the directionality is always mind, by which he also means soul and heart, to body. Welch writes, "this unity suggests that the heart or spirit will always be *represented* or *expressed* in the brain's chemical activity. When we choose good or evil, such decisions will be accompanied by changes in brain activity. ... It is as if the heart always leaves its footprints on the brain." Welch, *Blame It on the Brain*, 38, 44, 47–48. See also Welch, "Emotions are a Language."

21. Borgman, *Feelings and Faith*, 130.

Finally, emotional duty is the moral impetus for applying mental voluntarism to our occurrent emotional states. If I had thought or believed something different, I might have avoided this illicit emotion. I am now in a state of emotional culpability for my thought or unbelief. I might escape this culpability by choosing to think or believe differently. Therefore, I must now choose to think or believe differently. It is easy to see how this makes emotion morally relevant since this definition characterizes emotion as a sort of alterable mental state, which may or may not correspond to God's revealed will. For example, to be anxious is to bring about or allow a certain sort of attitude grounded in the deep belief that God is not trustworthy (Matt 6:25–34) to give good things to his children (Matt 7:9–11).

A Psychological View

A psychological point of view is quite different. Consider Joseph LeDoux's description of anxiety. This description is from his earlier work; we will address his more developed view in Chapter 8. LeDoux sees anxiety as what happens in the brain and nervous system. It involves a complex reaction system involving parallel brain transmissions "to the amygdala from the sensory thalamus and sensory cortex. The subcortical pathways provide a crude image of the external world, whereas more detailed and accurate representations come from the cortex."[22] LeDoux calls these parallel tracks the high road and the low road (Figure 1.2).[23]

According to LeDoux, the amygdala functions as a sort of "hub in the wheel of fear," getting input from the sensory thalamus (stimulus features), sensory cortex (objects), rhinal cortex (memories), hippocampus (memories and contexts), and medial prefrontal cortex.[24] The amygdala, in turn, activates the autonomic nervous system to adjust the body for the situation (e.g., heart rate, blood pressure, and adrenaline). These reactions of the body reciprocally reinforce the memory to automate future emotional responses to similar situations; adrenaline strengthens memories associated with emotional reactions. In sum, for LeDoux anxiety is a sort of fully bodily reaction that conditions us for future contexts. For LeDoux,

---

22. Joseph E. LeDoux, *The Emotional Brain: The Mysterious Underpinnings of Emotional Life* (New York: Simon & Schuster, 1996), 164–65.

23. Adapted from LeDoux, *Emotional Brain*, 164.

24. LeDoux, *Emotional Brain*, 170.

to label this anxious reaction as "sin" is inappropriate because the bodily responses of anxiety are responses of unconscious processing; it is merely a legacy of evolutionary processes, which is largely outside of our control.[25]

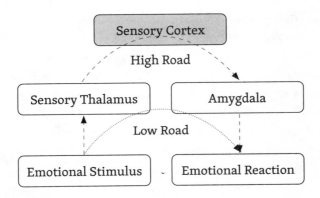

Figure 1.2, LeDoux's High and Low Road

Again, the two explanations of anxiety—one from theology and one from psychology—compete because they seem mutually eliminating. Moreover, choosing the right explanation is crucial for therapeutic recommendations; ontology underlies therapy. Each person will automatically adopt some explanation for the unwanted emotion. The explanation both helps us cope with the pain and governs strategy for coping. A significant benefit of counseling is reframing the story of what we are feeling. Counselors bring comfort because the way we explain our emotion to ourselves makes a great difference to how we experience it.[26] Competing assessments of the nature of emotion can add real distress to the sufferer.

25. Interestingly, LeDoux is very aware of the view he is rejecting. He writes, "Christian theology has long equated emotions with sins, temptations to resist by reason and willpower in order for the immortal soul to enter the kingdom of God." LeDoux, *Emotional Brain*, 24.

26. The first two steps of Jeffrey Schwartz's treatment of OCD are relabel and reattribute. In the first case, the person is to shift an urge like "I need to wash my hands again" to "I am having a compulsive urge." In the second case, a person is to attribute the urge to OCD. Jeffrey Schwartz, *Brain Lock* (New York: ReganBooks, 1996), xxi.

THE TREATMENT DILEMMA

Returning to our case study, suppose Mary goes to see her pastor. What sort of advice would she get? What if she goes to a clinical psychologist? The assumptions of the two stories yield very different therapeutic recommendations. I have no intention of framing these accounts as ultimately inconsistent but offer them as examples of the lay of the land when it comes to pastoral care within the American evangelical church. My examples, Brian Borgman and Joseph LeDoux, are in no way parallel in terms of expertise, but they perhaps can represent the real dilemma many parishioners face. I am not even suggesting that Borgman would address Mary's case exactly as his chapter on anxiety describes but present this chapter as an example of a typical moral and theological diagnosis of anxiety.

Brian Borgman treats anxiety in *Feelings and Faith*. While Borgman fails to give a definition of emotions, he describes them cognitively: "the emotions … express the values and evaluations of a person and influence motives and conduct."[27] So anxiety is sinful "most of the time" since our emotions "express our values and evaluations [and] … tell us what we really, really believe."[28] When Jesus addresses anxiety in Matthew 6:25–35, he diagnoses the problem with the words, "O you of little faith" (v. 30). Borgman adds, "Our *souls* are speaking, and our *innermost being is expressing* what we believe and whom we do not believe."[29] His prescription is likewise cognitive. We fight anxiety "by *knowing* what God has done for us and in us through his Son … [and] by *realizing* God did not give this fear to us."[30] We need to use biblical passages like Proverbs 18:10 and Psalm 56:3 to focus on the character of God. As Borgman writes, "I overcome anxiety by focusing on the consolations, the promises, you have given me in your Word."[31] The words "knowing," "realizing," and "focusing" seem to indicate that some cognitive work is needed—refocusing the mind on spiritual truths and expanding one's appreciation of the intensity or scope of them. I am using the word "work" here very intentionally, since anyone with any personal experience with chronic anxiety will understand that mental effort is work.

---

27. Borgman, *Feelings and Faith*, 103.
28. Borgman, *Feelings and Faith*, 128.
29. Borgman, *Feelings and Faith*, 128, emphasis added.
30. Borgman, *Feelings and Faith*, 129, emphasis added.
31. Borgman, *Feelings and Faith*, 130.

In the end, Borgman's advice to Mary might involve something like Calvin's notions of mortification, as self-conscious rejection of anxiety as sinful, and vivification, as giving mental attention to believing the promises of God.[32] To reiterate, anxiety for Borgman seems to be an intrusive mental state that shows how we truly disbelieve, and thus requires repentance.

Finally, to balance the picture, it is interesting to note the difference between Borgman's chapter on anxiety and his next one on depression. In this next chapter, he says that he takes depression "very seriously," and thinks, "It is a dangerous physician who throws a few Bible verses at those who are depressed and tells them just to have more faith." He adds, "The medical and physiological issues are complex."[33] This is not merely a difference in tone. What he has said about anxiety has assumed it is simply cognitive and related to the soul, while depression is assumed to be complex physiologically. Some of this difference may be accounted for by the fact that the term "depression" already has a chronic connotation; it is a technical psychological term.[34] However, Borgman seems to account for this by noting that the anxiety he is talking about includes "mental and emotional distress."[35]

What would Joseph LeDoux recommend for Mary? LeDoux would probably see Mary's condition as a sort of anxiety disorder, by which he means that anxiety has become "maladaptive" or "excessive in intensity, frequency or duration—causing the sufferer distress to the extent that his or her daily life is disrupted."[36] The problem is that Mary's combined brain and

---

32. Borgman, *Feelings and Faith*, 123. Obviously, I am not also considering the role of the Spirit in describing it this way. I am assuming that the Spirit is not more active in our thought work than in our offering our parts as "slaves to righteousness" (Rom 6:19). Borgman also writes, "As we come to this section, once again I pluck the same old string on the guitar of mortification: honestly evaluate any sinful emotions, patterns, or tendencies (Rom. 12:3). Be quick to confess and seek to forsake these patterns (Prov. 28:13)." Borgman, *Feelings and Faith*, 130.

33. Borgman, *Feelings and Faith*, 133. One wonders if perhaps the difference in tone arises from a personal encounter with serious depression but not with serious anxiety.

34. Borgman treats the following topics in Part 3 of *Feelings and Faith*: Mortifying Ungodly Emotions: (1) "An Introduction to Mortifying Ungodly Emotions," (2) "Sinful Anger," (3) "Unforgiveness and Bitterness," (4) "Fear, Anxiety, and Worry," and (5) "Depression."

35. Borgman, *Feelings and Faith*, 124.

36. Joseph E. LeDoux, *Anxious: Using the Brain to Understand and Treat Fear and Anxiety* (New York: Penguin Books, 2015), 11. LeDoux sees three contributing factors to anxiety disorders: biological factors, general psychological processes, and specific learning experiences (15–16).

nervous system is "doing what it is supposed to do—it's just doing it in the wrong context."[37] Mary, like other mammals, is equipped with "factory installed defenses" such as the "fight or flight [or freeze]" mechanism (sympathetic nervous system).[38] Anxiety is essentially when this system is triggered without the presence of real danger, but toward avoidance of the possibility of danger by some conditioned stimulus (e.g., a scream). Avoidance can become persistent because avoidance behaviors may seem to be rewarded by a person's not experiencing negative outcomes, which elicits an embodied false assumption of having prevented them.[39] Anxiety becomes a stimulus-response habit that works in conjunction with the sympathetic nervous system to create a physiological atmosphere of hypersensitivity to the mere possibility of dangers.[40]

Unlike some psychologists and psychiatrists, LeDoux would caution against chronic antidepressant treatment via SSRIs (selective serotonin reuptake inhibitors).[41] LeDoux's group found that "chronic but not subchronic [short term] administration" of SSRIs actually inhibited a crucial aspect of recovery.[42] While anxiety is not itself cognition, cognition can

---

37. LeDoux, *Anxious*, 16.

38. LeDoux, *Anxious*, 54. Cf. Walter Bradford Cannon, *Bodily Changes in Pain, Hunger, Fear, and Rage: An Account of Recent Researches into the Function of Emotional Excitement* (New York: Appleton, 1927), 187.

39. LeDoux, *Anxious*, 74.

40. LeDoux, *Anxious*, 313.

41. The popular level description of mental illness as a chemical imbalance is roundly dismissed by psychologists and psychiatrists on the grounds that it suggests a too simplistic assumption of the workings and etiology of mind-brain dysfunction. Most prefer an etiological account that is a blend between biological and psychosocial factors. Ronald Pies writes the following of the claim that, "Psychiatrists think all mental disorders are due to chemical imbalance": "In the past 30 years, I don't believe I have ever heard a knowledgeable, well-trained psychiatrist make such a preposterous claim, except perhaps to mock it." Ronald W. Pies, "Psychiatry's New Brain-Mind and the Legend of the 'Chemical Imbalance,'" *Psychiatric Times*, July 11, 2011, http://www.psychiatrictimes.com/couch-crisis/ psychiatrys-new-brain-mind-and-legend-chemical-imbalance. Robert Whitaker is on a veritable crusade against the psychiatric industry for this idea. See Robert Whitaker, *Anatomy of an Epidemic: Magic Bullets, Psychiatric Drugs, and the Astonishing Rise of Mental Illness in America* (New York: Broadway, 2010); Robert Whitaker and Lisa Cosgrove, *Psychiatry Under the Influence: Institutional Corruption, Social Injury, and Prescriptions for Reform* (New York: Palgrave McMillan, 2015).

42. Nesha S. Burghardt, Torfi Sigurdsson, Jack M. Gorman, Bruce S. McEwen, and Joseph E. LeDoux, "Chronic Antidepressant Treatment Impairs the Acquisition of Fear Extinction," *Biological Psychology* 73, no. 11 (June 2013): 1078; SSRIs are often used in conjunction with cognitive behavioral therapy (CBT) as a way of helping the patient to perform the necessary

have an impact on anxiety through memory.[43] LeDoux notes that when people consciously access memory, they actually form a new memory; this is a process called reconsolidation.[44] By revisiting triggers for anxiety, perhaps through a combination of talk and exposure therapy, it might be possible to dampen the memories—what LeDoux calls extinction—by integrating new cognitive content into them. Anxiety, on this view, is the nervous system's underlying defensive processes, which can be altered by cognition and experience. LeDoux says, "coping represents the cognitive planning of voluntary actions once we find ourselves in the midst of an involuntarily elicited emotional reaction."[45] Anxiety is morally neutral for views like LeDoux's; it is a physics problem with a psychological overlay. The overlay is the conscious explanation the feeling of physiological reactions. Treating it involves finding ways of reconfiguring the physics of the brain and nervous system.

The trouble for Mary is this: If she treats her anxiety as a direct manifestation of sin, she may find that the cycle of ineffective repentance from mental sin will very likely add a layer of spiritual anxiety to the other

---

mental adjustments in treating OCD. The most common type of cognitive behavioral therapy for OCD is exposure and response prevention (EX/RP). Very crudely, this is exposing the patient to triggers and asking them to suppress compulsive responses. Cf. Edna B. Foa et al., "Six-Month Outcomes from a Randomized Trial Augmenting Serotonin Reuptake Inhibitors with Exposure and Response Prevention or Risperidone in Adults with Obsessive-Compulsive Disorder," *Journal for Clinical Psychiatry* 74, no. 4 (April 2015): 440–46; Lindsay A. Bornheimer, "Exposure and Response Prevention as an Evidence-Based Treatment for Obsessive-Compulsive Disorder: Considerations for Social Work Practice," *Clinical Social Work Journal* 43 (2015): 38–49; Edna B. Foa et al., "Treatment of Obsessive Compulsive Disorder by Exposure and Ritual Prevention, Clomipramine, and Their Combination: A Randomized, Placebo-Controlled Trial," *American Journal of Psychiatry* 162 (2005): 151–61; E. B. Hembree, D. S. Riggs, M. J. Kozak, M. E. Franklin, and E. B. Foa, "Long-Term Efficacy of Exposure and Ritual Prevention Therapy and Serotonergic Medications for Obsessive-Compulsive Disorder," *CNS Spectrums* 8, no. 5 (2003): 363–71.

43. LeDoux sees the cognitive approach to emotion as problematic for two reasons. First, "much emotional processing occurs unconsciously and therefore ... there is more to an emotion than what we can glean from our introspections about it." For LeDoux, equating emotion with cognition is problematic both because different brain systems process cognition and emotion and because it is "possible for your brain to know that something is good or bad before it knows exactly what it is." He adds, "The hallmark of cognitive processing is flexibility of responses on the basis of experience. Cognition gives us choices." LeDoux, *Emotional Brain*, 69.

44. Karim Nader, Glenn E. Schafe, and Joseph LeDoux, "Fear memories require protein synthesis in the amygdala for reconsolidation after retrieval," *Nature* 406 (August 2000): 722–26.

45. LeDoux, *Emotional Brain*, 177.

sources. It literally adds iniquity to injury. One of the most common objects of OCD-type obsessions is a person's spiritual condition, i.e., scrupulosity.[46] If she is within the Reformed tradition, Mary will very likely begin to ask if she has been genuinely converted. Treating anxiety as willful sin often produces even more debilitating anxiety.[47] In cases like Mary's, the psychological story often becomes more compelling because the therapeutic recommendations of emotional voluntarism seem hopeless and false; many chronic sufferers simply cannot repent and believe their way out of the anxiety. In cases of serious distress, the dilemma is also more serious, psychology or Christian faith, but not both. There is a path out of the church that runs through the counselor's office.

As a redress to my concern, some biblical counselors embrace the dilemma, suggesting that emotion comes from the soul or heart unless it comes from the body, as with mental illness.[48] I do not wish to deny the

---

46. Religious OCD is categorized as scrupulosity. Statistics vary as to the prevalence of scrupulosity amongst OCD suffers (ranging from 5% to 33%), but it is a very common obsessional theme. In very religious societies, the rates of scrupulosity are as high as 50 to 60% in Saudi Arabia and Egypt, respectively; Jonathan S. Abramowitz and Ryan J. Jacoby, "Scrupulosity: A Cognitive-Behavioral Analysis and Implications for Treatment," *Journal of Obsessive-Compulsive and Related Disorders* 3 (2014): 140–49; cf. Jane L. Eisen, Wayne K. Goodman, Martin B. Keller, Meredith G. Warshaw, Lynne M. DeMarco, Douglas D. Luce, and Steven A. Rasmussen, "Patterns of Remission and Relapse in Obsessive-Compulsive Disorder: A 2-Year Prospective Study," *Journal of Clinical Psychiatry* 60, no. 5 (1999): 346–51; D. Mataix-Cols, I. M. Marks, J. H. Greist, and L. Baer, "Obsessive-Compulsive Symptom Dimensions as Predictors of Compliance with and Response to Behaviour Therapy: Results from a Controlled Trial," *Psychotherapy and Psychosomatics* 71 (2002): 255–62; Osama Mohamed Mahgoub and Hassan Babiker Abdel-Hafeiz, "Pattern of Obsessive-Compulsive Disorder in Eastern Saudi Arabia," *The British Journal of Psychiatry* 158, no. 6 (June 1991): 840–42. One study found that non-Catholics and Muslims are more likely to "endorse scrupulosity compared with other religious individuals." E. McIngvale, K. Rufino, M. Ehlers, and J. Hart, "An In-Depth Look at the Scrupulosity Dimension of Obsessive-Compulsive Disorder," *Journal of Spirituality in Mental Health* 19, no. 4 (2017): 295–305.

47. For example, many Christian OCD sufferers will develop grave concerns about their conversion. However, it is important to concede that from a traditional Protestant perspective, an inner state that is involuntary does not necessarily disqualify it from being called sin, or perhaps sinfulness. Denny Burk says, "All sinful desire springs spontaneously from our nature, but its unchosenness does not make it any less sinful." Denny Burk, "Is Homosexual Orientation Sinful?" *Journal of the Evangelical Theological Society* 58, no. 1 (2015): 110.

48. Again, I cite Edward Welch, "What about our emotions? Are they related more to the heart or the body? A brief response is that emotions are typically a response of the entire person, heart *and* body. But they can proceed from *either* the heart or the body. Depression, for example, when traceable to personal sin or guilt, is caused by the heart. Yet in future chapters we will see that depression can also be caused by bodily weakness." Welch, *Blame It on the Brain*, 44. This approach creates a guilty (sin) until proven innocent (illness) attitude toward negative emotion.

qualitative exceptionalism of mental illness, but the question is, how does one know if bodily illness is involved, especially in borderline cases? Just what is this illness? Is the body not always involved with emotion? To save the voluntarist theory, the theological approach seems to assume that we need to attend to how the body qualifies agency only when emotional dysfunction has reached a crisis.

Briefly, each side of this dilemma has problems. On the one hand, we must not abandon a theological framework that sees faith as in some sense opposed to anxiety.[49] Israel was to fear God and to take refuge in him (Ps 46:1-2). Isaiah 30:2-5 emphasizes that those who "take refuge in the protection of Pharaoh" will find that protection turn to shame. God's people were not to trust in military power (Ps 20:7), but to rest in "the Lord GOD, the Holy One of Israel," because "In returning and rest you shall be saved" (Isa 30:15). Anxiety is not trivial. Moreover, a materialist has only natural hope through natural channels of finding meaning (health, prosperity, achievement, etc.). Any psychology that cannot make sense of martyrdom is not adequately Christian.

On the other hand, emotional voluntarism has not adequately accounted for how the body qualifies agency. Anxiety is never merely a mental state. Mary's condition must be understood holistically. It simply cannot be understood apart from considering the functions of the sympathetic nervous system, including heart rate, epinephrine, and constricting of the arteries, and of the brain. Emotional voluntarism fails because it lacks two features: (1) tiered psychology and (2) a holistic relation between body and soul, which accounts for embodied plasticity.[50]

In the first place, our thoughts are not the same as the automatic judgments of our unconscious; we may disapprove of our being anxious, and our unconscious judgments are deeply intertwined with bodily inputs, including neurochemical conditions and inputs from the nervous system throughout the body. Emotions are quasi-independent of executive, conscious mental activity because they are responsive to inputs that are not directly cognitively mediated, via perception and our autonomic nervous

---

49. Our fear system is given by God for living in a fallen world where we will be exposed to danger. To be unafraid would be dangerous and foolish. I owe this insight to Eric Johnson. Danger, like the other aspects of the curse, was meant to drive humanity to dependence.

50. Again, my proposal is a sort of dualistic holism.

systems especially. Our psychology is tiered, possessing not merely conscious symbolic thought, but also the perceptive or adaptive unconscious
and physiological inputs. I will model how the two work together produc-
tively and reciprocally.

In the second place, emotional voluntarism fails to account for the durability of neurological plasticity. By plasticity, I simply mean the capacity to
take a shape (malleability) and hold that shape (durability). It is the capacity that enables habit formation. This use is somewhat idiosyncratic, since
the contemporary psychological literature assumes that plasticity refers to
the capacity to form new neuropathways. However, even this use assumes
that these new pathways perdure, that they are durable.[51]

Our bodies, especially our neurons, take a shape and hold that shape.
This is how memories form. So thinking itself takes place within physical
constraints. Every thought involves a neuropathway. The physicality of
our nervous system, including the brain, qualifies our emotions, making
them plastic, or capable of being habituated. The physicality of the body
plays an important role here by way of neuroplasticity, the nervous system's ability to form new, stable patterns of responsiveness to inputs.[52] It
takes time for us to form new memories and associations under the direction of our conscious thought.

Theologians who advocate emotional voluntarism tend to overestimate the power of thinking and underestimate the power of experience
to affect our emotions. Theologians might recognize how the body holistically qualifies how we think and make choices, leaving us open to emotional alteration and habituation by direct experience in a way that is not
entirely negative. By recognizing this, we may have the opportunity to

---

51. On my use of the term "plasticity," see Introduction, footnote 4n15.

52. Recent research on neuroplasticity, the brain's ability to change via connectivity, new
neurons, or neurobiochemical alterations, has been used effectively to treat psychological
disorders like obsessive compulsive disorder. Eberhard Fuchs and Gabriele Flügge give a
helpful overview of the last forty years of research in this area. Eberhard Fuchs and Gabriele
Flügge, "Adult Neuroplasticity: More Than 40 Years of Research," Neural Plasticity (2014): 1–10.
Jeffrey Schwartz has especially leveraged the notion that people can "change their own brain
chemistry" through "self-directed neuroplasticity" at the UCLA School of Medicine. Schwartz,
Brain Lock, xiv. Schwartz devotes a significant portion of his book The Mind and the Brain to
discussing the last few decades of research on neuroplasticity. He writes, "in what may be the
most remarkable form of neuroplasticity, scientists are seeing glimpses that internal mental
states can shape the structure and hence the function of the brain." The Mind and the Brain:
Neuroplasticity and the Power of Mental Force (New York: ReganBooks, 2002), 254.

value rightly the tangible ways the ministry of Jesus has inaugurated, but not consummated, kingdom life by his redemptive work and by the giving of the Spirit. We put on the reign of Christ progressively as we observe his commandments, limited by our finitude and by the lingering effects of sin, via natural and moral evil. We might have a robust eschatologically sensitive psychology, which brings nuance not only to our understanding of sin, but also of how God restores *shalom* within the triune economy.

RECOVERY PROJECT

This is a recovery project because, surprisingly, medieval theologians accounted for how the body qualifies agency better than many modern theologians have. The high medieval Christian tradition of Thomas Aquinas defended a tiered psychology comprising rational, sentient, and vegetative powers. The sentient powers are the middle tier between the higher rational powers, which are directly voluntary, and the lower vegetative powers, which are entirely involuntary. The two sentient powers are sense appetite and sense perception, such that these powers have a sort of cognition and volition (perception and passion) directly keyed to particular objects (experience) and independent of intellect and will.

The sentient powers operate holistically, as composite powers, involving material psychic spirits and the movement of the heart. According to the prevailing Galenist theory, the corporeal organ of the heart literally effects the movements of this passive power, i.e., passions.[53] Being a holistic function of a body-soul composite, passions might participate in humankind's rational nature, but only indirectly, or by persuasion. Aquinas said that they are governed only politically by the higher rational powers of intellect and will, not despotically.[54] In other words, these powers are only partly responsive to thinking and willing. Sense appetite naturally inclines and moves toward or away from particular goods or evils in direct response to the presentation of sense perception. But the sentient powers can become informed and habituated to move rationally over time by reason and will.

---

53. Thomas Aquinas, *ST*, 1.78.1. I will discuss Galenism more fully in the following chapter. I am referring to the prevailing medical theory inspired by Galen (AD 130–210), which persisted into the nineteenth century.

54. Aquinas, *ST*, I.78.1.

The proper subject of emotional habit for Aquinas was sense appetite. Because the sentient soul is a composite—functions holistically as body and soul—habit exists in both body and soul.[55] Medieval passions were plastic in this sense, possessing the capacity to form habits (*habitus*). Plasticity involves malleability and durability, the ability to be molded into a semi-permanent shape.[56] Habit (*habitus*), according to the mainstream medieval view, is a durable quality of these passions akin to character, by which human beings dispose well or badly toward their ends. Courageous people will not be moved immediately to fear by a daunting enemy because they possess a virtuous *habitus*. But how do they possess this? Again, the lower tier of the human psyche is directly responsive to experience. According to Aristotelian psychology, a courageous person becomes courageous by doing courageous things. In other words, a young Greek boy might be trained to overcome fear by killing spiders, then wolves, then by play-acting killing imagined enemies with blunt swords. The boy learns by experience to associate danger with the experience of overcoming it. Just as the plasticity of muscle grounds strength, so the plasticity of his lower psychological powers (sense appetite) grounds courage. He becomes well-disposed to overcome evil for the sake of some good. Sense appetite, a lower psychological tier, and habit were important categories with reference to sin and sanctification until relatively recently in theological psychology.

In the following chapter, I will describe this medieval tradition in more detail to set the stage for tracing how theological psychology developed up to the Reformation with the psychology of John Calvin. The point of this historical development covering the next few chapters is threefold: First, I aim to introduce a more nuanced set of conceptual categories that are the foundation of my constructive proposal. Perhaps surprisingly, the psychology of Thomas Aquinas is quite sensitive to the body's contribution to emotion. Second, I aim to contrast the holistic and tiered psychology of Aquinas with that of John Calvin. Third, I aim to suggest that the disappearance of psychological tiers and habit from Calvin's psychology does not arise from a deliberate rejection of the views of Thomas Aquinas.

---

55. Chapter 2 will clarify in what sense habit exists in the body for Aquinas.
56. See footnote 4n15.

2

THE PSYCHOLOGY OF
THOMAS AQUINAS

As just suggested, the first step in my argument is to get a more nuanced psychological language or conceptual system on the table, that of Thomas Aquinas. I wish to demonstrate how Aquinas's psychology is holistic, involving plasticity, and tiered. To do so, I explain his system in detail. I am focusing on Aquinas for two reasons. First, historically speaking, Aquinas's treatment of the passions is perhaps the most significant theological treatment of the passions. His importance so eclipses his contemporaries that Peter King calls it the "mainstream view."[1] It largely represents the thesis to which later medieval psychology is the antithesis, especially on the issue of sense appetite and its passions. Peter King notes, "Thomas Aquinas set the agenda for later medieval discussions of the passions: the masterful analysis in his 'Treatise on the Passions' (ST, IaIIae.22–48) largely eclipsed the work of his predecessors, discussing the material with such depth and clarity that later thinkers could do no better than to begin with his account, even when they disagreed with it."[2] The

---

1. Peter King, "The Inner Cathedral: Mental Architecture in High Scholasticism," *Vivarium* 46 (2008): 253.

2. Peter King, "Late Scholastic Theories of the Passions: Controversies in the Thomist Tradition," in *Emotions and Choice from Boethius to Descartes*, ed. Henrik Lagerlund and Mikko Yrjönsuuri, Studies in the History of the Philosophy of Mind 1 (Dordrecht: Kluwer, 2002), 229. Aquinas's influence continued into the early modern period. Susan James notes that in developing the context of the seventeenth century psychology of the passions, "the Scholastic interpreter who exerted the greatest influence on early-modern theorists of the passions was undoubtedly Thomas Aquinas." Susan James, *Action and Passion: The Emotions in Seventeenth-Century Philosophy* (Oxford: Clarendon, 1997), 30. However, it should also be conceded that certain details of Aquinas's psychology were almost immediately challenged and rejected

41

thoroughness of Aquinas's treatment of the passions is a unique feature, and this may be related to the importance of this topic to his overall theology. Alexander Pope recognizes that the *Summa Theologiae* is a sort of creative refashioning of the Neoplatonic *exitus-reditus* (emanation and return) theme, treating God (*Prima pars*), humanity (*Secunda pars*), and Christ and the sacraments (*Tertia pars*).[3] Moral theology lies at the center of the *Summa* and is the crucial hinge of the *exitus-reditus* theme. Mark Jordan writes, "I believe that Thomas wrote the *Summa* for the sake of the second part—that is, in order to situate the moral component of theology within a properly ordered account of the whole."[4] Moreover, the passions are at the center of his moral theology. So it is easy to see why his treatment of them is as detailed as it is.

Second, Aquinas's categories are valuable for contemporary theorizing in spite of their antiquity. His account of the passions is remarkably thorough and systematically integrated ethically, psychologically, physiologically, and theologically. I have already suggested that medieval psychology might be better positioned to integrate the discoveries of contemporary neuroscience than contemporary Reformed theology. Here I begin to substantiate this claim by showing how physiologically integrated Aquinas's theory is. His psychology is deeply intertwined with Galenist medicine. While I acknowledge that Galenism has been discarded as a medical theory, I am primarily interested in how Aquinas integrated the body into his psychology, however the body's actual workings may be described. The fact that medicine is integrated into Aquinas's view in a robust way contrasts

---

especially by influential Franciscans of the University of Paris and Oxford. Only three years after Aquinas's death in 1274, Étienne Tempier, the bishop of Paris, issued a ban of excommunication for teaching certain Thomistic and Averroist doctrines. Elsewhere King writes, "the native medieval tradition stemming from Augustine, supplemented by medical information from the Arabic commentators, were combined to produce a unique and comprehensive theory of the emotions. It was given its highest expression by Thomas Aquinas, who built on the work of many predecessors, most notably lean de la Rochelle and Albert the Great." Peter King, "Emotions in Medieval Thought," in *The Oxford Handbook on Emotion*, ed. Peter Goldie (Oxford: Oxford University Press, 2009), 174.

3. Alexander Pope, "Overview of the Ethics of Thomas Aquinas," in *The Ethics of Aquinas*, ed. Alexander Pope (Washington, DC: Georgetown University Press, 2002), 30.

4. Mark D. Jordan, "Ideals of *Scientia moralis* and the Invention of the *Summa Theologiae*," in *Aquinas's Moral Theory: Essays in Honor of Norman Kretzmann*, ed. Scott MacDonald and Eleonore Stump (Ithaca, NY: Cornell University Press, 1999), 97.

with more contemporary theological accounts of emotion. Moreover, Galenism was a good theory, at least formally speaking.[5]

I will also keep my heuristic question in view: How do these theologians account for the ways the body qualifies agency with their psychological categories, especially the faculties? I will offer brief evaluative comments on these questions following each major section of this chapter: (1) The Hylomorphic Powers of the Soul; (2) Aquinas's Physiology; (3) Acts and Passions; and (4) Habit and Virtue. In general, my argument is as follows: Aquinas's psychology is valuable because it is holistic, integrating physiological observations from Galenic medicine. The physiological aspect of his psychology, within his category of sense appetite, qualifies the extent to which emotions (i.e., passions) are rational and voluntary, but also establishes a top-down account of how virtue may be formed by reason's governance and the will's choice.

THE HYLOMORPHIC POWERS OF THE SOUL

Aquinas's view of the soul is composite, or hylomorphic, soul as form, body as matter; and tiered, distinguishing several levels of powers. His view of the soul, like that of his teacher Albert Magnus, is that the soul is the "first principle of life in those things around us that are alive" (*animata*; I.75.1; cf. I.75.5).[6] As the first principle of life, the soul is the form of the body and its mover. Together the body and the soul are one unified substance, rather than being the conjoining of corporeal and incorporeal substances.[7]

---

5. I mean that Galenism was actually a good theory in the sense that it saved the appearances, i.e., accounted for the empirical data. This phrase is from the Greek *sōzein ta phainomena*, which was first used of theories of celestial movement, attributed to Plato. In this sense the Ptolemaic theory of epicycles was formally a good theory, though it was also false. My concern is that appearances have to be accounted for in some way theoretically, and contemporary theological theories of emotion fail to do so with the physiological data. Cf. Pierre Duhem, *To Save the Phenomena*, trans. Edmund Dolan and Chaninah Maschler (Chicago: University of Chicago Press, 1985).

6. In-line citations are from Thomas Aquinas, *Summa Theologiae,* trans. Alfred J. Freddoso, updated 10 January 2018, https://www3.nd.edu/~afreddos/summa-translation/TOC.htm.

7. Richard Dales notes, "In order to save the unity of man, Aquinas sacrificed the completeness of the soul. He did not consider the soul and body as two existing substances; rather they have a common principle of existence given to the substance 'man' by the soul, as form." However, Aquinas is clear that, unlike the souls of animals, the human soul is subsistent (I.75.2, 6). He is clearly a dualist in this sense. Later Thomists wanted to preserve the language of substance for the soul itself in some sense but distinguished the soul as incomplete substance from the complete substance of body and soul. Richard C. Dales, *The Problem of*

Strictly speaking, a human being is not a soul, nor a body, but "the soul and body together" (I.75.4), a composite.

Aquinas argues that there are three types of souls: the souls of plants (vegetative soul), of animals (sensitive soul), and of human beings (rational soul). In human beings, these three souls are "numerically the same (*eadem numero*)" (I.76.3).[8] There are also four vital works that the soul performs: nourishment (*nutrimur*), sensory cognition (*sentimus*), movement (*motus*), and intellective understanding (*intelligimus*), both sense and movement being accomplished by the sensitive soul (I.76.1).[9] Nourishment is accomplished by the vegetative soul, which is the vital principle of plants. The sensitive soul of animals enables sensory cognition and appetition or perception and passions; the sensitive soul of animals subsumes the vegetative soul. Humans have a rational soul comprising intellect and will. The rational human soul subsumes both sensitive and vegetative souls and their powers.[10]

The relationship between the powers of the soul and the body is complex and tiered. As the soul is the form of the body, so the powers of the soul are the accidents of the soul's essence (I.77.6–7). The more imperfect and receptive the powers are, the more they are conjoined with the body. The intellective soul is not even exercised by means of a corporeal organ, since it must receive universal forms in its knowing (I.78.1). The sentient soul is exercised "by means of a corporeal organ, but not by means of any

---

the *Rational Soul in the Thirteenth Century* (Leiden: Brill, 1995), 108; Dennis Des Chene, *Life's Form: Late Aristotelian Conceptions of the Soul* (Ithaca, NY: Cornell University Press, 2000), 71.

8. Aquinas devotes Article 11 of *Questiones Disputate de Anima* to making this point. Daniel Callus goes into detail about the origin of the problem of multiple souls or multiple substances. Daniel A. Callus, "Origins of the Problem of Unity of Form," *Thomist* 24 (1961): 257–85.

9. Robert Miner, *Thomas Aquinas on the Passions: A Study of Summa Theologiae, 1a2ae 22–48* (Cambridge: Cambridge University Press, 2011), 13. Cf. Aristotle, *De Anima*, 413a21–416b31; all citations from Aristotle are from *The Complete Works of Aristotle: Revised Oxford Translation*, ed. Jonathan Barnes, 2 vols. (Princeton, NJ: Princeton University Press, 1984).

10. This arrangement corresponds nicely to the hierarchical spirit of the age where everything exists in the great chain of being and needs mediating links to everything else. The place of human beings was between the sentient animals and the immaterial angels. Human beings were the link between heaven and earth, possessing both the bodily characteristics of the animals and the perfective rational characteristics of God and the angels. In this sense a human being is a *microcosm*, a summing up everything animate, vegetative, animal, rational; and inanimate, the four elements in the cosmos. This language is from Nemesius of Emesa. Cf. E. Ruth Harvey, *The Inward Wits: Psychological Theory in the Middle Ages and the Renaissance*, ed. E.H. Gombrich and J.B. Trapp, Warburg Institute Surveys VI (London: Trinity Press, 1975), 2–3.

corporeal quality" (I.78.1). The corporeal qualities of hot, cold, moist, and dry are only required for appropriately disposing the sensitive organ. For example, in a Galenic view, bodily heat disposes the passions to anger. (More on Galenic medicine below.) Finally, the vegetative soul is exercised "by means of a corporeal organ and by means of a corporeal quality" (I.78.1). In sum, the lower the power, the more bodily involving, with the emotional capacities (sentient powers) being exercised by means of a corporeal organ and disposed by corporeal qualities (e.g., heat).

THE ARRANGEMENT OF THE POWERS

To understand how emotion arises within the psyche, it is crucial to understand the various powers and how they interact. The sensitive and intellective operate on external objects; they know, will, perceive, desire, etc. (I.78.1). These operations can be divided four ways by two disjunctions, intellective soul versus sensitive soul (higher versus lower faculties) and apprehensive powers versus appetitive powers (see Figure 2.1).[11] They are as follows: (1) intellect—the higher intellective power knowing being in general (*ens universale*); (2) will—sometimes called intellectual appetite; (3) sensitive apprehensive power—the cognitive power of the sensitive soul, sensing sensible bodies; and (4) the sensitive appetite—the appetite of the sensitive soul, responsive to the estimation of the sensitive apprehensive power. I will briefly describe the two lower powers and then the two higher.

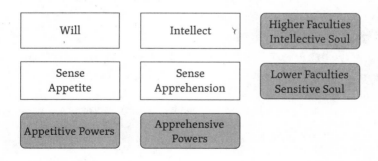

Figure 2.1, Peter King's Criss-Crossing Faculties

---

11. I am adapting Peter King's way of putting it. He metaphorically describes the mental architecture like a cathedral where the central area is "partitioned by two distinctions that criss-cross." Peter King, "Inner Cathedral," 254.

Sense apprehension is itself divisible into the powers of common sense, imagination, estimative power, and memory. Common sense merges the proper sensibles of each of the five external senses—e.g., color from the eyes, sound from the ears—into a perception of a single and unified thing. It enables the "reception of sensible forms" (I.78.4). This sensible form is captured and stored by the imagination (*phantasia*) by means of a phantasm, a material impression of an image, like a wax impression. Imagination is "a sort of treasury of forms that have been received through the sensory power" (I.78.4). The imagination is useful both for sensing what is present and for apprehending internally what is not present. The estimative power apprehends "non-sensory intentions" (I.78.4), and memory stores these. For example, the estimative power might apprehend something as harmful or agreeable (I.78.4). These four powers, common sense, imagination, estimative power, and memory, make up sense apprehension. But some further explanation is perhaps required about intention.

The word "intention" is akin to the more contemporary philosophical notion of intentionality,[12] which was derived from it. Intention in this sense expresses about-ness.[13] Intention in this older sense has nothing to do with the modern notion of intention as purposing to do something.[14] A mental state is about something if it represents an object, property, or state of affairs. It is possible to distinguish first-order intentions, simple representations of objects such as "wolf," from second-order intentions, such as "dangerous," involving a relation to the self.

In describing the estimative power, Aquinas speaks of its ability to capture non-sensible intentions, or second order intentions. These are properties of the object that are not available through mere perception, not through the five external senses, especially whether the object is to be pursued or shunned. The genius of this psychological feature is that it allows

12. I will use the two words, intention and intentionality, synonymously with no reference to purposiveness.

13. This medieval concept of intention received new life from the work of nineteenth century philosopher Franz Bretano (*Psychologie vom empirischen Standpunkte*, 1874). Bretano was a key transitional figure influential in both psychology and what came to be called phenomenology. Franz Bretano, *Psychology from an Empirical Standpoint* (Abingdon: Routledge, 2015); Alex Byren, "Intentionality," in *Philosophy of Science: An Encyclopedia*, ed. Sahotra Sarkar and Jessica Pfeifer (New York: Routledge, 2006), 405–410.

14. Nor has it anything to do with intension, a technical term in linguistics and formal logic.

Aquinas, and the Arabic philosophers before him, to explain the intelligent perception of animals apart from ascribing rationality to them. A favorite example cited from Avicenna is that of a sheep seeing a wolf as dangerous. The wolf is perceived through the senses and imagination, but perceiving it as dangerous comes from the estimative power. In the case of animals, the estimative power comes simply from natural instinct—though Miner suggests "[Aquinas] does not exclude the possibility" of animals learning.[15] Human beings differ in that they possess a special type of estimative power called the "cogitative power, which arrives at intentions of this sort through a certain comparison" (I.78.4). This comparative and instinctual[16] cogitative power is also called particular reason.[17] A key distinction between estimative power and cogitative power is that the latter apprehends an object but also apprehends the general notion of the end and the means to it (I–II.6.2) because it is informed by reason. In other words, particular reason can get beyond the apparent good to how the object fits within the broader arena of human good and the ends to achieve it. This distinction enables human beings to have more perfect voluntariness than animals.

The second lower power, sense appetite, is "an inclination that follows upon sentient apprehension" (I.81.2). It is made up of the concupiscible and irascible powers. By the concupiscible power, "the soul is simply inclined to pursue those things that are agreeable according to the senses and to avoid those things that are harmful." And by the irascible power, "the soul

---

15. Robert Miner, *Thomas Aquinas on the Passions*, 72. Miner might go beyond Aquinas on this point. He gives some examples of animal learning, but these are not examples that Aquinas himself cites. Miner sees himself as following Aquinas's example in "generating examples of the sort that Aquinas may or may not provide" (Miner, *Thomas Aquinas on the Passions*, 72n 12). Since Aquinas attributes the difference between human beings and animals to the collative power of human beings, this could imply that animals have no collative power. Since Aquinas does not specify with much detail the functions this power carries out for human beings, it might also be the case that animals possess merely a more rudimentary power of comparing intentions. In any case, it seems quite obvious that animals may learn from experience. To take an example from Miner, dogs begin to cower from masters who beat them, perceiving the master as dangerous.

16. Aquinas does seem to indicate that human beings have this collative power in addition to what animals have. In *ST* I.78.4, he writes, "man also perceives them through a certain comparison."

17. It is also important to note here that particular reason represents the mental processes that precondition the way we see particular items. The psychological function of particular reason is to saturate objects with second-level intentions. The term does not refer to discursive moral reasoning.

resists aggressors that pose obstacles to what is agreeable and that inflict harm" (I.81.2). The movements of the sense appetite are called passions or affections and involve bodily change (I–II.22.2–3). Among the concupiscible passions are love, hate, desire, aversion, joy, and sadness. Among the irascible powers are hope, courage, despair, fear, and anger. These powers obey reason, but only by political rule, that is by the persuasion of discursive reason through a practical syllogism.[18] In this way, the passions are sensitive to reason's rule, but not immediately and directly subject to its command.

Now to the two higher powers of the intellective soul, the intellect and the will, or intellective appetite. The intellect, unlike the sentient apprehensive power, pursues being in general (*ens in universali*). Its power to grasp universals enables it to make intelligible the presentations of the apprehensive power. The intellect has both active and passive aspects to it. Aquinas follows Aristotle in placing intelligibility not in things themselves, as Plato did, but in the power of the intellect to make things intelligible. The passive intellect receives from phantasms the forms of sensible objects, but it is the active intellect, which participates in the divine higher intellect, that gives these forms intelligibility. But even as the intellect gives intelligibility to phantasms, the phantasms are still necessary for any discursive reasoning, for "making use of already acquired knowledge" (I.84.7). Aquinas's view is not that of the Cartesian fully disembodied mind. The intellect may not operate "by means of a corporeal organ" (I.78.1), but it always operates in conjunction with sense.[19]

The will is an appetite to be distinguished from natural appetite, involving no cognition (e.g., nutritive appetite for health), and sentient appetite, involving the cognition of a singular sensible object. Just as the intellect knows being in general, the will pursues the good (*beatus*) in general as the ultimate end. The will is of course led toward singulars in its willing, but is to be distinguished from sense appetite because it does so "under some

---

18. We should note that Aquinas distinguishes between reason, which knows through the discursive syllogism, and intellect, which knows simply.

19. Aquinas rejected the Averroist doctrine that the active intellect is just a higher intellect that everyone shares, the unicity of the intellect, but argues instead that "within the human soul there is a power, derived from a higher intellect, though which it can illuminate phantasms" (I.79.4). A careful reader will notice that here Aquinas fails to be holistic by my definition but is far closer to it than Cartesian dualism.

universal notion" (*secundum aliquam rationem universalem*, I.80.2.ad.2). The
will is absolutely speaking a less noble power than the intellect; it follows
the intellect in its choosing. This view came to be called the intellectualist view.[20] Later Franciscan scholars especially criticized Aquinas for not
acknowledging the will's ability to choose against the intellect's approval.
But the will has some freedom in that it has the ability to move the intellect,[21] thereby preserving the will as mover of all the powers of the soul.
While the intellect dictates what the will pursues, the will also moves the
intellect to consider its object.

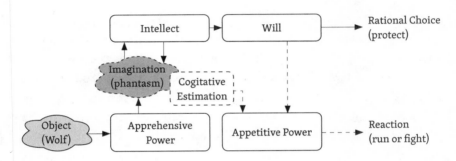

Figure 2.2, Thomistic Action Theory

Finally, to summarize Aquinas's action theory (Figure 2.2), sensitive
apprehension takes in and retains the form, not the matter, of the external
object as an individual phantasm. This phantasm is formed, evaluated, and
stored by a conjunction of the common sense, imagination, and estimative
power. The sentient appetite reacts in response to this apprehension, perhaps in accordance with reason and perhaps not, virtuously or viciously.

---

20. Bonnie Kent objects to this characterization of Aquinas as intellectualist. She sees
Aquinas's view as cooperative. Also, she notes that Aquinas differs from Aristotle in ascribing
the will a role in action theory. "Aquinas's theological works present an account of incontinence plainly inspired by Aristotle's teachings. The chief difference is that Thomas awards
a role to the will." Bonnie Kent, *Virtues of the Will: The Transformation of Ethics in the Late
Thirteenth Century* (Washington, DC: Catholic University of America Press, 1995), 105.

21. I–II.56.3: "Now it is possible for the intellect, like the other powers, to be moved by the
will; for an individual considers something in actuality because he wills to. And so insofar as
the intellect has an ordering to the will, it can be the subject of a virtue absolutely speaking."

The active intellect forms in the passive intellect an apprehension of this form by the means of the phantasm and submits its judgment to the will.[22] The will inclines and chooses what the intellect approves rationally unless drawn by the passions against reason to a merely apparent good. So, the person always acts in accordance with the will's dictates.

EVALUATION

The key points to recognize at this stage are three. First, by my definition, Aquinas's account of the human person is significantly more holistic than the Cartesian account, the thinking thing housed in the body. The soul is the form that vivifies and makes possible all human powers. Even the intellect, which functions without a bodily organ, to preserve the possibility of capturing universals, must rely on the lower embodied phantasms from the imagination for thinking. Aquinas's model of agency is also remarkably holistic. This holistic account of agency must account for the body's role in human action, and so promises intriguing prospects for incorporating plasticity. Second, his account of the powers of the soul is tiered, involving the higher intellectual powers and the lower sensitive powers. This distinction enables the possibility of internal conflict and contradiction, both appetitively and cognitively, respectively. I might perceive and desire something I think false and reprehensible, for example pixels in the form of sexual temptation. Third, I have mentioned already that the rational governance of the passions is political rather than despotic. In other words, since the lower powers are independent sources of cognition and appetite and can respond directly to objects, the intellectual powers do not have strict and direct control of the sentient powers. That the lower faculties possess some independence from the higher entails that an agent must govern the lower faculties indirectly, Aquinas's persuasion. I will suggest that this involves some combination of thinking, loading perception with framing concepts; and attention, governing the objects presented to the passions.

---

22. Gary Hatfield, "The Working of the Intellect: Mind and Psychology," *IRCS Technical Reports Series* 90 (1996): 10.

AQUINAS'S PHYSIOLOGY

So far, I have given only a general account of the soul and its powers. In order to clarify just how the body qualifies these powers, it is necessary to give some background on medieval medical theories. Doing so will illuminate some otherwise abstruse judgments Aquinas makes about the character of the passions, my primary interest. Aquinas's investment in Galenism is foundational to his account of how the body qualifies human agency. I will argue that the organic climate of the body qualifies the passions in a way that intertwines the moral and natural realms.

Aquinas's exact relationship to his physiological assumptions is difficult to discern for two reasons. First, while his teacher Albert Magnus shows quite a bit of interest in physiological exploration, Aquinas shows less interest in directly engaging the topic.[23] It is not immediately clear to what extent he assumes Albert's physiological convictions. Second, while Aquinas often cites a very important early advocate of Galen's medicine, Nemesius of Emesia (*De Natura Hominis*), he falsely attributes this work to Gregory of Nyssa. As a result, it is not clear whether Aquinas appreciates the physiological research of the kind Nemesius practiced, or whether he relies on Gregory of Nyssa's theological authority, as *auctor*.[24] In fact, if you add these citations to those from John of Damascene, twenty-three of which are copied or paraphrased from Nemesius,[25] the physician is the

---

23. George Reilly remarks, "[Aquinas] was not definitely interested in physiological psychology as such although he realized perfectly well the absolute necessity of an experimental basis for the rational psychology that was his chief concern; in fact, except for where necessary for clearness, or illustration he seems studiously to avoid any excursions into the physiological realm though many such opportunities were constantly presenting themselves." George Reilly, *The Psychology of Saint Albert the Great: Compared with That of Saint Thomas* (Washington, DC: Catholic University of America, 1934), 18.

24. As C. S. Lewis points out, the medievals were "very credulous of books. They find it hard to believe that anything an old *auctour* has said is simply untrue." C. S. Lewis, *The Discarded Image* (Cambridge: Cambridge University Press, 2012), 11. Emil Dobler writes, "dass Thomas Aquin Nemesius nicht einmal dem Namen nach gekannt haben dürfte – er zitiert immer Gregor von Nyssa und meint damit ein Werk des bekannten und angesehenen Kirchenvaters vor sich zu haben." Emil Dobler, *Indirekte Nemesiuszitate bei Thomas von Aquin: Johannes von Damaskus als Vermittler von Nemesiustexten* (Freiberg: Universitätsverlag Freiburg Schweiz, 2002), vii; cf. Emil Dobler, *Falsche Vaterzitate bie Thomas Von Aquin: Gregorius, Bischof von Nyssa oder Nemesius, Bischof von Emesa?* (Freiburg: Universitätsverlag Freiburg Schweiz, 2001), 121–27.

25. Dobler, *Indirekte Nemesiuszitate*, 99–127; 197–98. Dobler writes, "Das schmale und unscheinbare anthropologisches Bändchen *De natura hominis* wurde von seinem Landsmann Johannes von Damaskus eifrig benutz, so sehr, dass etliche Kapitel im II. Buch der *De fide*

third most cited source in the crucial *Sed contra* sections from I.71–102 to
I–II.6–89 of the *Summa*, only behind Aristotle and Augustine. What can be
stated positively is this: In the places where Aquinas's psychology touches
on physiological issues, he assumes a general Galenic physiology something
like that of Nemesius or of Albert Magnus, his teacher.[26]

The pre-Socratics had given a basic account of the four elements and
their opposable properties: earth (cold and dry), water (cold and moist), air
(hot and moist), and fire (hot and dry).[27] It was supposed that the human
body, along with all other material bodies, is composed of these four elements.[28] The elements combine to form the four humors: blood, choler or
yellow bile, melancholy or black bile, and phlegm, which are responsible
for the four complexions, "sanguine (hot and moist), choleric (hot and dry),
melancholic (cold and dry), and phlegmatic (cold and moist)."[29] The humors
are important for psychology because they were thought to have a direct
impact on psychological function by influencing the spirits (Greek *pnēuma*),
which performed various vital and psychological functions. Spirits, or air
once it has been inspired, represent the least material of material things,
and so sometimes were considered to be a crucial intermediary between
the material and immaterial world. They fulfill very important nutritive,
sensitive, cognitive, and volitional functions in Galenic psychology. They
act like Hermes to the Olympian gods; they are messengers and workers
for the entire compass of vital and psychological functions. The inhibition
or excitation of the spirits is a major channel through which physiology
encroaches on the control people have on their emotions.

---

orthodoxa eine wortgetreue Abschrift oder mindestens eine verkürzte Fassung der neme-
sianischen Vorlage darstellen." *Indirekte Nemesiuszitate*, ix.

26. Anthony Preus argues that a true Aristotelian action theory had almost completely
died out by this time, and that the prevailing theory was mixed with the Stoic conception of
pnēuma. This is consistent with my reading of Aquinas here. Preus notes the prevalence of
what he calls the Alexandrian synthesis of Aristotelian and Stoic theory that was proposed
by Alexander of Aphrodisias (c. AD 200), to which certain Renaissance Aristotelians reacted
wanting a purer peripatetic doctrine. Preus claims that the "Alexandrian synthesis was dominant in the [Aristotelian] tradition." Anthony Preus, "Intention and Impulse in Aristotle and
the Stoics," *Apeiron* 15 no. 1 (1981), 56.

27. Aristotle calls these the first order of the "three degrees of composition." The second
is bone, flesh, etc., and the third face, hand, etc. Aristotle, *Parts of Animals*, 646a13–24.

28. Harvey, *Inward Wits*, 4.

29. Jürgen Schäfer, "When They Marry: They Get Wenches," *Shakespeare Quarterly* 22 no.
3 (Summer, 1971), 205.

On a generic Galenic view,[30] spirits originate through respiration, literally inspiration, where air (*aer*) becomes spirit (*pnēuma*). When spirits are inspired, they are called natural spirits (*pnēuma physikon*) and are joined with the blood in the heart. Some of the spirits are transformed into vital spirits (*pnēuma zōtikon*) by the heart's fire as they pass into the right ventricle. Vital spirits provide the body vitality and warmth.[31] Some

---

30. Galen was by far the most important medical authority for almost a millennium and a half. The Galenic theory can be difficult to describe because Galen was unconcerned with systemically outlining the process of the circulation of *pnēuma*. When Michael Boylan gives his best effort at describing Galenic circulation, he concludes, "If this account is even close to being correct, then *pnēuma* can be understood as a vital entity that fulfills various mechanical functions that we now ascribe to: nutrition, natural vitality, assorted hormone-directed influences connected with desire, anger, quarrelsomeness, and generally all neurological activity." Michael Boylan, "Galen: On Blood, Pulse, and the Arteries," *Journal of the History of Biology* 40 (2007), 220.

31. The heart was thought either to be the center of thinking and willing, Aristotle's cardiocentric view, or merely the center of movement or willing, the brain accomplishing thinking, Hippocrates's cerebrocentric view. Aquinas does not clearly take sides on this issue, but is hesitant to criticize Aristotle's view (I–II.80.2). Moreover, Aquinas seems to affirm another corresponding Aristotelian doctrine, the cooling function of the brain. While explaining why man has the worst sense of smell, he notes that he has the largest brain (I.91.3). The idea is that for the brain to act as a radiator for the body, it must be cold and moist, but moistness is an impediment to smell. In this case, the most natural reading is that the brain operates as a radiator and is the location of the sense of smell, a reading which both affirms and contradicts Aristotle's view. While Aquinas does not commit himself to either view, he also reports the doctors' view for the location of the cogitative power, in "the middle part of the head" (I.78.4). Still, for Aquinas the heart is the "first principle of movement" (I.20.1 ad. 1) and plays a central role in the function of the virtues.

Hippocrates writes, "I hold that the brain is the most powerful organ of the human body, for when it is healthy it is an interpreter to us of the phenomena caused by the air, as it is the air that gives it intelligence. Eyes, ears, tongue, hands, and feet act in accordance with the discernment of the brain; in fact the whole body participates in intelligence in proportion to its participation in air." Hippocrates of Cos (460–377 BC), "The Sacred Disease," XIX, in *Hippocrates: With an English Translation*, trans. W.H.S. Jones, vol. 2 (Cambridge, MA: Harvard University Press, 1959), 179; Cf. Aristotle, *Parts of Animals*, 647a22–32: "Again, as the sensory faculty, the motor faculty, and the nutritive faculty are all lodged in one and the same part of the body ... it is necessary that the part which is the primary seat of these principles ... be one of the simple parts. ... For this reason it is the heart which in sanguineous animals constitutes this central part." There were also other defenders of the cardiocentric view including Praxagoras of Cos (fourth century BC), Zeno of Citium (third century BC), the Stoics of the second century BC, and Athenaeus of Attalia (first century BC). Enrico Crivellato and Domenico Ribatti, "Soul, mind, brain: Greek philosophy and the birth of neuroscience," *Brain Research Bulletin* 71 (2007), 330.

Manzoni writes, "early Christian theologians looked favorably at these cardiocentric theories and at the pneumatic, or spiritual, doctrines insofar as they were compatible with the Judeo-Christian beliefs contained in the Holy Scriptures." What made cardiocentric theories seem agreeable for theologians like Tertullian were biblical passages that seem to make the heart the seat of human character. T. Manzoni, "The Cerebral Ventricles, the Animal Spirits and the Dawn of Brain Localization of Function," *Archives Italiennes de Biologie* 136 (1998),

vital spirits are transformed into psychic spirits (*pnēuma psychikon*) at the stem of the brain, performing psychic functions and pulsing into the body to provide intelligence, movement, and sense to it.[32] The location for the functions of psychic spirits generally is the brain, and specifically its three ventricles or cells. The three ventricles, from front to back, were generally thought to house the (1) imagination or common sense, (2) cogitation or thought, and (3) memory.[33] This ordering of mental faculties represents the ordinary progression of knowing in Aristotle's *De anima*.[34] The functions of the internal senses are accomplished as the psychic spirits move through the ventricles.

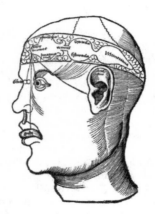

Figure 2.3, Ventricles for Psychic Spirits, Gregor Reisch, *Margarita Philosophica* (1503)

113; Tertullian, *De anima*, XV. He cites Ps 51:10; 139:23; Prov 24:12; Wis 1:6; Matt 5:28; 9:4; Rom 10:10; and 1 John 3:20.

32. The psychic spirits were transformed by means of the *rete mirabile* (lit. "wonderful net"). The *rete mirabile* is a cluster of veins and arteries found at the base of the brain in some animals, particularly large mammals, that Galen wrongly attributed also to human beings from his dissection of oxen. Manzoni goes into quite a bit more detail in "Cerebral Ventricles," 103–52. Cf. Chris Smith, Eugenio Frixione, Stanley Finger, and William Clower, *The Animal Spirit Doctrine and the Origins of Neurophysiology* (Oxford: Oxford University Press, 2012), 32–34; Stanley W. Jackson, "Galen—on Mental Disorders," *Journal of the History of the Behavioral Sciences* 5 (1969), 367.

33. Galen himself did not ascribe exact locations to these functions. This is first attested to Posidonius of Byzantium, but picked up by Nemesius. R. W. Sharples and P. J. van der Eijk, *Nemesius on the Nature of Man* (Liverpool: Liverpool University Press, 2008), 25.

34. Aristotle, *De anima*, III.2–4.

While Aquinas clearly held the traditional Christian view that spirit is incorporeal,[35] he also connected spiritual with Galenic processes. For example, Aquinas uses spiritual to refer to processes like vision in describing the spiritual change that takes place in the eye, "insofar as it receives the intention of a thing (*recipit intentionem rei*)" (I–II.22.2).[36] Aquinas explicitly references the material spirits of Galenic medicine. In the same place he rejects the spirit as mediator between soul and body, he affirms that the first instrument of the moving power is spirit, or breath (I.76.2, reply objections 2 and 3). There are also a number of passages where Aquinas talks about the workings of the material physiological spirits. For example, when he argues that violent heat is an effect of anger, he says, "since anger's movement … has the mode of incursion, which is what heat is proportioned to, the result is that anger's movement is a cause of a certain fervor in the blood and spirits that surround the heart, which is itself an instrument of the passions of the soul" (I–II.48.2).[37]

Finally, as I mentioned on the Galenic theory, the function of psychic spirit may be impeded by the quality of the body, particularly the quality of the humors (*chymos*, LSJ, "animal juices").[38] The humors were meant to be mixed harmoniously in the body, and this proper blend was referred

35. Aquinas asks, "Is an angel wholly incorporeal?" (I.50.1), to which he answers by citing Ps 104:4, "He makes his angels spirits." He contrasts corporeal and spiritual substances and beings throughout Question 50 of *Prima Pars*. Likewise there are a large number of instances throughout the *Summa* where the words "Spirit" and "spiritual" refer to the Holy Spirit and things pertaining to him.

36. Also, in a different sense, "A soul is both soul and spirit, a soul with respect to what is common to it and the other souls, viz., giving life to a body … it is called a spirit with respect to what is proper to itself and not to the other souls, viz., that it has an immaterial intellective power" (I.97.3); cf. I–II.72.2 reply obj. 3, "Even in the case of carnal sins there is some spiritual act, viz., an act of reason."
Moreover, Aquinas is clear that the soul is not "united to the body by the mediation of a corporeal spirit" (I.76.7). Since the soul is the substantial form of the body, not merely its mover, there is no accidental medium by which the soul is united to the body. If a mover and the moved can be thought of as distinct, then they might require a medium. But the soul and body are just one, which is to say being, and a medium is impossible with things that are one in a hylomorphic unity of form and matter (I.76.2).

37. See also I–II.44.1 on the effect of fear. In I–II.40.6, Aquinas says, "young people have high spirits, and so their hearts are bigger. But having a big heart makes one tend toward arduous tasks. And so young people are spirited and full of hope."

38. "[The spirits] can be altered by vicious humors and the badness of the surrounding air, and besides by noxious potencies or the poison of venomous animals." Temkin Owsei, "On Galen's Pneumatology," *Gesnerus: Swiss Journal of the history of medicine and sciences* 8 (1951), 186.

to by the Greek term *eukrasia* (LSJ, "good temperature," or literally "well mixed," as of a drink). In English, the word "temperament" captures it, but with the caveat that we remember the close connection to the qualities of cold, hot, dry, and wet. The humors themselves were of varying qualities like the seasons of weather: yellow bile (hot and dry), blood (hot and moist), black bile (cold and dry), and phlegm (cold and moist). Someone who was not well mixed would be described by the term *dyscrasia*. The ancient doctors considered this to work as follows: Things like inherited traits, seasons, exercise, or even food could impact the sorts of humors the body produced. If someone eats a cold and moist food like barley, this would tend to produce phlegm,[39] which might plug up or slow down the flow of spirit in the arteries and veins.[40] Furthermore, too much cold, and one might be inflicted by a cold disease, and likewise with too much hot. So vicious humors, bad air, bad weather, bad food, or even psychological passions, something like sudden emotion, can severely impact the proper functioning of psychic spirits.[41] The point is that the care of the body is an indirect way of governing the passions.

Aquinas definitely does echo the doctors' view that the qualities of the body, the humors, have an impact on the function of the sensitive appetite. He says that the sensitive soul operates by means of a corporeal organ, and "hot and cold and moist and dry and other corporeal qualities ... are required only for appropriately disposing the organ" (I.78.1).[42] Someone who is out of balance with respect to the humors is unhealthy (I–II.73.3),[43]

---

39. Galen, *Galen: On the Properties of Foodstuffs (De alimentorum facultatibus)*, trans. Owen Powell (Cambridge: Cambridge University Press, 2003), 474. He writes, "For he who knows that barley is cold and moist by nature, and also understands how to recognize the mixtures of bodies, both those that are innate and those that occur in an acquired condition, will use barley for food appropriately."

40. Interestingly, a phlegmatic temperament was not necessarily agreeable, since cold contributes to inactivity, and even femininity. Jürgen Schäfer illustrates how this connection works out in Shakespeare, especially in relation to the gender and characteristics of children. Schäfer, "When They Marry."

41. Jackson, "Galen," 367.

42. Aquinas explains that "the human body had to be made from the matter of the four elements in order that man might share something in common with the lower bodies, constituting, as it were, a certain middle ground between spiritual substances and corporeal substances" (I.91.1).

43. "[T]he good of health consists in a certain measure in the humors that is appropriate to an animal's nature" (I.73.3).

and will be more prone to certain passions, and by extension, certain vices. For example, "a man is disposed toward getting angry insofar as he has a choleric temperament. ... And so someone who is disposed by his natural temperament toward anger gets angry more readily" (I–II.46.5). Aquinas also mentions the humors along with the spirits when talking about "the devil's interior operation" (I–II.80.2). The manipulation of spirits and humors by the demons can give rise to temptation through the soul's perceiving and desiring.

In sum, Aquinas assumes a generic Galenist view of physiology. However, it must also be conceded that physiology is not a central focus of Aquinas's *Prima Secundae,* but an important background.

EVALUATION

The physiological background of Aquinas is important because it highlights the extent to which the lower powers were subject to bodily conditions like youth, temperament, and experience. Insofar as his moral theology was concerned with the habits of the passions, it is also conditioned by the organic climate of the body; the moral and natural realms are intertwined in the composite faculty. To cite just one example, Aquinas admits that someone with a choleric temperament, a high proportion of choler, is predisposed to anger (I–II.46.5). In today's language, this person might measure low in agreeableness and high in neuroticism according to the Big Five Inventory (BFI) personality taxonomy.[44] This person might also be diagnosed with some sort of disorder such as intermittent explosive disorder.[45] The DSM lists both environmental and physical risk factors: "Research provides neurobiological support for the presence of serotonergic abnormalities, globally and in the brain, specifically in areas of the limbic system (anterior cingulate) and orbitofrontal cortex in individuals with intermittent explosive disorder."[46] In other words, where Aquinas sees a

---

44. O. P. John and S. Srivastava, "The Big-Five Trait Taxonomy: History, Measurement, and Theoretical Perspectives," in *Handbook of Personality: Theory and Research,* ed. L. A. Pervin and O. P. John, vol. 2 (New York: Guilford, 1999), 102–38.

45. *DSM-V,* 466–69. Diagnostic criteria include recurrent behavioral, physical, or verbal aggression occurring twice a week for three months or involving damage or injury three times within a twelve month period; grossly out of proportion responses; unpremeditated outbursts; marked distress or impairment; and be at least six years old.

46. *DSM-V,* 468.

chronic case of too much choler, modern psychiatrists might see too little serotonin.[47] For now, I merely wish to note that the issue of temperament is a part of Aquinas's moral theology and that this is one way the body qualifies moral agency. In what follows I will describe the nature of the passions and the extent to which they are active or passive in light of this physiological background. What we will see is that the plasticity—habit forming capacity—of the sensitive appetite gives the passions a "curious in-between status" with regard to rationality and voluntariness.[48]

ACTS AND PASSIONS

Having covered human powers and the physiological background, we come to the core treatment, a consideration of a human being's acts (I–II.6–21) and passions (I–II.22–48). Generically acts are the ways a human person can function as an agent, or can do something, and passions are the ways a human person is a patient, having something done to them. These clear categories are a very helpful conceptual platform for understanding human emotion. Are emotions active or passive? Are they something a person does or something a person suffers? The answer requires both understanding Aquinas's notion of the passions and a consideration of how his understanding maps with contemporary terminology. I will argue that Aquinas's account of the passions categorizes them as neither purely passive nor purely active. His model preserves the essential bottom-up passivity of the passions but within an overall framework of agency that is top-down with some bottom-up reciprocity (e.g., emotion influences reason). Aquinas conceived of agency as coming from the choice of the higher faculties while acknowledging a certain independence of the lower faculties.

---

47. Lee Anna Clark and David Watson note the similarities between the ancient notion of temperament and modern trait psychology. They write, "Two aspects of this ancient formulation remain alive in current theories of temperament: (1) Biological factors are seen to underlie observable characteristics, and (2) emotions are seen as core and defining features of temperament. ... Researchers today investigate serotonin deficits, the noradrenergic system, and mesolimbic dopaminergic pathways rather than imbalances among the humors, but the recognition that behavior is partly a function of physical characteristics was a remarkable insight." Lee Anna Clark and David Watson, "Temperament: An Organizing Paradigm for Trait Psychology," in *Handbook of Personality*, ed. Oliver P. John, Richard W. Robins, and Lawrence A. Pervin, 3rd ed. (New York: Guilford, 2008), 265.

48. Robert Pasnau, *Thomas Aquinas on Human Nature* (Cambridge: Cambridge University Press, 2004), 257.

In the introduction to his section on action, Aquinas makes a distinction between acts that are proper to human beings and acts that are common to human beings and other animals. This distinction divides what are most properly called actions from passions. In other words, only acts that are perfectly voluntary—as opposed to imperfect voluntariness, which can exist in animals—are properly acts. And voluntariness involves, "(a) an apprehension of the thing that is the end, but also (b) a cognition of the concept of an end and (c) a cognition of the relation between the means ordered to an end (*quod ordinatur in finem*) and the end itself" (I–II.6.2). Only a human being can choose because only a rational agent can discern beyond the apparent good to the good end, and only a rational agent can situate a particular act within the ordered pursuit of beatitude. Acting involves understanding the proper end, discerning the means to it, understanding the circumstances, apprehending the proper order of goods, willing, commanding the execution, etc.

Passions are the acts of a passive power that are common to human beings and animals but do not involve rational voluntariness, at least in the occasion of acting (I–II.41.1). Like the tutored reflexes of a good pilot, human passions are regulated by reason because they may be habituated by longstanding voluntary intention. (More on this below.) Aquinas adopts the definition of passion of John of Damascus: "A passion is a movement of the sentient appetitive power upon one's imagining something good or bad" (I–II.22.3). Aquinas is quick to point out that "a passion properly speaking exists when there is a bodily change (*ubi est transmutatio corporalis*)," so this must take place in the sentient appetite, which is a composite of body and soul (I–II 22.3).

In what follows, I will analyze the nature of passions by addressing five questions: (1) How is sensitive appetite distinguished from intellectual appetite? (2) How are they ordered? (3) How does the body's involvement in passions impact their moral status? (4) What sort of motion is involved with passions? (5) How does the body condition the passions?

Sensitive and Intellectual Appetites

How is sensitive appetite distinguished from intellectual appetite? The first metaphysical clarification to make is how it is possible for the two appetites to be at odds with each other. The two appetites differ both with

respect to the sorts of goods toward which they incline and with respect
to the objects that move them.

First, sensitive and intellectual appetite incline toward different goods,
sensitive appetite toward apparent goods and intellectual appetite toward
universal good. In Aquinas's metaphysics, all appetite is simply inclination directed toward something under the aspect of good or toward good
itself (I-II.8.1). To the modern reader, the simple notion of inclination does
not adequately capture the degree to which appetite is metaphysically
freighted. For Aquinas, all things in the universe have inclination, even
a rock inclines downward, and each thing inclines toward its own good.[49]
Moreover, human inclination is toward perfection of human essence,
convertible with beatitude.[50] Within human nature, the various powers
contribute to human perfection and beatitude, but do so by inclining to
different ends. For example, the natural appetite of the vegetative soul
inclines toward nutrition, growth, and generation (I.78.1). While both
sensitive and intellectual appetite incline toward apprehended goods
(cognized goods, I-II.8.1), sense appetite inclines toward apparent goods,
apprehended objects of perception. Intellectual appetite inclines toward
the universal object good or some individual under the concept good (I.80.2;
ad. 2). Sense inclines toward tasty food; intellect reminds us that it is bad
for us.

Aquinas also distinguishes the two appetites by the objects that move
them. While sense appetite is moved by an external object, intellectual
appetite is moved by an internal principle, pursuing the object of a goal

---

49. Aquinas's argument for inclination being directed to the good is something like this:
Inclination is always toward something similar and appropriate to itself; a being is similar
and appropriate to some sort of being; inclination in a being is toward some sort of being;
and being is convertible with good (I.6.3 arg. 1); Therefore, inclination is toward the good.

50. Mere existence is the first act of being, but the act of inclination in the accidental
powers is toward the second act of being, perfect being. Only God's *esse* (act of being) is the
same as essential (what he is). For human beings to desire perfection is to desire God, who
is himself perfect *esse*. In I.6.1 ad. 2, Aquinas says, "In desiring their own proper perfections,
all things desire God Himself insofar as the perfections of all things are certain likenesses of
the divine esse." Aquinas writes in I-II.2.8, "But the object of the will, which is man's appetite,
is the universal good, just as the object of the intellect is universal truth. From this it is clear
that nothing can put man's will to rest except the universal good. But the universal good is
found only in God and not in any created good, since every creature has participated goodness.
Hence, only God can satisfy man's will—this according to Psalm 103:5 ('He satisfies your desire
with good things'). Therefore, it is in God alone that man's beatitude lies."

or end. What makes the movements of the sensitive appetite passions is that they require this external object for motion.[51] These appetites must be acted upon by an external object. But we must not think that the external object determines the passive power. The sensitive appetite is meant to be rightly ordered under the higher powers, informed and directed by them. In this way the passive powers, sense perception and appetite, are framed by the top-down ordering of the active powers, intellect and will, couching the passivity of the passions in the framework of general inclination and activity of the agent. The passions may be in the driver's seat in the moment, but overall the rational powers are.[52]

THE ORDERING OF SENSITIVE APPETITE

But how does this work? How are the rational active powers in the driver's seat? How do they bring agency to the passive powers? There are two key components enabling the active powers to exercise top-down rule on the passive ones: the intellect provides concepts and syllogisms to the cogitative power (i.e., practical reason), and the will directs all the powers.

First, passions are influenced by the sort of representations to which they respond. All passions are responsive to some kind of imagining, either by actual perception of a present object or by imagining in the absence of one. In both cases, passions respond to a *phantasia*, an image or appearance.[53] As I indicated above, the sensitive apprehensive powers—common sense, imagination, cogitative power, and memory—work together to form intentional representations (e.g., wolf as dangerous). Common sense encodes the impression of "wolf" in our imagination, which stores them. Cogitative power provides second-order intentions like "as dangerous," and memory stores these. The cogitative power is key because it brings together these

---

51. Peter King puts it this way: "Active potencies enable their possessor to 'do' something, whereas passive potencies enable their possessor to 'suffer' or 'undergo' something. This intuitive sense is captured in the idea that the reduction of a potency to act requires a cause or explanation: those potencies whose actualization is due to an internal principle are active potencies; those potencies whose actualization is due to an external principle are passive potencies." Peter King, "Aquinas on the Passions," in *Aquinas's Moral Theory: Essays in Honor of Norman Kretzmann*, ed. Scott MacDonald and Eleonore Stump (Ithaca, NY: Cornell University Press, 1999), 2

52. This is perhaps the crucial difference between ordinary and clinically disordered passions; in the latter case, reason is no longer governing overall.

53. A passion "follows upon an act of an apprehensive power" (*ST* I–II.46.2).

intentions (I.81.3) by the universals supplied by reason (e.g., the first order
intention, "wolf") and evaluates the objects with second order intentions
like "as dangerous." It does this immediately by a sort of quick judgment
(I–II.45.4). We do not merely see a wolf but see it as dangerous.

This is the temporal sequence. What the imagination apprehends
under the aspect of the cogitative power is prior to and independent of
the intellect's apprehending for any particular perception.[54] When persons
perceive objects under some aspect, good, evil, present, absent, arduous,
etc., the passions are immediately responsive to this aspect. The cogitative power responds without consulting the intellect. But this response
is also informed by reason prior to any particular apprehension. This is
why Aquinas states that particular reason (cogitative estimation) is "apt
to be moved and directed" by reason in applying its universal judgments
to particulars (1.81.3). In other words, human thoughts inform subsequent
quick judgments.

Second, the will plays a crucial role in modulating passions. It is not
reason alone that modulates passions, but the decisions and goals of the
will. A wolf is dangerous only because it threatens some prior inclination
toward good ends, e.g., life and happiness. This is the broader sense in
which the will directs all the powers of the soul to the good end in general
(I.82.4). We might call this the will's power to orient the soul. The will also
rules the sensitive appetite as regards execution. Unlike sheep, human
beings may stand unmoved in the face of a dangerous wolf—whatever
the passions may be doing—because the body awaits the command of the
will (I.81.3). This is why virtue exists in the will "more than in the irascible power or concupiscible power," though it exists too in these "insofar
as they participate in reason" (I.56.6, 4).

Let me illustrate with a brief example. Human beings are not determined to eat chocolate cake; we may resist our desire. But we also can

---

54. Aristotle, *Metaphysics*, 1010b1–3: "not everything which appears is true. Firstly, even
if sensation—at least of the object special to the sense in question—is not false; still appearance (*phantasia*) is not the same as sensation." The idea here is that while sensation never
errs, it is possible to misidentify a *phantasia*, either by obliteration of the impression in the
soul or by improperly identifying the impression. Cf. Aristotle, *De Anima* 428b18–25; Plato,
Theaetetus, 191c1–e1; Aquinas writes, "the sentient power does not collate and inquire into a
thing's singular circumstances, but instead makes a quick judgment" (I–II.45.4). All citations
of Plato are from *Plato: The Collected Dialogues including the Letters*, ed. Edith Hamilton and
Huntington Cairns (Princeton, NJ: Princeton University Press, 1961).

alter our desire for it. We may govern our desires by our rational powers by supplying concepts to cake such as "unhealthy" or by pursuing goals that are inconsistent with eating cake (e.g., losing weight). But this alteration of desire happens only with great difficulty. While our passions are still inclined to cake, the will needs to inhibit our eating of it. And it is imaginable that someone who has not tasted sugar for ten years may not even have the inclination to do so, reason and will having so thoroughly reinforced this intention. Within human persons the passive acts of sense appetite are framed within the active goals of human agency.

The distinction between rational appetite and sense appetite should now be clearer. The will in conjunction with reason orders all the powers to human good and provides for the senses both the concepts and the inclinations to order the passions properly. Sense appetite sits underneath rational appetite, not as an inherently irrational force to be eliminated, but rather as an integral aspect of the human pursuit of the human good, being rightly governed by the higher powers of reason and will. Sense appetite has its own inclinations, which are not dominated by rational appetite but governed politically by it. The distinction between the two permits the possibility of conflict even while the inclinations may each be pursuing genuine goods. This is what I mean by a tiered psychology. When sense appetite takes in an apparent good, such as a desirable fruit, it rightly desires the fruit as desirable, but this appetite may need governance by reason's "thou shalt not eat of it" (Gen 2:17 KJV), reason supplying the intention as unlawful. But when sense appetite is governed appropriately by reason, it performs a function within the virtuous person to aid the performance of the good consistently and with ease.

The Nature of a Passion

This structural ordering seems to make sense phenomenologically speaking, but there is still a mystery: the fact that a person possesses two appetites does not itself explain why the governance of the lower by the higher is merely political. The political metaphor assumes that emotions are somewhat difficult to change.[55] Just as people assume their own interests are

---

55. Again, I have defined plasticity as involving malleability and durability. Because our bodies can take durable new forms, plasticity grounds habit formation.

ultimate, so also the passions make apparent goods ultimate and need
governance. The question remains, why does it make sense that I might
overcome craving for chocolate cake only with difficulty and over time?
For Aquinas, embodiment has a morally significant role to play in emotion
because it contributes to the complex habits of virtue and vice. How does
the body's involvement in passions impact their moral status?

The following section will clear up confusion about passion being a
pejorative term for Aquinas and establish a preliminary description of
how the body is involved in passions. If we misunderstand how the body
is involved in passions, we will fail to recognize the true nature of holistic
human good. I am especially concerned to avoid both angelism and animalism. By angelism, I mean the failure to consider how human goodness
must be embodied, and by animalism, I mean the failure to consider how
the rational powers give quasi-rational agency even to our lower, more
embodied powers. In what follows I trace out how the body is relevant to
Aquinas's moral theology. We must attend to two paradoxical facts: (1) the
passions are the center of Aquinas's moral theology; and (2) the passions
can only exist per se in the body.

Passions and Virtue

First, the passions are at the center of Aquinas's moral theology. Aquinas
explicitly rejects the pejorative Stoic notion of passions as disturbances.
Not all passions are bad, only immoderate ones (I–II.24.2). He very diplo-
matically explains that the Stoics condemned all passions because they
failed to distinguish between the sentient and intellectual appetite. They
called reasonable movements of the appetitive part an act of will, and
unreasonable ones passions. So by definition, passions are "sicknesses of
the soul" (I–II.24.2).[56] If the Stoics had distinguished sentient appetite, they
might have recognized that it too may have reason-moderated passions.
Even though every passion involves something "added to or subtracted
from the heart's natural movement," passions "need not always depart from
the order of natural reason" (I–II.24.2 ad. 2). Unlike Augustine,[57] Aquinas

---

56. Aquinas here cites Tully in *De Tusculanis Quaestionibus*, 3.

57. Augustine—who notes that the words perturbations (*perturbationes*), affections (*affectiones*), emotions (*motus*), and passions (*passiones*) are sometimes used interchangeably—prefers to use *motus* and *affectiones* when describing "these emotions and feelings that spring from

often uses passions in a positive sense and sometimes interchangeably with affections (contra Dixon).[58]

In contrast to the Stoics, Aquinas suggests that passions are essential to virtue. Generically, passion simply refers to "the condition of being acted upon,"[59] responsiveness, or receptivity. This use may be expanded positively, as when medicine brings health, or negatively, as when disease brings illness (I–II.22.1; I.79.2). While the negative use is most properly a passion (I–II.41.1), Aquinas refers both to favorable and unfavorable movements of the sense appetite as passions. This positive use of passions enables Aquinas to connect them to virtue. He writes, "If, as the Stoics posited, what we are calling 'passions' are disordered affections, then it is clear that a perfect virtue exists without any passions. On the other hand, if what we are calling 'passions' are all the movements of sentient appetite, then it is plain that those moral virtues that have to do with the passions as their proper matter cannot exist without the passions" (I–II.59.5). Consequently, Aquinas often speaks of virtuous passions and suggests that virtue is seated

---

love of the good and from holy charity," preserving *passiones* for the "morbid and disordered passions." Augustine, *City of God*, XIV.9.

58. Thomas Dixon remarks, "These terms [*motus* and *affectus*], which can both be rendered as 'affections', referred to acts of will, both in Augustine and Aquinas, and are to be contrasted with *passiones*, which for both writers were not active movements of the will but passive movements of the lower, sensory appetite." Dixon adds that affections may be bad or good, and passions need not be sinful, but "there was rarely any reference to a positively virtuous passion." The picture here is that passions may be neutral insofar as they are controlled by reason, but when they exert themselves on the human agent, the effect is bad, similar to the Stoic view. Thomas Dixon, *From Passions to Emotions: The Creation of a Secular Psychological Category* (Cambridge: Cambridge University Press, 2006), 48.

Nicholas Lombardo notes that there are some "serious problems with [Dixon's] reading of Aquinas." In addition to passions being essential to virtue, Aquinas can sometimes use passion and affection interchangeably, even in instances where there is bodily modification. Yet because passions, strictly speaking, involve bodily change, they need to be differentiated somewhat. Lombardo summarizes, "all passions of the soul are affections but not all affections are passions." Nicholas E. Lombardo, *The Logic of Desire: Aquinas on Emotion* (Washington, DC: The Catholic University of America Press, 2011), 16n61, 76. There are affections that are not passions, like those of the intellectual appetite that Peter King calls "pseudopassions," since they "do not involve any somatic reactions or indeed any material basis at all." King, "Aquinas on the Passions," 105. Loosely, these are movements of the will. Like the passions, they rely on an object, but unlike them, they express immediate agency, since they are ordered to the universal rational conception of good, beatitude (I–II.6.2). Additionally, Lombardo claims that "[v]irtuous passions may well respond to abstract ideals, either by being shaped by rational considerations or by sharing by overflow in the affections of the will." Lombardo, *Logic of Desire*, 16–17n61, cf. 76. Aquinas claims that we desire some things "because of reason" (I–II.31.3; 34.1, 4).

59. *OED*, "passion," III.11.

in the passions, not merely the intellect or will (I–II.56.3–6).[60] Even the
virtue of justice, which Aquinas connects with the intellect, "cannot exist
without passion" (I–II.59.5).

Moreover, just as appetite plays a central role in drawing humanity
back to God in Aquinas's *exitus-reditus* scheme, so also the passions represent a sort of pinnacle of restoration and are essential for true beatitude.
Paul Gondreau eloquently argues that the emotions also play "a necessary
first step in our striving for happiness, in our attaining the end of seeing
God" by enabling us to enjoy "bodily goods," which, while not giving us
fulfillment, still are goods and can order us to the ultimate good.[61] The role
the passions play in Aquinas's moral theology is evident both in the size
of his treatment of the passions, the largest treatment in the *Summa*, and
in its location.[62] Gondreau writes, "[There is a] moral vision of human
affectivity implied in Aquinas's decision to place his systematic study on
emotion, the treatise on the passion ... in the part of the *Summa* that deals
with morals." Later Gondreau writes, "In order to break ranks with the
Stoic-inspired school of thought, then, and to stress that we cannot secure
a happy life—the goal of moral action—without the emotions, Aquinas
takes the unprecedented step of situating the passions at the heart of his
study on human morality."[63]

---

60. Lombardo, *Logic of Desire*, 16n61.

61. Paul Gondreau, "The Passions and the Moral Life," *The Thomist* 71 (2007), 427. This is
much like Lewis's notion that our desires for temporal goods "bear at best a symbolic relation
to what will truly satisfy. ... The books or the music in which we thought the beauty was
located will betray us if we trust to them; it was not in them, it only came through them. ... For
they are not the thing itself; they are only the scent of a flower we have not found, the echo of
a tune we have not heart, news from a country we have never yet visited." C. S. Lewis, "The
Weight of Glory," in *The Weight of Glory and Other Addresses* (New York: HarperOne, 2001), 30–31.

62. As Pinckaers has noted; Servais Pinckaers, "Reappropriating Aquinas's Account of
the Passions," in *The Pinckaers Reader*, ed. John Berkman and Craig Steven Titus (Washington,
DC: Catholic University of America Press, 2005), 273.

63. Gondreau, "Passions," 421, 430. He is corroborating the claim of Servais Pinckaers
that Aquinas's concern for the passions in the moral life marks a unique achievement "of
remarkable genius." Servais Pinckaers, *The Sources of Christian Ethics*, trans. Mary T.
Noble (Washington, DC: The Catholic University of America Press, 1995), 224; Pinckaers,
"Reappropriating Aquinas's Account," 273–74.

Passions and the Body

Second, the idea that passions are essential to virtue seems hard to recon-cile with the fact that Aquinas believes passions cannot exist in the soul per se, but only in body. It is the body that makes passions possible for human beings.[64] Passions can only belong to a substance that is open to contraries, that is, a material substance.[65] But Aquinas argues that pas-sions do belong to the soul on biblical grounds (Rom 7:5). If passions can be said to be sinful, and if sin exists in the soul, then the passions must exist in the soul (I–II.22.1 s.c.). Aquinas solves this by arguing that pas-sions belong to the soul per *accidens* because they occur in "the composite of body and soul by reason of the body."[66] And so just as sinful passions exist in the person (body-soul composite), so also virtuous passions exist. Unlike God and the angels, a human being's "good action exists with pas-sion, just as it exists with the help of a body" (I–II.59.5 ad. 3). To pursue good, insofar as it is human good, requires the passions. Because human beings are composite creatures with body and soul, knowing and enjoying the good is perfected by the overflow of joy into the senses (I–II.59.5); we must have our cake and enjoy it too. Aquinas makes a significant contribution to theological psychology by preserving this positive use of passions. This

---

64. In fact, Aristotle denies that movement itself can be an attribute of the soul, strictly speaking. "It is an impossibility that movement should be even an attribute of [the soul]" (*De Anima* I.3).

65. The soul cannot change "by an exchange of contraries" as the body can (*Questiones Disputatae de Veritate* 26.1 co.). Properly speaking, passions do not belong to the soul per se, since it is immaterial.

66. *Questiones Disputatae de Veritate* (QDV), 26.2 ad. 4. Passions, as being acted upon involving bodily change with respect to quality, belong only per *accidens* to the soul itself, but considered as a composite of soul and body per se to the sense appetite (I–II.22.1; ad. 3). In *Questiones Disputatae de Veritate* (QDV), Aquinas also distinguishes between psychical passions and bodily passions, only the former possessing the mover and moved structure (QDV 26.2 co.; ST I–II 44.1). Aquinas does not clearly distinguish psychical and bodily passions in the *Summa*. In the *Summa*, Aquinas's language for the passions is simply the passions of the soul (*passiones animae*; e.g., I–II.22 pr.). The distinction is that a bodily passion (*passio corporalis*) "begins with the body and ends with the soul," such as when the body is injured, and a psychical passion (*passio animalis*) is "aroused by the apprehension and appetency of the soul, and a bodily transformation (*corporis transmutatio*) follows upon [it]" (QDV 26.2). Sadness differs from pain in that sadness begins with "apprehension of a source of harm," whereas pain "is dependent on a bodily passion" (QDV 26.3 ad. 9). Cf. Lombardo, *Logic of Desire*, 46. I think this distinction threatens the coherence of his account, and will therefore not appeal to it; even bodily pain is felt by the soul, a sort of apprehension.

is remarkable given his philosophical context.[67] Lombardo notes, "One of the more remarkable aspects of his account is precisely his positive and balanced appraisal of the *passiones animae*."[68] Aquinas safeguards his theology against a latent gnostic streak that has haunted Christian theology. To the extent that the passions have a positive role in virtue, so the body has a positive role in virtue since the passions exist per se in the body-soul composite.

THE NATURE OF MOVEMENT IN A PASSION

We have seen that passions are movements of the passive power and sensitive appetite, and that they are subject to reason's political rule by way of the intellect's concepts and the will's goals and decisions. We have also discussed that the body is essential to the passions, which are themselves essential for the pursuit of beatitude. But we need to return to the essential issue of how the body qualifies emotional experience for Aquinas. In other words, what are our passions like by virtue of the fact that they are embodied? First, I will clarify the material and formal components of the movements. And in the following section, I will explain how the body qualifies the movements of the passions with a sort of hylomorphic interplay.

---

67. Aquinas reflects the mood of the day by admitting, "the passions have to do with defectiveness, since a passion belongs to something insofar as it is in potentiality. Hence, in things that are close to the first perfect thing, viz., God, there is hardly anything of the character of potentiality and passion" (I–II.22.2 ad. 1). Metaphysically speaking, the tendency to disparage passions is owing to the Platonic idea that the immaterial God is the highest good, and the contemplation of God is the highest beatitude of the Christian life. As Augustine writes in *On the Trinity*, "For this contemplation is held forth to us as the end of all actions, and the everlasting fullness of joy" (*On the Trinity* I.viii.17, NPNF[1] 3:26). Abstractly speaking, the general scheme is that the soul may be unified and made perfect by pursuit of God, since being is oneness is good, and may be fractured and distracted by the pursuit of worldly things, the objects of the passions. In *Of True Religion*, Augustine recommends that Christians "despise the world of sense" and come "called away from desire for temporal and transient goods to spiritual and intelligible goods and to the hope of eternal life" (Of True Religion IV.6, in *Augustine: Early Writings, Library of Christian Classics*, edited by J. H. S. Burleigh [Louisville, KY: Westminster John Knox Press, 2006], 229). Aquinas likewise says, "And so in the active life, which is occupied with many things, there is less of the character of beatitude than there is in the contemplative life, which is centered on one thing, viz., the contemplation of truth" (*ST* I–II.3.2 ad. 4).

68. Lombardo, *Logic of Desire*, 17n61.

Just as the composite body-soul possesses formal and material components, so also does the composite sensitive appetite.[69] These two components comprise the dual aspect movement of the passions. Aquinas follows
Aristotle in saying all movement is "fulfillment of what is potentially,"[70]
including alteration, increase or decrease, or locomotion.[71] But the formal
and material aspects of the movements of sensitive appetite seem to move
in different senses.

Formally speaking, the movement of sense appetite is teleological or
goal directed. The motion of sense appetite is a subset of the motion of the
person's appetite, which is a subset of appetite in general as an inclination toward the good. Humanity's return to beatitude (*reditus*) is thus the
meta-frame for passion as movement in metaphysical terms. In this sense,
a passion is the start of a moral progression from passion to action to beatitude.[72] The most obvious example of teleological language is found in how
Aquinas differentiates the types of passions in I–II.23.2. He mentions that
there is a contrariety among the *termini* of the sensitive appetite involving
(a) the good and the bad and (b) approach and withdrawal. Concupiscible
appetite involves contrariety in only the first sense, its objects are good
and bad (see figure 2.4):[73]

---

69. *QDV*, 26.2; Paul Gondreau says, "Though Aquinas's view on the intimate relation
between body and soul in human affectivity echoes the consensus opinion of many of his
predecessors—including Augustine, Damascene, Lombard, and, especially, Albert, as well as
Aristotle—no previous author describes the nature of this relation as that of a union between
a formal appetitive component and a material bodily component, or that the psychical action
of a passion is exercised by means of a bodily organ." Gondreau, *Passions of Christ's Soul*, 207.

70. Aristotle, *Physics*, 201a11.

71. Aristotle, *Physics*, 226a19–35; 201a9–14.

72. Simo Knuuttila notes the comparison between the passions as movements and the
"stages of natural processes"—inclination, movement, and rest. He says, "Only the middle part
seems to be movement." He notes the incongruity of speaking of movements of appetite in
behavioral terms. There is an inconsistency in "[e]quating desire with a movement which
is caused by desire." A human being may desire a pleasurable food, and the bringing of the
fork to the mouth is caused by the desire, but both are spoken of as movement. The conflict
is clearer in the case of pleasure, which by the definition of passion would be a movement
but is also called "the terminus of a movement" (I–II.31.2). But there need be no contradiction
here if we recognize this threefold framing. Simo Knuuttila, *Emotions in Ancient and Medieval
Philosophy* (Oxford: Oxford University Press, 2004), 249–51.

73. This is adapted from Carlo Leget, "Moral Theology Upside Down," *Jaarboek Thomas
Instituut* 18 (1999): 111.

	Good in itself	Bad in itself
Simple Inclination	Love (*amor*)	Hate (*odium*)
Movement	Desire (*desiderium*)	Aversion (*fuga*)
Rest	Pleasure/Joy (*delectatio*)	Sadness (*dolor*)

Figure 2.4, Table of Concupiscible Passions

The teleological idea is present along with stages of movement, inclination, movement, and rest. These are stages of the movement of sense
appetite, not stages of behavior. But it is clear that the natural movement
of sense appetite is teleologically oriented toward the good.[74] The very
structure of the scheme involves a culmination at the final passions of
either joy or sadness (I–II.25.4).

Materially speaking, Aquinas also talks about the physiological aspect
of sense appetite. This is particularly where Aquinas's reliance on Galenic
medicine becomes obvious. That this material alteration is no mere byprod-
uct can be seen by the fact that Aquinas speaks of the material change as
part of the definition of passion (I–II.22.3). He says that a natural change
is ordered per se toward an act of the sentient appetite, explaining, "This
is why a natural change in an organ is posited materially in the definition of movements of the appetitive part—as, for instance, when it is said
that anger is the heating of the blood around the heart" (I–II.22.2 ad. 3).
Formal and material movements are powerfully complementary. The material movement of the body is conformed and proportionate to the formal
movement of appetite (I–II.37.4). For example, just as fear draws a person
back from the object, so also there is "in the case of fear, on the part of the
body, a drawing of heat and spirits inward toward the interior parts of
the body" (I–II.44.1).

---

74. The irascible appetite involves two kinds of contrariety, the good and the bad and
approach and withdrawal. The irascible appetite concerns not just the good and bad considered simply, but the arduous or difficult good or bad. The irascible passions involve the
perception of a complex object, or two objects, i.e., the hated obstacle and loved thing (I–
II.46.2); therefore, it both attracts and repels. The object of the irascible power may be the
same as the concupiscible power, but with the non-sensible intention of arduous or difficult.

Aquinas applies various descriptors of the movement of sense appetite from the point of view of the body, but particularly dimension. Aquinas says, "In every passion of the soul something is either added to or subtracted from the heart's natural movement in the sense that the heart is moved either more intensely or less intensely by contraction and dilation; and accordingly the movement has the character of a passion" (I–II.24.2 ad. 2). Carlo Leget illustrates this movement with the four principal passions, joy, a species of pleasure; sorrow; hope; and fear (I–II.25.4). Joy expands the soul, since *laetitia* (gladness) is etymologically related to *latitia* (width; I–II.31.3 ad. 3).[75] Sorrow most harms the body since it is "opposed to human life because of the very species of the movement and not just because of its measure or quantity" (I–II.37.4 and 2). Sorrow weighs down the soul to the point that "sometimes even the exterior movement of the body is impeded, so that the man remains stupefied within himself" (I–II.37.4 and 2). Hope is linked with the enlarging of the heart, which comes along with high spirits. Aquinas says, "young people are spirited and full of hope" (I–II.40.6). Finally, fear is associated with contraction or being drawn inward (*cum contratione*, I–II.41.1). This is a passion in the fullest negative sense, where bad overcomes good. Fear is not as bad as sadness, since fear has to do with a future evil, not a present one as sadness does. Fear is also spoken of as a withdrawal of heat to the lower interior parts and from the heart, leaving the higher exterior parts cold and consuming interior moisture, causing thirst and a quivering of lips and jaw (I–II.44.3 c.; ad. 1, 3).

The Bodily Conditions of the Passions

But how does the body qualify the passions? What does it contribute to the moral tone of emotions? Emotions are neither simple and voluntary movements of the unencumbered soul, nor are they amoral, blind, irrational forces. They are moral movements of the soul within composite corporeal organs modulated by corporeal qualities. The body seems to contribute a certain thickness or viscosity to the passions of the soul.

So we have an intuition that embodiment brings some sort of plasticity or moldability to human moral agency. But just how does this work? A key to understanding this is paying attention to what Gondreau calls a sort of

---

75. Leget, "Moral Theology Upside Down," 112–18.

hylemorphic interplay, a two-way traffic between body and soul as form and matter and mover and moved.[76] The soul produces alteration in the body, and likewise the bodily conditions can cause the soul to undergo passion, influence the will, or even entirely obstruct one's reasoning capabilities. Again, the language of Aristotle may sound strange to the modern reader, but the framework anticipates remarkably the interplay between mind and body in affective neuroscience—e.g., the movement from cognition to the release of hormones by the sympathetic nervous system, which in turn modulates cognition. In what follows, I will address the ways the body qualifies the passions, and then trace this up to how passions even impact our rational faculties.

The Conditions of the Body

It must be noted that Aquinas mostly emphasizes how the body influences the soul negatively. However, not only can a more positive influence be inferred, but there are also some intriguing hints supporting this. For Aquinas, every act of a power using a corporeal organ depends not only on the soul's power but also "on the disposition of the corporeal organ" (I–II.17.7). This disposition may be related to health, natural temperament, or perhaps some lingering pre-existing passion (I–II.17.7 ad. 2). This disposition of the organ is prior to the passion (act of the passive power), and so is not subject to reason's command. Aquinas calls the impact of the body on the powers of the soul a "defect in the instrument" (I–II.44.4). For example, the corporeal aspect of fear, the coldness and withdrawal of the heart's natural movement, is apt to disturb the overall operation of the soul (I–II.44.4). The impact on the soul by the body in this way only happens incidentally, since neither apprehension nor reason is involved in bringing it about (I–II.6.1 ad. 2).[77]

There are two temporal frames when considering the sorts of bodily defects that can impact the proper functioning of the soul, a long-term and a short-term temporal frame. Considered in the long-term temporal frame,

---

76. Gondreau, *Passions of Christ's Soul*, 208.

77. Aquinas uses the word "indirectly" in *Questiones de Veritate*. He says, "when the body is injured, the union of the body is weakened; and so the soul, which is united to the body in its act of existing, suffers indirectly. ... Thus, when the body is transformed by an alteration, the soul itself is said to suffer indirectly." *QDV* 26.2.

the body influences the function of the soul through a person's health or temperament. Aquinas does not have much to say about the relationship between health and the soul, but says it consists of "a certain measure in the humors that is appropriate to an animal's nature" (I–II.73.3). But both health and temperament are just the characteristic balance of temperament for an individual person. So what Aquinas says about the influence of the humors on the function of the soul might be applied both to temperament and health. A predominance of an individual humor influences someone's characteristic appetites. He says, "a man is disposed toward getting angry insofar as he has a choleric temperament, where, among the humors, yellow bile (*cholera*) is the one that moves most quickly, since it is similar to fire" (I–II.46.5). This characteristic disposition arising from temperament is a natural habit and can be found in varying degrees among individuals (I–II.63.1).[78] Temperaments seem to be able either to aid or to impede the sentient powers,[79] partly influencing virtue and vice. "Accordingly, one man has a natural aptitude for scientific knowledge, another for fortitude, another for temperance" (I–II.63.1). Finally, there is a correlation between bodily changes and certain fixed times, seemingly indicating circumstances such as life stages, particular situations, etc., and proneness to certain sins (II–II.35.1 ad. 2).

On the other hand, in a short-term temporal frame, pre-existing physiological conditions impact the proper functioning of the soul. When a

---

78. Insofar as health and temperament are related, Aquinas may actually claim that an exterior principle like the aid of medicine can correct a disposition that is unhealthy. He says,

So, then, if we are talking about a habit insofar as it is a subject's disposition with respect to a form or nature, then it is possible for a habit to be natural in any of the ways just mentioned. For instance, there are natural dispositions which are fitting for the human species and which no man is found outside of. And this sort of disposition is natural in this sense has a certain latitude, it is possible for diverse degrees of this sort of disposition to belong to diverse men with respect to with the nature of the individual. Moreover, a disposition of this sort can be either wholly from nature or partly from nature and partly from an exterior principle, as was explained above with respect to those who are cured by art. (I–II.51.1)

He is here talking about health, but again, insofar as there is transference to temperament, there may be an inference to be made toward modern psychotropic drugs.

79. Aquinas writes, "[I]t is possible for some of the powers of the soul to be stronger in one individual than in another, because of their different bodily compositions (*propter diversas corporis complexiones*)" (I–II.82.4 ad. 1).

passion has not dissipated physiologically, this state can bleed over by way of bodily disposition to affect human action (I–II.17.7 ad. 2).

Bodily alteration impacts the entire soul. The overall operation of the soul has a unifying principle in its single essence, which means that there really is only one act of attention (*una intentio*) to which the various powers contribute (I–II.37.1). What this means is when the body undergoes a passion, the whole soul suffers. Aquinas makes this point explicitly when discussing the passion of Christ. He says, "all the powers of Christ's soul did suffer ... because all the faculties of Christ's soul were rooted in its essence, to which suffering extended when the body, whose act it is, suffered" (III.46.7).[80] When the body is defective in some way, the powers of the soul are impacted. The impact of the body on the function of reason and will is especially seen in the effect that the passions have on judgments that follow bodily transmutation. For example, Aquinas observes that fear disorders reason because of a "lack of heat," but concedes, "if the fear is moderate and does not disturb reason too much, then it contributes to operating well, insofar as it causes a certain carefulness and makes the man deliberate and act more attentively" (I–II.44.4).

As a parallel case, Aquinas notes the possibility of the devil tempting persons through the local motion of the body (I–II.80.2). Since "a corporeal nature naturally obeys a spiritual nature with respect to local motion," the devil can cause local motion in persons, by which Aquinas means the motion of the humors, the animal spirits, and the heart, explicitly mentioning all three. These motions can give rise to images in the imagination and movement of the sense appetite. In this passage we see definite causality; local bodily movement can impact the soul's perceiving and desiring, and perceiving and desiring can, in turn, cause bodily movement, as is well attested in many other passages. To put it briefly, Aquinas was committed to the view that humoral qualities impact the function of our lower faculties. And by extension, insofar as these lower faculties impact ratiocination—the

---

80. Aquinas also stipulates, "Christ's higher reason did not suffer thereby on the part of its object, which is God" (III.46.7).

intellect relies on phantasms for discursive reasoning (I.84.7)—the operations of intellect too may be affected (I–II.51.1).[81]

Finally, there are some suggestions that the body may positively contribute to the function of the soul. First, Aquinas thinks that certain temperaments may contribute to virtue, for example, to courage, to knowledge, or to temperance (I–II.63.1; I–II.82.4 ad. 1). Youthfulness, which is connected with having an expansive heart, is connected with hope (I–II.40.6)—though it is also connected with foolishness. Second, there are certain bodily functions that actually aid with emotional regulation, such as sadness (I–II.37.4). For example, tears and sighs lessen sadness by diffusing the soul's attention and because crying is pleasurable (I–II.38.2). Sleep also aids with sadness by overcoming the bodily defect of fatigue (I–II.38.1).[82] Third, Aquinas talks about the body as a cause of daring, saying "whatever builds up heat around the heart" may stimulate it, including the size of the heart and wine (I–II.45.3). Most significantly, the condition of the body following a passion aids the body in acting appropriately by preparing the body for action, helping the body to act with ease according to the direction of reason (I–II.17.7 ad. 2). The bodily movements associated with hope, for instance, may prepare the body for arduous exertion.

Passions and Reason

I have already discussed some basic ways that the intellectual powers govern the sensitive powers. I suggested that reason guides the cogitative power in its representations by providing it both with first and second order intentions (wolf as dangerous) and with practical syllogisms. Also, in addition to the will orienting the entire soul to good and directing all the powers, it also executes action as it chooses, such that except in the cases of a total absence of reason ("those who are furious or mindless"), the will chooses to make use of a habit and is not determined by it (I–II.76.3 arg. 3; 71.4 ad. 1). Having discussed how the body qualifies the passions, we are

---

81. Aquinas says here, "For one man, because of the disposition of his organs, is more apt than another man to understand well, insofar as the intellect's operation needs the sentient powers" (I–II.51.1).

82. Simon Harak notes this effect of sleep as evidence of the body's harmony with the soul, so that "something that affects the 'outer person' can affect the 'inner person' as well. In short, the whole self is moving in concert." G. Simon Harak, *Virtuous Passions: The Formation of Christian Character* (New York: Paulist Press, 1993), 80.

now in a better place to nuance the relationship between the passions and reason. The point is this: Passions occupy a sort of middle ground in terms of voluntariness. While passions that exist before our actions diminish our voluntariness, we still have some degree of control over them, especially over our final goals and the means we choose to reach them.

Robert Miner writes, "It is the very materiality of the sensory appetite that explains, most fundamentally, why we cannot entirely control them."[83] Our passions are not entirely rational; they have a "curious in-between status," as Pasnau suggests.[84] Since they are not entirely rational, they are not entirely voluntary. And if they are not entirely voluntary, then we are not entirely responsible for them, and they are not entirely moral. But insofar as they are rational and voluntary, then we are responsible for them, and they are moral. So there may be cases where responsibility is nil, and there may be cases of nearly full responsibility. It is for this reason that Aquinas says, "The passions of the sentient appetite both (a) are able to be venial sins in their own right, and (b) incline the soul toward mortal sin" (II–II.35.1 ad. 2). The difference here is that venial sins are a certain turning toward, fixing on a merely apparent good, while mortal sins are a certain turning away, rejecting God as the ultimate end of beatitude (I–II.72.5). In Aquinas's view, passions are moral, but the will's choice determines our ends. It is important to his psychology that he does not see voluntariness or responsibility for passions as all or nothing.

In I–II.23.4, Aquinas summarizes how passions are related to the judgment of reason, either antecedently or consequently. An antecedent passion "clouds reason's judgment," and thus diminishes the moral quality of the act that follows (I–II.24.3 ad. 3). On the other hand, consequent passion happens when a person chooses to be affected by an emotion or when a person chooses something so strongly that there is an overflow of passion.[85]

---

83. Miner, *Thomas Aquinas on the Passions*, 108.

84. Pasnau, *Thomas Aquinas on Human Nature*, 257.

85. Aquinas calls these either (a) by way of redundancy, some translations say "overflow," or (b) by way of choice. In the first case, the passion only follows and intensifies the will's movement toward something. In the second case, people may choose to be affected by some passion so that they may act more promptly "because of the sentient appetite's cooperation" (I–II.23.3). Both cases of consequent passions seem to be voluntary in the sense that they follow reason's judgment. The consequent passion by way of redundancy comes from a certain overflow of the passions from the will (I–II.24.1).

But we must consider that antecedent passions may also be consequent, and consequent passions may also be antecedent. This moment's consequent passion may be the next moment's antecedent one; we govern our emotions over time. So even antecedent passions might be somewhat within our control.

Take three instances where Aquinas admits that passions are not within our control. First, he suggests that sense appetite might be surprised or distracted. Sentient appetite's movement might be "suddenly aroused at an apprehension by the imagination or sensory power" (I–II.17.7).[86] We might envision sudden fright over a terrifying appearance. Even in this case, Aquinas suggests, "it could have been stopped by reason if reason had foreseen it" (I–II.17.7). A terrifying experience is unsurprising in a haunted house. Claudia Eisen Murphy suggests that this might be called "indirect counterfactual control," when a decision leads to an emotion especially when it could have been foreseen.[87] But notice, to avoid the haunted house in order to avoid sudden fright implies a certain inevitability in human nature for our passions to respond in characteristic ways to certain situations.

Second, Aquinas is also clear that "the condition and disposition of the body is not subject to reason's command." This is what prevents "the movement of sentient appetite from being totally subject to reason's command" (I–II.17.7). The body is not subject to habit except insofar as it is within the composite of sensitive appetite, i.e., virtue as a habit of the soul, and with respect to health, which is from nature (I–II.50.1).[88] Aquinas does admit that heath is rightly called a habitual disposition, an imperfect habit, because the body is disposed to the soul as form (I–II.50.1). If in light of what we now know about health, health and temperament is a sort of imperfect habit, then there may be a very indirect sense in which a person might have some control over even antecedent passions brought on by the body's condition,

---

86. This might even move the will indirectly to make decisions it would not have. Aquinas writes, "since all the powers of the soul are rooted in the single essence of the soul, when one power is intensified in its act, another has to become less intensified in its act or is totally impeded" (I–II.77.1).

87. Claudia Eisen Murphy, "Aquinas on Our Responsibility for Our Emotions," *Medieval Philosophy and Theology* 8 (1999): 190–91.

88. Aquinas assumes that the body is not subject to habit because a habit is only required when there is a potentiality for multiple effects, and "the natural powers [those of the body] are determined to a single effect" (I–II.50.1; I–II.49.4).

in spite of the fact that it is not directly commanded by reason. A person might, for example, fight depression or chronic anxiety with exercise.

Third, Aquinas suggests a case that is more troubling, that passions might actually distract or distort the judgment of reason such that the person is not even aware of the irrationality of their judgment. In these cases, "reason's judgment and apprehension, along with the estimative power's judgment, are impeded by vehement and disorderly apprehensions on the part of imagination" (I–II.77.1). This sounds quite a bit like mental illness. Aquinas says that these people have lost touch with rationality such that reason's judgment follows sense appetite and the will follows reason's judgment. He writes, "Hence, we see that men who are in a passion do not easily turn away from the things by which they are being affected." Under a passion many things seem "greater or smaller than they are in reality" (I–II.44.2). An OCD suffer sees a variety of non-threatening situations as dangerous.[89] It is unclear in this case to what extent entering into this passion could have been avoided.

However, even here where the "disorderly apprehensions on the part of the imagination" are involved, we recall that imagination may be used positively as well as negatively.[90] Imagination seems to be a useful way for managing the passions or for stimulating them. For example, displays of friendship make sadness easier to bear because the person "imagines that others are bearing that burden with him, trying, as it were, to make it lighter for him" (I–II.38.3).[91] As fear involves imagining some imminent evil (I–II.44.1), so also hope follows imagined victory, by our own power or with help (I–II.45.3). A believer may assent intellectually to future punishment, but it is through the forming of "phantasms of the pains" and imagining "the fire burning and worm gnawing" that passions follow (QDV 26.3 ad. 13).

Finally, I need to reiterate again the role that the will plays in orienting all the powers. Whereas animals have only passions, and no movements of will, angels and God have only movements of will and no passions, and human beings have both.[92] Humanity is made for communion with God.

---

89. There is also a range of more trivial examples; a lover sees nothing but good in the beloved, for example.

90. I owe this observation to Murphy, "Aquinas on Our Responsibility," 193.

91. Cf. Aristotle, *Nicomachean Ethics*, IV.5.

92. I–II.3.2 ad. 4; I–II.3.5 ad. 3; I–II.5.1 ad. 1; I–II.24.3 ad. 2.

When our wills settle on temporal goods without being properly ordered to God, we are guilty of animalism, living as if our need for temporal goods determine our actions. On the other hand, when we forget that we are dust and that human goodness is bound up with rightly ordered embodied passions, then we are guilty of angelism and will almost inevitably manage them badly. Human beings were made to manage their passion by ordering them to higher things. The beatitude to which human beings are ordered is similar to that which the angels experience where "man's mind will be joined to God by a single operation" (I–II.3.2 ad. 4; I–II.3.5). Aquinas writes, "[A] man's ultimate perfection will lie in the man's reaching the point of contemplating in the way that the angels contemplate" (I–II.3.7 ad. 3). But it differs from that of angels in that Aquinas rejects the notion that human beatitude is disembodied. Aquinas claims that humankind will be embodied in the final state, but the reasons for this are mysterious to him. He suggests that there is perhaps a natural desire in humanity to govern their bodies (I–II.4.5). In any case, in the final state "there will be an overflow of the soul's beatitude into the body, so that the body itself will have its own perfection" (I–II.4.6).

The will plays two roles in modulating our passions toward beatitude. First, our will orients all our powers, rightly ordering temporal goods to our true beatitude. This might be seen as a sort of unifying attention. The first and most essential affection is the appetite for God that is love. All human acts of will are ordered toward beatitude, which ultimately is love for God (I.19.3; I.20.1). In our earthly condition, we have a complex web of lesser goods that vie for our attention. The failures of the powers are often attributed to poor attention (I–II.77.1).[93] It is this most primary love that enables many to make rational and voluntary choices that are fit to be called human acts rather than merely acts of human beings, since all human actions are for the sake of an end (I–II.1.1). Human beings are properly the master of the acts only because they are rightly ordered by the affection of love (I–II.5.4 ad. 2). Second, our will perfects us through an

---

93. Cf. I–II.17.6 I–II.33.3; I–II.37.1; I–II–38.2; I–II.46.5.

overflow from higher to lower powers, producing the consequent passions
by its movements (I–II.3.3 ad. 3).[94]

EVALUATION

We are in a better place now to assess just how the body conditions agency
for Aquinas. In Aquinas's notion of the political rule of the passions, we see
the coming together of my two features of tiered psychology and holistic
plasticity. In the first case, Aquinas has clearly established the hierarchy
of powers and their assigned roles—reason rules the lower powers. In
the second case, the body contributes a variability of control—the rule is
political. Aquinas analogizes this rule to the power a ruler has over "free
men who are not totally subject to his command." Reason does not rule
despotically, as a master over a servant. Sense appetite has its own iner-
tia (I–II.17.7). Our emotions are, as Jonathan Haidt analogizes, like a man
riding an elephant.[95] Aquinas attributes this variability to embodiment
(I–II.17.7).[96] This variability of control is quite familiar to us; we all know
what it is to fight emotions we do not approve.

I have also hinted at two ways that the passions are habituated for
Aquinas. Using his distinction between perfect and imperfect habit, the
sense appetite may be perfectly habituated by means of the soul's movement (e.g., emotional habit), and the body itself may be imperfectly

---

94. When Nicholas Lombardo says, "all passions of the soul are affections but not all
affections are passions," he supposes that there are also affections, which Peter King calls
"pseudopassions," since they "do not involve any somatic reactions or indeed any material
basis at all." That there are such movements is clear from Aquinas's criticism of the Stoics,
that "they did not distinguish, in the way that the Peripatetics did, the passions of the soul
from other human affections" (I–II.59.2; cf. III.15.4). Loosely, these are movements of the
will, like the passions are the movement of sense appetite. Like the passions, they rely on an
object, but unlike them, they express agency, since they are ordered to the universal rational
conception of good, beatitude (I–II.6.2) and voluntary according to his requirements for
voluntariness: "(a) an apprehension of the thing that is the end, but also (b) a cognition of
the concept of an end, and (c) a cognition of the relation between the means ordered to an
end (*quod ordinatur in finem*) and the end itself" (I–II.6.2); Lombardo, *Logic of Desire*, 76; King,
"Aquinas on the Passions," 4.

95. Jonathan Haidt, *Happiness Hypothesis: Finding Modern Truth in Ancient Wisdom* (New
York: Basic Books, 2006), 27.

96. I–II.17.7, "The condition and disposition of the body (*qualitas et disposition corporis*) is
not subject to reason's command. And so this, on the other hand, prevents the movement of
the sentient appetite from being totally subject to reason's command."

habituated by means of the soul's form (e.g., health).[97] My only significant reservation with this scheme concerns the extent to which the passions may be perfectly habituated in this life, especially both in light of the weakness of our bodies and the influence of depravity.

Our analysis also uncovers an important implication of Aquinas's tiered psychology: the lower faculties have the unique feature of being directly and more strongly responsive to experience. The haunted house elicits fear in spite of how much we tell ourselves there is no danger. So experience has immense power to shape the habits. This is a crucial insight for literature and the arts. The imagination's power to stimulate emotion presents both an opportunity and a warning. The warning is that there is a certain inevitability of passion connected with our attention (i.e., the lust of the eyes, 1 John 2:16). Our sense appetite is easily distracted or engrossed in its objects, potentially indirectly moving the will and wrongly ordering us to the earthly world. This makes good sense in light of Colossians 3:2, "Set your minds on the things that are above, not on things that are on earth." We might say that where our attention is, there our hearts will be also. Fortunately, our wills direct all our powers, even our attention; this is the opportunity. Our will can rightly order our attention to perceive the world according to God's revelation. By the illumining grace of the Spirit, we can attend both in the right ways and to the right things, enabling a psychological reciprocity where our thinking frames our seeing and our seeing saturates our thinking, where experience reinforces God's word.

Finally, it would be easy to dismiss Aquinas's treatment of the physicality of the passions on the grounds that Galenism is factually wrong. But as I have suggested, this would miss both the larger point that Aquinas integrates medicine into his moral theology and the narrower point that his moral theology accounts for embodied plasticity. Moreover, Galenism does not import radically different intuitions about the psychological influence of the body on emotions. For example, the fact that we still use a

---

97. In evaluating the role of plasticity in Aquinas, it is important to distinguish the roles the soul and physicality play in plasticity. It is probably fairer to say that physicality accounts more for the recalcitrance and irrationality of emotion than for the malleability of emotion on his account. Aquinas ultimately attributes the possibility of habit formation to the soul. However, seen as a composite, the passions can be habituated, and their habituation is essential to virtue.

metaphor like heated for anger suggests that we recognize that anger dis-
sipates slowly just as heat does. Aquinas's psychological division between
higher cognitive powers and lower, more body-involving powers is actually
quite contemporary, as I will demonstrate in Chapter 8.

HABIT AND VIRTUE

Finally, having touched on the powers and how the body qualifies them, we
will briefly discuss what sort of habits virtue and vice are and how they are
formed. This is directly relevant because our inquiry covers the capacity
for and means of forming habits. The notion of habit (*habitus*) in Aquinas
poses two problems. On the one hand, it can be difficult for a modern reader
to disassociate the word "habit" from a notion of mechanical, mindless,
repetitive actions. Disassociating habit from mindless repetition is necessary to grasp Aquinas's metaphysically freighted use of the term. On the
other hand, it is also difficult to follow his treatment of the topic because he
attempts to reconcile traditions that have very different views of habit; i.e.,
Augustine is quite negative about it.[98] Bonnie Kent uses an apt metaphor
for Aquinas's reconciling work: "Thomas operates very much like a host
laboring to produce congenial, fruitful conversation among guests deeply
at odds with each other."[99] My overriding concern is Aquinas's explanation,
but his reconciling work will also necessarily be in view.

For Aquinas, habit (*habitus*) refers to "a disposition, in virtue of which
the thing which is disposed is disposed well or badly" (e.g., health, I–
II.49.1).[100] It is a having a particular arrangement of affairs in the middle
voice, that is, with respect to itself. This is the definition of "disposition."[101]

---

98. E.g., "But that which did for the most part afflict me, already made a slave to it, was
the habit of satisfying an insatiable lust." Augustine, *Confessions*, XII.22 (*NPNF*[1] 1:99). See
John Prendiville's excellent treatment of Augustine's views of habit. John G. Prendiville, "The
Development of the Idea of Habit in the Thought of Saint Augustine," *Traditio: Studies in
Ancient and Medieval History, Thought and Religion* 28 (1972): 29–99.

99. Bonnie Kent, "Habits and Virtues (Ia IIae, qq. 49–70)," in *The Ethics of Aquinas*, ed.
Alexander Pope (Washington, DC: Georgetown University Press, 2002), 116.

100. Habit may also refer to "an activity, as it were, of the haver and the thing had," such as
with "the man who has a garment." It is a "having" in the middle voice. Aristotle, *Metaphysics*,
1022b4–7. cf. Aquinas, I–II.49.1.

101. Aristotle, *Metaphysics*, 1022b1. The word *diathesis* derives from the verb *diatithēmi*,
meaning "arrange" (LSJ). According to Aquinas, disposition is "an ordering of something that
has parts" (a) "with respect to place," (b) "with respect to potentiality," or (c) "with respect

To be disposed is to be arranged in a certain way, which arrangement can contribute to the thing's end, the perfection of form, or can counteract it. When applied to persons, habit is a quality that perfects a rational agent. It is the bridge between the person's very nature and the achievement of that nature; it perfects the person's accidental *esse*, not the primary act of existence. Virtue is a type of habit that perfects a rational power in relation to its ends (I–II.55.1). Virtue refers to a habit of being well disposed toward the achievement of human perfection, the end of human nature, beatitude (I–II.49.4). Vice is its contrary, not a synonym for sin, but "a quality because of which the mind is bad" (I–II.71.1).[102] Habit is distinguished from a mere disposition because it is more stable, "irremediable or exceedingly hard to change."[103] Only perfect dispositions are qualified to be called habits, strictly speaking (I–II.49.1). So the habits of the body are only imperfect habits.

To this point, what Aquinas has to say about habit and virtue differs very little from the Aristotelian view: "habits are that according to which we have or bear ourselves (*nos habemus*) well or badly with respect to the passions" (I–II.49.2), and, "Virtue is what makes the one who has it good and renders his works good."[104] But as becomes clear, Aquinas is carefully negotiating between Aristotelian and Christian elements in his treatment of virtue. He provides a synthetic account of virtue that brings together Aristotle's ideas of habit with Augustine's notion that virtue deals with "good use of free choice,"[105] and Peter Lombard's definition of virtue as "a good quality of mind, by which one lives righteously, which no one uses

to species." The second refers to preparatory dispositions like inchoate knowledge or virtue; the third refers to perfect dispositions like virtue. These are habits (I–II.49.1).

102. Aquinas is citing Augustine here, which in context and in Latin reads, "*Sic et in homine interiore animus res est, rapina actus est, avaritia vitium est, id est, qualitas, secundum quam malus est animus*" ("So in the inward man the soul is the thing, theft is an act, and avarice is the defect, that is, the property by which the soul is evil"). Augustine, *A Treatise Concerning Man's Perfection in Righteousness* ii.4, NPNF¹ vol. 5, 160. Sin for Aquinas is "a bad act" rather than a quality (I–II.71.3). For Aquinas, vice is to sin as virtue is to merit.

103. Following Aristotle, Aquinas first defines the term "habit" generically as "a quality that is hard to change" (I–II.49.1). Habit (*hexis*), for Aristotle, often translated "state," differs from disposition (*diathesis*), translated "condition," in that habit is "more stable and lasting longer." Aristotle, *Categories*, 8b25–9a9; 8b29; 9a3.

104. Aristotle, *Nicomachean Ethics*, 1105b26–27.

105. Augustine, *Reconsiderations*, in *On the Free Choice of the Will, On Grace and Free Choice, and Other Writings*, Cambridge Texts in the History of Philosophy, ed. Peter King (Cambridge: Cambridge University Press, 2010), 132; I.ix.6.

badly, and which God works in us without us."[106] In negotiating between Aristotelian and Christian ideas, Aquinas makes two massive alterations to Aristotle's theory. First, citing Averroes, Aquinas says, "a habit is that whereby we act when we will" (I–II.49.3).[107] That Aquinas speaks of the will as a discrete power represents a departure from the Aristotelian tradition.[108] Second, Aquinas qualifies his statements about acquired virtue by saying that only infused virtues, that is virtues by grace, are perfect virtues and deserve to be called virtue absolutely speaking (I–II.65.2).[109] By making this qualification, Aquinas is aligning himself with the last clause of Lombard's definition as the true definition of virtue, "which God works in us without us." I will develop these two adjustments a bit more fully as I continue to fill out the picture.

First, with reference to the will's use of habits, it is helpful to understand how habits work within Aquinas's action theory. Habits are found in various powers of the soul, including reason, sensitive appetite, and the will. A habit exists in a single power but may influence other powers by diffusion or disposition (I–II.56.2). The powers of the soul work cooperatively to produce a good choice, the passions moderated by temperance and fortitude, reason supplying prudence, and the will pursuing justice (I–II.56.3–6). When the powers are perfected in this way and working together, they produce a good choice.

While there are other virtues, these are the four cardinal virtues: temperance, fortitude, prudence, and justice from Aristotelian virtue ethics. Temperance and fortitude involve the concupiscible and irascible powers of the sensitive appetite, respectively, and are moderated insofar as they participate in reason and are ready to obey it (I–II.56.4). Prudence is an intellectual virtue, not a moral virtue, involving practical reasoning (I–II.56.3).

---

106. "*Bona qualitas mentis, qua recte vivitur, qua nullus male utitur, quam Deus in nobis sine nobis operatur.*" Peter Lombard, *Libri IV Sententiarum*, Book 2. Distinction 27. Cap. 5 (Ad Claras Aquas [Quarachhi]: Typografia Collegii S. Bonaventurae, 1916), 446.

107. Aquinas references Averroes's commentary on *De Anima*, 3.

108. Bonnie Kent says, "Aristotle had nothing approximating the scholastic conception of the will." Kent, *Virtues of the Will*, 131.

109. Bonnie Kent writes, "Naturally acquired habits described as perfect, unqualified virtues by comparison with habits unrelated to a good will and uninformed by prudence gradually emerge as imperfect virtues and virtues only in a relative sense by comparison with God-given habits." Kent, "Habits and Virtues," 123.

Prudence relies on the appetite being rightly ordered, especially an upright will (I–II.56.2 ad. 3). Prudence cannot even begin to consider means if it is not already aligned to the proper human end, which is supplied by the will. Finally, justice exists more in the will than in the irascible and concupiscible power because the will moves these powers (I–II.56.6).

When the human person has the habits of pursuing justice prudentially with moderated passions, this person is able to choose good in accordance with these habits. Choosing always involves both (a) intending and (b) preferring a means (I–II.56.4. ad. 4). The former involves the moral virtues, those of appetition, and the latter involves the intellectual virtues, those of cognition. Intellectual virtues differ from moral virtues in that intellectual virtues merely enable facility and are thus only virtues in a certain respect. Intellectual virtues are not by nature used, but by nature facilitate use. The idea is that if people possess the habit of grammar, for instance, they need not always speak with grammatical correctness; they may "utter barbarisms or commit a solecism" (I–II.56.3). On the other hand, moral virtues—habits of appetition—are by nature used, and thus are virtues absolutely speaking (I–II.56.3).

Much of the above would be perfectly agreeable to Aristotle, but in situations where knowledge or habit contradicts choice, the difference is clearer. Aristotle suggests that when a person knowingly chooses the wrong action, "clear-eyed akrasia," this person possesses merely perceptual knowledge.[110] While Aquinas makes favorable remarks about Aristotle's explanation of akrasia (I–II.77.2 ad. 4; I–II.58.2), he also admits that the virtuous person can choose badly (I–II.71.4). Ultimately, for Aquinas, the source of sin is the will, not merely ignorance (voluntas est causa peccati; I–II.75.2 s.c.). For Aquinas, a virtue is always subject to ill use, or the wicked choice; it is possible even for a virtuous person to choose badly, since "a

---

110. Aristotle, Nicomachean Ethics, 1145b22–31. See Risto Saarinen for a full treatment of the history of this problem. Risto Saarinen, Weakness of Will in Renaissance and Reformation Thought (Oxford: Oxford University Press, 2011). Socrates flatly denied the possibility, ascribing the so-called akratic action to ignorance. Aristotle seems to agree with him but suggests that the type of knowledge the person possesses is merely perceptual knowledge. This perceptual knowledge then authorizes the person to act in a way which reason would forbid (Nichomachean Ethics 1147b9–18). The possibility of what Risto Saarinen calls "clear-eyed akrasia," knowingly doing the wrong thing, is effectively denied. Moreover, the incontinent person who acts akratically lacks perfect virtue since practical wisdom includes action for Aristotle (Nicomachean Ethics, 1146a7–8); Saarinen, Weakness of Will, 11.

man makes use of the habit when he wills to" (I–II.71.4; I–II.78.2).[111] What a bad choice reveals from a Christian perspective may be a failure in preferring a means, as in the case of venial sin, or also a failure in intending, as in the case of mortal sin. Ultimately the will is implicated, but especially in cases of mortal sin, which involve a turning away from God. These possibilities go far beyond Aristotle's ethics.

Second, Aquinas's theory of theological virtue departs from Aristotle's view far more markedly in what Aquinas calls virtue absolutely speaking. As Aquinas unfolds his theory of the virtues, he does not begin with virtue absolutely speaking, but something like mere human virtue.[112] These virtues are acquired by repetitive action as Aristotle describes: "excellences [virtuous habits] we get by first exercising them … we become just by doing just acts, temperate by doing temperate acts, brave by doing brave acts."[113] But these acquired virtues fall short of the definition of full virtue that Aquinas explicitly affirms. Lombard provides this definition: "a good quality of mind, by which one lives righteously, which no one uses badly, and *which God works in us without us*."[114] Eleonore Stump marks this dramatic departure from Aristotelianism, arguing that it is time to set aside "the view that Aquinas holds an Aristotelian virtue ethics."[115] The issue for Stump is that what Aquinas calls real virtues are not acquired by practice, nor are they realizable by agents acting in their own right.[116] The real vir-

---

111. Citing Thomas Aquinas, *De Malo*, Saarinen points out, "Aquinas maintains that although the akratic person does not sin 'from choice' (*ex electione*), he nevertheless sins 'while choosing' (*eligens*)." Saarinen, *Weakness of Will*, 28.

112. Or as is often attributed to Augustine, splendid vice. Terrance Irwin observes that Augustine never used the term *splendida peccata*, concluding, "Once we understand why Augustine reasonably takes pagan virtues to fall short of true virtue, we should also see why he must regard them as something more than splendid vices." T. H. Irwin, "Splendid Vices? Augustine For and Against Pagan Virtues," *Medieval Philosophy and Theology* 8 (1999): 106, 127.

113. Aristotle, *Nicomachean Ethics*, 1103a30–b1.

114. Peter Lombard, *Libri IV Sententiarum*, Book 2. Distinction 27. Cap. 5. Emphasis added.

115. Eleonore Stump, "The Non-Aristotelian Character of Aquinas's Ethics: Aquinas on the Passions," in *Faith, Rationality, and the Passions*, ed. Sarah Coakley (Malden, MA: Wiley-Blackwell, 2012), 93.

116. Bonnie Kent puts it somewhat differently: "Aquinas argued that only supernatural virtues are virtues simpliciter, that those virtues alone direct one to the ultimate end, that they alone are perfect virtues." Kent, *Virtues of the Will*, 27, 29; Michael Moriarty contrasts Aquinas's view on this question with Augustine's, concluding, "From a certain point of view, then, the overlap between the positions of Aquinas and Augustine is very extensive. … They both hold that, in virtue of the residual rationality that has survived the Fall, pagans are

tues come directly from God by infusion or union with him. Aquinas affirms only theological virtues as real virtues, along with the gifts of the Holy Spirit as "something like enzymes for the theological virtues." She analogizes that the gifts "catalyze a reaction which would go very imperfectly without the enzyme."[117] The gifts are the full form of the virtues arising from a personal union with God resulting in "a person's being attentive to God and apt to follow the inner promptings of God."[118] They enrich and complete the infused virtues by way of communion with God. Love, which is both an infused virtue and a gift, has a special role to play in human psychology in unifying the virtues—"all the moral virtues are infused simultaneously with charity" (I–II.65.3)—rightly aligning the will, which directs all the faculties to "our supernatural end" (I–II.65.2). Therefore, Stump relegates acquired virtue to the lowest rung in a three-tiered hierarchy on which the gifts of the Spirit are the fullest form of virtue.

It is worth noting how acquired virtues fall short of real virtue, and what their place is within Aquinas's psychology. For Aquinas, the acquired virtues are genuine perfect habits, but not true virtue. The efficient cause of true virtue is God, and in this sense the acquired virtues fall short. Since acquired virtues are realizable by agents acting in their own right, they do not come from God. But Aquinas argues that the formal cause of virtue is taken from its genus and its difference. Its genus is a quality or habit, and its difference, that which differentiates it, is its end (telos). The acquired virtues do qualify as virtues in terms of the genus, that is, they are indeed habits. But in terms of difference, acquired virtues are merely ordered toward proximal goods as their ends. Proximal ends are those within the grasp of mere human reason, rather than true beatitude, which "exceeds man's nature and which a man can attain only by God's power, through a

---

capable of performing some acts that are, in themselves, morally good, or even admirable. These acts will not, however, in the least improve their chances of salvation: they do not even amount to virtue in the full sense, since, lacking faith in the true God, pagans are unable to refer, or subordinate, their actions to him, as the supreme good for human beings; lacking grace, they cannot be actuated by charity." Michael Moriarty, *Disguised Vices: Theories of Virtue in Early Modern French Thought* (Oxford: Oxford University Press, 2011), 91.

117. Stump, "Non-Aristotelian Character," 94.

118. Stump, "Non-Aristotelian Character," 98.

certain participation in the divine nature" (I–II.62.1).[119] Theological virtues "have God as their object," are infused by him, and are "made known to us only through divine revelation" (I–II.62.1).

Aquinas seems interested in preserving acquired virtue in some sense while also affirming that this psychological state falls short of virtue that counts for anything before God. Aquinas seems less interested in the dark side of pagan virtues than he is interested in affirming the psychological existence of them as habits. The acquired virtues are real even if they are not wholly good. They are real in the sense that they are perfective habits; they are not wholly good in the sense that they are aimed only at lesser, merely natural goods. While this is a massive qualification, the point is that there is some sort of psychological similitude between infused virtues and acquired virtues, even if the former are the true virtues insofar as they are directed to supernatural ends and infused by God. Bonnie Kent writes, "By describing them as 'true but imperfect' virtues he was nonetheless able to make an important distinction Augustine did not: between those pagans with true, albeit imperfect virtues and those who have the appearance of virtue but are, in fact, motivated by secret vice."[120] Pagans may be good in a civic sense, not in any way that enjoins them to God. Acquired virtue can only "do what is good in relation to an end that does not exceed man's natural power" (I–II.65.2). The acquired virtues only "perfect man in accord with his common condition," not in accord with "some lofty condition" (I–II.65.1).

In the end, Stump is exactly right to say that Aquinas's ethics are not Aristotelian, though he incorporates Aristotelian elements into his psychology. If it is true that acquired virtues really are perfective habits ordered to proximal human goods, rather than ultimate supernatural goods, then we must not only take seriously the psychological existence of these acquired virtues, but we must ask how these imperfect virtues relate to the supernatural ones within the unified psyche. What do we make of the change of unregenerate people? Aquinas makes at least one interesting comment on this relation: "The acts that are produced by an infused habit do not cause any habit but instead strengthen the pre-existing habit, in the same way

---

119. Aquinas holds that beatitude is arrived at "though certain acts" (I–II.6 pr.). Theological virtues perfect these acts whose end is supernatural beatitude. Theological virtues alone produce merit. Virtue is to merit what vice is to sin.

120. Kent, *Virtues of the Will*, 29.

that medicine given to a man who is through his nature healthy does not cause health but instead strengthens the health that was had beforehand" (I–II.51.4 ad. 3). We must exercise care here. There is only one act of attention to which virtue applies, but we must not suggest that acquired virtue in any sense prepares one for the reception of grace.

Finally, while Aquinas gives a lot of attention to the formation of habits, he also talks about their "corruption and diminution" (I–II.53). They may be corrupted or diminished (I–II.53.1–2) by a variety of factors including forgetfulness, deception, ignorance, passion, and choice. A habit may fail either by cessation of act, as with forgetfulness (I–II.53.3), or by contrary action, as with deception and choice (I–II.53.1).

EVALUATION

I wish simply to make three observations about Aquinas's notion of virtue. First, his notion of virtue relies on his treatment of habit within his larger metaphysical scheme. Habit is not trivial but is the ontological ground of character building toward the realization of true humanity. If Aquinas is right about the metaphysical importance of habit, it is significant that Protestant theology has overlooked it. Protestant accounts of sanctification risk being metaphysically anemic, limiting themselves to the performance of moral duties. Second, for Aquinas, habit comes in different classes, perfect and imperfect with respect to their subject, body or soul, as in health or virtue; with respect to their means, acquired, infused, or by communion; and with respect to their source, from God or man. At the top of this hierarchy of virtues there is virtue from God that comes through his grace. At the bottom of this hierarchy is the imperfect habit of the body, which comes through exercise. However, since there is one composite being and one intention, the hierarchy of habits are intertwined—e.g., illness may influence hopefulness and mental distress may cause illness. Aquinas has very helpfully laid the groundwork for more sophisticated analysis of the phenomenological complexity of virtue. The category of acquired virtue could be significant to sufferers seeking to acquire emotional stability, but who might feel spiritually deficient. Many Christian mental health professionals distinguish between emotional and spiritual health for this very reason. However, Protestant theologians rightly recognize that even acquired virtue is not a human contribution, but the result of

God's common grace. This is a crucial theological caveat for appropriating Thomistic categories. Third, and finally, virtue is a helpful word because it refers not simply to doing right, but to the conditions for being disposed to the good, encompassing both moral and physiological aspects (perfect and imperfect).

CONCLUSION

We have not evaluated the full theological framework of Thomas Aquinas but have examined the mechanics of his psychology. We have attended both to the faculties and to how they are qualified by the body. Aquinas's account of humanity is holistic; human beings are composite of body and soul, but with a single intention. Phenomenologically speaking, we are unified. Aquinas offers a tiered psychology, with higher and lower powers, reason and will and sense perception and appetite. The higher powers govern the lower politically, and sense appetite responds directly to experience as mediated by bodily qualities. So Aquinas's psychology integrates medicine research. The special composite feature of sense appetite enables plasticity or moldability. These features—political rule, direct experiential responsiveness, and bodily mediation—account for the curious in-between status of the emotions with regard to rationality and voluntariness. Yet over time our higher powers have a significant degree of control over our lower powers by informing them cognitively and directing their motions volitionally. A key aspect of emotional control is attention, both in terms of how our wills orient all of our powers and in terms of what we perceive and imagine. Finally, Aquinas has a threefold hierarchy of virtue—acquired virtue, infused virtue, and the gifts of the Spirit—where acquired virtue is not even true virtue, but merely habit. We have asked how these virtues relate to each other within a unified psyche. The next chapter will look at four features of Aquinas's psychology:

1. Humankind is a holistic composite featuring plasticity (especially in the lower faculties).

2. Humankind possesses a tiered psychology involving higher and lower appetite and the possibility of cooperation or conflict between the two levels.

3. The higher powers govern the lower powers politically.

4. Humankind can possess imperfect virtue (civic virtue) apart from special grace but requires it for true virtue.

These four features were eclipsed by shifting priorities in the development of theological psychology between Aquinas and John Calvin.

3

—

DEVELOPMENTS IN MEDIEVAL AND RENAISSANCE PSYCHOLOGY

I n the previous chapter, I highlighted some of the advantages of Thomas Aquinas's psychology. We have seen that Aquinas accounts for the genuine involvement of the body in agency in a way that is not entirely negative. We have also seen that Aquinas's notion of the person is a holistic composite. Aquinas has a tiered psychology of higher and lower powers that enables genuine interaction between the powers under the political rule of the rational powers. The passions are independent from the rational powers in a way that is not purely passive; the passions have an in-between state with regard to voluntariness. Moreover, because people are holistic, passions are plastic. This insight is essential for virtue theory. Leveraging this plasticity via agency enables agents to plan what they will be, at least in some ways that fall short of true virtue. True virtue comes from the initiation of God's saving and restoring activity, opening up the path to true human beatitude. Aquinas's psychology, as I have mentioned, is characterized by four distinctive features:

1. Humankind is a holistic composite featuring plasticity, especially in the lower faculties.

2. Humankind possesses a tiered psychology involving higher and lower appetites and the possibility of cooperation or conflict between the two levels.

3. The higher powers govern the lower powers politically.

4. Humankind can possess imperfect virtue (civic virtue) apart from special grace but requires it for true virtue.

It is startling to note that all of these seem to be effectively eliminated in John Calvin's psychology, except perhaps the last feature. This chapter aims at giving a rough historical bridge from Aquinas to Calvin for a few reasons. First, this historical bridge suggests that Calvin is in no way explicitly rejecting the psychology of Thomas Aquinas. The conversation had shifted to such an extent that Aquinas's psychology is almost nowhere obviously behind Calvin's psychological assertions. This chapter will outline some major controversies that shifted the questions being answered in theological psychology. Second, this historical bridge also provides a partial explanation for two ways that Calvin's psychology seems distinct from Aquinas's: (1) it is much less holistic in terms of the body-soul relation; and (2) it seems to have little to no place for the lower passions in moral theology, which seems to yield an altered explanation for internal conflict. I hope to show here also that Calvin reflects the shape of the psychological conversation, rather than any particular rejection of Aquinas.[1]

I am asking the following questions: How did theological psychology get from Aquinas to Calvin? How did both the central questions and the answers of theological psychology develop during the intervening 235 years? The point is to trace how the discussion changed, not to fault Calvin for failing to answer questions that were not being asked. The aim is to provide a contextual lens for reading Calvin's psychology and to explain how

---

1. In saying this I am agreeing with Heiko Oberman's observation that major transitional figures have as many similarities with their interlocutors as differences. The tendency to see the history of theology only through the lens of major disagreements, not noting the continuities, can sometimes distort or idealize the theology of these major figures. Oberman writes,

> Reformation scholars have been inclined to view the later middle ages merely as the "background of the Reformation" and have too often been guided in their evaluation by statements of the Reformers – especially Martin Luther – which by their very nature tend to be informed by a conscious departure from particular developments in the medieval tradition. There is a tendency in this school to stress contrasts between Luther and late medieval theologians and in general to assign Luther more to the tradition of St. Paul and Augustine than to that of William of Ockham and Gabriel Biel.

Heiko Augustinus Oberman, *The Harvest of Medieval Theology* (Grand Rapids: Baker Academic, 1983), 1. Bonnie Kent adds, "We might fault modern scholars for having taken this announced too much at face value, but not for inventing it. In any case, the problem lies less with the story of decline, or disintegration, or rupture in itself than with the tendency to describe thirteenth- and fourteenth-century thought in anticipation of developments centuries later." Bonnie Kent, *Virtues of the Will: The Transformation of Ethics in the Late Thirteenth Century* (Washington, DC: Catholic University of America Press, 1995), 9.

he came to have no place for virtue as an inhering habit of the body-soul composite. This contextual lens is an interpretive frame for understanding the sparse explicit comments Calvin makes about his psychology, especially in *Institutes*, Book I, Chapter 15, Sections 6–8.[2] The following chapter will take up Calvin's psychology in more detail.

This chapter contains two major sections, each with two subsections. Under "The Nature of the Soul," I will discuss the development of the identity thesis of the essence of the soul and its powers and the immortality of the soul. In both of these sections, I am attempting to show how psychology moved away from Aquinas's holistic composite account of human nature toward a more Cartesian dualist account. Under "The Functions of the Soul," I will discuss the ascendency of the will in action theory in the late Middle Ages, including the development of the determined will. In these sections, I will trace how virtue came to have little to no role to play in action theory.[3]

THE NATURE OF THE SOUL

The Identity Thesis and the Essence of the Soul

Perhaps the most significant explanatory frame for Calvin's psychology is the development in the thirteenth and fourteenth centuries of what Adam Wood calls the identity thesis of the relation between the soul and its powers. There were two concurrent controversies during this period, the identity problem and the unicity problem. In the first case, many theologians came to think that the soul just is identical with its powers rather than distinct—e.g., Aquinas held the powers to be accidents of the soul and distinct from it. In the second case, many theologians came to think it unlikely that there is only one form within a human person (unicity), arguing instead for a plurality of forms.[4] The reason these two problems

---

2. My overwhelming focus on this section stems from the fact that Calvin seems to give explicit treatment of the topic only here. Irena Backus says, "Rather uncharacteristically for Calvin [his account of the soul] is condensed in one chapter of the *Institutes* where it is fully elaborated only in 1559. The reformer barely adverts to it in his Commentary and Sermons on the book of Genesis." Irena Backus, *Historical Method and Confessional Identity in the Era of the Reformation (1378–1615)* (Leiden: Brill, 2003), 85.

3. By action theory, I simply mean the study and account of the psychological processes and traits that culminate in bodily action.

4. Adam Wood, "The Faculties of the Soul and Some Medieval Mind-Body Problems," *The Thomist* 75 (2011): 588–89.

are relevant is that together they tended toward a more dualistic and less holistic understanding of body and soul. By affirming a plurality of forms and the idea that the soul is identical with its powers, Scholastic theologians tended to view the soul-body relation increasingly as instrumental and therefore began to prefer mechanistic explanations for how the body operates. There was also a tendency to reduce the number of the soul's powers to the disembodied rational powers, intellect and will. Again, I will call the first problem the identity problem and the second the unicity problem.

The unicity problem arises partly because of Augustine's dividing matter into spiritual matter and corporeal matter.[5] This division tends to lead Scholastics after Aquinas to affirm a plurality of substantial forms. If matter is already qualified as corporeal or spiritual, it has a sort of form. It makes sense then to suppose that another form is added to make it what it particularly is, be it a rock or living body. For example, if the incarnate Christ possessed only one form, his living soul, it seems difficult to affirm that his body was in death either a body or his, since his living soul was absent. The problem also perhaps arose from the difficulty in explaining the parts of the soul, the rational, sensitive, and vegetative, leading some Aristotelians to posit three forms.[6] Wood summarizes, "Most thirteenth-century Scholastics agreed that living things have multiple substantial forms."[7]

The identity problem is related to the unicity problem because most proponents of plurality of forms were identity theorists with regard to the soul and its powers,[8] affirming that the soul just is its powers. These Scholastics explained the diversity of powers that a person possesses by appealing to a diversity of forms. (See Figure 3.1). Thirteenth century

5. Wood, "Faculties of the Soul," 590.

6. Daniel Callus traces this inter-Aristotelian debate about whether or not the vegetative, sensitive, and rational souls are different substances, beginning with Avicenna and Avicebron. Callus distinguishes between the debate over multiple souls and multiple substances or forms. Callus, "Origins of the Problem of Unity of Form," 282.

7. Wood, "Faculties of the Soul," 591.

8. The unicity versus plurality question differs from the distinction versus identity question, and it was possible to affirm a unicity of forms and soul/faculty identity like William of Auvergne.

theologians en masse rejected the idea that the soul was distinct from its powers, even theologians who came to be suspicious of a plurality of forms.[9]

	Unicity of Forms	Plurality of Forms
Soul/faculty Distinction	(1) Thomas Aquinas	
Soul/faculty Identity	(3) William of Auvergne	(2) Robert Kilwardby, Peter John Olivi

Figure 3.1, The Identity and Unicity Problems

Aquinas, by contrast, explains the diversity of powers as the accidental forms, distinct from the soul's essence of the soul.[10] He writes, "since the soul's power is not its essence, it must be an accident contained within the second species of quality" (ST I.77.1 ad. 5).[11] Aquinas's conviction at least partly arises from the fact that the powers of the soul seem both to contradict each other at points and to be located bodily, perfecting certain bodily organs.[12] Since the soul singly cannot oppose itself "at the same time and in the same respect," the powers must be distinct.[13]

Aquinas's chief opponent, Henry of Ghent (1217–1293), appealed to the principle of parsimony in arguing that diverse operations could indeed

---

9. Wood, "Faculties of the Soul," 591–93; Wood writes, "even some thirteenth-century Scholastics who appear to have reservations about the plurality of substantial forms endorse the identity of the soul with its powers," (593). He cites Rufus of Cornwall and William of Auvergne as examples. See Ernest A. Moody, "William of Auvergne and his Treatise *De anima*," *Studies in Medieval Philosophy: Science and Logic* (Berkeley, CA: University of California Press, 1975), 1–110; Daniel A. Callus, "Two Early Oxford Masters on the Problem of the Plurality of Forms: Adam of Buckfield—Richard Rufus of Cornwall," *Revue neoscholastique de philosophic* 42 (1939): 411–45.

10. Wood, "Faculties of the Soul," 598–99.

11. For Aquinas, the powers of the soul are qualities (*proprietates*), not its essence. Wood translates this as accidental forms; ST I.77.1 ad. 5; I.77.1. ad. 1. QD De Anima 12.1; Wood, "Faculties of the Soul," 598.

12. Aquinas also appeals to the argument of Alexander of Hales of an analogy being *esse* and *operari* and *essentia* and *potentia*. Wood explains, "if a creature's capacities for operation were identical to its essence, then it would be like God, whose activity is identical to his being." Wood, "Faculties of the Soul," 600.

13. Wood, "Faculties of the Soul," 601.

come from the same subject, the soul. And what is historically significant is that it appears that most theologians were convinced by his argument. Wood notes that "Richard of Mediavilla, Peter John Olivi, John Duns Scotus, William of Ockham, John Buridan, and others all invoke versions of Henry's reasoning in their defenses of the identity thesis."[14]

Holding both the plurality of forms and the identity thesis tended to reduce the number of powers according to the principle of parsimony, to avoid multiplying forms. For example, John Duns Scotus (1266–1308) and William of Ockham (1285–1347) use Henry of Ghent's argument to argue for the identity thesis as well as to reduce the number of substantial forms in a living being. For the sake of simplicity, both Ockham and Duns Scotus argue that "the vegetative and sensitive souls are really identical."[15] By failing to distinguish the vegetative and sensitive powers, the sensitive powers are effectively downgraded into irrationality by theologians, thereby eliminating what I am calling tiered psychology. Ockham goes further than most in distinguishing two souls, the rational and the non-rational, the non-rational comprising the sensitive and vegetative powers.[16] He argues for two souls, in this case like Aquinas, on the grounds that the powers can oppose each other. It seems impossible for the intellectual part to be the same as the sensitive and vegetative parts since the intellectual part does not use a bodily organ. So Ockham neatly proposes a plurality of souls, not merely forms, but an identity between these souls and their powers. By comparison, Calvin denies the two souls view.

Other theologians of this period, such as Walter Chatton (c. 1290–1343), William Crathorn (fl. 1330s), Gregory of Rimini (c. 1300–1358), and John Buridan (1295–1363) also adopted the identity thesis, but with differing

---

14. Wood, "Faculties of the Soul," 609–10.

15. Wood, "Faculties of the Soul," 610. Duns Scotus, *Ordinatio* IV, d. 44, q. 1 (Wadding, ed., 10:98); Ockham, *Rep.* 3.4 (*Opera theologica* 6:130–48). Both men thought the soul is identical with its powers. Scotus recognized only a formal distinction, while Ockham saw a distinction only in name. Wood, "Faculties of the Soul," 611. For more on why Scotus holds a formal distinction, see Ian Christopher Drummond, "John Duns Scotus on the Role of the Moral Virtues" (PhD diss., University of Toronto, 2016), 12–17.

16. Vesa Hirvonen notes that "Ockham seems to think that the Paris Condemnation of 1277 required the plurality of forms in the human being." Ockham theorized that there are two souls and three forms: the corporeal, the sensitive (also a soul), and the intellectual (also a soul). Vera Hirvonen, *Passions in William Ockham's Philosophical Psychology* (Dordrecht: Kluwer Academic, 2004), 35.

views about the plurality of souls. Buridan held that the soul and its principle powers are identical, but added that the dispositions of bodily organs are used as instruments, positing a distinction between "principle and instrumental or dispositional powers."[17] This allowed Buridan to escape the difficulty that forced Ockham to posit two souls, namely, how the soul can be both "extended and unextended, material and immaterial."[18] Buridan suggested that while the instrumental powers are extended and material, the principle powers are not. The principle powers are not exercised by any bodily organ, while the instrumental powers are. The immaterial, principle powers are distinct from these bodily dispositions but identical with the soul.[19] The principle powers use the instrumental ones "as a blacksmith uses fire and a hammer."[20]

It is easy to see how Buridan's view is only a short step from that of René Descartes. It is only a short step from material instrumental powers to material mechanistic powers. Wood explains, "Instead of attempting to explain how an indivisible intellectual soul could be both the form of an extended body and the principle of its organic operations, Descartes gave up these Aristotelian essentials. The organic operations could be accounted for by mechanistic physics."[21] And if the soul is immaterial and unextended, it also remains difficult for Buridan to explain either how the intellect inheres in the body or how an unextended sensitive soul, being the same as the intellective soul, can achieve an act of sensation. Buridan says this problem is "truly miraculous and supernatural."[22] This is the exact problem that Descartes solved by appealing to the pineal gland as the seat of the soul. Buridan's psychology appears to be a movement toward a more

---

17. John Buridan, *Questiones in De anima*, 2.5. Cited in Wood, "Faculties of the Soul," 614n83; 617n91.

18. Wood, "Faculties of the Soul," 628.

19. Sander W. de Boer explains, "If by 'power' we refer to the required qualitative dispositions, then the powers are distinct from the soul and from one another [seemingly Aquinas's position]. If, on the other hand, we refer to power in the sense that the dispositions are not included, then all powers, including the vegetative and sensitive ones, are identical with the soul." Sander W. de Boer, *The Science of the Soul: The Commentary Tradition on Aristotle's De anima, c. 1260–1360* (Leuven: Leuven University Press, 2013), 246.

20. Buridan, *Questiones in De anima*, 2.5.

21. Wood, "Faculties of the Soul," 635.

22. Wood, "Faculties of the Soul," 628; Buridan, *Questiones in De anima*, 2.9.

rigid dualism within roughly Aristotelian Scholastic thought itself; instrumentalism is only a short step from Cartesianism.

As Wood narrates it, the debate over the identity thesis "gradually wound down toward a generally Buridan consensus."[23] Katharine Park writes, "more and more philosophers without any specific commitment to the *via moderna* began to move towards an assertion of the identity of the soul and its faculties and a corresponding emphasis on the organs of the body as the key to psychological function below the level of intellection."[24] She adds that there was an "increasing tendency to favour specific physiological over general philosophical explanations for organic functions."[25] In short, the vegetative and sensitive powers were relegated to the body and were thus out of the realm of philosophical or theological explanation.

Finally, Wood notes that both Gabriel Biel and John Mair adopted Buridan's view.[26] Martin Luther's relationship to Gabriel Biel is well-documented.[27] John Mair's influence on John Calvin was perhaps more tenuous,[28] but it seems reasonable to suppose that Calvin was familiar with this Buridian consensus about the soul and its powers.

What does the identity thesis mean for my tiered and holistic psychology? The turn away from psychological holism eliminated the crucial quasi-rational tier. In rejecting a holistic account of the body and soul, sensitive appetite was radically reconceived as a part of the lower, irrational aspect

---

23. Wood, "Faculties of the Soul," 632.

24. Katharine Park, "The Organic Soul," in *The Cambridge History of Renaissance Philosophy*, ed. Charles B. Schmitt and Quentin Skinner (Cambridge: Cambridge University Press, 1988), 478–79.

25. Park, "Organic Soul," 480.

26. Wood, "Faculties of the Soul," 634.

27. Oberman, *Harvest of Medieval Theology*; Leif Grane, *Contra Gabrielem: Luthers Auseinandersetsung mit Gabriel Biel in der Disputatio Contra Scholasticam Theologiam 1517* (Copenhagen: Gyldenhal, 1962); David Steinmetz, "Aquinas for Protestants: What Luther got Wrong," *Christian Century* 122, no. 7 (August 2005): 23–26; Lawrence Murphy, "Gabrield Biel as Transmitter of Aquinas to Luther," *Renaissance and Reformation* 19, no. 1 (February 1983): 26–41.

28. Anthony N. S. Lane gives a good summary of the speculated influence. Anthony N. S. Lane, *John Calvin: Student of the Church Fathers* (Grand Rapids: Baker Books, 1999), 16–25. Alister McGrath is a bit more sanguine about Mair's possible influence. At the least he says Calvin may have been influenced by the *schola Augustiniana moderna*, "There are ... excellent reasons for suggesting that Calvin was indeed influenced by such a school, whether directly or indirectly." Alister E. McGrath, "John Calvin and Late Mediaeval Thought: A Study in Late Mediaeval Influences upon Calvin's Theological Development," *Archiv für Reformationsgeschichte* 77 (1986): 71.

of human nature, a part of the body. Virtue, as we will see below, in order
to sustain its connection to rationality, was thus migrated to being a quality of the will alone.

The Immortality of the Soul

A second and related controversy that frames Calvin's psychology is the
debate concerning the immortality of the soul. This was no trivial issue.
Paul Richard Blum succinctly states that the "debate during the Renaissance
over the immortality of the soul encompassed epistemology, metaphysics,
and theology."[29] My reason for highlighting this controversy is to show that
more than one controversy promoted a more rigid dualistic conception of
human nature during this timeframe. The controversy over the immortality of the soul is related to the debate over the plurality and identity
problems in that both of these controversies tend to assume that the intellectual soul and the body cannot be as closely bound as Aquinas describes.

The doctrine of immortality came under attack from two points of view,
the Alexandrism and the Averroism. Platonic philosophy was the antithesis for both of these views. Neither view thought an eternal intellective
soul could be in the body—Alexandrism essentially eliminating the soul
and Averroism positing one unified eternal intellect. In both cases, there is
the same crisis: How can an eternal soul be embodied? I will briefly survey
the key characters of this debate.

As just mentioned, there were two general ways to deny the immortality
of the soul, Averroism and Alexandrism. According to Averroism, there is
one unified eternal intellect that all human beings share, which is taken
to preclude the intellect as the individual form of the body, and by implication the immortality of the individual human soul.[30] As Eckhard Kessler

---

29. Metaphysically the question is, is there something spiritual, unchangeable, and lasting that gives form, life, and real intelligence to human life, which exceeds that life of the
animals? If so, epistemically speaking, "what is the evidence for this, and what does it mean
for man to be essentially spiritual?" Theologically speaking, not only is the *imago* at stake,
but also the sense in which God enables human beings to have true knowledge (e.g., illumi-
nation). The question was bound up with an argument over the credentials of theology and
philosophy to know about the universe and humanity in particular. Paul Richard Blum, "The
Immortality of the Soul," in *The Cambridge Companion to Renaissance Philosophy*, ed. James
Hankins (Cambridge: Cambridge University Press, 2007), 211.

30. John Monfasani writes, "[Averroism] was the attribution to Aristotle of Averroes'
doctrine of the unity of the agent and possible intellects for all men and therefore the denial

notes, "immortality and individuality are mutually exclusive in principle." Since what is eternal is single, distinct individual human souls cannot be.[31] Alexandrism, by contrast, represents the view that the soul is a form arising from the potentiality of matter. It is purely material, the "highest development of the animalistic soul."[32] This is similar to the Galenic view that the soul is just a temperament of the body, a particular concoction of the humors and spirits.[33]

The controversy over the immortality of the soul had many layers and waves of controversialists. Julius Weinberg notes that the schism between faith and reason was partly the target of the Condemnations of Paris against Averroistic and Aristotelian doctrines in 1270 and 1277. He points to Siger of Brabant (1240–1280) and Boethius of Dacia (c. 1240–1284) as early controversialists in this fission, both men being targets of the condemnation of Averroism of 1277.[34] Blum states that the "real beginning of the immortality debate" was the Council of Florence in 1439. Here Georgius Gemistus, known as Plethon (d. 1452), "launched an attack on Latin Aristotelianism by accusing Aristotle ... of inconsistency by teaching in his book *On the Soul* that the human mind is eternal, but not endorsing

---

of the immortality of the individual human soul." John Monfasani, "The Averroism of John Argyropoulos and His 'Quaestio utrum intellectus humanus sit perpetuus,'" *Tatti Studies in the Italian Renaissance* 5 (1993): 165. See also Marco Sgarbi, "Benedetto Varchi on the Soul: Vernacular Aristotelianism between Reason and Faith," *Journal of the History of Ideas* 76, no. 1 (January 2015): 2.

31. Eckhard Kessler, "Alexander of Aphrodisias and his Doctrine of the Soul: 1400 Years of Lasting Signifiance," *Early Science and Medicine* 16 (2011): 21.

32. Kessler, "Alexander of Aphrodisias," 22. We might even say, anachronistically, emerging from the potentiality of matter.

33. Galen's actual view of the soul is only suggestively, not explicitly physicalist. He still gives some lip-service to the Platonic soul. Cf. Robert Hankinson, "Partitioning the Soul: Galen on the Anatomy of the Psychic Functions and Mental Illness," in *Partitioning the Soul: Debates from Plato to Leibniz*, ed. Klaus Corcilius and Dominik Perler (Berlin: De Gruyter, 2014), 85–106.

34. Citing Siger's view that Aristotle's arguments for the eternity of the world were conclusive, Julius Weinberg writes, "Thus, arguing by natural reason, one could produce irrefutable proofs of what is, according to the truth of the faith, false. From this one who held to faith could only conclude that human reason is not ultimately dependable." Julius Weinberg, *A Short History of Medieval Philosophy* (Princeton, NJ: Princeton University Press, 1964), 172. Bonnie Kent has quite a bit of detail related to this and on the reception history of Aristotle in *Virtues of the Will*, 39–93. Henry Nardone remarks that very little is known about their lives following the condemnation, with one source claiming that Siger was stabbed to death by a papal clerk in 1281; Henry F. Nardone, "St. Thomas Aquinas and the Condemnation of 1277" (Diss., Catholic University of America, 1964), 72.

that same doctrine in his *Ethics*."[35] Plethon's work is attributed with prompt-
ing Cosimo de' Medici to commission Ficino's translations of Plato, thereby
initiating a resurgence in Platonic thought.[36] Not long after this, George
of Trebizond and Cardinal Bessarion were participants in the debate.
George of Trebizond published his *Comparatio Philosophorum Platonis et
Aristotle* (1458), stimulating Cardinal Bessarion's very influential response,
In Columniatorem Platonis (1469).[37] In his book, George defends the claim
that Aristotle believed in the immortality of the soul.[38] Bessarion's rebuttal,
by contrast, "quickly won a widespread readership [and] … made a particularly lasting impact on contemporaries."[39] In it Bessarion includes an
attack on Aristotle's view of the immortality of the soul.[40]

But perhaps the most important controversialists were involved in
The Pomponazzi Affair,[41] Platonist Marsilio Ficino (1433-1499) and Pietro
Pomponazzi (1462-1525). In 1482, the Platonist Ficino called for a pious philosophy which would defend and explain Christian beliefs.[42] He argued for
the immortality of the soul, saying, "Were the soul not immortal, no creature would be more miserable than man."[43] He is emblematic of a "growing pressure from the alliance of Neoplatonism and the church" between

---

35. Blum, "Immortality of the Soul," 213.

36. Blum, "Immortality of the Soul," 213.

37. The *Comparatio* of George of Trebizond was itself not very influential, leading John
Monfasani to say, "one could argue that the major achievement of George's work was that
it provoked Bessarion into writing the *In Calumniatorem Platonis*." John Monfasani, "A tale
of two books: Bessarion's *In Calumniatorem Platonis* and Geroge of Trebizond's *Comparatio
Philosophorum Platonis et Aristotelis*," *Renaissance Studies* 22 no. 1 (2007): 4. Cf. Ludwig Mohler,
Kardinal Bessarion als Theologe, Humanist, und Staatsman: Darstellung (Darmstadt: Paderborn
1967), 346-83.

38. Monfasani, "tale of two books," 14.

39. Peter Schulz, "George Gemistos Plethon (ca. 1360-1454), George of Trebizond
(1396-1472), and Cardinal Bessarion (1403-1472): The Controversy between Platonists and
Aristotelians in the Fifteenth Century," in *Philosophers of the Renaissance*, ed. Paul Richard
Blum, trans. Brian McNeil (Washington, DC: Catholic University of America Press, 1999), 28.

40. Schulz, "George Gemistos Plethon," 30; *In Columniatorem Platonis*, 2.7.

41. So Eckhard Kessler, "The Intellective Soul," in *The Cambridge History of Renaissance
Philosophy*, ed. Charles B. Schmitt and Quentin Skinner (Cambridge: Cambridge University
Press, 1988), 504-7.

42. Jill Kraye, "Pietro Pomponazzi (1462-1525): Secular Aristotelianism in the Renaissance,"
in *Philosophers of the Renaissance*, ed. Paul Richard Blum, trans. Brian McNeil (Washington,
DC: Catholic University of America Press, 1999), 93.

43. Marsilio Ficino, *Platonic Theology*, 1.14 (1.1). Cited in Kraye, "Pietro Pomponazzi," 100.

1490–1520.[44] Eckhard Kessler remarks that this tendency and the resulting Aristotelian reaction mark this period. He writes that the Aristotelian reaction "led to a reassessment of natural philosophy as a mode of argument in its own right."[45]

Pietro Pomponazzi, an Italian contemporary of Ficino, was a part of this Aristotelian reaction.[46] He argued that there is simply "no way of maintaining man's individual unity as a rational mind composed of body and soul, and serving as the subject of cognition."[47] Since sustaining the possibility of universal knowledge was the only reason for positing an immaterial soul, Pomponazzi thought it was simplest to conclude that the soul is the highest material form, "attaining in its most elevated operations something beyond materiality," the Alexandrism position.[48] He denied that Aristotle taught the immortality of the soul even suggesting that he "never even thought of such non-sense."[49] However, Pomponazzi states that his belief in the immortality of the soul remained unshaken, since it was known by revelation and by faith. Effectively, Pomponazzi pitted reason and natural philosophy against faith, arousing a severe backlash from the church.[50]

---

44. Kessler, "Intellective Soul," 494–95.

45. Kessler, "Intellective Soul," 495.

46. Another key figure was Agostino Nifo (1473–1545). Nifo represents Neoplatonic eclecticism. (Kessler, "Intellective Soul," 496). While he began his career as an Averroist, he later adapted his view by a "superimposing of Neoplatonic participation metaphysics on the Aristotelian metaphysics of form and matter" (Kessler, "Intellective Soul," 498). For Nifo, the human soul is an intermediate form that participates in both celestial form, spiritual cognition, and in terrestrial, with regard to the human body. In this way he explains the soul as both being the substantial, individual form of the body and possessing universal knowledge. Participation language enables him to negotiate the Averroistic assumption that the soul cannot do both. The syncretic view attempts to bring together Averroistic Aristotelianism and Neoplatonism. Kessler notes that "[Nifo] concludes by proudly rejoicing in his agreement with Ficino, the founder of Renaissance Platonism" (Kessler, "Intellective Soul," 500).

47. Kessler, "Intellective Soul," 501.

48. Kessler, "Intellective Soul," 503.

49. Pomponazzi, *Tractatus de immortalitate animae*, 36. Cited in Kraye, "Pietro Pomponazzi," 100 (translation is her own).

50. Kraye writes, "Pomponazzi's first response to this onslaught was an *Apologia* (1518), cannily dedicated to Cardinal Sigismondo Gonzaga, in which he restated his position that immortality was not rationally demonstrable since it was contrary to the principles of Aristotelian natural philosophy. As an article of faith, it could—and should—be founded solely on divine revelation." Kraye, "Pietro Pomponazzi," 102. Wood identifies some other theologians who doubted whether the immortality of the soul could be proved by reason, including Scotus, Ockham, and Buridan. Wood, "Faculties of the Soul," 624–26. See also

Pomponazzi's view was decidedly rejected by the Fifth Lateran Council, 1512–1517. The council decreed that in spite of the assertion of some that the soul is mortal, "at least according to philosophy … we condemn and reject all those who insist that the intellectual soul is mortal, or that it is only one among all human beings."[51] The council further decreed, "And since truth cannot contradict truth, we define that every statement contrary to the enlightened truth of the faith is totally false and we strictly forbid teaching otherwise to be permitted."[52] The controversy over Pomponazzi's views led Bartolomeo Spina to write in 1519 that the doctrine of the immortality of the soul was "half-dead."[53]

Again, this is crucial context for understanding Calvin's claim that "not one of [the philosophers], with the exception of Plato, distinctly maintained its immortality" (I.15.6).[54] In a debate over the interpretation of Aristotle,[55] it is easy to see how Platonic psychology might be a safer alternative for philosophical formulation. There are two key points to make. First, we have an overlapping reason for the movement toward a more rigid dualism. A more holistic dualism like Aquinas's seemed dangerously susceptible to denying the immortality of the soul. But as I have noted, without a holistic account of human nature, it is hard to see how plasticity has a place in psychology, and how bodily emotion is anything but irrational. Second, as

---

Kessler, "Intellective Soul," 503–4; Duns Scotus, *Ordinatio* IV, d. 43, q. 2 in Allen Wolter, ed., *Philosophical Writings: A Selection* (Indianapolis: Hackett, 1987), 133–62; Ockham, *Quodibet* 1.10 (*Opera theologica* 9:63).

51. "Fifth Lateran Council 1512–17 A.D," *Papal Encyclicals Online*, http://www.papalencyclicals.net/ councils/ecum18.htm; Norman P. Tanner, ed., *Decrees of the Ecumenical Councils*, 2 vols. (Washington, DC: Georgetown University Press, 1990), 595–655.

52. "Fifth Lateran Council."

53. Bartolomeo Spina, *Propugnaculum Aristotelis de immortalitate*, Dedicatory Letter, cited by Dennis Des Chene, *Life's Form: Late Aristotelian Conceptions of the Soul* (Ithaca, NY: Cornell University Press, 2000), 46. See also Etienne Gilson, "Autour de Pomponazzi: Problematique de l'immortality de l'ame en Italie au debut de XVIC siecle," *Archives d'historie doctrinale et literaire du moyen age* 36 (1961): 198. See Eckhard Kessler for a fuller account of the Pompanazzi controversy. Kessler, "Intellective Soul," 504–7.

54. John Calvin, *Institutes*.

55. Bonnie Kent corrects Etienne Gilson's narrative of the rise of Neo-Augustinianism against Aquinas's Aristotelianism. She notes a tendency among theologians of the thirteenth century to cite Aristotle for support, but not directly to oppose him, excepting theologians like Peter Olivi. She summarizes, "Efforts to reconcile Aristotle with the faith were the rule, not the exception." Kent, *Virtues of the Will*, 63, 82–87, 93. It certainly seems like the desire to claim Aristotle's authority and to interpret him rightly continued well on into the fifteenth century.

we will see in the next chapter, Calvin does not explicitly reject Aquinas or even Aristotle, but finds the Aristotelian view troublingly ambiguous in light of the contest of interpretation especially among the Averroists.

Finally, the issue of the nature of the soul is also of great consequence to the fate of virtue, since as Franciscus Toletus (1532–1596) writes, "[if] the use of reason, as well as life and death, depends on temperament; from it too various habits come; and so the soul is nothing other than a temperament of qualities, and thus an accident."[56] If the soul is an accident, then it owes its ontological dependence to the body, not the other way around. As an accident it cannot be the first principle of life and motion, nor can it inhibit irrational appetites, since these appetites themselves are owing to the qualities of the body.

THE FUNCTIONS OF THE SOUL: THE ASCENDENCY OF THE WILL IN ACTION THEORY

I have described a general movement away from the composite holism of Thomas Aquinas. Now we turn to addressing the role of the passions in moral theory. The context of how the will came to have a more prominent place in action theory partly illuminates the diminished moral relevance of the passions. I am not claiming that this is an exhaustive or fully causal explanation for their role in Calvin, especially because many post-Reformation Reformed Scholastics do talk about the passions of sensitive appetite, though with a more rigidly dualistic perspective. I am merely suggesting that this philosophical context helps to explain how Calvin should not be seen as explicitly rejecting the view of Thomas Aquinas.

In what follows I will discuss the ascendency of the will in action theory and its resulting reconfiguration. By ascendency of the will, I mean two things. First, that the will is assigned an expanded role in action theory. And second, that the will is enhanced to accommodate this expanded role. Following the Condemnations of 1277 in Paris and William de la Mare's *Correctorium fratris Thomae* written in 1279, the will became the singular faculty of choice even over against the determination of the intellect. Then in order to accommodate this expanded role, the will was assigned a larger

---

56. Franciscus Toletus, *In de Anima* 2c1q1, *Opera* 3:39rb–va; cited in Des Chene, *Life's Form*, 70.

share in the affective element as well as being seemingly an independent source of rationality.

On the one hand, the will, rather than the composite faculty of sense appetite, was taken to be the seat of the passions. On the other, the will functioned somewhat like a *homunculus*,[57] operating independently of and even contrary to reason. I will further suggest that when the *homunculus* will is overlaid by the moral determination of the will, the psychological outcome is a will determined by sin that is at war with reason. This has troubling implications for my introspective dilemma of negative emotion. Elizabeth Agnew Cochran states this concern succinctly: "Reformed theology historically links the emotions with the will, which is subject to moral necessity. Contemporary Reformed reflection on the emotions must therefore grapple with questions about moral agency and accountability that arise from this account of necessity."[58]

VOLUNTARISM AND THE CHOOSING WILL

In order to illustrate the shift to the choosing will, it is necessary to distinguish voluntarism from intellectualism. By voluntarism I am referring to what Bonnie Kent designates ethical voluntarism, which is "a strong emphasis on the active character of the will, the claim that the will is free to act against reason's dictates, and the conviction that moral responsibility depends on this conception of the will's freedom."[59] Intellectualism can be neatly captured by the verbiage of the Condemnation of 1277 issued by Bishop Étienne Tempier: "That the will necessarily pursues what is firmly held by reason, and that it cannot abstain from that which reason dictates.

---

57. Latin, "little man." I am simply referring to the fact that the will is its own fully sufficient agent.

58. Elizabeth Agnew Cochran, "The Moral Significance of Religious Affections: A Reformed Perspective on Emotions and Moral Formation," *Studies in Christian Ethics* 28, no. 2 (2015): 150.

59. Bonnie Kent notes that there are three forms of voluntarism, which are related but need to be distinguished: (1) psychological voluntarism; (2) ethical voluntarism; and (3) theological voluntarism. According to Kent, the first signifies "little more than a general emphasis on the affective and volitional aspects of human nature, then it originated with the first Franciscan masters at Paris." The third represents an emphasis on God's absolute power (*potentia absoluta*) or freedom to act in a way not bound by metaphysical necessity. Kent, *Virtues of the Will*, 94–95.

This necessitation, however, is not compulsion but the nature of the will."[60] I want to argue that Aquinas held neither view. As a way into this debate, and to distinguish Aquinas's view from intellectualism, I will describe Aquinas's theory of how the will can go wrong—his vice theory—to act as a foil against the developing view.

Intellectualism after 1277

Aquinas is often said to have advocated a form of intellectualism. The difficulty with applying this term to him is that the term "intellectualism" only crystalizes its meaning against the voluntarist movement, which arose after his death. The controversy began in earnest at the Condemnation of 1277, three years after Aquinas's death. After this condemnation, Kent says, "the freedom of the will was the most common topic of debate."[61] Prior to the 1270s, free choice was talked about as an act (William of Auxerre), a joint power of reason and will (Peter Lombard), a habit of reason and will (Bonaventure), or even a distinct power in its own right (Albert the Great).[62] One reason why Aquinas is often credited with intellectualism is William de la Mare's *Correctorium fratris Thomae*. De la Mare was particularly unhappy with the fact that Aquinas designated the intellect as the best power.[63] For William, to be in accord with the condemnations of 1277, especially articles 158, 159, and 163, the will must be "lord of its acts."[64]

Voluntarists were concerned to guard against a type of intellectualism that has trouble assigning blame for sin to anything but ignorance in the intellect or compulsion in the passions. If the will simply followed the dictates of the intellect, then the will seems to have no role in sinful

---

60. Étienne Tempier, "Selections from the Condemnation of 1277," in *Medieval Philosophy: Essential Readings with Commentary*, eds. Gyula Klima, Fritz Allhoff, and Anand Vaidya (Malden, MA: Blackwell, 2007), 187–88. "Quod voluntaas necessario prosequitur, quod firmiter creditum est a ratione; et quod non potest abstinere ab eo quo ratio dictat." Cited in Henry F. Nardone, "St. Thomas Aquinas and the Condemnation of 1277" (Diss., Catholic University of America, 1964), 68. Kent, *Virtues of the Will*, 76–77.

61. Kent, *Virtues of the Will*, 99.

62. Kent cites Odin Lottin's observation that "Beginning with William of Auxerre, many Scholastics either defined free decision as 'a faculty of will and reason' or used the definition as a basis for their variants." This very vague definition could support a variety of views; Kent, *Virtues of the Will*, 99. Odin Lottin, *Psychologie et Morale aux XIIe et XIIIe Siècles*, Tome III (Gembloux: Duculot, 1959), 66–262.

63. Aquinas, *ST* I-II.3.5; cf. William de la Mare, *Correctorium fratris Thomae*, Article 2/50.

64. Mare, *Correctorium*, 8/56.

action theory, especially since on Aquinas's view the passions can affect reason's judgment. Aquinas seems to endorse the condemned view: "an act of willing is nothing other than a certain inclination that follows upon an understood form" (ST I.87.4). However, Bonnie Kent suggests that Aquinas did not advocate this sort of intellectualism. She writes,

> The problem for his [Aquinas's] followers was not that the master had advocated an extreme intellectualism: he surely had not. The problem was that he consistently treated freedom as the product of intellect and will working together. ... If the *Correctorium fratris Thomae* had never been written, perhaps Thomists would have rested content with traditional formulas. Free decision, a happy marriage between reason and will might conceivably have remained the topic of debate.[65]

From Aquinas's perspective, the problem with the condemnations is that they assumed an unhappy marriage, or perhaps too large a division, between intellect and will.

Vice Theory

To get a little clarity on the degree to which Aquinas holds the condemned view, it is important to understand the mechanics of his sinful action theory. If the will can go wrong, how does it? Aquinas is very clear that sin proceeds from the act of willing, not from ignorance. Where Aquinas differs dramatically from later medieval voluntarists is that Aquinas is less concerned with the will's immediate power of choosing right or wrong, and more concerned with long-standing psychological habits of virtue and vice. For later theorists like Ockham, the will must not be determined at the moment of choice. This view calls into question virtue and vice as habits of will. Why does an essentially free will need habits? For voluntarists, the will's freedom is its most essential characteristic. For Aquinas, the will's most essential characteristic is its disposition toward beatitude with God according to proper means.

For Aquinas, sin occurs when human beings follow merely their sentient nature to the negation of their rational nature, especially as

---

65. Kent, *Virtues of the Will*, 105.

illuminated by grace. The inclinations of sentient nature are meant to
lead, according to human rational nature, to the end of beatitude through
union with God. But the loss of original justice means that human beings
pursue objects independently of the governance of the rational powers,
mere apparent goods, rather than their highest good. Aquinas affirms that
the will naturally inclines to ultimate beatitude by a sort of necessity, a
natural inclination according to its first principles (ST I.82.1). But since
the rational powers of human beings may be directed toward opposites,
they are liable to sin when these powers do not recognize the connection
between particular goods and beatitude (ST I.82.2). When the will treats
means as ends, as is so often the case, human beings act contrary to their
own nature. In this case, the will chooses contrary to nature and orients the
whole person to inferior goods and is cut off from beatitude. Aquinas says,
"vices and sins proliferate among men because they follow the inclination
of their sentient nature in opposition to the order of reason" (ST I–II.71.2
ad. 3). While it is clear that in Aquinas's view sin seems to originate at the
instigation of sentient appetite, this is only the case because the loss of
original justice disorders the desires making the person's rational nature
susceptible to pursuing mere apparent goods. The will chooses evil, since
it is not in accordance with beatitude with God, under the guise of apparent good. Sin is clearly in the will.

Vice is that settled habit that orders the faculties in ways that are contrary to nature, especially when a person pursues the inclinations of sentient nature without carrying them through to the proper human end. Vice
subverts the proper ordering of a person's rational pursuit of beatitude in a
characteristic way (habitus). So, Aquinas has no trouble affirming a sort of
condition or limitation of the freedom of the choice in fallen human beings
(depraved habitus). While the consequence of original sin is the loss of
original justice, vice proliferates precisely because of the tendency toward
inferior happiness among men that settles as a semi-permanent disposition, or the habit of vice. However, vice does not force the will. Aquinas is
clear that people use a habit when they will (ST I–II.71.4). He is also clear
that grace is necessary for free choice (ST I.83.1 ad. 2–4). Vice is significant
for Aquinas's sin theory, since when original justice is lost, there is now
within human nature the potential for corruption among the faculties. The
point is that this settled ordering of the faculties sets Aquinas apart from

the voluntarists whose emphasis on the will's freedom calls into question both virtue and vice because of the radical freedom of the will.

Aquinas the Intellectualist?

If vice subverts the ordering of the faculties, how then should the faculties work? To put it otherwise, was Aquinas the intellectualist he is made out to be? Absolutely speaking, the intellect is the highest power. It obviously outranks the sentient faculties because it is rational. But even among the rational faculties, the intellect outranks the will because its object is simpler, the good itself, not the good via the intellect as with the will (ST I.82.3). The intellect leads the way by accepting the good by way of its idea of it. The will simply follows in choosing.

However, the will also has priority in a couple of senses. First, the will seeks the higher entity, the good, rather than the true. But second, and more importantly, the will can move the intellect as well as the other powers. There seem to be two basic functions the will possesses among medieval theologians: (1) the will as orienting power, or the orienting will, and (2) the will as chooser, or the choosing will. I have already mentioned that the choosing will simply follows the intellect, i.e., choosing follows apprehending. But the orienting will is primary since it orients the entire range of faculties toward their proper end, including reason. Aquinas writes, "the will moves all the powers of the soul to their acts in the manner of an agent—except for the natural powers of the vegetative part of the soul, which are not subject to our choice" (ST I.82.4). In terms of the function of the choosing will, Aquinas sounds like an intellectualist. But in terms of the function of the orienting will, Aquinas is Augustinian.

Put simply, Aquinas clearly affirms free choice from the cooperation of reason and will. The will orders the powers as its appetite for a person's rational end, but reason allows free judgment by way of comparison made by reason among particular actions (*ex collatione quadam rationis*). However, free choice may be conditioned by vice, or even the temperament of the body, the mix of humors and motion of the spirits. But these two considerations do not negate free choice since, by the power of God, it is within the powers of human beings to acquire virtue and vice or at any given moment to exclude them from a choice, since human beings use virtue and vice when choosing.

Consequently, Aquinas's view is possible only before the Condemnations of 1277 and the *Correctorium fr. Thomae*. Both of these documents assume a competitive relationship between the intellect and the will. In Aquinas's view, the will is intellectual appetite and is responsible for choosing in the same way that the intellect is responsible for reasoning, that is, within the sequence of action.[66] However, Aquinas's view is not competitive; the will just is what the intellect desires, and the intellect just is what the will knows.[67] The voluntarist view—which requires that the will be able to choose against the intellect—seems to assume that the faculties function as *homunculi* or independent rational agents, intellect possessing a separate appetite and the will possessing a separate rationality.[68] For example, Henry of Ghent proposes that the will can be considered as natural, as deliberative, and as free. He says, "the will as deliberative restrains its natural motion by deferring the pursuit of that good, and by impelling the cognitive [power] to examine from the circumstances whether it should be pursued or not."[69] The two faculties become *homunculi* able to stand at odds with each other.

So, what theological concerns drove this development? Bonnie Kent explains why this issue became so central; "If we are to be praised for virtue and blamed for vice, we must be master of our acts; and we cannot be master of our acts unless we have free decision."[70] A strong concern for

---

66. In *ST* I.83.4, Aquinas notes that intellective appetite : will : free choice : intellective apprehension : intellect : reason.

67. Aquinas cites Aristotle's definition of choice, "either an appetitive understanding or an intellective desire" [*intellectus appetitivus vel appetitus intellectivus*]; *ST* I.83.3, citing Aristotle, *Nicomachean* Ethics, 6.

68. Perreiah calls this the autonomous will. Alan Perreiah, "Scotus on Human Emotions," *Franciscan Studies* 56 (1998): 325.

69. Henry of Ghent, *Quodl.* IV q. 22 (Leuven 8:356–357); cited in Drummond, "John Duns Scotus on the Role of the Moral Virtues," 46.

70. Kent, *Virtues of the Will*, 110. Bonnie Kent objects to the common characterization of a voluntarist Neo-Augustinian theological school reacting to an Aristotelian school, especially in the area of late thirteenth century ethics. She asks, "What would it even mean for a thinker to be a Neo-Augustinian *in ethics*?" (emphasis in the original; Kent, *Virtues of the Will*, 16). She cites Fernand Van Steenberghen's criticism of Etienne Gilson, that "the great doctrinal conflicts of the thirteenth century were, for the most part, struggles between different forms of Aristotelianism" (Kent, *Virtues of the Will*, 12; citing F. Van Steenberghen, *La philosophie au XIIIᵉ siècle* [Louvain-Paris: Éditions Peeters, 1991], 407–11; 433–39). Kent further notes that many scholars "were working to reconcile Aristotle's teachings with Augustine's, as well as with the teachings of other 'authorities'" (Kent, *Virtues of the Will*, 34). She writes,

moral responsibility and particularly for culpability drove these controversies. As a result, the role of the will in action theory was increased. The
will became a quasi-reasoning *homunculus* which is best characterized by
its freedom. But what is most significant for understanding Calvin is that
the discussion shifted away from free choice as a function of the combined
faculties in conjunction with virtue and vice to a discussion about free will,
about the will's independent role in freely choosing.

The Appetites of the Will

However, there is another way of describing the freedom of the will that
is perhaps more persuasive. John Duns Scotus's account of the will proposes another possibility than a quasi-reasoning *homunculus*, namely,
that there are two appetites in the will. Duns Scotus's account illustrates
a mature outcome of the structural changes necessary to sustain the
choosing will. In what follows, I will describe his view and the questions
it raises for Aquinas's notion of appetite. I will suggest that with Duns
Scotus, we encounter a notion of appetite that is rather different than
that of Aquinas, a rational appetite that is by its very nature immoderate
and corrupt. Aquinas held that all appetite inclined toward the good, and
that evil was to be explained by appetite that lacks the proper order. Duns
Scotus seems to suggest that a stronger corruption of appetite is present
within the will itself.

It is widely noted that Duns Scotus adopted Anselm's terminology of
two affections to describe the will. For Anselm, to be an agent is to possess
voluntas, some sort of motive power. Anselm asserts that all agents desire
happiness; this is the chief motive power of the will.[71] But to be a moral

---

most of the late thirteenth-century masters presumed to be "Augustinian" tried
to establish that their own views were in harmony with Aristotle's. Modern scholars might justifiably fault them for distorting Aristotle's thought, for papering
over genuine conflicts between Aristotle's ethics and psychology, on the one hand,
and the teachings of Augustine and other Christian authorities, on the other. But
if we do fault them, let us bear in mind that Thomas Aquinas and other quasi-
"Aristotelian" masters of theology engaged in similar distortions. Efforts to reconcile
Aristotle with the faith were the rule, not the exception, in the theology faculty;
and what emerged, as we shall see was the transformation of classical virtue ethics.
(Kent, *Virtues of the Will*, 93)

71. Anselm, *De casu diaboli*, 12; *Complete Philosophical and Theological Treatises of Anselm of
Canterbury*, trans. Jasper Hopkins and Herbert Richardson (Minneapolis: Arthur J. Banning,
2000), 238.

agent, something more is required. The moral agent must possess another motive power, the motive power for justice.[72] The moral agent must possess two sources of motivation.

Duns Scotus adapted this insight for his own purposes to formulate his account of the human will. Where Anselm saw two distinct affections (motive powers), Duns Scotus saw two aspects of the same will, the affection for advantage (*affectio commodi*) and the affection for justice (*affectio justitia*). For Duns Scotus, the affection for advantage is the natural will, that is the will's natural inclination for its own happiness. Strictly, this affection does not by itself elicit any action, since the affection for justice, or the will as free, is the proper cause of elicited acts.[73] The affection for justice is the moderator (*prima moderatrix*) of the affection for advantage, ordering it according to the justice of God's law.[74] It is precisely Duns Scotus's concern for moral responsibility that leads him to posit the two affections in the will. The affection for justice enables the agent to will or to nil a proposed action, which enables the agent to be free.

There are two aspects of this account worth noting. First, while Duns Scotus's account can be seen to contrast advantage with justice, it also

---

72. I owe the simplicity of this explanation to Peter King, "Scotus's Rejection of Anselm: The Two-Wills Theory," in *John Duns Scotus 1308–2008: Investigations into His Philosophy*, ed. L. Honnefelder et al. (Münster: Aschendorff, 2011), 359–78. Speaking of the person without a will for justice, Anselm writes, "Therefore, insofar as [this will] is a being, it is something good. But as far as justice or injustice is concerned, [this will] is neither good nor evil [i.e., not a moral agent]." Anselm, *De casu diaboli*, 13.

73. John Duns Scotus, *Ordinatio* III, d. 17; II, d. 6, q. 2; cited in John Boler, "An Image for the Unity of Will in Duns Scotus," *Journal of the History of Philosophy* 32 (1994): 27. Cruz González-Ayesta argues against the standard view for a distinction between the *affectio commodi* and the natural will. There is enough overlap between the terms however that for simplicity I will assume the standard view. González-Ayesta argues for the following propositions: (1) The natural will does not elicit any act whatsoever. It is a mere inclination or first perfection. (2) The natural will is the will acting only with an affection for the advantageous and not with an affection for justice: it refers to an intellectual appetite. (3) There are two natural inclinations, one for the advantageous and one for justice, and both of them are perfections of the free will. Cruz González-Ayesta, "Duns Scotus on the Natural Will," *Vivarium* 50 (2012): 39; see also her previous article, where she argues for the standard view, Cruz González-Ayesta, "Scotus' Interpretation of the Difference Between Voluntas ut Natura and Voluntas ut Voluntas," *Franciscan Studies* 66 (2008): 371–412. Allan B. Wolter, trans., *Duns Scotus on the Will and Morality* (Washington, DC: Catholic University of America Press, 1986), 181–83.

74. I am not here distinguishing between moral and metaphysical freedom.

contrasts inclination with choice.[75] Affection for advantage is intellectual appetite passively considered. Affection for justice is the will's active power of self-determination. Cruz González-Ayesta admits that, "The doctrine of the two affections, for example, is taken from St. Anselm; and Anselm's background is not Aristotelian but rather Augustinian and possibly Stoic."[76] The tension that was possible for Aquinas between sense appetite and the will is now internal to the will itself. Second, depending on how one takes Duns Scotus's use of the term "natural will," there may be considerable revision to the reliability of rational appetite.[77] Whereas rational appetite for Aquinas is oriented toward ultimate beatitude with God, for Duns Scotus, the natural will seems to incline immoderately toward the advantageous, calling into question the goodness of the natural will, seemingly driving a wedge between metaphysics and morality. Duns Scotus says, "that nature is so inclined towards its object by this affection for the advantageous that if it had of itself an elicited act, it could not help eliciting it with no moderation in the most forceful way possible."[78]

---

75. Alan Perreiah remarks that Duns Scotus's moral philosophy is "a locus classicus for the crucial distinction between appetition and volition." Perreiah, "Scotus on Human Emotions," 325.

76. González-Ayesta, "Scotus' Interpretation," 394–95.

77. There is considerable controversy among scholars about the meaning of Duns Scotus's natural will and how it relates to freedom, either moral or metaphysical. Allan Wolter distinguished between moral and metaphysical freedom in 1986, reading the natural will both technically as act eliciting toward perfection or non-technically as a tendency toward advantage. Wolter, *Duns Scotus on the Will and Morality*, 39–45. Other relevant works include: John Boler, "Transcending the Natural: Duns Scotus on the Two Selections of the Will," *American Catholic Philosophical Quarterly* 67 (1993): 109– 112; Boler, "An Image for the Unity of Will in Duns Scotus" (1994), 23–44; Sukjae Lee, "Scotus on the Will: the Rational Power and the Dual Affections," *Vivarium* 38 (1998): 40–54.

78. Duns Scotus, *Ordinatio* II, d. 6 q. 2 nn 55-56, in Wolter, *Duns Scotus*, 300. It is useful to get context here:

> As for the first, the natural will is not of itself immoderate, since it inclines only after the manner of nature —and in this it is not immoderate, for it inclines as it was made to do, nor has it power to do otherwise. But to be so inclined or less inclined is in the power of the will as free, through an elicited act. When the natural will is taken to be orientated towards happiness, I grant this. But this will is not actually immoderate through an elicited act. For the inclination of a natural appetite is not an elicited act, but resembles a first perfection [i.e., something identical with the substance or being of the will]. And this is no more immoderate than is the nature to which it belongs. However, that nature is so inclined towards its object by this affection for the advantageous that if it had of itself an elicited act, it could not help eliciting it with no moderation in the most forceful way possible. But the natural will, as having only the affection for the beneficial, is not the cause

Taken together, these two features—the contrast between inclination and choice and the immoderate natural inclination—produce a quasi-Stoic posture of distrust toward the passive movements of the will.[79] We will discuss in more detail below the fact that there are passive movements in the will. For now, I simply point out that the moral life for Duns Scotus seems to be one of perpetual continence, choosing against immoderate desire. The natural will does not cease to be immoderately drawn to the advantageous, and so the affection for justice will perpetually fulfill its role in curbing it.

Changing Notions of Virtue

Finally, it is critical to notice the alteration of meanings for the words "virtue" and "vice," which come along with the choosing will. In Aquinas, virtue and vice have to do with being disposed with regard to all the soul's powers, higher and lower. As the will moves from being predominantly passive in choice, receiving its object from the intellect and awaiting the command of reason, to being predominantly active, virtue and vice come to refer only to the choosing of the will. Generically, virtue is a "perfection of a power" (ST I–II.55.1). But when virtue applies only to the will, it comes to refer to the morally good choice.[80] This development begins to call into question the very necessity of the category with Peter Olivi and John Duns Scotus.[81]

Duns Scotus argues that the proper subject of the virtues is the will. He claims, "the sole reason for postulating virtues in the powers is to regulate what of itself could act either rightly or not rightly."[82] What is properly a

---

of any elicited act; only the will as free can cause such, and therefore, qua eliciting an act, the will does have what is required to moderate passion.

79. There is actually a third item worth noting. Peter King raises a powerful objection to Duns Scotus's theory, namely that the affection for justice doesn't even seem to be a motive power on his account. It is rather an instrument for "subordinating one's will to a higher will, namely the Divine Will, through adopting from it the 'rule of justice'" (King, "Scotus's Rejection of Anselm," 15). If the affection for justice is an affection, the unity of the will seems threatened; if it is not, then it seems hard to differentiate it from a cognitive power, like practical reason. And, as King adds, "if the only motivational structure a human agent possesses is the affection-for-advantage. ... What would motivate a free agent to actually regulate its behaviour, since it is only ever motivated by its own advantage?" King, "Scotus's Rejection of Anselm," 18.

80. Cf. Drummond, "John Duns Scotus on the Role of the Moral Virtues," 19.

81. For a more detailed overview of these developments see Kent, Virtues of the Will, 68–149.

82. Duns Scotus, Ordinatio III, d. 33 n. 17, in Wolter, Duns Scotus, 325.

habit for Duns Scotus is "an elective habit."[83] But he admits, "the will on its own without a habit could perform an act that is right and morally good."[84] To understand the diminished role of virtue, it is helpful to ask a key question: What makes the morally good act good? While for Aquinas this has at least partly to do with the passions (*ST* I–II.24.3), for Duns Scotus it is "that the act be deliberately conformed to a rational judgment," that an act has "the right object, [is] directed to the right end, and [is] done at the right time and place in the right way."[85] Virtue is not strictly necessary for this. Ian Drummond concludes that "moral virtues have no necessary role in bringing about the moral goodness of acts."[86] He adds, "with Duns Scotus there has been a kind of hollowing out of the concept of moral virtue."[87] It is worth noting that Duns Scotus empties moral virtue of its role in the goodness of an action, but he does not empty the notion of habit. However, his notion of habit is not metaphysically freighted with terms like "perfection of a power" since the will is a free self-determining power.[88]

PASSIONS OF THE WILL

So to recapitulate, a concern for moral accountability led to an expanded role for the will in action theory. The will must hold the power of freedom and must be able to stand against the judgment of reason, or culpability is swallowed by ignorance. In consequence, the proper subject of virtue is the elective power. The elective power is made possible either by turning intellect and will into independent *homunculi* or by the existence of two motive powers within the will, the affection for advantage, which is naturally suspect because it tends toward immoderation, and the affection for justice, which enables free choice. In both cases, the will takes prominence in action theory because it possesses the ability to choose against

---

83. Duns Scotus, *Ordinatio* III, d. 33 n. 45, in Wolter, *Duns Scotus*, 335.

84. Duns Scotus, *Ordinatio* III, d. 33 n. 44, in Wolter, *Duns Scotus*, 333.

85. Drummond, "John Duns Scotus on the Role of the Moral Virtues," 230, 229.

86. Drummond, "John Duns Scotus on the Role of the Moral Virtues," 230.

87. Drummond, "John Duns Scotus on the Role of the Moral Virtues," 230.

88. It seems we could also cite Ockham's view here. Oberman remarks that Aureolusis (precursor to Ockham) was criticized by Ockham "for adhering to the necessity of the grace-habitus." Heiko A. Oberman, "Some Notes on the Theology of Nominalism: With Attention to Its Relation to the Renaissance," *The Harvard Theological Review* 53, no. 1 (January 1960): 53.

the determination of the intellect. Therefore, if virtue exists, it must have the will as its subject; virtues must be elective habits. In consequence, if moral virtues are in the will, then the passions that need to be moderated by the moral virtues are passions of the will rather than of sense appetite.

In what follows, I will discuss the Augustinian precedent for passions of the will before turning to how this alters the definition of a passion. Duns Scotus admits that there are both passions of the will and passions of the body but claims that only the passions of the will are morally relevant. This is in keeping with what was just mentioned about the moral life being one of continence. This also deepens the ambiguity about the body's role in psychology generally and in the passions particularly. Next, I will suggest that the existence of natural passions of the will only further calls into question the role of virtue in assisting free choice. Finally, Duns Scotus's account of the will at least sets up some possible irony in that the structure intended to preserve free will seems to be coopted by John Calvin to deny it.

Augustine, Stoicism, and the Passions of the Will

The idea of passions of the will is odd given Aquinas's assumptions about the nature of the soul. For him a passion in the strictest sense was only proper to matter, since to undergo a passion is to exchange one quality for the opposite. So, Aquinas concedes that passions belong to the soul only "per accidens—viz., insofar as the composite is acted upon" (I–II.22.1).[89] Yet the notion that passions can occur in the will is not entirely foreign to Christian theology; it has an Augustinian and Stoic history. Augustine's

---

89. Peter King points out that "there are analogues to the passions pertaining to the purely intellective part of the soul—call them 'pseudopassions.' These pseudopassions, unlike the passions, do not involve any somatic reactions or indeed any material basis at all. They are located in the intellective appetite as rational acts of will." King, "Aquinas on the Passions," 4–5n7. These movements of the will Aquinas calls affections: "all passions of the soul are affections not all affections are passions." Nicholas E. Lombardo, The Logic of Desire: Aquinas on Emotion (Washington, DC: Catholic University of America Press, 2011), 76. King suggests that the desire to stop smoking might be said to be a pseudopassion, but "quite unlike the passion (the craving) for nicotine." It is the bodily alteration that signals the true passion for Aquinas. King, "Aquinas on the Passions," 4–5n7.

City of God reveals a clear, if limited, link between his thought and that of Cicero's *Tusculan Disputations*.[90]

Cicero records Chrysippus's attempt to argue against determinism by distinguishing mere contributory causes of action, mere reactions to sense impressions, and principle causes, assent to sense impression.[91] Chrysippus argues that the latter remain in our control.[92] Augustine interacts at great length with the Stoic view in *The City of God*. He essentially agrees with the Stoic account of what passions are, mental disturbances (*phantases*), but disagrees with the Stoics and Platonists in two key areas. First, Augustine does not blame sin on the body by interpreting flesh as merely referring to the body.[93] Second, he thinks that all human beings may experience the full range of human emotion, even admitting that a righteous person may experience the fourth Stoic disorder of grief (*dolor*).[94] Overall, he rejects the Stoic notion of impassibility (*impassibilitas*; Greek *aptheia*), suggesting that for Christians, if "their love is right, all these feelings of theirs are right."[95] Finally, for Augustine, virtue is simply good passions, and vice is simply bad passions.[96]

---

90. For a fuller explanation, see Neil W. Gilbert, "The Concept of Will in Early Latin Philosophy," *Journal of the History of Philosophy* 1 (October 1963): 17–36. Gilbert traces the origin of the concept of the will, arguing that early Latin writers adapted Greek terminology for an even older notion.

91. Gilbert, "Concept of the Will," 21.

92. Chrysippus calls the two categories "perfect and principle causes" of action and "auxiliary and proximate causes." Cicero, *De Fato*, XVIII, in *On the Orator: Book 3. On Fate. Stoic Paradoxes. Divisions of Oratory*, trans. H. Rackham, Loeb Classical Library 349 (Cambridge, MA: Harvard University Press, 1942), 237–39. At this point in philosophical history, it is not clear that *voluntas* means anything but movement of the mind. This is why the Stoic tradition has fueled the contemporary cognitivist theory of emotion. Is a movement of the mind a false judgment or an appetite, a cognitive or appetitive mental state? But the point from a Stoic point of view is to avoid the unreasonableness of suggesting that the wise person is entirely free of passions.

93. Augustine argues that flesh is a synecdoche referring to the whole man. *The City of God*, trans. Henry Bettenson (New York: Penguin Classics, 2003), XIV.3. He admits that "we are burdened by the corruptible body, and yet, knowing that the cause of our burdening is not the true being and substance of the body but its decay, we do not want to be stripped of the body, but to be clothed with its immortality," citing, Wis 9:15; 2 Cor 4:16; 5:1–4. *City of God*, XIV.3.

94. Augustine notes, "The Apostle praises the Corinthians for having felt a godly grief." *City of God*, XIV.8.

95. Augustine, *City of God*, XIV.9.

96. Augustine, *City of God*, XIV.5, 9.

In sum, clearly here we have passions existing in some sense in the higher faculties.[97] And it is just this claim by Augustine that Duns Scotus cites in his argument for the passions of the will. He writes, "According to Augustine in *The City of God* XIV, chapters 5 and 6, there are passions in the will; for this reason, if virtue is to be posited on account of action and passion in the power in which the passion and action of the will are present, it follows that the virtues are placed there, since there are some passions in the higher part of the soul."[98] The precedent was set within Augustine, and as Bonnie Kent claims, "By the late thirteenth century, passions of the will were routinely acknowledged."[99]

Duns Scotus and the Passions of the Will

So, what are these passions of the will for Duns Scotus? For Aquinas, the passions, strictly speaking, are movements of a passive power, sense appetite, which is composite (body and soul) and involves bodily changes. For Duns Scotus, the notion of passions is redefined to be inclusive of passive movements of appetite both in the will and in sense appetite. Ian Drummond summarizes that for Duns Scotus, "the passions are qualities that are distinct from the acts of their subject, and can be caused in any appetitive power by an object towards which that power is inclined or disinclined."[100] Again, from a Thomistic perspective, this is very odd, since passions are movements (acts) of a passive power.[101] For Aquinas, habits,

---

97. It is not clear that these passions are even the same sort of thing, since Augustine cites with seeming to approve of Aulus Gellius's claim that for the Stoics, passions are "mental visions which they call phantases." *City of God*, IX.4. This would obviously make passions a cognitive phenomenon, which seems odd, since passions seem to be an alteration of movement of some sort by definition. This trend has seemingly been picked up by the philosophers of emotion called cognitivists.

98. Duns Scotus, *Ordinatio* III, d. 33 n. 34: "In voluntate sunt passiones, secundum Augustinum XIV De civitate cap. 5 et 6; et propter hoc, si propter actionem et passionem ponenda sit virtus in illa potentia in qua est passio et actio voluntatis, sequitur quod cum passiones aliquae sint in suprema parte animae, quod ibi ponantur virtutes." Quoted in Drummond, "John Duns Scotus," 24.

99. Kent, *Virtues of the Will*, 212.

100. Ian Drummond, "John Duns Scotus on the Passions of the Will," in *Emotion and Cognitive Life in Medieval and Early Modern Philosophy*, ed. Martin Pickavé and Lisa Shapiro (Oxford: Oxford University Press, 2012), 60.

101. For Duns Scotus, sensitive appetite is an active power. Drummond, "John Duns Scotus on the Passions of the Will," 64; *Ordinatio* I, d. 17, n. 76, V 5, 177: 'Ille [sc. appetitus sensitivus] habet rationem principii aliquo modo, licet non active libere.'

not passions, are qualities. However, for Duns Scotus, passions are just inclinations that are stimulated by an external active principle.[102] Since this very general definition contains no material component, it can apply equally well to sense appetite and to the will.[103]

What motivates Duns Scotus to posit passions in the will at all? Again, he does so because the will is that power which most needs virtue. Drummond explains,

> Scotus agrees with Aquinas that passions and the virtues that moderate them must belong to the same subject, but reverses his argument: whereas Aquinas argues that the moral virtues are in the sensitive appetites because that is where the passions of the soul occur, Scotus has an independent reason for holding that the moral virtues are in the will, namely, because they are habits of choice. He thus concludes instead that the passions that are moderated by the moral virtues are in the will.[104]

Since virtues involve both free choice and moderating passions, and assuming virtue and passions must be in the same subject, then there must be passions in the will. Where Aquinas begins by assessing where passions occur, and then assigns the location of the virtues, Duns Scotus flips the argument because moral virtues must be about free choice.[105] It is not clear that this is a good reason for positing passions in the will. Finally, Duns Scotus does provide two other reasons for positing passions in the will. First, "According to Augustine in *The City of God* XIV, chapters 5 and 6, there are passions in the will."[106] And second, there is a theological reason, that Christ's passions must have been voluntary.[107]

---

102. They are a passive principle inclined to an active principle, which seems to make them actively responsive.

103. Drummond, "John Duns Scotus on the Passions of the Will," 64.

104. Drummond, "John Duns Scotus on the Passions of the Will," 59.

105. Drummond, "John Duns Scotus on the Passions of the Will," 59.

106. Duns Scotus, *Ordinatio* III, d. 33 n. 34; cited by Drummond, "John Duns Scotus on the Role of the Moral Virtues," 24.

107. Duns Scotus, *Ordinatio* III, d. 15, nn. 14–15, V 9, 481–482. Drummond writes, "But if his pain occurred only in the sensitive part of the soul, then there cannot have been any merit in it, since it would be a merely natural occurrence not imputable to him as a rational agent." Drummond, "John Duns Scotus on the Role of the Moral Virtues," 24.

So, what about the passions of the sensitive appetite? Scotus preserves a place for them in his theory. Even if passions exist in the will, they may also equally exist in the sensitive appetite. But the passions of sensitive appetite are not relevant to virtue. They may also acquire a sort of habit, but this is not properly called virtue.[108] Drummond suggests that this may be merely a "verbal concession to the traditional way of speaking about moral virtue."[109] The sensitive appetite or body has no special moral status for Duns Scotus.

Before turning to the implications of this for virtue, I simply note that Duns Scotus's account creates ambiguity over the body's relation to the passions of the will. Since the body has no place in the definition of passion, the passions of the will do not seem to involve it except by the will's command.[110] Ian Drummond seems to suggest that body involvement is a mark that they are not passions of the will. He writes, "Those passions that do involve bodily change, he claims, are passions not of the soul as such, but of the body and soul together."[111]

Finally, a few words can be said about the implications of virtue's role in action theory in light of the passions of the will. As we have already noted, in the late thirteenth and early fourteenth century, the free choice of the will became a theological priority to preserve culpability. But if the free choice of the will at any particular time is important to culpability, then this calls into question any positive function not only of virtue, but

---

108. Drummond, "John Duns Scotus on the Role of the Moral Virtues," 39; *Ordinatio* III d. 33 n. 45 (Vat. 10:163).

109. Drummond, "John Duns Scotus on the Role of the Moral Virtues," 39.

110. Duns Scotus writes,

> By nature, the will chooses before it or reason commands anything to the sensitive appetite. For reason seems to affect the sensitive appetite only by the mediation of the will, which is properly the rational appetite; the will also wills something in itself before it commands something concerning it, for it is not because it commands the lower power that it wills that, but vice versa. Therefore, in that prior [instant] the will is able to generate in itself from its right acts of choice (since it is just as much indeterminate and determinable as the intellect) a habit that will incline it to choosing rightly; and this habit will most properly be a virtue, since a habit of choice most properly inclines to acting just as it was generated from right acts of choice.

Ordinatio III. d. 33 n. 44; cited in Drummond, "John Duns Scotus on the Role of the Moral Virtues," 20.

111. Drummond, "John Duns Scotus on the Passions of the Will," 53.

also of passions. The very existence of passions seems to call into question the will's self-determination. Duns Scotus might respond by arguing that the only passions the will suffers are those that follow "from a freely elicited act of the will."[112] But then, we are left with a dilemma. On the one hand, if to preserve freedom Duns Scotus claims that the inclinations of the will follow from a freely elicited act, then the passions seem never to run contrary to the will, which is false. There are also passions that arise from natural necessity. On the other hand, if, as Duns Scotus concedes, passions may also arise by natural necessity, then the very freedom of the will is threatened.[113] Furthermore, why should any passions be necessary for moral goodness? If there are natural passions and these are outside of our responsibility, then they must not have definite bearing on choice. While virtues seem unnecessary for free choice, passions seem to possess the capacity to inhibit it.

Finally, even if Duns Scotus can make sense of an undetermined will existing with natural passions that run contrary to it, Duns Scotus seems also to have dichotomized the passions into those someone has no responsibility for—natural passions, passions of sense appetite—and those someone has full responsibility for. This is precisely the sort of dichotomy that does not account for the plasticity of emotion. The notion of virtue as enabling a person to act consistently and with ease (i.e., temperance) has been discarded in favor of a continence as the highest aspiration.[114]

All of this might set up for a striking irony. Duns Scotus places the passions into the will—because the will must be the subject of virtue—and distinguishes two appetites. He is motivated to affirm the free choice of the will. Calvin might be seen to preserve the basic structure of this will while suggesting that the passions of the will inhibit free will. Might the existence of the passions in the will work against what Duns Scotus was trying to do? It would be very hard to establish definite lineage to Calvin on this point. It is probably not the case that Calvin explicitly relies on Duns

---

112. Drummond, "John Duns Scotus on the Passions of the Will," 65.

113. Drummond, "John Duns Scotus on the Passions of the Will," 68.

114. In the traditional language of virtue ethics there are four possible states: (1) temperance, desiring good, approving good, and doing good; (2) continence, desiring evil, approving good, and doing good; (3) incontinence, desiring evil, approving good, and doing evil; and (4) intemperance, desiring evil, approving evil, and doing evil.

Scotus's account of the will, nor his view of moral virtue. It is rather that Duns Scotus is representative of the way the question of moral virtue had shifted by Calvin's time. But this shift may contribute to the explanation of Calvin's simple psychology—intellect and will—since by the time of his writing, for many theologians these were the only morally relevant faculties.

Determination of the Will

Finally, I will illustrate in the following chapter that Calvin's negativity toward virtue partly arises out of his concern for guarding against pride. Calvin is known to have a bleak view of the will's capabilities. This may be the strongest reason why virtue does not feature in Calvin's moral theology. However, we will see that Calvin's view of the will also did not occur in a vacuum. It is not that Calvin is a dreary cynic about humanity, seeing at every turn only and always malicious motives. Calvin and Luther's treatises on the bondage of the will also have a context. In what follows I will trace this context. I am suggesting that in addition to the narrowing of the notion of willing already discussed, the role of human virtue was diminished by a commitment to God's *potentia absoluta* in salvation with an overlay of predestination and depravity. God freely predetermines to accept Christ's atoning work to justify those whose wills are morally determined to sin.

First, the more remote context for Calvin's determined will involves Ockham, Duns Scotus, and the *via moderna* with its commitment to the *potentia absoluta*.[115] This commitment meant that God was not bound by some metaphysical necessity to create and govern the world in just this way. What God could have done *de potentia absoluta* is above us, as the Socratic proverb says, "*Quae supra nos, nihil ad nos*" (That which is above us, is nothing to us).[116] Oberman notes that what drives this commitment is a concern for God's sovereignty, for Ockham in this case, but without suggesting that

---

115. Heiko Oberman summarizes the distinction between the *potentia ordinata* and *potentia absoluta*: "The basic argument is that what God actually has chosen to do *de potentia ordinata* in creation and recreation—i.e., in the realms of natural philosophy and theology—he very well could have chosen to decide differently *de potentia absoluta*." Heiko A. Oberman, "Via Antiqua and Via Moderna: Late Medieval Prolegomena to Early Reformation Thought," *Journal of the History of Ideas* 48, no. 1 (January-March 1987): 27.

116. Quoted in Oberman, "Via Antiqua and Via Moderna," 33.

God's will is arbitrary.[117] So in the centuries prior to Calvin, schools developed that were both interested in and divided over this important category of *potentia absoluta*.

We also have in Duns Scotus and Ockham a transition from Thomas Aquinas's view that merit is based on divine justice to merit depending on divine free will.[118] Duns Scotus affirms, "every created offering is worth exactly what God accepts it for, and not more."[119] This also seems to be Calvin's view, who writes in *Institutes* II.17.1, "In discussing Christ's merit, we do not consider the beginning of merit to be in him, but we go back to God's ordinance, the first cause. For God solely of his own good pleasure appointed him Mediator to obtain salvation for us. ... Christ could not merit anything; but did so because he had been appointed to appease God's wrath with his sacrifice."[120] This development also goes a long way toward explaining the diminished emphasis on a *habitus* of grace, since God is free to regard as meritorious whatever he chooses, at least according to *potentia absoluta*.[121]

Charles Trinkaus draws the following conclusion from the absence of any meaningful relationship between virtue and merit: "The consequences of this position is to give man free will in the realm of secular life but in

---

117. Calvin acknowledges that God's will does sometimes appear to be capricious, but adds, "if we had quiet and composed minds ready to learn, the final outcome would show that God always has the best reason for his plan: either to instruct his people in patience, or to correct their wicked afflictions and tame their lust, or to subjugate them to self-denial, or to arouse them from sluggishness; again, to bring low the proud, to shatter the cunning of the impious and to overthrow their devices" (*Institutes* I.17.1).

118. But this is not strictly justice. McGrath clarifies that this is *iustitia secundum praesuppositionem divinae ordinationis* rather than on *iustitia secundum absolutam aequalitatem*. McGrath, "John Calvin," 74.

119. Duns Scotus, *Ordinatio* III, dist. 19 q.1 n.7, "Dico, quod omne aliud a Deo, ideo est bonum, quia a Deo volitum, et non est converso: sic meritum illud tantum bonum erat, pro quanto acceptabatur," quoted in McGrath, "John Calvin," 74. François Wendel writes, "In his great commentary upon the Sentences of Peter Lombard, Duns Scotus had declared that the passion of Christ was, in itself, of no particular value or special efficacy; that value and efficacy had been conferred upon it by the Divine will, which had deigned to accept the passion of Christ as sufficient, and had destined it to the work of redemption." François Wendel, *Calvin: Origins and Development of His Religious Thought*, trans. Philip Mairet (New York: Harper & Row, 1950), 129.

120. Calvin, *Institutes* II.17.1. McGrath writes, "Calvin clearly adopted a Scotist solution to the problem of the merit of Christ." McGrath, "John Calvin," 76. Likewise, Alex Gordon writes, "It is worth noting that, on the first point [salvation through the merits of Christ], Calvin adopted a Scotist solution." Alex Gordon, "The Sozzini and Their School," *The Theological Review* 66 (July 1879): 315.

121. McGrath, "John Calvin," 75.

effect to deny the validity of freely willed morality for attaining salvation except when God happens to accept it as valid."[122] The absolute freedom of merit then opened the door for philosophical questions both about human moral freedom in relation to natural fortune and in relation to God's will. The severing of virtue and merit combined with a rapidly shifting economic landscape to produce a grim pessimism about moral ability. A sort of natural determinism arising from a lack of control over economic goods was embraced by humanists such as Francesco Petrarch, Marsilio Ficino, and Pico, who often recommended a withdrawal from worldly concerns for personal salvation.[123] The Reformers then took the next step in denying human power over salvation. Trinkaus writes, "The reformers, particularly Luther, also denied that there was any possibility of morality in business or politics but took the further step of denying man the power of achieving either virtue or justification by his own free will."[124]

Second, and more immediately, two Italian Renaissance humanists, Pietro Pomponazzi and Lorenzo Valla, put forward a bleaker view of humanity just prior to the Refomers. We will discuss briefly the latter because of his connection to the Reformers. Lorenzo Valla's *Dialogue on Free Will* (*De libero arbitrio*, 1439) predates Luther's *On the Bondage of the Will* (*De servo arbitrio*, 1525) by about eighty-five years. In it, Valla portrays a dialogue between himself and a man named Antonio. He begins his treatise with a warning against trusting philosophy, "I would prefer ... that other Christians and, indeed, those who are called theologians would not depend so much on philosophy or devote so much energy to it, making it almost an equal and sister of theology."[125] After arguing that foreknowledge does not cause necessity, Valla argues that the will of God does. He tells a fable of a man named Sextus who receives a prophecy from Apollo of the evils he will commit. Valla notes that it is not Apollo's knowledge that makes

122. Charles Trinkaus, "The Problem of Free Will in the Renaissance and the Reformation," *Journal of the History of Ideas* 10, no. 1 (January 1949): 55.

123. The rapidly changing economic conditions contributed to this pessimism about fortunes.

124. Trinkaus, "Problem of Free Will," 58.

125. Lorenzo Valla, "Dialogue on Free Will," in *The Renaissance Philosophy of Man*, ed. Ernst Cassirer, Paul Oskar Kristeller, and John Herman Randall Jr. (Chicago: University of Chicago Press, 1948), 155.

Sextus bad, but Jupiter's will.[126] Finally, he refers Antonio to Romans 9 for an explanation of this.

In his discussion of Valla's determinism, Anders Kraal argues that Valla's discourse anticipated and may have influenced Luther's *De servo arbi-trio* (1525). It is well known that Luther compliments Valla in 1532, saying, "[Valla] disputes ably on free will."[127] But as Kraal points out, Melanchthon had already complimented Valla in 1519 or 1520 for refuting the position of the schools. Kraal notes, "This claim makes it very probable that not only Melanchthon but also other Wittenberg Reformers, including Luther, were acquainted with Valla's *De libero arbitrio* already in the early 1520s."[128] Finally, Calvin remarks in the *Institutes* III.23.6, "But it seems to me that Valla, a man not otherwise much versed in sacred matters, saw more clearly and wisely, for he showed this contention to be superfluous, since both life and death are acts of God's will more than of his foreknowledge." Calvin continues:

> If God only foresaw human events, and did not also dispose and determine them by his decision, then there would be some point in raising this question: whether his foreseeing had anything to do with their necessity. But since he foresees future events only by reason of the fact that he decreed that they take place, they vainly raise a quarrel over foreknowledge, when it is clear that all things take place rather by his determination and bidding. (*Institutes* III.23.6)

While it is not clear that Valla drew any clear ethical or psychological conclusions from this stronger determinism, Calvin and Luther certainly did, neatly overlaying divine sovereignty on human depravity—theological determinism on top of moral determinism. God must be Lord over all human goodness as he is Lord over all the cosmos. The outcome was the

---

126. Valla writes, "Jupiter as he created the wolf fierce, the hare timid, the lion brave, the ass stupid, the dog savage, the sheep mild, so he fashioned some men hard of heart, others soft, he generated one given to evil, the other to virtue." Valla, "Dialogue on Free Will," 173.

127. Martin Luther, *Tischreden*, Bd. I, WA., 1912, #259; cited in Trinkaus, "Problem of Free Will," 60, translation his; Valla is also the topic of banter between Luther and Erasmus over this question. Luther claims Wycliffe and Valla on his side. Martin Luther, *Bondage of the Will*, ed. J. I. Packer (Grand Rapids: Baker Academic, 1957), 109.

128. Anders Kraal, "Valla-Style Determinism and the Intellectual Background of Luther's *De servo arbitrio*," *Harvard Theological Review* 108, no. 3 (July 2015): 416. Kraal also gives other arguments for dependence.

final blow for any positive place for virtue in theological ethics. God's election and free grace, not human virtue, is the basis of salvific merit.

However, moral determinism is softer than theological determinism. After all, there is, at the very least, more than one way to go wrong. If this is true, there are still questions to be asked about psychology. Might there be a sort of virtue, even one that is not properly virtue, which God works in all human beings by common grace? For now, we have merely seen how these psychological alterations converged to squeeze out a place for virtue in theological psychology.

CONCLUSION

In sum, there were significant shifts in the psychological conversation that diminished the importance of virtue. These shifts are very suggestive in explaining the degree to which Calvin departed from the four features of Aquinas's psychology that have been highlighted. In the first place, psychology was gradually moving toward a more mechanistic and irrational conception of the human body. The composite holism was cast aside in the debates about body-soul relation and the immortality of the soul. Moreover, tiered psychology was discarded as the body was downgraded into irrationality, and morally relevant passions were ascribed only to the will. Yet the will seems to have no use for virtue, since it becomes most essentially free. Finally, a new appreciation for divine freedom and sovereignty further minimized any role virtue might play in theology. Virtue came to be seen as a threat to sovereign grace.

Since we need to read Calvin as he is situated, we can avoid blaming him for not answering questions that were not being asked. But we also might avoid assigning too much consequence to his way of organizing his psychology. In all of this, it is not clear that Calvin is directly objecting to the views of Thomas Aquinas. The theological disputes that occurred between Aquinas and Calvin produced a general psychological inheritance for Calvin, a core of four tendencies according to which, as we will see, Calvin psychology generally conforms:

1. Body/soul dualism: A tendency to hold a more dualistic approach to the body-soul relation which attributes the lower faculties to the body, owing both to the arguments over the

identity of the soul and its powers and over the immortality
of the soul.

2. Ascendency of the will in action and affective theory: A tendency to see the will and its passions as the morally relevant
   faculty, along with a corresponding tendency to see the passions of sense appetite as mere bodily passions, natural and
   irrational.

3. Curtailing of virtue in action theory: A tendency to curtail the
   importance of virtue for the ethical life in action theory.

4. Continence as highest ethical state: A tendency to see continence, rather than virtue, as the maximal ethical state for
   persons. I have already remarked that the additional contribution of the Reformers is a tendency to overlay God's volitional
   determinism on human psychological determinism as a way
   of minimizing the importance of human virtue.

In the next chapter, I will lay out Calvin's psychology in light of these
four tendencies. I will argue that Calvin's psychology generally reflects
these shifting priorities, and consequently, does a poor job at describing
how the body qualifies human agency. Before turning to his view, it is
worthwhile to record his words about the study of psychology: "But I leave
it to the philosophers to discuss these faculties in their subtle way. For the
upbuilding of godliness a simple definition will be enough for us. I, indeed,
agree that the things they teach are true, not only enjoyable, but also profitable to learn, and skillfully assembled by them. And I do not forbid those
who are desirous of learning to study them" (*Institutes* I.15.6).

4

—

THE PSYCHOLOGY OF JOHN CALVIN

This chapter has two aims. First is to describe John Calvin's psychology. Second is to evaluate how well his psychology attends to how the body qualifies agency, especially emotional agency. I will treat his sources; his general views of soul and body, the powers of the soul, and emotions and their qualities; and his attitude toward virtue. Evaluation will follow each major section. There are two key features from Aquinas that clarify how the body qualifies emotional agency: his holistic account of body and soul and his tiered psychology. The first feature enables Aquinas to incorporate plasticity in the entire agent, but especially in the composite sensitive appetite, the location of quasi-rational passions. The second feature enables Aquinas to theorize about the political governance of emotions by the higher powers. The focus of this chapter is how the body qualifies emotional agency for Calvin.

Building on some of the themes traced in the previous chapter, I will show how the medieval and Renaissance background illuminates Calvin's psychology. Theological disputes between Aquinas and Calvin that contributed to a decline in virtue ethics will also be traced.[1] These disputes

---

1. Bonnie Kent puts it this way: "Was it only Scotus and his fellow travelers who began the transformation of classical virtue ethics that eventually produced the Kantian good will? Or was the transformation already taking place, albeit more subtly, in the works of Aquinas? If there was indeed some dramatic rupture in the history of Western ethics, did it occur in the late thirteenth century, between Aquinas and Scotus, or at least between Aquinas and Ockham? Or did it occur between Aristotle and the Stoics, or at least between Aristotle and Augustine? Were scholastic efforts to reconcile Christian doctrine and classical virtue ethics admirable but misguided? Were the hybrid theories produced in this period so fraught with internal tensions that they were doomed to languish and die? Or was the project of synthesis a feasible one, undermined only by so many historical accidents?" Bonnie Kent, *Virtues of the Will: The Transformation of Ethics in the Late Thirteenth Century* (Washington, DC: Catholic University of America Press, 1995), 254.

are then summarized as producing four tendencies: (1) body/soul dualism; (2) ascendency of the will in action and affective theory; (3) curtailing of virtue in action theory; and (4) continence as the highest ethical state. This chapter will link Calvin's psychology with these tendencies, not as establishing explicit lineage, but as pointing to some clues for understanding his account. My aim, again, is to provide context to give relief to Calvin's view. To do this, I simply want to establish a framework for viewing Calvin; the point is to understand him. Calvin's psychology will also be evaluated for how well it accounts for plasticity (malleability and durability) in emotions.

To approach Calvin, I am relying primarily on his explicit description of his psychology in the *Institutes* and on his commentaries, especially with respect to emotion.[2] Book I, chapter 15, sections 2–8 of the *Institutes* is especially important because only here does Calvin seems to give direct attention to psychology in philosophical terms. Irena Backus says, "Rather uncharacteristically for Calvin [his account of the soul] is condensed in one chapter of the *Institutes* where it is fully elaborated only in 1559. The reformer barely adverts to it in his Commentary and Sermons on the book of Genesis."[3] Because this section in the *Institutes* is so short, I appeal to his commentaries and a few other writings to unpack his views on emotions (passions, affections).

---

2. All inline citations in this chapter are from John Calvin, *Institutes of the Christian Religion*, 2 vols., ed. John T. McNeill, trans. Ford Lewis Battles (Louisville: Westminster John Knox, 2006).

3. Irene Backus, *Historical Method and Confessional Identity in the Era of the Reformation (1378–1615)* (Leiden: Brill, 2003), 85. The 1536 edition has very little to say about psychology. There is not a single section devoted to it. In his treatment of Christology, Calvin distinguishes soul and body, and somewhat cryptically remarks the characteristics of each may be transferred to the other. Ford Lewis Battles, *Institutes of the Christian Religion: 1536 Edition* (Grand Rapids: Eerdmans, 1975), 52. Calvin also connects the Socinian view of incarnation with the Manichean view that "man has his soul by derivation from God," through God's breath. Battles, *1536 Edition*, 53. Calvin seems at this point to be talking about heart in very general terms as the source of loving, and mind as the source of thinking. He's drawing from biblical language without superimposing a rigid psychology. For example, "we may understand that the essentials of prayer are set in the mind and heart, or rather that prayer itself is properly an emotion of the heart within, which is poured out and laid bare before God, the searcher of our hearts [cf. Rom 8:27]." Battles, *1536 Edition*, 73. However, by the 1543 version of the *Institutes*, these sections are largely in place, though arranged a bit differently, e.g., I.5.2 follows after I.15.8; Battles, *1536 Edition*, 52. See also Ioanne Calvino, *Institutio Christianae Religionis* (Argentorati: Wendelinum Ribelium, 1543), 20–22 [Book I, Chapter 2]; Ioanne Calvino, *Institutio Totius Christianae Religionis* (Geneva: Ioannis Gerardi, 1550), 30–33 [I.2.17–22].

CALVIN'S SOURCES

The topic of sources for Calvin's psychology raises two issues. First, there is a question about Calvin's orientation toward his sources biblical and otherwise. To what extent did he explicitly depend on human authorities other than the Bible? And second, to what extent is psychology a biblical concern? This section is aimed at getting some high-level assumptions made explicit rather than making a contribution on these points. There have been many books and articles written on the topic of Calvin's sources.[4]

In reference to the second question, it seems overall that Calvin thinks psychology is a biblical concern insofar as theology and doctrine is immediately concerned with the essence, powers, and qualities of the soul. He is less eager to contribute speculations about what he deems to be psychological minutiae. For example, on the one hand, Calvin considered the substance and immortality of the soul to be of vital theological importance. He wanted to prove the soul's substance and immortality "by clear passages of Scripture."[5] On the other hand, when speaking of the powers of the soul, he somewhat inconsistently warns against speculation "unless we want to torture ourselves in trivial and useless matters," while admitting that the subtleties of the philosophers "are true, not only enjoyable, but also profitable to learn, and skillfully assembled by them" (*Inst.* I.15.6). He did

---

4. Here is just a sampling of sources that contribute to this discussion: Backus, *Historical Method*; Roy W. Battenhouse, "The Doctrine of Man in Calvin and in Renaissance Platonism," *Journal of the History of Ideas* 9, no. 4 (October 1948): 447–71; T. Robert Baylor, "'With Him in Heavenly Realms': Lombard and Calvin on Merit and the Exaltation of Christ," *International Journal of Systematic Theology* 17, no. 2 (April 2015): 152–75; William J. Bouwsma, "The Quest for the Historical Calvin," *Archiv für Reformationsgeschichte* 77 (1986): 47–57; Quirinus Breen, *John Calvin: A Study in French Humanism* (Hamden, CT: Archon, 1968); Anthony N. S. Lane, *John Calvin: Student of the Church Fathers* (Grand Rapids: Baker Books, 1999); Alister E. McGrath, "John Calvin and Late Mediaeval Thought: A Study in Late Mediaeval Influences upon Calvin's Theological Development," *Archiv für Reformationsgeschichte* 77 (1986): 58–78; Edward F. Meylan, "The Stoic Doctrine of Indifferent Things and the Conception of Christian Liberty in Calvin's *Institutio Religionis Christianae,*" *Romantic Review* 8 (1937): 135–45; Heiko A. Oberman, "*Initia Calvini*: The Matrix of Calvin's Reformation," *Nederlands Archief voor Kerkgeschiedenis* 72, no. 2 (1992): 113–54; Charles Partee, *Calvin and Classical Philosophy*, ed. Heiko Oberman, Studies in the History of Christian Thought (Leiden: Brill, 1977); Jill Raitt, "Calvin's Use of Bernard of Clairvaux," *Archive für Reformationsgeschichte* 72 (1981): 98–121; Karl Reuter, *Vom Scholaren bis zum jungen Reformato Studien zum Werdegang Johannes Calvins* (Neukirchen: Neukirchener Verlag, 1981); and David C. Steinmetz, "Calvin as Biblical Interpreter Among the Ancient Philosophers," *Interpretation* 63, no. 2 (2009): 142–53.

5. John Calvin, *Psychopannychia*, in *Selected Works of John Calvin: Tracts and Letters*, ed. Henry Beveridge and Jules Bonnet, trans. Henry Beveridge, 7 vols (Grand Rapids: Baker Book House, 1983), 3:420.

not forbid the study of them but avoided speculation himself. He wanted to teach the clear teachings of Scripture while avoiding what is useless.

So, if Calvin affirmed studying psychology in a limited sense, what does it mean for Calvin to be biblical about psychology, and how do other sources relate to the Bible? In *Psychopannychia* he writes that human wisdom can find no certainty with regard to the soul, nor can philosophers agree "on any single point!"[6] He compliments Plato for talking "nobly of the faculties of the soul," adding that Aristotle "has surpassed all in acuteness."[7] But philosophers can say nothing about what the soul is or whence it comes. This seems to be an indication that, at least early in his career, Calvin wanted to be biblical in his approach to psychology rather than philosophical.

Continuing to take cues from *Psychopannychia*, we may observe Calvin's own explanation of his method. He was reluctant to put too much weight on the concepts without attending to their use. He recognized the possibility of taking a particular usage and applying it too generally. He says, "By Scripture usage different meanings are given to these terms [soul and spirit]; and most people without attending to this difference, take up the first meaning which occurs to them, keep fast hold of it, and pertinaciously maintain it ... and will not allow themselves to be convinced of the contrary."[8] But Calvin did not wish to "raise disputes about mere names, but [to] attend to the thing itself."[9] Instead, Calvin begins with an analysis of human nature from Genesis 1:26, where God creates human beings after his own image and likeness. Calvin argues that since God is a spirit, the image and likeness must refer to something that is not body, and this is just the breath of life that was introduced into the clay body that housed it. Calvin concludes, "nothing can bear the image of God but spirit, since God is a Spirit" (cf. Eph 4:24; Col 3:10).[10] To substantiate this account of the soul, Calvin cites numerous passages including Job 4:19; 2 Corinthians 7:1; Hebrews 12:9, 23; 1 Peter 1:9, 13, 22; 2:25. In Job 4:19, for instance, human beings are said to "dwell in houses of clay." From 1 Corinthians 2:11, Calvin

---

6. Calvin, *Psychopannychia*, in *Selected Works*, 3:420.

7. Calvin, *Psychopannychia*, in *Selected Works*, 3:421.

8. Calvin, *Psychopannychia*, in *Selected Works*, 3:420.

9. Calvin, *Psychopannychia*, in *Selected Works*, 3:422; CO 5:180.

10. Calvin, *Psychopannychia*, in *Selected Works*, 3:424.

further gathered that the human spirit is the part "in which the power of thinking and understanding resides."[11]

But does this mean Calvin was strictly biblical and uninfluenced by philosophy or the natural world? Had he taken his own counsel that we "ought to unlearn all that we have learned apart from Christ, if we wish to be his disciples"?[12] Several commentators have argued over the extent to which Calvin relied on philosophical sources. For example, whereas Roy Battenhouse sees heavy philosophical influence on Calvin's anthropology, Charles Partee cautiously emphasizes his differences with the Platonic tradition especially.[13] Citing Calvin's argument for the soul from 1 Peter 1:9, John Cooper thinks that it is clear that Calvin "is a legitimate target for the charge that his philosophical prejudice caused him to misconstrue the biblical text."[14]

It is perhaps helpful here to distinguish between philosophical influences as explicit, conscious sources of theorizing and as implicit, unconscious sources of theorizing. This is not to make a particular judgment about Calvin's unconscious mind, but merely to point out that any scholar traffics in concepts and intuitive judgments that are not always made explicit. The concepts a scholar inherits are products of cultural, philosophical, or theological development. Quirinus Breen acknowledges the difficulty of throwing off a mental set once it has been established. He suggests that Calvin never quite threw off humanist impulses, especially the humanist disengagement from "reverence for the teachings of the medieval doctors."[15] Likewise Battenhouse suggests that Calvin never quite

---

11. Calvin, *Psychopannychia*, in *Selected Works*, 3:426.

12. Calvin, *Commentary on 2 Timothy 3:14*. All citations of Calvin's commentaries are from Jean Calvin, *Calvin's Commentaries*, 45 vols., translated by John King, et al. (Edinburgh: Calvin Translation Society), 1844–56.

13. Battenhouse writes, "the conclusion toward which the evidence seems to point is that Calvin's so-called Biblical theology is not quite so Biblical as its nuggets of quotation would like to impress upon us." Battenhouse, "Doctrine of Man in Calvin," 469; Partee, *Calvin and Classical Philosophy*, 56. Breen, *John Calvin* (1968).

14. John Cooper, *Body, Soul, and Life Everlasting*, 2nd ed. (Grand Rapids: Eerdmans, 2000), 104–5.

15. Breen argues that the humanists show contempt for the medieval fathers "by not even quoting them," and found it "more stimulating to spend an hour with Plato than a month with Thomas or Duns Scotus." Breen, *John Calvin*, 146–47. Calvin contrasts Paul's citation of Aratus in Acts 17:28 with the way Papists use "testimonies of men" for "authority's sake" (Calvin, *Commentary on Acts 17:28*). Irena Backus points out, "Augustine does constitute an

"freed himself from the outlook of his early reading [Platonism]."[16] David Steinmetz asserts succinctly, "In Calvin's case, Jerusalem never parted company with Athens."[17]

Calvin seems to have been influenced quite a bit by both Stoicism and Platonism but not always explicitly. In the case of Stoicism, he often explicitly rejected some tenets while implicitly assuming others (more below).[18] Much has also been made of Calvin's use of the Platonic term "prison house" of the soul, referring to the body (I.15.2).[19] The term originates from Plato's *Phaedo* where he writes,

> Every seeker after wisdom knows that up to the time when philosophy takes it over his soul is a helpless prisoner, chained hand and foot in the body, compelled to view reality not directly but only through its prison bars, and wallowing in utter ignorance. And philosophy can see that the imprisonment is ingeniously effected by the prisoner's own active desire, which makes him first accessory to his own confinement.[20]

Alida Sewell notes that Calvin both "likely read [*Phaedo*] personally" and uses the term "prison house" in his writings more often than Plato, a total of ninety-one times.[21] She doubts that this pervasive usage could arise from

authority, albeit in a limited sense, especially for Calvin. ... Only the Bible provides Calvin with the proof that the true Church are God's elect who have existed from time immemorial." Backus, *Historical Method*, 52.

16. Battenhouse, "The Doctrine of Man in Calvin," 448.

17. Steinmetz, "Calvin as Biblical Interpreter," 143. Edward Adams makes a similar claim: "Calvin attempts to develop an approach to natural theological knowledge which is philosophical informed as well as biblically based." Edward Adams, "Calvin's View of Natural Knowledge of God," *International Journal of Systematic Theology* 3, no. 3 (November 2001): 292.

18. Alida Sewell writes, "Boisset considers Calvin's thinking to be anti-Stoic, whereas Schaff concluded the opposite. Although it would be too much to say, with Schaff, that Calvin was 'a Christian Stoic,' some Stoic tendencies can be found in Calvin's work also." Sewell cites an example of a Stoic tendency, the idea of virtue as following the dictates of reason rather than the passions. Alida Leni Sewell, *Calvin, the Body, and Sexuality* (Amsterdam: VU University Press, 2011), 23. Cf. E. F. Meylan, "The Stoic Doctrine of Indifferent Things and the Conception of Christian Liberty in Calvin's *Institutio Religionis Christianae*," *The Romantic Review* 28 (1937): 135–45.

19. *a carnis ergastulo anima*, cf. *Inst.* II.7.13; III.3.14, 19; III.6.5; III.9.4; IV.1.1; IV.15.11–12; IV.16.19; IV.17.30; OS 2:135–136; 2:178; 3:442–43, 449; 6:89.

20. Plato, *Phaedo*, 82d–e in *Plato: The Collected Dialogues including the Letters*, ed. Edith Hamilton and Huntington Cairns (Princeton, NJ: Princeton University Press, 1961), 40–98.

21. Sewell, *Calvin, the Body, and Sexuality*, 57, 63.

mere thoughtlessness, though the terminology might have been a popular idiom at the time.[22] Jean Boisset, likewise, sees in Calvin an intimate
familiarity and recourse to Plato: "These statistics show that Calvin never
ceased, from 1536 to 1560, to have recourse to the Platonic sources, that he
clarified his borrowings, and that he augmented them in the last edition
[of the *Institutes*] in comparison with those of 1543 and 1550."[23]

In spite of this, Calvin avoided explicit citations from philosophers
as primary justification for his claims, and he pushes back on relying on
philosophers.

> Here, too, let Philosophers give place, since on almost all subjects
> their regular practice is to put neither end nor measure to their dis-
> sensions, while on this subject in particular they quarrel, so that you
> will scarcely find two of them agreed on any single point! Plato, in
> some passages, talks nobly of the faculties of the soul; and Aristotle,
> in discoursing of it, has surpassed all in acuteness. But what the
> soul is, and whence it is, it is vain to ask at them, or indeed at the
> whole body of Sages, though they certainly thought more purely
> and wisely on the subject than some amongst ourselves, who boast
> that they are the disciples of Christ.[24]

The problem with relying on Plato, or even on the church fathers, is that
human authorities, the medieval *auctores*, often get things wrong. We see
Calvin's notion of depravity here. Calvin explicitly criticizes the "Papists"
for citing masters "for authority's sake" so to "lean on the testimonies of
men."[25] So overall, it is best to admit that Calvin was foremost a biblical

---

22. Sewell, *Calvin, the Body, and Sexuality*, 67. Sewell also notes that Augustine rejected the
term. Steinmetz notes the personal appeal this metaphor would have had to Calvin in light of
his pervasive health problems. He says, "He knew from bitter experience how imprisoning the
human body can be. But at the same time, he was firmly committed to the Christian doctrine
of resurrection." Steinmetz, "Calvin as Biblical Interpreter," 145.

23. Jean Boisset, *Sagesse et Sainteté dans la Pensée de Jean Calvin* (Paris: Presses Universitaires
de France, 1959), 227; cited and translated by Sewell, *Calvin, the Body, and Sexuality*, 63. "Cette
statistique montre que Calvin n'a jamais cessé, de 1536 à 1560, de recourir à la source platonicienne,
qu'il a précisé ses emprunts, et qu'il les a augmentés, dans la dernière édition, par rapport à celles
de 1543 et de 1550."

24. Calvin, *Psychopannychia*, in *Selected Works*, 3:420.

25. John Calvin, *Commentary on Acts 17:28*. He adds that human beings "have naturally
some perseverance of God" and so "draw true principles from that fountain."

scholar who may have implicitly assumed some philosophical prejudices or concepts. While not inclined to rely explicitly on philosophical sources for psychological theorizing, the concepts he inherited were roughly Platonic. Calvin's psychology was developed insofar as it was necessary for him to treat related theological issues. Charles Partee's comment is apt: "Calvin looks at the subject of soul and body, immortality and resurrection through the 'spectacles of Scripture.' The lens of Calvin's spectacles were certainly tinted by Platonism here, but the source of Calvin's view of soul and body is the Scripture."[26]

Additionally, even in his eagerness to be biblical, Calvin also made introspective or experiential arguments about psychology to bolster his theological views. For example, he points to the fear of spiritual judgment as an "undoubted sign of the immortal spirit," since "the body is not affected by the fear of spiritual punishment" (*Inst.* I.15.2).[27] He often supplemented his arguments with appeals to general revelation, famously with his *sensus divinitatis* (*Inst.* I.3.1).[28] For example, "How detestable, I ask you, is this madness: that man, finding God in his body and soul a hundred times, on this very pretense of excellence denies that there is a God? ... They see such exquisite workmanship in their individual members, from mouth and eyes even to their very toenails" (I.5.4).[29]

---

26. Partee, *Calvin and Classical Philosophy*, 65.

27. Another activity of the soul apart from the body is the "investigation of heavenly things" (*Inst.* I.5.5). Cf. Paul Helm, *John Calvin's Ideas* (Oxford: Oxford University Press, 2005), 130–31.

28. Cf. *Inst.* I.3.3. Edward Adams claims, "It seems to me to have been established beyond any serious doubt that Calvin draws his theory of the *sensus divinitatis* from the Hellenistic philosophical dogma of the 'preconception' (prolepsis) of God. The doctrine of the preconception originated with Epicurus, but was taken over and developed by the Stoics. The notion of the preconception is prominent in Cicero's dialogue *On the Nature of the Gods* and it is from this source that Calvin derives it." Edward Adams, "Calvin's View of Natural Knowledge of God," *International Journal of Systematic Theology* 3, no. 3 (November 2001): 284–85. See also Egil Grislis, "Calvin's Use of Cicero in the *Institutes* I:1–5: A Case Study in Theological Method," *Archiv für Reformationsgeschichts* 62 (1971): 5–37; Cicero, *De natura deorum*, 1.16.43–44, in *On the Nature of the Gods. Academics*, trans. H. Rackham, Loeb Classical Library 268 (Cambridge, MA: Harvard University Press, 1933), 45; Steinmetz, "Calvin as Biblical Interpreter," 151.

29. *Inst.* I.5.1, "Lest anyone, then, be excluded from access to happiness, he not only sowed in men's minds that seed of religion of which we have spoken but revealed himself and daily discloses himself in the whole workmanship of the universe. As a consequence, men cannot open their eyes without being compelled to see him ... upon his individual works he has engraved unmistakable marks of his glory, so clear and prominent that even unlettered and stupid folk cannot plead ignorance."

Finally, we have already noted that Aquinas was unwittingly and indirectly influenced by Galen's medicine. What about Calvin? To what extent did Galen influence his theology? That Calvin was a Galenist is almost a truism since it was the reigning medical paradigm.[30] It hardly would have been possible for him not to espouse these medical views. It is true that a direct contemporary of Calvin, Andreas Vesalius (1514–1564), began to challenge some of Galen's views.[31] But as a popular scientific theory, Galenism persisted well into the nineteenth century.[32] It was not until germ theory in roughly 1880 that scientists found a satisfactory answer for what causes diseases. Alida Sewell also points out that Calvin was a friend of the sons of Dr. Guillaume Cop (d. 1532), who was the personal physician to the French king, Francis I.[33] Guillaume Cop possibly introduced Calvin to Galen and Hippocrates, since Cop produced a French translation of them both. What is certain is that Calvin read Galen.[34] To cite just one example, in Calvin's commentary on 2 Timothy 2:17, he writes, "Now Galen, in many passages throughout his writings, and especially where he lays down definitions in his small work 'On unnatural swellings,' distinguishes the one [gangrene] from the other [cancer]."[35] It is necessary for now only to note this background. We will return to the topic later when discussing Calvin's views of the body and soul. As with his philosophical views, there is no prolonged attempt to integrate medicine and theology.

THE SOUL, THE BODY, AND THE *IMAGO DEI*

That Calvin supposed that human beings consist of soul and body is beyond controversy, defining soul as "an immortal yet created essence, which is [a

---

30. The notion of a reigning paradigm comes from Thomas Kuhn, *The Structure of Scientific Revolutions*, 3rd ed. (Chicago, IL: University of Chicago Press, 1996). Sewell writes, "In common with his contemporaries, Calvin held to the theories of the traditional medical authorities [i.e., Galenism]." Sewell, *Calvin, the Body, and Sexuality*, 69.

31. Servetus also challenged Galen's theories on circulation.

32. There are countless instances of Galenism in the novels of Jane Austen (1775–1817), Charles Dickens (1812–1870), Anthony Trollope (1815–1882), and even George Eliot (1888–1965). To cite just one example from Jane Austen, "[Lydia] had high animal spirits, and a sort of natural self-consequence." The language of colds and fevers continues today, even the Galenic recommendation to dress warmly lest we "catch a cold." Jane Austen, *Pride and Prejudice* (Sweden: Winehouse Classics, 2016), 29.

33. Sewell, *Calvin, the Body, and Sexuality*, 27.

34. Sewell, *Calvin, the Body, and Sexuality*, 70.

35. Calvin, *Commentary on 2 Timothy*, 2:14–18.

human being's] nobler part" (*Inst.* I.15.2).[36] The body is the prison house of the soul. Calvin argues for an immortal spirit from the human fear of judgment, from the human ability know God and angels (immaterial things), and even from sleep, which can suggest thoughts of things that never happened or will happen to human beings (I.15.2). A person can only know an immaterial thing such as immortality if this knowledge arises in something that goes beyond the body. The soul is the principle of a knowledge that cannot have arisen from irrational material.[37] This sense of immortality is one of the pre-eminent gifts engraved on the human mind. Furthermore, biblically speaking, when the Bible refers to a human being as a soul, it indicates "it to be the principle part" (I.15.2; cf. Heb 13:17; 1 Pet 2:25, etc.).

This principal part of a human being is also the "the proper seat of [God's] image" (I.15.3). In the soul's relation to the body, we see something of Calvin's respect for Stoic ethics.[38] In *De Clementia*, we read, "Nothing apter or more appropriate could be devised for the comparison [than the comparison of mind and prince] ... the mind (*animus*) of man is a tiny thing, minute, discernible to no eyes ... the members of the body have indeed from themselves a vigor and natural force, but the moderation thereof is in the mind's power."[39] By comparison, in the *Institutes* Calvin calls the mind or soul (*animus*) the nobler part (*Inst.* I.15.2). Like a prince, the function of the nobler part here is to direct or to rule, so it is called the *hēgemonikon* (*to hēgemonikon*) (I.15.8). In Adam's original state, the affections were "kept within the bounds of reason, all his senses tempered in right order" (I.15.3).

---

36. Calvin adds that the soul can also be called spirit in the biblical text. He additionally argues that the common metonymy of spirit (2 Cor 7:1) or of soul (1 Pet 2:25) for human beings testifies that it is the principal part (*Inst.* I.15.2). See also Matt 10:28; Luke 12:5; Heb 13:17; 1 Pet 2:11.

37. Of this argument Paul Helm writes, "This argument's gaps are obvious enough. More interesting is whether Calvin sees such an argument as having premises that do or do not depend upon Scripture. It is not very clear." Helm, *John Calvin's Ideas*, 130–31.

38. Battles writes, "Calvin recognized Seneca's supreme gift to be in ethics, and this judgment is certainly borne out in the course of the Commentary." Ford Lewis Battles, "The Sources of Calvin's Seneca Commentary," in *John Calvin*, ed. Basil Hall (Grand Rapids: Eerdmans, 1966), 48.

39. *Calvin's Commentary on Seneca's De Clementia*, Renaissance Text Series, III, ed. and trans. Ford Lewis Battles and André Malan Hugo (Leiden: Brill, 1969), 91: *nihil ad similitudinem poterat aptius aut propius excogitari. ... ita animus hominis pusillum est quiddam & minutulum, nullis oculis conspicuum. ... membra corporis habent quidem à se vigorem & naturalem impetum, sed penes animum est temperatura.*

Calvin goes on to say that the mind and heart or soul and its powers is the "primary seat of the divine image" (I.15.3). This is significant because it is the soul primarily that can reflect God's own "attributes and excellencies."[40] Jason Van Vliet summarizes that the image of God is "an attributive similarity which the Triune God imprinted upon the human soul from the beginning."[41] And since God is spirit, it is the spiritual aspect of humankind that has the ability to reflect him—and by inference also, can fully reflect him as spirit.[42] Calvin even analogies the difference between body and soul with the difference between the concerns of Christ's spiritual kingdom and the civil jurisdiction, which are completely different.[43]

Calvin does not deny "that our outward form, in so far as it distinguishes and separates us from brute animals, at the same time more closely joins us to God" (I.15.3). He does not "contend too strongly" with those who wish to include in the image of God that human beings stand upright, ready to gaze into the heavens, "provided it be regarded as a settled principle that the image of God, which is seen or glows in these outward marks, is spiritual" (I.15.3). Calvin is here objecting to the view of Andreas Osiander, who claimed that the image of God extends to body and soul indiscriminately. The discrimination that Calvin makes here seems to be that the *imago* properly pertains to the soul, but it may be seen or "glows" in the outward man. While the soul is not human being, the image of God is manifest in it.

Again returning to the theme of the soul's governance of the body, Calvin insists that original integrity of soul included the fact that Adam "had full possession of right understanding, when he had his affections kept within the bounds of reason, all his senses tempered in right order, and he

40. Jason Van Vliet, *Children of God: The Imago Dei in John Calvin and His Context* (Göttingen: Vanderhoeck & Ruprecht, 2009), 116.

41. Van Vliet, *Children of God*, 253. Calvin says we are the "most remarkable example of his justice, wisdom, and goodness" (*Inst.* I.15.1).

42. Van Vliet explains, "The logic behind this interpretation is relatively straightforward: God has no physical body since he is spirit. Therefore, his similitude must reside in the spiritual, not the physical, component of human beings, namely, the soul." Van Vliet, *Children of God*, 43.

43. *Institutes* (1536), OS 1:228; *At vero, qui inter corpus et animam, inter presentem hanc fluxamque vitam et futuram illam aeternamque discernere noverit, neque difficile intelliget, spirituale Christi regnum et civilem ordinationem, res esse plurimum seposita.* "But whoever knows how to distinguish between body and soul, between this present fleeting life and that future eternal life, will without difficulty know that Christ's spiritual Kingdom and the civil jurisdiction are things completely different." Translation Battles, *1536 Edition*, 207.

truly referred his excellence to exceptional gifts bestowed on him by his Maker" (I.15.3).[44] Here we have a preliminary indication of a two-faculty, three-part psychology: intellect (right understanding), will (affections), and senses (the bodily component).

Van Vliet claims that in spite of his rebuttal to Osiander, "Calvin eventually came to include the body as part of the *imago Dei*."[45] This would be very surprising considering not only Calvin's rejection of Osiander but also that almost no earlier theologian did so, not even Melanchthon, who was otherwise more concerned with the body.[46] I think even on Van Vliet's own evidence that his conclusion is too strong. Calvin returns repeatedly to the metaphor of light and darkness in describing God's relation to the human faculties. So on Van Vliet's reading, God's light is reflected in human creatures. In the original state of human beings, "there was no part of man, not

---

44. Van Vliet writes,

> Since Paul singles out "righteousness and holiness" as key components of the restoration, Calvin also identifies these as "the chief part" of God's image in man at creation. At the same time, there is more to the image than just the chief part. In addition to possessing the gifts of righteousness and holiness, Adam "was endued with right judgment, had affections in harmony with reason, had all his senses sound and well-regulated, and truly excelled in everything." Words such as "harmony" and "well-regulated" indicate that being created in the likeness of God is not merely a matter of reflecting certain divine attributes, but also possessing those qualities in a unified and integrated manner. *Imago Dei* contains *integritas definita*.

(Van Vliet, *Children of God*, 93.)
He adds, "the mature Calvin sees the *imago Dei* not only as a spiritual reflection of certain divine attributes, but also as the integrity of the soul, a word which connotes both soundness and concord. At creation, the faculties of the soul are not only free from any taint of sin, but they also cooperate with each other in a harmonious fashion." Van Vliet, *Children of God*, 113. Cf. Aquinas "original justice":

> "Through original justice reason perfectly restrained the lower powers of the soul, and reason itself was perfected by God and subject to Him. But as has already been explained (q. 81, a. 2), this original justice was taken away because of the sin of the first parent. And so all the powers of the soul remain in some way deprived of the proper ordering by which they are naturally ordered toward virtue, and this deprivation is itself called a wounding of the nature. … Thus, insofar as reason is deprived of its ordering toward the truth, there is the wound of ignorance; insofar as the will is deprived of its ordering toward the good, there is the wound of malice; insofar as the irascible power is deprived of its ordering toward the arduous, there is the wound of weakness; and insofar as concupiscence is deprived of its ordering toward the pleasurable as moderated by reason, there is the wound of concupiscence. So, then, there are four wounds inflicted on the whole of human nature by the sin of the first parent." (*ST* I–II.85.3)

45. Van Vliet, *Children of God*, 258.
46. Van Vliet, *Children of God*, 258.

even the body itself, in which some sparks did not glow" (I.15.3). Van Vliet is nearer to the mark when he says, "beginning with his commentary on Genesis he opens the door slightly to include some scintillations of the image in the human body as well."[47] It is most consistent with Calvin's view to say that the body reflects the *imago Dei* only secondarily as the sparks from the soul—as the principle of divine likeness—fall on it by governing it.

Finally, it is important to understand the redemptive historical plot of Calvin's assessment of the body and soul, here and below with respect to the powers. The state of the soul and body differed dramatically prior to and after the fall. The soul's ability to reflect God is "so vitiated and almost blotted out that nothing remains after the ruin except what is confused, mutilated, and disease-ridden." The image "was not totally annihilated and destroyed in [Adam], yet it was so corrupted that whatever remains is frightful deformity" (I.15.4). What is this deformity? Again, Calvin primarily directs his attention to the deformity of soul—since "whatever has to do with spiritual and eternal life is included under 'image'" (I.15.4)—that is, the intellect and the will. The remedy for the psychological corruption, the darkness of intellect and the perverseness of the will, is regeneration and renewal (2 Cor 3:18; Eph 4:24; Col 3:10, etc.). We simply note again that since the soul is the subject of the image, it is also the subject of the restoration. As far as the body is concerned, resurrection seemed to be Calvin's chief hope.

EVALUATION

What have we seen so far about how the body qualifies agency for Calvin? Insofar as Calvin tends to align the soul with the *imago Dei* and connect with the spiritual concerns, he seems to segregate the two parts of human nature. Calvin's stress that the soul is the seat of the *imago* carries with it the danger of angelism without a corresponding emphasis that humankind is a holistic composite of body and soul.[48] Calvin does admit that the whole human being is body and soul but seems to imply that the body is of almost

---

47. Van Vliet, *Children of God*, 116.

48. Battenhouse writes, "What Maritain has called the heresy of angels would seem to be here [in Ficino] foreshadowed more than a century before Descartes." He explains in a footnote, "The heresy traces back, actually, to the psychological dualism of Plato, as Maritain recognizes in his *An Introduction to Philosophy*." Battenhouse, "Doctrine of Man in Calvin," 451. See Jacques Maritain, *Three Reformers: Luther, Descartes, Rousseau* (New York: Scribner, 1936), 53; Jacques Maritain, *An Introduction to Philosophy* (New York: Longmans, 1930).

no concern in spiritual matters. We also seem to observe a directionality for the *imago* that runs from the soul to body ("sparks ... glow"). The soul governs the body in only a top-down sort of way. It is not obvious that the body works back on the soul reciprocally, at least not in a way that is positive. This tiered reciprocity as important to psychology, but between the higher and lower powers. Even the language of governance (hegemony) begins to suggest a dominance relationship between the two. Calvin also seemed principally interested in the corruption and restoration of the soul, rather than the body. Calvin placed the blame for sin principally on the soul rather than the body— see his comments on flesh in Romans 7—but in exculpating risks neglect. We have already seen signs of several of the developments we traced in the previous chapter, especially a more rigid dualism between body and soul.[49]

THE NEGLECTED BODY

What does Calvin have to say about the body, if it is of secondary importance in reflecting the *imago Dei?* The initial difficulty here is that Calvin was just not very concerned with this topic. Again, he saw spiritual matters as principally pertaining to the soul and its powers. As a result, his comments on the body and its relation to the spiritual life are scattered and not well formed. Alida Sewell summarizes,

> Calvin's own thinking about the body is not to be found in one handy chapter in the *Institutes*, or anywhere else. That in itself says something about the importance or lack thereof, of the human body in Calvin's mindset. For him, the mind and reason feature much more prominently than does the body. The idea of a "theology of the body" would be a foreign concept for him.[50]

In the absence of systematic treatment, we will first investigate Calvin's familiarity and endorsement of Galenism. Second, we will see how his Galenic and late medieval notions of the body and soul underlie his scattered comments about the body.

---

49. Per above: (1) body/soul dualism; (2) ascendency of the will in action and affective theory; (3) curtailing of virtue in action theory; and (4) continence as the highest ethical state.
50. Sewell, *Calvin, The Body, and Sexuality*, 7.

As already illustrated, "In common with his contemporaries, Calvin held to the theories of the traditional medical authorities."[51] Even without speculating about the level of Calvin's interaction with the medical doctor Guillaume Cop, the father of his friend Nicholas Cop, we have strong evidence of Calvin's intimate acquaintance with Galenic medicine and its theories about spirits, the four humors, and even physiological aspects of personality.

In general terms, Calvin expresses a high respect for doctors and even dedicated his commentary on 2 Thessalonians to his own doctor, Benedict Textor.[52] He also expresses this sort of high regard for Galen himself: "in regard to the structure of the human body one must have the greatest keenness in order to weigh, with Galen's skill, its articulation, symmetry, beauty, and use. But yet, as all acknowledge, the human body shows itself to be a composition so ingenious that its Artificier is rightly judged a wonder-worker" (*Inst.* I.5.2).[53] Calvin apparently read Galen and at least one other Galenist medical doctor, Paul Aegineta (Paul of Aegina, c. 625–c. 690). In his commentary on 2 Timothy 2:17, Calvin cites Galen's "On Unnatural Swellings" and the sixth book of Aegineta where he defines cancer on Galen's authority.[54]

Specifically, Calvin integrates Galen's views on the spirits and humors in many places. In *De Clementia* he writes,

---

51. Sewell, *Calvin, The Body, and Sexuality*, 69.

52. Calvin writes, "To that distinguished man, Benedict Textor, Physician. While you are reckoned to excel in the knowledge of your profession by those who are competent judges in the matter, I for my part, have always regarded as very high excellence that strict fidelity and diligence which you are accustomed to exercise, both in attending upon the sick, and in giving advice. ... you were influenced not so much by regard to a particular individual, as by anxiety and concern for the common welfare of the Church." "Dedication," *Commentary on 2 Thessalonians*. William J. Bouwsma also cites Textor's personal advice on biblical medical terminology in *Commentary on 2 Timothy* 2:17. Bouwsma, *John Calvin: A Sixteenth Century Portrait* (Oxford: Oxford University Press, 1989), 243. In a letter to Melanchthon, Calvin calls doctors "men of no common skill in their profession, persons of good sense," adding, "[I] willingly permitted myself to be guided by such masters." *Selected Works*, 6.483. Sewell, *Calvin, The Body, and Sexuality*, 73.

53. Calvin may have been referring to Galen's work *Peri chreia moriōn* (*De Usu Partium Corporis Humani*, On the Usefulness of the Parts of the Body).

54. *The Medical Works of Paulus Ægineta* was translated into English by Francis Adams in 1834. Paulus Ægineta, *The Medical Works of Paulus Aegineta, The Greek Physician*, trans. Francis Adams (London: J. Welsh, Treuttel, Würtz, 1834), https://archive.org/stream/medicalworksofpa01pauluoft#page/n4/mode/1up.

Still, it is truer to say that all living beings consist of four elements
and divine spirit. This was clearly Aristotle's opinion. For they
derive flesh from earth, humor from water, breath from air, heat
from fire, and natural disposition from divine spirit. The astrolo-
gers, however, think otherwise: that when we are born our spirit
derives from the sun, our body from the moon, blood from Mars,
natural disposition from Mercury, desire from Jupiter, carnal passions from Venus, humor from Saturn. It is not unreasonable, then,
that Seneca applies to SPIRIT the epithet VITAL.[55]

Later, when commenting on the biblical text, Calvin writes that "the vital
spirits chiefly reside in the blood … a token which represents life," and
"excessive grief not only consumes the vital spirits, but dries up almost
all the moisture which is in our bodies."[56] This latter text is significant
because of the connection between emotion and physiological changes.[57]
Like Aquinas, Calvin seems to assume emotions involve bodily changes.
Vital spirits are connected with life in his commentary on Genesis 15:15, and
he feels the need to point out that soul does not refer to them in Psalm 34:2
but to the affections instead—unlike Luke 12:13–21. Lastly, Calvin makes
a significant theological analogy between the vital spirits and the Holy
Spirit in *The Interim, or the Declaration of Religion, of His Imperial Majesty
Charles V*, IX.3:

Whoso, therefore, is not in the communion of the body, is no more
quickened by the Holy Spirit unto eternal salvation, than any

---

55. Calvin, *De Clementia*, 103–5.
56. *Commentary on Genesis 9:4*; *Commentary on Psalm 22:15*.
57. Here are two other examples.

It appears to me that David rather means to say, that his affections were, as it
were, melted within him, whether it were from joy or sorrow. As the soul of man
sustains him, so long as it keeps its energies collected, so also it sinks within him,
and, as it were, vanishes away, when any of the affections, by excessive indulgence,
gains the ascendancy. Accordingly, he is said to pour out his soul, who is so excited,
that his affections lose their vigor, and begin to flow out. David's language implies,
that his soul melted and fainted within him by the greatness of his sorrow, when
he thought of the condition from which he had fallen. *Commentary on Psalm 42:4*

For we know that passions appertain not to him [God]; but he is set forth as a father,
who burns with jealousy when he sees his son ill-treated; he acknowledges his own
blood, his bowels are excited. *Commentary on Joel 2:18–19*

natural member cut off and torn away from its body is quickened unto natural life, because it is no longer invigorated by the vital Spirit flowing from its one head. Wherefore, we must believe that no one out of the Christian Church and its spiritual communion can obtain eternal life.[58]

Calvin also echoes the Galenic theory of humors in his commentary on Matthew 6:22. He analogizes the function of the eye to the members of the body as the mind to the affections. Just as an eye diseased with a humor guides the foot wrongly, so also the mind can lead the affections astray.[59] In the *Institutes*, Calvin analogizes the corruption of physical food by the presence of "evil humors" to the corruption of spiritual food by a soul corrupted by "malice and wickedness" (*Inst.* IV.17.40).[60] In a letter to William Farel, Calvin explains the buildup of humors in his head and the consequent "defluxion":

On that day, when I was preaching, as usual, and found great dif-ficulty in speaking, owing to the nostrils being blocked up with mucus and the fauces [the passage between the back of the mouth and the pharynx] choked with hoarseness, all of a sudden I under-went a strange sensation; the cough, to be sure, ceased, but rather unseasonably, while the head continued to be crammed with evil humours.[61]

Likewise to Melanchthon, Calvin complains that his doctors "wanted to kill me outright with the heating fumes of Malmsey and Muscat wine" and that "only once [they] attempted to expel the bilious humours from my spleen."[62] Calvin even cites the humoral personality theory, writing to Monsieur de Richebourg of a certain Louis: "as he was of a more san-guine temperament, was also more lively and cheerful. Charles, who has

---

58. Calvin, *The Interim, or the Declaration of Religion, of His Imperial Majesty Charles V*, IX.3 in *Selected Works*, 3:202. See also Chapter XVIII of *The Adultero-German Interim*, "Of the Sacrament of the Eucharist" in *Selected Works*, 3:214.

59. *Commentary on Matthew 6:22; Commentary on Luke 11:34–36; 16:13.*

60. Calvin also mentions the build-up of "fetid humors" among the Persians in *Inst.* IV.12.22.

61. Cited in Sewell, *Calvin, the Body, and Sexuality*, 74; *Selected Works*, 4:204.

62. *Selected Works*, 6:483.

somewhat of melancholy in his disposition, is not so easily drawn out of himself."[63] This is significant because this is one area where we see a body to mind relation in Calvin's medical references. Happiness here is not merely a way of seeing the world or circumstances but is at least partly precipitated by the blending of bodily humors.

To summarize, physiologically speaking, Calvin was invested in Galenism. He even speaks of the connection between emotion and physiological alteration. Moreover, he applied Galenic humor theory to personality, opening the door for a body to mind relation. We are now in a position to draw some conclusions about Calvin's attitudes toward the body in light of this background.

First, Calvin saw the organization of the body, like the hierarchy of the world itself, as an eloquent vehicle for revealing God's "power, goodness, and wisdom" (*Inst.* I.5.1, 3). The medieval world picture was a well-ordered hierarchy from the lowest forms of organic life (plants) to the highest (human beings), from various forms of spiritual life to God as the highest being. A human being operates both as a bridge between organic animals and the spiritual world and as an image of the universe.[64] Like his ancient and medieval predecessors, Calvin was comfortable with calling a human being a *microcosm*, an analogy of the universe. As the wise providential rule of God is to the world, so is the mind of a human being to the body— at least in the created state. Calvin reacted quite strongly to heliocentric theory. In a sermon on 1 Corinthians 10:19–24, he says,

> and let us not be as like those fantasizers, who, having a spirit of bitterness and contradiction, find fault with everything, and pervert the order of nature. We will see certain ones of them so frenzied, not only in religion, but to show above all that they have a monstrous nature they will say that the sun does not move, and that it is the earth which migrates and which turns.[65]

---

63. *Selected Works*, 4:252; Sewell, *Calvin, the Body, and Sexuality*, 75.

64. See Eustace M. Tillyard, *The Elizabethan World Picture* (New York: Vintage, 1959); C. S. Lewis, *The Discarded Image* (Cambridge: Cambridge University Press, 1964).

65. John Calvin, "Huitieme Sermon, 1 Cor. Caput. X v. 19–24," CO 49:677; Fr.: *et ne soyons pas semblables à ces fantastiques, qui ont un esprit d'amertume et de contradiction, pour trouver à redire par tout, et pour pervertir l'ordre de nature. Nous en verrons d'aucuns si frénétiques, non*

Calvin's concern to affirm God's orderly governance of the world is reflected in his statements about the orderly composition of human beings at creation.

Moreover, even in spite of the fallen state of human beings, Calvin was quick to praise not only the natural world but also the body. Both are the objects of arguments from general revelation for the wisdom, power, and goodness of God. On at least three occasions, Calvin expresses his admiration for the beauty of mothers with their babies:

> God needs no other orators to illustrate his power than infant children who are still at their mother's breasts. They themselves are dumb, but the marvelous providence of God that shines in them speaks with eloquence and sonority. Anyone who considers how a fetus is begotten in the womb of its mother, is nourished there for nine months until it is brought forth into the light, and from the moment of birth finds ready food, must feel not only God's work in the world but also be carried away in admiration of him.[66]

Again in the *Institutes*, Calvin writes, "the human body shows itself to be a composition so ingenious that its Artificer is rightly judged a wonder-worker" (I.5.2). In a sermon on Job 10:7–15, Calvin says,

> Yet it is humankind who is the chief work and the most excellent of all the creatures, God willed to unfold that which he had put in only small portions in heaven, in earth, and in the animals: so much that humankind is called a "microcosm" (*un petit monde*), which we see so many admirable things that we are astonished. Then this being the case, we must always be persuaded, that God in contemplating his work in us, be moved and inclined to do good to us, to sustain us. ... of humankind we see that they are elegant from the top of

---

pas seulement en la religion, mais pour monstrer par tout qu'ils ont une nature monstrueuse, qu'ils diront que le soleil ne se bouge, et que c'est la terre qui se remue et qu'elle tourney. Translation mine.

66. *Commentary on Matthew 21:16*; See also *Inst.* I.5.3: "Indeed, he not only declares that a clear mirror of God's works is in humankind, but that infants, while they nurse at their mothers' breasts, have tongues so eloquent to preach his glory that there is no need at all of other orators."

In his *Commentary on Isaiah 49:15*, he writes, "how incredible the affection of a mother is for the infant whom she warms in her bosom and nurses and watches over with care, so that she passes sleepless nights, worries continually, and forgets herself!"

their head to soles of their feet, ... that no one could find a fault to the end of a toenail.[67]

Indeed human beings are "the infinite wisdom of God declared in the human form."[68] Calvin heaps more praise on the body later in the sermon before adding, "but still the principal [part of man] is in the soul."[69] In a later sermon on Job, he clarifies that both the body and the soul are God's good creation in essence, but just as with the soul, the body is also perverted.[70] As a good creation, Calvin affirmed that caring for the body is part of Christian obedience. Commenting on Paul's counsel for Timothy to use a little wine for the stomach's sake, Calvin imagines an objection: "Is that the road by which we rise to heaven?" He does not affirm this Neoplatonist censure, affirming instead temperance so that "every person should attend to his own health," avoiding "excessive parsimony" or "cramming their belly."[71]

We might add to this that Calvin distanced himself from a Neoplatonist distrust of the material world. This makes perfect sense in light of his medieval background and its tendency to see the material world as part of an ordered hierarchy. Calvin rejected the Augustinian formula *utor non frui* (use but do not enjoy).[72] He warns against those things "which are injurious to godliness" and counsels believers to "enjoy God's temporal favors,

---

67. CO 5:481; *Or est-il ainsi que l'homme est le principal ouvrage et le plus excellent qui soit entre toutes les creatures, Dieu a voulu là desployer ce qu'il n'avoit mis qu'en petites portions et au ciel, et en la terre, et en tous animaux: tellement quel'homme est appelle comme un petit monde, que là nous voyons tant de choses admirables qu'il faut qu'on en soit estonné. Puis qu'ainsi est, nous devons tousiours estre persuadez, que Dieu contemplant son ouvrage en nous, sera esmeu et enclin à nous bien faire, à nous maintenir. ... de l'homme nous voyons qu'il est poly depuis le sommet de la teste iusques à la plante des pieds ... et qu'on ne sauroit point trouver à redire au bout d'un ongle* (Translation mine). Calvin seems to have a special fascination with the perfection of fingernails, mentioning the topic twice in this sermon. He also returns to the subject in his *Commentary on Psalm 139:15*, "When we examine it, even to the nails on our fingers, there is nothing which could be altered, without felt inconveniency, as at something disjointed or put out of place; and what, then, if we should make the individual parts the subject of enumeration?"

68. CO 5:481, *exprimer la sagesse infinie de Dieu, laquelle se declare en la forme humaine.*

69. CO 5:488, *Mais encores le principal est en l'ame.*

70. CO 5:781. We will say more later about the sense in which human beings are corrupted, essence or quality.

71. Calvin, *Commentary on 1 Timothy 5:23.*

72. Augustine develops the idea in *On Christian Doctrine* I.3–5. He writes, "We have wandered far from God; and if we wish to return to our Father's home, this world must be used, not enjoyed, that so the invisible things of God may be clearly seen, being understood by the things

as if they did not use them."[73] Calvin writes in his commentary on Psalm 104:15, "It is permissible to use wine not only for necessity, but also to make us merry."[74] Even sex, the generation of human beings, is not unclean in and of itself (*Inst.* II.8.4).[75]

And yet just as Calvin speaks quite harshly about the powers of the soul after the fall, he can do so with the body. The order of the microcosm has been radically altered. For example, he references the infection of our minds from the "boiling" of lust's enslavement of senses (III.10.3). In a sermon on Job, Calvin says, "Here is the cause that must sting us and provoke a desire for death, it is to know, to be finally stripped of this mortal body, which is as a haven full of all stench and infection, we are fully reformed into the image of God, and it will reign in us, and that which is corrupt in our nature, will be totally annihilated."[76] However, Calvin is very careful not to blame sin on the body. God's law is "not only to suppress our bodies" but in all things "guards our souls."[77] God's law is the vehicle of his governance for those who stand between the fall and God's final restoration.

---

that are made—that is, that by means of what is material and temporary we may lay hold upon that which is spiritual and eternal." Augustine, *On Christian Doctrine*, I.4, NPNF¹ 2:523.

73. *Commentary on Matthew 13:44–52*. Here, as also in his commentary on 1 Timothy 4:5, the key for Calvin is the confluence of the regenerated faculties and the law of God, not as much a specific psychological attachment to temporal things as competitors with God for our love. It is not obvious that Calvin's view goes very deep beyond a linguistic disagreement with Augustine. It might be suggested that the term "use" for Augustine meant "use for enjoying God," which might suggest that there is a sort of delight in the object, but as a signpost as C. S. Lewis might say. Lewis also uses the wandering metaphor; the signposts are things that produce joy: "When we are lost in the woods the sight of a signpost is a great matter." C. S. Lewis, *Surprised by Joy: The Shape of My Early Life* (Orlando: Harcourt, 1955), 238.

74. Calvin, *Commentary on Psalm 104:15*. In *Inst.* III.10.2, Calvin writes, "Now if we ponder to what end God created food, we shall find that he meant not only to provide for necessity but also for delight and good cheer." See also III.19.9.

75. See also *Inst.* III.10.2, "Let this be our principle: that the use of God's gifts is not wrongly directed when it is referred to that end to which the Author himself created and destined them for us, since he created them for our good, and not for our ruin."

76. CO 5:170, *Voila di-ie, la cause qui nous doit piquer et soliciter à désirer la mort, c'est a savoir, afin qu'estans despouillez de ce corps mortel, qui est comme une loge pleine de toute puantise et infection, nous soyons pleinement reformez à l'image de Dieu, et qu'il regne en nous, et que ce qui est de corruption de nostre nature, soit du tout anéanti.* (Translation mine)

77. CO 1:337, *Celuy-la en sa Loi n'a point voulu seulement reprimer nos corps: mais il a sur tout regardé nos âmes.* (Translation mine)

Finally, Calvin's attitude toward inferior or secondary causes may be relevant to our investigation. That Calvin seemed to connect physiological change with emotion (e.g., of grief in *Commentary on Genesis 9:4*) makes it strange that he did not seem to be interested in this or give it much attention in his ethics. It is at least plausible that this can be traced to his distrust of inferior or secondary causes. He writes, "Philosophers think not that they have reasoned skillfully enough about inferior causes, unless they separate God very far from his works. It is a diabolical science, however, which fixes our contemplations on the works of nature, and turns them away from God."[78] Again, on the analogy of the microcosm, if God ultimately governs nature, it is plausible that Calvin's interest would be chiefly in the role the human mind plays in governing the natural elements of the composition of human beings, their spirits and humors. Bouwsma speculates that this aversion may be tied to Calvin's dislike of confusion or mixture.[79] Speaking generally, this may be speculative, but it may provide at least a clue for his lack of interest in composite faculties like in Aquinas. Furthermore, Calvin tended to ascribe direct divine causality for natural phenomena like thunder or clouds. Again, given the analogy assumed in human being as microcosm, we may have a clue to his reluctance to talk about the causal chain from physiological to psychological (e.g., sleep deprivation).[80]

EVALUATION

What does Calvin have to say about the body? While he seemed to hold similar physiological assumptions to Aquinas, he gave almost no effort to integrating them into his theology. Calvin often speaks positively about the body, marveling at how it displays the glory of its creator; he respected doctors and the benefit of their art. He also endorsed the benefit of good

---

78. *Commentary on Psalm 29:5.*

79. Bouwsma, *John Calvin*, 34–35. T. F. Torrance says Calvin has "nothing to do with second causes." T. F. Torrance, *Calvin's Doctrine of Man* (London: Lutterworth, 1949), 13.

80. One possible exception is in Calvin's *Commentary on Daniel 6:10*, speaking of why Daniel opened his window to pray: "There is no doubt that the Prophet used this device as a stimulus to his fervor in prayer. For when praying for the liberation of his people, he directed his eyes towards Jerusalem, and that sight became a stimulus to enflame his mind to greater devotion. ... Let us learn, therefore, when we feel ourselves to be too sluggish and cold in prayer, to collect all the aids which can arouse our feelings and correct the torpor of which we are conscious."

health for the spiritual life. It is surprising given Calvin's use of the prison metaphor that he was quite affirming both of the body and of material things, provided they be ordered or within bounds. He may have been neglectful of the body generally, but he was not Neoplatonic.

However, as his analogy between sickness and depravity shows, he seemed to assume that the soul has to do with sin and the body with sickness. His reticence to integrate physiology with moral emotions was because if he assumed that the body is irrational, then it would naturally follow that reason cannot govern its inclinations, and therefore they cannot be moral. And this may have been related to his general reticence to endorse secondary causes. In any case, Calvin's view of moral agency is a sort of top-down hegemony. Yes, the body was influenced by the fall, and will also be influenced by the restoration. But this restoration happens through the renewal of the mind and will by the regeneration of the Spirit. Calvin seemed to underestimate the possibility of the body contributing something either to sin or to restoration. But Gnosticism can come in the back door by doing a very un-gnostic thing, denying the body's unique role in sinfulness. The reason is this: by denying the body's role in sin, Calvin also minimizes its role in restoration. This division of realms between body and soul shows how little Calvin saw the person as a holistic composite.[81]

SUBSTANCE AND IMMORTALITY OF THE SOUL

The substance and immortality of the soul were an important interest for Calvin, especially given that he treats these two points in his first theological work, *Pyschopannychia*. In this volume, he wanted to demonstrate: (1) that the soul is a substance and (2) that "after the death of the body [the soul] truly lives, being endued both with sense and understanding."[82] These topics are important for my concerns because Calvin's concern to preserve the immortality of the soul distances him from a holistic or tiered

---

81. Again, by holistic I mean that the body qualifies the range of psychological functions, even thought, such that none of people's functions are abstracted from their metaphysical constituents, body and soul. The soul and body function concurrently, the soul accounting for the vitality and structure of the entire living organism. Interactions between mind and body are within a holistic framework and do not represent soul and body interaction, as if the soul just were the mind.

82. Calvin, *Pyschopannychia*, in *Selected Works*, 3:419–420.

psychology. For Calvin, the soul must be a distinct immaterial substance—
rather than mere form or vital spirits—for it to survive death.

Calvin seems to have two distinct groups in mind in this treatise, two
types of *psychoktonoi* (Greek, soul-murderers).[83] There are those who
"imagine that it sleeps in a state of insensibility from Death to the The
Judgment-day, when it will awake from its sleep," and those who "will
sooner admit anything than its real existence, maintaining that it is merely
a vital power which is derived from arterial spirit on the action of the lungs,
and being unable to exist without the body, perishes along with the body,
and vanishes away."[84] The first group—clearly identified—are "the nefari-
ous herd of Anabaptists"[85] who advocated soul sleep.[86] But the second seems
to a Galenist or Alexanderist, he cites Epicurus, tendency to style the soul
as mere matter. In the *Institutes* I.5.5, Calvin remarks that his opponents
"willingly drag forward ... that frigid statement of Aristotle [that the soul
is actuality of a natural body] both to destroy the immortality of the soul
and to deprive God of his right." He continues, "For, since the soul has
organic faculties, they by this pretext bind the soul to the body so that it
may not subsist without it." Calvin seems to admit the soul's governance
over the so-called nutritive powers, while also emphasizing that this "in
no way obscures God's glory, but rather illumines it" (I.5.4). He writes, "Let
Epicurus answer what concourse of atoms cooks food and drink, turns
part of it into excrement, part into blood, and begets such industry in the
several members to carry out their tasks, as if so many souls rule one body
by common counsel!" (I.5.4).

Calvin's famous opponent Michael Servetus advocated something like
this view, but with a pantheistic twist. While Servetus is widely known
for his connection to Calvin, his medical contributions were significant.
He was among the first to reconfigure Galen's ideas of circulation when
he published his *Christianismi restitutio*. Servetus combined innovations in
medicine with a pantheistic notion that the vital spirits are divine essence.

---

83. Calvin, *Psychopannychia*, in *Selected Works*, 3:414.

84. Calvin adds, "and becomes evanescent till the period when the whole man shall
be raised again," showing that he is referring to Christian advocates for this Galenist or
Alexanderist view. *Pyschopannychia*, in *Selected Works*, 3:419.

85. *Pyschopannychia*, in *Selected Works*, 3:418.

86. Van Vliet, *Children of God*, 67.

His view amounted to saying that the soul is in the blood, but that the soul is divine substance.[87]

For Calvin this was no "trifling difference."[88] The issues at stake go beyond the possibility of intermediate or eternal beatitude. He also was concerned to protect the status of human beings as image bearers. There is likeness, not equality, as Servetus claimed, between God and human beings, and "it follows that the image of an immortal God is reflected in the immorality [sic] of the human soul."[89] Calvin's defense of immortality in *Psychopannychia* begins with this very point. The image of God must be separate from the flesh, otherwise it cannot be immortal and cannot properly reflect the image and likeness of God.[90] Moreover, a body cannot be partaker of the "wisdom, justice, and goodness of God."[91]

IMMORTALITY

Calvin describes the soul as immortal substance (*Inst.* I.15.6). We reference again Bartolomeo Spina's comment in 1519 that the doctrine of the immortality of the soul was "half-dead." This helps to frame the intensity of Calvin's theological interest in the topic.[92] Furthermore, the controversy

87. This view has similarities to Averroism. See Stephen Mason, "Religious Reform and the Pulmonary Transit of the Blood," *History of Science* 41 (2003): 459–71.

Calvin responded in *Declaration Povr Maintenir La Vraye Foy que Tiennent tous Chrestians de la Trinité des persones en vn seule Dieu* (Geneve: Jean Crispin, 1554), 89–90: "For [Servetus] said that all creatures are of the proper substance of God, just as all things are full of infinite gods. This is the language which he was not embarrassed to use, and even put down in writing. I being fascinated by an absurdity so serious, replied to the contrary. 'How could any man if he strike this pavement here with his foot, and if he say, that he treads on your God, would you not be horrified to see the majesty of God subjected to such a reproach?' Then he says, 'I have no doubt that this bench, this table, and anything you can show me, is the substance of God.'"

> Car pour ce qu'il disoit que toutes creatures sont de la propre substance de Dieu, ainsi que toutes choses sont pleines de dieux infinis; c'est le langage qu'il n'a point eu honte de prononcer, et mesme coucher par escrit: moy estant fasché d'une absurdité si lourde repliquay à encontre, Comment povre homme, si quelcun frappoit ce pavé icy avec le pied, et qu'il dist, qu'il foulle ton Dieu, n'aurois tu point horreur d'voir assubietti la maiesté de Dieu à tel opprobre? Alors il dit, Ie ne fay nulle doute que ce banc, & ce buffet, & tout ce qu'on pourra monstrer, ne soit la substance de Dieu. (Translation mine)

88. *Psychopannychia*, in *Selected Works*, 3:418.

89. Van Vliet, *Children of God*, 68.

90. *Psychopannychia*, in *Selected Works*, 3:423.

91. *Psychopannychia*, in *Selected Works*, 3:424.

92. Bartolomeo Spina, *Propugnaculum Aristotelis de immortalitate*, Dedicatory Letter; cited by Dennis Des Chene, *Life's Form: Late Aristotelian Conceptions of the Soul* (Ithaca, NY: Cornell University Press, 2000), 46.

over Pomponazzi's view of the soul, which was finally rejected by the Fifth
Lateran Council (1512–1517), also helps to frame Calvin's conviction that
"not one of [the philosophers], with the exception of Plato, distinctly maintained [the soul's] immortality" (I.15.6).[93] When read against the controversies about Aristotle, especially the Averroistic and Alexanderist tendencies,
Calvin's uneasiness with the Aristotelian view makes perfect sense. To the
Alexanderist, the intellect is really just a production of the accidents of
the body, and therefore "passes away with the dissolution of the body."[94]
Aristotle's idea that the soul is the form of the body could easily be read in
this way, and often was.[95] Calvin himself references "that frigid statement
of Aristotle" (*Institutes* 1.5.5). Aristotle writes in *De Anima* II.1 (412a20), "the
soul is an actuality of the first kind of a natural body having life potentially
in it."[96] Calvin does not explicitly object to Aristotle—other than calling the
statement frigid—but to those who "drag [it] forth" to equate the soul and
body (*Inst.* I.5.5). He says, "Others so attach the soul's powers and faculties
to the present life that they leave nothing to it outside the body" (I.15.6).
Calvin denies that the soul is "merely a vital power which is derived from
arterial spirit on the action of the lungs, and being unable to exist without
body, perishes along with the body, and vanishes away and becomes evanescent till the period when the whole man shall be raised again."[97]

　　In addition to Calvin's biblical arguments, especially in *Psychopannychia*,
he seemed to endorse a view that the soul immediately knows its immortality (*Inst.* I.15.2). Calvin believed that there are "unfailing signs of divinity
in man," but that we must recognize the creature and Creator distinction
(I.5.5). There is a "sense of divinity which can never be effaced … engraved
upon men's minds" that we are ever engaged in forgetting (I.3.3). God's
wisdom is on display both in the heavens and on earth (I.5.2). For Calvin,
the study of the stars is itself "an activity of the soul distinct from the

93. Plato, *Phaedrus*, 245c in *Plato: The Collected Dialogues*, 492.

94. Eckhard Kessler, "The Intellective Soul," in *The Cambridge History of Renaissance Philosophy*, ed. Charles B. Schmitt and Quentin Skinner (Cambridge: Cambridge University Press, 1988), 487.

95. Daniel A. Callus, "The Origins of the Problem of the Unity of Form," *Thomist* 24 (1961): 258.

96. See Aristotle, *De Anima*, 412a27, in *The Complete Works of Aristotle: Revised Oxford Translation*, ed. Jonathan Barnes, 2 vols. (Princeton: Princeton University Press, 1984).

97. *Psychopannychia*, in *Selected Works*, 419–20.

body," and along with memory and precognitive or predictive dreams, are "unfailing signs of divinity in man" (I.5.5). These, by extension, are signs of human immortality, since they cannot be explained by mere bodily functions.[98] Immortality, and our murky awareness of it, was clearly an important concern for Calvin. So it is easy to see why this pushed him away from the Aristotelian view.

Substance Language

Calvin is clear that the soul is immortal, but he adds that it is also an incorporeal substance (*substantium incorporeum*). He demonstrates this from Scripture first by noting that the soul, or sometimes spirit, "returns to God who gave it" (Eccl 12:7). Indeed the Scripture teaches, "we dwell in houses of clay" (*Inst.* I.15.2; cf. Job 4:19). This shows that the incorporeal substance is joined with the body as a habitation (I.15.6). The substance of the soul is also a human being's principle part, since Scripture uses soul as a metonymy for human being (1 Pet 1:9; 2:25; *Inst.* I.15.2).

In discussing the philosophers' views, Calvin adds that the soul, though "not spatially limited," is "set in the body, it dwells there as in a house; not only that it may animate all its parts and render its organs fit and useful for their actions, but also that it may hold the first place in ruling man's life" (I.15.6). Certainly, the language here is Platonic and Augustinian; Calvin does not use the language of "form" here.[99] But there are also perhaps some echoes of an Aristotelian, entelechist model, i.e., the soul as vital principle, especially Calvin's terminology of animating its parts and rending

---

98. *Institutes* 1.5.5 bears very strong resemblance to the argument against a materialistic view of the soul in Cicero's *Tusculan Disputations* I.24–27. Cicero writes, "M. Again, can you think, pray, those views of less importance which pronounce that there are divine elements in human souls? Could I discern how such elements could come into being I should also see how they came to an end. For it seems to me that I can tell from what the blood, bile, phlegm, bones, sinews, veins, in fact all the framework of the limbs and the whole body have been compounded and how they were fashioned: as for the soul itself, if it had no characteristic except that through it we have life, I should think that the life of men was supported by natural process much as the life of a vine or a tree is, for such things we say have life. Also, if man's soul had no characteristic except that of seeking out or avoiding things, that also it would share with the beasts." Cicero, *Tusculan Disputations* I.24, in *Tusculan Disputations*, trans. J. E. King, Loeb Classical Library 141 (Cambridge, MA: Harvard University Press, 1927), 65–67.

99. Augustine, *The Greatness of the Soul*, 13–14, in *St. Augustine: The Greatness of the Soul, The Teacher*, ed. Joseph Colleran (Mahwah, NJ: Paulist Press, 1978), 39–42.

its organs useful.[100] It is useful to remember that, philosophically speaking, the line between Platonists and Aristotelians was somewhat ambiguous during this time particularly in light of the movement toward a more instrumental soul-body relation in the Buridan consensus.[101] As we have seen, Buridan is likewise clear that the soul animates sensitive substance instrumentally, and this is exactly what he claims the so-called sensitive soul is, just the instrumental extension of the soul to the body.[102] These terms—animate, render, ruling—evidence again not only a Platonic view, but also echo a widespread and broadly instrumental view of the soul's relation to the body within a generally Aristotelian tradition. The relation of body and soul in Calvin's psychology is not perfectly transparent. It is fair to say he was more Platonic than Aristotelian. But given Calvin's immediate Scholastic context, it is difficult to make a rigid demarcation. The instrumental view of body-soul relation is a good sign, however, that Calvin was not a Thomist with regard to mind and body.

However, it is also worth noting that Calvin was not here directly addressing the sixteenth-century Thomists.[103] Aquinas specifically said that the rational powers of the intellect and will do not depend on a corporeal organ, and therefore survive the body.[104] The sixteenth-century Thomists likewise upheld this distinction and spoke of the soul as substance—immaterial, indivisible, and not spatially extended. In Scholastic

---

100. Backus says, "There is room in Calvin's theology for the entelechist view." Backus, *Historical Method*, 93. From his *Psychopannychia*, we also see another common element in the tradition of medieval theological psychology, that the soul is the cause of life. The difference between an animate object and inanimate is precisely the existence of an *anima*. Calvin points out that the Scripture even speaks of the soul "metonymically for life" (Job 13:14; Ps 119:109; Matt 6:25; Luke 12:20). Calvin, *Psychopannychia*, in *Selected Works*, 3:421.

101. Adam Wood, "The Faculties of the Soul and Some Medieval Mind-Body Problems," *The Thomist* 75 (2011): 628.

102. Cited and translated by Wood, "Faculties of the Soul," 615–18; Buridan writes, "any of these parts is a sensitive animated substance, since it is composed of a body and a soul, and none other than a sensitive soul." *Questiones in De anima* 2.7.

103. Calvin apparently read Themistius' *Commentary on De Anima*. Themistius explains that for Aristotle, the productive intellect (active intellect) survives death, but the surviving soul cannot remember the person's earthly thoughts since the passive intellect perishes with the body. This may have added to the confusion. Backus, *Historical Method*, 88–89.
  It is worth remembering that even if Aristotle was concise and ambiguous about the immortality of the intellectual part of the soul, he specifically rejected the notion of the soul as a harmony in *De Anima* 407b26–408a34 in *Complete Works of Aristotle*.

104. Thomas Aquinas, *Summa Theologiae*, trans. Alfred J. Freddoso, updated January 10, 2018, https://www3.nd.edu/~afreddos/summa-translation/TOC.htm. I.78.1.

terms, "substance" was roughly synonymous with "form." The soul is the form of the body in the sense that it is the active principle of its existence, the substantial first principle upon which all bodily accidents depend.[105] While they were reluctant to discard the language of substance for the soul, they said it was incomplete substance — since strictly speaking, substance is the *hylomorphic* compound of form (soul) and matter (body).

Thomistic philosophers of the Renaissance were besieged on two sides, as it were. They fought on the one hand the Platonist view that the soul is an independent substance, and on the other hand the Alexanderist or Galenist materialism, the tendency to conceive of the intellect as arising from the potentiality of matter, or that the soul is a bodily temperament. Thomistic philosophers held that the soul is the form of the body against the Platonists, who held that the soul only uses the body instrumentally, and that the soul is substance against the Galenists or Alexanderists, who held that the soul is an accident of the body, a harmony of its qualities. The Thomists wanted to "bind the human soul as tightly to the body as possible" while "granting the possibility of immortality."[106]

TWO SOULS

Finally, Calvin repudiates "those persons who affirm more than one soul in man, that is, a sensitive and a rational soul" (*Inst.* I.15.6). This is probably a reference to Plato's *Republic*, since Calvin references the conflict between organic motions and the soul's rational part as armies at war. Plato writes of "two factions that are fighting a civil war."[107] However, even this is not certain, since Plato speaks of parts of the soul, rather than souls. More immediately, William of Ockham defended two souls, not merely forms, on the grounds that the parts can oppose each other.[108] While this is speculative, Calvin may not have been entirely familiar with the nuances of this question, dismissing it as something "trivial and useless" (*Inst.* I.15.6). The comment certainly reflects a current debate "whether human beings were

---

105. Des Chene, *Life's Form*, 69–75.

106. Des Chene, *Life's Form*, 69.

107. Plato, *Republic*, IV.439c–440e in *Plato: The Collected Dialogues*.

108. See above, chapter 3, p. 97; William of Ockham, cited in Vera Hirvonen, *Passions in William Ockham's Philosophical Psychology* (Dordrecht: Kluwer Academic, 2004), 23–46.

informed by sensitive souls in addition to intellective souls."[109] Katharine
Park also remarks that this view somewhat revived in the sixteenth century with a renewal of interest in Averroes.[110] Calvin preferred the view
that there is only one unified, immortal, intellective soul. It seems that
Calvin took something like Buridan's view of intellect and sense, since he
explicitly ascribes sense to the soul, but seemingly in an instrumental way.

Park specifically connects holding the single immortal and intellective
soul with the preference for physiological explanation for the sensitive
and vegetative powers, and Calvin seems to fit within this general stream,
which was "by far the more common throughout the early Renaissance."[111]
Calvin's inattention to the soul's interaction with its powers falls in line
with a growing number of Renaissance scholars who were not interested in
quibbling over the distinctions of powers when speaking of the soul, since
the distinctions are bodily distinctions.[112] For example, Phillip Melanchthon
saw the organic powers as material. In his *Liber de anima*, he outlines a physiological account of the organic powers: "There has been a great and foolish
battle in the schools about the distinction of the faculties. Concerning the
organic powers, it is clear that they are distinguished by their organs; for as
the soul produces different operations in different organs, just as different
sounds are produced in different pipes."[113] This instrumental distinction

109. Katharine Park, "The Organic Soul," in *The Cambridge History of Renaissance Philosophy*, ed. Charles B. Schmitt and Quentin Skinner (Cambridge: Cambridge University
Press, 1988), 475.

110. Park, "Organic Soul," 483. Backus assumes "he expresses disapproval of Plato's subdi-
vision of the soul" here. However, this seems unlikely since Plato divided the soul into three
parts with only the higher being rational. In favor of Backus's position is that perhaps both
the irrational parts are lumped, and this is a reference to the charioteer allegory in *Republic*
IV. Backus, *Historical Method*, 92.

111. Park, "Organic Soul," 483.

112. It is worth noting that a connection of Calvin, Jacques Lefèvre d'Étaples, worked
together with Josse Clichtove and Nifo of Padua on "questioning the validity of the real distinction between the soul and its faculties." Park, "Organic Soul," 479.

113. Philip Melanchthon *MO* 13:20, quoted in Park, "Organic Soul," 479. In fact, Melanchthon
integrated Galenic ideas about spirits with a material view of the indwelling of the Holy Spirit.
Sachiko Kusukawa explains, "Melanchthon argued that the Holy Spirit or the Devil could mix
with these medical spirits. In pious men, the Holy Spirit would mix with the medical spirits
and render knowledge of God clearer; evil spirits on the other hand could also mix with the
medical spirits and impeded judgement and cause the limbs to perform the cruellest of deeds,
such as when Medea killed her own children." Sachiko Kusukawa, ed., *Melanchthon: Orations
on Philosophy and Education* (Cambridge: Cambridge University Press, 1999), xx; Melanchthon,
Liber de anima, *MO* 13:88. Melanchthon shows familiarity also with Nemesius of Emesa's *De*

is very friendly with Platonic thought, and because of this philosophical advantage, it represents something of a rough consensus view until the even more mechanized physiology of René Descartes.

EVALUATION

In terms of the medieval developments highlighted in the last chapter, Calvin's views on the immortality and substance of the soul are easily recognizable. In an effort to defend the immortality of the soul, Calvin appeals to the nature of the soul as incorporeal substance on both biblical and experiential grounds. He uses the term "substance" over against the term "form," presumably because it more clearly affirms the immortality of the soul. It seems clear enough that the theological and biblical concerns drove the philosophical theorizing, not the other way around. Calvin is not inclined toward the holistic framework of the Thomists, who bound "the human soul as tightly to the body as possible," while "granting the possibility of immortality."[114]

In terms of body-soul relation, he seems to have a roughly instrumental view like most of his contemporaries. Insofar as the medieval development tended toward dualism, Calvin's position is not surprising in the least. Calvin simply reflected the common psychological trends of his time. Overall Calvin seems inclined toward simplicity and gets into psychological questions only in so far as it is useful for the Christian. He admits only one intellective soul, which raises a natural question about how he accounts for internal conflict. We will return to this in the following section.

FACULTIES

Calvin's faculty psychology is very simple, involving the intellect and the will. This is first a consequence of Calvin's view of the *imago*. Because Calvin viewed our intellectual faculties as the chief seat of the image of God, his simple psychology merely expands on the *imago*. This is significant because this qualifier rules out, in principle, a discussion of composite faculties, which incorporate the body. As Calvin writes in the *Institutes*

---

natura hominis. He notes that "Gregory of Nyssa, the brother of Basil, has written a book on the soul," most probably referring to Nemesius's book, which was commonly attributed to Gregory. Melanchthon, *MO* 13:6–7.

114. Des Chene, *Life's Form*, 69.

I.15.3, "the primary seat of the divine image was in the mind and heart, or in the soul and its powers." Calvin's simple psychology also arose from his humanist reluctance to enter into meaningless quibbles over psychological minutiae. However, he did make allowance for "any who are inclined to prosecute the study" to investigate these matters fully (I.15.6).

Calvin's most focused treatment of psychology is in book I, chapter 15. In brief, Calvin's approach begins with a dismissal of Augustine (I.15.4), proceeding to a treatment of the "Manichean error of the soul's emanation" (I.15.5), before treating the opinions of the philosophers (I.15.6–8). In addressing Augustine, Calvin curtly dismisses his speculation that the faculties of the soul mirror the Trinity—understanding, will, and memory—saying that this view is "by no means sound" (I.15.4).[115] Likewise, Calvin dismisses the Manichean view that the soul derives from God's substance, since this would mean "God's nature is subject not only to change and passions, but also to ignorance, wicked desires, infirmity, and all manner of vices" (I.15.5). We see clearly here first that Calvin ascribes depravity to the higher faculties; the image of God is corrupted. He says, "Contrary motions stir up and variously distract [man's] soul. Repeatedly he is led astray by ignorance. He yields, overcome by the slightest temptation. We know his mind is to be a sink and lurking place for every sort of filth" (I.15.5).

When Calvin gets to the "true," "enjoyable," and "profitable" teachings of the philosophers on this matter, he produces an intentionally synthetic account. While he does cite Plato's *Theaetetus*, he engages more with Aristotle than Plato. Calvin's account of the faculties explicitly relies on *De anima*. Irena Backus connects Calvin's account of the five senses with *De anima* III.1 (425a13–426b21); his account of the imagination with *De anima* III.3 (427a15–429a9); his account of reason with III.4 (429a10–430a9); his account of the passive and active intellect with III.5–6 (430a10–430b25); and his distinction between the three appetitive and cognitive faculties with *Eudemian Ethics* II.7 (1223a21–27).[116] Calvin also seems quite flexible with

---

115. In so doing he parts ways with a major stream of the Christian tradition including Anselm, Abelard, Peter Lombard, Bernard of Clairvaux, etc. Van Vliet, *Children of God*, 42; see also John E. Sullivan, *The Image of God: The Doctrine of St. Augustine and Its Influence* (Dubuque, IA: Priory Press, 1963), 209-10.

116. Backus, *Historical Method*, 95. Backus notes that the division of three somewhat aligns with Plato's division.

Aristotle's opinion of there being "three things in the soul which control action and truth—sensation, thought, desire;"[117] Calvin calls them "sense, understanding, and appetite" (*Inst.* I.15.6).[118] He adds that even when philosophers—in this case Themistius—try to speak "most plainly," they still needlessly complicate the picture. Overall Calvin seems relatively indifferent to how these matters are sorted out, objecting chiefly that the philosophers "always imagine reason in man as that faculty whereby he may govern himself aright" and are "ignorant of the corruption of nature that originated from the penalty for man's defection" (I.15.6–7).

Calvin closes his description with a working definition for the *Institutes*, that the soul consists of just two faculties: "understanding [or intellect, *intellectum*] and the will [*voluntas*]" (I.15.7). In the following section, I begin to develop his treatment of these two faculties. But before doing so, I want to make a few observations about shadowy comments Calvin makes about sense and about a possible physiological backdrop behind the will as the heart.

First, it is important to remark that Calvin does seem to admit the existence of sense, while not treating it as a faculty of the soul. As I have briefly mentioned, the faculties of the soul are those by which we reflect the *imago*, and the body is therefore excluded. Sense seems to be a merely bodily power. In this discussion, we see Calvin's dualism work out pointedly. On the one hand, "while the whole man is called mortal, the soul is not thereby subjected to death; nor does reason or intelligence belong to the body merely because man is called a 'rational animal'" (I.15.3). And again with reference to sense:

> For the sense perception inhering in brute animals *does not go beyond the body*, or at least extends no further than to material things presented to it. But the *nimbleness of the human mind* in searching out heaven and earth and the secrets of nature, and when all ages have been compassed by its *understanding and memory*, in arranging each thing in its proper order, and in inferring future events from the

117. Aristotle, *Nicomachean Ethics*, 1139a17–18, in *Complete Works of Aristotle*.

118. Paul Helm remarks, "Here we see Calvin's admiration for Aristotle coupled with a tendency to cut him short when he suspects that some Aristotelian distinction is not profitable and may lead to speculation." Paul Helm, "Vermigli, Calvin, and Aristotle's Ethics," *Unio Cum Christo* 3, no. 2 (October 2017): 92.

past, *clearly shows that there lies hidden in man something separate from the body*. (I.15.2, emphasis added)

Calvin elaborates the philosophers' views in the *Institutes* II.2.2. Here he distinguishes between sense as a dim cognitive capacity, "entangled in baser things," against the higher light of reason. He adds, somewhat incoherently, generic appetite as a third faculty, speaking of its capability to be molded into will or as sense appetite to draw human beings off into error. Calvin is not perfectly lucid here, but he clearly saw the sense appetite of the philosophers as problematic and needing to be "tamed and gradually overcome by reason's rod."

Second, it may be the case that Calvin saw a physiological backdrop to the soul's powers. Like Buridan, Calvin seems to admit that the soul has organic faculties in I.5.4–5. The difficulty here is that he seems to be doing so for the sake of argument. Calvin either has no settled consistent view on the question or he simply means that the organic parts are the parts of the body to which the soul has special reference.[119] He says, "to establish that there is something organic in the soul that should correspond to its several parts in no way obscures God's glory, but rather illumines it" (I.5.4). In the Renaissance, it was sometimes supposed that the soul infuses "the parts of the body with its powers." Des Chene writes, "The motive power [the will], for example, resides primarily in the heart."[120]

Des Chene's example of the heart also raises the question of whether Calvin assumed correspondence between the heart as the will and the heart as a physiological organ. This is an interesting and undeveloped

---

119. Another text in favor of organic faculties is Calvin's *Commentary on Genesis 2:7*: "I do not hesitate to subscribe to the opinion of those who explain this passage of the animal life of man; and thus I expound what they call the vital spirits by the word breath. Should any one object, that if so, no distinction would be made between man and other living creatures, since here Moses relates only what is common alike to all: I answer, though here mention is made only of the lower faculty of the soul, which imparts breath to the body, and gives it vigor and motion: this does not prevent the human soul from having its proper rank, and therefore it ought to be distinguished from others."

120. Des Chene, *Life's Form*, 78. This tendency persisted even into the twentieth century. The heart is spoken of as the seat of the affections and the physical organ in James Joyce's *Ulysses*, for example. "Your heart perhaps but what price the fellow in the six feet by two with his toes to the daisies? No touching that. Seat of the affections. Broken heart. A pump after all, pumping thousands of gallons of blood every day." James Joyce, *Ulysses* (New York: Random House, 1986), 87.

question. It may be that Calvin would admit that the heart is a biblical, psychological, and medical word, that heart corresponds both to the will and to the internal organ.[121] One piece of evidence for this may come from Calvin's personal motto, *Cor meum tibi offero, prompte et sincere*, "My heart

I give you, promptly and sincerely," which is represented in this emblem from 1547 by an anatomically accurate representation of it on Galenic theory.[122] The correspondence between emotion and physiological response, as for example in Calvin's *Commentary on Psalm 22:15*, seems to illustrate some sort of volitional-physiological parallelism: "excessive grief not only consumes the vital spirits, but dries up almost all the moisture which is in our bodies."[123] If so, his comment that "the body is not affected by the fear of spiritual punishment" would seem to be inconsistent (*Inst.* I.15.2). Yet Calvin probably does not mean that the body is totally unaffected, but rather that the body is unaffected in the absence of the soul—i.e., the affect comes from the soul.

Figure 4.1, John Calvin's Seal, 1547

Commenting on Romans 10:10, Calvin contrasts the seat of faith as not in the brain (*cerebro*), but in the heart (*cordes*), before adding, "I would not contend about the part of the body in which faith is located: but as the word 'heart' is often taken for a serious and sincere feeling, I would say that faith is a firm and effectual confidence."[124] There is one other text that

---

121. Perhaps also known as the bowels, as in *Commentary on 2 Corinthians 7:15*, "As the bowels are the seat of the affections, the term is on that account employed to denote compassion, love, and every pious affection."

122. The motto and translation are taken from Herman J. Selderhuis, *Calvin's Theology of the Psalms*, Text and Studies in Reformation and Post-Reformation Thought (Grand Rapids: Baker Academic, 2007), 26. The illustration is from Barbara Carvill, "The Calvin Seal," *Calvin University*. Excerpts from the Fall 2005 Faculty Conference Address, https://calvin.edu/about/history/calvin-seal.html. For an anatomic history of the shape of the heart, see Pierre Vinken, *The Shape of the Heart* (New York: Elsevier, 1999).

123. *Commentary on Psalm 22:15*.

124. *Commentary on Romans 10:10*; *Verum observemus, fidei sedem non in cerebro esse, sed in corde: neque vero de eo contenderim, qua in parte corporis sita sit fides: sed quoniam cordis nomen pro serio et sincero affectu fere capitur.* CO 21:202. See also *Commentary on Ephesians 3:17*: "He points to that part in which Christ peculiarly dwells, in your hearts—to show that it is not enough if the knowledge of Christ dwell on the tongue or flutter in the brain." Calvin seems here to be referencing the physiological organ.

indicates that Calvin did perhaps assume some sort of psycho-physical parallelism. He cites the bowels as the "seat of the affections," saying Titus "had been, at that time, more vehemently stirred to love [the Corinthians]; and that, from the innermost affections of his heart."[125] The fact that Calvin elsewhere claims the heart is the seat of the affections, and here uses the more physiological term "bowels," is suggestive. However, the issue of correspondence or parallelism is speculative, and I am unable to settle the matter here, at least partly because Calvin does not seem to have settled the issue in his own mind.[126]

THE INTELLECT AND WILL

How does Calvin's psychology function? Calvin distinguishes the faculties of intellect and will in the following way. The part of the intellect is to "distinguish between objects, as each seems worthy of approval or disapproval" and to be the "leader and governor of the soul." The part of the will, on the other hand, is to "choose and follow what the understanding [intellect] pronounces good, but to reject and flee what it disapproves" and "in its own desire [to await] the judgment of the understanding" (*Inst.* I.15.7). So far this sounds like an intellectualist treatment. While he is unwilling again here to be delayed by "those minutiae of Aristotle ... that the mind has no motion in itself, but is moved by choice," Calvin claims to affirm Aristotle's conception of the will. Finally, he states his preference for the simpler designation of will for all appetite (I.15.7), disregarding the distinction of the philosophers between sense appetite, which "inclines to pleasure" and "becomes inordinate desire and lust," and will.

It is necessary to take a brief aside about Calvin's faculty psychology and biblical terminology. It might be that Calvin preferred these two terms because they have biblical precedent and superimposed his psychology on them. The question is, to what extent does Calvin equate the biblical terms "heart" and "mind" with the faculties of will and intellect, respectively? Bouwsma sees a problem here:

---

125. *Commentary on 2 Corinthians 7:15.* Calvin is commenting on the connection between the affections and the Greek term *splanchna* (bowels).

126. Calvin seems to prefer not to iron out the subtleties. For instance, commenting on Psalm 26:2, he suggests that the distinction between higher affections and the sensual, corresponding with heart and loins (*reins*), is "more subtle than solid." *Commentary on Psalm 26:2.*

[Calvin] struggled to come to terms with a conception of the human being as a mysterious psychosomatic unity dependent on the "heart." Although he recognized the importance of the biblical heart, his effort to identify it with one or another of the traditional faculties, as we have seen, suggests that he often failed to understand that it represented a radically different conception of the personality.[127]

Calvin identifies "the mind and the heart" (*mente et corde*) as the soul's powers in I.15.3 and II.2.2.[128] He explicitly aligns the four terms respectively in II.2.12.[129] In *Bondage and Liberation of the Will*, Calvin likewise flatly admits, "I myself also acknowledge, the heart signifies the will."[130] When speaking of Ezekiel 36:26, "I will ... give you a heart of flesh," Calvin writes, "Who shall say that the infirmity of the human will is strengthened ... when it must rather be wholly transformed and renewed?" (*Inst.* II.3.6).[131] Calvin argues for the depravity of the entire soul on this basis. He was concerned to distance himself from the views either that Adam's sin was caused by sense appetite or that it continues to impact humankind only through sense appetite. Of Adam's sin, Calvin writes, "[A]ll parts of the soul were possessed by sin after Adam deserted the fountain of righteousness. For not only did a lower appetite seduce him, but unspeakable impiety occupied the very citadel of his mind, and pride penetrated to the depths of his heart" (II.1.9).[132] By appealing to Ephesians 4:17–18, 23, Calvin proves that "none of the soul [mind and heart, not just sensual appetites] remains pure or untouched by that mortal disease" (II.3.1). He argues that both the

---

127. Bouwsma, *John Calvin*, 131–32.

128. See also *Commentary on Psalm 103:1; 119:80*.

129. *Inst.* II.2.12, "On the other hand soundness of mind (*mentis*) and uprightness of heart (*cordis*) were withdrawn at the same time. This is the corruption of the natural gifts. For even though something of understanding (*intelligentiae*) and judgment remains as a residue along with the will (*voluntate*), yet we shall not call a mind (*mente*) whole and sound that is both weak and plunged into deep darkness. And depravity of the will is all too well known. ... Therefore, so that the order of discussion may proceed according to our original division of man's soul into understanding (*intellectum*) and will (*voluntatem*), let us ..."

130. John Calvin, *Bondage and Liberation of the Will*, ed. A. N. S. Lane, trans. G. I. Davies (Grand Rapids: Baker Academic, 1996), 6.378.

131. See also *Inst.* II.3.2; III.3.6; *Commentary on Romans 6:13*.

132. Hence, Calvin rejected the idea (he cites Peter Lombard) that original sin is "kindling" (*fomes*), chiefly connected with sensuality.

intellect and the will are corrupted on the basis of the following text: "all the Gentiles walk in the vanity of their minds, being darkened in their understanding, alienated from the life of God, because of the ignorance which is in them, and their blindness of heart" (II.3.1). Calvin also argues that first movements or pre-passions are sin by appealing to Deuteronomy 6:5 and Matthew 22:37, "we are bidden to 'love God with all our heart, with all our soul, and with all our faculties'" (III.3.11).[133] He argues that any slight inclination or vain thought, even sudden emotions, show persons to be "in such a degree empty of the love of God." For this reason, to say that tinder is a mere "wellspring of sin" is to deny that "the transgression of the law is sin" (III.3.11). Generally speaking, the heart fulfills the role of the will in being the seat of the affections.[134]

On the other hand, Calvin distinctly recognizes the fact that the term "heart" is not used this way exclusively, biblically speaking. His favorite example to cite is Deuteronomy 29:4, concerning which he writes, "The word *heart* is not here used for the seat of the affections, but for the mind itself, which is the intellectual faculty of the soul."[135] He cites this text in making a similar explanation at least eight times in his commentaries.[136] He seems to explain his rationale in two texts. First, in his *Commentary on Ezekiel 18:32*, Calvin explains that when spirit and heart are together, heart takes its normal usage as "the will, or the seat of the affections." Second, in his *Commentary on Ephesians 1:18*, he explains, "The Hebrews frequently employ [heart] to denote the rational powers of the soul, though more strictly, being the seat of the affections, it means the will or desire." It is worth asking whether Calvin's reading of the biblical word "heart" is not unduly influenced by his identification of it with the psychological notion

---

133. We will discuss this issue again later. See Knuuttila, *Emotions in Ancient and Medieval Philosophy*, 176–195; Scotus had argued that it was possible even for the will to have "pre-passions" for which it was not morally culpable. Drummond, "John Duns Scotus on the Passions of the Will," 70–71.

134. *Inst.* II.3.10; II.8.52; III.2.8; III.3.6, 16; III.6.5; III.19.4; *Commentary on Psalm 119:80; Commentary on Isaiah 33:20* (contrasted with bodily senses); *Commentary on Jeremiah 17:1, 19; Commentary on Ezekiel 18:32; Commentary on Matthew 15:19; Commentary on John 2:23–25; Commentary on Romans 7:5, 14; Commentary on 2 Corinthians 7:15; Commentary on 2 Peter 1:1–4;* etc.

135. *Commentary on Deuteronomy 29:4 (On the Harmony of the Law).*

136. *Commentary on Exodus 35:33; Commentary on Deuteronomy 2:14–16; 24:7; Commentary on Matthew 14:24; Commentary on John 7:48; 12:40; Commentary on Romans 2:15–16; Commentary on Ephesians 1:18.*

of the will. We will take up this question later. In general, when Calvin had faculties in view, he saw the biblical term "heart" referring to will and the term "mind" to intellect, but this is not without exception.

INTELLECTUALISM AND VOLUNTARISM

We have seen that Calvin's description of the relationship between intellect and will in the *Institutes* I.15.7 sounds like an intellectualist treatment. Was Calvin an intellectualist? Dewey Hoitenga has identified what he calls an inconsistency in Calvin's psychology as it pertains to his affirmation of both intellectualism and voluntarism. He notes how Calvin first describes his psychology in intellectualists terms, but then "forsakes his intellectualist account of our created state as soon as he describes the fall. He describes the fall, however, in the same chapter (1.15) in which he describes the created state."[137] So, we have inconsistent accounts within one chapter of the *Institutes*. Hoitenga summarizes, "The inconsistency in Calvin's account of the human will as God created it is this: he claims that the intellect governs the will and yet clearly implies that it does not."[138] Richard Muller, who wrote the preface to Hoitenga's book, suggests a solution: Calvin may be "pointing at a symmetrical model of movement from primacy of the intellect (pure nature) to primacy of the will (fallen), primacy of the will (redeemed), and primacy of the intellect (glorified)."[139] This solution—which seems to be right—will perhaps not satisfy Hoitenga, since the crux of his complaint is how it is possible for the will to fall in the first place.

In general, in spite of his affirmation of intellectualism, Calvin inclines toward voluntarism. There are three things to note: first, it seems to be essential to Calvin's psychology not only that the will is fallen in desiring evil, but also that it is fallen in rejecting the intellect's rightful rule. Second, understanding the redemptive-historical states of the faculties is essential for reading Calvin rightly. Third, Hoitenga rightly recognizes that both Calvin and Aquinas appeal to what he calls a "voluntarist lapse," appealing to the will, especially for the fall, in an otherwise intellectualist

---

137. Dewey Hoitenga, *John Calvin and the Will: A Critique and Corrective* (Grand Rapids: Baker, 1997), 45.

138. Hoitenga, *John Calvin and the Will*, 23.

139. Richard Muller, "Preface," in Hoitenga, *John Calvin and the Will*, 6.

theory. The voluntarist lapse is the will's ability to "avert the attention of the intellect from its better knowledge."[140]

EVALUATION

Calvin had a simple psychology comprising only intellect and will largely because they are the chief seat of the *imago Dei*. This connection functionally rules out a tiered and composite psychology where higher and lower faculties can interact, cooperate, or conflict with each other. Calvin did admit that the philosophers teach about sense perception and appetite, but suggests that they are connected with the body, concerned with baser things, and draw us into error. There are two potential issues here. First, Calvin's limiting of the faculties, since they reflect the *imago*, to purely soulish faculties threatens angelism. Calvin so far raises the bar for humanity that it reaches the point where we aspire to live as if we did not have a body. What Calvin seems to overlook is that the body contributes limits to human agency that are not entirely negative. Plasticity is key because it is the quality that grounds the formation of the habits of vice and virtue. Second, Calvin must explain internal conflict in some other way. We have already briefly touched on one possible solution: it may be that in the fallen state, the faculties war against each other—lapsarian voluntarism against prelapsarian intellectualism. Obviously, this possibility means that, like his medieval predecessors, Calvin would hold to a *homunculus* theory of the faculties. We will investigate this possibility further below.

Calvin's psychological use of the biblical and physiological word "heart" also raises questions about his exegesis and his view of the body-soul relation. Exegetically speaking, Calvin risks eisegesis on a key argument for the depravity of the whole soul from Ephesians 4:17–23. He equated mind with intellect and heart with will to make this argument in spite of his acknowledgement that they are not always used this way (*Inst.* II.3.1; cf. Deut 29:4; Rom 2:15).[141] The exegetical concerns are perhaps mitigated by the fact that even if the concepts do not entirely align, his reading may reflect good judgment. The physiological question of what Calvin means

---

140. Hoitenga, *John Calvin and the Will*, 48.

141. *Commentary on Romans 2:15*, "He means not that [the law] was so engraven on their will, that they sought and diligently pursued it, but that they were so mastered by the power of truth, that they could not disapprove of it."

by heart is tantalizing, but perhaps unsolvable. As we have seen, he consistently speaks of the powers of the soul dualistically in the sense that the soul governs the body hegemonically without reference to how the body might qualify them holistically.

CALVIN ON THE WILL

Calvin's account of the human will is very familiar to Reformed theologians. However, as the heart (will) is the seat of the affections, we need to dig a bit deeper into its structure and its corruption. Both of these areas have implications for his account of emotion. If the heart is corrupt, then human emotion will always be suspect. This raises a number of questions: Does the heart always and only desire evil things? To what extent are these desires corrupted, and how do we distinguish between good and corrupt desires? In what follows, we examine the structure and corruption of the will in more detail.

THE STRUCTURE OF THE WILL

Dewey Hoitenga claims, "Like his medieval predecessors, Calvin affirms that the will was created with two main components, inclination and choice." It may be that the components Hoitenga identifies originate with John Damascene's *thelēsis* and *boulēsis*, which refer to appetite generally considered, or the actual activation of willing with a cognitive object.[142] Cruz González-Ayesta also notes another Scholastic distinction between the *voluntas ut natura* (will as to nature) and the *voluntas ut ratio* (will as to reason). The former is the will directed to a final end, the latter to means.[143] However, John Duns Scotus is a nearer antecedent here and provides a helpful foil for Calvin's view. Duns Scotus rejected the distinction of *voluntas ut natura* and *voluntas ut ratio* as a distinction between willing ends and means. He did distinguish two types of willing, or appetites, which are really "the same power considered under two perspectives."[144]

---

142. F. J. Adelmann, *The Quest for the Absolute* (The Hague, Netherlands: Martinus Nijhoff, 1966), 24.

143. There is some ambiguity here about how this distinction should be described. Cruz González-Ayesta alerts the reader to the fact that the end-means interpretation may be the Thomistic interpretation. Cruz González-Ayesta, "Scotus' Interpretation of the Difference Between Voluntas ut Natura and Voluntas ut Voluntas," *Franciscan Studies* 66 (2008): 374.

144. González-Ayesta, "Scotus' Interpretation," 379.

The natural will is the will considered passively as an inclination to the *affectio commodi* (affection for the advantageous). The free will is the will as the active, rational power of free choice that considers not only the *affectio commodi*, but also the *affectio justitiae* (affection for justice). For Duns Scotus, the will is the only rational power. These two appetites allow it to exercise its freedom, the freedom to look beyond the advantageous, to moderate natural inclinations in service of action that does not transgress God's laws.

This is a helpful foil in two respects. First, Duns Scotus's *affectio commodi* is a radical revision to the longstanding theological tradition of natural appetite—all human beings are naturally oriented to the good, since in Duns Scotus's view the affection for advantage is immoderate.[145] As we will see, Calvin repeatedly calls for moderation and bridling of the affections. Second, what for Duns Scotus preserved free will, the *affectio justitiae*, is precisely what Calvin denied fallen humanity possesses. The chief problem for Calvin was that we no longer have any means by which to bridle, a favorite term for Calvin, our appetites. In fact he writes, "if you consider the character of this natural desire of good in man, you will find that he has it in common with animals" (*Inst.* II.2.26). For human beings, the moderating choice of the will is necessary for free choice (II.2.26). Calvin writes, "Then was choice added, to direct the appetites and control all organic motions, and thus make the will completely amenable to the guidance of reason" (I.15.8). In the fallen state, it is not clear how much of this power remains.

So, was Calvin a Scotist with regard to the will? Might it be possible that he preserved the structure of Duns Scotus's will, natural appetite and moderating choice, without affirming his rationale, Duns Scotus's proposal of two affections to preserve free will? The answer is probably not, or at least not explicitly. Calvin was aware of the older Scholastic tradition of free choice versus free will, arising from the cooperation of both intellect and will, and even assumed this framework in the *Institutes*, at the very least for the sake of argument. In the *Institutes* II.2, where Calvin discusses free choice, he begins with opinions of the philosophers and church fathers

---

145. As I noted earlier, Duns Scotus says, "that nature is so inclined towards its object by this affection for the advantageous that if it had of itself an elicited act, it could not help eliciting it with no moderation in the most forceful way possible." *Ordinatio* II, d. 6 q. 2 nn 55–56, quoted in Allan Wolter, *Duns Scotus on the Will and Morality* (Washington, DC: Catholic University of America Press, 1986), 300.

on the matter. He summarizes that theologians have traditionally taught that the power of free decision resides "in the reason and the will," but "inclines more to appetite" (II.2.4). In sections 2–12, Calvin discusses the opinions of others, the Scholastic "it seems" (*Videtur quod*). Sections 13–17 cover the intellect's ability to know "things terrestrial," such as civic polity or the arts. Sections 18–25 cover its ability to know "things celestial," such as God, salvation, the law, etc. Finally, only one article (II.2.26) is given to the examination of the will, before concluding that the Scholastics are refuted (II.2.27). This rhetorical approach may suggest that free choice for Calvin involved both the intellect as darkened and "the will, which is the chief seat of sin" (II.2.pr). In light of the approach to the question, and his description of pre-fall humanity as intellectualist, he may have held a generic cooperation of the powers view, with inclination more to appetite in our post-fall state. Richard Muller's suggestion that if Calvin were thoroughly Scotist, "his voluntarism would have been more thoroughgoing," supports to my reading.[146]

The Corruption of the Will

Dewey Hoitenga also raises a second inconsistency in Calvin's thought: "The second inconsistency in Calvin's account of the will is that he denies, for the most part, that the will as so created persists into the fallen state." Hoitenga cites Calvin's affirmation of the Augustinian principle that "the natural gifts in man were corrupted, but the supernatural taken away."[147] Calvin affirms the principle, saying, "that common opinion which they have taken from Augustine pleases me." He continues to distinguish between humankind's natural gifts and supernatural gifts, the latter being "the light of faith and righteousness" (II.2.12). The natural gifts are corrupted, the supernatural ones stripped away, so that human beings have no "hope of eternal salvation" and are "banished from the Kingdom of God." In fact, Calvin even goes so far as to say that "something of understanding and judgment remains as a residue *along with the will*" (II.2.12, emphasis added).

---

146. Muller, "Preface," in Hoitenga, *John Calvin and the Will*, 9.

147. Hoitenga, *John Calvin and the Will*, 70. John T. McNeill clarifies, "This sentence, much in Augustine's style and based upon his thoughts, is of medieval formulation. Lombard has 'alia sunt corrupta per peccatum, id est naturalia ... alia subtracta' (*Sentences* II. Xxv. 8; MPL 192. 207)." *Institutes of the Christian Religion*, II.2.4, n42.

On the other hand, Hoitenga claims that Calvin "ascribes nothing but depravity to the fallen will."[148] It is easiest to see the problem when we contrast what Calvin says about the intellect with what he says about the will. In the *Institutes* II.2.12, we read that the intellect is "partly weakened and partly corrupted ... some sparks still gleam," which "show [man] to be a rational being differing from brute beasts."[149] By contrast, Calvin says almost nothing positive about the functions of the will. Yes, humans still have a will, but "it cannot strive after the right" (II.2.12); "the will remains, with the most eager inclination disposed and hastening to sin. ... [man] was not deprived of will, but of soundness of will" (II.3.5). There is a polarization in the language about the will that is not present in that concerning the intellect.

The problem for Hoitenga goes beyond a mere rhetorical overshot. The problem for Hoitenga is precisely that Calvin ascribes no good inclination whatsoever to the will, such that "there can be no motive left in the will for choosing a morally good alternative instead of an evil one; every choice is doomed from the start to be a choice of evil."[150] Recall, Duns Scotus had posited two affections for precisely this reason, to account for the possibility of an alternate choice. According to Calvin, even animals desire their advantage, and humans exceed them in possessing reason (II.2.26). Hoitenga protests that Calvin denies "that there is even any desire in the will for distinctively human happiness."[151] Calvin was guarding against a view that puts virtue "within our power."[152] But in doing so, he fails to distinguish the sense in which human beings differ from animals, that humans beings can develop some sort of character through reflective decision making, that we may become just by doing just things (Aristotle) even if this is only imperfect justice. And justice, in this sense, does refer to the inclination of the will. Hoitenga concludes by stating that Calvin's voluntarism is so

---

148. Hoitenga, *John Calvin and the Will*, 73.

149. Calvin returns frequently to this point, that reason distinguishes human beings from beasts. He echoes Augustine with this argument. Augustine writes, "Just as we are superior to the beasts by reason of our powers of reason and intelligence . ... [we must be] more careful to cultivate the faculties in which we surpass the beasts than to develop the body." Augustine, *City of God*, trans. Henry Bettenson (New York: Penguin Classics, 2003), 320.

150. Hoitenga, *John Calvin and the Will*, 77.

151. Hoitenga, *John Calvin and the Will*, 78.

152. Hoitenga, *John Calvin and the Will*, 80; cf. *Inst.* II.2.4.

radical "that the will has power not only to do wrong, and thereby corrupt itself, but also nearly to destroy its very own essence."[153]

How might Hoitenga's complaint be answered? It certainly helps but does not answer to say that Calvin was concerned about the semi-Pelagian idea that people may choose God unaided by grace. When Calvin says that "[we] run counter to the experience of common sense" to say that the intellect has "no perception of any object whatever," surely this sort of argument applies to the will as well.[154] Might it be possible to say that the will does desire a good object—say marital fidelity—even if this good is not rightly ordered under the lordship of Christ? I think this is precisely Calvin's position, though it must be inferred.

To answer Hoitenga, a few points must be established. First, contrary to Hoitenga's suggestion that the will nearly destroys its very essence, Calvin is very clear that what is corrupted in the fall is the will's habit, its quality. It is the accidental property that is affected. In *The Bondage and Liberation of the Will*, Calvin writes,

> Or is Pighius still so uneducated as not to recognise anything in between the substance of the will, or the faculty of willing, and its actions or its actual effects? ... Bernard I proposed three things for consideration: to will per se, that is, simply to will; then to will badly; and [to will] well. The first is the faculty of willing or, if preferred, the substance. To will well and badly are qualities or opposed habits which belong to the power itself. I had omitted its acts, because they contribute nothing relevant. Having defined these three things, I had taught that the will is perpetually resident in our nature, that the evil condition of the will results from the corruption of that nature, and that by the regeneration of the Spirit the evil condition is corrected and in that way the will is made good instead of evil.[155]

In writing this, Calvin is exactly in line with medieval theology.

---

153. Hoitenga, *John Calvin and the Will*, 89.
154. *Institutes* 2.2.12
155. Calvin, *Bondage and Liberation of the Will*, 6.378.

Second, as I have already mentioned, Calvin's conception of free choice may prioritize but not entirely depend on the will. By following the argument of *Institutes* Book II, chapter 2, we can trace the capabilities of the intellect and the will. If human intellect can approve "earthly things ... which have their significance and relationship with regard to the present life," and if a person may actually will and execute these things, even developing civic virtue of a sort (II.3.3), then, by inference, the will must have some inclination or ability to choose them.

Calvin did admit that a person is free to choose earthly or civic goods. Muller writes, "the hyperbolic character of Calvin's argument against free choice (in *Institutes*, II.v) can give the impression that he did not believe that any good acts of any sort could be performed by fallen human beings outside of grace."[156] Yet, Calvin did in many instances. In his preface to Melanchthon's *Loci Communes*, Calvin writes, "he [Melanchthon] concedes to a man a degree of liberty in that which does not go beyond this earthly life" and "to this liberty, which he calls civil, he puts a bridle to restrain it, saying that God always rules over it. There is not much problem with this."[157] Calvin writes something similar in his treatise *Against Anabaptists and Libertines*: "man's soul is [...] endowed also with will, in order to choose and desire those things that his life [i.e., this earthly life] wants."[158] He seems to explain his disinterest in clarifying this point in *Bondage and Liberation of the Will*, where he writes,

> Likewise when the wording of the Augsburg Confession needed to
> be produced, [Melanchthon] desired to linger only on that teaching

---

156. Muller, "Preface," in Hoitenga, *John Calvin and the Will*, 8.

157. *CO* 9:849 (translation mine). This is Melanchthon's statement: "If you relate human will (*voluntas*) to predestination, there is freedom neither in external nor internal acts, but all things take place according to divine determination. If you relate the will (*voluntas*) to external acts, according to natural judgment there seems to be a certain freedom. If you relate the will (*voluntas*) to the affections, there is clearly no freedom, even according to natural judgment. When an affection has begun to rage and seethe, it cannot be kept from breaking forth." Philip Melanchthon, *Loci Communes* in *Melanchthon and Bucer*, ed. Wilhelm Pauck (Philadelphia: Westminster, 1969), 30.

158. *CO* 7:183, *Against Anabaptists and Against the Libertines*, 237; translation Van Vliet, *Children of God*, 181; cf. *CO* 2:33; *OS* 3:32–33; *Inst.* I.1.2. *Commentary on Ephesians* 2:1; "Some kind of life, I acknowledge, does remain in us, while we are still at a distance from Christ; for unbelief does not altogether destroy the outward senses, or the will, or the other faculties of the soul. But what has this to do with the kingdom of God?"

which alone is peculiar to the church and necessary to know for salvation, namely that natural powers by themselves have no ability to conceive faith, to obey the divine law, and [to attain] entire spiritual righteousness. What they can do in public affairs and outward behaviour he did not want to discuss in too much detail, because it is not of great importance for faith.[159]

Third, Calvin's position on Augustine's dictum is clearer if we understand it in context. Paul Helm compares Calvin's view favorably with those of Augustine and Aquinas. He cites Aquinas's description in the *Summa* I–II.85.1. Aquinas argues that sin diminishes the good of human nature in three ways:

1) "First, the very principles of nature ... such as the powers of the soul." He adds, "the first good of the nature is neither destroyed nor diminished by sin."

2) "Second ... man has by his nature an inclination toward virtue, this inclination toward virtue is itself a certain good of the nature." He adds, "the second good of the nature, viz., the natural inclination toward virtue, is diminished by sin."

3) "Third, one can call the gift of original justice a certain good of the nature that was given to the whole of human nature in the first man." He adds, "The third good of the nature, on the other hand, was completely taken away because of the sin of the first parent."[160]

That is, the essence remains, the quality (accident) is diminished, and the supernatural gift of original justice is removed. By comparison, Calvin claims that the supernatural gifts of "the light of faith as well as righteousness" are "stripped from him."[161] And again, we have already seen how Calvin affirms that the quality of the faculties is corrupted, rather than the essence. Helm calls this an "organic view of human nature," pointing

---

159. Calvin, *Bondage and Liberation of the Will*, 1.251.
160. Paul Helm, *Calvin at the Center* (Oxford: Oxford University Press, 2010), 310, 312, 316.
161. *Institutes* 2.2.12.

both to a pathogen metaphor of corruption and vital connectedness.[162] Taken together with the point about willing earthly goods, it is possible to affirm Calvin's consistency on this point, but with a generous reading of his account of the human will.[163]

Finally, one difficulty in seeing Calvin's position is that Calvin sometimes describes the intellect and will as *homunculi*, as his late medieval voluntarist predecessors had done. By *homunculi*, I mean that both the intellect and the will are like independent agents in that they both seem to possess independent cognition and volition. For example, when Calvin speaks of the "disagreement between organic motions and the soul's rational part," which some philosophers had explained by appealing to a rational and sensitive soul, Calvin adds, "As if reason itself did not also disagree with itself and were not at cross-purposes with itself, just like armies at war" (*Inst.* I.15.6). To point out the obvious, motion may run contrary to motion, and cognition may contradict cognition, but the types do not run contrary to each other. The Stoic idea that an emotion is a judgment is wrong precisely because emotion is a type of movement, not a form of cognition. If reason is like "armies at war," then reason has volitional power. Reason may contradict itself, but not hate itself. This leads to a more serious exegetical point. In spite of Calvin's usual interpretation of heart as will, he denies that heart can mean will in Romans 2:15, which reads, "They show that the work of the law is written on their hearts, while their conscience also bears witness, and their conflicting thoughts accuse or even excuse them." He writes, "He means not that [the law] was so engraven on their will, that they sought and diligently pursued it, but that they were so mastered by the power of truth, that they could not disapprove of it." Yet, clearly, Calvin has something more than intellectual self-contradiction in mind when he writes a few paragraphs later, "those who are conscious of having done evil,

162. Helm, *Calvin at the Center*, 312, see also 310–16.

163. Helm notices that Bavinck thinks that Calvin was working in opposition to the Augustinian principle. It is "quite extraordinary that Bavinck should say that the Reformation view is the precise opposite." He explains the misreading as Bavinck and others "working with a Counter-Reformation view of nature and grace, taken over not from the patristic and medieval organic-essentialist view, but from Cajetan and as adopted by Bellarmine, and read back into medievalism and into Calvin's own situation: a classic case of anachronism." Helm, *Calvin at the Center*, 331, 333.

are inwardly harassed and tormented."[164] Either the intellect has its own inclinations (a *homunculus*) or the will is also involved in the conscience. It is hard to find a consistent view here.

EVALUATION

Are we in a better position to understand how the intellect and will worked for Calvin, or where he sourced internal conflict? It is not clear that we are. Muller's suggestion that Calvin's psychology is intellectualist pre-fall and post-restoration and voluntarist post-fall and pre-restoration seems apt. Yet this also seems to confirm my suggestion that Calvin's faculties are *homunculi* like his medieval predecessors. While this may serve to account for introspective conflict, it threatens the coherence of what the terms "intellect" or "will" might mean. In fact, I reject the *homunculi* view as incoherent. We are left wondering still how Calvin accounted for internal conflict. He needed to recognize that internal conflict must be volitional conflict—since cognitive conflict is just contradiction. Of course, Calvin explains internal conflict also as a case of sinfulness versus Spirit. But if internal psychological conflict is possible for the unregenerate—so it cannot be spirit versus flesh—then there must be a psychological source for the ambivalence. Calvin seems not to understand the point of distinguishing sense appetite from the will, or in the case of later medieval theologians, of distinguishing two affections of the will.

Calvin's reluctance to enter into the minutiae of psychology causes problems. When pressed, Calvin gives a more considered account of depravity. He admits that the will is merely corrupted, by which he means that its quality not its essence is destroyed. He also admits with Melanchthon that

---

164. *Commentary on Rom 2:14–15.* My point here is the Calvin is inconsistent even on his own terms. It seems obvious enough that his viewpoint is also inconsistent with experience. It surely is possible for non-Christians to have mixed feelings about moral issues that somewhat map their Christian counterparts. Hoitenga makes this same point.

> A fourth consequence follows from the third. If fallen human beings cannot feel the struggle between good and evil in their lives, there will be no analogy in their fallen experience by which they can even understand the gospel itself. For the gospel poses the special (indeed, ultimate) conflict that fallen human beings need to feel between the evil of their having rejected (and thereby lost) the supernatural gifts of trusting and loving God and enjoying his favor, and the good of their possessing these supernatural gifts once again through faith in the gospel.

Hoitenga, *John Calvin and the Will*, 90.

the will can incline toward and choose civic goods and that its object may be good if not absolutely good. This is in line with the medieval tradition and is a very important concession for Calvin's psychology. It might be that the will inclines toward some genuine but secondary goods, and that a person need not mistrust every negative internal impulse. If the will can desire good, then Calvin was already part of the way to affirming a sort of imperfect virtue.

Finally, in this section we also begin to see real shortcomings in terms of how Calvin accounted for plasticity. He appeals to the quality of habit in explaining corruption, but without reference to how it develops. The subject of the vice (corrupt habit) must be both the body and soul. But since Calvin was not concerned with the body, he gives the impression that the corruption and sanctification of the soul is unrelated to it. We will have to wait to see what else Calvin says about habit when discussing virtue.

AFFECTIONS, PASSIONS, AND VIRTUE

AFFECTIONS AND PASSIONS

Finally, we will provide some basic contours of Calvin's position about the emotions and emotional development. As stated above, just as with his medieval predecessors, the seat of the affections is the heart, or the will. Affections are a phenomenon of the soul. Admittedly, there is some ambiguity on this, but insofar as the body is involved in affections, the direction of causality is soul to body. Calvin says, "For although the body, strictly speaking, is not of itself influenced by desire, we know that the feelings of the soul intimately and extensively affect it."[165] He notes also that "the bowels are the seat of the affections," using Galenic physiological terms for the effects of passions, "the more they restrain themselves, the more strongly they are inflamed; they burn and boil within" (*Inst.* II.7.10).[166]

Calvin uses the terms "passions" and "affections" somewhat interchangeably, since they both are seated in the will, but passions are very often morally negative and excessive. In some cases, the terms are interchangeable. For example, Calvin talks about "all those sinful passions and

---

165. *Commentary on Psalm 63:1.*
166. Bouwsma, *John Calvin,* 133.

affections of the soul, to which we are by nature guided and led."[167] Sinless passions are even ascribed to Christ.[168] However, most references to passions are negative.[169] Human beings are "impelled by unruly passions"; passions are compared with disease and Plato's horses, which throw off the charioteer (i.e., reason, II.2.3).[170]

The term "affections," likewise, is used in mostly negative contexts. Calvin was concerned with affections that are disordered, excessive, or beyond bounds especially.[171] He speaks of them predominantly negatively because post-fall affections lack the regulation and harmony of pre-fall affections. Calvin says Adam "had affections in harmony with reason" and there was "tempering in the several parts of the soul."[172] He had "his affections subordinated to reason" (*Inst.* I.15.4) and "a right judgment and a proper government of the affections prevailed."[173] And yet even Adam failed to keep his affections "under due restraint" and fell (II.1.4).

By far, the most significant single feature of Calvin's theory of emotion is the need for restraint or regulation; our post-fall emotions are excessive and disordered, and therefore sinful. What we need is twofold: Initially, the law bridles both on our emotions and our acting on them. However, since we cannot keep the law perfectly, the gospel bids us to renounce ourselves and trust in God and the means he supplies in the grace we have in Christ and by the Spirit. Spiritual emotions are regulated by God's power and by God's law.

For example, in his *Commentary on Jeremiah 30:9*, Calvin writes that without a bridle for our emotions, "the condition of wild beasts would be better and more desirable." Calvin says, "the passions of the godly are laid under restraint by the Word."[174] In his preface to his *Commentary on the*

167. *Commentary on 1 Peter 2:11.*

168. *Commentary on Matthew 26:27; Commentary on Mark 3:5; 11:33.*

169. See Calvin's commentaries on Gen 43:11; Exod 5:20; 17:1; Lev 10:3; Num 4:4, 17; Ps 17:15; Isa 38:10; Jer 2:24; Dan 3:13–16; Hos 7:11–12.

170. Plato, *Phaedrus* 246a–254e in *Plato: The Collected Dialogues.*

171. *Commentary on John 11:33; Commentary on Jonah, Lecture 97; Commentary on Mark 3:5; Commentary on 1 Corinthians 7:6–9; Commentary on Ephesians 4:26; Commentary on 1 Thessalonians 4:13.*

172. *Commentary on Genesis 1:1–31.*

173. *Commentary on Genesis 2:1–25.*

174. *Commentary on Leviticus 31:1.*

Psalms, Calvin urges that Christians "renounce the guidance of our own affections and submit ourselves entirely to God, leaving him to govern us, and to dispose of our life according to his will, so that the afflictions which are the bitterest and most severe to our nature, become sweet to us, because they proceed from him."[175] Commenting on Psalm 22:1, Calvin advises Christians to "repress the very commencement of disordered affections."[176] David is said to contend "courageously against his own affections."[177] Other words used to describe the task are govern, subdue, curb, correct, bridle, moderate, lay aside, renounce, deny, and regulate.[178] Calvin summarizes the situation in a well-known passage, "there are disorderly affections of an inward kind which require to be restrained. What a busy workshop is the heart of man, and what a host of devices is there manufactured every moment!"[179] Calvin even claims that "if our affections were properly regulated, there would be no other cause of just hatred among us."[180] And it is the peace of God that is the bridle for New Testament Christians—this word is used at least thirty-five times in the commentaries.[181]

What gives special significance to the fight for emotions is that God particularly "calls for the affections of the heart, that He alone may be spiritually worshipped."[182] As we have already shown, to love with less than all a person's faculties is to be a transgressor of the law. The excesses of the affections are a constant reminder of indwelling sinfulness. Calvin says, "nothing is gained without beginning with the internal affections of the heart" (III.3.16). He echoes Joel 2:13, "rend your hearts and not your garments."

---

175. *Commentary on the Psalms.*

176. *Commentary on the Psalms 22:1.*

177. *Commentary on the Psalms 41:1–3.*

178. *Commentary on Gen 16:5; Deut 10:16; Ps 28:3–5; 39:1–2; Mic 4:3; Hag 2:10–14; Matt 16:24; Phil 1:8.*

179. *Commentary on the Psalms 141:1–4.*

180. *Commentary on Matthew 10:21.*

181. For example, *Commentary on Colossians 3:15*, "As, however it is difficult to restrain them, he points out also the remedy, that the peace of God may carry the victory, because it must be a bridle, by which carnal affections may be restrained."

182. *Commentary on Exodus 20:3.*

So to recapitulate, human beings must not be wise in their own prudence, but "subdue his own depraved affections and submit them to God."[183]
Repentance involves acknowledging "all their thoughts, affections, and
pursuits, are corrupt and vicious; and that, therefore, if they would enter
the kingdom of God they must be born again" (*Inst.* III.19.3). For the believer
the gospel should "penetrate the inmost affections of the heart, fix its seat
in the soul, and pervade the whole man a hundred times more than the
frigid discourses of philosophers" (III.6.4).

The Holy Spirit instills "his holiness into our souls" and inspires "new
thoughts and affections" (II.3.8). When the Spirit is regulating affections,
we can be assured that our emotions are righteous.[184] To be engrafted into
Christ's body means that it is fitting for us "to withdraw our affections from
the earth, and with our whole soul aspire to heaven" (III.6.3). The Spirit
enables us by giving us "all virtues, all proper and well regulated affections" with the renewed nature we have from Christ.[185] So, "It must be our
study ... to imbue our minds with such reverence and obedience to God as
may tame and subjugate all affections contrary to his appointment. In this
way, whatever be the kind of cross to which we are subjected, we shall in
the greatest straits firmly maintain our patience" (III.8.10).

Finally, the emotions of Christ seem to present some difficulty for
Calvin. Calvin contrasts our emotions with his:

As no moderation can be seen in the depravity of our nature, in
which all affections with turbulent impetuosity exceed their due
bounds, they improperly apply the same standard to the Son of God.
But as he was upright, all his affections were under such restraint
as prevented every thing like excess. Hence he could resemble us in
grief, fear, and dread, but still with this mark of distinction. Thus
refuted, they fly off to another cavil, that although Christ feared
death, yet he feared not the curse and wrath of God, from which
he knew that he was safe. But let the pious reader consider how far
it is honourable to Christ to make him more effeminate and timid
than the generality of men. (II.16.12)

183. *Commentary on Daniel* 4:27.
184. *Commentary on Deuteronomy* 18:37–40.
185. *Commentary on Galatians* 5:22.

As we noted earlier, Christ was subject to passions, just as other human beings.[186] But we see that Christ's affections were restrained and avoided excess.

Calvin recognized the difficulty involved with attributing "trembling and sadness" to Christ in the garden of Gethsemane. To his credit, he embraces Christ's humanity as he says, "For he took upon him not the appearance, but the reality, of incarnation."[187] But, again, Christ's grief was within "due bounds" and "regulated," though Calvin does not explain how this sorrow can be regulated and be "even to death." Moreover, Christ did not grieve over death but "because of our sins ... pressed down on him with their enormous weight."[188] Calvin admits that Christ's prayer that "this cup pass from me" was emotionally motivated and explains that prayers are "not always arranged even in a distinct order, but, on the contrary, are involved and confused." He likens this to a vessel tossed in tempests. Yet, inconsistently, he also reemphasizes that "Christ had not confused emotions," but "so far as the pure and innocent nature of man could admit, he was struck with fear and seized with anguish, so that, amidst the violent shocks of temptation, he vacillated—as it were—from one wish to another." It is not clear how Calvin can hold these strands together. He follows this up by emphasizing again that Christ "restrains himself" and "corrects and recalls that wish which had suddenly escaped him."[189] Later he adds, "We see how Christ restrains his feelings at the very outset, and quickly brings himself into a state of obedience."[190]

Calvin's explanation is worth marking. He asks, "How was his will pure from all vice, while it did not agree with the will of God? For if the will of God is the only rule of what is good and right, it follows, that all the feelings

---

186. *Commentary on the Psalms* 22:1, 14: "By the way, it should be marked, that Christ, although subject to human passions and affections, never fell into sin through the weakness of the flesh; for the perfection of his nature preserved him from all excess. ... The perfect purity of his nature did not extinguish the human affections; it only regulated them, that they might not become sinful through excess. The greatness of his griefs, therefore, could not so weaken him as to prevent him, even in the midst of his most excruciating sufferings, from submitting himself to the will of God, with a composed and peaceful mind."

187. *Commentary on Matthew* 26:37.
188. *Commentary on Matthew* 26:37.
189. *Commentary on Matthew* 26:37.
190. *Commentary on Matthew* 26:39.

which are at variance with it are vicious."[191] The assumed premise here is Augustine's dictum, "if [the will] is wrong, these motions of the soul will be wrong, but if it is right, they will be not merely blameless, but even praiseworthy."[192] Yet Calvin distinguishes here between wanting and wanting, so to speak. He says there is "a certain kind of indirect disagreement with it which is not faulty."[193] In other words, it is possible for a person to desire in an ultimate sense what is good, but to recoil at the immediate means. This is a very significant opening in what otherwise seems to be a high emotional bar.

Augustine concludes, "We see how those prayers are holy, which appear to be contrary to the will of God; for God does not desire us to be always exact or scrupulous in inquiring what he has appointed, but allows us to ask what is desirable according to the capacity of our senses."[194] While his explanation addresses one major concern—how Christ could feel something contrary to the will of God to such an extent that he prayed for that contrary thing—it is still difficult to swallow that Christ's emotion was within due bounds and with restraint when he was sweating drops of blood (Luke 22:44). What would excess look like? It certainly seems like it would be easier to affirm that even extreme emotion can be sinless in some cases.[195]

CALVIN AND STOICISM

Kyle Fedler objects to the characterization of Calvin as legalistic and Stoic. He cites "two misguided notions concerning Calvin's ethics": (1) "that Calvin was a Stoic in his treatment of the emotions, advocating a Christian life characterized primarily by an elimination of the emotions," and (2) that "Calvin is a legalist in terms of his ethics."[196] For Fedler, Calvin's treatment of the first concern also addresses the second. It is precisely "Calvin's repeated emphasis on the affective dimension of the moral life" that puts to bed the

---

191. *Commentary on Matthew 26:37.*

192. Augustine, *City of God,* 14.6.

193. Calvin, *Commentary on Matthew 26:39.*

194. Augustine, *City of God,* 14.6.

195. See Calvin, *Commentary on John 11:33.*

196. Kyle Fedler, "Calvin's Burning Heart: Calvin and the Stoics on the Emotions," *Journal of the Society of Christian Ethics* 22 (Fall 2002): 155.

concern over legalism.[197] In this section, I want to make just two observations that partly confirm and partly question Fedler's conclusion.

First, Fedler is right to point out that Calvin was not an advocate of Stoicism. He rejected Stoicism on a number of occasions. For example, in his *Commentary on Exodus*, 31:14, he writes, "By the praise which is given to the anger of Moses, the imagination of the Stoics is refuted, with whom indifference (*apatheia*) is the highest of virtues" (*Inst.* III.8.9). As Fedler demonstrates, Calvin was neither Stoic about fate nor about *apatheia*.[198] However, on the issue of emotion, Calvin never really rid himself of his Stoic sensibility. Fedler also recognizes strong resonances. Risto Saarinen writes, "Augustinian models that employ the interplay of desire and consent still display some Stoic features."[199] For example, Saarinen highlights the Stoic runner who cannot stop running as an analogue to the Reformation's *simul iustus et peccator* and undergirds the Christian's wrestling with sin throughout life. The Stoic sensibility is especially pronounced in Calvin's language of bridling emotions.[200] Uncomfortable with the emotive expression of the Psalms, Calvin seemed to think that the chief value of the Psalms is to uncover hypocrisy.[201] Bouwsma remarks that Calvin's reading of Job is very curious:

---

197. Fedler, "Calvin's Burning Heart," 156.

198. Fedler, "Calvin's Burning Heart," 139–47.

199. Risto Saarinen, "Weakness of Will: Reformation Anthropology between Aristotle and the Stoa," in *Anthropological Reformations: Anthropology in the Era of Reformation*, ed. Anne Eusterschulte and Hannah Wälzholz (Göttingen: Vandenhoeck & Ruprecht, 2015), 20.

200. To list just a very few selections from Calvin's *Commentary on the Psalms*, he suggests bridling affections in commenting on Psalms 21:1; 36:1; 37:8; 39:1–2; 82:1–4; 85:8; 119:147. For example, in *Commentary on Psalm 119:147* he writes, "[Paul] admonishes us, while engaged in the exercise of prayer, to bridle our turbulent affections ... for it is only by having the Word of God continually before our eyes, that we can bridle the wanton impetuosity of our corrupt nature." And in *Commentary on Jeremiah 30:9*, "It would, indeed, be better for us to be wild beasts, and to wander in forests, than to live without government and laws; for we know how furious are the passions of men. Unless, therefore, there be some restraint, the condition of wild beasts would be better and more desirable than ours. Liberty, then, would ever bring ruin with it, were it not bridled and connected with regular government."

201. *Commentary on the Psalms*, "Preface": "But here the prophets themselves, seeing they are exhibited to us as speaking to God, and laying open all their inmost thoughts and affections, call, or rather draw, each of us to the examination of himself in particulars in order that none of the many infirmities to which we are subject, and of the many vices with which we abound, may remain concealed. It is certainly a rare and singular advantage, when all lurking places are discovered, and the heart is brought into the light, purged from that most baneful infection, hypocrisy."

But his almost deliberate insensitivity is nowhere more in evidence than in his reading of the book of Job. It interested him deeply; he devoted one of his longest sermon sequences to it; and, baffled by its contrast between the faith and humanity of Job and the moralism of Job's friends, he hardly knew what to make of it. He finally came to the remarkable conclusion that Job's friends, although their "arguments and reasons" were good and their teachings "holy and useful," had mysteriously defended the wrong cause.[202]

Second, while I disagree with Fedler's claim that for Calvin emotions are judgments, since they are movements, Calvin did have difficulty sorting out the exact nature of internal conflict in a way that aligns him with the Stoics. If emotions were judgments for Calvin, then these judgments could be inconsistent with the judgments of reason. The problem with this view is that Calvin does not typically talk about emotions in terms of beliefs but as movements of the will. In this sense Calvin does fall prey to what Aquinas saw as the error of the Stoics. Aquinas writes, "For the Stoics did not distinguish between the sensory power and the intellect and, as a result, they did not distinguish between the sentient appetite and the intellective appetite."[203] The problem here is that by conflating the two sources of appetite, some other explanation is necessary for the common human experience of internal conflict, which is common also to unregenerate people. Calvin seemed to struggle with this explanation—giving a conflict within reason as one possibility (Inst. I.15.6) and a conflict between reason and the will as another. Again, I have already suggested that the difficulty here is that to have genuine internal conflict requires two appetitive drives, not simply cognitive contradiction.

EVALUATION

Calvin's rhetoric only confirms what his psychological structure implies, that there is no room for responding to negative emotion other than suppressing it. Given his account of the faculties, Calvin was understandably alarmed at negative emotion. When emotions are quasi-volitions of the

---

202. Bouwsma, John Calvin, 94–95.
203. Aquinas, Summa Theologiae, I–II.24.2.

will, they will be classed in the same basic category as other volitional acts. First movements themselves are sin. While Calvin declaimed Stoic *apatheia*, his recommendations for bridling and repressing emotion seem to leave no tolerance whatsoever for experiencing emotion that runs contrary to the will of God. He seems to represent the ideal post-fall Christian life as striving to be bridled and tranquil in the face of continuing internal disturbance.[204] Again, this raises the question of consistency for the emotions of Christ. The problem with not distinguishing higher from lower appetite is that a person must identify deviant emotion as volitional, and therefore subject to the same sort of moral censure as a deliberate, external act. By distinguishing higher and lower appetite, a tiered psychology, it might be possible to acknowledge deviant emotion without it being a person's truest expression of will, or without it being based on a person's truest belief.

I acknowledge that this is a critique about Calvin's theory of emotion and the way it works in his biblical commentary. I am very much aware that he exercised pastoral sensitivity and displayed an experiential awareness of the difficulty of grief, for example, over the death of his own wife.[205] Only someone with some experience with anxiety could write these words, "Those who are extremely anxious wear themselves out and become in a sense their own executioners."[206]

VIRTUE AND VICE

For what is more consonant with faith than to recognize that we are naked of all virtue, in order to be clothed by God? That we are

---

204. See for example *Commentary on Luke* 1:73: "We can only worship God properly with tranquil minds."

205. "Although the death of my wife has been bitterly painful to me, yet I restrain my grief as well as I can. ... You know well enough how tender, or rather soft, my mind is. Had I not exercised a powerful self-control, therefore, I could not have borne up so long. And truly mine is no common grief. I have been bereaved of the best companion of my life, who, if any severe hardship had occurred, would have been my willing partner, not only in exile and poverty but even in death. As long as she lived she was the faithful helper of my ministry. From her I never felt even the slightest hindrance. During the whole course of her illness she was more anxious about her children than about herself. Since I was afraid that she might torment herself needlessly by repressing her worry, three days before her death I took occasion to mention that I would not neglect my duties [to her children]. She spoke up at once: 'I have already committed them to God.' " "Letter to Viret, Apr. 7, 1549," CO 13:226–231 (translation from Bouwsma).

206. *Commentary on Jeremiah* 12:13.

empty of all good, to be filled by him? That we are slaves to sin, to be freed by him? Blind, to be illumined by him? Lame, to be made straight by him? Weak, to be sustained by him? To take away from us all occasion for glorying, that he alone may stand forth gloriously and we glory in him? (*Inst.*, "Preface")

Calvin speaks largely negatively about virtue. He does grudgingly concede at times that there are sorts of excellences that win praise "in the political assembly," but adds that these "deceive us" and are of "no value to acquire righteousness" (II.3.4). In fact, the situation is worse than this since these sorts of virtue actually make it difficult to approach God with humility and repentance. He says that "it is not less to our advantage than pertinent to God's glory that we be deprived of all credit for our wisdom and virtue" (II.2.1).

There are two interesting instances worth considering where Calvin seems to admit some sort of goodness in pagan or civic virtue. First, Calvin poses a problem: "in every age there have been persons who, guided by nature, have striven toward virtue throughout life. I have nothing to say against them even if many lapses can be noted in their moral conduct." He acknowledges that there is a caveat in these examples, that they "seem to warn us against adjudging man's nature wholly corrupted" (II.3.3). Nevertheless, Calvin sees even these cases as evidences of "some place for God's grace" in this "corruption of nature." He seems even willing to say that Camillus is better than Catiline provided that we also recognize that God sometimes gives "special graces" on human beings who are "otherwise wicked" (II.3.4).

The other interesting case is III.14.3, where Calvin cites Augustine's comments on splendid vice. He admits that the men of virtue are "God's instruments for the preservation of human society in righteousness, continence, friendship, temperance, fortitude, and prudence, yet they carry out these good works of God very badly." We see here positively represented the four cardinal virtues. The problem for Calvin (and Augustine) is that "they are restrained from evil-doing not by genuine zeal for good but by mere ambition, by self-love, or by some other perverse motive" (III.14.3).[207]

---

207. It is speculative but interesting to consider whether Calvin's youthful ambition may have conditioned his distaste for the semblance of virtue. He writes that ambition is the

He adds, "duties are weighed not by deeds but by ends." This is a fascinating comment because it reveals a teleological commitment underlying the denial of pagan virtues. Virtue ethics, at least since its reemergence, has been distinguished by its teleological framework. It seems that Calvin's primary problem with virtue ethics was that it has nothing to do with genuine righteousness before God. But in addition, we see that Calvin refused to consider seeming proximal goods as goods without reference to their ultimate *telos*. That the Boy Scout helps the old lady to cross the street should not be judged on his immediate motive (e.g., sympathy), but on his ultimate motive, which may be ambition or self-love.

Finally, while Calvin is reluctant to appeal explicitly to habit in the *Institutes*—either regarding virtue or vice—he does explicitly cite it in explaining the corruption of the will in *Bondage and Liberation of the Will*. Arguing against the Roman Catholic theologian, Albert Pighius, Calvin writes,

> Or is Pighius still so uneducated as not to recognise anything in between the substance of the will, or the faculty of willing, and its actions or its actual effects? ... no one is so unlearned as not to set habit in between. For what is the point of these forms of speech, "someone of a good or evil mind," if not to indicate his quality? ... To will well and badly are qualities or opposed habits which belong to the power itself.[208]

Calvin and Pighius agreed that habit mediates substance and willing. They disagreed as to the source, extent, and the severity of the *habitus* of sin. Calvin objected to the notion that corruption applies only to those who have habitually sinned, suggesting rather (as above) that "the whole race is said to be troubled" by the transmission of Adam's sin.[209]

"mother of many evils in human society, especially in the church." *Commentary on Galatians* 5:26. Yet just after his Seneca commentary was released, in a letter to François Daniel he wrote, "write as soon as you can and let me know with what favor or coldness it has been received." "Letter to François Daniel, 1532," CO 10:21; translations by Bouwsma, *John Calvin*, 18, 49.

208. Calvin, *Bondage and Liberation of the Will*, 6.378.

209. Calvin, *Bondage and Liberation of the Will*, 6.380. He writes, "Pighius limits it to those who have been corrupted by evil habit. ... Pighius declares that the hardness was incurred through bad habit. Just as if one of the philosophers' crew should say that by evil living a person had become hardened or callous towards evil."

On the issue of virtuous habit, Calvin had less to say. Paul Helm suggests that he took a motivational view, by which Helm means that Calvin rejected Aristotle's idea that we become just by doing just acts for "having the *habitus* of our minds redirected, a redirecting that, at least in its first stages, must be done for us and to us rather than our doing it."²¹⁰ Intriguingly, Helm thinks that Calvin was not quite fair to Aristotle since Aristotle also taught that, "The agent must be in a certain condition when he does [virtuous acts]." Helm also contrasts Calvin's view with the Reformed theologian Peter Martyr Vermigli, which incorporates acting into the formation of virtue, God being the "primary and most powerful cause of all the virtues."²¹¹

EVALUATION

In what follows, I will briefly comment on Calvin's account of virtue and vice before making general evaluative comments about Calvin's psychology. First, Calvin was largely negative toward virtue especially because he wanted to avoid any hint of Pelagianism, either in terms of humankind's ability to approach God or in meriting anything but condemnation. All human actions need to be judged by their ends, not by their acts, and in this way are damnable. Second, as we have seen, Calvin did appeal to the Scholastic notion *habitus* to explain the corruption of the heart. However, Calvin disconnected it from the practice of sinning, insisting that the *habitus* applies to all humankind from Adam. Likewise, he disconnected action from virtue by taking, as Helm says, a motivational view. In both of these cases, it seems that Calvin might have been more sensitive to how human beings are altered by their actions. In the first case, humankind seems to have progressed in corruption through idolatry (Rom 1:18–32). In the second case, why should affirming a motivational view, as not only Calvin but all Reformed theologians do, be inconsistent with affirming that God can change us through our actions as he works concurrently in us? The Reformed tradition has often used the word "cooperation," or synergism, with respect to sanctification while maintaining that justification is monergistic; the establishment of motive may be monergistic while the

210. Helm, "Vermigli, Calvin, and Aristotle's Ethics," 97.
211. Helm, "Vermigli, Calvin, and Aristotle's Ethics," 98.

development of it may be cooperative.[212] What seems clear is that Calvin had no need for plasticity, since he had little interest in the habit of virtue or how our actions change us.

Conclusion

More generally speaking, Calvin mirrors four themes we traced through the medieval transition: (1) Calvin was dualistic; (2) his account of the will seems to depend on later medieval developments within voluntarism; (3) he saw little to no value in virtue, seeing it instead as an obstacle to the acceptance and working of God's grace; and (4) since sin is ever present in the believer, he saw continence as the highest ethical state.

Calvin's psychology is not holistic. By connecting the soul with the *imago*, he was primarily interested in the faculties of the soul, assuming that the body plays little to no role in Christian formation. This risks angelism. His concern for the immortality of the soul may have some role to play in his dualism, though it is in common with his theological context (Thomists excepted). The faculties Calvin was interested in, intellect and will, are not significantly qualified by the body, since they merely produce top-down physiological effects. Calvin did not tier the faculties as Aquinas did, but accounts for internal conflict by citing hostility in the intellectual powers themselves, arising either from the contrary movements of sin or by conflict between the intellect and the will. Only conflict

---

212. Frances Turretin writes, "The question [about monergism] does not concern the second stage of conversion in which it is certain that man is not merely passive but cooperates with God (or rather operates under him). Indeed, he actually believes and converts himself to God; moves himself to the exercise of new life. Rather the question concerns the first moment when he is converted and receives new life in regeneration. We contend that he is merely passive in this, as a receiving subject and not as an active principle." Frances Turretin, *Institutes of Elenctic Theology* (Phillipsberg, NJ: P&R, 1997), 2.17.1. Charles Hodge writes,

> When Christ opened the eyes of the blind no second cause interposed between his volition and the effect. But men work out their own salvation, while it is God who worketh in them to will and to do, according to his own good pleasure. In the work of regeneration, the soul is passive. It cannot coöperate in the communication of spiritual life. But in conversion, repentance, faith, and growth in grace, all its powers are called into exercise. As, however, the effects produced transcend the efficiency of our fallen nature, and are due to the agency of the Spirit, sanctification does not cease to be supernatural, or a work of grace, because the soul is active and coöperating in the process.

Charles Hodge, *Systematic Theology*, vol. III: Soteriology (Grand Rapids: Eerdmans, 1940), 215.

between powers can explain conflict in unregenerate people, but this is impossible unless Calvin makes intellect and will *homunculi*. In general, Calvin's description of intellect and will are weakened by his reluctance to go into the minutiae. The consequence of his view for emotion is that a person predominantly interprets contrary motions as sinful and need-ing to be suppressed, without reference to health. Because emotion is seated in the will and the will is bound, Calvin seemed to take the move-ments of the will as sinful quasi-choices. Negative emotions are guilty until proven innocent. Because Calvin had not developed an account of how the soul and body come together in emotion, he was left assessing emotions strictly morally, rather than morally and naturally as with a composite faculty. With regard to plasticity, Calvin seemed to have no role for acquired habit in his psychology, though he appealed to *habitus* to explain corruption.

Finally, it may be heuristically helpful to distinguish between the three functions that the will performs from Aquinas to late medieval theology: (1) orientation, (2) choice, and (3) inclination. We can reasonably state that with regard to orientation, Calvin thought that the will is fundamen-tally earth-bound and cannot reach beyond the temporal goods (i.e., evils) of this earth. Since Calvin assessed virtue according to the ultimate *telos*, this state of the will produces only evil inclinations and choices from the heart. In terms of orientation, Calvin's view is similar to that of Aquinas in two ways. First, Aquinas also thought that vice proliferates and that grace is required for free choice. Second, Aquinas also thought that the will is responsible for ultimate orientation. Psychologically speaking, the principle differences are three: (1) degree about the extent of orientation, perhaps a rhetorical difference; (2) what baptism does to correct it; and (3) the efficiency of grace to effect a settled state of good will. This last point is significant because Calvin understood the pervasive impact of sin more acutely than Aquinas. Calvin was surely right to see continence as the highest aspiration in this life. It is not that Christians make no prog-ress in virtue by the grace of God. It is rather that Christian psychology on this side of the resurrection will always be an inaugurated psychology, never fully reaching a state of perfection as "we wait eagerly for adoption as sons, the redemption of our bodies" (Rom 8:23).

HISTORICAL POSTSCRIPT

Unfortunately, the limits of this project preclude me from giving the rest of the story through the Puritans to Jonathan Edwards to the nineteenth century where the next chapter picks up. But I want to say a few words as a historical post-script for three reasons. First, I want to clarify what I am and am not saying about Calvin. Second, I do not want to give the impression that this is a neat, linear, "just-so story" to fully explain the fall of holistic and tiered psychology. Third, I want to reiterate why so much historical grounding is necessary.

BLAMING CALVIN

In evaluating Calvin, it is essential to recognize three things. First, Calvin was a biblical theologian who was regularly engaged in pastoral work. He was not a university professor and, therefore, not bound to produce the sort of work that Aquinas or even Turretin wrote.[213] Second, Calvin is not the last word in Reformed theology. Muller writes, "Reformed theology cannot be reduced to Calvin's perspective and Calvin's theology cannot be reduced to the *Institutes*."[214] He adds, "The absence of particular themes or issues from Calvin's *Institutes* not only must lead a Reformed philosopher or theologian either to seek elsewhere in the Reformed tradition for a precedent or to develop his own approach to the theme or issue."[215] I am well aware that the issues I am investigating, while not absent, are not of central importance to Calvin. Part of the point of evaluating him is to make this apparent. Calvin's psychology is neither complete nor entirely consistent. "Calvin cannot properly function either as the sole guide or even the primary determiner of the Reformed tradition on certain points."[216] Third, and related, it is possible that we expect too much of our theological heroes. Jason Van Vliet writes, "Every author strives for coherence, yet no author attains it perfectly in his manuscript, let alone in a large corpus of writings. In this regard John Calvin is no exception. Hence it is advisable to ask whether modern readers sometimes expect too much of the

---

213. See Carl R. Trueman, *History and Its Fallacies: Problems Faced in the Writing of History* (Wheaton, IL: Crossway, 2010), 123.

214. Muller, "Preface," in Hoitenga, *John Calvin and the Will*, 5.

215. Muller, "Preface," in Hoitenga, *John Calvin and the Will*, 10.

216. Muller, "Preface," in Hoitenga, *John Calvin and the Will*, 10.

theologians of yesteryear."[217] Finally, I take solace in the fact that Calvin seems to authorize my critique: "I do not forbid those who are desirous of learning to study them [the subtleties of the faculties]. ... I shall not strongly oppose anyone who wants to classify the powers of the soul in some other way" (*Inst.* I.15.6).

"Just-So Story"

To avoid giving the wrong impression of linear development, there are two caveats. First, it may be the case that Calvin was less determinative of the shape of Reformed theology just after his death than he is today among evangelicals. In the first place, there is a longstanding debate over the relationship between Calvin and later Calvinism.[218] While the question is quite complex, there are reasons for speculating that the Reformed Scholastics and Puritans did depart somewhat from Calvin on the issue of psychology. Perry Miller has suggested that the Puritan position on the passions "was essentially that of Thomas Aquinas" and that "they framed sentences which, taken by themselves, could come as well from any scholastic or Aristotelian treatise."[219] More specifically, David Sytsma has demonstrated that the Reformed treatment of the affections during the period of early orthodoxy (ca. 1565–1640) "grew within the broad framework of Aristotelian psychology."[220] Specifically, a majority of Reformed theologians draw "on a generally Thomistic approach to the nature and division of the affections, although not without a dissenting Scotistic minority."[221] The "majority of Reformed authors in early orthodoxy favor the placement of

---

217. Van Vliet, *Children of God*, 22.

218. See Basil Hall, "Calvin against the Calvinists," in *John Calvin: Courtenay Studies in Reformation Theology*, ed. G.E. Duffield (Abingdon: Sutton Courtenay, 1966), 19–37; R. T. Kendall, *Calvin and English Calvinism in 1649*, Studies in Christian History and Thought (Eugene, OR: Wipf & Stock, 1997); Paul Helm, "Calvin and Calvinism: The Anatomy of a Controversy," *Evangel* 2, no. 10 (1984): 7–10.

219. Perry Miller, *The New England Mind: The Seventeenth Century* (Boston: Beacon, 1961), 254. Miller's understanding of Aquinas here might be questioned, but there is a more general point to be made about the categories of passions versus affections and will versus sense appetite.

220. David Sytsma, "The Logic of the Heart: Analyzing the Affections in Early Reformed Orthodoxy," in *Church and School in Early Modern Protestantism: Studies in Honour of Richard A. Muller on the Maturation of a Theological Tradition*, ed. Jordan J. Ballor, David S. Sytsma, and Jason Zuidema, Studies in the History of Christian Thought (Leiden: Brill Academic, 2013), 472.

221. Sytsma, "Logic of the Heart," 473.

the affections in the sensitive appetite."[222] Sytsma sees Jonathan Edwards as an advocate of a minority view here.

So, if Calvin's view was not determinative for Reformed orthodoxy, why am I focusing on Calvin? There are at least two reasons. First, insofar as Richard Muller expresses concern that "Reformed theology cannot be reduced to Calvin's perspective," it seems fair to infer that it sometimes has been.[223] Second, the view that emotions are composite movements of body and soul seems not well represented within contemporary Reformed theology. And since Calvin is so important to the Reformed tradition and his view seems to be at odds with the more integrated view, it is necessary to assess his view with a proper historical footing.

While ideas about the soul's interaction with the body were largely circumscribed to Descartes' thinking being, other elements of Renaissance psychology evolved more slowly and unevenly as alternate medical paradigms developed. A good example is the fate of Galenism. Galenism first came under fire from Andreas Vasalius (1514–1564). But the theory declined piecemeal as different aspects came under scrutiny into the nineteenth century. At least on a popular level, Galenism continued to have prominence into the nineteenth century. Germ theory eventually explained diseases better than heats, colds, or bad airs following John Snow's observations of the Broad Street cholera outbreak of 1854 and the work of Louis Pasteur and Robert Koch in the 1860s. The development was uneven.

As already mentioned, there is some evidence that Reformed theologians of the seventeenth century were more invested in physiology than

---

222. Sytsma, "Logic of the Heart," 478. He cites Puritan William Fenner as a minority advocate for the view that affections are "kinds of willing." Fenner writes, "therefore *Austen*, and *Galen*, and *Scotus*, and why say I them, the scriptures say the affections are motions in the heart." Fenner, *Treatise*, 6. This is also a confirmation of my tentative psychological and physiological alignment of will and heart above. Sytsma cites Scultetus, Weemes, Du Moulin, and Reynolds as majority advocates. "Logic of the Heart," 482. He writes, "We can conclude, however, that the Reformed tradition prior to the spread of Descartes' concept of the soul, which denied a sensitive part, generally placed the affections in the sensitive appetite with a minority favoring a Scotist view." "Logic of the Heart," 479.

223. Richard Muller, "Preface," in Hoitenga, *John Calvin and the Will*, 5. Elsewhere he writes, "all [of the theologians noted here] represent Calvin as one among several important founders of the Reformed faith and none identify Calvin as their absolute predecessor. ... None of the writers were entirely comfortable with the label of 'Calvinist.'" Richard Muller, "The 'Reception of Calvin' in Later Reformed Theology: Concluding Thoughts," *Church History and Religious Culture* 91, nos. 1–2 (2011): 273.

Calvin was.[224] For example, the Scottish theologian John Weemse writes with a thoroughgoing physiological integration in his *The Portraiture of the Image of God in Man*. He writes,

> All the passions are seated in the *heart*, we see in *Feare*, such as are transported therewith, call backe the blood to the *heart*, as to the place where feare exerciseth her tyrannie. ... The *heart* is the first mover of all the actions of man; for as the first mover carryeth all the spheres of the Heaven with it, so doth the *heart* of man carry all the members of the body with it.[225]

He adds that in natural generation, the heart is framed, but in spiritual regeneration, the heart is reformed. He even suggests that a wise heart is more on the right side of human beings' body, while a foolish one is on the left.[226] Since the lungs are near the heart, we see that "speech is but the interpreter of the heart."[227]

With these caveats, I hope to reinforce the point that we are seeking to understand Calvin and to assess the extent to which his psychology can account for habit, especially with regard to my twofold account of plasticity—malleability and durability. The narrative is in place to reinforce the contours of Calvin's thought diachronically.

HISTORY AS (RE)CONSTRUCTION

Finally, there are at least three reasons why I have spent so much space developing history. First, theological reasoning must take up the mantel within the context of the tradition of the Spirit's work in teaching us to read God's word within the church. To honor a properly theological understanding of the development of doctrine requires paying attention to theological history. Second, and more to the point for me, it was extremely odd to me that medieval theological psychology was actually more physiologically

---

224. E. M. W. Tillyard says the views of humankind immediately following Calvin's death were "in the purest medieval tradition." The world picture of the medieval universe and its microcosm was oddly very much alive and precarious on the heels of Copernicus (d. 1543) and Vesalius; Tillyard, *Elizabethan World Picture*, 3.

225. John Weemse, *The Portraiture of the Image of God in Man in His Three Estates of Creation, Restauration, Glorification*, 3rd ed. (London: John Bellamie, 1636), 21.

226. Weemse, *Portraiture*, 22.

227. Weemse, *Portraiture*, 23.

integrated than contemporary theology. If this surprised me, it seemed likely to surprise other Protestant theologians, and therefore to need unpacking. The mere fact of this odd state of affairs seems to be an argument for contemporary theologians to take notice. Third, and finally, any discourse requires shared grammar. If theological psychology is to be reintroduced as a viable theological locus, we must remember its grammar.

5
—

MODERN REFORMED PSYCHOLOGY

What has come before this may have felt like a journey into strange lands for some readers. Generally, my rationale for this journey is that it is irresponsible to approach theological questions, or questions of biblical interpretation, as if they have never been answered before. If theologians have lost touch with the heritage of psychological reflection, then it would be irresponsible to theorize without some attempt at re-inhabiting the catholic (universal) tradition. But more specifically, the story told so far serves at least three functions. First, the story shows that questions about psychology, the body and soul, their powers, and the plasticity assumed by the notions of virtue and vice were very important to the church's theological development. Second, the story allows us to contrast Calvin and Aquinas constructively on the key psychological issues. By situating their theological psychological concepts within their native context, I am enabled to use them in flexible ways without risking anachronism. Third, the story has partly explained why habit, and embodied plasticity, was not an essential element at the headwaters of Reformed psychology, as it had been earlier in the Christian tradition.

In the following chapters, I want to provide a model of a holistic psychology that takes embodiment seriously. I will argue that affirming a holistic and tiered psychology enriches Reformed theology both with respect to the book of nature, e.g., integrating neuroscience, and with respect to Scripture, e.g., illuming how the Bible assumes embodied agency. This chapter picks up the thread of theological psychology from the time psychology became its own empirical discipline. It will highlight an already existing turn toward anthropological holism in Reformed theology, but one accompanied by a reluctance to address issues of essence or nature, the whatness of human nature, body, and soul. Chapter 6 suggests that Thomistic-like holism may still be the best way of addressing body-soul relations. Chapter 7 traces embodiment biblically and theologically and suggests that there is a crucial psychological tension between body and mind, biblically speaking. Chapter 8 proposes a Thomistic-like model of emotion. Finally, Chapter 9 provides a psychologically holistic reading of Matthew 6:25–34 within its theological and canonical context.

REFORMED THEOLOGICAL CONTEXT

Why might a transdisiplinary treatment of psychology be necessary at this moment for Reformed theology? There seems to be a tension between the importance of psychology for theology and the level of engagement on issues of human nature within the Reformed tradition. While Reformed accounts of human nature have psychological assumptions deeply embedded in them, recent Reformed theologians make measured comments on human nature, generally avoiding engagement with neuroscientific advances. What follows will develop this tension by highlighting the importance of psychological assumptions for Reformed theology and briefly surveying what Reformed systematic theologians have had to say about human nature roughly since psychology became a discipline (c. 1879). I will first show how Reformed theology has turned toward a more holistic account of human agency, though precisely what this means is not clear. This presents an opportunity for expanding on how the body qualifies agency. Second, I will show that the tradition has shied away from speculating on human nature, perhaps partly because of the challenges of modern science, but also because of increasing skepticism about whether the Bible gives us a psychology.[1] I want to argue that it is important to make claims

---

1. For example, F. LeRon Shults recounts this history while advocating for a thoroughly relational anthropology. He is particularly annoyed by the few (he cites one) Reformed attempts at reforming faculty psychology. He writes of Dewey Hoitenga's commonsense view that "for every noetic or volitional function of a human being there is a faculty of the soul that possesses that function, by which it produces that noetic or volitional state in question." Shults suggests, "They [Hoitenga] appear to be unaware of the scientific and philosophical reflection that has led to the obsolescence of this model already in the nineteenth century." When he turns to criticizing Hoitenga's view, he makes two notes: "first, that this view emerged only in Western cultures with male-oriented conceptions of the power of the soul. This is not the 'commonsense' view of human knowing in most cultures. Second, and more importantly, in the late sixteenth and early seventeenth centuries when these anthropological terms became fossilized in Protestant theology, it was also 'common sense'

about human nature because these doctrines matter for other important Reformed doctrines.

EMBEDDED PSYCHOLOGICAL ASSUMPTIONS

There is a threefold logic that organizes Reformed thought on the doctrine of humanity: (1) human beings as agents, essence, accidents, and responsibilities; (2) human beings as related and relatedness to God, others, and nature; and (3) the redemptive stages of human beings, especially pertaining to their accidental qualities.[2] Psychology is directly concerned with all of these elements. For example, there are quite a few psychological assumptions in what Charles Hodge writes here:

> We are no longer the objects of God's displeasure, his favour having been propitiated by the death of his son, ver. 10. As a consequence of this we have conscious peace with God, that is, we have neither any longer the present upbraidings of an unappeased conscience, nor the dread of divine vengeance. Both of these ideas are included in the peace here spoken of.[3]

Hodge assumes that there is a connection between our awareness of God's pleasure in us and the conscious experience of peace. Just how does this

---

to think that the sun revolved around the earth. Today, not only in cosmology but also in psychology, we know better." Shults does not seem to feel the need to explain the scientific and philosophical reflection that made faculty psychology obsolete. F. LeRon Shults, *Reforming Theological Anthropology: After the Philosophical Turn to Relationality* (Grand Rapids: Eerdmans, 2003), 185. See Dewey Hoitenga, *John Calvin and the Will: A Critique and Corrective* (Grand Rapids: Baker, 1997), 16.

2. I am roughly rephrasing Anthony Hoekema's proposal for treating the doctrine of humanity in *Created in God's Image*. He writes, "I will present the image of God as having both a structural and functional aspect, as involving man in his threefold relationship—to God, to others, and to nature—and as going through four stages—the original image, the perverted image, the renewed image, and the perfected image." Anthony A. Hoekema, *Created in God's Image* (Grand Rapids: Eerdmans, 1986), ix.

By using the word "accidental" here, I am referring to the medieval category to be distinguished from *essence*, just as Calvin himself does in *Bondage and Liberation of the Will*. So, Kelly Kapic, "To employ classical language, sin and its consequences are accidental rather than essential to being human, a point that Scripture reinforces both in terms of the goodness of the original creation and the promise of glorification." Kelly M. Kapic, "Anthropology," in *Christian Dogmatics: Reformed Theology for the Church Catholic,* ed. Michael Allen and Scott R. Swain (Grand Rapids: Baker Academic, 2016), 184.

3. Charles Hodge, *Commentary on the Epistle to the Romans* (Philadelphia: Grigg and Elliot, 1835), 162, https://books.google.com/books?id=VpMXAAAAYAAJ&dq.

work? Does the experience of peace only apply to the pangs of conscience and fear of judgment, or to fear more generally? How might a pastor counsel someone who is not experiencing peace? Is peace a feeling? Can persons with depression also experience this peace? How does this peace relate to embodiment and the action of the sympathetic nervous system? The claim assumes some answer to these questions.

To cite an example that is more to the point, Kelly Kapic draws some Christological conclusions from the *imago Dei* that are relevant to my concerns. He notes that the phrase *imago Dei* has "often served as shorthand for the whole doctrine of humanity."[4] Throughout Christian history, theologians have assumed that God's determination to "make man in our image" (Gen 1:26) implies some sort of similarity between God and human beings, either in nature (essence or accidents) or in function, or perhaps both of these things (e.g., reason, holiness, or dominion). Kapic believes any complete account of humankind must include all of these things. He writes, "By including human faculties, representation, and relationality in our discussion, we can have a robust anthropology that is recognizable to Christians across the centuries as well as faithful to the key biblical and contemporary concerns."[5] Citing a concern for a "holistic account of the human creature," Kapic argues that Reformed theologians would be wise "to turn to early Christian debates about the Son's assumption of a full human nature, thus connecting anthropology with Christology."[6] Kapic cites Gregory of Nazianzus, who wrote, "The unassumed is the unhealed," arguing, "we do not always appreciate how important physicality is to being human. ... The Son becomes incarnate to save, and those he saves are 'fleshly' creatures, unquestionably physical beings."[7] Here we see that "anthropology and Christology go together."[8] He summarizes, "With the Son's assumption of a human nature, the significance and value of our physicality is profoundly affirmed, and in his life we encounter the embodiment of the call to 'love

---

4. Kelly M. Kapic, "Anthropology," in *Christian Dogmatics: Reformed Theology for the Church Catholic*, ed. Michael Allen and Scott R. Swain (Grand Rapids: Baker Academic, 2016), 169.

5. Kapic, "Anthropology," 170.

6. Kapic, "Anthropology," 170, 172.

7. Kapic, "Anthropology," 175; Gregory of Nazianzus, "To Cledonius the Priest against Apollinarius."

8. Kapic, "Anthropology," 175.

the Lord your God' with our full creaturely selves, including our hearts, souls, minds, and strength (Matt. 22:37; cf. Mark 12:30; Luke 10:27)."[9] Kapic is pushing us to Christology in order to take our responsibility to image God seriously; and to do this, we must also take embodiment seriously.[10] Therefore, Kapic urges theologians to consider psychological faculties.

I will make more connections between Christology and embodiment in the next chapter, but it is worth noting that Kapic assumes psychological work must be done for the sake of other important doctrinal loci. Psychological theorizing plays a key role in understanding the *imago Dei*. As I have suggested, Reformed accounts of human nature have psychological assumptions deeply embedded in them. But just how thoroughly have modern Reformed theologies considered these psychological assumptions, especially issues involving human nature? I will show that while there is a movement toward holism, psychological theorizing about the essence of humankind has not been an important concern for recent Reformed theologians.

REFORMED FORMULATIONS OF BODY AND SOUL

CHARLES HODGE

Charles Hodge (1797–1878) is a useful starting point for this survey because I want to rehearse what Reformed theologians have written about the soul since the beginning of modern experimental psychology. Hodge published his *Systematic Theology* from 1871–1873, less than a decade before Wilhelm Wundt, the father of experimental psychology, opened the first psychological laboratory in Leipzig in 1879.[11] Hodge tersely states that God breathes the breath of life into human beings from the dust of the earth, and "he became ḥayâh nepeš, a living soul." He expands this by appealing to two principles, body and soul, material and immaterial. The soul is a substance

---

9. Kapic, "Anthropology," 192.

10. It may be human embodiment has been underdeveloped precisely because the *imago Dei* has set the agenda for most Reformed accounts. That there is a question whether human beings image God in their body at all has perhaps contributed to the topic's neglect. For background on this question, see Jason Van Vliet, *Children of God: The Imago Dei in John Calvin and His Context* (Göttingen: Vanderhoeck & Ruprecht, 2009), 34–62.

11. Alan Kim, "Wilhelm Maximillian Wundt," *Stanford Encyclopedia of Philosophy*, September 10, 2016, https://plato.stanford.edu/entries/wilhelm-wundt/.

distinct from the body.[12] Hodge simply asserts, naïvely to modern readers, "the idea of substance" is "one of the primary truths of the [sic] reason."[13] He gets this notion of primary truths from Gottfried Leibniz, who sees these as fundamental philosophical axioms such as the law of non-contradiction.[14] Hodge seems to take an Aristotelian view of substances from Leibniz, who writes, "I consider the notion of substance to be one of the keys to the true philosophy."[15] Hodge is affirming the older Scholastic view in the face of modern mechanistic conceptions of bodies as extension.[16] He adds that substance is "in the consciousness of every man, and is therefore a part of the universal faith."[17] The soul is real subsistence, the entity that grounds the act. Moreover, mind and matter are two distinct substances, and this is "sustained by the constant representations of the Bible," though the Scriptures do not "formally teach any system of psychology."[18] Hodge supports his position by appealing to biblical passages that distinguish the soul and body, to passages that say the body is discarded at death, and to the common belief and biblical teaching that the soul subsists after death.

On the other hand, while a human being is spirit (or soul) and body, "The relation between these two constituents is admitted to be mysterious. That is, it is incomprehensible."[19] Hodge makes three claims about this mysterious union: (1) that the soul is the source of life in the body; (2) that states of body produce states of mind (e.g., perception), and vice versa (e.g., emotion); and (3) that certain operations of the body are independent of

---

12. Charles Hodge, *Systematic Theology*, vol. II: Anthropology (Grand Rapids: Eerdmans, 1940), 42.

13. Hodge, *Systematic Theology*, vol. II, 42.

14. The following is a brief clipping of Leibniz's argument: "*in nature, there cannot be two individual things that differ in number alone.* ... And thus, perfect similarity is found only in incomplete and abstract notions, where things are considered [*in rationes veniunt*] only in a certain respect. ... It also follows that *there are no purely extrinsic denominations*, denominations which have absolutely no foundation in the thing denominated. ... The complete or perfect notion of an individual substance contains all of its predicates, past, present, and future." Gottfried Leibniz, "Primary Truths," in *Philosophical Essays*, trans. Roger Ariew and Daniel Garber (Indianapolis: Hackett, 1989), 32, emphasis original.

15. Leibniz, *Philosophical Essays*, 286.

16. See Brandon C. Look, "Gottfried Wilhelm Leibniz," *SEP*, ed. Edward N. Zalta, updated July 24, 2013, https://plato.stanford.edu/entries/leibniz/.

17. Hodge, *Systematic Theology*, vol. II, 42.

18. Hodge, *Systematic Theology*, vol. II, 43.

19. Hodge, *Systematic Theology*, vol. II, 44.

the will (e.g., breathing) while others are dependent on it (e.g., moving the body). He explicitly affirms a causal relationship that runs two directions, what he calls realistic dualism, as opposed to parallelism (Leibniz's pre-established harmony), materialism, and idealism.[20] In assuming a parallel between soul and mind, Hodge seems to put body and soul in a non-holistic causal relation.[21] On the other hand, he also views the soul as the source of life and identity.

Finally, Hodge does not develop his account of human faculties systematically, but treats them briefly only as necessary. He mentions three in passing when speaking of evolution: "emotion [or sensibility], intellect, and will."[22] Hodge explicitly mentions them again when speaking of sanctification. He is careful not to assert that there is any real distinction between soul and spirit or heart and conscience, using the word "heart" as the location of the feelings.[23] The clearest arrangement he gives of the faculties is a set of parallels he makes between the body, the lower faculties,

---

20. Hodge, *Systematic Theology*, vol. II, 45–46. Realistic dualism seems to refer to the difference in kind between mind (consciousness) and material objects. Hodge is rejecting both materialism and idealism by positing a real distinction between these sorts of things. As he writes, "neither is the body, as Delitzsch says, a precipitate of the mind, nor is the mind a sublimate of matter" (46). We can compare this to the definition of dualistic realism from James Bissett Pratt in 1917,

> [the realistic dualistic view] maintains that consciousness and the world of physical objects in space are essentially different from each other in kind; and that the physical may be defined as consisting of non-physical entities which, though they may be spatial, are not in space, and which exist only as functions of one or more individual persons or organisms. This view is so simple and so commonly held that it needs little elucidation. It involves two factors, namely, an empirical view of the make-up of consciousness, and the double thesis that there is real, three-dimensional space, common to different minds, and that consciousness is not in this space, but is only and always the function of persons or organisms.

James Bissett Pratt, "A Defense of Dualistic Realism," *The Journal of Philosophy, Psychology and Scientific Methods* 14 no. 10 (May 10, 1917): 253.

21. A holistic account would see consciousness as arising from the holistic body-soul composite. Hodge transitions between using soul, spirit, and mind seamlessly, for example in *Systematic Theology*, vol. II, 44–45 under the heading "Relation of the Soul and Body."

22. Charles Hodge, *Systematic Theology*, vol. II, 9. The following comments on free will seem to confirm this arrangement. "We have terms to express the *operations of the intellect*, others to designate *the feelings*, and others again for the *acts of the will*; but thousands of our acts include the exercise of the intellect, the sensibility, and the will, and it is absolutely impossible to find words for all these complex and varying states of mind." However, elsewhere he describes the three as "understanding, will, and conscience." Charles Hodge, *Systematic Theology*, vol. II, 279; emphasis added.

23. Hodge, *Systematic Theology*, vol. II, 50.

and the heart on the one hand, and the soul, the higher faculties, and the intellectual powers on the other.[24] He also refers to the lower faculties of the body by the term "sensuous faculties."[25]

Finally, Hodge makes a very important distinction between the two uses for the term "will," a broader and a narrower sense. In the broad sense the will is all "desires, affections, and even emotions."[26] In the narrower sense, the will refers to the power of self-determination by which we decide on our acts, imperative volitions. There will be a problem if an author affirms freedom only in the narrower sense, that we have power over our volitions, but is understood to mean the broader, that we have power over our desires. Hodge applies this criticism to Jonathan Edwards's "celebrated work": "He starts with a definition of the term, which makes it include all preferring, choosing, being pleased with, liking and disliking, and advocates a theory which is true, and applicable only to the will in the restricted sense of the word."[27] This is tantalizingly incomplete. Hodge seems to suggest that emotions are outside our control, being aligned with the body, in a way that goes beyond even Jonathan Edwards. In sum, we see some evidence of tiered faculties, but the lower faculties seem outside the scope of rationality.

Geerhardus Vos

Geerhardus Vos (1862–1949) follows Hodge's material closely, but more concisely. Like Hodge, he affirms two substances, which are distinct, claiming not that Scripture explicitly teaches these truths, but "by assuming and presupposing them everywhere."[28] While the relation between body and soul is mysterious, he asserts realistic dualism. By this he means that the union between the two is a life-unity, with certain functions of each being both dependent and independent of the other.[29] Finally, he refutes trichotomy citing both biblical and philosophical reasons. He concludes,

---

24. Hodge, *Systematic Theology*, vol. II, 231; cf. 49, 169.
25. Hodge, *Systematic Theology*, vol. II, 239.
26. Hodge, *Systematic Theology*, vol. II, 288.
27. Hodge, *Systematic Theology*, vol. II, 289.
28. Geerhardus Vos, *Reformed Dogmatics*, vol. 2: Anthropology, ed. and trans. Richard B. Gaffin Jr. (Bellingham, WA: Lexham Press, 2014), 1.
29. Vos, *Reformed Dogmatics*, 1–2.

"The soul is spirit and the spirit is soul, depending on whether one considers it from one side or the other. Spirit refers to the life-power that sets the body in motion."[30] Vos holds the same basic view as Hodge on the faculties, speaking of the intellect, the will, and the "capacity for emotions."[31] Vos also reaffirms Calvin's statement that the will is depraved by means of a sinful *habitus*.[32]

HERMAN BAVINCK

Herman Bavinck represents a turning point in this discussion. His psychological legacy is the most unique of the authors in this survey. What has and has not been translated from Bavinck helps make my point.[33] A reader of his *Reformed Dogmatics* could get the impression that Bavinck is even less concerned with the human nature than the authors above; he does not actually treat the essence of humankind in it. His section on "Human Nature" merely covers what it means to be created in the image of God.

However, Bavinck was interested in theological psychology. He wrote to William Kuyper on September 20, 1897, about the doctrine of humanity in *Reformed Dogmatics*: "The doctrine of man is incomplete. Therefore, in a couple of months I shall publish a small, separate work: *Beginselen der Psychologie* [*Foundations of Psychology*]."[34] In this small, separate work, Bavinck turns to a scientifically integrated treatment of human nature.[35] Intriguingly, in 1920, he turns to the subject again in a separate volume, *Bijbelsche en Religieuze Psychologie* [*Biblical and Religious Psychology*], but this time writing from a more conscientiously biblical and religious point of

---

30. Vos, *Reformed Dogmatics*, 3.

31. Vos, *Reformed Dogmatics*, 26; cf. 60.

32. Vos, *Reformed Dogmatics*, 59.

33. Bavinck's two books on psychology have been translated by students but remain unpublished. I spoke with an editor at an evangelical publishing house who suggested that one of the translations is not a suitable scholarly translation, and, at least in the opinion of one expert, Bavinck's views are not helpful for the contemporary counseling conversation.

34. Herman Bavinck, *Foundations of Psychology (Beginselen der Psychologie)*, trans. Jack Vanden Born (Master's Thesis, Calvin College, 1981), vii. Vanden Born translated Bavinck's second edition: Herman Bavinck, *Beginselen der Psychologie*, 2nd ed. (Kampen: J. H. Kok, 1923).

35. He describes what he conceives psychology to be, its methods, its account of the soul, and its account of its powers. Psychology, according to Bavinck, is "the science of the powers and activities of the human psyche." He affirms such methods as introspection, the historical method, including the Bible as a source, and experimentation. Bavinck, *Foundations of Psychology*, 3.

view. The earlier book seems to be an attempt to provide a psychology that is conversant both with contemporary psychology and with the Christian tradition, especially the psychology of Aquinas, yet contains less than ten biblical references.[36] In the latter book, Bavinck is more obviously engaged in biblical reasoning.

While Bavinck was interested in psychology, he seems to have judged it too cumbersome to develop within his systematic theology. No doubt this has to do with the increasing complexity of working across disciplinary lines—Bavinck devotes a significant portion of *Beginselen der Psychologie* to the theories of Johann Friedrich Herbart, Wilhelm Wundt, and association psychology, which he attributes to David Hume and John Stuart Mill. In fact, the mere existence of a science of psychology leads Bavinck to admit that Scripture "is not suitable for nor intended to be a textbook or a scientific handbook," adding that "it will be impossible to draw from the Bible a psychology which supplies us with something in our need" and that "the words which Holy Scripture employs, such as spirit, soul, heart, feeling, etc., have been borrowed from the Jewish idiom, have usually another intention than that which we associate with it, and are by no means always used in the same wider or narrower sense."[37] Nevertheless, special revelation speaks extensively to the concerns of human life. Bavinck cites a "threefold benefit" from the Bible for psychology. First, "it teaches us to know man as he is and as he shall always remain, in his origin, essence and destiny." Second, Scripture gives us insight into the soul that we can get nowhere else, chiefly the changes produced by sin and grace and deep insights into its motives. Third, Scripture does this with concreteness, especially in putting "persons on the stage for us, which are worthy of each one's consideration ... and among them, or better, high above them, Christ stands, the unique One among men, full of grace and truth."[38]

---

36. Jack Vanden Born makes the comment that Valentin Hepp deleted many Scripture references when he prepared the second edition. He writes, "The revised edition that has been translated in these pages was prepared by Valentin Hepp, Bavinck's biographer and successor at *Vrije Universiteit.* He deleted many of the references to Biblical texts and included such revisions as were contained in Bavinck's papers." Vanden Born, "Translator's Introduction," Herman Bavinck, *Foundations of Psychology*, ix.

37. Herman Bavinck, *Biblical and Religious Psychology*, trans. H. Hanko (Grand Rapids: Protestant Reformed Theological School, 1974), 10.

38. Bavinck, *Biblical and Religious Psychology*, 10–11.

Briefly, Herman Bavinck holds to a theistic theory of the soul, which "takes the soul to have its own spiritual independence and to have its own origin, essence and duration"; there are two substances.[39] We can recognize the soul by its activities, that is, draw metaphysical inferences from empirical observation. While all psychic events "demand a spiritual soul as carrier," the activity of knowing especially implies that the soul does not wholly depend on the body.[40] He echoes a Thomistic argument here by asserting that the soul must "be free from the material" to capture universals.[41] However, Bavinck draws a surprising conclusion from the fact that the Bible describes the creation of human beings as the "in-blowing of the breath of life." He writes, "when the Scriptures have man become a living soul with the in-blowing of the breath of life, they cut off all possibilities of Platonic or Cartesian dualism. The person as soul cannot be outside of the body. This applies to his essence as well and, thus, to the image of God. Spiritualism and asceticism must be rejected no less than materialism."[42] He affirms a Thomistic view of the soul as "the form, the moving power, the beginning of the body," and conversely, "the body is the material, the stuff and possibility of the soul."[43] Finally, he likewise says it is possible to "ascribe a soul to plants and animals," but "in man the soul reaches its highest development with reason and will. Man is rational."[44] As Jack Vanden Born notes, Bavinck is heavily invested in Scholastic thought. Vanden Born writes, "Having recently read in St. Thomas' *Summa Theologica*, I sometimes wondered if I was in the wrong book."[45]

By contrast, Bavinck offers a more straightforward analysis of biblical psychological categories in his *Biblical and Religious Psychology*. He warns that in the Bible we always deal with "the language of life." He writes, "Man is not described philosophically in the dissection of his parts, but is viewed in his unity."[46] Bavinck warns that the psychology of the body "appears to

---

39. Bavinck, *Foundations of Psychology*, 27.

40. Bavinck, *Foundations of Psychology*, 28.

41. Bavinck, *Foundations of Psychology*, 29.

42. Bavinck, *Foundations of Psychology*, 30.

43. Bavinck, *Foundations of Psychology*, 31. He adds, "They are as earnestly united as is the figure and the marble in a statue."

44. Bavinck, *Foundations of Psychology*, 31.

45. Jack Vanden Born, "Translator Notes," Bavinck, *Foundations of Psychology*, xxxiv.

46. Bavinck, *Biblical and Religious Psychology*, 21.

us to be, not an abstract, dogmatic concept-psychology";[47] this means for
him that biblical concepts do not yield a fully delineated scientific system,
but still a valuable general outline of human nature, both "theoretically
and practically."[48] In this sense the Bible's psychology is timeless.[49] Much of
this work is devoted to conceptual analysis, tracing the referents for biblical concepts like soul, spirit, heart, and inner being according to their *usus
loquendi*.[50] While emphasizing the unity of human beings, Bavinck defends
the same basic hylemorphic (form and matter) psychology but in this case
by interacting with biblical terminology. He writes, "the Israelites did not
think of this as a contrast between an immortal soul and a mortal body; but
as something which was in man from below and as something which was in
man from above."[51] He talks about the soul as "another name for that which
we call life or also the power of life," which human beings have in common
with animals, as Thomas argued.[52] The body is called tent or instrument,
like Cartesian or Platonic dualism, not to indicate the relationship between
body and soul, but only to acknowledge that the body "can be temporarily
cut off from the soul without the man himself ceasing to exist."[53] Following
biblical terminology, Bavinck also distinguishes the biblical use of the
terms "spirit" and "soul" by saying, "spirit designates the principle and the
power [of human life and higher consciousness]; while soul, on the other
hand, designates the seat and the subject of life. Man *has* a spirit, but *is* a
soul, while the angels are only spirits, and the animals only living souls."[54]
But considered from the perspective of scientific psychology, "there can be
no essential, substantial difference between them. Spirit and soul denote
the same inner man, but viewed from a different aspect."[55] Bavinck also
makes no attempt like Calvin to line up the heart with the will of faculty

---

47. Bavinck, *Biblical and Religious Psychology*, 62.

48. Bavinck, *Biblical and Religious Psychology*, 63.

49. Bavinck says that the psychology of the Bible is does not change "under the influence
of scientific insights" and thus "retains force as long as man remains the same in all times
and in all places." Bavinck, *Biblical and Religious Psychology*, 62.

50. Bavinck, *Biblical and Religious Psychology*, 25.

51. Bavinck, *Biblical and Religious Psychology*, 20.

52. Bavinck, *Biblical and Religious Psychology*, 27.

53. Bavinck, *Biblical and Religious Psychology*, 26.

54. Bavinck, *Biblical and Religious Psychology*, 50; emphasis original.

55. Bavinck, *Biblical and Religious Psychology*, 50.

psychology, arguing instead that the heart is something like the source of human agency, that from it "as a hidden, underground fountain, the life of ideas, affections, and emotions flows forth," and that it "pays attention."[56]

Bavinck addresses the faculties more directly in *Foundations of Psychology*. He tells a brief history of the organization of the faculties ranging from the Greeks to present day. Of particular note are his discussions of the demotion of the vegetative and sensitive orders and the establishment of the feeling faculty. He writes, "the Enlightenment made understanding the essence of man. Vegetative and sensitive life did not belong to the soul, but it was of a lower order, and anything that arose from this order was distrusted." The Romantic movement was a sort of reaction to this: "Sensitive man took center stage. Sentimentality reigned. Men doted on natural life. Fashionable men dressed à la Franklin in crude costumes and promenaded on thick soles aided by knotted walking canes. ... The final argument for God, virtue and immortality was feeling."[57] Bavinck rejects the feeling faculty, opting instead for two faculties, divisible into higher and lower divisions: higher knowing comprising understanding and reason and lower knowing comprising perception, memory, and imagination; higher desiring comprising the will and lower desiring comprising a "rich life" of "unconscious striving" including the motions of vegetative life (nourishment, etc. cf. Aquinas), reflexes, innate drives, etc.[58] The lower desiring division of human beings also includes sensitive life, desires that are responsive to the lower knowing abilities. Following Aquinas, Bavinck holds that in animals these are natural instinct, and not free. However, human beings may govern their sensual life. He writes, "But in man the lower knowing ability rises to the higher and, similarly, the desiring ability rises to will. And with higher understanding, reason and will, an individual can govern his lower sensual life." Human beings have drives in addition to instincts. A drive is "an enduring, habitual desire, a disposition to desire specific goods, and it raises the same desire again and again. Drives may be

---

56. Bavinck, *Biblical and Religious Psychology*, 55.

57. Bavinck, *Foundations of Psychology*, 44–45.

58. Here Bavinck echoes Aquinas's metaphysical notion of appetite. Bavinck writes, "The desiring faculty was designed so that it can only strive for its good. The good must be understood subjectively as that which we assume will enhance us and agree with our nature." Bavinck, *Foundations of Psychology*, 124.

innate or they may develop gradually."[59] Moreover, Bavinck's psychology is genuinely tiered. He differentiates lower sensual representations from higher conceptualizations and lower desiring from higher willing. These are differentiated to such an extent that they can be in conflict. He writes,

> Thus a significant difference exists between desiring and willing, just as there is between sensual representations and conceptualizations. While there is more within the desiring faculty, desiring and willing are two important activities. They are different from one another, so much so that it is possible for them to be in conflict. Frequently the will simply follows desire and takes it over, as it were, because it has no ground or power to oppose desire. As a rule we eat, drink and sleep when the need becomes manifest. But sometimes drives for drunkenness or drugs, for example, are so strong that reason and will are completely pushed aside.[60]

Bavinck's psychology is Thomistic-like but with slightly different terminology. His psychology contains both of the elements I have suggested are necessary to correct the inadequacies of emotional voluntarism. First, his psychology is genuinely holistic, endorsing Aquinas's hylemorphic dualism. Bavinck writes, "Suggesting only that emotions cause physical change is just as wrong as only saying physical changes cause emotions. The body is not a machine brought into motion by the soul and neither is the soul the reflex of the body. The soul and body together make the essence of a person, a peculiar sensory-spiritual essence that is called man."[61] Second, it is genuinely tiered, embracing the possibility of conflict between higher and lower powers even in the unregenerate.[62] He writes, "The Reformation taught that sensual desire, even if not a sin in itself and even if it existed fully harmoniously with the psychic-life of both the first human beings and of Christ, was disordered by sin, thus establishing conflicts between the

---

59. Bavinck, *Foundations of Psychology*, 127–28. I have already suggested that perhaps affections could be a useful term if it refers to these sorts of drives.

60. Bavinck, *Foundations of Psychology*, 130.

61. Bavinck, *Foundations of Psychology*, 143.

62. Bavinck's psychology deserves fuller treatment. For example, he very helpfully distinguishes between moods, feelings, emotions, and passions while holding that they are all movements of the same lower faculty. I will have to develop his psychology in more detail elsewhere.

lower and higher nature of man."[63] He even accounts for habit formation in his comments about psychological drives. Bavinck's two volumes on psychology represent the most developed attempt at a scientifically conversant biblical psychology in the Reformed tradition in the last one hundred and fifty years. Bavinck's attempt at describing a Thomistic-like psychology in conversation with contemporary psychology inspires my own.

Louis Berkhof

After covering the origin of humankind, Louis Berkhof (1873–1957) turns to his constitutional nature in his *Systematic Theology*. He covers trichotomy and dichotomy, the "constituent elements of human nature" (body and soul), and the relation of body and soul, before turning to the other traditional topics of the origin of the soul and the image of God. He states simply, "The prevailing representation of the nature of man in Scripture is clear dichotomy." He clarifies that a human being is not a duality, but unity. "It is not the soul but man that sins; it is not the body but man that dies; and it is not merely the soul, but man, body and soul, that is redeemed in Christ."[64] When God creates human beings, they become a "living soul," which describes the human being as a whole. Berkhof warns against reading later Greek philosophy into the Old Testament text. He further suggests that spirit refers to the "principle of life and action" while soul refers to the same element of the human being, but "as the subject of action in man, and is therefore often used for the personal pronoun in the Old Testament."[65]

Concerning the body-soul relation, Berkhof rejects both types of monism, materialism and idealism, in favor of dualism. He likewise argues for realistic dualism, by which he means, "body and soul are distinct substances, which do interact, though their mode of interaction escapes human scrutiny and remains a mystery for us."[66] He calls the body the instrument of the soul, acknowledging that some functions of the body are dependent on the conscious activity of the soul and that the soul continues to function after death.[67] He concludes ominously, "A great deal of

---

63. Bavinck, *Foundations of Psychology*, 132.

64. Louis Berkhof, *Systematic Theology* (Carlisle, PA: Banner of Truth, 2005), 192.

65. Berkhof, *Systematic Theology*, 194.

66. Berkhof, *Systematic Theology*, 195.

67. Berkhof, *Systematic Theology*, 195–96.

present day psychology is definitely moving in the direction of materialism. Its most extreme form is seen in Behaviorism with its denial of the
soul, of the mind, and even of consciousness."[68]

Like Hodge and Vos, Louis Berkhof affirms three faculties: intellect,
will, and affections.[69] Unlike Calvin, he does not align the heart with the
will, but calls it "the central organ of the soul, out of which are the issues
of life."[70] Like Calvin, Berkhof includes in the image of God only human
rational or moral powers, intellect, and will.[71] Berkhof argues that regeneration is necessary to correct the faculties, but that it must reach the whole
heart, perfecting human nature as a whole—intellect, will, and feeling. He
sees regeneration as implanting the principle of spiritual life in human
beings instantaneously. However, when he speaks of faith, he remarks that
the exercise of faith "gradually forms a *habitus*, and this acquires a fundamental and determining significance for the further exercise of faith."[72]

G. C. BERKOUWER

With G. C. Berkouwer, we notice a decided shift in confidence about the
degree to which the Bible teaches an anthropology or psychology. He writes,

There is a growing consensus among theologians that the Scriptural
data on man do not render superfluous research directed at the various aspects of man. Or, in other words, the theological investigation
of man cannot seek a solution along the lines of a scientific anthropology, or a Biblical psychology and physiology, as if the intention
of Scripture were to give us information about the various aspects
of man, or the details of the composition of man.[73]

---

68. Berkhof, *Systematic Theology*, 196.
69. Berkhof, *Systematic Theology*, 233.
70. Berkhof, *Systematic Theology*, 233.
71. Berkhof, *Systematic Theology*, 207.
72. Berkhof, *Systematic Theology*, 503.
73. G. C. Berkouwer, *Man: The Image of God* (Grand Rapids: Eerdmans, 1962), 194.
Berkouwer thinks it noteworthy that Herman Bavinck claims it is impossible to "obtain a
psychology from the Bible," but titles his book *Bijbelsche en religieuze Psychologie*, explaining
that Bavinck must "have some different meaning in mind when he uses the term 'Biblical
psychology.'" Berkouwer, *Man*, 194, citing Herman Bavinck, *Bijbelsche en religieuze Psychologie*
(Kampen: J. H. Kok, 1920), 13. Surely Bavinck does have a different meaning in mind. Bavinck's
psychology utilizes and criticizes contemporary psychological research while consciously
submitting to Scripture and building within the theological tradition.

Berkouwer seems uncomfortable with the word "psychology" because of its tendency to abstract just one component of human beings, the soul, taking the word literally, the study of the soul.[74] He prefers anthropology, which refers to the whole human being, "keeping in mind, however, that we do not encounter in Scripture a scientific description of man." On the other hand, Berkouwer does want to affirm that "man stands in the very center of the Biblical witness!"[75]

The problem with biblical psychology for Berkouwer is simply that "we never encounter in the Bible an independently existing, abstract, ontological, structural interest in man."[76] The Bible never intends or intended to talk about the parts of human beings, but "directs our glance towards man in his totality, in his relation to God."[77] While there are distinctions between the biblical terms, the Bible is primarily concerned with the whole of human beings in their unity. So, are we to discard the traditional Reformed formulation that human beings are composed of two substances, soul and body? Berkouwer makes several points here. First, he points out that dichotomy is not more unified than trichotomy. Second, he marks how dichotomy has come under sharp attacks, for example by Herman Dooyeweerd. These attacks raise the question of whether this criticism runs counter to the confessions of the church, e.g., the Council of Chalcedon, the Heidelberg Catechism (Q. 1, 11, 26, 36, 57), and the Belgic Confession (A. 18).[78] Berkouwer counters that these confessions do not intend to give "positive statements on the composition of man" by the use of their concepts. In fact, he argues, the Council of Vienne actually intended to reject dualism; it was "undoubtedly intended to emphasize the unity of man."[79] This is a subtle misrepresentation of the decrees of the council, since both Olivi and the council

74. Berkouwer, *Man*, 194–95.

75. Berkouwer, *Man*, 195.

76. Berkouwer, *Man*, 196.

77. Berkouwer, *Man*, 199.

78. Article 18 of the Belgic Confession concerns what Christ assumed: "And Christ not only assumed human nature, as far as the body is concerned, but also a real human soul, in order to be a real human being. For since the soul had been lost as well as the body, Christ had to assume them both to save them both together." "The Belgic Confession (2011 Version)," Christian Reformed Church, accessed February 2018, https://www.crcna.org/welcome/beliefs/confessions/belgic-confession.

79. Berkouwer, *Man*, 219.

affirmed forms of dualism; both affirmed that the entire soul was the form of the body. Olivi simply objected to saying it was the rational part.[80] Finally, and seemingly conceding the criticisms of dualism, Berkouwer states, "The dichotomy of soul and body seems inevitably to produce an ontological emphasis which throws its shadows over the Scriptural witness to man as he actually is sought and found by God. In Scripture we hear no ontological explanations, but rather a religious affirmation, that Christ died for us 'while we were yet sinners' (Rom. 5:8)."[81] He quips that we ought not to abstract the real human beings from the body.

ANTHONY HOEKEMA

In his *Created in God's Image*, Anthony Hoekema (1913–1988) builds on the insights of Bavinck and Berkouwer, asserting, "Though we cannot derive an exact, scientific psychology or anthropology from the Bible, we can learn from Scripture many important truths about man."[82] He adds, "the Bible also focuses our attention on man as he is related to others and to creation. In other words, the Scriptures are not primarily interested in the constituent 'parts' of man or in his psychological structure, but in the relationships in which he stands."[83] However, because Reformed theologians have commonly treated these subjects, Hoekema discusses trichotomy and dichotomy in turn. He sees both as illicitly dividing humankind, arguing instead that the Bible "describes the human person as a totality, a whole, a unitary being."[84] Hoekema defends embodiment by characteristically rejecting Greek dualism: "The Bible, however, does not teach any such sharp antithesis between spirit (or mind) and body. According to the Scriptures matter is not evil but has been created by God. The Bible never

---

80. The declaration of the council reads: "In order that all may know the truth of the faith in its purity and all error may be excluded, we define that anyone who presumes henceforth to assert [sic] defend or hold stubbornly that the *rational or intellectual soul* is not the form of the human body of itself and essentially, is to be considered a heretic." "Council of Vienne 1311–1312 A.D.," Papal Encyclicals Online, https://www.papalencyclicals.net/councils/ecum15.htm, emphasis added. It is true that Olivi supposed that Aristotelianism amounted to something like materialism, making the body responsible for thinking. Cf. Robert Pasnau, "Olivi on the Metaphysics of Soul," *Medieval Philosophy and Theology* 6 (1997): 109–32.

81. Berkouwer, *Man*, 229.

82. Anthony A. Hoekema, *Created in God's Image* (Grand Rapids: Eerdmans, 1986), 204.

83. Hoekema, *Created in God's Image*, 204.

84. Hoekema, *Created in God's Image*, 210.

denigrates the human body as a necessary source of evil but describes it as an aspect of God's good creation, which must be used in God's service."[85] Finally, Hoekema supports his claim that the Bible treats human beings in their unity and wholeness by surveying the biblical uses of Hebrew words like *nepeš*, *rûaḥ*, *lēb*, and *bāśār*, and Greek words like *psychē*, *pneuma*, *kardia*, *sōma*, and *sarx*. He cites Karl Barth's description of a human being as a "besouled body" favorably.[86]

Hoekema does see two sides to humankind, citing the "physical and nonphysical," or body and personality, or mind, by which he means both the mental and spiritual sides.[87] While recognizing two sides, he prefers the term "psychosomatic unity" to dualism or duality. He cites Donald MacKay's description of the unity between mind and brain as "two equally real aspects of one and the same mysterious unity."[88] However, Hoekema also defends the continued existence of believers in the intermediate state following death: "But we must acknowledge that, according to biblical teaching, believers can exist temporarily in a state of provisional happiness apart from their present bodies during the 'time' between death and resurrection. This intermediate state is, however, incomplete and provisional."[89]

Hoekema concludes by describing some implications of a whole person approach for church, school, family life, medicine, and psychology and counseling. In this section, he cites the psychological emphasis on the organism, rather than the dichotomies of dualism and faculty psychology. He notes that organismic theory has been widely accepted and that it teaches there are "no separate compartments" in humankind.[90] Hoekema admits that the will is not a separate kind of faculty in this sense, otherwise we would be treating it as if it were a *homunculus*. In his words, "When one asks whether the 'will' is free, one assumes that the will is a separate

---

85. Hoekema, *Created in God's Image*, 206.

86. Hoekema, *Created in God's Image*, 216; Karl Barth, *Church Dogmatics*, The Doctrine of Creation, vol. III.2, ed. G. W. Bromiley and T. F. Torrance, trans. H. Knight et al. (Edinburgh: T&T Clark, 1960), 351.

87. Hoekema, *Created in God's Image*, 216–17.

88. Hoekema, *Created in God's Image*, 218; Donald M. MacKay, *Brains, Machines and Persons* (Grand Rapids: Eerdmans, 1980), 14.

89. Hoekema, *Created in God's Image*, 222.

90. Hoekema, *Created in God's Image*, 225; citing Calvin S. Hall and Gardner Linzey, *Theories of Personality*, 2nd ed. (New York: John Wiley, 1970), 298–337.

agent in a person that may or may not be free in its actions."[91] Hoekema
rejects faculty psychology since willing is just a function of the person.[92]
What Hoekema seems not to realize is that if there are no separate compartments (functions) within the human psyche, then internal conflict is
impossible. On this point, Aquinas's tiered psychology is substantiated by
empirical research.

MICHAEL HORTON

Finally, the work of Michael Horton (1964–) represents another relational
or covenantal impulse within some Reformed anthropological formulations. Horton asserts, "Human identity can be discerned only by attending closely to the unfolding covenant drama in which human beings play
a supporting role. Just as biblical faith does not speculate on the 'whatness'
of God's hidden essence but on the 'whoness' (i.e., the character, actions,
and purposes) revealed in the script, the same may be said of the way in
which the faith describes humanity."[93] For Horton, Platonism and materialism represent two contrasting accounts of trying to understand humanity through attending to whatness. Neither of these views "is prepared to
receive selfhood, humanity, and personhood from another—especially
from God—as a gift and as a responsibility."[94] While Horton wants to affirm
a biblical distinction between body and soul, to preserve the soul's living
presence after death, he prefers the term "psychosomatic holism, since
dichotomy implies that the distinction between soul and body is more basic
than its unity."[95] The soul is "validated not by any speculation concerning
essences but on the basis of the economy of grace in which believers are
promised that their souls will not share in their bodily death. Beyond this,

---

91. Hoekema, *Created in God's Image*, 227.

92. Hoekema appeals to John Locke's argument in *An Essay Concerning Human
Understanding* for support. Locke's argument amounts to suggesting that faculties bring about
a "confused notion of active things in us," that the word does not have "a clear and distinct
sense." I cannot see how this criticism amounts to anything more than metaphysical skepticism, ironically grounded in a metaphysical optimism that reason has certain knowledge
when it has clear and distinct ideas. John Locke, *An Essay Concerning Human Understanding*
(Oxford: Clarendon, 1894), II.21.6, 14–17.

93. Michael Horton, *The Christian Faith: A Systematic Theology for Pilgrims on the Way*
(Grand Rapids: Zondervan, 2011), 373.

94. Horton, *Christian Faith*, 373.

95. Horton, *Christian Faith*, 377.

we should not speculate about the human essence any more than about the divine essence."[96] Horton remarks, "A biblical anthropology has nothing to lose—in fact, everything to gain—from the dissolution of ancient and modern mind-body dualism," adding, "Criticism of dualism in general and soul-body dualism in particular is a recurring motif in Reformed theology up to the present day." Instead he treats human nature from a relational or covenantal perspective, focusing on "the inherently relational and ecstatic (outward-going) character of human existence rather than on the introspective quest for the inner light."[97] To be is to be in relation to God; "We exist because we are addressed [by God]."[98] Finally, since Horton rejects speculation on human essence, he also avoids speculating on any faculties.[99]

EVALUATION

The principal aim of this survey is to demonstrate the development of the treatment of the essence of the soul within the contemporary Reformed tradition. We can make the following observations: First, we note a consensus developing that the concepts of Scripture underdetermine any fixed scientific conceptual schema. We see a tendency among Reformed theologians to move from explicitly affirming substance dualism on the grounds of biblical concepts to chastened claims about essence along with caveats that the Bible is not a philosophical book. Second, we see a pronounced turn toward holism when it comes to addressing human agency. All the more recent authors seem to agree that the Bible does not speak of human agency through dichotomy of body and soul. Third, especially with Hoekema and Horton, we see evidence of a turn toward more relational anthropology.[100] Horton pushes back on speculating about whatness

---

96. Horton, *Christian Faith*, 377–78.

97. Horton, *Christian Faith*, 397.

98. Horton, *Christian Faith*, 396. He cites Robert Jenson, who writes, "to be is to be heard of; and it is this interpretation that is demanded by the doctrine of creation." Robert W. Jenson, *Systematic Theology*, The Works of God, vol. 2 (Oxford: Oxford University Press, 1999), 35–36.

99. In a footnote Horton writes, "Following Abraham Kuyper and Herman Bavinck, G. C. Berkouwer explicitly defends a relational view of humanity over against abstract consideration of the nature or being of humanity as identified with the soul, heart, mind, or other faculties." He seems not to be aware of Herman Bavinck's treatment of psychology. Horton, *The Christian Faith*, 378.

100. Dewey Hoitenga remarks, "Reformed theologians, as I said earlier, have backed away from the topic of our noetic and volitional faculties." Hoitenga, *John Calvin and the Will*, 16.

toward speaking of whoness, on personhood as being constituted by relation, especially humankind's covenantal relation.[101] Fourth, we see a pronounced indifference toward the faculties with the exception of Herman
Bavinck.[102] Older Reformed theologians tend to endorse three faculties,
intellect, will, and some faculty for accounting for emotions. More contemporary Reformed theologians rejected faculties altogether in favor of
a more holistic view of the person. It is not clear how someone like Horton
might explain internal conflict.

How do we evaluate this survey? First, even if the concepts do not determine a philosophical view of human essence, it might be that the judgments of Scripture govern our concepts even in ways that the concepts
of Scripture do not.[103] We need to ask a further question about whether
Scripture guides our theology on these grounds. We are in danger of conceding any authority Scripture may legitimately have in psychological
discussions by avoiding speculation on the grounds that the concepts are
not decisive. Second, the move toward relational anthropology should not
justify neglecting essence. With Kapic, I want to affirm that all aspects of
theological anthropology need to be considered. It is important, for example, that Jesus was sent "in the likeness of sinful flesh" (Rom 8:3). Finally,
the movement toward holism is encouraging for a theology interested in
how the body qualifies human agency. A holist will already be motivated to
pay attention to this contribution. However, at least in Reformed systematic

---

101. This coincides with a relational turn in theological anthropology generally. See
John D. Zizioulas, *Being as Communion: Studies in Personhood and the Church* (London: Darton,
Longman & Todd, 1985); Edward Russell, "Reconsidering Relational Anthropology: A Critical
Assessment of John Zizioulas's Theological Anthropology," *International Journal of Systematic
Theology* 5, no. 2 (July 2003): 168–86; Ray S. Anderson, *On Being Human: Essays in Theological
Anthropology* (Grand Rapids: Eerdmans, 1982); David F. Ford, *Self and Salvation: Being
Transformed* (Cambridge: Cambridge University Press, 1999); Colin E. Gunton and Christoph
Schwöbel, eds., *Persons, Divine and Human: King's College Essays in Theological Anthropology*
(Edinburgh: T&T Clark, 1991); Colin E. Gunton, *The Promise of Trinitarian Theology* (Edinburgh:
T&T Clark, 1991); Anthony C. Thiselton, *Interpreting God and the Postmodern Self: On Meaning,
Manipulation and Promise* (Edinburgh: T& T Clark, 1995); and Stanley J. Grenz, *The Social God
and the Relational Self: A Trinitarian Theology of the* Imago Dei (Louisville: Westminster John
Knox, 2001).

102. This may be changing. At the time this book was published, I could not read Paul
Helm's new book, *Human Nature from Calvin to Edwards* (2018). He treats faculty psychology
extensively. Paul Helm, *Human Nature from Calvin to Edwards* (Grand Rapids: Reformation
Heritage, 2018).

103. David Yeago, "The New Testament and Nicene Dogma: A Contribution to the Recovery
of Theological Exegesis," *Pro Ecclesia* 3, no. 2 (1994): 152–64.

theorizing, the notion of holism has not been fully defined or developed. Without further explanation of what holism means, the term will bear little weight for theological theorizing. In the next chapter, I will propose a model of embodied dualistic holism that can bear more theoretical weight, at least in terms of the significance of embodiment. In the following chapter, I will try to demonstrate the biblical theological concern for the body to give biblical substance to the notion of holism.

6

—

BOOK OF NATURE: BODY AND SOUL

The last chapter showed how Reformed theology has moved toward anthropological holism, which is important for making sense of emotional plasticity. However, Reformed theologians have also been reticent to specify what holism means or what it entails for moral agency and psychological powers. In order to fight what I have called emotional voluntarism, we need a compelling model of how the body qualifies agency.[1] We need to say more about what sort of holism this is. I want to suggest that a holistic psychology of the body and soul is one that stresses the interaction between the psychological tiers (discussed in Chapter 8) rather than the interaction of soul and body as metaphysical constituents. Soul and body always function holistically in the composite person. Again, to cite Bavinck, "Suggesting only that emotions cause physical change is just as wrong as only saying physical changes cause emotions. The body is not a machine brought into motion by the soul and neither is the soul the reflex of the body. The soul and body together make the essence of a person, a peculiar sensory-spiritual essence that is called man."[2] I will argue for a holistic model in

---

1. I have summarized emotional voluntarism by the following characteristics: (1) emotion as judgment: emotion is strictly or first a mental state; (2) emotions of the heart: since emotions are morally significant, the proper subject of emotion is the heart, though perhaps some emotions are sourced in or influenced by the body; (3) deep belief associationism and legitimacy: emotion is a mental state that arises when a deep belief is elicited into consciousness; the beliefs that surface unbidden are also our truest; (4) mental voluntarism: emotions as mental states are changeable by shifting attention, mainly through internal speech (e.g., repenting of false beliefs), to bring about new mental states; (5) emotional duty: people are duty bound to address any emotional aberrance as quickly as possible, since this is within their power.

2. Herman Bavinck, *Foundations of Psychology (Beginselen der Psychologie)*, trans. Jack Vanden Born (Master's Thesis, Calvin College, 1981), 143.

this chapter. Chapter 8 will build on this one by a providing a model of emotion that accounts for internal psychological conflict.

What follows will first pick up the philosophical debate about the nature of the soul by rehearsing the arguments of John Cooper and Nancey Murphy. I will suggest that J. P. Moreland's Thomistic-like dualism is a good holistic model that enables theologians to account for all the data, empirical and theological. Moreland's position allows theologians to endorse and integrate neuroscientific data without disenchanting the person, especially with regard to identity and moral agency, preserving the possibility of genuinely free interaction between the psychological tiers. Murphy's position, by contrast, seems unable to avoid two consequences—the dissolution of identity and a physicalist determinism that dissolves agency. Moreland's position seems fitting to Christian theology and to the biblical text, and in this way honors my methodological commitment to giving attention to what God says is in Christ. My aim is to recover something similar to Aquinas's version of embodied holism to be able to specify how the body qualifies agency.

THE STATE OF THE SOUL IN REVIEW

What is the status of metaphysical dualism? Must we abandon the soul? Certainly, there are various ways that the traditional doctrine has been chipped away from its high medieval formulations. I will sketch a brief summary. The soul for medieval Scholastics was both form and substance. As form, it explained the life, properties, and powers of an organism; all these come from the form of the living form-matter composite substance. As independent substance, it was capable of existing independently of the body, at least temporarily. Substance metaphysics was crucial to the intelligibility of the soul in the Renaissance. Yet the generic notion of substance was already being abandoned by the late Renaissance. René Descartes (1596–1650)—who needs to be understood against the background of Scholasticism—was a key figure here.[3] Descartes was explicitly rejecting

---

3. Brandon L. Rickabaugh makes this same point in "Responding to N. T. Wright's Rejection of the Soul," *The Heythrop Journal* (2016): 6: "Descartes adamantly rejects the dualism of Plato. The soul, says Descartes, does not simply reside in the body 'as a pilot resides in a ship,' but rather forms a kind of natural unity 'most closely joined' and 'as if intermixed' with it. Arguably, Descartes' view has more in common with scholastic-Aristotelian theories of soul-body union than is popularly portrayed."

Aristotelian substance dualism with his form of dualism. Cartesian dualism conceives of the body as not needing the soul for its fundamental vitality, thereby opening the way for rejecting animal and vegetative souls; the soul, is the Cartesian mind, relates to the body only through the pineal gland. Descartes had no need for positing substantial forms. In a letter to Regius in January of 1642, he writes,

> I fully agree with the learned Rector that those "harmless enti-ties" called *substantial forms* and *real qualities* should not be rashly expelled from their ancient territory. And I haven't outright rejected them; I merely say that they aren't needed in explaining the causes of natural things; and I think it's a positive merit in my arguments that they don't depend at all on uncertain and obscure notions of that sort. Now in matters like this, saying "I'm not willing to use these supposed entities" is very close to saying "I do not accept them", because the only reason anyone accepts them is the belief that the causes of natural effects can't be explained without them. So, all right, I confess that I do wholly reject them.[4]

The problem for Descartes is that these forms were postulated in the first place to explain "how natural things behave." And yet citing them "amounts to saying that it proceeds from something they don't understand—which doesn't explain anything!"[5]

The process of disentangling the body from metaphysical explanations is still ongoing. The soul's power to give life seems to have been finally discarded in the debates over vitalism, which subsided around 1930.[6] The

---

4. René Descartes, "Letter to Regius, i. 1642," in *Selected Correspondence of Descartes, 1641–1644*, vol. 3, ed. and trans. Jonathan Bennett (2010–2015), 150, online: http://www.earlymodern texts.com/assets/pdfs/descartes1619_3.pdf

5. Descartes, "Letter to Regius, i. 1642," 151.

6. For a background of vitalism in scientific context, see William Bechtel and Robert C. Richardson, "Vitalism," in *Routledge Encyclopedia of Philosophy*, ed. Edward Craig, vol. 9 (London: Routledge, 1998), 639–42. Ernst Mayr writes, "considering how dominant vitalism was in biology and for how long a period it prevailed, it is surprising how rapidly and com-pletely it collapsed. The last support of vitalism as a viable concept in biology, disappeared in about 1930." He cites at least four reasons: that it was seen as a metaphysical concept; the abandonment of ideas of a special living substance; failure of positive arguments for a nonma-terial vital force; and new explanations for things that had been proof of vitalism. Ernst Mayr, "What is the meaning of 'life'?" in *The Nature of Life: Classical and Contemporary Perspectives*, ed. Mark A. Bedau and Carol E. Cleland (Cambridge: Cambridge University Press, 2010), 94.

arguments against vitalism are merely a special case of the arguments against the soul. Essentially the argument goes like this: Vitalism was posited to explain facets of life that were then unexplainable by mechanistic processes, by inference to the best explanation. These explanations have since been provided. Therefore, we have no other independent reasons for supposing vitalism is true, since nothing more needs to be explained and the supposed power (*elan vital*) does not explain anything. Further, all the supposed powers of the soul were explained gradually as the study of the human body as a mechanism uncovered how biological processes work.

More recently, the properties and powers of the body have been explained by a combination of genetics and developmental epigenetics, roughly nature and nurture at a chromosomal level. The Human Genome Project has provided the blueprint of properties, a window into how biological bodies are built and sustained. The mere existence of a blueprint also goes a long way to overturning the purposiveness of the soul, that the soul provides teleology.[7] However, the debate continues over to what extent DNA determines biological formation and over the precise ways that genes express. Are we determined by nature? By nuture? Or are we free in any sense? Does "the genotype determine the phenotype"?[8] For substance ontology, these questions were somewhat simpler since each kind of soul pursued its own distinctive kind of *telos*, which, for human beings, could be pursued or not by our rational self-determination. The soul accounted both for the existence of living kinds and individuals and for the whole process of formation from embryo to maturity.

So much for substance, but what about thinking? The Cartesian soul was a stripped-down version of substance, a sort of thinking thing. The final frontier, so to speak, is brain mapping, that is, identifying specific neuropathways that link the various parts of the brain. This project is underway, the Human Connectome Project.[9] By tracing neuropathways, the researchers hope to understand various mental disorders and illnesses.

---

7. It might seem that evolution has a sort of teleology, that life pursues life. But for Darwin, these processes were supposed to be stochastic (random) at least on a cosmic level. This remains an interesting question.

8. Peter G. H. Clark, "Determinism, Brain Function and Free Will," *Science & Christian Belief* 22, no. 2 (2010): 134.

9. The Human Connectome Project is a collaborative project between the Laboratory of Neuro Imaging at the University of Southern California and the Martinos Center for

The assumption taken for granted by the researchers is that brain activity explains mental states. Nancey Murphy summarizes aptly, "In short, all of the human capacities once attributed to the immaterial mind or soul are now yielding to the insights of neurobiology."[10]

THEOLOGICAL AND PHILOSOPHICAL
ARGUMENTS FOR DUALISM

Historically speaking, substance dualism seems cornered. On the one hand, the metaphysical framework that gave it intelligibility has collapsed, and on the other, even the final frontier of the mental is under attack from reductionist materialism. What can be said positively for dualism? What follows will cover a few important interlocutors in this conversation. It will become clear that I consider the burden of proof to be on those wishing to part ways with centuries of Christian tradition on this point.[11] While I find monist materialism theologically and philosophically unconvincing, there is a serious need to learn from empirical observations about human nature.

The most significant theological defense of dualism in the last thirty years is John Cooper's *Body, Soul and Life Everlasting* (1989). Cooper argues "that some sort of 'dualistic' anthropology is entailed by the biblical teaching of the intermediate state, a doctrine that is affirmed by the vast majority in historic Christianity."[12] The central issue for Cooper is "whether the soul

---

Biomedical Imaging at the Massachusetts General Hospital and Harvard University. See http://www.humanconnectomeproject.org/about/.

10. Nancey Murphy, "Science and Society," in *Witness: Systematic Theology*, ed. James Wm. McClendon Jr. and Nancey Murphy, vol. 3 (Nashville: Abingdon, 2000), 126.

11. John Cooper finds it disturbing to suggest that "a doctrine affirmed by most of the Christian church since its beginning is false." Cooper, *Body, Soul, and Life Everlasting*, 2nd ed. (Grand Rapids: Eerdmans, 2000), 1.

12. Cooper, *Body, Soul, and Life Everlasting*, xv. In the second edition of his book, Cooper surveys recent affirmations of some sort of dualism, the traditional Christian position. He cites the Catholic Catechism, historians, biblical scholars, and Christian philosophers: *Catechism of the Catholic Church* (Mahwah, NJ: Paulist Press, 1994); Joseph Ratzinger, *Eschatology: Death and Eternal Life*, ed. A. Nichols, trans. M. Waldstein (Washington, D.C.: Catholic University of America, 1988); N. T. Wright, *The New Testament and the People of God* (Minneapolis: Fortress, 1992); Robert H. Stein, *Luke*, The New American Commentary, vol. 24 (Nashville: Broadman, 1992); Luke Timothy Johnson, *The Gospel of Luke*, Sacra Pagina Series, vol. 3 (Collegeville, MN: Liturgical, 1991); Ben Witherington III, *Conflict and Community in Corinth: A Socio-Rhetorical Commentary on I and 2 Corinthians* (Grand Rapids: Eerdmans, 1995); Alvin Plantinga, "On Heresy, Mind, and Truth," *Faith and Philosophy* 16, no. 2 (April 1999): 182–193; Richard Swinburne, "Body and Soul," in *The Mind-Body Problem: A Guide to the Current Debate*, ed. R. Warner and T. Szubka (Oxford and Cambridge, MA: Blackwell, 1994), 311–16;

can survive and function apart from the human body."[13] Cooper outlines the same sorts of challenges to dualism from materialism that I have just outlined.[14] In addition, he summarizes the challenges from biblical scholarship, from historical scholarship, and from poor practical applications of dualism. He thinks that biblical scholarship in particular poses a "greater threat to traditional Christian anthropology and eschatology than philosophy and science."[15]

For Cooper, to decide for dualism comes down to taking into account all relevant factors, biblical, historical, scientific, etc. For Cooper, the question is not settled by whether or not we have scientific grounds for positing a soul, but by whether, given all the relevant data—including biblical data—a dualistic reading is the best explanation. And so, for him, the biblical data is decisive since it is not "silent or confused or polyvocal on the issue."[16] Moreover, in his view, there is nothing inconsistent with holding this view, scientifically speaking. Cooper is primarily interested in proving the biblical claim, and secondarily in stressing dualism's consistency with empirical research.

In *Body, Soul, and Life Everlasting*, Cooper treats the Old Testament in two chapters, highlighting both its holistic emphasis and its dualistic implication. He admits that "the Hebrew view of human nature strongly

Richard Swinburne, "Dualism Intact," *Faith and Philosophy* 13, no. 1 (January 1996): 68–77; Keith Yandell, "A Defense of Dualism," *Faith and Philosophy* 12, no. 4 (October 1995): 548–66; Charles Taliaferro, *Consciousness and the Mind of God* (Cambridge: Cambridge University Press, 1994); Charles Taliaferro, "Animals, Brains, and Spirits," *Faith and Philosophy* 12, no. 4 (October 1995): 567–81; Stephen Davis, *Risen Indeed: Making Sense of the Resurrection* (Grand Rapids: Eerdmans, 1993); Gary Habermas and J. P. Moreland, *Beyond Death: Exploring the Evidence for Immortality* (Wheaton, IL: Crossway Books, 1998); J. P. Moreland and Scott Rae, *Body and Soul: Human Nature and the Crisis in Ethics* (Downers Grove, IL: InterVarsity, 2000); John Foster, *The Immaterial Self A Defense of the Cartesian Dualist Conception of the Mind* (London and New York: Routledge, 1991); and Eleonore Stump, "Non-Cartesian Substance Dualism and Materialism Without Reduction," *Faith and Philosophy* 12, no. 4 (October 1995): 505–31.

13. Cooper, *Body, Soul, and Life Everlasting*, 1.

14. Materialism presents two challenges that are regarded as disproof of the existence of the soul. First, there is the fact that the mind seems to be dependent in some sense on the brain. Second, any justification for positing the existence of the soul seems to have been discarded. Cooper, *Body, Soul, and Life Everlasting*, 23.

15. Cooper, *Body, Soul, and Life Everlasting*, 24.

16. Cooper, *Body, Soul, and Life Everlasting*, xxvi.

emphasizes living a full and integrated existence before God in this world."[17]
The important Hebrew concepts are holistic, even sometimes used interchangeably with physical referents.[18] The analysis of Old Testament terminology leads Cooper to conclude, "the variety and interchangeability
of terminology simply do not provide a footing for a clearly dualistic
reading."[19] However, Cooper also draws attention to the fact that the Old
Testament clearly refers to the disembodied beings—or perhaps "ethereal
bodily being[s]"—with the term rĕpā'îm. Cooper cites Isaiah 14:9-10, which
reads, "Sheol beneath is stirred up to meet you when you come; it rouses
the shades (rephaim) to greet you."[20] Finally, he cites two undisputed passages that reference the hope of resurrection, Isaiah 26:19 and Daniel 12:2.[21]

In the end, Cooper concludes that the Old Testament is neither strictly
holistic nor dualistic. People are separable from their bodies in that they
can continue to exist after death without them. But people are also fully
integrated. He writes, "Biological processes are not just functions of the
body as distinct from the soul or spirit, and mental and spiritual capacities
are not seated exclusively in the soul or spirit. All capacities and functions
belong to the human being as a whole, a fleshly-spiritual totality."[22] This
is a very good summary of holism.[23]

Cooper also sees continuity both between the Old Testament and the
intertestamental period and between the intertestamental period and the
New Testament. There is merely a shift in emphasis. He writes, "With
the possible exception of the Sadducees, therefore, all the varieties of
intertestamental personal eschatology appear to entail a dualism of some

---

17. Cooper, *Body, Soul, and Life Everlasting*, 37.

18. The Hebrew concepts of *nepeš*, *rûaḥ*, *bāsār*, *qereb*, and *lēb* all are used with physiological references. For example, the Hebrew word often glossed as "soul," *nepeš*, is used in
Psalm 105:18 to refer to the neck: "his neck was put in a collar of iron." Even *rûaḥ*, which is
glossed "spirit," refers to the "breath of life" or "a vital force, the power of life." Cooper, *Body,
Soul, and Life Everlasting*, 39–40.

19. Cooper, *Body, Soul, and Life Everlasting*, 43.

20. Moreover, a number of texts forbid the consultation of spirits (Deut 18:11; Lev 19:31;
20:6; Isa 8:19), including the narrative of Saul's consultation of Samuel and the medium of
En-dor in 1 Samuel 28.

21. See also Job 19:25-27; Ps 49:15; 16:10; 73:26; Ezek 37.

22. Cooper, *Body, Soul, and Life Everlasting*, 70.

23. It is somewhat surprising to me that Reformed theologians have not more thoroughly
developed this.

sort, a dualism often more pronounced than that associated with the Old Testament conception of Sheol."[24]

At this point in the argument, Cooper makes a key concession—at least for the sake of argument, echoing the development of the Reformed tradition: "[T]here is no simple way to move directly from Scripture to philosophical anthropology, psychology, biology, or sociology. The Bible is neither theoretically clear in its mode of expression nor is [sic] interested in addressing such philosophical issues as the number of substances of which human beings are composed."[25] However, Cooper is reluctant to say that the Bible "contains no philosophy." He suggests that it is "wiser to recognize a certain complexity of the question than to demand a simple yes or no." The Bible may express a certain view of human nature that "presupposes or implies positions on philosophical issues."[26] He admits that there is difficulty moving from the use of concepts straight to a psychology. Moreover, on the grounds of conceptual use alone, if there were no cases "which seem to imply dualism," then monism might be a reasonable guess "about the implicit anthropology of the New Testament."[27] However, the Bible's teaching on the intermediate state clearly implies dualism.

Cooper proposes a test where he looks at key biblical passages in light of three views: the traditional view of the intermediate state, the immediate resurrection view, and the extinction and re-creation view. Cooper again runs through the New Testament concepts of spirit and soul, citing key passages like Matthew 10:28 and Luke 24:37. Other non-Pauline texts assume either a future resurrection or continued existence after death (Luke 20:37-38; 23:42-43; John 5:28-29). Turning to Pauline texts, we have more evidence both for a future resurrection (1 Cor 15; 1 Thess 4:13-18) and for an intermediate or disembodied state (2 Cor 12:1-4; Phil 1:21-24).

On the grounds of this analysis, Cooper clarifies the dualism he is advocating: "We are constituted in such a way that we can survive 'coming

---

24. Cooper, *Body, Soul, and Life Everlasting*, 92.

25. Cooper, *Body, Soul, and Life Everlasting*, 96. He adds later, "we have endorsed the nontheoretical nature of the biblical message and denied that it teaches a philosophical anthropology. Instead we have insisted that Scripture presents a nontheoretical, 'commonsense' vision of the afterlife which nevertheless has ontological presuppositions and implications." Cooper, *Body, Soul, and Life Everlasting*, 180.

26. Cooper, *Body, Soul, and Life Everlasting*, 101.

27. Cooper, *Body, Soul, and Life Everlasting*, 104.

apart' at death, unnatural as this may be. This is all that I mean by 'dual-ism.'"[28] This does not entail Platonic, Cartesian, or even two-substance dualism. But it does require that personhood not be entirely bound up in the body, which dies. And again, this affirmation of dualism is only half the truth since the biblical picture is also holistic. "Only some combination like 'holistic dualism' will tell the whole story."[29]

Finally, Cooper addresses objections to his view. It is one thing to work out a comprehensive and coherent interpretation of a teaching of Scripture. It is another to assert the compatibility of that position with current sci-ence and philosophy. There may be a dilemma where the Christian is forced to act in bad faith either toward the Bible or science. However, Cooper asserts, "If it turns out that holistic dualism is compatible with contem-porary science and philosophy, the dilemma does not exist."[30] Cooper does not think that the correlation between brain states and mental events ren-ders dualism incompatible with science.[31] Correlation between mental events and brain activity has led scientists to conclude that brain states cause mental events, precluding an understanding of the human agent as a "self-activating entity."[32] In other words, we—understood as self-con-scious mental agents—are not the source of our own actions, since con-sciousness itself is causally predetermined by what happens in the brain. Consciousness just does reduce to brain activity. Cooper objects to this characterization for a couple of reasons.

First, he is dubious about the way mental states and brain activity are correlated, that is through localization. Localization refers to the theory that certain locations of the brain accomplish certain mental functions. Localization is key for correlation since it is possible to correlate brain and mental states only if we have some idea which brain activity corre-sponds to the mental state. Cooper demurs, "it is not even certain whether there is complete correlation between brain events and specific states of

28. Cooper, *Body, Soul, and Life Everlasting*, 163.

29. Cooper, *Body, Soul, and Life Everlasting*, 164.

30. Cooper, *Body, Soul, and Life Everlasting*, 205.

31. Cooper concedes "one of the severest blows to classical dualism," the "discovery that states of consciousness and mental events are heavily dependent on what goes on in the brain." Cooper, *Body, Soul, and Life Everlasting*, 205.

32. Cooper, *Body, Soul, and Life Everlasting*, 206.

consciousness. The brain seems to function like a vast corporation in which millions of specific events all connected in large networks are required for a single thought or feeling."[33] He additionally cites evidence from Donald MacKay that suggests that when a part of the brain is damaged, another part may take over to make a process possible, i.e., cross-modal reassignment.[34]

Second, Cooper points to the fact that brain states and mental states seem to interact, that we seem to observe a two-way correlation. Manipulation of the brain is coincidental with altered experience, and conversely, "if subjects initiate some mental act like thinking or imagining something, changes in brain activity can be discerned."[35] He adds that the "data are consistent with various philosophical theories," dualistic interactionism, dualistic parallelism (with no causal interaction), dual-aspect monism, or even idealism or materialism.[36] The point is that brain physiology underdetermines a philosophical point of view. However, he finds materialism to be the most troubling because it assumes that the brain system is closed; the two-way correlation is not two-way causality.

---

33. Cooper, *Body, Soul, and Life Everlasting*, 206.

34. Cooper, *Body, Soul, and Life Everlasting*, 206; Donald M. MacKay, *Brains, Machines and Persons* (Grand Rapids: Eerdmans, 1980), 33–34. The term "cross-modal reassignment" is from Jordan Grafman, "Conceptualizing functional neuroplasticity," *Journal of Communication Disorders* 33 no. 4 (August 2000): 345–56. Jeffrey Schwartz writes,

> As far as scientists can tell, then, a young brain can usually compensate for injury to a particular region by shifting the function of the damaged region to an unaffected region. ... Grafman offers the example of an adolescent boy whose brain had been injured years before in a freak childhood accident. His right parietal lobe, a structure that supports visual and spatial skills, suffered a lesion. Yet despite the injury, the boy developed normal visual and spatial skills. Oddly, however, he had great difficulty with math, which is normally a function of the left parietal lobe.

Jeffrey Schwartz, *The Mind and the Brain: Neuroplasticity and the Power of Mental Force* (New York: ReganBooks, 2002), 100. Brain localization is called into question by Joseph LeDoux. He makes the point that the visual cortex is not the location of vision, but rather that it is a necessary part of a complex system "that makes seeing possible." Joseph LeDoux, *The Emotional Brain: The Mysterious Underpinnings of Emotional Life* (New York: Simon & Schuster, 1996), 76.

35. Cooper, *Body, Soul, and Life Everlasting*, 207. Neuroscientist Jeffrey Schwartz is deeply invested in examining mental causation. See Jeffrey M. Schwartz, *Brain Lock* (New York: ReganBooks, 1996) and Jeffrey M. Schwartz, "A Role for Volition and Attention in the Generation of New Brain Circuitry: Toward A Neurobiology of Mental Force," *Journal of Consciousness Studies* 6, nos. 8–9 (1999): 115–42.

36. Cooper, *Body, Soul, and Life Everlasting*, 207.

Materialism leaves "no role for mysterious causality of the mind."[37] Cooper speculates that there may be some physical indeterminacy (e.g., subatomic particles) that allows the mental to influence brain events "without violating any law of physics."[38] This precludes a priori exclusion of dualism by materialism; dualism need not be inconsistent with physics. He concludes that a holistic-dualism "is not obviously incompatible with the findings of establishment science or with various contemporary approaches to philosophy."[39]

Finally, in his preface to his second edition, Cooper reinforces this conclusion that "there is no conceptual need to abandon a doctrinally required dualism in favor of monism." He notes that even "Nancey Murphy is candid about this. After surveying the advances in brain science she admits: 'it is still possible to claim that there is a substantial mind and that its operations are neatly correlated with brain events. ... It follows, then, that no amount of evidence from neuroscience can prove a physicalist view of the mental.'"[40]

I want to make a few observations about this survey. First, Cooper has given convincing evidence that some form of intermediate state is assumed and taught by Scripture, that this view fits best with dualism, and indeed, that it is difficult to square this with monism. He does not claim that substance dualism is the only way to accommodate the intermediate state, but doubts there is another way.[41] One possible exception that he cites is William Hasker's emergent dualism.[42] The difficulty for any physicalist

---

37. In other words, Cooper thinks that non-reductive materialism is impossible. Cooper, *Body, Soul, and Life Everlasting*, 208.

38. Cooper, *Body, Soul, and Life Everlasting*, 208.

39. Cooper, *Body, Soul, and Life Everlasting*, 230.

40. Cooper, *Body, Soul, and Life Everlasting*, xxvi, citing Nancey Murphy, "Non-Reductive Physicalism: Philosophical Issues," in *Whatever Happened to the Soul? Scientific and Theological Portraits of Human Nature*, ed. Warren Brown, Nancey Murphy, and H. Newton Malony (Minneapolis: Fortress, 1998), 139.

41. Cooper writes, "Perhaps there are physicalistic theories of human nature that are compatible with an intermediate mediate state. ... I do not claim that substance dualism is the only way to meet this condition. However, I do not seriously consider whether a materialist anthropology could meet it." Cooper, *Body, Soul, and Life Everlasting*, xxvii.

42. William Hasker, "The Case for Emergent Dualism," in *The Blackwell Companion to Substance Dualism*, ed. Jonathan J. Loose, Angus J. L. Menuge, and J. P. Moreland (Hoboken: Wiley, 2018), 61–72. Peter Clarke calls William Hasker's emergent dualism "a nontraditional form of substance dualism." Peter Clarke, "Neuroscience and the Soul – A Response to Malcolm Jeeves," *Science and Christian Belief* 21, no. 1 (2009): 61–64.

theory is that affirming an intermediate state is tantamount to being a dualist, since only for a dualist position is a person divisible from the body. Second, Cooper's response to brain science avoids implicit inconsistency by showing the following proposition to be unnecessary: there is no possible way to reconcile dualism with the determinacy of physics.[43] But he seems to fall short of being fully persuasive on this point. Is subatomic indeterminacy a convincing way to avoid this inconsistency?[44] Third, Cooper's final conclusion in this work is not a confident affirmation of two-substance dualism, but rather a defense of a dualism of some sort that would make the intermediate state possible. He writes, "My own philosophical position continues to waffle between substance dualism and the soul-matter holism of the Thomistic tradition."[45] In the second edition, he suggests that dualistic holism captures his view as well or better than holistic dualism, since this "might be more consistent with the biblical picture."[46]

---

43. Alvin Plantinga distinguishes explicit, formal, and implicit inconsistency as follows: (1) explicit, "a set of propositions is explicitly contradictory if one of the members is the denial or negation of another member;" (2) formal, "[a] set is one from whose members an explicit contradiction can be deduced by the laws of logic;" and (3) implicit, "a set S of propositions is implicitly contradictory if there is a necessary proposition p such that the result of adding p to S is a formally contradictory set." Alvin Plantinga, *God, Freedom, and Evil* (Grand Rapids: Eerdmans, 1974), 13, 14, 16.

44. Peter Clarke makes an intriguing argument. He calls Heisenbergian uncertainty "a kind of cloud cover in which small perturbations can occur 'unnoticed' by the watchful eye of nature's laws." He suggests that Heisenbergian uncertainty is simply too weak to influence synaptic firing. Clarke writes that the uncertainty in energy is "200,000 times too small to disrupt even a single Van der Waals interaction, the weakest of all the chemical bonds." Peter G. H. Clarke, "Determinism, Brain Function and Free Will," *Science and Christian Belief* 22, no. 2 (2010): 144. Michael Brownnut offers a rejoinder where he says, among other things, that Heisenbergian uncertainty is only a part of quantum uncertainty. Michael Brownnut, "Response to Peter Clarke on 'Determinism, Brain Function and Free Will,'" *Science & Christian Belief* 24, no. 1 (2012). Jeffrey Schwartz worked with Henry Stapp to produce an explanation for how this could work in *The Mind and the Brain* (2002). What makes the argument from Schwartz and Stapp prima facie compelling is that Schwartz is a clinical psychologist. His success as a clinician rests on his assumptions about the efficacy of mental effort. See Henry P. Stapp, "Quantum Interactive Dualism: An Alternative to Materialism," *Zygon* 41, no. 3 (September 2006): 599-616. The most fundamental point Schwartz and Stapp make seems to be the following: "Contemporary basic physical theory differs profoundly from classic physics on the important matter of how the consciousness of human agents enters into the structure of empirical phenomena." Jeffrey M. Schwartz, Henry P. Stapp, and Mario Beauregard, "Quantum physics in neuroscience and psychology: a neurophysical model of mind-brain interaction," *Philosophical Transactions of the Royal Society B* 360 (2005): 1309.

45. Cooper, *Body, Soul, and Life Everlasting*, xxvii.

46. Cooper says this way of putting it was suggested to him by John Kok, a philosopher at Dordt College. Cooper, *Body, Soul, and Life Everlasting*, xxvii.

THEOLOGICAL AND PHILOSOPHICAL
ARGUMENTS FOR MONISM

If John Cooper focuses his attention on biblical exegesis over neuroscience, then Nancey Murphy represents the inverse. Murphy's volume *Bodies and Souls, or Spirited Bodies?* comprises four chapters: the first covers biblical and theological material; the second focuses on scientific issues; and the third and fourth deal with the philosophical problems for the physicalist. In the first chapter, Murphy defends the view that "there is no such thing as the biblical view of human nature insofar as we are interested in a partitive account."[47] While the "Hebraic scriptures know nothing about body-soul dualism, it is surprisingly difficult to settle the issue of what the New Testament has to say."[48] Moreover, she argues that the Bible does not teach that human hope lies in an immortal soul, but in the resurrection.

Murphy directly addresses John Cooper's book only very briefly in her book. She suggests that there are problems with taking Old Testament and New Testament texts on Sheol at face value,[49] pointing to Joel Green's treatment of these texts. Murphy explains that for Green, paradise does not refer to an intermediate resting place of the dead, but rather the "final reward of the righteous."[50] Green contests Cooper's position on the grounds (1) that he "erroneously supposes that Jewish thought as it developed in [the intertestamental] period simply draws out the message present in embryonic form in the Hebrew Bible, and on this shaky foundation rests his assertion that these later Jewish texts provide us with faithful commentaries on Old Testament perspectives," and (2) that Cooper shows "insufficient nuance with regard to the nature and diversity of perspectives on death and the afterlife represented in the literature of Second Temple Judaism."[51]

---

47. Nancey Murphy, *Bodies and Souls, or Spirited Bodies?* (Cambridge: Cambridge University Press, 2006), 22.

48. Murphy, *Bodies and Souls,* 17.

49. Murphy, *Bodies and Souls,* 20.

50. Murphy, *Bodies and Souls,* 20.

51. Joel B. Green, "Eschatology and the Nature of Humans: A Reconsideration of Pertinent Biblical Evidence," *Science and Christian Belief* 14, no. 1 (April 2002): 41, 46. Cooper objects to Green's treatment generally: "In general, Green plays down the evidence for the intermediate state and dualism in Scripture instead of either refuting it or providing an alternative reading that is shown to be as comprehensive and coherent as the traditional view." Cooper, *Body, Soul, and Life Everlasting,* xxii.

However, Murphy merely reports this argument, thereby "showing the difficulty in determining what a New Testament author has in mind on this particular issue."[52] She finds it unlikely that Christians would need a far-reaching knowledge of intertestamental literature to understand a key aspect of biblical interpretation. She suggests, to the contrary, that the New Testament authors "are not intending to teach *anything* about humans' metaphysical composition."[53] She writes, "So I conclude that there is no such thing as *the* biblical view of human nature *insofar as we are interested in a partitive account* ... [so] contemporary Christians are free to choose among several options."[54]

So summarily dismissing biblical considerations, Murphy turns to theological considerations, especially the doctrine of God, Christology, and soteriology. Murphy's treatment is frustratingly terse here. Essentially Murphy questions the assumption that Christ must have a soul to be divine, pointing to James McClendon's survey of Christological options for dealing with a physicalist anthropology that "has been widely accepted among theologians for at least a half century."[55] Murphy offers no help for putting together a coherent view of Christology apart from pointing to an existing tension in Trinitarian thought between "those who emphasize the unity of God and those who emphasize the three-ness."[56] Both in this section and in those that follow, Murphy assumes the position she is supposed to be defending without offering much help in integrating it theologically. She admits she "can only be suggestive."[57]

Murphy closes with a helpful delineation of the problems of the "excessive inwardness of the Platonists."[58] She seems to be arguing that the correction of these problems is additional support for her own view.[59] This

---

52. Murphy, *Bodies and Souls*, 21.

53. Murphy, *Bodies and Souls*, 21.

54. Murphy, *Bodies and Souls*, 22. She goes on to say that only the radical dualism of Plato and Descartes are ruled out, not dualism per se.

55. Murphy, *Bodies and Souls*, 25; see James W. McClendon Jr., *Doctrine: Systematic Theology*, vol. 2 (Nashville: Abingdon, 1994), 250–79.

56. Murphy, *Bodies and Souls*, 25.

57. Murphy, *Bodies and Souls*, 27.

58. Murphy, *Bodies and Souls*, 37.

59. Murphy, *Bodies and Souls*, 35, "So the strongest point I can make here is to claim, as I did in the preceding section, that physicalism—along with an eschatological hope for resurrection

is a weak argument for two reasons. First, it is questionable that dualism, even of a Platonic sort, by itself entails Augustinian inwardness. Second, even if this were true, it is not obvious that Platonic dualism is the only alternative to physicalism.

If there is no such thing as the biblical view of human nature, then Christians are free to prioritize general revelation in considering the essential nature of humankind. Murphy tells a story of three major scientific influences on the soul: the replacement of Aristotelian physics by modern physics, the Darwinian revolution, and contemporary neuroscience. She suggests that "the developments in physics and neurosciences have both been as much *or more* significant in reshaping theories of human nature."[60] Whereas physics created a problem for the relation between body and soul by rejecting forms, neuroscience accounts for "all of the human capacities once attributed to the mind or soul ... [as] processes involving the brain, the rest of the nervous system and other bodily systems" (e.g., thinking, feeling, self-maintenance, growth, reproduction, etc).[61] She notes that vitalism is "the last gasp of the ancient and medieval idea of the soul as a life force."[62] Ultimately, she concludes, "Humans are not hybrids of matter and something else, they are purely physical organisms."[63]

Murphy is aware that with this claim comes a significant difficulty: How is it possible to avoid reductionism from a physicalist point of view? She addresses this problem in two steps, first arguing for top-down causation, and second contrasting machines with even the simplest biological organisms.[64] In the first case, Murphy distinguishes laws from boundary conditions. Contra Pierre Simon de Laplace, knowing the laws of nature and the state of the universe at one time is not sufficient for knowing future states. One must know also the conditions (structural and environmental) governing the transitions between states, the boundary conditions.[65]

---

of the body—leads more *naturally* to a concern for the physical world and its transformation than does dualism."

60. Murphy, *Bodies and Souls*, 40.

61. Murphy, *Bodies and Souls*, 56.

62. Murphy, *Bodies and Souls*, 57.

63. Murphy, *Bodies and Souls*, 69. This story of scientific explanations eclipsing theological speculations is compelling as a narrative.

64. Murphy, *Bodies and Souls*, 73.

65. Murphy, *Bodies and Souls*, 79.

Murphy thinks that this provides a way of thinking about top-down and bottom-up causation: "top-down determination of structural conditions is entirely compatible with the uninterrupted operation of lower level laws once those structures are in place."[66] The conditions exert downward causation on the effects, especially by selection.[67] Intriguingly, as an example of "downward causation by selection," she cites the "effect of the environment on a developing brain."[68] On a "neural Darwinism" account, the connections that "turned out to be useful" are reinforced, plasticity in turn giving rise to new structural conditions.[69]

To illustrate more concretely, Murphy gives the example of a jet operating on autopilot. Structural conditions like shape are important, as are environmental ones like headwinds. And the jet is also goal determined by the programming of the autopilot feature. While this is not a perfect example for free will since the jet is programmed by someone, it calls "attention to the fact that it is possible to design a system that uses information about its own states and about its environment in such a way as to alter its own behavior in pursuit of a goal. Once such systems have come into existence, new regularities, new laws of nature, come into existence with them."[70]

This takes Murphy to her second step, to demonstrate the spectrum of goal-orientation that exists among all living organisms, and how "complex organisms come to have the ability to modify their own goals."[71] This strategy is very effective in that it enables her to fix humankind firmly on a biological, goal-seeking spectrum with animals. The principle of parsimony suggests that if the soul is unnecessary for complex, even self-directed, goal pursuit in animals, and most theologians already think this, it is also likely the case for humans.

---

66. Murphy, *Bodies and Souls*, 80.

67. Murphy explains, "a larger system of causal factors can exert downward efficacy on lower-level entities by means of *selection*." She cites Donald Campbell's example, natural selection. Murphy, *Bodies and Souls*, 81.

68. Murphy, *Bodies and Souls*, 83.

69. Murphy, *Bodies and Souls*, 83–84.

70. Murphy, *Bodies and Souls*, 85.

71. Murphy, *Bodies and Souls*, 85. She writes, "All living organisms are intrinsically active and goal-directed, at least to the extent that they pursue the goals of survival and reproduction."

If top-down causality is intelligible, biologically speaking, the major task remaining for Murphy is to explain the higher-level principles that make human choices meaningfully free. Her analogy seems to force us to conclude that we are cleverly designed automatons. For Murphy, human freedom involves five cognitive abilities that humans uniquely possess: (1) "a concept of self"; (2) "the ability to run behavioral scenarios and predict the outcome of possible actions;" (3) "the capacity for self-transcendence"; (4) "sophisticated enough language to make a description of that which moves me to act [sic] the subject of evaluation"; and (5) "the ability to evaluate my prior reasons in light of the abstract concept of goodness as such."[72]

In her final chapter, Murphy addresses some philosophical challenges to her view: the problem of establishing the truth of physicalism, the problem of human distinctiveness, the problem of how God acts in the world, and the problem of personal identity. With regard to the first question, she admits that in spite of the successes of cognitive neuroscience, "science can never prove there is no soul, a soul whose capacities are simply well correlated with brain functions." But neither can philosophical arguments prove dualism true.[73] She suggests that a good way forward is to consider physicalism "as a central component of a variety of well confirmed scientific theories."[74] Physicalism is the hard core of a wildly successful scientific research program. To this, I merely add that this does very little to advance her argument, since other philosophical theories of the body and soul could equally well form the hard core of this scientific research

---

72. Murphy, *Bodies and Souls*, 97.

73. Murphy writes, "The important question for philosophy, then, is the source of linguistic resources, and whether those habitual or newly minted forms of language are congruent with the way things really are. This requires, in turn, that one ask whether the theories of, say, Plato or Aristotle are better supported than contemporary neuroscientific theories about the sources of our capacities for cognition, emotion, and all of the other faculties that earlier theorists had attributed to the soul or mind." Murphy, *Bodies and Souls*, 114–15. However, it might also be worth asking about the extent to which contemporary neuroscientists are attempting to offer philosophical or psychological theories about human capacities. Surely, philosophy of any sort needs to be accountable to reality, but science differs formally from philosophy. There are some neuroscientists who are attempting to do philosophy, e.g., Jesse Prinz and Daniel Dennett, but it is not obvious that they are better at philosophy than trained philosophers are.

74. Murphy, *Bodies and Souls*, 111.

program. Moreover, she seems to be confusing the jurisdictions of scientific and philosophical work.

Murphy is more helpful in addressing the next two problems, that of human distinctiveness and that of the possibility of divine intervention in the natural world. With regard to human distinctiveness, she notes that while chimpanzees do seem to have something like self-awareness, they do not have a "symbolic self-concept." She adds, "Animals can be angry, but cannot experience righteous indignation."[75] I might add that the self-concept human beings possess is not merely symbolic, but narrative shaped.[76] With regard to divine intervention in the natural world, Murphy again emphasizes that not all causation is bottom-up and that it is possible to integrate divine action and natural causation. The two strategies for doing this are by asserting "that God works solely in a top-down manner," as Arthur Peacocke claims, or by giving an account of God's action "by means of action at the quantum level."[77] Murphy writes, "It is possible from a theistic perspective to interpret current physics as saying that the natural world is intrinsically incomplete and open to divine action at its most basic level."[78]

Finally, Murphy gives an account of identity which denies that the "body *qua* material" constitutes identity, "but rather the higher capacities that it enables: consciousness and memory, moral character, interpersonal relations, and, especially, relationship with God."[79] This approach is similar to the relational anthropology cited earlier. Murphy speaks of identity in exclusive terms, not what but who and why.

75. Murphy, *Bodies and Souls*, 118. Cf. Endel Tulving, "Episodic Memory and Autonoesis: Uniquely Human?" in *The Missing Link in Cognition: Origins of Self-Reflective Consciousness*, ed. Herbert S. Terrace and Janet Metcalfe (New York: Oxford University Press, 2005), 3–56.

76. See Paul Ricoeur's distinction between *idem* (self-sameness) and *ipse* (self-constancy). Paul Ricoeur, *Oneself as Another* (Chicago: University of Chicago Press, 1992).

77. Murphy, *Bodies and Souls*, 130–31; summarizing Arthur Peacocke, "God's Interaction with the World: The Implications of Deterministic 'Chaos' and of Interconnected and Interdependent Complexity," in *Chaos and Complexity: Scientific Perspectives on Divine Action*, ed. Robert J. Russell, Nancey Murphy, and Arthur Peacocke (Vatican City State and Berkeley, CA: Vatican Observatory and Center for Theology and the Natural Sciences, 1995), 263–88.

78. Murphy, *Bodies and Souls*, 131.

79. Murphy, *Bodies and Souls*, 132.

EVALUATION

While this defense is impressive, there is still much that is deeply mysterious here. First, if Murphy wants to explain mental causation by means of "downward causation by selection," then the solution has done very little to untangle the problem.[80] Murphy seems to be suggesting that we need to recognize more than one chain of efficient causes, those leading up to some effect, such as flying in the autopilot analogy, and those leading up to the conditions under which the effect comes to be, such as building the plane.[81] Yet no matter how many chains of efficient causes are present, it is still difficult to see how mental causation transcends efficient causality in a way that goes beyond quasi-teleology. For genuine teleology there must be some agent acting according to teleological ends, not merely top-down efficient causes. There would need to be genuine mental causation. Here it is striking how reliant Murphy's account is on the quasi-teleological assumption of Darwinism. When providing explanation for why adaptations occur, the explanation is teleological; these are for survival. However, Darwinism strictly relies on efficient causes, since selection occurs by stochastic (or random) processes within populations, not individual organisms. Any individual adaptation is random but looks teleological post facto when it proves adaptive to a surviving set of organisms. On this view, it is hard to make sense either of "neural Darwinism" or of real teleological mental causation.

So metaphysically, we are faced with some real problems if Murphy wants to avoid materialistic determinism through emergent conditions. The explanatory principles may be different (lower vs. higher), but they are still efficient causes. A person is still not self-directed, but only apparently self-directed. The theological issue is this: if real freedom is not possible given materialist determinism, then moral agency is only apparent. Murphy marks out three forms of freedom: (1) liberty of spontaneity;

---

80. See Jaegwon Kim, *Essays in the Metaphysics of Mind* (Oxford: Oxford University Press, 2010); William Hasker, "Nonreductive Physicalism: A Constitutional Response," in *In Search of the Soul: Four Views of the Mind-body Problem*, ed. Joel B. Green and Stuart L. Palmer (Downers Grove, IL: InterVarsity, 2005), 88–89; Roger Philip Abbott, *Sit on Our Hands, or Stand on Our Feet? Exploring a Practical Theology of Major Incident Response for the Evangelical Catholic Christian Community in the UK* (Eugene, OR: Wipf & Stock, 2013), 141.

81. Murphy puts it this way, "we need to think of *two* series of events: those leading up to the triggering of the effect and also those leading up to the condition under which the triggering cause is able to cause the effect." Murphy, *Bodies and Souls*, 81, emphasis original.

(2) free will as autonomy (acting for a reason); and (3) libertarian or incompatibilistic freedom.[82] She argues that her account of freedom satisfies the criteria for the first two types. I am suggesting that it does not satisfy even type (2), since someone is only apparently acting teleologically.

The key issues are these: In what sense is physicalist compatibilist freedom free? And does this freedom account for how the Bible speaks of persons? It makes sense to suggest that more complex organisms possess more complex biological feedback loops to navigate their environment in smarter and more adaptive ways. It might also make sense to suggest that the highest feedback loops enable language, philosophy, literature, Jerry Seinfeld, nuclear warfare, and R. Mutt's "Fountain." In these cases, these people are intending to do things at least in the sense that their intentions seem to precede and often follow as explanations of their actions. What is not clear is that these people qualify as moral agents. It would seem that a basic requirement of being a moral agent is that people are the source of their own actions—never mind, for now, the ability to do otherwise. James Stump makes a similar critique of Murphy's position by targeting the issue of supervenience. Supervenience is very difficult to define in a way that makes downward causation anything but illusory.[83] Moreover,

---

82. Murphy, *Bodies and Souls*, 104–5.

83. Stump suggests that the concepts of levels of reality, supervenience, emergence, and downward causation, upon which this theory depends, are incoherent. In the case of supervenience, he writes, "A-properties strongly supervene on B-properties if and only if things that are alike in B-properties must be alike in A-properties ... but now there is something about the B-properties which necessarily gives rise to A-properties." But just what is this relation? Stump argues that since these theorists are materialists, there must be some "materialistically acceptable explanation of how A-properties strongly supervene on B-properties; it must be taken as a brute fact." However, the supervenience relationship between the brain and mind is anything but obviously materialistically respectable. The relation must either just be physical (as with reductive supervenience) or, as Stump explains, explained by some other facts that either also supervene on B-properties (causing a regress) or are further B-properties (not explaining the relation).

But there remains another problem: even though the higher level depends on the lower (it supervenes), it is "able to exercise causal influence back down on those lower levels" (supervenience becomes emergence). The problem here is that if A-properties depend on B-properties, then a change in A-properties depends on a change in B-properties making downward causation illusory. Stump writes,

> For instance, say that I am going to make a decision either to raise my right hand or my left hand. Let us say that mental state R is the decision to raise my right hand, and mental state L is the decision to raise my left hand. Then according to the thesis of downward causation, R has a different effect on the lower level electrical circuitry which causes arms to move about than does L. It is at the higher level of

frequently cited examples that make supervenience seem obvious, like an
image supervening on pixels, often smuggle in external mental causation;
the mind makes the image. Stump writes, "Murphy is left with baldly
asserting that the mental-level descriptions as explanations for human
behavior are compatible with the causal determinism which exists at the
neuronal level and that free will probably comes somehow from 'the multiple interacting layers of information processing in the brain.' This does
not resolve the problem."[84]

Moreover, physicalist determinism is morally repugnant to Christian
theology in ways that other so-called determinisms are not. This sort of
determinism brings an immediate threat to human moral agency. We can see
this by evaluating the determining mechanism of the types of determinism
that are common among theologians. There are at least three: (1) determinism arising from the knowledge of God; (2) determinism arising from the
will of God; and (3) determinism from moral turpitude or depravity. In the
first and second case, it is not clear how God's knowledge or God's willing of
an action would make it psychologically determined. Contemporary theologians typically do not appeal to physicalist determinism as the determining
mechanism for how God's will makes something so. Typically, the determining mechanism is itself mysterious. In the third case, moral determinism, considered separately from theological or materialistic determinism,
seems to be a soft sort. It is not the sort of psychological determinism that
entails that nothing else could have happened. If we consider any particular

---

mental properties that the decision is made. And the causal powers of the mental
realm really have an effect on the physical. But according to the supervenience
theory, there must have been a difference in the lower level neuronal properties
in order for R to emerge rather than L at my moment of decision. Then is it not the
case that it is the difference in neuronal properties that is ultimately responsible
for which arm gets raised?

Mental causation is illusory, as is genuine mental interaction, leaving no psychological
difference between Murphy's view and reductive epiphenomalism. The rigidity of the presumed supervenience relation precludes Murphy from appealing to levels as an explanation
of downward mental causation. Stump relies on Jaegwon Kim's description of strong supervenience. James B. Stump, "Non-Reductive Physicalism – A Dissenting Voice," *Christian Scholar's
Review* 36, no. 1 (Fall 2006): 68–72; Jaegwon Kim, "Supervenience, Emergence, Realization,
Reduction," in *Oxford Handbook of Metaphysics*, ed. Michael J. Loux and Dean W. Zimmerman
(Oxford: Oxford University Press, 2010).

84. Stump, "Non-Reductive Physicalism," 72; Murphy, "Nonreductive Physicalism:
Philosophical Issues," 139.

choice, Augustinian orthodoxy merely requires that apart from grace, it cannot attain superlative moral purity, especially of the type that would achieve merit before God. But if a choice always goes wrong, there is at least more than one way to go wrong. Given the choice between A (good) and B (evil), we can at least choose B_1, B_2, or B_3, etc. So, moral determinism of the sort required for Augustinian orthodoxy need not affirm that nothing else could have happened, but just that nothing merit worthy or entirely morally pure could have happened. Calvin remarks that what he objects to is the idea that the will "has both good and evil within its power," by which he means "that it is put within our power whether or not to obey the commandments, to refrain from evil and to do good."[85]

Physicalist determinism is of a much stronger type than depravity, or what I have called determinism of moral turpitude. With physicalist determinism, nothing else could have happened because the origin of the act derives ultimately from a set of efficient causes, not from an agent acting for teleological reasons. This is a sort of determinism that Calvin strongly denied. Calvin would identify these types of lower material laws as coercion or an external impulse, since to be internal in Calvin's sense is to be psychologically internal. So in *The Bondage and Liberation of the Will*, he writes, "Therefore we describe [as coerced] the will which does not incline this way or that of its own accord or by an internal movement of decision, but is forcibly driven by an external impulse."[86] Calvin positively affirms freedom from psychologically external coercion: "I both acknowledge and consistently maintain that choice is free, and I hold anyone who thinks

---

85. Calvin, *Bondage and Liberation of the Will*, ed. A. N. S. Lane, trans. G. I. Davies (Grand Rapids: Baker Academic, 1996), 1.246. It may be objected that Reformed moral determinism (total depravity) is a stronger type than that of Augustinian orthodoxy, of a type which requires that the only available inclination of the will is an evil inclination, thereby limiting choice more severely from within the agent's psychology. Yet this is precisely the inconsistency that Dewey Hoitenga objects to in *John Calvin and the Will: A Critique and Corrective* (Grand Rapids: Baker, 1997). Calvin himself affirms Augustinian orthodoxy on this point, but then incautiously pushes his assertions about the will beyond it. On Hoitenga's reading, Calvin claims the will is merely corrupted, but inconsistently portrays it as destroyed, since it can only incline toward evil. And again, if—as Reformed theologians often admit—common grace restrains the will from inclining and choosing the worst possible end, then it must incline and choose some gradation of goodness (as noted in Chapter 4). If the will is free to choose a lesser evil, then again Reformed moral determinism is not of the sort that nothing else could have happened.

86. Calvin, *Bondage and Liberation of the Will*, 2.279–80. See also 3.293–94, 302–3, 310–13, 315–19; 4.329, 340; 5.357–58.

otherwise to be a heretic."[87] The point is that the person is acting as an agent. At the very least, Reformed theologians want to affirm that the soul is the source of its acts.

Second, there is an interesting lack of parallelism between Murphy's integrated and quantum level account of divine action in the world and her rejection of the soul. My point is this: What does not seem to bother her about God's relation to and intervention in the world seems to bother her about proposals for a soul. It seems reasonable to posit atheism as the hard core of a materialistic, scientific paradigm that is doing rather well. Why should "spooky stuff" seem implausible in human nature but not with respect to the divine nature?[88] Murphy has suggested that God may interact with the world at a quantum level. Why not the human soul?[89]

Third, and finally, as a general observation about Murphy's method, she is not obviously situating her theological reasoning within the larger history of the Spirit's teaching ministry within the church (Isa 40:13–14; John 16:13–15; Rom 11:33; 1 Cor 2:10–11).[90] This inattention to the Triune God's revealing and instructing activity in the church is especially apparent when Murphy argues for physicalism on the grounds that it is the hard core of a successful scientific research program. Surely, one of the marks of a good theory is comprehensiveness, that it accounts for all the relevant data. A theological theory that does not give pride of place to the revealing and teaching activity of the triune God seems presumptive. This is not to suggest that a theologian is slavishly subject to tradition, but rather that the burden of proof is shifted to innovators. Moreover, her claim that the tradition is ambiguous is quite misleading. This book is written at least

---

87. Calvin, *Bondage and Liberation of the Will*, 2.279.

88. I am taking the terminology from Patricia Smith Churchland as cited by Nancey Murphy in "I Cerebrate Myself: Is there a little man inside your brain?," *Books and Culture: A Christian Review* 5, no. 1 (January–February 1999): 24–26, http://www.booksandculture.com/articles/1999/janfeb/9b1024.html; Patricia Smith Churchland, "Can Neurobiology Teach Us Anything about Consciousness?" in *The Nature of Consciousness: Philosophical Debates*, ed. Ned Block, Owen Flanagan, and Güven Güzeldere (Cambridge, MA: MIT Press, 1997), 127.

89. This is not the only theological problem Murphy faces. David Siemens claims that "nonreductive physicalism apparently makes the Incarnation impossible." He explains, "if the human soul is only a function of the physical body, we cannot join it to the nonphysical divine substance." David F. Siemens Jr., "Neuroscience, Theology, and Unintended Consequences," *Perspectives on Science and Christian Faith* 57, no. 3 (September 2005): 189.

90. Michael Allen and Scott Swain, *Reformed Catholicity: The Promise of Retrieval for Theology and Biblical Interpretation* (Grand Rapids: Baker Academic, 2015), 22–33.

partly to argue for paying attention to neuroscience; yet to begin an argument with a cursory dismissal of the biblical testimony on any topic, as Murphy does by stating, "there is no such thing as the biblical view," is theologically reckless.[91]

Positively speaking, Murphy makes some real contributions. First, she warns us to take materialist reductionism as a real threat. Second, Murphy is sensitive to the complexity of the relation of human beings to animals. Her delineation of the differences is quite helpful.[92] Third, Murphy rightly criticizes the all or nothing approach to human free will. She is right to point out that there are gradations of freedom. And fourth, Murphy is making a serious attempt to interact with the ways scientists encounter reality through empirical research. Yet in light of my concerns with Murphy's work, we need to ask if it is possible to frame an account of the body and soul that takes seriously both the Bible and the tradition of biblical and theological reasoning.

THOMISTIC DUALISM

There are a few scholars who are advocating a Thomistic view of the body and soul.[93] J. P. Moreland defends what he calls a Thomistic-like view. He rejects Murphy's claims that neither tradition nor the biblical witness manifests a consensus on the question of dualism. With regard to tradition, Moreland replies, "For nineteen and a half centuries, everyone interpreted

---

91. Murphy, *Bodies and Souls*, 22.

92. Recall that Thomas Aquinas posited plant and animal souls because the soul did not merely explain the mind. Murphy is right to point out the continuity between human beings and animals.

93. J. P. Moreland, "A Critique of and Alternative to Nancey Murphy's Christian Physicalism," *European Journal for Philosophy of Religion* 8, no. 2 (2016): 107–28; J. P. Moreland, "In Defense of a Thomistic-like Dualism," in *The Blackwell Companion to Substance Dualism* (Oxford: Blackwell, 2018), 102–22; J. P. Moreland, "Tweaking Dallas Willard's Ontology of the Human Person," *Journal of Spiritual Formation & Soul Care* 8, no. 2 (2015): 187–202; Rickabaugh, "Responding to N. T. Wright," 1–20; Brandon Rickabaugh, "A Combination Problem for Emergent Dualism and a Neo-Aristotelian Solution," paper presented at 2017 Dominican Colloquium in Berkeley: Person, Soul and Consciousness, Dominican School of Philosophy and Theology, July 2017; C. Stephen Evans and Brandon Rickabaugh, "What Does It Mean to Be a Bodily Soul?" *Philosophia Christi* 17, no. 2 (2015): 315–30; C. Stephen Evans and Brandon Rickabaugh, "Neuroscience, Spiritual Formation, and Bodily Souls: A Critique of Christian Physicalism," in *Christian Physicalism? Philosophical and Theological Criticisms*, ed. R. Keith Loftin and Joshua R. Farris (Lanham, MD: Lexington, 2017).

the Christian faith to entail dualism."[94] With regard to Scripture, he notes the lower view of Scripture among theological liberals and counters, "where there is ambiguity that does not result from revisionist eisegesis, it is due to confusions about dualism on the part of biblical and theological scholars."[95] Moreland cites N. T. Wright's paper "Mind, Spirit, Soul and Body: All for One and One for All Reflections on Paul's Anthropology in His Complex Contexts" as an example.[96] Brandon Rickabaugh agrees, suggesting that what Wright seems to be attacking is extreme anthropological dualism (EAD). Rickabaugh defines EAD as follows: "(i) the soul is special to God, but the body isn't, (ii) the afterlife is valuable, but this life is not, and (iii) the soul is autonomously immortal."[97] In fact, Wright's own view of the intermediate state seems to demand a view that is virtually indistinguishable from that of Moreland or Rickabaugh. Moreland makes this point explicitly: "in the same paper he [Wright] affirms a dualist reading of II Corinthians 5:1–10, Acts 23:6–9 and II Corinthians 12:2–4 in keeping with his thesis that the Jews of Jesus' day, and the New Testament, affirm life after death: death, followed by a disembodied intermediate state followed by a general resurrection."[98]

Moreover, Moreland does not think that dualism arises either as an explanation for the biologically unexplained, nor from a syncretistic borrowing from Greek philosophy. He sees dualism as common sense to most of humankind, even properly basic,[99] as well as a straightforward reading of biblical texts like Matthew 22:23–33, Acts 23:6–9, and 2 Corinthians 12:2–4. Moreland suggests, "[T]he Fathers turned to Greek philosophy to provide tools to flesh out what they already saw in scripture independently of and prior to their employment of Greek philosophy."[100]

So far, Moreland echoes Cooper's insistence that dualism is the most natural reading of the biblical text. But how does it stack up philosophically?

---

94. Moreland, "A Critique," 109.

95. Moreland, "A Critique," 109.

96. Moreland, "A Critique," 109; N. T. Wright, "Mind, Spirit, Soul and Body: All for One and One for All Reflections on Paul's Anthropology in His Complex Contexts," paper presented to the Society of Christian Philosophers: Regional Meeting, Fordham University, March 18, 2011.

97. Rickabaugh, "Responding to N. T. Wright," 9.

98. Moreland, "A Critique," 109.

99. Moreland, "A Critique," 114.

100. Moreland, "A Critique," 109.

Moreland also draws attention to Murphy's concession that science cannot prove there is no soul.[101] He argues that Murphy fails to see that her concession implies that the theories are "empirically equivalent," a point he eagerly wants to affirm.[102] If Murphy wants a psychology that is genuinely holistic, Moreland feels he can provide her one with his Thomistic-like dualism. C. Stephen Evans agrees, asking, "What, exactly, is it about these findings [of neuroscience] that are supposed to create problems for dualism?"[103]

It might be supposed that, given empirical equivalence, theoretical simplicity would decide for physicalism. But are the theories equivalent? Moreland sees seven areas of explanatory advantage that his dualistic view has over physicalism: synchronic unity of consciousness, diachronic unity of the human person, free will, ontological grounding of kind, unity of kinds, the development of an organism, and near-death experiences. I will focus on just three of these.

First, Moreland claims that the binding problem is in principle unsolvable for the physicalist. The binding problem is as follows:

> Objects have different features such as color, shape, sound, and smell. Some, such as color and sound, are represented separately from the instant they hit our sensory receptors. Other features, such as color and shape, are initially encoded together but subsequently analyzed by separate areas of the brain. Despite this separation, in perception the brain must represent which features belong to the same object. This is the binding problem.[104]

If no single part of the brain is responsible for consciousness, "There is literally nothing that is aware of the state as a whole, nothing to serve as unifier for the state and, a fortiori, for synchronic consciousness in general."[105] An appeal to mind makes the problem more mysterious. Moreland

---

101. Murphy, *Bodies and Souls*, 112.

102. Moreland, "A Critique," 111.

103. C. Stephen Evans, "Separable Souls: Dualism, Selfhood, and the Possibility of Life After Death," *Christian Scholar's Review* 34 (2005): 333–34.

104. Alex O. Holcombe, "Binding Problem," in *The Sage Encyclopedia of Perception*, ed. E. Bruce Goldstein (Thousand Oaks, CA: Sage, 2010), 205. Holcombe also discusses the problem of temporal binding.

105. Moreland, "A Critique," 120.

is likewise unimpressed by an appeal to emergent properties, suggesting that this is "not a solution, but a name for the problem to be solved"; we have "magic without a Magician."[106] By contrast, Moreland explains the dualistic view:

> Various arguments solve the causal pairing problem, but in my view, the most effective finds a connection between soul/body or mind/brain more primitive than causation which grounds the latter. Such a connection is at the very heart of my Thomistic-like dualism. The soul animates, unifies, forms, informs and is holenmerically present to its body. My mind and brain, then, causally interact with and only with each other, because my mind is a faculty of my soul, my brain is an inseparable part of my body, and my soul relates to my body in the ways just specified.[107]

Second, dualism has an advantage in explaining how human persons maintain diachronic identity. For a physicalist, the person is never more than a "mereological aggregate," or "a particular whole that is constituted by (at least) separable parts and external relation-instances between and among those separable parts."[108] Murphy's suggestion that identity is bound up in memory, consciousness, moral character, and relationships is merely "a way of taking the object to be the same." It does not really ground identity.[109]

Finally, dualism has an explanatory advantage with respect to real moral agency, the self-apparent fact that human beings are the source of their own choices via mental causation. Moreland objects that Murphy's position "turns human agents into smart bombs, equipped with self-directed feedback and self monitoring systems that enable a sort of reasons-responsive guidance control."[110] Moreland writes, "While Murphy's views may allow her to avoid biological determinism, they do not permit an avoidance of physical determinism," since in her view a person's actions

---

106. Moreland, "In Defense of a Thomistic-like Dualism," 23.

107. Moreland, "In Defense of a Thomistic-like Dualism," 23.

108. Moreland, "A Critique," 121.

109. Moreland, "A Critique," 123.

110. Moreland, "A Critique," 125.

are determined by "overall physical structure and environmental inputs" (top-down conditions).[111]

So, what is Thomistic-like dualism? Moreland also refers to it by the name organicism.[112] This theory is basically Aristotelian hylomorphism (form and matter) with a late medieval overlay. Moreland describes the soul as a "thin particular," the exemplification of an essence that "sub-stands" its accidental features.[113] The soul is "a simple (containing no separable parts), spatially unextended substance that contains the capacities for consciousness and for animating, enlivening, and developing teleologically its body."[114] It is mereologically complex. The soul is "holenmerically present throughout the organism's body."[115] This is precisely the sort of dualism that is well correlated, which Murphy seems to think is empirically equivalent with respect to neuroscience.

Besides being the formal or essential cause of the body, Moreland adds that the soul is also "an internal efficient first-moving cause of the development and structure of the body" and "the teleological guide for that development and structure."[116] The physical constituents of protein synthesis (DNA, RNA, ribosome, helicase, polymerase, etc.) are merely tools (instrumental causes) for the biological powers or functions of the soul.[117] These are like the materials in constructing a house, patterns that stabilize but do not generate the order. Moreland cites Richard Lewontin, saying, "DNA is a dead molecule, among the most nonreactive, chemically inert molecules in the living world."[118] DNA transcription and translation require the "coordinated activity of numerous complex molecules."[119]

---

111. Moreland, "A Critique," 125.

112. Moreland, "In Defense of a Thomistic-like Dualism," 7.

113. Moreland, "In Defense of a Thomistic-like Dualism," 4. See also Robert Pasnau, *Metaphysical Themes, 1274–1671* (Oxford: Clarendon, 2011), 99–134.

114. Moreland, "Tweaking Dallas Willard's Ontology," 198.

115. Moreland, "In Defense of a Thomistic-like Dualism," 5.

116. Moreland, "In Defense of a Thomistic-like Dualism," 7.

117. Moreland, "In Defense of a Thomistic-like Dualism," 7. The difference between this instrumental language and that of the Buridan consensus from Chapter 3 is that here the soul inheres in the whole body. Instrumental language refers not to organs, but to the most basic level of materiality.

118. Richard Lewontin, "The Dream of the Human Genome," *New York Review of Books* 39, no. 10 (May 28, 1992): 31–40; cited in Moreland, "In Defense of a Thomistic-like Dualism," 11.

119. Moreland, "In Defense of a Thomistic-like Dualism," 11.

In this way, the body is a mode of the soul, and the mind is a faculty of the soul; as such, they can causally interact. The soul-body connection is more primitive than the mind/brain connection.[120] Since the mind is a faculty of the soul, and since the whole body has a "soulish aspect,"[121] it is not surprising that there would be conscious aspects throughout the body by the instrumentality of the nervous systems. Moreover, as the body is a mode of the soul, so the body is crucial to conscious experience. As Moreland succinctly states it, "the body qua soul contains the conscious state."[122] So, for example, when one's mirror neurons suffer damage, we should not be surprised that empathetic feelings are altered, since "a feeling of empathy is an irreducible state of consciousness in the soul whose obtaining depends (while embodied) on the firing of mirror neurons."[123] Just as a CD, strictly speaking, contains no music but grooves (or bumps) that play with "the right retrieval system," so also the body is a physical structure that qualifies agency. It does not literally store conscious memories, only the grooves by which memories are retrieved, since the conscious properties belong to the soul.[124]

CONCLUSION

Moreland's proposal is promising for offering a dualism that coheres with the biblical record and that offers empirical equivalency with the data of neuroscience. Moreland helps to bridge the impasse between Cooper and Murphy in a way that does not succumb to physicalist determinism. I have been advocating holism, but in this chapter clarify that the holism is a dualistic holism. On the one hand, holism takes seriously the way the body qualifies agency (bottom-up); on the other, dualism takes seriously the way the symbolic mind actively governs agency (top-down politically). Moreland's brand of dualistic holism, a term which Cooper endorses, is a better theory than Murphy's because it is more comprehensive and takes moral agency seriously. If there were no need to account for consciousness, identity, especially after death, and free will, then physicalism might be

---

120. Moreland, "In Defense of a Thomistic-like Dualism," 23.
121. Moreland, "In Defense of a Thomistic-like Dualism," 11.
122. Moreland, "Tweaking Dallas Willard's Ontology," 201.
123. Moreland, "Tweaking Dallas Willard's Ontology," 201.
124. Moreland, "Tweaking Dallas Willard's Ontology," 201–2.

an equivalent theory. But especially since the entire narrative of Scripture, and nearly all moral discourse, assumes that human beings are at least the source of their own actions and will be morally responsible after death, then I prefer Moreland's dualistic holism.

It might be objected that Moreland's organicism is just a return to vitalism, which has been thoroughly rejected by scientists. But it is worth recognizing that vitalism has also been rejected for philosophical, not strictly scientific, reasons. Dennett has claimed that if one argument "for the irreducibility of consciousness were to succeed, [then] an analogous argument would establish the truth of vitalism."[125] Moreover, philosopher Brian Jonathan Garrett argues that this analogy succeeds. Garrett suggests that the hard problem of consciousness arises from the fact that it seems to require an explanation that goes beyond the physical. He points out that the vitalist controversy was a controversy because there was an analogous "hard problem," namely, why life from movement?[126] Garrett suggests that if this question needed no answer, perhaps consciousness needs no answer either. Obviously, I want to flip the argument and suggest that questions about the nature of life, consciousness, identity, and freedom still do need an answer. We do not make them disappear by pointing out that most scientists have treated them as easy problems.

Finally, Moreland's Thomistic-like dualism is able to integrate the two most significant contributions Murphy makes to this discussion. First, Moreland's theory takes the way that our bodies qualify our human agency seriously. A Thomist-like, organicist account of the soul, where the soul inheres in the body holistically, enables something like empirical equivalence with physicalist theories. We are not left searching for how soul and body causally relate; the soul just is the substantial form of the body. And by implication, we need not equate the soul only with the conscious, reflective thought. The soul enables even bodily awareness. And it is precisely this

---

125. Daniel Dennett, "Facing Backwards on the Problem of Consciousness". This way of summarizing Dennett's claim is from Brian Jonathan Garrett, "What the History of Vitalism Teaches Us About Consciousness and the 'Hard Problem,'" *Philosophy and Phenomenological Research* 72, no. 3 (May 2006): 576.

126. Garrett cites Nehemiah Grew (1641–1712) and summarizes in more contemporary terms, saying that Grew found it difficult to see how apart from a vital principle that "an organized, subtilized, moving body is anything more than a puppet ... that is, a lifeless 'zombie.'" Garrett, "What the History of Vitalism Teaches," 583.

awareness at a lower register that contributes to the conscious experience of inner conflict by way of tiered psychology. The psychological relation that matters is the top-down and bottom-up reciprocity of what people colloquially call mind and body, considered as psychological principles. In Chapter 8, I will suggest that what we call mind and body maps roughly on what Aquinas calls rational and sensitive faculties and on what I will call symbolic conscious awareness and adaptive unconscious.

Second, Murphy has clarified freedom by clarifying the relation between humankind and animals. There exists a gradation of complexity between the mental capacities of humankind and the lowest rung of the animal kingdom and a corresponding gradation of freedom. Apes are free to do things bacteria are not. However, true moral freedom, choice arising from self-determination, requires thought, especially symbolic self-awareness. Murphy has helpfully suggested that this means at least that human beings have a self-concept, to which I only add that this is narratival. This gradation suggests that human beings are not differentiated from animals by possessing a soul, but by their capacities. Moreland heartily agrees because, along with Aquinas, he affirms that all living organisms are ensouled, the soul differing between species.[127] For most of the Christian tradition, it was assumed that the form or soul gave living things their unique self-sustaining appetite.[128] The difference between human beings and animals is still what the medievals said it was, that human beings are rational.[129] Human persons often experience emotional responses to narratival downturns in their self-concept. Likewise, our freedom differs from

---

127. Personal email from J. P. Moreland, December 6, 2017.

128. Jaak Panksepp points out that higher consciousness is always based on a certain sort of "action-readiness" within the lower systems. The simplest organisms have drives for survival which Panksepp calls simple ego-type life form or SELF. Jaak Panksepp, "The Neuro-Evolutionary Cusp Between Emotions and Cognitions: Implications for Understanding Consciousness and the Emergence of a Unified Mind Science," *Evolution and Cognition* 7, no. 2 (2001): 153.

129. I do not say that this is the only difference or that being rational is the *imago Dei*, just that, psychologically speaking, this is a significant difference. It seems reasonable to suggest that man differs from animals, with which he shares a soul, by *possessing reason* (God speaks to man), and from computers, with which he shares language, by *possessing a soul*, the living and active power for self-determination through the will. Selmer Bringsjord argues that cognitive engineers will never build persons on the grounds that persons are not automatons. Selmer Bringsjord, *What Robots Can and Can't Be*, Studies in Cognitive Systems (Dordrecht: Springer, 1992).

animals along these same lines. Language enables abstract and self-directed conscious intentionality for framing new possibilities not just for
action, but for narrative self-concept. Animals may desire and plan, but
they seem not to be able to plan their desires. In other words, human beings
are free in the sense that we are self-reflectively aware of what we are and
can fashion ourselves otherwise, at least to some extent. Theologically
speaking, as God speaks, so human beings listen and respond. What sets
us apart is precisely that we are rationally communicative in response to
his initiation. Emotionally speaking, the internal dialogue between our
higher and lower processes is differentiated by the interplay between the
tacit and explicit elements of human consciousness. We can say no to at
least some of our impulses.

The next chapter will provide a biblical theological account of agency
in three vignettes. I will argue that a biblical account of agency assumes
a sort of dialogical relationship between the linguistically oriented mind
of a human being and the experientially oriented body (as psychological principles), which are governed by the speech of God, especially his
commands meant to bring about flourishing. The chapter will proceed as
follows: (1) embodied, disobedient, and cursed agency in the creation and
fall narrative (Gen 1–3); (2) embodied faithfulness in Gethsemane (Matt
26:1–46); and (3) the application of Christ's faithfulness for human embodiment in Christ and by the Spirit (Rom 5:12–8:27; 12:1–21).

7
—

BOOK OF SCRIPTURE: THE BODY IN BIBLICAL THEOLOGY

This chapter looks back to the previous one by validating theological movement toward holism from the biblical narrative and forward to the next chapter by highlighting and nuancing the psychological distinction between body and mind in the New Testament. I will argue that they are best viewed as psychological terms at least in some Pauline contexts.[1]

I will sequence three biblical-theological vignettes on human embodiment, Genesis 1–3, Matthew 26, and Romans 5–12, and will argue that the garden temptation narratives of Adam and Jesus assume a responsibility to govern our bodies as a gardener does a garden. The mind and the body are in dynamic interplay as psychological principles; thinking governs seeing, and willing governs desiring. The word of God informs our minds and enables embodied flourishing. This responsibility to govern our bodies by the Spirit toward sanctification is explicit in Romans 5–12.

From Romans 5–12, I want to suggest that a typical discussion of body or flesh in the Bible, Hebrew *bāsār* and Greek *sōma* and *sarx*, tends to miss important psychological nuances.[2] I will show how in some Pauline texts,

---

1. Ellen Charry cites Romans 7, saying that Paul emphasizes "inner conflict between an irrational part of the soul and an rational part." Ellen T. Charry, *God and the Art of Happiness* (Grand Rapids: Eerdmans, 2010), 11.

2. E.g., John A. T. Robinson rightly emphasizes the importance of the body for Pauline theology. He writes,

> One could say without exaggeration that the concept of the body forms the keystone of Paul's theology. In its closely interconnected meanings, the word σῶμα (*sōma*) knits together all his great themes. It is from the body of sin and death that we are delivered; it is through the body of Christ on the Cross that we are saved;

there is an important psychological distinction between body and mind rather than between body and soul, a metaphysical distinction.[3] Especially Romans 6–12 assumes an account of agency with an interplay between the more linguistically oriented mind, which is responsive to the commands of God, and the experientially oriented body. This text applies mind and body/flesh in a psychological hierarchy. The mind embraces the truth of the new regime in Christ and presents its bodily members toward habituated enslavement to righteousness. This less abstract psychological level of the body, embodied and experiential perception, is the source of psychological input that is potentially enslaved, plastic or receptive to habit, whether to sin or righteousness.[4] The application of the benefits of Christ in sanctification, especially in Romans 6, relies on this possibility. The body is habituated to the habits of the reign of sin or grace.

So, thinking and acting mutually reinforce each other. The connection between body and mind is porous; language frames our experience, and experience saturates our concepts.[5] I will argue that new covenantal obedience is liturgical in the sense that it is participatory, reflexive practice of the life of communion with God by the power of the Holy Spirit. New covenant obedience is directed at formation, made possible by plasticity, the first fruits of the glorification of our bodies.

---

it is into His body the Church that we are incorporated; it is by His body in the Eucharist that this Community is sustained; it is in our body that its new life has to be manifested; it is to a resurrection of this body to the likeness of His glorious body that we are destined.

John A. T. Robinson, *The Body: A Study in Pauline Theology* (Philadelphia: Westminster John Knox, 1952), 10.

However, Robinson disavows a psychological reading of flesh by conflating it with the Greek idea that matter is evil. He seems to think that the mere existence of good passions (*epithymia* of the Spirit) is an argument against the psychological view. It is better to see the psychological nuance that is present in the text and divorce it from the Greek idea of evil matter.

3. A key assumption here is that the soul is responsible for life, not merely for human thinking.

4. My argument parallels but does not directly rely on the work of Dallas Willard. He seems to make almost identical judgments about flesh, and plasticity, and the role of practices in sanctification. See Dallas Willard, *The Spirit of the Disciplines* (New York: Harper Collins, 1988), 90–92.

5. I am conscientiously riffing on Kant's famous quote, "Thoughts without content are empty, intuitions without concepts are blind." Immanuel Kant, *Critique of Pure Reason*, ed. and trans. Paul Guyer and Allen W. Wood (Cambridge: Cambridge University Press, 1998), 193–94.

BIBLICAL THEOLOGICAL REFLECTIONS
ON HUMAN AGENCY

The First Adam in the Garden of Eden

It is no longer possible simply to cite Genesis 2:7 and infer dualism with-out further explanation: "then the LORD God formed the man of dust from the ground and breathed into his nostrils the breath of life, and the man became a living creature."[6] But neither should we ignore some essential biblical lines of thought that originate here. We do have a sort of proto-psychology displayed in humankind's land-dependent materiality and God-dependent vitality. I provisionally state it this way: (1) the life and agency of human beings is uniquely related to the breathing and speaking God; (2) the life and agency of human beings is uniquely related to the earth. What follows will unpack those relations, beginning with the second point.

Human beings are groundlings, or "from the ground" (min-hā'adāmāh, Gen 2:7), just like all the plants and animals (Gen 2:9, 19). This means that humans share the same organic nature with them. Like the animals, the LORD God crafted (yṣr) the man (hā'ādām). The term "crafted" is used of a potter or metallurgist.[7] Humankind being made of dust or clay is a repeated theme in the Old Testament.[8] Human beings are said to be made of clay (ḥōmer) and will return to dust ('āfār), as when Job tells God, "Remember that you made me like clay; and will you return me to the dust?" (Job 10:9). The psalmist states that God "remembers that we are dust" (Ps 103:14).

Not only is human nature organic, but so also is their work. Human beings were to cultivate the earth to eat and enjoy its fruits to sustain God's craft. Genesis 2 says the man was placed in the garden to work or to till (lĕ'āvdāh) and to sustain or keep it (ûlĕšāmrāh, Gen 2:15). Both God and human beings are concerned with the proper stewardship of material things. God planted (wayiṭa', Gen 2:8) a garden and made the man his

---

6. Green sees word studies as deeply flawed, since "the Old and New Testaments develop no technical vocabulary to denote human essences." He adds, "the Bible knows nothing of a speculative or philosophical interest in the definitions of the human person." Joel Green, *Body, Soul, and Human Life: The Nature of Humanity in the Bible* (Grand Rapids: Baker Academic, 2008), 14–15.

7. L. Koehler, W. Baumgartner, and J. J. Stamm, *The Hebrew and Aramaic Lexicon of the Old Testament* (HALOT), ed. and trans. M. E. J. Richardson, G. J. Jongeling-Vos, and L. J. De Regt, 5 vols. (Leiden: Brill, 2000), יצר.

8. Job 4:19; 10:8–9; Ps 90:3; 103:14; 104:29; 119:73; 146:4; cf. Gen 18:27.

undergardener. This stewardship involved an ongoing responsibility to the organic productivity of the land. And the man and woman's organic responsibility also extends to caring for their own bodies and to bearing children. Humankind's cultural mandate is phrased in terms of the organic metaphor, "Be fruitful and multiply" (Gen 1:28).

This organic stewardship is bestowed within covenantal communion. God speaks to the man first with the command not to to eat of the tree of knowledge of good and evil. Not only God's crafting, but God's speech in Genesis 2:16–17 implies a covenantal relationship. Kevin Vanhoozer emphasizes that speaking has both covenantal and transformative aspects.[9] While language minimally implies a commitment to shared understanding, God's words in verses 16–17 bestow gifts and call for obedience, implying also a relation of beneficent covenantal authority. This language is also transformative. It is an instance not merely of moral testing, but also of moral instruction, since human beings are asked to be good without full access to knowing good, the knowledge that the tree promised. This moral instruction involves not merely knowledge, but the practical experience of doing the good that has been revealed. The tree of life is also in the garden, which may have promised the possibility of being initiated into deeper communion with God. See Revelation 2:7, "To the one who conquers I will grant to eat of the tree of life, which is in the paradise of God."[10] The man and woman possessed agency because the command of God raised in them an awareness of God's loving authority, their capacity to fulfill God's commands, the possibility of alternative actions, and consequences for their lives. Each of them came to have a self-concept, a sense of who "I am," where they could shape their own narrative toward life or death (Gen 2:17, "you shall surely die"). If God speaks limits only to human beings, then it is probable that only human beings need them. God's command establishes

---

9. Kevin Vanhoozer, "From Speech Acts to Scripture Acts: The Covenant of Discourse and the Discourse of the Covenant," in *After Pentecost: Language and Biblical Interpretation*, ed. Craig Bartholomew, Colin J. D. Greene, and Karl Moller, Scripture and Hermeneutics Series, vol. 2 (Grand Rapids: Zondervan, 2001), 9–10.

10. Kevin Vanhoozer suggests, "The tree of life has perhaps a sacramental significance. It symbolizes the deeper communion with God that would have been possible after their probation. Rev 2:7 'To him who overcomes, I will grant to eat of the tree of life, which is in the Paradise of God.'" Class Notes: Lecture 10: Original Sin, Theology II. *Trinity Evangelical Divinity School.*

covenantal agency; human beings are entrusted with responsibilities that imply real moral agency.

The narrator tells us next that woman (*'iššah*) was taken from man (*'îš*) as Adam (*'ādām*) was taken from the ground (*min-hādamāh*).[11] There is perhaps something of a parallel in the man's responsibility to the ground from which he comes and the responsibility that the woman (*ḥawwāh*) has to the man from which she comes. But the mutuality of this covenant is emphasized by the conclusion of Genesis 2:24, "leave ... hold fast ... and they shall become one flesh (*lĕbāšār 'eḥād*)."[12]

Dru Johnson argues that the temptation narrative is a conflict of interpretation.[13] The serpent takes God's place as epistemic authority by reinterpreting his speech; the issue is not autonomy.[14] If, as I have mentioned, God's command in the garden represented an initiation into knowing the good by experience, then the language of God functions to tutor humankind into goodness by way of linguistically framed free agency. The speech of God was meant to act as a top-down guide for embodied perception to initiate the man and the woman into a greater experience of *shalom*. Language has a remarkable power to bring form; it enables moral agents to take new forms of being. Language enables the body to take shape. The serpent's alternate way of framing their vision produced desire. Johnson describes the problem, "It was in listening that [the woman] saw and it was through the serpent's hermeneutical lens that she saw."[15] The interpretation of the serpent reframed her embodied perception of the fruit so that the woman saw, desired, took, and ate. Notice how the verbal framing generated embodied psychological responses, altered vision and altered desire.

---

11. Victor Hamilton suggests that the narrator picks the Hebrew word *'išša* "based on assonance" with the Hebrew word for man, *'îš*; the roots are not identical. Victor P. Hamilton, *The Book of Genesis: Chapters 1–17*, The New International Commentary on the Old Testament (Grand Rapids: Eerdmans, 1990), 180.

12. See also 1 Cor 6:16; Eph 5:31.

13. Dru Johnson, *Biblical Knowing: A Scriptural Epistemology of Error* (Eugene, OR: Cascade, 2013), 50. See also Kevin Vanhoozer's comment, "Satan, insofar as he interprets God's speech for his own devices, may perhaps be viewed as the first radical reader-response critic—the first to replace the author's voice with his own: 'Did God say?' Theological non-realism is ultimately a rebellious protest against having to answer to any other voice than our own." Kevin J. Vanhoozer, *Is There a Meaning in This Text? The Bible, The Readier, and the Morality of Literary Knowledge* (Grand Rapids: Zondervan, 1998), 361n240.

14. Johnson, *Biblical Knowing*, 52.

15. Johnson, *Biblical Knowing*, 54.

There is a rational failure to govern the body. In Genesis 3:17, we see this interpretive indictment repeated as Adam is condemned for "listen[ing] to the voice" of his wife rather than the voice of God's commands. When God confronts the couple, he asks, "Who told you that you were naked?" (Gen 3:11).[16] It seems that awareness of shame must come from a verbal source.

God's curse, like his creation, is verbal. He speaks to the serpent, the woman, the man, and the ground. Being from the ground, Adam participates in its curse in at least two ways. Genesis 3:17 says that the ground is bound with a curse, which causes pain to Adam in the production of the food. And Genesis 3:19 adds that Adam will again participate in the cursed ground ('adāmāh) by returning to it. It reads starkly,

> By the sweat of your face, you will eat your bread
> until you return to the ground (el-hā'adāmāh)
> for you were taken from it,
> for you are dust ('āfār) and to the dust (el-'āfār) you will return[17]

Adam, being from the ground, was to be frustrated by it until he returned to it. Insofar as his entire being was qualified by materiality, the curse on materiality affected him holistically—the curse did not leave his mind untouched. The procession is as follows: the man was taken from the ground by God; the man, in turn, cultivated and received from the ground to sustain himself; then he returned to the ground or dust.[18] The whole process was frustrated by the curse.[19] Heinrich Holziger writes that the entire relationship between hā-'ādām (Adam) and hā-'adāmah (the ground) became a "hostile one."[20] Similarly, the covenantal responsibility between

---

16. Johnson, *Biblical Knowing*, 60.

17. Translation mine.

18. Frank Spina notes this symbiotic relationship between the tiller and the ground. Frank Anthony Spina, "The 'Ground' for Cain's Rejection (Gen 4): 'ᵃdāmāh in the Context of Gen 1–11," *Zeitschrift für die alttestamentliche Wissenschaft* 104, no. 3 (1992): 319–32. See also Bruce D. Naidoff, "A Man to Work the Soil: A New Interpretation of Genesis 2–3," *Journal for the Study of the Old Testament* 3, no. 5 (1978): 4.

19. Spina develops also Cain's relationship to the cursed ground, that Abel's blood cries out from it, that Cain is cursed "from the ground" which opened to receive Abel's blood, and that the ground would no longer yield for him (Gen 4:10–12). Spina, "The 'Ground' for Cain's Rejection," 327.

20. "das Verhältnis des Erdbodens zu ihm ein anderes, ein feindseliges sein werde (besonders v. 18)"; H. Holziger, *Genesis* (Freiburg: J.C.B. Mohr [Paul Siebeck], 1898), 36. https://books.google.com/books?id= NiZVAAAAYAAJ&q.

man and woman was spoiled by the curse (Gen 3:16). *Shalom* was broken and replaced with enmity between God and humankind, the man and the ground, humankind and their own bodies, the woman and the man, and the woman and the serpent. *Shalom* was broken at every level of creation. The command of God, given to tutor humankind into *shalom*, brings death by sin. This original sin has corrupted what T. F. Torrance calls the triadic relation of God, human beings, and world.[21]

But God did not abandon his people. The history of salvation demonstrates God's renewal of his care to his groundlings by his word. God promises a land (*ereṣ*), which is often referred to as Israel's ground (Exod 20:12; 23:19; Deut 11:9; Jer 23:5), the firstfruits consecrating its produce. To his people God promises to "forgive their sin and heal their land" (2 Chr 7:14). In the second case, God is said to remember that human beings are from the ground. Job's prayer, "Remember that you have made me like clay" (Job 10:9), is echoed in Psalm 103:11–19. In verse 14 we read, "For he knows our frame; he remembers that we are dust." The immediate context of this is the Lord's fatherly compassion to "remove our transgressions from us" (103:12–13) and his steadfast love "to those who keep his covenant and remember to do his commandments" (103:18). In Psalm 119:73, the psalmist also connects God's responsibility of fashioning with a prayer for understanding directed at God's commands: "Your hands have made and fashioned me; give me understanding that I may learn your commandments." R. R. Reno connects the original inbreathing of breath (*nešamah*) with Jesus breathing on his disciples, giving them the breath of life (John 20:22). R. R. Reno writes, "In breathing his Spirit upon us the Father 'remembers that we are dust' (Ps 103:14) and his Spirit renews 'the face of the ground' (104:30)."[22]

In sum, in creation we see organic human beings tied to organic relations with both the land and each other but made alive and governed by God. Human beings have three sorts of implied covenantal responsibilities, as subject to God, to each other, and to the land. The relation to God was to

---

21. T. F. Torrance, *Reality and Evangelical Theology: The Realism of Christian Revelation* (Downers Grove, IL: InterVarsity, 1999), 27. Torrance draws epistemic and ontological inferences from this triadic relationship. But more to the point, he continues, "it also implies that we are not really engaged in theology in the proper sense, and are not scientifically engaged with theology, if we restrict it to the God/man or man/God relationship."

22. Reno, *Genesis*, 68.

obey; God exercised top-down authority with his words over their bodies as related to the fruitfulness. But God's rule is "not antinatural tyranny but more like the authority of the gardener who husbands creation to its fullness."[23] By his word, God cultivates flourishing in his creatures. Human beings are to listen to his voice; this is a major theme of the Bible.[24] The relationship among the man and the woman was directly related to the fact that she was bone of his bones and flesh of his flesh. This relationship grounds the marriage covenant where the two become one flesh. They are to exercise mutual care for bearing fruit. The relationship to the land was also aimed at the cultivation of its fruitfulness.

The curse frustrates all three of these relationships. Humankind is exiled from the place of covenantal communion with God. For the woman, the pain of fruitfulness (childbearing) is increased and the relationship with the man is strained. For the man, the fruitfulness of the land is cursed; he will earn and eat his bread in pain and frustration. All the life and agency of human beings are qualified by their organic nature and their participation in the curse on the land. They are dust, and to dust they shall return (Gen 3:19). So, all the creation responsibilities for free human agents are touched by the curse. The fall frustrates humankind by means of corrupted desire and results in further corruption.

THE SECOND ADAM IN THE GARDEN OF GETHSEMANE

Jesus in the Likeness of Sinful Flesh

In Romans 8:3 we read, "For God has done what the law, weakened by the flesh, could not do. By sending his own Son in the likeness of sinful flesh and for sin, he condemned sin in the flesh."[25] We have here in brief the story of the frustration by the flesh of the commands of God to preserve *shalom*. But we also have a brief summary of the bodily conditions the Son of God assumed to make us children of God; Jesus Christ overcame sinful flesh

---

23. James K. A. Smith, *Awaiting the King: Reforming Public Theology* (Grand Rapids: Baker Academic, 2017), 67.

24. Exod 15:26; Deut 4:1; 7:12; Josh 3:9; Ps 95:7–9; Isa 51:1; Jer 11:4; Matt 7:24–26; Heb 3:15.

25. Thomas Schreiner claims that *katekrinen*, translated condemned here, conveys the meaning "break the power of sin." Thomas R. Schreiner, *Romans*, Baker Exegetical Commentary on the New Testament, ed. Moisés Silva (Grand Rapids: Baker Academic, 1998), 402. See also Romans 5:6, "For while we were still weak, at the right time Christ died for the ungodly."

by coming "in the likeness of sinful flesh." It seems that cleanly capturing the sense of the term "flesh" continues to frustrate interpreters.[26] The gravest difficulty is not routinely addressed: How does Paul connect flesh with the body and human sinfulness without specifying the connection between these ideas?[27] It seems that commentators do little to connect the dots between the characteristic usage of flesh as pertaining to a physical body and the Pauline usage as sinful human nature. Without an alternate explanation, the most obvious hypothesis is that these ideas are connected by a cosmological dualism that sets spirit and matter against each other.[28]

I am proposing an alternate connection by taking Romans 6:6 as the closest thing to a definition of flesh, especially the phrase "the body ruled by sin" (CSB, *to sōma tēs 'amartias*) and the infinitive of purpose that clarifies it, enslaved (*douleuein*). Flesh in this context represents the vicious dispositions (a *habitus*, a having) of the body, with its organic plasticity, by sin and under the law.[29] I am referring both to the term's anthropological

---

26. For example, Anthony Thiselton presents a dizzying array of possibilities in ranging from "man as sinner" to "human considerations" to the "human body." Anthony C. Thiselton, "Flesh," in *The New International Dictionary of New Testament Theology*, ed. Colin Brown (Grand Rapids: Zondervan, 1975), 671–83. Richard Erickson recognizes six semantic fields: (1) physical matter; (2) human body; (3) human person; (4) human relationships in a morally neutral sense; (5) human relationships in a morally negative sphere; and (6) "Paul's most characteristic use of *sarx*," sinful human nature. Richard J. Erickson, "Flesh," in *The Dictionary of Paul and His Letters*, ed. Gerald F. Hawthorne and Ralph P. Martin (Downers Grove, IL: InterVarsity, 1993), 303–6.

27. Thiselton points to the usage of the term "flesh" in Hellenistic cosmological dualism. Thiselton, "Flesh," 674. Erickson rightly notes, "The ontological dualism of Hellenistic thinkers is ruled out in Paul's view, since while the fleshly body, and humanity generally, are weak and open to defilement, they are nonetheless redeemable and subject to resurrection." Erickson, "Flesh," 305.

28. A cosmic dualistic approach often appeals to Hellenistic parallels, setting flesh against spirit. However, Robert Jewett sees a better precedent in the cosmic and apocalyptic dimensions of the term in the Qumran. Robert Jewett, *Paul's Anthropological Terms: A Study of their Use in Context Settings* (Leiden: Brill, 1971), 92–94. Jörg Frey assesses the use of *bāśār* (flesh) in these and pre-Essene sapiential literature. In both cases, this literature is similarly "characterized by a kind of cosmic and eschatological dualism." Jörg Frey, "The Notion of 'Flesh' in 4QInstruction and the Background of Pauline Usage," in *Sapiential, Liturgical & Poetical Texts from Qumran*, Proceedings of the Third Meeting of the International Organization for Qumran Studies, Published in Memory of Maurice Baillet, ed. Daniel K. Falk, F. García Martinez, and Eileen M. Schuller (Leiden: Brill, 2000), 217.

29. Vicious meaning "of the nature of vice," that is, vice as a quality of habit. OED Online, s.v., "vicious,-adj," accessed May 8, 2018, I.1. www.oed.com/view/Entry/223179. Robert Gundry makes a similar claim about the term "body," not that the body is evil, but that it is "caught in the middle [of sin and mind] and dominated by sin rather than the mind." However, Gundry thinks that Paul only "*associates* sin with the body and makes redemption consist in the

and redemptive-historical aspects in Romans. In the redemptive-historical sense, those who are in the flesh are "under the dominion of the powers of the old era," in contrast to those in the Spirit (Col 1:13; Rom 8:2).[30] In the anthropological sense, sin corrupts humankind holistically as a habit of being. It is not that sin impacts only the body and not the soul or mind (see Eph 2:3), but rather that flesh captures the way sin and evil leave their mark on the embodied agent by way of plasticity under the leading of the depraved mind. In Romans 6:6 the word "body" is not set against the soul, as if mere physicality is in view, but against the mind. But physicality is an aspect of the term's use here. Unlike cosmological dualism, my reading sees body as a psychological division that makes no assumptions about the evil of matter.[31] The connection is rather that flesh instantiates sin's rule in individual human by way of bodily plasticity.[32] The quality of plasticity is what makes flesh, a disposition or *habitus*, possible, ontologically speaking.[33]

---

resurrection." Gundry seems not to recognize that the text assumes that the body is a source of psychological inputs and the location of habit (i.e., slavery). Robert H. Gundry, *Sōma in Biblical Theology, with Emphasis on Pauline Anthropology*, Society for New Testament Monograph Series 29 (Cambridge: Cambridge University Press, 1976), 58, 138, emphasis original.

30. Schreiner, *Romans*, 354.

31. Jay Adams, *A Theology of Christian Counseling: More Than Redemption* (Grand Rapids: Zondervan, 1979), 106–8. Jay Adams seems to take a similar position to the one I am advocating. He writes, "It is true that the material creation was cursed following man's sin, and that both the natural world and sinfully habituated human flesh now cause problems for the counsel, but that is not because the materiality of the earth or of the body" (106–7). However, Adams takes the body as a metaphysical term, simply referring to physicality in contrast to the soul or heart "that causes the aggravating habituation of the material body" (108). I see the reference to body in this text not as a reference to metaphysical makeup, but to a psychological division.

32. This view has precedence in medieval theology. Thomas Aquinas considers *fomes* (inclination) and *consuetudo* (habit) as located in the lower faculties. The *reatus* (debt) and *macula* (stain) are washed away in baptism, but the *fomes* and *consuetedu* are only diminished. These are disordered in the sense that they are not aligned to their proper ends. Unlike Aquinas, I am not suggesting that only the lower appetites are impacted by sin. I simply see the lower psychological principle as chiefly in view in this passage. See Charles Raith II, *Aquinas and Calvin on Romans: God's Justification and Our Participation* (Oxford: Oxford University Press, 2014), 150–57.

33. Henri Blocher thinks the medieval idea of *habitus* captures this best: "*habitus*, a disposition, a 'having' (which is the verbal form!) may still be the most convenient one here." There seems to be a gap in the English language that does not cover this term. The word "habituated" doesn't quite capture original sin as *habitus*. It seems to imply a process of habituation by active, repetitive volitional movement. But what I mean here is perhaps more subtle. I am searching for a word that captures the accumulation of embodied cultural baggage that is non-linguistic and is perhaps even written into our material makeup. Blocher helpfully highlights the term "cultural heredity." But even this term does not capture the extent to which original sin is bound up in our bodies. Blocher also recognizes this: "The highest of

Just as the world in 1 John 2:16 represents the plasticity or sedimentation of human culture in its practices, structures, beliefs, etc., so also the flesh represents this sort of mode with an eye to how we embody sin.[34]

Whereas the children of Adam possess both souls that do not naturally seek God apart from his gracious initiation and the cultural and bodily habits of enslavement, Jesus did not assume a fallen soul, but did assume the "defects of the body," in Aquinas's language (*ST* III.3.14–15). He argues that the defects of the body are contracted by humanity as a consequence of the fall, but that these were assumed by Christ. On Aquinas's view, the soul of Christ does not possess the *fomes,* or the inclination, toward concupiscence. These bodily defects may involve genetic components, e.g., genetic mutations involving predispositions to anxiety or depression. So, when Jesus came "in the likeness" (*en homoiōmati,* Rom 8:3) of sinful flesh, he at least participated in the fight against the grain of bodily plasticity that we face in embodied existence.[35] Metaphysically speaking, his soul is sinless,

---

our religious affections or emotions affect the chemical balance in our cells, and the reverse is also true. We are spiritual down to our toes, or to our instincts; we are living bodies right up to our mental activities, our longings, our loves. If original sin involves both, it is human indeed." Blocher also criticizes the "false antimony (sic) between nature and freedom. ... a *distinction* is certainly to be made between bodily processes and personal freedom, but no *separation.*" Henri Blocher, *Original Sin: Illuminating the Riddle,* New Studies in Biblical Theology (Downers Grove, IL: IVP Academic, 2000), 128, 123, 122.

34. In my judgment the interpretations of following passages are improved by my reading flesh as at least connoting physicality: John 1:13–14; 3:6; 6:51–56; 6:63; Rom 3:20; 1 Cor 1:29; 5:5; 15:39, 50; 2 Cor 4:11; Eph 2:11–14; Col 1:22–24; 2:11–13; Heb 2:14; 10:20; 1 John 4:2; 2 John 7; Jude 8. The following passages are compatible with my reading: Matt 19:5; 26:41; John 8:15; Rom 13:14; 2 Cor 11:18; 12:7; Gal 3:3; 4:23–29; 5:13–24; Phil 3:3; 1 Pet 3:18; 4:1–2, 6; 2 Pet 2:10, 18; Jude 23. The following texts may pose problems for my reading: Matt 16:17; Rom 9:3–8; 1 Cor 7:28; 2 Cor 7:1; Gal 3:3; Col 2:23. There are also passages which just refer the body: Luke 24:39; Acts 2:31; Rom 1:3; 1 Cor 6:16; 2 Cor 10:2; Gal 1:16; Phil 1:22, 24; Col 2:1, 5; Rev 17:16; 19:18, 21.

35. The Greek word *omiōma* translated "in the likeness" is a point of debate, especially whether it conditions sinful flesh toward similarity or dissimilarity. Following Ugo Vanni, Vincent Branick argues that *omiōma* "by no means marks a distinction or a difference between Christ and sinful flesh. ... [he] comes as the full expression of that sinful flesh." Vincent Branick, "The Sinful Flesh of the Son of God (Rom 8:3): A Key Image of Pauline Theology," *Catholic Biblical Quarterly* 47 (1985): 250. Florence Morgan Gillman contests this reading showing examples where only similarity is meant. However, the stress on the word is similarity, even if not identity, and particularly in a context where flesh is overwhelmingly negative, the point seems clear: Jesus is sent in the flesh to redeem flesh. Florence Morgan Gillman, "Another Look at Romans 8:3: In the Likeness of Sinful Flesh,' " *The Catholic Biblical Quarterly* 49 (1987): 598–600.

but he shared our inherited bodily conditions (Heb 2:14–18).[36] To return to J. P. Moreland's analogy in the prior chapter, Christ's assumption of a human body may be likened to a scratched CD, but his retrieval system is perfect, enabling its healing. Jesus did not sin, but perhaps he participated in the bodily conditions that contribute to sin for human beings without a divine nature.[37] The overall point is this: Romans 8:3 leads us to expect that the body of Jesus might be a crucial antagonist in the narrative of the Messiah's victory. This is precisely what we find in the climax of the Gospel of Jesus as told by Matthew.

Overcoming Weak Flesh

The Gethsemane narrative is a part of what might be called the betrayal narrative: Matthew 26:1–27:2. The section begins with a prediction that "the Son of Man will be delivered up to be crucified" (26:2) and ends with Jesus being "delivered ... over" to someone with the power to do so (27:2). The characters of this narrative are the leaders of the Jews, Jesus, Judas, Peter, and strangely an unnamed woman. In 26:6–35, we see two contrasts involving Judas. First, in 26:6–13, we see Jesus being extravagantly anointed as Messiah by this unnamed woman who values his life as it ought to be valued; Jesus calls her deed a beautiful deed. By contrast, Judas sells Jesus' life for thirty pieces of silver (26:14–16). Second, in 26:17–29, Judas is contrasted with Jesus. Jesus shares not only the Passover meal, the cup and the bread with his disciples, but also his own life: "Drink of it, all of you,

---

36. This perhaps helps us to nuance the ongoing debate between those who hold that the Son assumed an unfallen human nature and those who hold that he assumed a fallen one. Kallitos Ware highlights the difficulty of the debate, suggesting that while we need to hold "the first alternative, that Jesus took unfallen human nature, we need also uphold the second, that he lived out his human life under the conditions of the fall." Kallistos Ware, "The Humanity of Christ: The Fourth Constantinople Lecture," in *Journal of Anglican and Eastern Churches Association* (1985): 4. Kelly Kapic surveys the history of taking "sinful flesh" to mean fallen human nature. Kapic shows that even as this view gained more prominence in early twentieth century theology, two readings of the precedent for this view in Christian history developed. Kelly Kapic, "The Son's Assumption of a Human Nature: A Call for Clarity," *International Journal of Systematic Theology* 3, no. 2 (July 2001): 154–66.

37. Additionally, sin was not credited to him under the headship of Adam. Schreiner takes this to mean "that the Son did not merely resemble human flesh but participated fully in sinful flesh," but then clarifies this with the examples of "the powers of old age: sickness and death." Schreiner, *Romans*, 403. I agree with Schreiner's general statement but am going to argue that the sinfulness of flesh is precisely the body's ability to take the form, via plasticity, of rebellion against God.

for this is my blood of the covenant, which is poured out for many for the forgiveness of sins" (26:27–28). As he shares this meal with them, Jesus reveals that one of the disciples will betray him, the one who "dipped his hand in the dish" with him (26:23). Whereas the woman is extravagantly hospitable to Jesus, Judas violates hospitality by repaying the sharing of a meal with betrayal.

Jesus returns to the theme of betrayal in Matthew 26:31, and Peter promises never to fall away, saying, "Even if I must die with you, I will not deny you!" (26:35). So, the Gethsemane narrative itself (26:36–46) is situated on the heels of Peter's denial as a sort of test case both of the disciples' ability to be alert (Matt 25:1–13) and of Peter's disavowing threefold denial.[38] Peter fails three times in Gethsemane just as he does in his denials. Gethsemane represents a contrast then between Peter and Jesus, the one who overcomes sorrow and anxiety and the one who is overcome by the weakness of the flesh (Matt 26:37–43). Peter is in focus not only because he is the only disciple mentioned by name in verse 37, but also because he is the addressee of the central command of the section. In 26:40–41, Jesus says to Peter, "So, could you not watch with me one hour? Watch and pray that you may not enter into temptation. The *spirit* indeed is willing, but the *flesh* is weak" (emphasis added). Spirit here is used with a psychological nuance, referring to mental or conscious willingness.[39]

In terms of biblical theology, we have the second, greater Adam undergoing a test of obedience to the will of God.[40] In this case, Jesus was wrestling through being made to drink from the cup of God's wrath on behalf of his true children. This second Adam not only endured temptation in a garden, but he did so on the Mount of Olives (Luke 22:39), which Stanley Hauerwas marks "as the mount on which the Lord will stand to save his

---

38. Of Matthew 25, Stanley Hauerwas writes, "Jesus's use of Daniel is not an attempt to invite his disciples to 'think ahead,' but to discern the present. ... The disciples' task is to stay awake, to be ready, exactly because they do not and cannot know the day and hour of the triumph of the Son of Man. Disciples are not in the game of prediction. Rather, they are called to be ready and prepared." Stanley Hauerwas, *Matthew*, Brazos Theological Commentary on the Bible (Grand Rapids: Baker, 2006), 206.

39. W. Bauer, F. W. Danker, W. F. Arndt, and F. W. Gingrich, *Greek-English Lexicon of the New Testament and Other Early Christian Literature*, 3rd ed. (Chicago: University of Chicago Press, 2000), πνεῦμα, 3b, "as the source and seat of insight, feeling, and will."

40. I owe this observation to Caleb Thompson.

people" in Zechariah 14:1-5.[41] The nature of Jesus' temptation is emotional turmoil, characterized within a typically emotionally opaque narrative by the words "sorrowful and troubled [anxious, *adēmon*]" (Matt 26:37). Jesus explicitly says to his disciples, "My soul is very sorrowful, even to death" (26:38). Whereas Adam and Eve faced illicit desire, Jesus faced its natural correlate, the sorrow of loss. We know a bit more about the nature of this grief from Luke's account, which records that "his sweat became like great drops of blood falling down to the ground" (Luke 22:44).[42] The general object of Christ's sorrow is made clear by the fact that he prayed for the passing of "this cup" (Matt 26:39). Jesus remembered the judgment of God for sin where Adam and Eve failed to, and Jesus' act of obedience involved the very punishment promised for Adam's disobedience. As N. T. Wright highlights, the cup Jesus drank from is also the baptism with which he was baptized, which both signal Jesus' awareness of his vocation (Mark 10:38-40), "to take upon himself the suffering predicted for the people."[43] In contrast to Peter, however, Jesus overcame the weakness of the flesh; in contrast to Adam, he submitted to the will of God. By Matthew 26:42, the battle seems to have climaxed, as Jesus prays his resolve, "your will be done." He would drink the cup that was offered to him by his betraying and kissing friend in verses 47-50. By contrast, Peter cut off the ear of the servant of the high priest (Matt 26:51; John 18:10).

Psychologically speaking, we have a moment of great internal conflict.[44] B. B. Warfield notes the tension present in this expression of angst. He says,

---

41. Hauerwas, *Matthew*, 201.

42. Claire Clivaz gives a helpful reassessment of the external evidence on this passage. I regard the data as yet inconclusive. Clivaz ably argues that the passage was even inserted, with reference, into the liturgical reading of Matthew in early lectionaries. Clair Clivaz, "The Angel and the Sweat Like 'Drops of Blood' (Lk 22:43-44): 𝔓⁶⁹ and *f*¹³," *Harvard Theological Review* 98, no. 4 (2005): 414-40. Cf. Christopher M. Tuckett, "Luke 22,43-44: The 'Agony' in the Garden and Luke's Gospel," in *New Testament Textual Criticism and Exegesis: Festschrift J. Delobel*, ed. Adelbert Denaux, BETL, vol. 161 (Leuven: Leuven University Press, 2002), 131-44. See also J. N. Birdsall, "A Fresh Examination of the Fragment of the Gospel of St. Luke in ms. 0171 and an Attempted Reconstruction with Special Reference to the Recto," in *Philologia Sacra: Biblische und patristische Studien für Hermann J. Frede und Walter Thiele zu ihrem siebzigsten Geburtstag*, ed. Roger Gryson, Vetus Latina (Freiburg: Herder, 1993).

43. N. T. Wright, *Jesus and the Victory of God*, Christian Origins and the Question of God, vol. 2 (Minneapolis: Fortress, 1996), 573.

44. Jesus says, "My *soul* is very sorrowful, even to death" (Matt 26:38). BDAG suggests that the word "soul" refers here to the "seat and center of the inner human life," especially of "feelings and emotions." BDAG, ψυχή.

"He had come into the world to die; but as he vividly realizes what the death is which he is to die, there rises in his soul a yearning for deliverance, only however, to be at once repressed."[45] Warfield adds, "the clearly realized approach of his death ... threw him inwardly into profound agitation."[46] As mentioned above, the body makes a significant contribution to the poignancy of this situation. Luke 22:44 records, "And being in agony [*en agōnia*] ... his sweat became like great drops of blood falling down to the ground." Clair Rothschild highlights the Greek word *agonia*, used only in the New Testament, writing, "it is also well attested as a reference to psychological anguish accompanying a moment of fear, as in what we might think of as a panic attack."[47] Commentators have suggested that "sweat ... like great drops of blood" refers to a rare medical phenomenon called hematidrosis where the capillaries surrounding the sweat glands burst.[48] Both hematidrosis and excessive sweating are associated with very strong reactions in the sympathetic nervous system. It is not that Jesus secretly and inwardly did not want to obey his Father, as if the emotion has finally revealed the true nature of his faithlessness, but rather that the poignancy of the situation caused great emotional turbulence. The emotion displayed here is not a quasi-choice for which Christ would be morally culpable since it

---

45. B. B. Warfield, "On the Emotional Life of our Lord," *Biblical and Theological Studies*, ed. B. B. Warfield et al. (New York: Charles Scribner's Sons, 1922), 72–73.

46. Warfield, "On the Emotional Life," 73.

47. Clair K. Rothschild, "Holy Sweat: Interpreting Luke's Portrait of Jesus in the Garden," *The Bible Today* 55, no. 3 (2017): 189.

48. One article in the *Indian Journal of Dermatology* reports, "The severe mental anxiety activates the sympathetic nervous system to invoke the stress-fight or flight reaction to such a degree as to cause hemorrhage of the vessels supplying the sweat glands into the ducts of the sweat glands." The article also records, "Acute fear and intense mental contemplation are the most frequent causes, as reported in six cases in men condemned to execution, a case occurring during the London blitz, a case involving fear of being raped, a case of fear of a storm while sailing, etc." H. R. Jerajani, Jaju Bhagyashri, M. M. Phiske, and Nitin Lade, "Hematohidrosis – A Rare Clinical Phenomenon," *Indian Journal of Dermatology* 54, no. 3 (2009): 290–92. "Seventy-six cases were studied and classified. ... Acute fear and intense mental contemplation were found to be the most frequent inciting causes." J. E. Holoubek and A. B. Holoubek, "Blood, sweat, and fear. 'A classification of hematidrosis," *Journal of Medical Chemistry* 27, no. 3-4 (1996): 115–33. See also J. Manonukul, W. Wisuthsarewong, R. Chantorn, A. Vongirad, P. Omeapinyan, "Hematidrosis: A pathologic process or stigmata. A case report with comprehensive histopatholic and immuoperoxidas studies," *American Journal of Dermatopathology* 30, no. 2 (April 2008): 135–39; Zhaoyue Wang et al., "A Case of Hematidrosis Successfully Treated with Propranolol," *American Journal of Dermatopathology* 11, no. 6 (2010): 440–43. Other articles have connected hematidrosis with trauma.

runs contrary to the will of God. Surely, to the contrary, it establishes the possibility—even if only for him—of a person being sinlessly divided. It is precisely the fact that Christ was overcoming the weakness of the flesh that makes sense of this situation.[49]

This is where Calvin's overly simplistic psychology causes him trouble. Calvin conducts elaborate verbal gymnastics to affirm that Jesus' emotions in Gethsemane were within bounds and that his prayer to "take this cup from me" was not a transgression. Calvin writes, "the strength and violence of grief suddenly drew this word from his mouth, to which he immediately added a correction."[50] Calvin seemed to be assuming that emotions, in spite of the fact that they come from the heart (will), in spite of the fact that they may run contrary to God's will, and in spite of the fact that they may provoke words that run contrary to God's will, are still blameless provided they are not too strong. This runs contrary to the whole tenor of the narratives of the four Gospels, which emphasize the intensity of the struggle. Wright calls Gethsemane "the moment when [Jesus'] vocation was tested to the limit."[51]

An easier explanation for Jesus' turmoil in the garden is that it is simply part of the fallen embodied human condition to experience emotional turmoil under stress; the Son came "in the likeness of sinful flesh" (Rom 8:3). But Jesus overcame sinful flesh by fulfilling "the righteous requirement of the law" (Rom 8:4) and "condemned sin in the flesh" (Rom 8:3). Jesus was not corrupted by the sinful moral orientation of humanity, but did experience the same emotional turbulence that comes through our agency being qualified by embodiment, by internal natural weakness in the face of stress. Jesus knew very well the weakness of the flesh. Calvin may have overcorrected out of a concern for avoiding Gnosticism by minimizing the role of the body in sinfulness. The problem is this: every assertion a theologian makes about the doctrine of sin can have an equal and opposite reaction in the doctrine of sanctification.[52] By minimizing the role of the body in sinfulness, Calvin may have set a trajectory within the Reformed tradition of

---

49. Cf. "The indeed spirit is willing, but the flesh is weak" (Matt 26:41).

50. John Calvin, *Calvin's Commentaries*, 45 vols, translated by John King, et al. (Edinburgh: Calvin Translation Society, 1844-56).

51. Wright, *Jesus and the Victory of God*, 606.

52. From a private conversation with Kevin Vanhoozer, June 30, 2017, Libertyville, IL.

minimizing the role of the body in moral agency generally. And neglecting the body in agency also carries the consequence of neglecting the tangible ways our experiences affect and form us. The body is formed by our own moral evil, the moral evil of others against us (e.g., generational abuse or neglect), and even natural evils like natural inability or weakness from genetic predispositions.[53]

This is a point that Christian psychologist Eric Johnson makes in stressing the importance of the biblical concept of weakness. Johnson clarifies that this term "can be used to refer to all kinds of limitations: physical, psychological, moral, and spiritual," adding by way of example, "Jesus ... told his sleepy disciples in the Garden of Gethsemane that the spirit is willing, but the flesh is weak (Matt 26:41)."[54] The relevant point is that weakness is a natural adjective for embodied existence and covers multiple types of falling short of completeness or wholeness.[55] The term encompasses a range of meanings from literally speaking of the body, as with a lack of physical strength (1 Pet 3:7) and sickness (John 4:46), to a more figurative powerlessness (Rom 8:3, 26; 1 Cor 1:27, etc.), and even poverty (Acts 20:35).[56] What is significant about this word is that it most literally refers to physicality and has a strong connection with sin (Rom 5:6). In the Gospels, weakness contrasts with health and wholeness, and in Paul with power (1 Cor 1:17–2:4).[57] In Hebrews, weakness evokes sympathy but is also connected with temptation and the tendency to be "ignorant and wayward" (Heb 5:2). We are told that we have a priest who can "sympathize with our weakness" (Heb 4:15). If what I am saying about the body is true, then weakness is a perfect term for capturing the ways that moral and natural evil leave their mark on human persons.

---

53. It is often the case that natural evil contributes to moral evil—famine may cause theft.

54. Eric L. Johnson, *God and Soul Care: The Therapeutic Resources of the Christian Faith* (Downers Grove, IL: IVP Academic, 2017), 278.

55. "Weakness in the Bible refers to the state of being 'less than' in some respect, either less than some ideal—less than complete and whole—or less than what is typical for human beings, and so deficient in some respect to most other people, or both." Johnson, *God & Soul Care*, 279.

56. Gustav Stählin, "ἀσθενής," in *Theological Dictionary of the New Testament*, ed. Gerhard Kittel and Gerhard Friedrich, trans. Gerhard Friedrich (Grand Rapids: Eerdmans, 1964), 1:490–93.

57. Johnson, *God & Soul Care*, 278.

THE BENEFITS OF THE SECOND ADAM

Having made the biblical theological parallel between Adam and Christ, we will resume the narrative in Romans 5:12. In Romans 5–12, we see a theological account of the hope that is extended "through our Lord Jesus Christ" (Rom 5:1, 11, 21; 7:25) by making peace with God and giving life in the Spirit. I will trace how the benefits of the second Adam are applied with respect to the flesh. Overall, this text presents how the Christ inaugurated the reign of grace and life over the reign of sin and death where the body or flesh is the key battleground for the new regime. Will the body be ruled by sin or by grace? There are four key considerations: (1) Is the reign of grace in Christ superior to the reign of death in Adam? (2) Will that reign of Christ be realized in our bodies? How does the believer think and act to participate bodily in this reign? (3) What role did the law play in forming our fleshly passions and in bringing about hostility within ourselves? (4) What role does the Spirit play in enabling the reign of grace and restoring our bodies?

The Superiority of the Reign of Grace in Christ

Romans 5:12–21 presents an analogy between the reign or regime inaugurated by the first Adam and that of the second. Structurally, verse 12 begins the analogy between Adam and Jesus, but verses 13–14 break off the analogy with a parenthetical comment. Verse 12 reads, "just as sin came into the world through one man, and death through sin, and so death spread to all men because all sinned." Verses 13–14 are a parenthetical comment explaining that there is evidence that sin reigned between Adam to Moses because all human beings died, explaining that in spite of the fact that the law of Moses had not been given, sin was in the world even if the transgressions were not like that of Adam, an explicit violation of a clear command, "you shall not eat" (Gen 2:17).[58]

---

58. Here I am following the exegesis of Henri Blocher in *Original Sin*. How was it possible to sin before the law was given to Moses? Paul makes two assertion-concession statements. First, "sin indeed was in the world before the law was given," even if it "is not counted" (Rom 5:13). And second, Paul repeats the same assertion, rephrased, "death reigned from Adam to Moses," with a similarly reworded concession, "even over those whose sinning was not like the transgression of Adam, who was a type of the one who was to come" (Rom 5:14). This second assertion-concession seems to be saying the same thing as the first but with a different emphasis. Blocher's position is that "God sees [persons before Moses] in Adam and through Adam, in the framework of the covenant of creation. Therefore, he sees their sins as committed against the Genesis 2 command, as grafted onto Adam's sin in Eden." Blocher

Romans 5:5–17 clarify the nature of this analogy between Adam and Jesus. These verses mark three ways that the free gift of grace resulting in life is better than the one man's trespass resulting in death and condemnation. First, whereas Adam's transgression brought death to many, Jesus Christ, far from merely settling the score, brought a superabundance of grace for many. The situation is a total reversal from debt to abundance (5:15).[59] Second, whereas one trespass brought condemnation, the gift of justification covers many trespasses (5:16). Third, whereas the trespass brought the devastating and enslaving regime of death, the gift brings the abundance of grace offered by the regime of life in Jesus Christ (5:17). Adam and Christ are representative of competing kingdoms, and those under their sway of sin or grace will taste the fruits of their enslavement, death or life. Finally, the section closes by again noting the outcome of this regime change, that grace is enabled to "reign through righteousness leading to eternal life through Jesus Christ our Lord" (5:21).

The passage stresses the free gift of righteousness, abundant grace, and reigning in life. To understand the free gift, we must look back to Romans 3–4. However, to understand the abundance of grace and reigning in life, we must look forward. Romans 5:9 illustrates the double grace: "we have now been justified by his blood, much more shall we be saved by him from the wrath of God." This apodosis is paralleled by the phrase in 5:10, "much more, now that we are reconciled, shall we be saved by his life." What salvation is still being anticipated? The most probable answer is remaining sin, namely, the weakness (*asthenōn*) of 5:6, which is also called sin or ungodliness. Romans 5:8 states, "but God shows his love for us in that while we were still *sinners*, Christ died for us" (emphasis added). Weakness here emphasizes the powerlessness of humanity to fulfill the righteous demands of the law.

Reigning in Union with Christ

How then do we experience the reign of Christ in our bodies? How is the reign of Christ actualized? In Romans 6, we see that our participation or

---

paraphrases Romans 5:13b, "so death reigned even over people who had not sinned, as Adam had done, by violating a precept directly given to them." Blocher, *Original Sin*, 77–78.

59. The language of grace is so profuse in this verse that the construction is somewhat awkward: "*to charisma ... pollō mallon hē charis tou theou kai hē dōrea en chariti tē tou henos anthrōpou Iēsou Christou eis tous pollous eperisseusen.*"

union with Christ in baptism has profound implications for the life in our mortal bodies. We are baptized into his death and raised with him so that "we too might walk in newness of life" (Rom 6:4; cf. 5:17–21). What does it mean to walk in newness of life? There is a disjunction between grace reigning (5:21) and enslavement to sin in 6:6–19. Human beings are enslaved to that which is reigning, either grace or sin. To be enslaved to sin is to let it reign; to be free from sin's dominion is to be obedient to God and under the reign of grace (6:15–17).

In the first place, the point of our being baptized into Christ's death, or being "crucified with him," was so that the "body of sin might be brought to nothing, so that we would no longer be enslaved to sin" (Rom 6:6). This point will be reiterated with respect to the law in 7:4–12. Commentators have struggled to know how to take the word "body" in 6:6, seemingly to avoid the gnostic implications of translating it as the CSB does, "the body ruled by sin." However one takes the word "sōma" in verse 6 bears on its use in verse 12 and the repeated use of the word "members" in verses 13 and 19. Some aspect of physical embodiment is in view throughout.

Schreiner explains how sōma is used in Romans 6:6: "the body of sin ultimately refers to the whole person (see esp. the comments on Rom 6:12–13). Nonetheless, the word sōma is used because the body is the means by which sin is concretely accomplished (cf. 6:12–13). The purpose is not to say that the body is intrinsically evil, nor that sin exists because of sinful bodies."[60] He seemingly grounds his case for taking body in verses 6 and 12 as the whole person because of the parallel to "yourselves" in verse 13.[61] Douglas Moo also cites this rationale only adding, "sin certainly influences more than just the physical side of people."[62] Schreiner then extends his reasoning by highlighting the additional parallel between "yourselves" and "members." He writes, "'Members' and 'yourselves' are apparently

---

60. Schreiner, *Romans*, 316.

61. Schreiner, *Romans*, 323. Schreiner claims that this reference to the mortal body cannot refer to the physical body because of the parallel to "yourselves" in Rom 6:13. By contrast, I see body in verse 12 as clarifying the more general term "yourselves" in verse 13. He provides no additional rationale for his reading. Yet this reading forces him to see members not as referring to the body, nor desires as being related to the body. He gives no rationale for why Paul includes the word "mortal."

62. Douglas Moo, *The Epistle to the Romans*, The New International Commentary on the New Testament, ed. Gordon D. Fee (Grand Rapids: Eerdmans, 1996), 383n156.

synonymous, and this suggests that 'members' refers not only to the body, but to the whole person with all its capabilities. Moreover, the 'desires' of verse 12 cannot be limited to bodily ones alone."[63] In defense of this reading, Schreiner asserts that sins such as strife, jealousy, or coveting are said to come from the flesh (Rom 7; 13:13–14; Gal 5:19–20).

The logic seems to be as follows: (1) the passions of the body must refer to things mentioned in the context, strife, jealousy, and coveting; (2) since strife, jealousy, and coveting require cognition, they cannot come from the body, but must come from some principle beyond the body; (3) in spite of its connections to physicality, the best candidate for this principle is the notion of flesh in the cited passages; (4) since flesh does not implicate the body (or Gnosticism), "mortal body" in Romans 6:12 must refer to something beyond physicality. However, the assumption that the body cannot be the source of desires like jealousy and strife is psychologically dubious.[64] One problem here is that Schreiner's reading of flesh bleeds into his interpretation of body.

On the other hand, if the body can be the source of strife, jealousy, and coveting, then we can read mortal body straightforwardly. Robert Gundry has argued convincingly that *sōma* never refers to the whole person, as Bultmann has claimed, but rather refers to the physical body. To prove this, Gundry reviews uses in extrabiblical literature and the Septuagint (LXX) and throughout the New Testament and especially in Pauline literature. I am following Robert Gundry and John Murray in taking *sōma* (body) not as referring to the whole person (so, Rudolf Bultmann), but as referring to the physical body within a framework of psychological duality.[65] John Murray writes,

---

63. Schreiner, *Romans*, 323.

64. If the body means whatever is happening under the surface of consciousness, as I am suggesting, then it most certainly does respond in intelligent ways unconsciously. See Karlijn Massar, Abraham P. Buunk, and Mark DeChesne, "Jealousy in the blink of an eye: Jealous reactions following subliminal exposure to rival characteristics," *European Journal of Social Psychology* 39 (2009): 768–79; David Terburg, Nicole Hooiveld, Henk Aarts, J. Leon Kenemans, Jack van Honk, "Eye tracking unconscious face-to-face confrontations: Dominance motives prolong gaze to masked angry faces," *Psychological Science* 22, no. 3 (March 2011): 314–19; and Larissa Z. Tiedens, Miguel M. Unzueta, and Maria J. Young, "An Unconscious Desire for Hierarchy? The Motivated Perception of Dominance Complementarity in Task Partners," *Journal of Personality and Social Psychology* 93, no. 3 (2007): 402–14.

65. Gundry, *Sōma in Biblical Theology*.

These references suffice to show the extent to which the apostle thought of sin and sanctification as associated with the body. The expression "the body of sin" would mean the body as conditioned and controlled by sin, the sinful body. If this is the meaning how can he speak of "the body of sin" as being brought to nought? … The body is an integral part of personality and since the old man has been crucified the destruction of the body of sin is an indispensable aspect of that radical transformation of the entire person which the crucifixion of the old man connotes. The body of the believer is no longer a body conditioned and controlled by sin.[66]

To Schreiner's argument regarding the parallel between the words "body," "members," and "yourselves" in Romans 6:12–13, Gundry rightly points out, "We may ask why the reverse understanding—viz., that *sōma* delimits the personal pronouns ["yourselves"] to man as physical body—is not equally possible. In the parallel statement 'She slapped his face' and 'She slapped him', 'face' and the personal pronoun 'him' interchange. But their interchangeability does not imply that 'face' has here become a technical term for the whole man."[67] Even while holding Schreiner's position, Douglas Moo concedes that the use of the words "mortal," "passions," and "members" are in support of taking body to be referring to the physical. Gundry also appeals to the opposite line of reasoning from 2 Corinthians 4:10–11, "always carrying in the body the death of Jesus, so that the life of Jesus may also be manifested in our bodies. … so that the life of Jesus also may be manifested in our mortal flesh." Gundry writes, "the persecution clearly was physical—thus the two references to *sōma* and the one reference to 'mortal flesh.'"[68] It is far simpler to see "body" in Romans 6:12 giving nuance to "yourselves" in verse 13. This reading maintains a consistent

---

66. John Murray, *Epistle to the Romans* (Grand Rapids: Eerdmans, 1997), 221. Moo registers his agreement that Murray's reading "seems to fit this verse well," but opts for body as referring to the whole person on the grounds that it refers to the whole person in Rom 6:12–13. It is not obvious that these uses of body cannot also refer to the physical body. However, Moo helpfully notes, "the qualification 'of sin' would not mean [on Murray's reading] that the body is inherently sinful (a Greek notion rejected by the Bible) but that the body is particularly susceptible to, and easily dominated by, sin." Moo, *Epistle to the Romans*, 375.

67. Gundry, *Sōma in Biblical Theology*, 29–30.

68. Gundry, *Sōma in Biblical Theology*, 32.

line of reference along the six uses of the words "body" and "members" in Romans 6:6–19 and genuinely accounts for the adjective "mortal."[69]

So, on this reading, the Christian's being crucified with Christ somehow enables the "body ruled by sin" (CSB) to be "brought to nothing," or made powerless,[70] to the end that the Christian is no longer "enslaved to sin" (Rom 6:6). This dying implies both freedom from the mastery of sin and new life in Christ Jesus. Yet this freedom from mastery seems to require a new reckoning from the Christian. This is perhaps a new way of mentally framing how we experience the enslaving desire in order to overcome it, because the injunction to "consider yourselves dead to sin" (6:11) is directly followed by the words, "Let not sin therefore reign in your mortal body" (6:12). Literally speaking, to let sin reign is to present the parts (melē) of our body as tools for practicing unrighteousness. The force of the command might be better captured by saying stop letting sin reign. That sin and death have been reigning is clear from the phrase "no longer" of 6:6 and 6:9. So also then, to be alive and under grace implies a responsibility now to "present your members as slaves to righteousness" (6:19).

I want to make three other psychological observations from this section. First, psychologically speaking, to be under grace impels an obedience from the heart that is full of thanksgiving (Rom 6:17). Second, the mortal body is clearly a psychological principle in the sense that it is a source of passions.[71] This is also evident in Ephesians 2:3 where flesh and body are paralleled, "we all once lived in the passions of the flesh, carrying out the desires of the body and the mind." Third, there is an expectation that this command to present your members "as instruments for righteousness" (Rom 6:13) is in some sense good making, or at least "leads to righteousness" (6:16), which leads to sanctification (6:19) and eternal life (6:22). What we do forms us into what we are becoming.

---

69. BDAG, μέλος.

70. BDAG, καταργέω.

71. Likewise, flesh (sarx) is a source of psychological inputs. For instance Epicurus writes, "Pleasure in the flesh admits no increase when once the pain of want has been removed" (Ouk epauxetai en tē sarki hē hēdonē, epeidan hapax to kat' endeian algoun exairethē). In Diogenes Laertius, Lives of Eminent Philosophers, trans. and ed. R. D. Hicks, Loeb Classical Library, vol. 2 (Cambridge, MA: Harvard University Press, 1995), 10.144; "sarx," LSJ, "the flesh, as the seat of the affections and lusts, fleshly nature." (II.1); this is also consistent with New Testament usage: Gal 5:16, 24; 1 Pet 2:11; 2 Pet 2:18; 1 John 2:16.

The Law and the Flesh

What role did the law play in forming our fleshly passions and in bringing about hostility within ourselves? Paul moves smoothly into a discussion of the law without transition. The abrupt topic change reminds us that the law has always been in mind where Paul has been referencing slavery to sin. In the old covenant, the law worked with sin to arouse passions in our members (Rom 7:5). There is a definite connection between the law and what the law produces in sinful humanity, namely the "body of sin" (6:6), what I have called the best definition of flesh in the text. Romans 7:5–12 illustrates perfectly the habituation of flesh by sin and under the law. Nowhere is there a clearer statement of what the medievals meant by depravity as *habitus*, "while we were living in the flesh, our sinful passions, aroused by the law, were at work in our members to bear fruit for death" (7:5). And again in 7:8, "But sin, seizing an opportunity through the commandment, produced in me all kinds of covetousness."

This is not a gnostic reading of flesh for two reasons. First, it is not flesh itself that frustrates humankind but its enslaving quality—we are slaves of the one we obey. Disobedience leads to slavery through *habitus*—"you once presented your members as slaves to impurity and to lawlessness leading to more lawlessness" (Rom 6:19). So flesh as physicality is not the origin of sin, but rather flesh is the disposition (*habitus*) that sin and evil have engraved on embodied agency since Adam. Second, if the *habitus* of flesh is an obstacle to righteousness, the plasticity of the body is also an opportunity. Paul commands believers not to "let ... sin ... reign in your mortal body, to make you obey its passions" (6:12) but to "present your members as slaves to righteousness" (6:19). And the presentation of our members (bodies) also leads to a new sort of slavery or *habitus* "leading to sanctification" (6:19). On the other hand, ironically, to remove any bodily aspect from the term "flesh" can produce a somewhat gnostic position because the body would have no positive role to play in sanctification. These texts have a clear line of physicality. It is reasonable to suppose that the reason this emphasis on physicality is obscured is because commentators see no way of affirming the role of the body in sin while avoiding Gnosticism. By suggesting that flesh captures the way our plasticity aids both sin and sanctification, we can make sense of this language and push further away from Gnosticism because we affirm the body's role in sanctification.

Craig Keener connects the struggle between flesh and spirit in Romans 7 with the struggle between reason and passion within Paul's philosophical context.[72] He agrees with the majority of commentators who see in this passage "the life under the law," adding, "I will further argue that this is only life under the law without life in Christ," and, "I deny that 7:7–25 depicts Paul's current experience as a Christian."[73] This section serves a psychological function within the argument of Romans, which may not illegitimately be applied even to Christian experience because the text represents human experience.[74] Keener highlights how the fall of humankind involved a sort of vicious cycle of misuse of the mind, devolving into idolatry and yielding to passions, which further corrupt the mind (Rom 1:18–32). The Jews, also being idolaters, have not benefited from possessing the law, which was to bring "light to those who are in darkness" and aid them to "approve what is excellent" and "know [God's] will" (2:18, 19). Romans 7:7–25 vividly describes how the law was powerless to fight the corruption of the flesh. In spite of the genuine knowledge it provided, the essential power to keep the law was missing. The conflict lies between the way the mind is instructed by the law and the way the corruption of the flesh (bodies, members) wars with the mind. This conflict is familiar to all people; even the Gentiles "show that the work of the law is written on their hearts" (Rom 2:15).[75] But the special means of grace available to those who are in Christ is the life-giving power of the Spirit (Rom 8). Keener also explicitly connects the contrast between mind and flesh in Romans 7 with the physicality of the body. He notes that ancient interpreters have recognized, "Paul connected the mortal body with vulnerability to vice," concluding, "Even if Paul is simply playing on an idea in his culture, in

---

72. Craig Keener, *The Mind of the Spirit: Paul's Approach to Transformed Thinking* (Grand Rapids: Baker Academic, 2016), 88.

73. Keener, *Mind of the Spirit*, 56.

74. Again, I do think Paul is talking to believers when he commands them not to let sin reign "since you are not under law but under grace" (Rom 6:14) and "to put to death the deeds of the body" (8:13) since they are not debtors "to live according to the flesh" (8:12). The very presence of these commands seems to legitimize the continuance of this internal conflict into the state of grace.

75. The language of Romans 2:15 is jarring in light of Jeremiah 31:33, "For this is the covenant that I will make with the house of Israel after those days, declares the LORD: I will put my law within them, and I will write it on their hearts. And I will be their God, and they shall be my people."

this context Paul does in some sense connect sin with the behavior, desires, and mortality of the body."[76]

We see flesh (Rom 7:14, 18), members (7:23), and body (7:24) all implicated as the location in which sin dwells. Sin wages war in our members (7:23); these are the same members we are commanded to present as instruments to righteousness in 6:13. So also the terms law of the mind (noos) and the law of sin are an approximation for mind and flesh because flesh is the body habituated by sin and under the law. All this raises a very natural question for anyone who knows the embodied dominion of sin: "Who will deliver me from this body of death? Thanks be to God through Jesus Christ our Lord!" (7:24–25). The deliverance here is no gnostic release of soul from body, but rather the proper ordering of human agency (1:26–27; 6:12; 7:5) by the "Spirit of life" (8:2), who brings life to our mortal bodies.

The Spirit Who Gives Life

How exactly does Jesus Christ deliver us from this body of sin and death? The question brings us back to where we started prior to considering the Gethsemane narrative: "For God has done what the law, weakened by the flesh, could not do. By sending his own Son in the likeness of sinful flesh and for sin, he condemned sin in the flesh, in order that the righteous requirement of the law might be fulfilled in us, who walk not according to the flesh but according to the Spirit" (Rom 8:3–4). We clearly see the liabilities of embodied human existence in sin and under the law. Christ has overcome those liabilities and delivers us from the reign of sin and death by making us alive in him by the Holy Spirit.

And what role does the Spirit play in enabling the reign of grace and restoring our bodies? Those who belong to Christ are indwelt by the Holy Spirit, who enables the law to be fulfilled in them (Rom 8:4). In Romans 8:7, Paul remarks how the "mind that is set on the flesh is hostile to God" and *cannot* submit to God (*oude gar dunatai*). Recall Paul's description of

---

76. Keener, *Mind of the Spirit*, 99. He lists nine evidences: (1) "the 'body of sin' (6:6)"; (2) "the 'desires' of the 'mortal [death-destined] body' (7:5)"; (3) "'sinful passions' working in bodily members (7:5)"; (4) "sin related to the 'flesh' (7:18, 25)"; (5) "'the body of this death' (7:24)"; (6) "the present body is 'dead because of sin' (8:10)"; (7) "resurrection hope for 'mortal bodies' (8:11)"; (8) "death for those who live according to the 'flesh' (8:13a; cf. 8:6)"; (9) "hope of life if one puts to death the body's works (8:13b)."

our ungodliness in 5:6, "still weak" (*asthenōn*). Here Paul remarks that the Spirit "helps us in our weakness [*astheneia*]" (8:26). The Spirit gives us the power to fulfill "the righteous requirement of the law" (8:4).[77] The Spirit gives life (8:2), peace (8:6), and righteousness (8:10). In Christ, the Spirit enables us to present our members for sanctification. Sanctification, considering ourselves alive and presenting our members, is participatory not only because we are in Christ, but also because we have the Holy Spirit (8:9).

The characteristic of "those who live according to the Spirit" is that they "set their minds on the things of the Spirit" (Rom 8:5). Schreiner connects this with the new orientation of the human will made possible by the Spirit.[78] So in Romans 8:10, where we see the contrast between Spirit and body, we see that the Spirit enables a sort of internal tension between the plasticity of rebellion and the new mind that the Spirit brings into reality. Whereas those who are in the flesh cannot please God, those who are in the Spirit can, in spite of being in our mortal bodies. Paul explains, "But if Christ is in you, although the body is dead because of sin, the Spirit is life because of righteousness" (8:10). Commentators struggle to make sense of what it might mean for the body to be dead.[79] Yet the interpretation is easy given what I have said so far: the dead body is just like the "likeness of sinful flesh" (8:3) that Christ assumed, the body formed via plasticity by sin and under the law, or the body under the curse. Insofar as the body still participates in the habits of death, it is dead and awaits its full redemption. Paul then reiterates the command from 6:12 in 8:12–14 when he says, "So then, brothers, we are debtors, not to the flesh, to live according to the flesh. For if you live according to the flesh you will die, but if by the Spirit you put to death the deeds of the body, you will live. For all who are led by

---

77. Schreiner, *Romans*, 405–7. He writes, "The notion that verse 4 is forensic, however, should be rejected. There are good reasons for saying that Paul has in mind actual obedience of Christians. … The last clause of verse 4 also suggests that the actual keeping of the law by believers is contemplated: τοῖς μὴ κατὰ σάρκα περιπατοῦσιν ἀλλὰ κατὰ πνεῦμα. … Those who confine obedience to forensic categories in 8:4 seem to miss rather badly the scope of Paul's argument."

78. He writes, "Strictly speaking, φρονεῖν and φρόνημα (*phronēma*, mind-set, vv. 6–7) signify the direction of the will in human beings." Schreiner, *Romans*, 411.

79. For instance, Schreiner asks, "what precisely does this sentence mean? … More likely, the reference is to the physical death believers must endure because they are sinners." This sentiment echoes Schreiner's comments about the flesh Christ assumed. Schreiner, *Romans*, 414.

the Spirit of God are sons of God." Notice the direct parallel between flesh and body.[80] But notice also the key difference between the commands of Romans 6 and 8, namely that the Spirit is the one who vivifies our practice. It is only by his power that we can put on the Lord Jesus Christ, not gratifying the flesh (cf. 13:14). I am drawing from a very important Pauline notion of concurrence in labor (1 Cor 15:10), which produces legitimate boasting in the Spirit's work in and through us (Rom 15:17–19), which is just a boast in the gospel itself (Rom 1:16; 5:2).

Next, we see a vivid picture of the lack of *shalom* for body and earth, even for those in Christ, even for those who have the Spirit. There is an eschatological tension between the inauguration of the new covenant and the consummation. Just as creation groans and waits for freedom from its bondage to corruption under the curse (Gen 3:17–19), so we also, "the firstfruits of the Spirit," groan as we wait for "the redemption of our bodies" (Rom 8:23). The call to present ourselves is forward-looking because our "sufferings of this present time are not worth comparing with the glory that is to be revealed to us" (8:18). This glory is the end of slavery (8:15) and the coming into heirship by adoption (8:17, 23).

By highlighting the role of the body in sin and sanctification, the stakes for the embodiment of our faith are raised and moderated. On the one hand, the stakes are raised by the fact that the presentation of our bodies—leading to sanctification—is central to the economy of the Spirit. He brings life to our mortal bodies (Rom 8:11). On the other hand, the stakes are perhaps moderated by our continued expectation of groaning as we await the redemption of our bodies (8:23)—the already and not yet. One way of putting this is that our plastic bodies will always be formed by natural

---

80. This is the one place where Gundry's analysis of *sōma* seems quite strained. Gundry is concerned to demonstrate that *sōma* does not designate the whole self but the physical body. He recognizes that one way of reading Romans 8:10, "the body is dead because of sin," is as a "periphrasis for 'the flesh.'" But he judges taking it this way would mean that the body cannot be physical, because the flesh "does not denote materiality" (p. 38). So, instead of admitting that flesh and body both denote an aspect of physicality, Gundry attempts to demonstrate that "the body is dead because of sin" is not parallel to flesh. He explains that the deeds of the body are ultimately sourced in the flesh but are merely instrumentally worked out in the body. He explains that the dead body cannot equal flesh because then the body would need casting off as the flesh does rather than quickening. But again, if Gundry has already decided that flesh cannot have a physical nuance, then he cannot see how the flesh needs quickening as I am arguing. He sustains this strained distinction for his treatment of Rom 6:6; 7:24; Gal 5:16–17, 24; and Col 1:22; 2:11. Gundry, *Sōma in Biblical Theology*, 38–46.

and moral evil. We may keep experiencing mental anguish from bodily dysfunction (e.g., mental illness) as we await our redemption. Moral and natural evil are deeply intermingled in the very form of our fleshly experience at least between the fall and final restoration. The Spirit brings life to our mortal bodies—giving power over moral evil—but does not entirely rescue us from the presence of sin in ourselves or in society.

Finally, we see the interplay between our minds and plastic bodies, and the Spirit's presence, summarized nicely in the oft cited command of Romans 12:1–2: "I appeal to you therefore, brothers, by the mercies of God, to present your bodies as a living sacrifice, holy and acceptable to God, which is your spiritual worship. Do not be conformed to this world,[81] but be transformed by the renewal of your mind, that by testing you may discern what is the will of God, what is good and acceptable and perfect." The language of presenting ties this command back to Romans 6 and the entire discussion of body, members, and flesh throughout Romans 6–8. There is also an assumption of plasticity in the terms "conformed" and "transformed."[82] And notice that the term "worship" (latreian) is a cultic term that along with "sacrifice" (thusian) suggests that the practice of righteousness is the proper offering in the inaugurated kingdom.[83] If, as James K. A. Smith suggests, our liturgy forms us, then we must not forget the liturgy of obedience, "which leads to righteousness" (Rom 6:16). That our body qualifies our existence is important not just for the doctrine of sin, but also as we present our bodies to righteousness, as we practice the liturgy of obedience.

---

81. BDAG, "συσχηματίζω," "to form according to a pattern or mold, form/model after something."

82. I do not deny that this use of the term "body" looks backward and forward to the body of Christ in the rest of this chapter. As Servais Pinckaers writes, "The term 'body' (soma) employed here [in Romans 12:1] evokes the body of Christ offered in the Eucharist and the body that forms the Church (12.1–2)." I do not have space to develop this here, but I see a very obvious connection between the experience necessary to form the body and the concrete commands for how the members of the body of Christ are to interact. The body of Christ heals our body by the mutual exchange of gifts. Servais Pinckaers, Morality: The Catholic View, trans. Michael Sherwin (South Bend, IN: St. Augustine's Press, 2001), 12.

83. Schreiner writes, "Paul's application of the OT is of immense importance here. Activity and language that focused on the cult in the OT is now extended to embrace every facet of the believer's existence. ... He understands the OT cult as now being fulfilled because the new age is inaugurated. In other words, Paul's understanding of the cult is fundamentally eschatological." Schreiner, Romans, 646.

CONCLUSION

To this point, I have shown three things: (1) the biblical theological relevance of the body through three vignettes; (2) the assumption of a tiered psychology, our minds governing our bodies, nourished by the very words of God (Ps 1:3); and (3) the psychological division that runs along the lines of mind and body rather than body and soul in Romans 5–12. This is an important clarification because, while the New Testament only occasionally differentiates soul or spirit from the body metaphysically (Matt 10:28; Luke 24:39), there is another sort of distinction made when it differentiates the body and mind. This psychological distinction is often missed (Rom 1:24–25; 7:23–25; 12:1–5; Col 2:11–23).

I want to draw two conclusions from this analysis. First, human existence is organic, not in the sense that human beings are merely material, but in the sense that their entire agency is qualified by embodied existence. I hope that this analysis has helped to illuminate the importance of the body for biblical theology. Human essence involves minimally organic matter and agency. Human beings share organic life with plants and animals but have the additional responsibility of covenantal agency, a trust of care and obedience.

Humankind's betrayal of that trust stems from an alternate linguistic framing of desire. The altered understanding of Adam and Eve transformed their vision, producing desire. Flesh took the form not of covenantal flourishing but of transgression, covenant breaking. Flesh is not the ultimate source of sin; human willing agency is. But flesh plays a crucial role. By contrast, Jesus assumed human flesh in order to heal it. As Gregory of Nazinanzus has written, "the unassumed is the unhealed." This makes possible the power of new covenant already/not yet life by the Spirit of life (Rom 8:11). By the Spirit we are enabled to present ourselves as slaves to righteousness, which is our sanctification. And yet we "groan inwardly as we wait eagerly for the adoption as sons, the redemption of our bodies" (Rom 8:23). This is not a full description of creation, fall, and redemption, but merely the story as it pertains to human embodiment.

Second, the psychology of Romans is roughly tiered according to mind and body (higher and lower powers) as psychological principles. The next chapter will elaborate how this rough distinction maps on psychological categories. This treatment has also highlighted this important psychological fault line. While this division aligns with the common experience of humanity, of everyday internal psychological conflict, the biblical treatment of it in Romans additionally nuances the division with the redemptive-historical categories of law and grace and sin and Spirit. The body is a source of psychological inputs in a sort of dialectic with the mind. In the terms of Romans, the body is enslaved by sin under the law in this epoch of redemptive history. But mind and body are being renewed by the Spirit under grace. Our bodies are not to remain enslaved by sin. The habit-forming capacity of the body can also contribute to sanctification. The Spirit inaugurates and enables a renewal of our embodied existence such that our renewed mind, by the hearing of faith, saturates our embodied practice by the Spirit's power. The Spirit administers his power both in faith and in practice, as Romans 12–15 assumes. This is a tiered account of agency that takes seriously how we are politically governed top-down with bottom-up reciprocity. We order our lives by the language of God and experience this order by the liturgy of obedience, faith and practice.

8
—

BOOK OF NATURE:
EMBODIED EMOTION

I n the previous chapter, I suggested that an important psychological dividing line, biblically speaking, is the body and mind division. To substantiate this, I constructed three biblical theological vignettes to emphasize the role of the body in redemptive history and to highlight the key psychological struggle between mind and body.[1] I agree with contemporary Reformed theologians that the Bible does not present us with a complete psychology. However, this assumed tiering of psychological inputs in the biblical picture raises an important empirical question: How might the book of nature fill out the biblical concepts concerning this division? In this chapter, I overlay this biblical distinction with a psychological one in conversation with the contemporary debate over the nature of emotion. By roughly mapping a contemporary neuroscientific model onto the rough biblical tiers of body and mind, I hope to bring additional texture to how the body qualifies agency via plasticity by leveraging certain empirical observations. The book of nature can thicken our reading of the Bible's treatment of anxiety, which will be discussed in Chapter 9. In what follows I will suggest that the key psychological tiers are roughly what Aquinas called higher and lower powers, both of which involve a cognitive and appetitive (or affective) component. I will raise the question of the relationship between emotion and thought, suggesting that we do not need a new definition of emotion, but rather a model for understanding the elements

---

1. Again, I am not suggesting that the mind is unaffected by depravity, rather that in the context of Romans, flesh represents the way the body takes the form of the sin that reigns in it, and that this is a key spiritual battle ground.

involved.[2] What is often overlooked by theologians is the role of the unconscious in emotional life. What contemporary psychologists mean by the
unconscious differs quite considerably from the Freudian unconscious,
and functions remarkably similar to Aquinas's lower faculties. It has often
been supposed that emotions must arise from conscious cognition or they
are irrational. But just as Aquinas's holistic and composite lower powers
were only rational by participation, so also is the unconscious, the source
of emotional cognitive processing. I will argue that these lower powers are
dense with meaning and important for understanding human finitude. I
will also try to tease out a basic framework for how the tiers of my model
interact within a single act of attention.

SETTING THE STAGE: EMOTION
AND COGNITION

In any emotional experience, there might be "thoughts, bodily changes,
action tendencies, modulations of mental processes such as attention, and
conscious feelings. But which of these are emotion?" asks Jesse Prinz.[3]
Generally speaking, the theories of emotion foreground some aspect
which is essential to emotion. These theories have been somewhat polar-
ized between viewing emotions as feelings or as judgments, designated by
the terms "non-cognitive" and "cognitive," though some neuroscientists
have insisted the best way to understand them is by way of the underlying circuits. Non-cognitivist accounts, or feeling theories, pioneered
by William James, suggest that emotion is the feeling of bodily changes.
Anthony Damasio's *Descartes' Error* (1994) represents a typical defense of
this sort of theory.[4] The strength of this view is its ability to account for the
affective component of emotion, and especially the ways emotion seems
to run contrary to or exceed thought.

---

2. Joseph LeDoux takes this tack in his "Rethinking the Emotional Brain." He writes, "What
follows is *not* an attempt at explaining or defining emotion. Instead, the aim is to offer a
framework for thinking about some key phenomena associated with emotion (phenomena
related to survival functions) in a way that is not confounded by confusion over what emotion
means." Joseph LeDoux, "Rethinking the Emotional Brain," *Neuron* 73 (February 2012): 653.

3. Jesse Prinz, *Gut Reactions: A Perceptual Theory of Emotion* (Oxford: Oxford University
Press, 2006), 1.

4. William James, "What is an Emotion?" *Mind* 9 (1884): 189–90. Antonio R. Damasio,
Descartes' Error: Emotion, Reason, and the Human Brain (New York: Putnam, 1994).

Robert Solomon represents a pioneer of the cognitivist view, or judgment theory. In his view, an emotion is a sort of self-involved judgment
about something—emotions possess intentionality or aboutness—geared
to perception, which may be episodic or long term and conscious or unconscious.[5] The object makes an emotion what it is, not its physiology.[6] Anger
is thus a judgment that I have been wronged by X person, or thinking X
person as culpable. Martha Nussbaum represents another advocate of this
view, calling emotions "geological upheavals of thought," or a sort of assent
to an appearance that is value laden.[7] The value of the cognitive perspective its ability to account for the variety of emotions, and by putting them
in cognitivist terms, to assess their meaning or morality. We have strong
intuitions that both of these poles are correct about the aspects of emotions they describe—feeling and judging.[8]

This fact partly explains why there are also many theories of emotion
that represent hybrid or impure versions of these theories.[9] These theories hold that emotions are made up of either a combination of states,
such as cognitive and bodily, or a single state with a precondition, such

---

5. Robert Solomon, "Emotions, Thoughts and Feelings: What is a 'Cognitive Theory' of
the Emotions and Does It Neglect Affectivity," in *Royal Institute of Philosophy Supplement*, ed.
A. Hatismoysis, (Cambridge: Cambridge University Press, 2003), 10; Robert Solomon, *The
Passions: The Myth and Nature of Human Emotion* (Notre Dame: University of Notre Dame
Press, 1983), 111–52.

6. Solomon, *Passions*, 124. Jesse Prinz writes that there are three hypotheses that all cognitive theories hold: (1) conceptualization hypothesis, "that cognitive aspects of our emotions
are highly structured"; (2) disembodiment hypothesis, "that the cognitive components bound
to our emotions are disembodied"; and (3) appraisal hypothesis, that emotions are to be
identified either with appraisals, "representations of an organism-environment," typically
psychologists, or propositional attitudes. Prinz, *Gut Reactions*, 24–25.

7. Martha Nussbaum, *Upheavals of Thought: The Intelligence of Emotions* (Cambridge:
Cambridge University Press, 2003), 90.

8. The American Psychological Association defines emotion as follows:

a complex reaction pattern, involving experiential, behavioral, and physiological
elements, by which an individual attempts to deal with a personally significant
matter or event. The specific quality of the emotion (e.g., fear, shame) is determined by the specific significance of the event. For example, if the significance
involves threat, fear is likely to be generated; if the significance involves disapproval from another, shame is likely to be generated. Emotion typically involves
feeling but differs from feeling in having an overt or implicit engagement with
the world.

American Psychological Association Dictionary of Psychology, ed. Gary R. VandenBos, 2nd ed.
(Washington, DC: American Psychological Association, 2015), 362.

9. Prinz, *Gut Reactions*, 10.

as cognition.[10] Because of the complexity of emotion, it seems clear that some sort of hybrid theory must be put forward to accommodate both our intuitions. And most contemporary treatments of emotion do offer some sort of hybrid theory, while emphasizing one pole or the other. Instead of giving my own encapsulated theory of emotion including a full definition, I relate a model of the elements involved in emotion from neuroscientist Joseph LeDoux before simplifying it and comparing it to the psychology of Thomas Aquinas. I am not attempting to answer definitively what is an emotion, but rather to present a rough model of which states and functions are occurrent in emotion and how they interact. The point of providing this model is to clarify my psychological tiers within a holistic framework.

LEDOUX'S NEW MODEL

Emotional Higher-Order Representations

Chapter 1 presented Joseph LeDoux's treatment of fear and anxiety in typical behaviorist terms: humans, like animals, are reactive to threatening external stimuli. These reactions to stimuli of our subcortical defense systems just are the emotions. Signals travel both the high road through the sensory cortex and the low road directly from the sensory thalamus to the amygdala. Just as with other higher primates, the amygdala—the hub of fear—produces an emotional response by activating the sympathetic nervous system, also conditioning the memory for future eliciting conditions.[11]

---

10. Prinz, *Gut Reactions*, 18–19. Prinz lists a third type, "multifunction hybrid," which "identifies emotions with a single kind of state but argues that states of that kind correspond to two or more different items on the list of emotional components."

11. It is worth pointing out that the limbic system plays no role in LeDoux's theorizing about emotion. He spends chapter 4 evaluating the existence of this system in *The Emotional Brain: The Mysterious Underpinnings of Emotional Life* (New York: Simon & Schuster, 1996), 73–102. LeDoux concludes the chapter as follows:

> The general theory, that the brain has a limbic system and that our emotions come out of this system, took on a life of its own and has survived, and even thrived, independent of its conceptual origins. Even as research has shown that classical limbic areas are by no means dedicated to emotion, the theory has persisted. Implicit in such a view is that emotion is a single faculty of mind and that a single unified system of the brain evolved to mediate this faculty. While it is possible that this view is correct, there is little evidence that it is. A new approach to the emotional brain is needed.

Emotional Brain, 102.

LeDoux even writes that "[t]he conscious feelings that we know and love (or hate) our emotions by are red herrings, detours, in the scientific study of emotions," and "[t]he brain states and bodily responses are the fundamental facts of an emotion, and the conscious feelings are the frills that have added icing to the emotional cake."[12]

But in an interview in 2012, the behaviorist neuroscientist made a startling admission: "After 30 years, I've decided that I haven't been studying fear or emotion at all."[13] He now sees emotion as higher order states of consciousness with the underlying subcortical defense systems only providing inputs. He writes, "An emotion [of fear] is the conscious experience that occurs when you are aware that you are in particular kind of situation that you have come, through your experiences, to think of as a fearful situation."[14] He suggests that the sorts of reactions a behaviorist neuroscientist studies are simply the way the "brain detects and responds to danger," adding that "even bacteria do these things." He suggests that basic survival functions are common to all living things but only contribute to emotion. Only when you "put one of those [survival] systems in a brain that has other capacities such as self-reflection and awareness of its other activities, then you get emotions."[15]

LeDoux's new model of emotional consciousness is groundbreaking among neuroscientists.[16] In a paper titled "A Higher-Order Theory of Emotional Consciousness," he and Richard Brown explain and defend a model that specifies that emotions arise in cortically situated general networks of cognition; the cerebral cortex is the outer layer of the brain

---

12. LeDoux, *Emotional Brain*, 18, 302.

13. LeDoux, quoted in Margaret Emory, "On Fear, Emotions, and Memory: An Interview with Dr. Joseph LeDoux," *Brain World*, June 6, 2020, http://brainworldmagazine.com/on-fear-emotions-and-memory-rock-starneuroscientist-joseph-ledouxs-new-terms/.

14. Joseph E. LeDoux and Richard Brown, "A Higher-Order Theory of Emotional Consciousness," *Proceedings of the National Academy of Sciences* 114, no. 10 (January 2017): E2016–25.

15. LeDoux, quoted in Emory, "On Fear, Emotions, and Memory."

16. For example, writing for *Psychology Today*, Christopher Bergland calls the new paper by Joseph E. LeDoux and Richard Brown, "A Higher-Order Theory of Emotional Consciousness"—"potentially earth-shattering." Christopher Bergland, "Joseph LeDoux Reports: Emotions Are 'Higher-Order States,'" *Psychology Today*, February 15, 2017, https://www.psychologytoday.com/us/blog/the-athletes-way/201702/joseph-ledoux-reports-emotions-are-higher-order-states.

responsible for processing complex mental functions.[17] Many neuroscientists have assumed that emotions are feelings arising directly from or
identical to the reactions of the subcortical survival circuits, often referred
to as the limbic system, which are common to both humans and animals.[18]
LeDoux agrees that these systems are common to many vertebrates, especially mammals, but is reluctant to call the outputs of these systems emotions, either in humans or animals. In the case of fear, for example, the
amygdala is the hub of a sort of defensive survival circuit that is separate
from the circuits that give rise to the experience of fear. What does account
for human fear? LeDoux and Brown cite three aspects: "[1] higher-order
representations (HORs) of [2] lower-order information by [3] cortically
based general networks of cognition (GNC)."[19] I will briefly summarize
these aspects.[20]

---

17. LeDoux and Brown, "Higher-Order Theory," E2016.

18. E.g., the fear circuit, amygdala to medial hypothalamus and dorsal periaqueductal
gray (PAG). For the other systems, see Jaak Panksepp, "The Neuro-Evolutionary Cusp Between
Emotions and Cognitions: Implications for Understanding Consciousness and the Emergence
of a Unified Mind Science," *Emotion and Cognition* 7, no. 2 (2007): 147.

19. LeDoux and Brown, "Higher-Order Theory," E2016.

20. LeDoux's view is important because it represents the most sophisticated account of
embodied emotion from arguably the most significant neuroscientist theorist on the topic
of emotion. My theory assumes that the body is normally involved in any paradigm case of
emotion. There is some debate about whether it is possible to have an emotion that does not
involve physiological arousal. For example, Nico Frijda writes, "Sometimes, to all evidence,
there are no signs of autonomic arousal while subjects say they are, or feel, happy or anxious
or angry. It is as well to take such subjects at their word, as long as their behavior does not
contradict them. Emotion can be there, it appears, without physiological upset of any note,
according to the criteria of subjective experience and expressive behavior." Nico H. Frijda,
The Emotions, Studies in Emotion & Social Interaction (Cambridge: Cambridge University
Press, 1986), 172–73.

Robert Roberts picks up on this to argue that "it follows that emotion cannot be the sensations of that (missing) bodily disturbance." Robert E. Roberts, *Emotion: An Essay in Aid of Moral
Psychology* (Cambridge: Cambridge University Press, 2003), 154. I do not wish to mediate this
dispute about definitions other than to say that the states that I am talking about are more
obvious cases of emotions because they command attention; they are intrusive mental states.
There are all sorts of bodily changes that are not registered as feelings (e.g., stress can go
undetected), but in the normal case of emotions, we are aware of them (e.g., when we say "I
am getting emotional"). It is possible that some emotions involve physiological change and
are not felt. As odd as it sounds, it is possible to push from working memory, to forget that
you are in pain, that is, to have unconscious pain. Again, my purpose is not to delimit what
is and what is not emotion, but rather to present a model of ordinary emotional experience.

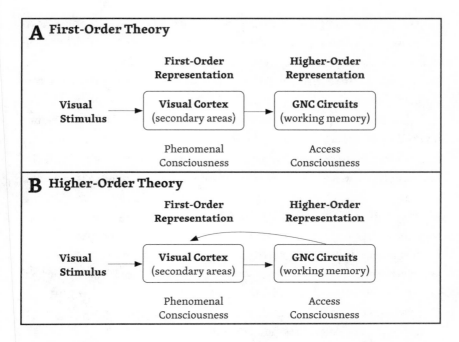

Figure 8.1, Higher-Order Theory (HOT), LeDoux and Brown[21]

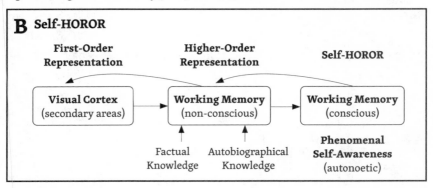

Figure 8.2, Self-HOROR, LeDoux and Brown

LeDoux and Brown affirm a higher-order theory (HOT) of consciousness, meaning that they do not believe that phenomenal consciousness of a visual stimulus, in the visual cortex, is enough for conscious awareness. There must be also additional higher-order representations (HORs), which

21. Figures 8.1–8.3 adapted from Joseph E. LeDoux and Richard Brown, "A Higher-Order Theory of Emotional Consciousness," Proceedings of the National Academy of Sciences 114, no. 10 (January 2017): E2016 [E2016–E2025]

are taken to be thoughts or images (see Figure 8.1).[22] LeDoux and Brown also make an adjustment to higher order theory. They distinguish between non-conscious higher-order representations in working memory (HOR) and those that are conscious.[23] In essence, to be phenomenologically conscious is not merely to have a HOR, but also to be introspectively aware of it, a higher order representation of a representation, or HOROR [B] (Figure 8.2).[24] This merely distinguishes two types of awareness, non-conscious and conscious. In making this distinction between HORs and HORORs, LeDoux and Brown are also accounting for the self-knowledge involved in an introspective higher-order representation; a HOROR, which they amend to self-HOROR. The point is that human conscious awareness depends on self-knowledge (e.g., of identity, goals, etc.).[25] LeDoux and Brown call these self-representations "integrated hubs for information processing, a kind of 'associative glue.'"[26] They write, "Without the self, there is no fear or love or joy. If some event is not affecting you, then it is not producing an emotion. When your friend or child suffers you feel it because they are part of you."[27] Emotional awareness is a sort of self-representation.

Whereas first-order theories of emotion involve two neurological circuits for consciousness—the subcortical and cortical—LeDoux and Brown suggest that "only one circuit of consciousness is required: the GNC [general networks of cognition]."[28] Against the views of most behaviorist neuroscientists, the subcortical processing merely provides inputs for the

---

22. LeDoux and Brown, "Higher-Order Theory," E2018.

23. This clarification enables the authors to account for Charles Bonnet Syndrome, where subjects that lack first-order representations can have "rich and vivid visual experiences in hallucinations." LeDoux and Brown, "Higher-Order Theory," E2020.

24. LeDoux and Brown, "Higher-Order Theory," E2020.

25. LeDoux and Brown, "Higher-Order Theory," E2020–21.

26. LeDoux and Brown, "Higher-Order Theory," E2021; citing J. Sui and G. W. Humphreys, "The integrative self: How self-reference integrates perception and memory," *Trends in Cognitive Science* 19, no. 12 (October 2015): 719–28. Sui and Humphreys try to demonstrate that self-reference: "(1) helps bind memories to their source, (2) increases perceptual integration, (3) makes it difficult to re-bind a new association to a stimulus formerly linked to the self, (4) modulates the coupling between attention and decision making and (5) increases interactions between brain regions. Self-reference provides a form of associative 'glue' for perception, memory and decision making and, through this, acts as a central mechanism in information processing." Sui and Humphreys, "The integrative self," 719.

27. LeDoux and Brown, "Higher-Order Theory," E2021.

28. LeDoux and Brown, "Higher-Order Theory," E2021.

more complex GNC circuits. Subcortical processes are not emotions. They only "indirectly influence the higher-order assembly of conscious feelings by the GNC."[29] The key points for the theory of emotion are two: (1) emotions are cortical constructions that arise from unconscious processes; and (2) this means that emotions are not just the activity of the lower survival systems, as with animals. LeDoux and Brown are skeptical that animals have emotions.[30]

So, how does this higher-order theory work for feelings of fear? Suppose you see a snake at your feet (see Figure 8.3).[31] First, a visual stimulus is processed both by the visual cortex and by the subcortical survival circuit, the high and low road from earlier. Simultaneously, the subcortical survival circuit via the amygdala triggers bodily responses while the visual cortex interfaces with long-term memory to contribute to a multimodal representation within a cortical convergence zone of the brain.[32] Since this representation is a function of the unconscious working memory by way of the HOR, it is unconscious unless it is selected by attention.[33] The amygdala likewise functions unconsciously, but by stimulating emotional

29. LeDoux and Brown, "Higher-Order Theory," E2019. So, for example, "damage to first-order subcortical circuits, such as defensive survival circuit or body-sensing circuits, should mute but not eliminate feelings of fear. Evidence consistent with this exists," E2021.

J. S. Feinstein et al. write, "Surprisingly, we found that inhalation of 35% CO_2 evoked not only fear, but also panic attacks, in three rare patients with bilateral amygdala damage. These results indicate that the amygdala is not required for fear and panic, and make an important distinction between fear triggered by external threats from the environment versus fear triggered internally by CO_2." J. S. Feinstein et al., "Fear and panic in humans with bilateral amygdala damage," *Nature Neuroscience* 16 (2013), 270. A. K. Anderson and E. A. Phelps write, "The findings of the present study suggest that neither patients with unilateral nor bilateral amygdala damage characterize their emotional life differently than that of normal, healthy controls." A. K. Anderson and E. A. Phelps, "Is the human amygdala critical for the subjective experience of emotion? Evidence of intact dispositional affect in patients with amygdala lesions," *Journal of Cognitive Neuroscience* 14, no. 5 (2002): 715.

30. This contrasts with the view of Jaak Panksepp. "In his view, core phenomenal states of emotional consciousness, such as feelings of fear, are innate experiences that arise in humans and other mammals from evolutionarily conserved subcortical circuits." LeDoux and Brown, "Higher-Order Theory," E2019. In other words, human emotion is a sort of evolutionary leftover that only arises from more primitive brain circuits (those lower down toward the brain stem). See Panksepp, "Neuro-Evolutionary Cusp"; Jaak Panksepp, *Affective Neuroscience: The Foundations of Human and Animal Emotions* (Oxford: Oxford University Press, 2004).

31. LeDoux and Brown, "Higher-Order Theory," E2021.

32. Joseph LeDoux, "Emotional Colouration of Consciousness: How Feelings Come About," in *Frontiers of Consciousness: The Chichele Lectures*, ed. Lawrence Weiskrantz and Martin Davies (Oxford: Oxford University Press, 2008), 74.

33. LeDoux, "Emotional Colouration," 74.

arousal brings attention to the representation. It pushes the representation into conscious working memory, much like physical pain does, since arousal demands attention.

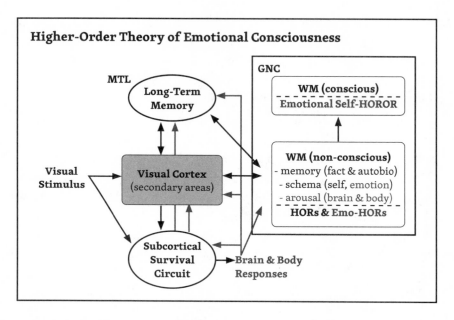

Figure 8.3, Higher Order Theory of Emotional Consciousness, LeDoux and Brown

The higher order representation is conditioned by memory. There are two types of explicit memories that condition it, semantic, in our example facts about the snake, and episodic memories, memories of snakes and autonoetic memories, e.g., a prior snake bite.[34] Since autonoetic consciousness (awareness of the self) is unique to human experience, animals do not strictly experience emotion: "no self, no emotion."[35] The amygdala is also conditioned by implicit memory, which is of the sort that "cannot be directly and explicitly retrieved and experienced consciously."[36] Implicit

---

34. These memories are associated with the hippocampus and surrounding cortical areas. Joseph LeDoux, *Anxious: Using the Brain to Understand and Treat Fear and Anxiety* (New York: Penguin, 2015), 184.

35. LeDoux and Brown, "Higher-Order Theory," E2023.

36. LeDoux, "Emotional Colouration," 73.

memory includes knowing how, associative conditioning, and priming.[37] Associative conditioning happens when an unconditioned stimulus, for example a desire for savory food, is paired with a conditioned stimulus, the sight of your favorite steakhouse. So, the representation of the snake in unconscious working memory is conditioned by semantic (e.g. rattle-snake or garter) and episodic memory integrating autobiographical knowledge (e.g., a prior snake bite). The collection of unconsciously processed knowledge is called a schema, which is applied not through ratiocination, but automatically and unconsciously, like Aquinas's cogitative estimation. The bodily reactions are simultaneously influencing the entire system of long-term memory, visual circuits, and the subcortical survival circuits in a feedback loop. Future memories of this snake incident are reinforced by the release of neuromodulator chemicals.

Because the amygdala has triggered an aroused state, the person becomes self-consciously aware of experiencing an emotion, an emotional self-HOROR, because arousal demands attention. The emotional feelings enter conscious working memory, which involves four aspects: (1) inputs that operate automatically, "articulatory loops and a visuospatial scratchpad"; (2) long-term memory providing meaning; (3) an episodic buffer, which binds representations to produce a unified representation; and (4) executive control or attention.[38] These four aspects map remarkably well on Aquinas's sub-faculties for perception.

What sort of theory of emotion do we have? It is significant that LeDoux speaks of emotional feelings as "emotionally colored cognitions."[39] For LeDoux, for any emotional state, the brain is doing two things: (1) detecting that the survival circuit is active; and (2) appraising and labeling the state.[40] This view is similar to a modified Jamesian theory, in that cognition

37. Priming is a sort of cognitive preference on the basis of some association or subliminal cue. For instance, LeDoux writes, "Consider the word fragment '_urse.' I can bias you to complete this fragment as "nurse" or "purse" by priming you with a story about either doctors or wallets prior to showing you the fragment. You don't have to be thinking about the prime for this to occur, and you don't even have to be aware of the prime, as it can be delivered subliminally, thus bypassing consciousness." LeDoux, *Anxious*, 189–90.

38. LeDoux, "Emotional Colouration," 92.

39. LeDoux, "Emotional Colouration," 69, 72. This is not dissimilar from Robert Roberts's "concern-based construals." Roberts, *Emotion*, 64.

40. LeDoux, "Rethinking the Emotional Brain," 664.

is responsive to feelings of bodily changes, but also an appraisal theory (e.g., Richard Lazarus), which has sometimes been categorized as a cognitive view. LeDoux says that there is "clearly overlap" between the cognitive theory (appraisal theory) and his own central theory. By central theory, he simply means to say that the appraisals are largely unconscious cognitive processing in the cortical areas of the lower subcortical processing.[41] Finally, as we will see below, his view is highly qualified by our human verbal capacity since words are not only the foundation to self-awareness, via the symbolic self-concept, but also make elaborate schema possible. Language may also elicit emotion through its power to bring about "as-if loops,"[42] leading to emotional self-regulation or greater de-regulation, as with rumination.[43]

The Unconscious

Lack of attention to the function of the unconscious is perhaps the most egregious oversight of theologians who theorize about emotion. Theologians may be wary of the unconscious because of the speculative theories of Sigmund Freud. The Freudian unconscious was a developed and speculative system that explained a person's hidden but dominant drives. Contemporary theorists are often complementary to Freud's perspicacity in examining it, but not for his treatment of it.[44] John Kihlstrom narrates how the study of the unconscious was pioneered by figures such as Eduard von Hartmann (1842–1906) and Hermann von Helmholtz (1821–1894) prior to the dynamic psychiatry of Sigmund Freud (1856–1939) and Josef Breuer (1842–1925). Interest in the unconscious waned during the behaviorist

---

41. LeDoux, "Emotional Colouration," 88.

42. Damasio, *Descartes' Error*, 174. See also LeDoux and Brown, "Higher-Order Theory," E2022.

43. Rumination is intense and lasting attention to one's own distress including possible causes and consequences. Rumination is largely unproductive because it does not focus on solutions. Timothy Wilson writes, "Rumination caused depressed participants to become even more depressed." Timothy Wilson, *Strangers to Ourselves: Discovering the Adaptive Unconscious* (Cambridge, MA: Harvard University Press), 176.

44. "Freud was right on the mark when he described consciousness as the tip of the mental iceberg." LeDoux, *Emotional Brain*, 17. As Timothy Wilson writes, "the modern, adaptive unconscious is not the same as the psychoanalytic one." Wilson, *Strangers to Ourselves*, 4.

revolution but returned with the cognitive revolution beginning in the 1950s.[45]

This new cognitive unconscious is very different from the Freudian dynamic unconscious. Blakey Vermeule calls this new interest in the unconscious "aggressively antipsychoanalytic."[46] The new "cognitive unconscious includes all the mental processes that are not experienced by a person but that give rise to a person's thoughts, choices, emotions, and behavior."[47] Timothy Wilson defines the unconscious as all those "mental processes that are inaccessible to consciousness but that influence judgments, feelings, or behavior."[48] These unconscious processes are the very foundations of consciousness.[49] There is a twin danger either to overestimate or to underestimate the unconscious. Is it smart or dumb? Is it primary or secondary to conscious thought and choice? Overestimating the unconscious tends toward seeing it as, in the words of John Kihlstrom, an "automaticity juggernaut," quietly and automatically pulling the strings of human agency.[50] However, my concern is that we do not underestimate it. John Bargh and Ezequiel Morsella write, "The unconscious mind is still viewed by many psychological scientists as the shadow of a 'real' conscious mind, though there now exists substantial evidence that the unconscious is not identifiably less flexible, complex, controlling, deliberative, or action-like

---

45. If psychology was to be a respectable science, it had to abandon the mental in favor of the observable. John F. Kihlstrom, "The Rediscovery of the Unconscious," in *The Mind, The Brain, and Complex Adaptive Systems*, ed. Harold J. Morowitz and Jerome L. Singer, SFI Studies in the Sciences of Complexity, vol. 22 (Reading, MA: Addison-Wesley, 1995), 123–29.

46. Blakey Vermeule, "The New Unconscious, A Literary Guided Tour," in *The Oxford Handbook of Cognitive Literary Studies*, ed. Lisa Zunshine (New York: Oxford University Press, 2015), 463. Anthony Greenwald writes, "Unconscious cognition is now solidly established in empirical research, but it appears to be intellectually much simpler than the sophisticated agency portrayed in psychoanalytic theory." Anthony G. Greenwald, "New Look 3: Unconscious Cognition Reclaimed," *American Psychologist* 47 (June 1992): 766. On the other hand, Matthew Erdelyi defends Freud's psychoanalysis as bona fide cognitive psychology. Matthew H. Erdelyi, *Psychoanalysis: Freud's Cognitive Psychology* (New York: Freeman, 1985).

47. Daniel L. Schacter, Daniel T. Gilbert, and Daniel M. Wegner, *Psychology*, 2nd ed. (New York: Worth, 2011), 188.

48. Wilson, *Strangers to Ourselves*, 23.

49. Panksepp, "Neuro-Evolutionary Cusp," 150.

50. John F. Kihlstrom, "The Automaticity Juggernaut—or, Are We Autonomous After All?," in *Are We Free? Psychology and Free Will*, ed. J. Baer, J. C. Kaufman, and R. F. Baumeister (New York: Oxford University Press, 2008), 155–80.

than is its counterpart."[51] Some psychologists see unconscious processes
as comprising more than 90 percent of our cognitive processing, including priming, filtering, selective attention, subliminal activation, unconscious learning, implicit memory, and even goal setting.[52] While the field
is dynamic and complex, I will present some evidence below from those
who see the unconscious as playing a significant role in human experience.

Like most theorists on emotion, LeDoux's account relies on cognitive processing that is almost entirely unconscious, except when it is the
focus of attention.[53] LeDoux writes, "The most straightforward way to
distinguish mental state consciousness from nonconscious processes that
control behavior is via language—by verbal self-report."[54] We may be conscious that the face we are seeing is of a man named Dan, but the cognitive
appraisals that ground this impression are complex and mysterious.[55] So,
the unconscious is also the foundation of emotional consciousness. Peter
Carruthers writes, "all affective states result from assessments of the relevance of environmental or bodily events, either to previously formed goals,
or to one's underlying values stored subcortically as dispositional properties of reward-systems in the basal ganglia. These appraisals are generally
swift and unconscious, operating at many different levels of processing of
the sensory input."[56] For example, "humans can recognize certain emotions
[in others] by the [whites of the] eyes alone and do not need to process the
face as a whole."[57] LeDoux points to substantial evidence for unconscious

51. John A. Bargh and Ezequiel Morsella, "The Unconscious Mind," *Perspectives on Psychological Science* 3, no. 1 (January 2008): 73.

52. Timothy Wilson writes, "We take in 11,000,000 pieces of information per second, but can process only 40 of them consciously." Wilson, *Strangers to Ourselves*, 23. See also Greenwald, "New Look 3," 766–79; Wilson, *Strangers to Ourselves*, 6, 17–42; and John F. Kihlstrom, "The Motivational Unconscious," *Social and Personality Psychology Compass* 13, no. 5 (2019): 1–18.

53. Jaak Panksepp writes, "It has long been obvious to critically minded observers that many of the emotional acts that humans and animals exhibit reflect no conscious intent." Panksepp, "Neuro-Evolutionary Cusp," 142.

54. LeDoux, *Anxious*, 149.

55. This is Michael Polanyi's example of the tacit in *The Tacit Dimension* (Chicago: University of Chicago Press, 1966), 149.

56. Peter Carruthers, "Valence and Value," *Philosophy and Phenomenological Research* 9, no. 1 (2017): 52.

57. LeDoux, "Rethinking the Emotional Brain," 659.

processing underlying emotion.[58] If the processing underlying emotion is unconscious, then we must pay attention to how this differentiates it from explicit thought.

BODILY INPUTS

Because theologians typically view emotion cognitively, they also tend to minimize the role the body plays in everyday emotions. There are certain aspects to emotional experience that are difficult to understand from the standpoint of the subjective logic, that is, a person's thoughts or desires. There are certain ways our psychological states are qualified by the body that may be deeply mysterious even to the one experiencing them. I will develop these as follows. First, I will discuss how physiology influences what we consider to be rational by leading us to confabulate, unknowingly falsely attribute, our feelings. Physiology can be a sort of cognitive interference keeping us from the reasons for our feelings. Second, our physiology enables emotional plasticity within the entire nervous system. Third, experience may leverage this neuroplasticity to bring about habits (states or traits) of emotional reactions. Fourth, these traits rely on embedded or implicit memory, which operates very differently from our explicit memory. Finally, I will illustrate these things by appealing to developmental trauma.

But first I want to clarify what I mean by bodily changes. As Joseph LeDoux has clarified, the amygdala is not straightforwardly responsible for fear, but rather is the hub for the bodily reactions triggered by a threat, which contribute to a conscious feeling of fear along with other cognitive elements (appraisal and valence). This is not different from Aquinas's notion that passions are movements of the soul, based on quick judgments, accompanied by bodily changes, such as heating or the quickening of

---

58. The articles that could be cited here from neuroscience, psychology, social psychology, etc. are overwhelming. This is only a very select few: Erdelyi, *Psychoanalysis*; Greenwald, "New Look 3"; Philip M. Merikle, Daniel Smilek, and John D. Eastwood, "Perception Without Awareness," *Cognition* 79 (2001): 115–34; John F. Kihlstrom, "The Cognitive Unconscious," *Science* 237 (1987): 144–52; Robert Zajonc, "Feeling and Thinking: Preferences Need No Inferences," *American Psychologist* 35 (1980): 151–75; and Larry L. Jacoby, "A Process-Dissociation Framework for Investigating Unconscious Influences: Freudian Slips, Projective Tests, Subliminal Perception, and Signal Detection Theory," *Current Directions in Psychological Science* 1, no. 6 (December 1992): 174–79.

spirits. In the case of anxiety, LeDoux specifies bodily alterations triggered by threats:

> bodily responses include [1] behavioral reactions (i.e. freezing, facial postures), [2] autonomic nervous system responses (i.e. changes in blood flow distribution accompanied by changes in blood pressure and heart rate; increased respiration; sweat gland activity) and [3] endocrine responses (release of pituitary-adrenal hormones). Reactive brain responses include [4] activation of arousal systems that release modulatory chemical signals throughout the brain and regulate the level of activation and receptivity to stimulation of neurons in target regions.[59]

The most significant physiological alterations arise within the sympathetic nervous system (SNS), often referred to as the fight or flight (or freeze) system. The sympathetic nervous system is responsible for a whole host of physiological reactions including dilating pupils, inhibiting salivation, increasing heart rate, constricting arteries, expanding the lungs, releasing various hormones and glucose, inhibiting digestion, etc. Generally speaking, the sympathetic nervous system routes energy away from long-term functions like digestion and toward the emergency functions of muscles and respiration. This is why chronic stress often causes digestive issues.[60]

Cognitive Interference

Our physiological inputs often mean that emotion subverts what we might consider to be rational. The body itself, especially the autonomic nervous system, plays a significant role in the emotional life. LeDoux's model of emotional representation recognizes that an object of fear, be it an external thing or a thought, may simultaneously activate bodily responses and

---

59. LeDoux, "Emotional Colouration," 76.

60. More recently, two systems have been recognized as part of the alarm response, the sympathoadrenal system (a part of the SNS) and the pituitary-adrenal system. The former "releases epinephrine and norepinephrine into the bloodstream, allowing these hormones to influence many of the [various] organs and tissues." These hormones are in the blood and do not affect the brain directly. The pituitary-adrenal system releases cortisol "from the adrenal cortex," which is routed throughout the brain and body. These hormones modulate cognition. Generally, neurotransmitters belong to the nervous system, hormones to the endocrine system, and cytokines to the immune system. LeDoux, *Anxious*, 56–60. See also Gabor Maté, *The Stress Disease Connection* (Hoboken, NJ: Wiley, 2011).

perceptual processing via the subcortical survival circuits, especially the amygdala. The brain and bodily responses (bodily inputs) that are triggered provide information to all levels of mental activity, but especially the less abstractable unconscious. By contrast, conscious attention is more abstract because of symbolic thought. Physiological changes are often felt by the agent in cognitively ambiguous ways.

Timothy Wilson writes about a study conducted in British Columbia where an attractive woman asked men to fill out a questionnaire, explaining that it was for her class project. When the men completed the survey, she gave them her phone number, explaining that she would be happy to discuss it further with them. The researchers kept track of how many men called her to ask her for a date. The researchers divided the experiment between male subjects who were in a park and those standing on a 450-foot-long suspension bridge over a gorge, the Capilano Suspension Bridge. The researchers predicted that more men would call for a date from the group on the bridge than those in the park, assuming, as Wilson notes, "that these men would be mixed up about exactly why they were physiologically aroused."[61] Sixty-five percent of the men on the bridge called, while only thirty percent of those in the park did.[62]

In a similar study, Stanley Schachter and Jerome Singer injected subjects with epinephrine or placebo.[63] In both cases the subjects were told that they were being injected with "Suproxin," which they claimed to be a vitamin that aids vision. Epinephrine almost exactly mimics the arousal of the sympathetic nervous system. Some subjects were informed of the epinephrine's effects, some were misinformed of its effects, and some were ignorant. The study demonstrates that those who were ignorant of any supposed effects of the shot and had received epinephrine were far more likely to get angry and to confabulate about its cause. By confabulation, I mean a misrepresentation of one's own memory or other mental states without the intent to deceive. Schachter and Singer make three claims

61. Wilson, *Strangers to Ourselves*, 101.

62. Wilson, *Strangers to Ourselves*, 101–2. See also Donald G. Dutton and Arthur P. Aron, "Some Evidence for Heightened Sexual Attraction Under Conditions of High Anxiety," *Journal of Personality and Social Psychology* 30, no. 4 (1974): 510–17.

63. Stanley Schachter and Jerome E. Singer, "Cognitive, Social, and Physiological Determinants of the Emotional State," *Psychological Review* 69, no. 5 (September 1962): 379–99.

from their findings: (1) "Given a state of physiological arousal for which an individual has no immediate explanation, he will label this state and describe his feelings in terms of the cognitions available to him." (2) "Given a state of physiological arousal for which an individual has a completely appropriate explanation, no evaluative needs will arise, and the individual is unlikely to label his feelings in terms of the alternative cognitions available." (3) "Given the same cognitive circumstances, the individual will react emotionally or describe his feelings as emotions only to the extent that he experiences a state of physiological arousal."[64] Again, this labeling of physiological arousal is confabulation. People spontaneously imagine reasons for feelings that are clearly physiological. This raises a related difficulty, which I call emotional bleed. People in an aroused state find it easy to make additional emotional construals in unrelated spheres. In instances of emotional arousal, one instance of anger— for example, "Individual S has culpably offended in the important matter of X and is bad"—easily bleeds into, "Individual S has also culpably offended in the important matter of Y," or "Individual P has culpably offended in the matter of Z," etc.[65] This sort of arbitrary transference of arousal is familiar to married people.

Plasticity

If emotion can interfere with rationality, it is also true that these interfering emotions can become habitual via plasticity. With regard to plasticity, there is plasticity at the level of neurological pathways, and there is the more general state or trait conditions of neurochemical hormones. With regard to neuroplasticity, there is the very well-known Hebb's rule: neurons that fire together wire together.[66] LeDoux puts it this way: "Donald Hebb proposed that when weak and strong stimuli activate the same neurons, the strong stimulus changes the chemistry of the neurons in such a

---

64. Schachter and Singer, "Cognitive, Social," 398.

65. I am borrowing Robert Roberts's propositional formula for anger; Roberts, *Emotions*, 204.

66. This is a rough summary of the following statement: "Let us assume that the persistence or repetition of a reverberatory activity (or 'trace') tends to induce lasting cellular changes that add to its stability. ... When an axon of cell A is near enough to excite a cell B and repeatedly or persistently takes part in firing it, some growth process or metabolic change takes place in one or both cells such that A's efficiency, as one of the cells firing B, is increased." D. O. Hebb, *The Organization of Behavior: A Neuropsychological Theory* (New York: Wiley, 1949), 62.

way as to enable the weak stimulus to activate the neurons more strongly in the future."[67] Jeffrey Schwartz, a neuroscientist and OCD specialist, wants to leverage neuroplasticity for sufferers, claiming, "you can physically change the way your brain works"; or you can rewire your brain.[68] This is particularly important for psychological habits because neural plasticity of the entire nervous system underwrites learning by association.[69]

Neuroplasticity is also related to chemical imbalances because neurological pathways are reinforced by the neurochemical or hormonal climate. It is widely recognized that psychological arousal releases hormones like adrenaline to enhance long-term memory.[70] Neurons wire together strongest during emotional states.[71] We have clearer memories of the day of our wedding and of September 11, 2001, than of three days before these dates. I will return to the topic of memory and arousal in discussing implicit memory.

The notion of a longstanding hormonal climate is captured by the often cited chemical imbalance. Because emotional reactions elicit the release of hormones, hormonal climates, like reactions, seem to become habitual or typical. But just what sort of habit is this? The answer is not clear. LeDoux differentiates between state anxiety and trait anxiety. Trait anxiety is often spoken of as a chemical imbalance, chronic, perhaps partly genetic, something like Aquinas's temperament, a habit of the body. The

---

67. LeDoux, *Anxious*, 92.

68. Jeffrey Schwartz, *Brain Lock* (New York: ReganBooks, 1996), xv. See also Jeffrey Schwartz, *You Are Not Your Brain: The 4-Step Solution for Changing Bad Habits, Ending Unhealthy Thinking, and Taking Control of Your Life* (New York: Penguin, 2011). Schwartz explains free will by the fact that the mind makes active choices.

69. "The plasticity of the nervous system—its ability to be molded in diverse ways by environmental inputs—is increasingly being recognized and acknowledged." Panksepp, "Neuro-Evolutionary Cusp," 157. Panksepp gives three examples involving stress, especially one regarding maternal bonding. Alvaro Pascual-Leon et al. writes, "plasticity is not an occasional state of the nervous system; instead, it is the normal ongoing state of the nervous system throughout the life span. ... a brain [is] undergoing constant change triggered by previous events or resulting from intrinsic remodeling activity." Alvaro Pascual-Leone, Amir Amedi, Felipe Fregni, and Lotfi B. Merabet, "The Plastic Human Brain Cortex," *Annual Review of Neuroscience* 28, no. 1 (July 2005): 379.

70. J. L. McGaugh and M. L. Hertz, *Memory Consolidation* (San Francisco: Albion, 1972); L. Cahill and J. L. McGaugh, "Mechanisms of Emotional Arousal and Lasting Declarative Memory," *Trends in Neurosciences* 21, no. 7 (1998): 295.

71. This is not true of explicit memory during traumatic events. This is why implicit memory often produces disturbing flashbacks of otherwise repressed events.

exact line between states and traits is quite difficult to determine.[72] Even the notion of chemical imbalance has come under fire for not adequately accounting for experience and implicit memory. There is an increasingly vocal resistance to the notion.[73] Psychiatrist Ronald Pies writes,

> I am not one who easily loses his temper, but I confess to experi-
> encing markedly increased limbic activity whenever I hear some-
> one proclaim, "Psychiatrists think all mental disorders are due to
> a chemical imbalance!" In the past 30 years, I don't believe I have
> ever heard a knowledgeable, well-trained psychiatrist make such a
> preposterous claim, except perhaps to mock it. On the other hand,
> the "chemical imbalance" trope has been tossed around a great deal
> by opponents of psychiatry, who mendaciously attribute the phrase
> to psychiatrists themselves.[74]

If chemical imbalance is not quite right, LeDoux suggests that there may be a better way of looking at it. LeDoux thinks that trait anxiety might be a habit of the entire nonconscious processing system. Instead of aiming at the feelings as drug companies do, any successful treatment of anxiety must "alter the nonconscious brain systems that process present and antic-ipated threats, as well as trigger behavioral and physiological responses that help cope with these threats."[75] LeDoux suggests that a major prob-lem with anxiolytics, drugs that reduce anxiety, is that they have only

---

72. Chaplin, John, and Goldberg write, "Although the distinction between traits and states is fuzzy, it is hardly arbitrary." William F. Chaplin, Oliver P. John, and Lewis R. Goldberg, "Conceptions of States and Traits: Dimensional Attributes with Ideals as Prototypes," *Journal of Personality and Social Psychology* 54, no. 4 (1988): 541–57.

73. Elliot Valenstein, *Blaming the Brain: The Truth About Drugs and Mental Health* (New York: Free Press, 1988); Robert Whitaker, *Anatomy of an Epidemic: Magic Bullets, Psychiatric Drugs, and the Astonishing Rise of Mental Illness in America* (New York: Broadway, 2010); and Irving Kirsch, *The Emperor's New Drugs: Exploding the Antidepressant Myth* (London: Bodley Head, 2009).

74. Ronald W. Pies, "Psychiatry's New Brain-Mind and the Legend of the 'Chemical Imbalance,'" *Psychiatric Times*, July 11, 2011. http://www.psychiatrictimes.com/couch-crisis/psychiatrys-new-brain-mind-and-legend-chemical-imbalance. To get a picture of the real complexities of the physiological component of depression, see R. H. Belmaker and Galila Agram, "Major Depressive Disorder," *New England Journal of Medicine* 358, no. 1 (January 2008): 55–68.

75. Joseph LeDoux, "What's Wrong with Antianxiety Drugs? A Possible Path Towards Better Options," *Psychology Today*, August 16, 2015, https://www.psychologytoday.com/us/blog/i-got-mind-tell-you/201508/whats-wrong-antianxiety-drugs.

been tested in states of anxiety, such that their impact on trait anxiety is not well understood.[76] Elliot Valenstein cautions, "There is a tendency to confuse the giant strides that have been made in our knowledge of brain chemistry and neuropharmacology with our still primitive understanding of the causes of mental illness and knowledge of how drugs can produce psychological changes."[77] LeDoux even co-authored a recent study that showed that chronic antidepressant use can actually impair learning.[78] So the drugs seem only to mask the feelings rather than to repair the error in the unconscious and bodily processes. The important point is that the body develops longstanding conditions that are difficult to alter, which may involve inherited traits, but these traits may be related to unconscious learning. To understand this sort of learning, it is necessary to distinguish between the types of memory, especially explicit and implicit.

Implicit Memory

A key to understanding how physiology features in conscious experience is the notion of implicit memory. We have already briefly discussed the distinction between explicit (semantic and episodic) and implicit memory. But how do these forms of memory work together in experience? How might implicit memory interfere with cognitive function? LeDoux suggests a sort of dependence relation where explicit episodic memory (experiential memory) depends on explicit semantic memory of facts, which depends on implicit memory. They are autonoetic (self-aware), noetic (aware), and a-noetic (unconscious), respectively. When we experience something, the experience is maintained in working memory for only a short period of time. If it is to be explicitly retrieved later, it must be stored

---

76. LeDoux, *Anxious*, 242.

77. Valenstein, *Blaming the Brain*, 4.

78. Numerous studies have investigated whether the combination of antidepressant treatment and extinction-based CBT is more effective than either monotherapy alone for treating anxiety disorders. Although some find a modest benefit of combining treatment in the short-term (32–35), others report no short-term advantage (36–38, 106, 107). However, there is evidence that combined treatment impedes the long-term benefits of exposure therapy. For example, when panic disorder patients were evaluated after treatment discontinuation, the outcome of those previously treated with CBT and imipramine (32) or alprazolam (33) was worse than patients who received CBT alone.

Nesha S. Burghardt, Torfi Sigurdsson, Jack M. Gorman, Bruce S. McEwen, and Joseph E. LeDoux, "Chronic Antidepressant Treatment Impairs the Acquisition of Fear Extinction," *Biological Psychiatry* 73 (2013): 1086.

via consolidation, by which LeDoux means that it is stored in long-term memory, the medial temporal lobe memory system. These memories are merely preconscious and capable of being retrieved into working memory (prefrontal cortex).[79] The ease with which we retrieve a memory is related to how strongly it was encoded and what it is associated with; memories can be heightened by arousal or by repetition. The stronger the synaptic connections between the long-term and working memory systems, the easier it is to make memories conscious again. This is the basis of all learning. However, just as consciousness depends on unconscious processes, so also explicit memories have implicit correlates.[80] For example, LeDoux describes how we may become conditioned even to the context of an emotional experience, which can trigger arousal in the absence of conscious cognitive processing. LeDoux writes,

> Consider another example. You are walking down the street and notice someone running toward you. The person, upon reaching you, hits you on the head and steals your wallet or purse. The next time someone is running toward you, chances are a set of standard fear responses will be set into play. You will probably freeze and prepare to defend yourself, your blood pressure and heart rate will rise, your palms and feet will sweat, stress hormones will begin to flow through your bloodstream, and so on. The sight of someone running toward you has become a conditioned fear stimulus. But suppose you later find yourself on the street where you were mugged. Although there is no one running toward you, your body may still be going through its defense motions. The reason for this is that not only did you get conditioned to the immediate stimulus directly associated with the trauma (the sight of the mugger running toward you), but also to the other stimuli that just happen to have been there.[81]

---

79. LeDoux, *Anxious*, 186.

80. Implicit memories are separate but related to explicit memories in healthy individuals. They are involved even in explicit memory recall. Bessel van der Kolk, *The Body Keeps the Score: Brain, Mind, and Body in the Healing of Trauma* (New York: Penguin, 2014), 178.

81. LeDoux, *Emotional Brain*, 165–66.

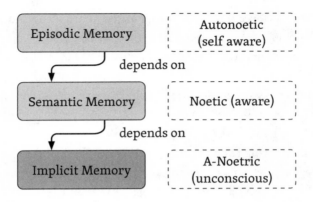

Figure 8.4: Explicit and Implicit Memory

LeDoux explains that one of the functions of the hippocampus is to create an unconscious representation of the context, not merely the stimulus.[82] Implicit memory is responsible for unconscious associations, general habits, motor skills, and affective priming.[83] Neuroplasticity underwrites implicit associations, often in very strong ways with traumatic events. We cannot begin to understand things like panic attacks and the highly erratic behavior of trauma survivors without understanding how implicit memory forms. In the case of panic attacks, implicit memory can trigger severe arousal which is debilitating. In the case of trauma, implicit memory can function like a ghost that haunts the consciousness of a person trying to forget (flashbacks). In certain cases, the explicit memory system is over-whelmed and breaks down, triggering extreme arousal in the body. Trauma fractures the working relationship between implicit and explicit memory and creates a condition of extreme emotional volatility for sufferers. Bessel van der Kolk writes,

> Under ordinary conditions these two memory systems—rational and emotional—collaborate to produce an integrated response. But high arousal not only changes the balance between them but also disconnects other brain areas necessary for proper storage and integration of incoming information, such as the hippocampus and the

---

82. LeDoux, *Emotional Brain*, 168.
83. LeDoux, *Anxious*, 189–90.

thalamus. As a result, the imprints of traumatic experiences are organized not as coherent logical narratives but in fragmented sensory and emotional traces; images, sounds, and physical sensations.[84]

Because the lower implicit memory system is so closely tied to the body, even taking certain yoga positions can precipitate intense panic in those who have been abused. For example, rape victims can have strong physiological reactions to the position happy baby, where a person lies on their back, knees bent with feet above.[85] LeDoux's theory of extinction of memories has both explicit and implicit facets. Because "explicit and implicit memories of the same situation are formed and stored separately," it may be that each system needs different treatment.[86] He writes, "Successful therapy thus involves changes in explicit (conscious) and implicit (nonconscious) cognition." And "if only the explicit or only the implicit system is treated, the untreated system can reinvigorate the fear."[87] This is at the core of cognitive-behavioral (talk and experience) therapy, and is important to why I am recommending a tiered psychology. It may be that theologians have not recognized the extent to which lived experience is vital to our sanctification and the extent to which the church as a social body ministers health and holiness to its members.

Developmental Trauma

Finally, to give full concreteness to the role of the body in emotional experience, I want to discuss the issue of child development. I raise this issue because it is perhaps the clearest way to illustrate how the body responds directly to its environment without mediation of language, forming implicit memories about the world that frames adulthood. In *The Boy Who Was Raised as a Dog*, Bruce Perry and Maia Szalavitz tell the story of Leon, a young boy who at the age of sixteen brutally murdered two teenage girls and subsequently raped their dead bodies. Perry writes, "Leon would teach me more about how much damage parental neglect—even

---

84. van der Kolk, *Body Keeps the Score*, 178.
85. van der Kolk, *Body Keeps the Score*, 274. I have spoken with a trauma survivor who was unable to finish her first yoga session because she could not control her sobbing.
86. LeDoux, *Anxious*, 269.
87. LeDoux, *Anxious*, 267, 275.

unintentional neglect—can inflict, and how modern Western culture can erode the extended family networks that have traditionally protected many children from it."[88] Leon, unlike his elder brother, was a classic sociopath. When asked what he might have done differently, he remarked, "I don't know. Maybe throw away those boots?"—which linked him to the crime.[89] Perry and Szalavitz recount just how Leon differed from his older brother Frank. The two boys had been raised by a mentally impaired mother in two very different circumstances. Frank had been surrounded by care, attention, and support during his first few years from his extended family. Leon had been born after the family had moved hundreds of miles from family to secure work. Unable to cope with the demands of two children, Leon's mother had left the house to walk with her elder son for most of the day, leaving Leon to cry in his bed. Because Leon had "stopped crying so much," she had assumed that her solution had worked. However, as Perry and Szalavitz explain, "Leon had been deprived of the critical stimuli necessary to develop the brain areas that modulate stress and link pleasure and comfort with human company."[90] Perry and Szalavitz are careful to caution that disorders like Leon's involve decreased impulse control, but not a complete lack of free will, and that the course of Leon's life was a "butterfly effect" of "escalation of small, in-themselves-inconsequential negative decisions made by him and for him that gradually led to a horrendous outcome for his victims, his family and himself."[91] What is clear from this example is that the neglect of Leon at a prelinguistic time of his life had significant moral consequences for the rest of his life. My point is this: we tend to think that moral governance happens only through the explicit use of language. However, we need a theological anthropology that sees a mother rocking her baby as a deeply spiritual act that knits *shalom* into the brain and nervous system of the child.

A large part of the work of Bessel van der Kolk also deals with developmental trauma. Like LeDoux, van der Kolk is critical of the brain-disease

---

88. Bruce Perry and Maia Szalavitz, *The Boy Who Was Raised as a Dog: What Traumatized Children Can Teach Us About Loss, Love, and Healing* (New York: Basic, 2006), 99.

89. Perry and Szalavitz, *Boy Who Was Raised as a Dog*, 105.

90. Perry and Szalavitz, *Boy Who Was Raised as a Dog*, 112.

91. Perry and Szalavitz, *Boy Who Was Raised as a Dog*, 119.

or chemical imbalance model of mental illness. He cites "four fundamental truths":

> (1) our capacity to destroy one another is matched by our capacity to heal one another. Restoring relationships and community is central to restoring well-being; (2) language gives us the power to change ourselves and others by communicating our experiences, helping us to define what we know, and finding a common sense of meaning; (3) we have the ability to regulate our own physiology, including some of the so-called involuntary functions of the body and brain, through such basic activities as breathing, moving, and touching; and (4) we can change social conditions to create environments in which children and adults can feel safe and where they can thrive.[92]

A sense of safety is one of the greatest moral bequests a parent can give a child. Van der Kolk has researched borderline personality disorder, which is characterized by the following traits, among others:

1. Frantic efforts to avoid real or imagined abandonment.

2. A pattern of unstable and intense interpersonal relationships characterized by alternating between extremes of idealization and devaluation.

3. Identity disturbance: markedly and persistently unstable self-image or sense of self.

4. Impulsivity in at least two areas that are potentially self-damaging.

   ...

8. Inappropriate, intense anger or difficulty controlling anger.[93]

Van der Kolk and his research team found that "81 percent of the patients diagnosed with [borderline personality disorder] at Cambridge Hospital

92. van der Kolk, *Body Keeps the Score*, 38.

93. *Diagnostic and Statistical Manual of Mental Disorders*, 5th ed. (Washington, DC: American Psychiatric Association, 2013), 663.

reported severe histories of child abuse and/or neglect; in the vast majority the abuse began before age seven."[94] One in four said that they could
not recall a single adult that made them feel safe as a child.[95] Van der
Kolk writes, "Over the years our research team has repeatedly found that
chronic emotional abuse and neglect can be just as devastating as physical
abuse and sexual molestation."[96] Again, without a model of how the body
reacts to its environment and works from the bottom-up on thinking, we
miss the crucial significance of social engagement on moral formation,
especially in child development. My model can perhaps open the door for
theologians to think better about this.

GOVERNANCE AND LANGUAGE

Finally, there is an obvious question lurking. If the unconscious has its own
appraisals (cognitions), which possess valence (appetite) and bring about
bodily arousal, then how does it relate to explicit conscious life? Jonathan
Haidt has analogized human agency as a "man riding an elephant."[97] But
do we have reins? Is consciousness purely epiphenomenal? Can we exercise downward governance of our emotions?[98] Anthony Greenwald and
Mahzarin Banaji suggest that there are three categories for expressing the
relation between consciousness and the unconscious: (1) superordinate,
where the unconscious possess "a high level of unconsciously operating
intelligence, capable of guiding the person's thought and actions" (e.g.,
Freud); (2) coordinate, where it is "operating in parallel with but independently of conscious cognition"; and (3) subordinate, where it functions
"prior to conscious attention, as in information-processing stage theories."
Greenwald and Banaji suggest that the third option is a useful starting

---

94. van der Kolk, *Body Keeps the Score*, 140. See also Judith Lewis Herman, John Christopher
Perry, and Bessel van der Kolk, "Childhood Trauma in Borderline Personality Disorder,"
American Journal of Psychiatry 146, no. 4 (April 1989): 490–95.

95. van der Kolk, *Body Keeps the Score*, 139.

96. van der Kolk, *Body Keeps the Score*, 87–88.

97. Jonathan Haidt, *The Happiness Hypothesis: Finding Modern Truth in Ancient Wisdom*
(New York: Basic Books, 2006), 27.

98. Timothy Wilson writes, "Wegner and Wheatley acknowledge that conscious will is
not always an illusion, just that it *can* be. The most reasonable position, I believe, is between
the extremes of consciousness-as-chief-executive and consciousness-as-epiphenome-
nal-press-secretary. If consciousness were purely epiphenomenal, then a book on self-insight
would not be very satisfying." Wilson, *Strangers to Ourselves*, 47.

point.[99] However, just as the debates over the priority of the intellect and will in the Middle Ages have two temporal frames, so does this question: the immediate frame within action theory and the comprehensive frame within personal agency. It may be that while the unconscious mostly sets the course of our lives and emotions in the immediate frame, except during deliberate choices, that conscious decision at least ideally accounts for who we are becoming in a comprehensive sense.

It must be admitted from the outset that there are reasons to doubt the efficacy of our thoughts to penetrate into our character. Timothy Wilson cites a penetrating line from George Bernard Shaw's *Pygmalion*, "You know, Pickering, that woman has the most extraordinary ideas about me. Here I am, a shy, diffident sort of man. I've never been able to feel really grown-up and tremendous like other chaps. And yet she's firmly persuaded that I'm an arbitrary overbearing bossy kind of person. I can't account for it."[100] The problem is both that we tend not to know ourselves and that we tend not to be who we intend to be. Timothy Wilson suggests that our true personality lies in two places, "in the adaptive unconscious and in conscious construals of the self."[101] He writes, "The constructed self consists of life stories, possible selves, explicit motives, self-theories, and beliefs about the reasons for one's feelings and behaviors. As John Didion says, 'We tell ourselves stories in order to live.'"[102] But what is the precise relationship between our explicit self, the language we use about ourselves, and our unconscious self?

One theory of the relation between our explicit and unconscious selves is the interpreter theory of consciousness. On this theory, consciousness is unified in the sense that our explicit consciousness constructs an ongoing narrative of the causes of mental states.[103] Michael Gazzaniga and Joseph LeDoux were attracted to this model because of studies they performed on

---

99. Anthony G. Greenwald and Mahzarin R. Banaji, "The Implicit Revolution: Reconceiving the Relation Between Conscious and Unconscious," *American Psychological Association* 72 no. 9 (2017): 869.

100. George Bernard Shaw, *Pygmalion* (New York: Penguin, 2003), 40–41; cited in Wilson, *Strangers to Ourselves*, 67–68.

101. Wilson, *Strangers to Ourselves*, 72.

102. Wilson, *Strangers to Ourselves*, 73.

103. LeDoux, "Emotional Colouration," 101.

split brain patients.[104] These patients had undergone a surgical operation to sever the corpus callosum, which allows communication between the hemispheres of the brain, as an attempt to prevent severe epileptic seizures. In one iteration of the study, the researchers flashed an image of a snow scene to the right hemisphere and a chicken to the left. A male subject was then asked to select a card that matched the image with each hand. With his left hand, controlled by the right hemisphere, he selected a shovel to match the snow, and with the right hand, controlled by the left hemisphere, he selected a chicken. The subject was then asked why he chose this card. Since the speech center is in the left hemisphere, the subject replied, "I saw a claw and picked a chicken, and you have to clean out the chicken shed with a shovel" (Figure 8.5).[105] The subject was unaware that his response was a spontaneous confabulation. Timothy Wilson argues that this sort of confabulation is extremely common in ordinary emotional life.[106] We often come up with explanations for how we are feeling that may or may not be accurate.

Figure 8.5, Split Brain Experiment, Gazzaniga and LeDoux

However, the mere existence of confabulation in any immediate case does not entail that our entire self-conscious mental life is confabulation, nor that language has no downward force. It merely awakens us to the possibility that we may be wrong about particular unconscious states. It seems that, comprehensively speaking, language helps us govern ourselves. LeDoux notes that the Sapir-Whorf hypothesis—that language shapes how we think, perceive, and behave—has recently come back into favor, at least in a chastened form.[107] One reason why LeDoux's model is groundbreaking is that

104. Michael S. Gazzaniga and Joseph E. LeDoux, *The Integrated Mind* (New York: Plenum, 1978). See also Wilson, *Strangers to Ourselves*, 95–96.

105. Gazzaniga and LeDoux, *Integrated Mind*, 148–49.

106. Wilson, *Strangers to Ourselves*, 93.

107. LeDoux, "Emotional Colouration," 102. Melissa Bowerman and Stephen Levinson write, "Indeed, quite a bit of recent fact and theory, both inside and outside the study of human development (Gumperz & Levinson 1996), suggests that some very moderate form of 'Whorfianism' may be unavoidable. The implications for human development are potentially

he partly opens the door for reconsidering this hypothesis for emotion. Dedre Gentner and Susan Goldin-Meadow write, "the view that language is a separate system from general cognition and with a de-emphasis of the semantic area, discouraged any search for a relation between language and cognition."[108] LeDoux's cortical model of emotion opens the door for language playing a more prominent role in the experience of emotion. He highlights "the long tradition of research showing that culture, and the language used by a culture, influences the emotions that are commonly experienced in that culture,"[109] adding, "the emotion concepts that a culture has can influence the way members of that culture experience situations and *make judgments* about how to act in those situations, and can be perplexing to members of other cultures who do not have those words and concepts."[110] The strongest version of the Sapir-Whorf hypothesis is that language determines the way we perceive the world. A much more reasonable version is that language conditions self-talk, which in turn has some influence on unconscious processing. I take it that this is what LeDoux is suggesting. For example, he adds, "Labeling of an emotional experience in a certain culturally defined way can influence the degree to which that experience is viewed as manageable or not."[111]

The issue of how language conditions unconscious emotional processing is somewhat undeveloped by LeDoux, but tantalizing. Since LeDoux believes that an emotion is a function of higher cortical processing and involves explicit information about the world and ourselves, the explicit information precedes any given experience in this sense; it is preloaded into emotional schemata within the comprehensive frame of emotional experience. The significance of this for the intelligence of unconscious

---

far-reaching." Melissa Bowerman and Stephen C. Levinson, eds., *Language Acquisition and Conceptual Development*, Language Culture and Cognition, Book 3 (Cambridge: Cambridge University Press, 2001), 13. See also Dedre Gentner and Susan Goldin-Meadow, eds., *Language in Mind: Advances in the Study of Language and Thought* (Cambridge, MA: MIT Press, 2003).

108. Gentner and Goldin-Meadow, *Language in Mind*, 5.

109. LeDoux, "Emotional Colouration," 102.

110. LeDoux, "Emotional Colouration," 103, emphasis added. See also Shinobu Kitayama and Hazel Markus, *Emotion and Culture* (Washington, DC: American Psychological Association, 1994); Anna Wierzbicka, "Does Language Reflect Culture? Evidence from Australian English," *Language in Society* 15, no. 3 (September 1986): 349–73; Rom Harré, ed., *The Social Construction of Emotions* (New York: Blackwell, 1986).

111. LeDoux, "Emotional Colouration," 103.

processing is underappreciated. For example, I recently walked out of the grocery store, looked to the right, and panicked. Only after I panicked did the cause of my panic become transparent to me. What I had seen and processed without conscious cognition was a green van parked where I normally park, the door open, and a person rummaging around on the driver's side. Clearly my unconscious processing was preloaded with a schema that might be expressed explicitly: (1) the concept of van; (2) that this green van is my van; (3) that my van is valuable to me and contains valuable things; (4) that an open door suggests that someone else has entered my van; (5) that the person behind the open door had opened it and was entering my van; (6) that the most plausible explanation for his doing so is that he wished to steal the van or my possessions; (7) that these facts inhibit certain goals that are meaningful to me, like retaining my possessions;[112] and (8) that therefore, this situation was alarming. None of this was explicit, and my reaction happened within a fraction of a second. And a fraction of a second later, I realized that I parked had somewhere else. All of these things will seem quite obvious to a cognitive point of view like that of Robert Roberts, for example, i.e., the subjective logic of emotion. What is intriguing is that LeDoux's model opens the door for a holistic framework for understanding how language, the unconscious, and the body interact.

If language works this way to modulate emotional experience, then the possibilities for targeted conditioning through language and experience are significant. Timothy Wilson writes, "'The do good, be good' principle is one of the most important lessons psychology has to offer."[113] This is simply a restatement of Aristotle's assertion that we become just by doing just things. But now we are perhaps in a better place to understand how this works. Classic behaviorist conditioning works by the association of an unconditioned stimulus (US, which are species specific) with a conditioned stimulus. So far this is possible for human beings and rats and a whole host of other animals. Pavlov's famous experiments with dogs relied on this sort of conditioning. Panksepp calls this sort of learning valence taking, the

---

112. See the structure of Richard Lazarus's dimensional appraisal theory. Richard S. Lazarus, *Emotion and Adaptation* (New York: Oxford University Press, 1991). Jesse Prinz lists four dimensions in Lazarus's appraisal theory: (1) goal relevance; (2) goal congruence; (3) type of ego-development; (4) blame or credit. Prinz, *Gut Reactions*, 15.

113. Wilson, *Strangers to Ourselves*, 215.

ability of brains to "imbue initially neutral environmental events [like a bell ringing] with values."[114] Again, we have discussed the plasticity that underlies this habit formation. But if, in human persons, language can modulate even unconscious emotional processing, then the possibilities of altering emotional reactions by way of language and experience are enormous. LeDoux recommends this very approach for treating anxiety. He acknowledges the value of cognitive therapy for maladaptive beliefs that have "become habitual" and are "carried out automatically by non-conscious processes." He writes, "Several top-down cognitive tools are used. The therapist helps the person introspectively recognize the auto-matic thoughts and uncover the beliefs they reflect. Through a process of reevaluation, or reappraisal, the beliefs come to be seen from a different perspective."[115] Yet he also argues that exposure therapy naturally comple-ments cognitive therapy because "therapeutic procedures that target sys-tems that work implicitly are best at changing implicit memories, whereas procedures that engage explicit processes and working memory are best at changing explicit processes."[116] It seems that the key to understanding Aristotle's insight is that executive and linguistic intentionality is neces-sary for reframing experience, which in turn reinforces the change. Only a treatment that directly engages both our lower, implicit systems and our higher, explicit mind will prove effective: reckoning and presenting, faith and practice.

A MODEL

I am not the first scholar to align the psychology of Thomas Aquinas with contemporary psychology. Giuseppe Butera asserts that Thomas Aquinas "anticipated all the major principles and methods of cognitive therapy (CT) in his philosophical psychology. This fact has gone largely unnoted by philosophers and psychologists alike."[117] Moreover, Butera suggests that

---

114. Panksepp, "Neuro-Evolutionary Cusp," 148.

115. LeDoux, *Anxious*, 266.

116. LeDoux, *Anxious*, 273.

117. Butera lists this framework:

(1) Emotions are caused by evaluative thoughts, typically called "automatic thoughts"; (2) Rules for evaluating our experiences operate without our consciously being aware of them; (3) The application of these rules to stimuli results in auto-matic thoughts; (4) Automatic thoughts are accessible to the person experiencing

Aquinas grasped the "dynamic structure of the human psyche."[118] I only hope to substantiate Butera's claims further by making this comparison. I am proposing a simple, rough model for a tiered psychology that captures the core impulses of LeDoux's model, but which is perhaps translatable between disciplines. I will briefly describe it, making comparisons with the insights from Thomas Aquinas's psychology.

I map Aquinas's higher powers, intellect and will, with executive consciousness. An easy way to distinguish our conscious awareness from our unconscious is our ability to put things into words. As LeDoux notes, consciousness and language are sidekicks.[119] Executive consciousness is symbolically framed and processes self-reflective thought. We make our decisions here. This is the level of conscious working memory, the level of our attention. We can conscientiously alter our mental gaze. This is the primary aspect of mind, though I think mind also applies to unconscious processing (see Figure 8.6). I see no insuperable reason for denying the existence of faculties of the soul, at least as they are understood holistically.[120] However, I have termed this executive consciousness, preferring to maintain the happy marriage of reason and will that Aquinas did, where the intellect just is the will's intelligence, and the will just is the intellect's desire, so that they cannot be distinguished introspectively. As Aquinas rightly remarks, there is only "one act of attention" (*una intentio*), to which

the emotions caused by them; (5) The specific content of an automatic thought leads to a specific emotional response; (6) Emotional disorders are caused by incorrect automatic thoughts, which can be modified through rational considerations; and (7) Habituation, in addition to awareness of such automatic thoughts, is necessary to change incorrect automatic thoughts and to inculcate correct ones.

Giuseppe Butera, "Thomas Aquinas and Cognitive Therapy: An Exploration of the Promise of Thomistic Psychology," *Philosophy, Psychiatry, & Psychology* 17, no. 4 (December 2010): 347, 349. See also George Mora, "Thomas Aquinas and Modern Psychology: A Reassessment," *Psychoanalytic Review* 64, no. 4 (Winter 1977): 495–530; and Frank J. Moncher, "A Psychotherapy of Virtue: Reflection on St. Thomas Aquinas' Theology of Moral Virtue," *Journal of Psychology and Christianity* 20, no. 4 (2001): 320–41.

118. Butera, "Thomas Aquinas," 347.

119. Ledoux, *The Emotional Brain*, 71, 300.

120. Hoitenga writes, "The common sense approach is that for every noetic and volitional function of human being there is a faculty of the soul that possesses that function, by which it produces the noetic or volitional state in question." I am not inclined to appeal to common sense for this but am willing to provisionally grant that the soul must be that by virtue of which reflective thinking and desiring exists, especially in light of the biblical and theological tradition on this point. Dewey Hoitenga, *John Calvin and the Will: A Critique and Corrective* (Grand Rapids: Baker, 1997), 16.

the various powers contribute (*ST* I–II.37.1).[121] This is deeply consistent with the focused ability of conscious working memory to accomplish only a few informational tasks.

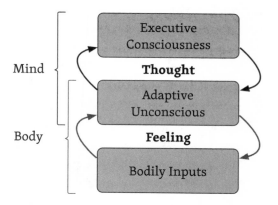

Figure 8.6, A Tiered Model of Emotional Consciousness

Functions	LeDoux	Aquinas
automatic representative input	visuo-spatial scratchpad	imagination
automatic articulatory input	articulatory loops	practical reason
memory providing meaning via schemata	long-term memory	memory & cogitative estimation
unified representations	episodic buffer	common sense
executive control	attention	attention

Figure 8.7, A Functional Comparison

I map Aquinas's lower powers with the adaptive unconscious. With regard to sensitive apprehension (perception), the functions of working

---

121. All references to *Summa Theologiae* (*ST*) are from Thomas Aquinas, *Summa Theologiae*, trans. Alfred J. Freddoso, updated January 10, 2018, https://www3.nd.edu/~afreddos/summa-translation/TOC.htm.

memory map extremely well with its capacities. I am not suggesting that all these features need have a strong one-to-one correspondence; rather I am highlighting the striking comparison between Aquinas's lower powers and how they have been mapped by contemporary neuroscience. LeDoux has suggested that working memory has four functions: (1) inputs that operate automatically, "articulatory loops and a visuo-spatial scratchpad"; (2) long-term memory providing meaning; (3) an "episodic buffer," which binds representations to produce a unified representation; (4) executive control or attention.[122] The visuo-spatial scratchpad seems to do the same representative work as imagination. Long-term memory conflates Aquinas's memory and cogitative estimation, which store and supply intentions respectively (e.g., wolf as dangerous). Peter Carruthers talks about emotional valence being aimed at the "nonconceptual representations" of "seeming good" or "seeming bad."[123] This is similar to Thomistic language. The episodic buffer performs the same basic function as common sense. Finally, executive control, as stated above, is similar to Aquinas's notion of one act of attention. With regard to sensitive appetite and its passions, in terms of contemporary cognitive science, "it is widely agreed ... that all affective states share two dimensions of valence and arousal."[124] These have an analogy with Aquinas's notions of the soul's movement and bodily change. In fact, even the two aspects of valence, approach and avoidance, are akin to Aquinas's primary notion of the movement of the soul, appetite toward the good and away from the bad.[125] Again, we need not adopt Aquinas's scheme, but I wish to emphasize the work our unconscious does and the sagacity of his system.

At the bottom level of my tiered psychology is bodily inputs. By this I am referring to the subcortical circuits that initiate especially alterations in the autonomic nervous systems and the release of hormones. In spite of the fact that Galenism was factually wrong, it is remarkable how similar the features of the two systems are. In both cases, there are physiological conditions of the body, humors and hormones, operating in characteristic and short-term ways to disrupt the functions of what moves the body, spirits and neurotransmissions. Aquinas explains how the body can impact

---

122. LeDoux, "Emotional Colouration," 92.
123. Carruthers, "Valence and Value," 63.
124. Carruthers, "Valence and Value," 51.
125. LeDoux, "Rethinking the Emotional Brain," 660.

decision making within two temporal frames. First, the health and temperament or personality of a person is a sort of humoral predisposition to certain emotions. Choleric persons are quick to be heated, for example (ST I–II.46.5). Life stages (ST I–II.40.6) or particular events can bring proneness to certain emotional virtues or faults (ST II–II.35.1 ad. 2). Long standing virtues may also positively impact tendencies to certain emotions (ST I–II.63.1; I–II.82.4 ad. 1). These elements of embodiment bring limits to human agency that are both a liability and a benefit. On the one hand, human beings may be overwhelmed by their environment and may experience interference in rational processing. On the other hand, these limits contribute to rationality and provide the grounds for stable character via plasticity. Just like Aquinas first proposed, the prevailing view among neuroscientists is that habits form both at a higher cognitive (e.g., memory or patterns of thought) and emotional level by pairing the amygdala with the ventral striatum.[126]

Finally, according to my model, what we often call thought is our executive consciousness coming to terms with our adaptive unconscious. What we call feeling is our adaptive unconscious reading our bodies by way of our schemata. Thought and feeling work in tandem to enable a sort of top-down governance within the psychological tiers, but with bottom-up reciprocity. This is what Aquinas called a political governance, which I have also analogized with the biblical metaphor of the gardener. Just as gardens are subject to flood, pestilence, and draught, so we also are touched not only by our own moral evil, but also by the natural evil in which our bodies participate by being from the ground (the flesh) and by experiencing our fallen environment (the world). Each level of my model reciprocally interacts with the other levels—neuroscientists have explained the feedback mechanisms biologically. On my model, mental illness is not strictly biological, nor is it strictly psychological. Mental illness is a vicious psycho-physio feedback loop producing distress. It is also social, as our experience with others is the single most important experiential factor in mental health. I cannot develop this here. This conception of mental illness collapses the

---

126. In the caudate nucleus. Jeffrey Schwartz calls this the habit center of the brain. Schwartz, *You Are Not Your Brain*, 321.

disjunction between illness and wickedness, yielding a more complex picture of ourselves as both sinful and dysfunctional.

THE SUBJECTIVE LOGIC

My aim has been to show how the body qualifies agency, with one eye to how the body is conditioned by executive consciousness and language. However, I do want to say a word in defense of philosophical treatments of emotions. We must understand the subjective logic of emotion—Why am I feeling this way?—and philosophical accounts help us to do this. Only by truly understanding the special nature of human agency can we endorse a moral account of emotion. I am not trying to replace the moral view with a medical view, but merely to modulate the moral view by how the body qualifies agency. If emotion is moral, then it cannot be studied simply from a biological perspective; physiology needs psychology, and psychology needs theology. The neuroscientists help explain many things (memory, plasticity, mental illness, etc.), but also have blind spots. I will focus on just one.

Neuroscientists seem to underestimate just how cognitive emotion is. The entire canon of literature relies on a deeply cognitive assumption about human emotion, as Martha Nussbaum in her book *Love's Knowledge* illustrates very well. For example, Nussbaum highlights two "features of Maggie Vervor's moral life," a character from *The Golden Bowl* by Henry James: "One is this assiduous aspiration to perfection, especially moral perfection. The other is the exclusive intensity of her love for her father, the oddness of her marriage to the Prince which ... has permitted her to gratify, to an extraordinary degree, her 'wish to remain, intensely, the same passionate little daughter she had always been.'"[127] Nussbaum evaluates the subjective logic of Maggie's emotional states, especially her drive toward moral perfection connected with pleasing her father. Emotion works cognitively on several levels here. First, James writes linguistically, framing his narrative by the interplay of Maggie's emotion and her internal dialogue. Nussbaum picks up what drives Maggie by this interplay, suspecting her self-deception. Second, the act of criticism assumes common human experience about how that emotion arises; the narrative is written to connect

---

127. Martha Nussbaum, *Love's Knowledge: Essays on Philosophy and Literature* (Oxford: Oxford University Press, 1990), 126.

with the way the reader sees and feels the world. The reader easily empathizes with the characters because the narrative brings about an imaginative emotional response in the reader. Finally, Henry James's exhaustive description of the self-awareness of his characters suggests a third aspect. He is not even remotely plausible as a writer without some assent to two contrasting points: (1) his streams of consciousness are unbelievably fantastical—no one thinks this way; and (2) they represent something real and complex about the way we interact with the world emotionally. We are constantly construing the world and modulating our feelings. In another literary example, we immediately understand how the pride of Elizabeth Bennet produces an erroneous construal of Mr. Darcy in Jane Austen's *Pride and Prejudice*. And it is stirringly obvious how Orual's resentment produces the sort of self-oriented love that consumes in *Till We Have Faces* by C. S. Lewis. The novel is simply not possible if emotions are not deeply cognitive. The subjective logic of emotions is indispensable.

And finally, if literature suggests a cognitive view, so also emotional responsibility is implied by biblical commands and by our participation in the biblical narrative. On this point, Robert Roberts writes,

> There is a necessary connection between the Christian emotions and the Christian story, because emotions are construals, and construals always require some knowledge, and the knowledge required by the Christian emotions is provided by the Christian story. So people who do not want to think of the spiritual life in terms of emotions and feelings because they believe that emotions are subjective and cut off from doctrine and thinking, can lay their fears to rest. Emotions are no less tied to concepts than arguments and beliefs are.[128]

In the same vein, Kevin Vanhoozer robustly defends the role of doctrine in identity formation, by which he means "summary statements of salvation history," or rather "the way we come to understand the [theo]drama and our role in it."[129] He conceives of salvation history in dramatic terms,

---

128. Robert Roberts, "Emotions and the Fruit of the Spirit," in *Psychology and the Christian Faith: An Introductory Reader*, ed. Stanton L. Jones (Grand Rapids: Baker, 1985), 87.

129. Kevin Vanhoozer, "Forming the Performers: How Christians Can Use Canon Sense to Bring Us to Our (Theodramatic) Senses," *Edification: The Transdisciplinary Journal of Christian*

as the theodrama, the drama of "what God has done in Christ through the Spirit ... what God has done, is doing, and will do with words, and with the Word and Spirit of life."[130] Words are important to Vanhoozer, not simply because they inform, as though all communication were assertion, but because they are the script that initiates participants into intellectual habits that, in conjunction with the imagination, "enable us to see this world in other-worldly—which is to say eschatological—terms so that our hearts may be aligned with the heart of God."[131] This is a very compelling vision for how theology engages emotion, especially in light of what I have already said about the relationship between construals and language. The language of Scripture appeals to our imaginations, not merely by asserting or commanding, but in various ways (poetry, aphorism, parable, etc.)[132] it forms our narrative sense of self within the larger theodrama. The aim of Christian teaching is to foster construals that align with who God says we are. Vanhoozer explicitly uses the language of perception. He suggests that Scripture is what brings the "power of synoptic vision," by which he simply means, "the ability to see together and connect apparently unrelated elements into a meaningful pattern."[133] Synoptic vision is an apt descriptor for the way that doctrine ought to shape the Christian mind. Drawing on the psychological model I have proposed, the sort of vision that best characterizes Christian faithfulness is saturated by what Vanhoozer calls canon sense.[134] I do not mean this in a metaphorical sense. Quite literally, emotion is responsive to seeing as, or perceiving as; doctrine can saturate our vision and emotion.

Psychology 4, no. 1 (2010): 5, 8.

130. Vanhoozer, "Forming the Performers," 7.

131. Vanhoozer, "Forming the Performers," 13.

132. Galatians 3:1 is a fascinating text that perhaps illuminates Paul's own appeal to the imagination of the Galatians. The text reads, "Foolish Galatians! Who has bewitched you? It was before your eyes that Jesus Christ was publicly portrayed as crucified." Bewitched (*ebaskanen*) has a primary meaning of "to exert an evil influence through the eye" (BDAG). It appears that Paul is condemning them for being deceived by the eyes of their imagination, which had formerly "seen" Christ as "publicly portrayed as crucified."

133. Vanhoozer, "Forming the Performers," 6.

134. Vanhoozer, "Forming the Performers," 12.

Conclusion

My model is a tiered psychology that assumes a distinction between higher and lower powers, referred to as executive consciousness and the adaptive unconscious. I am claiming that these powers can be mapped roughly with the psychological tiers that Romans 6–8 refers to as mind and body. The lower register is particularly important not only because it is regularly ignored, but also because it is less abstractable and deeply affected by physiological changes. My model is also thoroughly holistic in that it helps us to understand how the body qualifies agency. And yet it also helps us to understand how the body is not blind and irrational but governed politically by our executive powers. Having presented a model of emotion that integrates plasticity, I want to return to Matthew 6:25–34 to provide an alternate reading to the emotionally voluntaristic one already mentioned, and hope to raise a compelling holistic call to fight anxiety by seeking the kingdom.

9

—

BOOK OF SCRIPTURE: COMMANDING EMOTION

Finally, I will offer a reading of Matthew 6:25–34 in light of human embodiment as a rival to an emotional voluntarist reading. I have suggested that emotional voluntarism is the view that we are responsible for emotions as intrusive mental states that show what we truly believe. According to this view, emotional regulation and change is roughly within our reach since emotion just is cognition and can be addressed directly via cognitive intervention or voluntary mental work. This way of reading Matthew 6:25–34 would see Jesus' words "do not be anxious" as a categorical prohibition where any particular anxiety is a transgression. I object to this emotional voluntarist reading of Matthew 6:25–34 because it does not pay attention to the encyclopedic context of the directive. In what follows, I will reiterate what I mean by an emotional voluntarist reading before offering my interpretation of the command within its historical and exegetical contexts.

ELLIOTT'S PSYCHOLOGICAL ASSUMPTIONS

Matthew Elliott writes, "Worry, like fear, is the opposite of hope. ... [it is] the negative expectation of the future with an emphasis on the fact that the future outcome is not sure."[1] This cognitive reading of worry leads him to cite, seemingly with approval, the words of Hans Dieter Betz regarding Matthew 6:25–34: "The prohibitive imperative 'Do not worry' (*mē merimnate*) is meant to be categorical with no exceptions allowed; it is repeated

---

1. Matthew A. Elliott, *Faithful Feelings: Rethinking Emotion in the New Testament* (Grand Rapids: Kregel, 2006), 203.

in 28, 31, and 34, and thus constitutes the major exhortation of the passage."[2] On the other hand, Elliott concedes that worry is not always wrong. He explains, "worry is most often felt over things of this world which the Christian is not to value. Following Paul's example, anxiety over the state of a specific person or church is sometimes legitimate, where a pervasive attitude is not."[3] To substantiate this claim Elliott explains, "Jesus emphasizes the sovereignty of God in response to worrying about the daily cares of life. The major point for us is the clear cognitive basis for not worrying." He adds, "A belief in God, his care for his people, and his activity in history on behalf of his people give freedom from worry."[4]

I am concerned that Elliott has perhaps smuggled in some emotional voluntarist assumptions. Earlier, I suggested that there are five common assumptions about emotions among ecclesially-minded Reformed evangelical theologians:

1) Emotion as judgment: Emotion is strictly or first a mental state.

2) Emotions of the heart: Since emotions are morally significant, the proper subject of emotion is the heart, though perhaps some emotions are sourced in or influenced by the body.

3) Deep belief associationism and legitimacy: Emotion is a mental state that arises when a deep belief is elicited into consciousness; the beliefs that surface unbidden are also our truest.

4) Mental voluntarism: Emotions as mental states are changeable by shifting attention, mainly through internal speech (e.g., repenting of false beliefs), to bring about new mental states.

5) Emotional duty: People are duty bound to address any emotional aberrance as quickly as possible, since this is within their power.

---

2. Hans Dieter Betz, *The Sermon on the Mount*, Hermeneia (Minneapolis: Augsburg Fortress, 1995), 469.

3. Elliott, *Faithful Feelings*, 203.

4. Elliott, *Faithful Feelings*, 204.

Do we find evidence of these five assumptions in Elliott's work? It seems we have evidence of at least some of these. First, Elliott is professedly a cognitivist, by which he means that the "belief, judgement or evaluation is the only factor that can be universally used to differentiate emotions."[5] Second, when Elliott treats the biblical concept of heart, he emphasizes the heart as "the place where faith takes root in both mind and emotion."[6] He does emphasize that the Bible speaks holistically about humans, but by this he simply means that mind and heart or emotion and reason are interdependent.[7] Elliott pays very little attention to the role of the body in emotion, though he does briefly mention neuroplasticity: "By forcefully changing our focus to the things of God, we can rewire our emotional responses."[8] Ultimately, he never connects the heart to the body, but he argues, "The condition of the heart determines a person's standing before God."[9] Third, while Elliott is not clear about how emotions arise, he is clear that emotion differs in some way from deliberate thinking. For example, he writes, "Emotion serves to direct our attention and influence our thoughts. Emotion and cognition are constantly interacting."[10] His language throughout the book assumes emotion happens to us without explaining how.

Fourth, Elliott is somewhat voluntarist about emotion, if not a thoroughgoing mental voluntarist. For example, he admits that in addition to changing our beliefs, prayer and changing our environment may change emotions.[11] He writes, "We are often told in church to do the loving thing and the emotions will come. However, we learned that behaviour can change emotion but this is not a necessary result. It depends on how doing the right thing influences or does not influence our thinking."[12] Thought is paramount for Elliott. He adds that beliefs may be changed by talking

---

5. Elliott, *Faithful Feelings*, 32.

6. Elliott, *Faithful Feelings*, 131.

7. Elliott, *Faithful Feelings*, 133.

8. He writes in full, "Neurological pathways are built and reinforced as a result of what we choose to concentrate on. ... By forcefully changing our focus to the things of God, we can rewire our emotional responses." Elliott, *Faithful Feelings*, 255.

9. Elliott, *Faithful Feelings*, 133.

10. Elliott, *Faithful Feelings*, 47.

11. I affirm the value of prayer for coping with anxiety but also wish to demonstrate that there are additional theological resources that Elliott overlooks. Elliott, *Faithful Feelings*, 38.

12. Elliott, *Faithful Feelings*, 239.

to ourselves or facing our fears.[13] This last point vaguely echoes exposure therapy—though his example is a somewhat trivial one, of a person discovering that he likes roller coasters after riding one.[14]

Still, Elliott seems to have mental voluntarist tendencies nonetheless. There seems to be a lack of cohesion between his idea of how "doing the right thing" changes emotion and how he connects cognition and control elsewhere.[15] In defending the idea that emotions can be commanded, he gives three arguments. First, he cites Mark Talbot's notion of an indirect command. If we cannot alter emotion by sheer force of will, perhaps we can do it indirectly: "That is, the cognition behind the emotion must be changed to change the emotion."[16] Second, Elliott cites John Piper's argument that, "To know that a certain affection ought to exist is a sufficient condition for being the object of a reasonable command to experience that affection"; no assumption of ability is necessary.[17] This is just a rejection of Pelagius's assertion that ought implies can. Third, Elliott flatly states, "emotions can be commanded because they are cognitive."[18] The addition of this point seems to suggest mental voluntarism in a way that runs counter to what Elliott has said about circumstances or behavior. Finally, emotional duty seems to be what is motivating Elliott, since he wants to emphasize that emotions "provide us with a picture of our true values."[19]

How do these tendencies affect Elliott's reading of Matthew 6:25–34? For Elliott, worry has an implied propositional judgment; for example, it is troubling to me that my church is apostatizing. In the case of church apostasy, Elliott grants an exception for worrying, saying, "anxiety over the state of a specific person or church is sometimes legitimate." However, by citing Betz's statement of no exceptions about other cases, Elliott is emphasizing that Christians have a duty not to worry because of "the clear cognitive

---

13. Elliott, Faithful Feelings, 38.

14. This is a bad example because it is trivial and does not demonstrate awareness of more serious examples of how anxiety develops and is especially tied to social relations.

15. I am not saying Elliott cannot be consistent, but rather that he has not demonstrated how these ideas are consistent.

16. Elliott, Faithful Feelings, 143.

17. Elliott, Faithful Feelings, 263; John Piper, "Hope as the Motivation of Love: 1 Peter 3:9–12," New Testament Studies 26, no. 2 (1980): 216.

18. Elliott, Faithful Feelings, 263.

19. Elliott, Faithful Feelings, 39.

basis for not worrying" in Matthew 6:25–34.[20] Overall, he seems to read this passage as a simple command not to worry, with emotion's cognitive nature providing the basis for suggesting that emotion is in our control. A belief in God's care ought to free believers from worry, exceptions granted.

AN ALTERNATE READING OF
MATTHEW 6:25-34

What follows presents a reading of Matthew 6:25–34 that is not emotionally voluntarist, that sees this passage as a directive with an advising and induc- ing nuance for pursing a course of action that fights anxiety by pursuing a kingdom that is both already and not yet. The kingdom of God is marked by a tension between flourishing and suffering that leads us to expect not total psychological tranquility, but a growing embodiment of the peace of God with groaning (Rom 8:23; Phil 4:7). To substantiate this reading, I will address the following questions: What sort of speech act is the directive of Jesus in Matthew 6:25? Next, what sort of fulfillment does this directive assume both in terms of temporal frame—when is it to be accomplished?— and completeness—how thoroughly is it to be accomplished?

THE SPEECH ACT OF MATTHEW 6:25

So, what kind of a speech act is the directive of Jesus in Matthew 6:25, "do not be anxious about your life"? Asking questions about the speech act of this passage reveals, in the first place, a rejection of a code model of com- munication where meaning is exhausted by what is encoded and under- standing is exhausted by what is decoded.[21] Speech-act theory highlights how we use words or do things with them. Take the following example from Kevin Vanhoozer: "Coffee would keep me awake." It takes more than a code to recognize the meaning of this phrase; it also takes the "unencoded cir- cumstances of language."[22] At minimum, this sentence can express either a wish for coffee to stay awake or a wish for no coffee to sleep better. The

---

20. Elliott, *Faithful Feelings*, 204.

21. Kevin Vanhoozer, "From Speech Acts to Scripture Acts: The Covenant of Discourse and the Discourse of the Covenant," in *After Pentecost: Language and Biblical Interpretation*, ed. Craig Bartholomew, Colin J. D. Greene, and Karl Moller, Scripture and Hermeneutics Series, vol. 2 (Grand Rapids: Zondervan, 2001), 8.

22. Vanhoozer, "From Speech Acts to Scripture Acts," 9.

question for Matthew 6:25–34 is what is the author doing? As a prima facie evaluation, it looks as though he is commanding emotional control on the basis of certain promises.

Vanhoozer also pushes speech-act theory in a theological direction by considering speech in light of God's overall communicative action. Vanhoozer makes two key claims about language from a theological perspective that bear on this passage. First Vanhoozer says, "Language has a 'design plan' that is inherently covenantal."[23] Language implies a commitment to understand and be understood, to lovingly participate in an act of communion. Second Vanhoozer writes, "We affirm that language is transformative as well as informative."[24] Even the most mundane informative language has the transformative effect of altering our vision or understanding. We say the word "hot!" to our toddlers to transform their vision of stove-top pans as dangerous. So, we need to pay attention to the covenantal and transformative aspects of this act.

The question is what sort of transformation is expected from this speech act? Is it meant to communicate warning and to bring alarm as a "prohibitive imperative … with no exceptions allowed"?[25] Or is it rather meant to bring comfort to someone who is experiencing anxiety? With regard to this passage, we want to know the intention of the communicative act, and so we are looking for formal and informal contextual clues that suggest how it is to be taken. By informal clues, I mean the tone of the communication. By formal, I mean the specific type of speech act that is used.

First, informally, we notice the immediate context. Jesus commands his hearers, "Do not lay up for yourselves treasures on earth, where moth and rust destroy and where thieves break in and steal, but lay up for yourselves treasures in heaven. … For where your treasure is, there your heart will be also. … No one can serve two masters" (Matt 6:19–24). This context raises

---

23. Vanhoozer, "From Speech Acts to Scripture Acts," 10.

24. Vanhoozer, "From Speech Acts to Scripture Acts," 6. Vanhoozer writes, "For the sending is not simply a conveying of information, but a conveying of God's very person (i.e., a conveying of one's communicative as well as informative intentions). For what God proposed in sending the Son (and later, the Holy Spirit) involved much more than conveying information. The purpose of sending of God's Word was as much transformative as it was informative." Vanhoozer, "From Speech Acts to Scripture Acts," 11.

25. Betz, *Sermon on the Mount*, 469.

the very natural question: I have legitimate needs such as food, drink, and clothing for my very life; am I not to care about them at all?

To this we have a direct answer: "do not be anxious about your life, what you will eat or what you will drink, nor about your body, what you will put on" (Matt 6:25). In what follows, Jesus asks a rhetorical question and gives two examples. First he asks the rhetorical question, "Is not life more than food?" (6:25). This seems to be connected with verse 33, where he says, "seek first the kingdom of God and his righteousness." Life is about more than food; it is about the kingdom of God and the righteousness he is establishing in his kingdom. Next, Jesus gives two examples of God's knowing provision of temporal needs: (1) that God feeds the birds (6:26); (2) that God clothes the flowers (6:28). Rhetorically these examples communicate not merely by appealing to the mechanical fact of God's provision, but also by the force of the metaphors. We can imagine the fragility of handling a flower or small bird; even the wind can take the lives of flowers and birds. As an argument from the lesser to the greater, because God cares about fragile things that are insignificant, he will also care for fragile people who are his children.

Jesus' reference to God as "your heavenly Father" in Matthew 6:26 and 32 evokes multiple layers of context, including a variety of Old Testament references to the fatherhood of God such as Psalm 68:5; 89:26; 103:13; Isaiah 63:15–16; 64:8; and Malachi 2:10. It most significantly echoes the Davidic promise and in so doing prefigures the Isaianic fulfillment (Isa 53) of Christ's substitutionary death in Matthew 27.[26] As 2 Samuel 7:14 reads, "I will be to him a father, and he shall be to me a son. When he commits iniquity, I will discipline him with the rod of men, with the stripes of the sons of men." But the analogy is also experientially relevant for anxiety and perhaps fundamental to the human psyche.[27] To cite just two examples: first, psychological research has demonstrated that fathers play a key role

---

26. Isaiah 22:19–22 links "my servant" with the Davidic promise.

27. Deut 32:6; I could cite Freud's or Jung's father complex. There are also contemporary psychoanalytic treatments of this: Guy Corneau, *Absent Fathers, Lost Sons: The Search for Masculine Identity*, C. G. Jung Foundation Books Series, Book 4 (Boston: Shambhala, 1991); James M. Herzog, *Father Hunger: Explorations with Adults and Children*, 3rd ed. (New York: Routledge, 2013); Lila J. Kalinich and Stuart W. Taylor, eds., *The Dead Father: A Psychoanalytic Inquiry* (New York: Routledge, 2009).

in moderating anxiety.[28] John Gottman said, "Mothers stroke, and fathers poke."[29] Both make children feel safe in different ways, mothers by soothing and fathers by exciting their children while also setting limits. God is also analogized as a comforting mother (Isa 66:13; Matt 23:37).[30] Children learn from mothers that they will be safe when things go wrong, and from fathers that the world is safe enough to take risks. Fathers also constrain, and by constraining protect.[31] Second, Bessel van derk Kolk has highlighted the therapeutic value of merely conceiving of the ideal father who does not abuse his children, but loves and cares for them.[32]

Formally, there are two reasons not to worry in Matthew 6:25–34. Worrying is both useless and unnecessary because we cannot add a single hour to our own lives and because God knows what we need and will provide (6:27, 33). Here Jesus promises the help of the heavenly Father. Then Jesus further displaces responsibility for our needs by suggesting that tomorrow will worry about tomorrow, so we need not (6:34).

David Harris very helpfully taxonomizes speech acts into rough families, genera, and species. He sees two basic families, asserting and directing, divided "by the kind of mental attitude that features in their m-intended effect."[33] He also makes a helpful distinction between the species of directives:

1) A request for A to ψ is a directive for A to ψ backed by an expression of a desire for A to ψ.

28. For a review of the literature, see Susan Bögels and Vicky Phares, "Fathers' Role in the Etiology, Prevention, and Treatment of Child Anxiety: A Review and New Model," *Clinical Psychology Review* 28 (2008): 539–58.

29. Quoted in Bessel van der Kolk, *The Body Keeps the Score: Brain, Mind, and Body in the Healing of Trauma* (New York: Penguin, 2014), 112; van der Kolk references hearing Gottman say this.

30. Bögels and Phares, "Fathers' Role," 540.

31. I am emphasizing gender differences, but obviously parents overlap somewhat in these roles.

32. van der Kolk, *Body Keeps the Score*, 303.

33. David W. Harris, "Taxonomizing Speech Acts: Intention & Acts of Meaning Seminar, Week 6." Class notes at Hunter College, New York, NY, March 10, 2016. Posted online: http://danielwharris.com/teaching/spring16/handouts/Taxonomy.pdf. Accessed January 18, 2018, 1–8.

2) A command for A to ψ is a directive for A to ψ backed by a conditional threat to harm A unless A ψ's.

3) An inducement for A to ψ is a directive for A to ψ backed by a conditional promise to help A if A ψ's.

4) Advising A to ψ is a directive for A to ψ backed by an indirect assertion that it is A's interest to ψ.[34]

The two reasons not to worry in Matthew 6:25–34 are the uselessness of it and the promise of help. These reasons suggest that this passage is not strictly a command according to Harris's taxonomy. Instead, we seem to have a mix between advising and inducing. The passage answers a question about how a person may disavow earthly treasures and still live without worrying.

The overall point here is that the context of Jesus' prohibition of worry includes several elements: (1) a recognized need for temporal things; (2) rhetorically comforting examples that emphasize like fragility and greater importance; (3) rhetorically comforting references to our heavenly Father; and (4) multiple layers of displacement of personal responsibility, including God's promises for provision. Both informally and formally, the directive is best read as advising and inducing those who are inclined to anxiety to see their situation in a different light. In terms of the transformational aspect of the speech act, the passage is meant to bring comfort rather than to raise alarm. This hardly has the feel of the comment of Hans Dieter Betz, "The prohibitive imperative 'Do not worry' (*mē merimnate*) is meant to be categorical with no exceptions allowed."[35]

I do not mean to minimize the seriousness of this directive. In fact to the contrary, I consider the climactic comment in Matthew 6:33—"seek first the kingdom"—as the central thrust of the entire sermon. Jonathan Pennington asks, "The big question that the argument of 6:25–34 raises is,

---

34. Harris, "Taxonomizing Speech Acts," 6.
35. Betz, *Sermon on the Mount*, 469.

why is this such a big issue? … And especially, why does Jesus up the ante so high in 6:32 by making anxiety a matter of who is a true follower (those with the heavenly Father) and who is an outsider (gentile)?" His answer is that "anxiety is an example of double-souledness; it is the opposite of the singleness that marks the whole-person virtue of the follower of Christ."[36] I am perfectly happy with this answer. What I am pointing out is how the directive is delivered, that is, the contextual elements that clarify the covenantal and transformative intention of this passage. If Jesus is not only directing but also promising, then the serious responsibility to seek the kingdom is voiced with covenantal consolation.

EXPECTED FULFILLMENT

Next, to what sort of action is Jesus calling his hearers? What sort of fulfillment does this directive assume? First, how long will it take to fight anxiety? Second, how complete a victory over anxiety ought the Christian expect? To get a clearer picture of this issue, we must develop "encyclopedic competence" regarding the Sermon on the Mount. Jonathan Pennington borrows this term "encyclopedic competence" from Umberto Eco to refer not merely to a dictionary understanding of the words of a text, but a "knowledge of the real world [of the author]—its culture, history, beliefs."[37] Moving outward, the communicative act of Matthew 6:25–34 is nestled within the larger communicative act of the Sermon on the Mount, the Gospel of Matthew, first-century Judaism within the Greco-Roman world, and biblical theology.[38] There are many interpretive questions regarding the Sermon that are not answered by fine-grained exegesis.[39] Pennington

---

36. Jonathan T. Pennington, *The Sermon on the Mount and Human Flourishing: A Theological Commentary* (Grand Rapids: Baker Academic, 2017), 251.

37. Pennington, *Sermon on the Mount*, 21, citing Umberto Eco, *Semiotics and the Philosophy of Language* (Bloomington: Indiana University Press, 1984), 46–86.

38. Biblical theology raises the issue of canonical competence, as coined by Kevin Vanhoozer. Kevin Vanhoozer, "Scripture and Theology: on 'Proving' Doctrine Biblically," *The Routledge Companion to the Practice of Christian Theology*, ed. Mike Higton and Jim Fodor (New York: Routledge, 2015), 151, 157.

39. Pennington notes that this feature of the sermon makes it a good litmus test for many theological commitments: "The Sermon … reveals much about how one understands several issues of theology and Christian practice. Views on a wide range of the issues are revealed in one's reaction to the Sermon, including the role of the law in the new covenant, what role virtue plays in one's ethical system (if any), the importance of acts of piety in the Christian

suggests that Eco's encyclopedic competence "helps us to see that the best readings of the Sermon will be sensitive to its encyclopedic context while seeking to appropriate the experience of the Model Reader."[40] In what follows I will put Matthew 6:25–34 in three different contexts: (1) its first-century ethical context; (2) its immediate context within the Sermon on the Mount; and (3) its biblical-theological context of the kingdom. These contexts qualify both the time and completeness that Christians should expect with regard to this command.

Before proceeding to this analysis, I wish to make one final distinction between the simple fulfillment of a directive and a course of fulfillment. A directive with a simple act of fulfillment assumes that the sufficient conditions necessary for fulfillment are met except for the volitional decision. For example, someone may direct another person to pass the carrots, the carrots being on the table within reach, and the person possessing the power to lift and to move them. On the other hand, a directive with a course of fulfillment assumes that there may be other conditions that require effort, discipline, improvement, time, or even luck prior to the directive being fulfilled. For example, someone may direct another person to grow some carrots, assuming arable land, expertise, time, and external conditions like the right mix of rain, light, and temperature for fulfilling the command. It is necessary to consider whether the directive of Jesus assumes a simple act of fulfillment or a course of fulfillment. A key question about this text is this: Why might we expect this directive to assume a course of fulfillment rather than a simple act of fulfillment?

Historical Context: The Greco-Roman Virtue Tradition

Jonathan Pennington suggests two historical contexts that are crucial to encyclopedic competence for Matthew 5–7: "the story of Israel and second temple Jewish wisdom literature" and "the Greco-Roman virtue tradition."[41] I want to focus especially on the latter because the modern philosophical

---

life, the relationship between faith and works, one's eschatological orientation or lack thereof, the function of suffering in the Christian life, and the idea of God as Father, to name a few." Pennington, *Sermon on the Mount*, 3.

40. Pennington, *Sermon on the Mount*, 24.

41. Pennington, *Sermon on the Mount*, 25–35, quoting chapter headings on pp. 25, 29.

tradition of ethics may provide a crucial distortion to understanding Matthew 6:25. What follows is mainly an exercise in clearing away the potentially distorting context of modern ethics.

I want to distinguish between what I will call a Kantian ethical imaginary and a first-century one. It is possible that a typical Reformed evangelical reading of New Testament commands is distorted by a sort of Kantian ethical imaginary.[42] I suggest that there are two related elements to a Kantian ethical imaginary, a deontological approach to ethical decisions and a non-intrinsic relation between morality and happiness. By a deontological approach to ethical decisions, I simply mean that ethics operates by categorical imperatives; every ethical duty conforms to the rule always to act in such a way that you could be legislating universally.[43] By non-intrinsic relation between morality and happiness, I simply mean that happiness does not inhere in performing ethical duty either as an expected correlate of duty or as a proper motivation for it.

Kant argues that ethical laws are universally binding regardless of their contextual frame. As Alasdair MacIntyre writes, "Kant conceived his task as the isolation of the a priori, and therefore unchanging, elements of morality."[44] What is basic, unchanging, and universal for Kant is the moral precept. This quality of the moral precept is what grounds an individual's sense of moral duty; the moral law alone grounds duty for Kant. For Kant, to proscribe the moral law from duty alone eliminates considerations of happiness from moral reasons. Morality is not for happiness but stands independently grounded on the basis of reason alone. Happiness as a motive would jeopardize the universality of the moral law since happiness is subject oriented and context dependent. So, happiness

---

42. Alasdair MacIntyre writes, "Kant stands at one of the great dividing points in the history of ethics. For perhaps the majority of later philosophical writers, including many who are self-consciously anti-Kantian, ethics is defined as a subject in Kantian terms. For many who have never heard of philosophy, let alone of Kant, morality is roughly what Kant said it was." Alasdair MacIntyre, *A Short History of Ethics: A History of Moral Philosophy from the Homeric Age to the Twentieth Century*, 2nd ed. (Notre Dame: University of Notre Dame Press, 1998), 190.

43. One statement of Kant's categorical imperative is, "I should never act except in such a way that I can also will that my maxim should become universal law." Immanuel Kant, "Grounding for the Metaphysics of Morals," in *Classics of Western Philosophy*, ed. Steven M. Cahn, 7th ed. (Indianapolis: Hackett, 2006), 989.

44. MacIntyre, *Short History of Ethics*, 192.

is not a motive for duty, but a sort of effect.[45] Kant postulates God as the one who crowns duty with the reward of eternal happiness. Virtue is not itself the reward, but that which makes us worthy of reward, mediated by the "Author of nature."[46]

The notion of laws in Kantian ethics is easily transferrable to the biblical picture of God as lawgiver. As a result, twentieth-century Christian ethics had a strong Kantian tone to it. We can observe the deontological element in the oft-repeated phrase, "It is never right to do wrong in order to get a chance to do right."[47] We also observe the non-intrinsic relation between goodness and happiness.[48] John Piper's *Desiring God* was explicitly written to combat this assumption. He writes,

> When I was in college I had a vague, pervasive notion that if I did something good because it would make me happy, I would ruin its goodness.
>
> I figured that the goodness of my moral action was lessened to the degree I was motivated by a desire for my own pleasure. At the time, buying ice cream in the Student Center just for pleasure didn't bother me, because the moral consequences of that action seemed so insignificant. But to be motivated by a desire for happiness or pleasure when I volunteered for Christian service or went to church—that seemed selfish, utilitarian, mercenary.[49]

---

45. To say that virtue effects happiness is false for Kant, but only conditionally false. It is only false according to the form of causality in the world of sense. Immanuel Kant, *Critique of Practical Reason*, trans. Lewis White Beck, 3rd ed. (Upper Saddle River, NJ: Prentice-Hall: 1993), 121.

46. Kant, *Critique of Practical Reason*, 121.

47. This phrase is often attributed to Bob Jones Sr.

48. Alasdair MacIntyre traces these themes in modern moral philosophy from G. E. Moore (1873–1958) to H. A. Prichard (1871–1947), R. M. Hare (1919–2002), etc. MacIntyre's complaint is that by divorcing goodness from its end (happiness), we lose all grounds for applying or critiquing moral rules within a society. He writes, "Kant ... stands at the point at which the loss of moral unity means that morality can be specified only in terms of the form of its rules, and not of any end which the rules may serve. Hence his attempt to derive the content of moral rules from their form." The ultimate conclusion of divorcing goodness from its end is to devolve ethics into individualistic theories like emotivism and prescriptivism. MacIntyre, *Short History of Ethics*, 267.

49. John Piper, *Desiring God: Meditations of a Christian Hedonist* (Sisters, OR: Multnomah, 1986), 15–16.

I will cite just one other example. In *God in the Whirlwind*, David Wells writes, "In a psychological world, we want to be happy. In a moral world, we want to be holy. ... God stands before us not as our Therapist or our Concierge. He stands before us as the God of utter purity to whom we are morally accountable."[50] Nineteenth and twentieth century evangelicals often seemed to assume that obeying God is doing our duty without reference to happiness, with an expectation that there is a happiness to come. This is what Nietzsche was referring to when he called Christians nihilists.[51]

It might be that some evangelicals see the command against anxiety in Matthew 6:25–34 in this strong universally binding sense, that anxiety is always and everywhere a violation of God's universal moral command. To say this is to apply a deonotological approach to ethics to emotion. There are a few problems with the Kantian deontological approach to ethics being applied to emotion. The notion of emotional duty has a dual absurdity. In the first place, it is absurd to talk as if we have emotional duties, since emotions have no place in Kant's ethics. In the second place, Kant himself thought emotions could not be commanded.[52] In order to set ethics on a firm epistemological grounding, Kant disconnected it from its psychological, physiological, or social contexts. Kant had no room for virtue in his ethics, neither habits nor the passions they regulate, because the will is not the determining ground for ethics. Reason alone is the ground of ethics by way of the categorical imperative: always act in such a way that you could be legislating universally. So, habit, feeling, and circumstances (e.g., social contexts) are all equally irrelevant for Kant's ethics.[53] The point is that Kant rightly recognizes that emotions might be highly skewed by

---

50. David F. Wells, *God in the Whirlwind: How the Holy-love of God Reorients Our World* (Wheaton, IL: Crossway, 2014), 126.

51. Nietzsche writes, "The saint in whom God delights is the ideal eunuch. ... Life has come to an end where the 'kingdom of God' begins." He also writes that Schopenhauer sanctioned the "great cultural facts of humanity ... in a Christian, that is, a nihilistic sense." Friedrich Nietzsche, *Twilight of the Idols*, trans. Richard Polt (Indianapolis: Hackett, 1997), 28, 63.

52. Allen Wood writes, "The love of human beings must be *pathological* love, and not practical love. For he [Kant] is explicilty discussing *feelings* which *cannot* be commanded or obligatory. Pathological love is the only love that cannot be commanded or obligatory, while practical love is not a feeling, and it can be commanded." Allen Wood, "The Final Form of Kant's Practical Philosophy," in *Kant's Metaphysics of Morals: Interpretive Essays*, ed. Mark Timmons (New York: Cambridge University Press, 2000), 18.

53. MacIntyre, *Short History of Ethics*, 196.

physiology or social context. Insofar as Reformed evangelicals emphasize emotional responsibility in a voluntarist way, they seem to be swallowing one ethical assumption of the Kantian imaginary— the deontological approach irrespective of habit, context, and physiology—in correcting the other— non-intrinsic relation between morality and happiness. They legislate feeling without habit and context. Again, this produces an ironic reading of the anxiety command where it is taken to be a universal law (a Kantian reading) directed at feelings (anti-Kantian). However, Kant's warning about the nature of feelings is apt.

How does a Kantian ethical imaginary differ from a first-century one? It is precisely on this point: first-century ethics did account for virtue (habits of the passions) and for context because virtue just is the rational (*logikon*) pursuit of happiness (*eudaimonia*) within the complex circumstances of life. The principal concern of first-century ethical theory, be it Stoic, Epicurean, Aristotelian, etc., is what makes a good person, which is just the same as saying "what makes people truly happy."[54] First-century ethical thought takes into account not only the education of the intellect, but also the tutoring (intelligent habituation) of the passions by practical reason. A good man is one who reliably acts in ways that are rational and produce happiness in himself and in others. But perfect happiness is contingent on circumstances. Aristotle was quite clear that misfortune may destroy the happiness of the excellent man.[55] Aristotle writes, "[we should say that a person] is happy who is active in conformity with complete excellence and is sufficiently equipped with external goods, not for some chance period but throughout a complete life."[56] Again, Kant himself thought it is absurd that ancient philosophers could find "happiness in very just proportion to virtue in this life."[57] Kant rejected the notion that virtue is its own reward in favor of the idea that virtue, acting by duty, will merit the reward of happiness from God. So again, according to the Kantian imaginary, the only legitimate motivator for obedience, what actually moves the

---

54. Pennington, *Sermon on the Mount*, 31.

55. Aristotle, *Nicomachean Ethics*, 1100a10–1101a21 (I.10) in *The Complete Works of Aristotle: Revised Oxford Translation*, ed. Jonathan Barnes, 2 vols (Princeton: Princeton University Press, 1984).

56. Aristotle, *Nicomachean Ethics*, 1101a13–15 in *Complete Works*.

57. Kant, *Critique of Practical Reason*, 122.

will, is future eschatological reward. This is a very different sort of view to the ancient conception where virtue was universally assumed to have an intrinsic relation to happiness.

Pennington suggests that the Greco-Roman ethical tradition is an important context for early Christian ethics. He writes, "there is a consistent thread in the Greco-Roman tradition that rested the goal of human flourishing on the pursuit of virtue."[58] He suggests that a failure to attend to this first-century ethical perspective fundamentally misrepresents what the Sermon on the Mount is doing. My point is that we should not read the emotional directive as moral duty, but as aimed at cultivating virtuous character.

In what follows we will tease out this ethical context a bit more through what Pennington calls the "two conceptual rails" upon which the sermon runs.[59] We will see that within the context of Matthew, the righteousness of the kingdom of God is quite distinct from Kantian duty; it is an invitation into a paradoxical life of wholeness and flourishing with suffering. This kingdom is the God-oriented, already and not yet foretaste of blessedness. The already and not yet kingdom pushes us to expect an already and not yet psychology, where our emotional states are neither over- nor under-realized.

Immediate Context: Two Conceptual Rails for the Sermon

Within the immediate context, two relevant passages frame the imperative "do not be anxious": the aphorism "For where your treasure is, there your heart will be also" (Matt 6:21) and the aphorism "But seek first the kingdom of God and his righteousness, and all these things will be added to you" (6:33). Conjunctively, these aphorisms signal an important theme of the sermon—the kingdom of God is for those who wholeheartedly seek it. Confirmation of this theme is found in the broader context of the sermon where we see Jesus stipulating, "unless your righteousness exceeds that of the scribes and Pharisees, you will never enter the kingdom of heaven" (5:20). The Pharisees failed to achieve the wholehearted righteousness to which Jesus calls his disciples.

---

58. Pennington, *Sermon on the Mount*, 31.
59. Pennington, *Sermon on the Mount*, 41.

The righteousness that counts for the kingdom is wholeness (Matt 5:48, *teleios*). Jonathan Pennington sees this as one of two conceptual rails that are the track to understanding the sermon.[60] Pennington translates *teleios* as "wholeness" because translating it as "perfect" causes significant problems. He writes, "[it] communicates to the contemporary English ear the ideas of moral perfection, absolute purity, and even sinlessness."[61] Again, read through the Kantian lens, we might see perfection as emphasizing our absolute duty to fulfill moral laws without exception. However, the ethics of the Greco-Roman world was the virtue ethic tradition, which was concerned with prudent human action within a web of social commitments, such as a commitment to the good of the city or community.[62] Wholeness is not just personal integrity, but judging by the extensive treatments of interpersonal issues such as murder, adultery, divorce, promise keeping, loving your enemies, etc., also refers to the to the sort of communal *shalom* that the law was intended to initiate, the lack of which the prophets condemned (Isa 1:16-17; Jer 22:1-4; Amos 5:10-13; Mic 3:1-10). Jesus is inviting his hearers into the dawning of the kingdom of flourishing for all people. Like Israel, his church is to be a light for all peoples (Isa 42:6; 49:6; Matt 5:14-16), a community that embodies righteousness to the glory of God and for the good of humankind. The kingdom represents a reversal of Eden's shattered *shalom*: the relationships of human beings to God, to each other, and to the earth.

By contrast, the Pharisees in their hypocrisy lacked wholeness of heart, which is why the righteousness required for the kingdom of heaven must exceed theirs. We must not trivialize this sort of righteousness by suggesting that the Pharisees said one thing and did another, as one definition of hypocrisy suggests. The Pharisees were famous and beloved for their righteousness. Josephus writes that the Pharisees were extremely influential among the Jewish people, and that any excellence in the people's living and speaking was a "great tribute ... to the excellence of the Pharisees."[63] While it is true that eventually what is in the cup will overflow (Matt 12:34-37),

60. Pennington, *Sermon on the Mount*, 70.

61. Pennington, *Sermon on the Mount*, 70.

62. The word "human" is key here because the Greek tradition assumed that human beings uniquely possess rationality, but are also qualified by the body and finiteness.

63. Josephus, *Antiquities*, trans. Louis H. Feldman, Loeb Classical Library, vol. 8 (Cambridge, MA: Harvard University Press, 1965), 18.2-3.

the real problem with the Pharisees is that they achieved merely external righteousness, which was only apparent and calculated (Matt 6:2–5, 16; 23:1–36). They were divided internally and externally, not wholehearted, because they served "two masters"; that is, they loved the praise of people while externally serving God.[64] Moreover, the real fruit of the Pharisees was displayed in how their righteousness impacted their community. They imposed heavy burdens on others but refused to bear them themselves (Matt 23:4); they "devour widows' houses and for a pretense make long prayers" (Mark 12:40).[65] They tithed on even their mint, dill, and cumin, but neglected mercy, justice, and faithfulness (Matt 23:23).

Pennington's other conceptual rail is the Greek work *makarios*, which Pennington translates as flourishing—the subject of the Sermon's Beatitudes. There is a certain amount of paradox that is often missed in the Beatitudes because of the usual translation of *makarios* as "blessed." The problem with this translation is that it conflates two distinct connotations: (1) "a state of happiness" and (2) "being ... favored as the recipient of blessing from the Lord."[66] Pennington writes, "The English term 'blessed' is so heavily loaded with the narrower sense of 'divine favor' that the sense of human flourishing is almost always lost."[67] The contrast might be crudely captured by the two alternatives "blessed will be ..." versus "flourishing are ..." The former reinforces the Kantian imaginary, which separates virtue and happiness by making happiness only the eschatological reward of virtue. The latter represents a paradox in that it is precisely the poor in spirit, the mourning, the meek, and the persecuted that seem not to be flourishing.

This paradox is the point of the Beatitudes. To miss the paradox in the blessing statements is to miss the already and not yet aspect of kingdom ethics. Pennington writes, "Because the end has not yet come, human flourishing will only be experienced in a paradoxical way that combines loss, longing, suffering, and persecution with true happiness, joy, satisfaction, and peace."[68] Pennington argues that these statements are exclamatory

---

64. Pennington, *Sermon on the Mount*, 84.

65. This may be an interpolation from Luke 20:47, but both their love of money and their desire to hide this is well documented (e.g., Mark 7:9–13; Luke 16:14–15).

66. Pennington, *Sermon on the Mount*, 49.

67. Pennington, *Sermon on the Mount*, 50.

68. Pennington, *Sermon on the Mount*, 296.

descriptions of the state of happiness: "Proclaiming [a blessing statement] is to make a *value judgment* upon another member of the community's behavior and commitments."[69] John Nolland writes, "Beatitudes verge on the congratulatory: a category of persons is singled out, and their good fortune is proclaimed."[70] This is precisely the sort of kingdom Jesus is announcing not only in the sermon, but also in the book of Matthew as a whole. In the kingdom of Jesus, it is the sufferers—the poor in spirit, those who mourn, those who hunger and thirst for righteousness, etc.—who are "the greatest in the kingdom of heaven" (Matt 18:4). How fortunate to be last in a kingdom where the last are first (19:23–30).

Biblical-Theological Context: The Kingdom

The paradox of blessing statements raises the paradox of the kingdom in the broader context of Matthew. The ideal first-century reader of Matthew would have been sensitive to the eschatological expectations of restoration especially as presented by the prophets. The Isaianic vision, for example, promises an everlasting salvation for Israel (Isa 45:17) where all people from the ends of the earth will turn to God and every knee will bow (Isa 45:23). This restoration will bring peace and righteousness to his people (Isa 54:11–17). The Lord will offer water to everyone who is thirsty (Isa 55:1–2); he will revive the lowly (Isa 57:15); and he will break the chains of evil and oppression (Isa 58:6–12). These are the promises of the new covenant, which promises an outpouring of the Spirit who will preserve the words of the Lord in the mouths of his people (Isa 59:21). No passage in Isaiah is as striking as the promise of the new heaven and new earth in Isaiah 65:17–18: "For behold, I create new heavens and a new earth, and the former things shall not be remembered or come into mind. But be glad and rejoice forever in that which I create; for behold, I create Jerusalem to be a joy, and her people to be a gladness."

Within the overall narrative arc of Matthew, the Sermon on the Mount is a sort of invitation into this kingdom, but with a surprising twist. The climax of the book of Matthew displays the contrast in great vividness. In

---

69. Pennington, *Sermon on the Mount*, 49.

70. John Nolland, "Blessing and Woe," *Dictionary of Jesus and the Gospels*, 2nd ed., ed. Joel B. Green, Jeannine K. Brown, and Nicholas Perin (Downers Grove, IL: InterVarsity, 2013), 87.

Matthew 16:17, Peter is praised for proclaiming Jesus to be "the Christ, the Son of the living God" (16:16). Six verses later, Peter is castigated for denying that the Messiah should suffer with the following words: "Get behind me, Satan! You are a hindrance to me" (16:23). Jesus makes the lesson very plain, "If anyone would come after me, let him deny himself and take up his cross and follow me. For whoever would save his life will lose it, but whoever loses his life for my sake will find it" (16:24–25). The invitation into the kingdom is an invitation into an already and not yet life of flourishing with suffering. The kingdom in Matthew vividly represents this tension between the already and the not yet. As Kevin Vanhoozer writes, "A new age—characterized by the Spirit's ministry of the new covenant—has dawned, but the dawn has yet to give way to full daylight."[71] This new creation involves both the regenerating work of the Spirit through union with Christ for believers (already—2 Cor 5:17) and an expectation of heirship as children of the Father of the glory that will be revealed to us and in the new creation of the cosmos (not yet—Rom 8:18–25). Our covenantal participation in the life of God through the Spirit is a foretaste (firstfruits) of the not yet fully dawned eschatological promises.

What I want to suggest is that it is necessary to apply this already and not yet tension to our psychological expectations. Emotion seems to be an area of profound eschatological confusion. What I am advocating is an eschatologically sensitive psychology. I am suggesting that the Kantian imaginary may have produced both an under-realized and an over-realized assessment of our psychological states. Some scholars exhibit an under-realized expectation for our psychological states by assuming that commands in no way apply to our current emotional states and that emotional tranquility is only a reward for present continence. Matthew Elliott rightly criticizes C. H. Dodd for holding this view when he separates love as action and love as feeling. Dodd writes, "[Love] is not primarily an emotion or an affection; it is primarily an active determination of the will. That is why it can be commanded as feelings cannot."[72] Other scholars exhibit an over-realized expectation for psychological states by applying duty to

---

71. Kevin J. Vanhoozer, *Drama of Doctrine: A Canonical Linguistic Approach to Christian Theology* (Louisville: Westminster John Knox, 2005), 111.

72. C. H. Dodd, *Gospel and Law* (Cambridge: Cambridge University Press, 1951), 42. Elliott, *Faithful Feelings*, 138.

feelings without an acknowledgement of variable experience or our holistic, embodied nature. They rightfully emphasize the moral implications of emotion, but with an implied mental voluntarism and a too assured expectation that the Spirit will produce a rich psychological tranquility in this life. By contrast, the Sermon on the Mount seems to represent an invitation to flourishing with suffering, a communion of joy with the heavenly Father that is marked by profound suffering. Because emotion is qualified by embodiment within a groaning world (Rom 8:19–23), the Christian will always experience the spiritual life as already and not yet.

The already and not yet aspect of psychology is apparent not only by the continuing struggle against sin and its effects, personal and social, but also by our continuing struggle with illness or dysfunction. As noted, weakness (Latin, *vitium*) captures both the notion of sin and fragility. Virtue and happiness are in this life constantly conjoined with natural and moral evil. There is no easy way to disentangle the effects of sin and bodily weakness within our conscious experience; for example, neglected or abused children are often anxious and angry. But just as virtue and happiness are mixed with evil and despair, so also evil and despair are always qualified by the hope that is found in communion with the heavenly Father.

Philippians 4:6–7

In the spirit of Scripture interpreting Scripture, I want to make a few brief comments about Philippians 4:6–7: "Do not be anxious about anything, but in everything by prayer and supplication with thanksgiving let your requests be made known to God. And the peace of God, which surpasses all understanding, will guard your hearts and minds in Christ Jesus." First, just as I have been suggesting for Matthew 6:25–34, we need not to read either this directive or its corresponding promise in a psychologically rigid way. It may not be the case that prayer and thanksgiving will immediately banish every anxiety, but that the practice of prayer and thanksgiving is like watering the garden of our embodied selves toward the sort of maturity that enables Paul to say, "to live is Christ and to die is gain" (Phil 1:21), or "Even if I am to be poured out as a drink offering upon the sacrificial offering of your faith, I am glad and rejoice with you all" (Phil 2:17).

Second, the command "do not be anxious" (Phil 4:6, *mēden merimnate*) not only assumes that worries will come, but the promise concerning God's peace is formulated to suggest that the sort of peace that keeps us lies just beyond our experiential comprehension: the peace that "surpasses all *understanding* [*nous*]" (Phil 4:7) will "guard your ... [understanding] [*noēma*]." G. Walter Hansen reads this as "the peace that God himself has," which makes good sense of how it "surpasses all [human] understanding."[73] We experience life moment by unpredictable moment, but his peace can uphold us in anxiety. We are not to give ourselves over to worry, but to rest in God's peace.

The reference to God's peace also strikingly reminds us of the Matthean context of the command in the Sermon on the Mount, where we see that the already and not yet psychological suffering within the kingdom is manifest in the anxiety and sorrow of God incarnate in the garden (Matt 26:36–46). In this battle with the flesh, we do not see perfect Stoic tranquility or Aristotelian temperance, but moral courage in the face of the flesh (Rom 8:3–4). God's peace guarded Jesus' heart and mind so as to give him victory over the flesh. In overcoming the flesh, he invited us into his victory and into the vivification of our mortal bodies through his Spirit (Rom 8:11). And yet, this is not hope which is seen, but hope which is experienced as firstfruits (Rom 8:23–25); we wait with patience for the redemption of our bodies.

What Sort of Action?

We return to the question that began this section: To what sort of action is Jesus calling his hearers in Matthew 6:25–34? Within the context of first-century ethics, the Sermon on the Mount, and God's redemptive work in inaugurating the kingdom, Jesus is inviting us into a course of fulfillment that, in light of subsequent canonical revelation, involves embracing wholehearted righteousness through union with him in his death and resurrection and through the Spirit's enabling power to put to death the deeds of the body. This invitation is to put off anxiety by seeking the kingdom. To seek the kingdom is to be initiated into a relationship with God (communion) that yields already and not yet wholeness and flourishing

---

73. G. Walter Hansen, *The Letter to the Philippians*, Pillar New Testament Commentary (Grand Rapids: Eerdmans, 2009), 292.

through the care of the heavenly Father. Seeking is a holistic orientation that aims toward reversing the brokenness of the fall, since we are both reconciled to God and to each other, and therefore participate in putting on the new self (Gal 3:27; Eph 4:24; Col 3:10) in Christ's body through the mutual exchange of gifts of the Spirit (Rom 12; 1 Cor 12). The fulfillment of the directive of Jesus is accompanied both by the provision of the heavenly Father (covenantal consolation) and by inducements connected with our flourishing. This is not strict legislation, but the gentle coaxing of a shepherd. The disciples of Jesus are not to do as Israelites did, who failed to enter the rest of God. Israelites grumbled in their anxiety over God's provision (Exod 16:1–3), did not remember Egypt's bondage, and ran to Egypt for protection (Isa 30:1–15; Jer 42:14–44:27). Instead, we might learn the lessons of remembering God's redemption (Exod 13) and the practices of love (Deut 6) to participate in the life of trust. By attending to the redemptive context, we see that the problem of anxiety runs much deeper in biblical theology than we supposed. Trust is opposed to anxiety, and this trust will produce either boasting or shame. The psalmists repeatedly extol trusting the Lord (Ps 4:5; 9:10; 13:5; 20:7; 22:8, etc). For Paul it is crucial not to be ashamed of the gospel (Rom 1:16; 2 Tim 1:8) because faith gives us access to grace which warrants boasting in hope, and even in our sufferings (Rom 5:2–3) — the already and not yet.

CONCLUSION

In sum, the aim of this chapter has been twofold: (1) paying attention to the biblical theological context raises the bar for the directive of Jesus in Matthew 6:25–34, we must not be anxious but rather seek the kingdom; and (2) paying attention to the biblical theological context qualifies our expectations for fulfillment away from facile mental voluntarism to an encompassing course of fulfillment within the already and not yet life between inauguration and consummation. The inverse of anxiety in Matthew 6 is seeking the kingdom (6:33). In other words, we are to submit ourselves to the care and governance of our Father's rule. What brings us comfort is the surety of his ruling care; he is the gardener of his good creation and of us. As James K. A. Smith writes, "God's rule is not an antinatural tyranny but more like the authority of the gardener who husbands creation to its fulness."[74] Likewise, we are under-gardeners, having dominion not only over ourselves but over this world. I have tried to show the value of a psychology which is holistic and tiered, that is, a psychology where we possess the relationship of a gardener to our bodies. Our bodies are simply one sphere of our political rule over all creation under the curse. We must treat our bodies with the same sort of creational care that our Father does. And if we do, we might learn patience as he is patient with his creation. We often fail to see why patience is fitting to the created order. God's gardener rule over his organic creation can be a metaphor that governs the Christian struggle to overcome anxiety. Gardening and shepherding are both part of husbanding, and this metaphor leads us to Christology, to the example of the faithful second Adam who overcame the flesh to offer us forgiveness and hope by the bestowal of his Spirit. In Christ we see the faithful husband and head, who governs his bride by enfolding us into his body, nourishing and cherishing us (Eph 5:25–29). By the Spirit we likewise govern our bodies and those we are responsible for within the body of Christ. We are embodied creatures within a body whose political head is the chief shepherd and husband. Our experience will inevitably be marked by the presence of anxiety, like our Lord, but we seek the kingdom with an orientation of trust that at the very least hopes against hope (Rom 4:18) and rests in the peace of a God who sees the course of all things and shepherds us into its mystery.

74. James K. A. Smith, *Awaiting the King: Reforming Public Theology*, Cultural Liturgies, vol. 3 (Grand Rapids: Baker Academic, 2017), 67.

CONCLUSION

—

REVISITING MARY

What difference does my proposal make for Mary's anxiety? An emotionally voluntarist counselor might listen to Mary to gauge whether the issue is spiritual or physical. This assumes a too dualistic understanding of human nature: if the counselor determines that the issue is physical, Mary may need medication; if it is spiritual, Mary may need to repent of her sinful anxiety. And since anxiety straightforwardly reveals the nature of the heart, Mary's anxiety is guilty until proven innocent. Little attention is paid to the logic of the body, how Mary's unconscious is engaged with her environment.

By contrast, my holistic and tiered psychology judges her anxiety to arise primarily from her unconscious assessment of her situation. It also involves embodied aspects such as neuropathways, chronic bodily states, and patterns of brain development. This does not take Mary's anxiety out of the realm of the moral, for we are stewards of our bodies. The Christian faith demands us to set our hope in God's work in Christ by participating in kingdom life. And this participation in the gift of salvation—justification and sanctification by union with Christ—is also qualified by inaugurated eschatology. While we are *already* clothed in Christ's righteousness, our bodies are *not yet* released from their bondage to corruption. Psychologically speaking, we expect to live with a foretaste of the ultimate victory that we await with groaning at the restoration of all things. Christians are not promised unbroken psychological tranquility but are offered peace with God as grounds for hope against hope (Rom 4:18; 5:1-2).

A Christian counselor must first listen wisely to assess the constellation of causes for distress. The counselor would need to know about family history to determine any possible genetic influences; childhood experiences to

347

account for developmental challenges that may have lasting negative influence; current stressors; patterns of life; and unmet expectations (Figure 10.1). The causes of emotion are complex, difficult to identify, and only partly within our control.

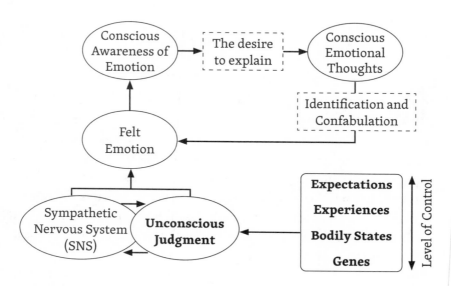

Figure 10.1, Emotions Reveal

The counselor should approach the anxiety with curiosity. Asking questions explores the unconscious processes, contributing to the emotional reactions. The unconscious tracks stressors that frustrate our goals.[1] For example, at various times of our lives we may face joblessness, strained relationships, death, illness, financial difficulties, loneliness, or the birth

---

1. For example, social psychologists have investigated the link between social anxiety and unconscious assessments of hierarchy. Politeness theory studies how people use negative politeness (i.e., avoiding imposition) and positive politeness (i.e., complementing) to negotiate social rank. Those who rank lower socially tend to employ more negative politeness toward social superiors. Jonathan Oakman, Shannon Gifford, Natasha Chlebowsky, "A Multilevel Analysis of the Interpersonal Behavior of Socially Anxious People," *Journal of Personality* 71, no. 3 (June 2003): 397–434; Peter Trower, Paul Gilbert, and Georgina Sherling, "Social anxiety, evolution, and self- presentation: An interdisciplinary perspective," in *Handbook of Social and Evaluation Anxiety*, ed. Harold Leitenberg (New York: Plenum, 1990), 11–45; Akio Yabuuchi, "Hierarchy Politeness: What Brown and Levinson Refused to See," *Intellectual Pragmatics* 3, no. 3 (2006): 323–51. We both track rank and negotiate it largely unconsciously.

of a child. Our capacity to manage stress—our resiliency—might be likened to the size of a box that we all carry. When this box overflows with stressors, anxiety, anger, or depression occur. Often cognitive, behavioral, or social aspects of these stressors can be addressed. Asking questions may uncover some of these stressors, which Mary may not even have been conscious of due to self-deceit or shame.

The cause of Mary's anxiety may be quite complex. Perhaps anxiety is a family trait—partly biological and partly learned. She may have inherited heightened sensitivity to stressors. Or perhaps a family tragedy such as divorce or a death marked her childhood at a crucial time of development, disposing her to expect unconsciously that the world is dangerous and unpredictable.[2] Childhood trauma may also make her nervous system even more reactive.[3] Trauma has been extensively linked to anxiety sensitivity.[4] These experiences of trauma and tragedy may amplify the ordinary difficulties of raising a very young child. Her anxiety may be increased by the responsibility of childcare or the weight of her husband's coldness. Unconsciously Mary may be balancing a complex web of worries related to her altered role as a new mom.

She may have ultimate concerns that are not deeply informed by the biblical narrative. She may find ultimate hope in things that are not ultimate, like financial gain, social standing, or physical health. She may have idealized family life so that her expectations are easily frustrated. Her

---

2. Andres G. Viana, Eric C. Berenz, Laura J. Dixon, and Flint M. Espil, "Trauma and Deliberate Self-Harm Among Inpatient Adolescents: The Moderating Role of Anxiety Sensitivity," *Psychological Trauma* 9, no. 5 (2017): 509–17; and Andrei C. Miu, Mirela I. Bîlc, Ioana Bunea, Aurora Szentágotai-Tătar, "Childhood Trauma and Sensitivity to Reward and Punishment: Implications for Depressive and Anxiety Symptoms," *Personality and Individual Differences* 119 (2017): 134–40.

3. For example, trauma makes children more reactive to noise. Tanja Jovanovic, Nineequa Q. Blanding, Seth D. Norrholm, Erica Duncan, Bekh Bradley, and Kerry J. Ressler, "Childhood Abuse is Associated with Increased Startle Reactivity in Adulthood," *Depression and Anxiety* 26, no. 11 (2009): 1018–26.

4. Brittany B. Kugler, Vicky Phares, Alison Salloum, and Eric A. Storch, "The Role of Anxiety Sensitivity in the Relationship Between Posttraumatic Stress Symptoms and Negative Outcomes in Trauma-Exposed Adults," *Anxiety, Stress, and Coping* 29, no. 2 (2016): 187–201; Bunmi O. Olatunji, Thomas Armstrong, Qianqian Fan, and Mimi Zhao, "Risk and Resiliency in Posttraumatic Stress Disorder: Distinct Roles of Anxiety and Disgust Sensitivity," *Psychological Trauma* 6, no. 1 (2014): 50–55; Erin C. Berenz, Salpi Kevorkian, Nadia Chowdhury, Danielle M. Dick, Kenneth S. Kendler, and Ananda B. Amstadter, "Posttraumatic Stress Disorder Symptoms, Anxiety Sensitivity, and Alcohol-Use Motives in College Students with a History of Interpersonal Trauma," *Psychology of Addictive Behaviors* 30, no. 7 (2016): 755–63.

ideals may be idols, so that she finds it difficult to see communion with
God as producing hope. These ultimate concerns may be deeply habituated into her ways of life. Again, no biological or environmental fact can-
cels Mary's responsibility to fight anxiety by pursuing the kingdom; they
merely give it proper context.

Finally, the goal of my project is not to endorse specific treatments for
anxiety, but to expand our understanding of anxiety and to push Christians
toward compassionate curiosity in light of how our bodies qualify emotions.[5] A Christian is a person who hopes in God. But we must wait with
patience for what we do not see, for these bodies of dust to be raised incor-
ruptible (Rom 8:18–25). In the meantime, we might remain compassionately
curious about the logic of our bodies. We might ask why we feel what we
feel and how the means of grace grant help and health. Six theses summarize my core contribution. They strengthen our sensitivity to the logic
of the body.

SIX THESES ON THERAPY AND EMBODIMENT

1. *The saving grace of God is the beginning, middle, and end of Christian therapy.*
God has a therapeutic agenda.[6] God's reconciling work is aimed at glo-
rifying himself by restoring our fellowship with him and restoring our
proper relations with each other and with creation. God's therapeutic
agenda is accomplished by grace alone. The triune God glorifies himself
according to his grace, by sharing his goodness in creation, by uniting us
to himself in his Son, and by governing his world with common kindness.
(These might be called creation grace, saving grace, and common grace.)
All of God's kindnesses to us come from his initiative and for his glory. In

---

5. The phrase "compassionate curiosity" is from Gabor Maté. He asks, "If I examine my
addictive behaviors without judgment and ask 'Why?' in the spirit of compassionate curiosity,
what do I find? More to the point, whom do I find? What is the full truth of me?" Gabor Maté,
In the Realm of Hungry Ghosts: Close Encounters with Addiction (Berkeley, CA: North Atlantic,
2010), 354.

6. Eric Johnson opens his book *God and Soul Care* with an axiom and its corollary: "Axiom
1: The triune God is the greatest Being there is, and he made humans in his image, so that
reflecting and participating in his glory is their transcendent, final goal. Corollary: The Proper
Flourishing of humans is therefore an immanent, subordinate goal in God's design." Eric L.
Johnson, *God and Soul Care: The Therapeutic Resources of the Christian Faith* (Downers Grove,
IL: IVP Academic, 2017), 21.

addition to word and sacrament, God graciously gives us nature, exercise, self-awareness, cognitive habits, sleep, friendship, and medication. We need not choose between resting in God in sleep and resting in God by meditating on his word, but we must give thanks. God achieves his therapeutic agenda solely by his grace.

2. *Because we are embodied beings, physicality always qualifies our agency.*
God formed us from the ground and enlivened us with his breath. We are not mere souls, but embodied beings. Our entire agency is qualified by physicality. If so, pastors and theologians need to develop a basic knowledge of how the body functions in emotional experience.[7] For example, if we know how the sympathetic nervous system involves our body, we know why our anxious moods persists and so we choose more effective means of dealing with them. Understanding how neural pathways are strengthened helps us to see how habits are formed and why they are durable. Our thoughts are not unencumbered by neurons. While Christian pastors and theologians are not therapists, there is no principled reason why they should ignore empirical research about the natural world, and especially about human beings. Theologians especially need to do some cross-disciplinarily work to assist pastors in this task.

3. *Our physicality puts limits on our change, but God renews us.*
We are physical. And so we are bound by time and space. Change is not instant. Consider how the Bible uses organic metaphors for Christian maturity. We grow abiding in the true vine (John 15:1–11). We are planted as the seeds of the kingdom (Matt 13:3–9; 1 Cor 3:5–9). We are grafted into his life (Rom 11:17–24). Just as in Eden, we are to cultivate fruitfulness, producing the fruit of the Spirit, "love, joy, peace, patience, kindness, goodness, faithfulness, gentleness, self-control" (Gal 5:22–23). We are governed by the

---

7. I recommend Bessel van der Kolk, *The Body Keeps the Score: Brain, Mind, and Body in the Healing of Trauma* (New York: Penguin, 2014); Joseph E. LeDoux, *Anxious: Using the Brain to Understand and Treat Fear and Anxiety* (New York: Penguin, 2015); Joseph E. LeDoux, *The Emotional Brain: The Mysterious Underpinnings of Emotional Life* (New York: Simon & Schuster, 1996). I also recommend pastors and theologians read about child development and addiction. For example, Bruce D. Perry and Maia Szalavitz, *The Boy Who Was Raised as a Dog* (New York: Basic Books, 2017); Maté, *In the Realm of Hungry Ghosts*; Kent Dunnington, *Addiction and Virtue: Beyond the Models of Disease and Choice* (Downers Grove, IL: IVP Academic, 2011).

word of God like trees planted by streams of water that yield their fruit in season, and whose leaves do not wither (Psalm 1:3).

These metaphors teach us that we need patience with ourselves and others, just as God is patient with us: "See how the farmer waits for the precious fruit of the earth, being patient about it, until it receives the early and the late rains" (Jas 5:7). We are to be steadfast in our sufferings (Jas 5:11), knowing that God is bringing about the first fruits of "maturity and completeness" in us (Jas 1:4, 18). We must have realistic expectations while we wait for our deliverance from the curse. Suffering arising from the curse teaches us to hope in God; this hope will not put us to shame (Rom 5:4–5). Because the hope of embodied creatures is ultimately our renewed and imperishable bodies in the new heavens and earth, we do not despise the limits that our physicality brings. We embrace our limits as expressions of our finitude. Our limits and our sufferings teach us how to depend on God.

Our emotions tell us whether we are flourishing or wilting. But changing our emotions may be slow. We have responsibility, but not total control over our bodies. Paul's example in his letter to the Philippians teaches us that we need not be buffeted by circumstances. Paul is like a mighty oak while we are saplings. Through long experience of God's faithfulness in trial, Paul learned the secret of contentment. This secret is that Paul could rejoice or boast even in his weakness and shame (2 Cor 12:9) because God's grace is enough, and his strengthening presence is near (Phil 4:9, 13).

4. God grants us the capacity to think, choose, see, and feel in order that we receive new life in Christ.
Our faculties are part of God's created wisdom. Our mental capacities enable us to imagine our lives as "hidden with Christ in God" (Col 3:2–3). We can endure intense psychological pain knowing that we have "every spiritual blessing in the heavenly places" (Eph 1:3). We must use our capacities to put on this way of seeing. Paul prays our imaginations would reflect this way of seeing the world, "having the eyes of your hearts enlightened" (Eph 1:18).

We also embody this perspective by our capacity to choose. Paul says to put to "death therefore what is earthly in you" and to put on the new life we have in Christ (Col 3:5, 12–17). Choosing to put on the life of Christ allows us to experience a foretaste of the joy of the new creation. We experience new creation life when we participate in it by the Spirit. Paul calls this life one of peace, wisdom, and gratitude. Our choices are an opportunity to experience more of the richness of God's saving grace.

5. *Our bodies are burdened by spiritual and bodily failings, weakness, and trials.* We must not forget those who are weary. Many Christians bear wounds from abuse or neglect. These wounds often produce chronic depression or anxiety. To place a burden of emotional duty on the shoulders of these people adds iniquity to their injuries.[8] Personal sin is not the only source of our suffering. Suffering comes from original sin, from personal sin, from the sins of others, and from the curse on the natural world. We are embedded in the social and cultural *kosmos*. The term *kosmos* (world) is a constellation of sinful cultural habits that often cause us deep wounds and pull us into sinful ways of relating to ourselves and others. Moral and natural evil are deeply intertwined in our personal and social habits.

The Bible calls us to an alternate social world, a new city. The church is to function as a body, each member ministering the nourishment of Christ to others (Eph 4:16; Col 2:19).[9] Too often, however, churches are not a place of spiritual nourishment and emotional healing. Shame is a significant problem in many churches, especially in churches where it is risky to be open about difficulties.[10] Yes, guilt and shame are part of the human condition because of original and personal sin.[11] The gospel addresses our shame because God takes our shame and offers us adoption.

---

8. Paul says that he was granted a "thorn in the flesh" (2 Cor 12:7). This thorn was a messenger of Satan to harass him. The language perhaps echoes the "thorns and thistles" from the curse that frustrate the created order (Gen 3:18) and perhaps the thorns Jesus wore as he overcame sin in the flesh (John 19:5).

9. In Colossians 2, Paul contrasts the shadow of "human tradition" (v. 8)—"questions of food and drink" (v. 16) and "asceticism" (vv. 18, 23)—with the body of Christ (*to de sōma tou Christou*; v. 17). Those who pursue the shadow, he writes, are "not holding fast to the Head, from whom the whole body, nourished and knit together through its joints and ligaments, grows with a growth that is from God" (v. 19).

10. Eric Johnson writes, "members of churches with the highest ethical standards often have the greatest difficulty in opening up with one another about their imperfections." Johnson, *God and Soul Care*, 448–49.

11. Harold Senkbeil differentiates guilt and shame as follows, "Guilt is sin committed; shame is sin suffered." In this sense, Adam and Eve were both violators and victims. He adds later, "Guilt has to do with behavior, while shame is a matter of identity." Harold L. Senkbeil, *The Care of Souls: Cultivating a Pastor's Heart* (Bellingham, WA: Lexham Press, 2019), 137–38. Curt Thompson puts it this way, "Guilt is something I feel because I have *done* something bad.

Harold Senkbeil offers the image of the waiting father from the prodigal son parable, who embraces his son, forgives him and restores his honor.[12]

Still shame is a relentless pest for many of the weakest in our congregations. Some of these people are overwhelmed by shame and incapable of seeing their way out of it. Research into child development only deepens our appreciation for the generational scars that patterns of abuse or neglect can leave. Curt Thompson records shame's disintegrating effect:

> For instance, when I experience shame, I find it virtually impossible to turn my attention to something other than what I am feeling. I can become overwhelmed with the activity of my brainstem (the no-clutch phenomenon), and my [prefrontal cortex] goes offline. I am not able to think coherently. ... Shame is overtaking me. I then begin to construct a narrative that predicts a bleak and pessimistic future. I am unable to tell the whole story, certainly not one in which I am loved by God unconditionally and life, in the end, will be okay.[13]

These experiences of shame often arise in the context of mundane interactions with others, especially for those with difficult childhood experiences.

Eric Johnson argues that the body of Christ is a means of grace for combating shame.[14] We reenact how our waiting father restores honor to his children when we "Outdo one another in showing honor" (Rom 12:10).[15] Johnson cites the Puritan Divine Richard Sibbes, "There is sweet sight of

---

Shame is something I feel because I *am* bad." Curt Thompson, *The Soul of Shame: Retelling the Stories We Believe about Ourselves* (Downers Grove, IL: IVP Books, 2015), 63.

12. Senkbeil cites Luke 15:22, "Bring quickly the best robe, and put it on him, and put a ring on his hand, and shoes on his feet." Senkbeil, *Care of Souls*, 140.

13. Thompson, *Soul of Shame*, 67.

14. Johnson writes, "The therapeutic value of belonging to a community that seeks to cultivate genuine friendship is manifold. Such support can help to undermine a legalistic/perfectionist orientation that afflicts many Christians, especially in early adulthood. It can also help to resolve shame by means of face-to-face acceptance of one another (Rom 15:7)." Johnson, *God and Soul Care*, 452.

15. Johnson writes, "As church members celebrate God's goodness in one another and on behalf of Christ, by practicing mutual respect and affirmation, recognizing and practicing their gifts, challenging each other, yet overlooking and enduring each other's sins, weaknesses, and mistakes, they give each other new kinds of social experiences—which are also concrete experiences of the Spirit of Christ in one another." Johnson, *God and Soul Care*, 451.

God in the face of a friend."[16] We need to bestow greater honor on our weaker members (1 Cor 12:23) to help release them from their shame; they are God's "glorious inheritance" (Eph 1:18).[17]

God's people must also minister the comfort of Christ by entering empathetically into the suffering of others. We must "bear one another's burdens, and so fulfill the law of Christ" (Gal 6:2); we must "weep with those who weep" (Rom 12:15). This means that we absorb some of the emotional burden of others.[18] It means we listen with compassionate curiosity, not supposing that anxiety comes only from personal sin.

6. *Habits are a grace, corrupted by the curse, renewed by the Spirit.*
Not only are our faculties gifts from God, but also our capacity to form habits. Apart from grace, human habits are corrupt both individually and culturally. In *East of Eden*, John Steinbeck illustrates how the sin of Cain persists and blossoms into a thousand varieties from generation to generation. And yet in the midst of this darkening (Rom 1:21) the light and love of Christ breaks into history to redeem human beings from their sins and to offer a new humanity in his body. The Spirit of Christ enables the body of Christ bear fruit of new habits (Gal 5:16), to be transformed into a mature humanity (Eph 4:13). By faith, Christians are united with Christ, and by faith we walk into this new humanity (2 Cor 5:7). So by the Spirit we put on the new self (Eph 4:24; Col 3:10) and present our bodies as instruments for righteousness (Rom 6:13-19) to establish these habits of righteousness.

We are plastic; we can take new forms. This enables us to experience transformation. We had been conformed to the world, and now we are to be transformed by the word (Rom 12:1-2). And as the Spirit forms in us the firstfruits of this new life, we also recognize in our groaning the hunger pains for a feast of glory that we cannot yet imagine. And so we hope: "we

---

16. Johnson, *God and Soul Care*, 452; citing Richard Sibbes, "The Soul's Conflict with Itself," in *Works of Richard Sibbes*, vol. 1 (Edinburgh: Banner of Truth Trust, 1973), 192.

17. Johnson warns of a sort of "caste system" which develops in churches between the more honorable members and the weaker members. He writes, "A little investigation, however, usually reveals that the weaker have often had fewer advantages in life, perhaps having been exposed to more childhood abuse or neglect than the more honorable." Johnson, *God and Soul Care*, 458.

18. But we do not take full responsibility for the burdens of others, "For each will have to bear his own load" (Gal 6:5).

ourselves, who have the firstfruits of the Spirit, groan inwardly as we wait eagerly for adoption as sons, the redemption of our bodies. For in this hope we were saved. ... [and] we wait for it with patience" (Rom 8:23-25).

APPENDIX

—

ON THE HEART

E motional voluntarism relies on three assumptions about the biblical word "heart": (1) it just is the human soul in exclusion to the body, metaphysically speaking, and (2) it is the ultimate source of our emotions, which (3) reveal our true beliefs. Consequently, we need to evaluate these points biblically. I cannot do justice to the topic here, but want to argue that these assumptions are by no means necessary.

First, some authors take "heart" to refer to the soul to the exclusion of the body, metaphysically speaking. For example, Ed Welch's argument in "Sinner's Learning to Act the Miracle" depends on this disjunction. He writes,

> The differences between body and soul can be summarized this way: the soul is the moral epicenter of the person. In our souls or hearts, we make allegiances to ourselves and our idols or to the true God. In our souls, we follow the Lord's commands or turn from them. The soul is called righteous or unrighteous, obedient or disobedient, willing or unwilling. The body is our means of service in a physical world. It is never described in moral terms. Instead, it is either strong or weak. This means that though the body cannot make us sin, its weaknesses can make our lives complicated, difficult, and painful.[1]

---

1. Ed Welch, "Sinners Learning to Act the Miracle," in *Acting the Miracle: God's Work and Ours in the Mystery of Sanctification*, ed. John Piper and David Mathis (Wheaton, IL: Crossway, 2013), 70.

In Old Testament terms, according to HALOT, the heart (*lēv*) has a wide range of possible meanings:[2] the physical organ (1 Sam 25:37); the "seat of vital force" (Ps 22:26); the inner self (Jer 4:18); moral inclination (Gen 6:5); determination (Gen 42:28); of the will (Num 16:28); attention, awareness, or reason (Exod 9:14); the mind generally (Gen 8:21); the conscience (1 Sam 25:31); generally in the middle of something (Prov 23:34); God's heart (Jer 32:39). The term does not neatly map on any traditional categories of faculty psychology.

Generally, the heart is what is inward in a person or thing,[3] even the physical organ itself.[4] In the Old Testament the heart (*lēv*) can refer to the power of thought, of understanding, or of inner monologue.[5] It also refers to the power of deliberate personal intention.[6] Prominently, it refers to a sort of source for various emotions or virtues. To have a strong heart is an idiom for courage or resolve.[7] The heart can be glad, fearful, contemptuous, angry, sorrowful, compassionate, or stirred to generosity.[8] The heart is also connected with attention and even perceiving, like seeing and hearing.[9] Finally, the heart seems most distinctly to be the source of moral orientation. To be in opposition to God is to be stubborn or to turn the uncircumcised heart away from God.[10] Sin is said to be engraved on the heart, which is deceitful.[11] By contrast, the true follower of God has a new or soft heart, which is turned toward God and others.[12] God's people are to devote

---

2. *Hebrew and Aramaic Lexicon of the Old Testament* (HALOT), ed. Ludwig Koehler, et al., trans. M. E. J. Richardson, G. J. Jongeling-Vos, and L. J. De Regt, 5 vols (Leiden: Brill, 2000), lēv, 1–13.:

3. Heart of the sea: Exod 15:8; Ezek 27:25. Heart of heaven: Deut 4:11.

4. Exod 28:29; 2 Sam 18:14; 2 King 9:24.

5. Gen 6:5; 17:17; 24:45; 27:41; Exod 7:22; Deut 29:4; 29:19; Judg 5:15; 1 Sam 1:13; 1 Kgs 3:9; 10:24; Isa 33:18; 46:8; 47:10.

6. Gen 8:21; Num 16:28; 24:13; Judg 9:3.

7. Gen 42:28; Num 32:7–9; Judg 19:5; 1 Sam 17:32; 2 Sam 7:27; 17:10; Amos 2:16.

8. Gladness: Exod 4:14; Judg 16:25; 18:20; 19:22; 1 Sam 2:1; 25:36. Fear: Deut 28:65; 1 Sam 4:13; Isa 35:4. Contempt: 2 Sam 6:16. Anger: 2 Sam 13:33. Sorrow: 2 Sam 13:20; Jer 8:18; 48:36. Compassion: Gen 34:3; 50:21; Judg 5:9; 2 Sam 14:1; Isa 15:5; Hos 11:8. Generosity: Exod 35:5, 21.

9. Exod 9:21; 1 Kgs 9:3; Isa 6:10; 44:18; Jer 5:21–23; Ezek 40:4.

10. Exod 8:15; Josh 11:20; 1 Sam 6:6; 1 King 11:3–7; Isa 44:18; 63:17; Jer 5:21–23; 46:12; Ezek 3:7; Zech 7:12; Mal 2:2.

11. Jer 17:1, 9.

12. 1 Sam 10:9, 26; Isa 57:15; Jer 24:7; 31:33; 32:39; Ezek 11:19; 36:26; Mal 4:5–6.

their whole hearts to God, who tests them.[13] The prophets especially are concerned with the orientation of the hearts of Israel. Isaiah 29:13-14 is representative:

> And the Lord said:
> "Because this people draw near with their mouth
> and honor me with their lips,
> while their hearts are far from me,
> and their fear of me is a commandment taught by men
> therefore, behold, I will again
> do wonderful things with this people,
> with wonder upon wonder;
> and the wisdom of their wise men shall perish,
> and the discernment of their discerning men shall
> be hidden."

In the New Testament, the Greek terms *kardia* (heart) and *psychē* (soul) have quite a bit of semantic overlap. But the heart does not overlap with the soul as a metaphysical term in opposition to the body.[14] According to BDAG, the heart (*kardia*) has two primary meanings, (1) "the seat of all physical, spiritual, and mental life" and the heart as the "interior" or "center" of something (e.g., the sea, Ezek 27:4).[15] The first definition encompasses both physical life (Ps 101:5 LXX; 103:15 LXX) and a wide range of psychic dimensions, not merely willing: the entire inner life (Luke 16:15); conscious awareness (Eph 1:18); thinking (Luke 1:51); comprehending (Acts 16:14); remembering (Luke 2:19) ; the will (2 Cor 9:7); moral character (Jas 4:8); source of emotion and desires (Luke 24:32); and a dwelling place of heavenly powers (Rom 5:5).

---

13. Deut 6:5; 1 Kgs 8:23; Ps 9:1; 27:8; 28:7; Isa 38:3; Jer 3:10; 4:14; 20:12.

14. According to *A Greek-English Lexicon of the New Testament and Other Early Christian Literature* (BDAG), rev. and ed. Frederick William Danker, 3rd ed (Chicago: University of Chicago Press, 2000) (BDAG), there are three primary definitions for *psychē*: (1) "life on earth in its animating aspect making bodily function possible;" (2) the "seat and center of the inner human life in its many and varied aspects;" and (3) "an entity with personhood." In the first case, the soul is the "life-principle" (Acts 20:10) or "the condition of being alive" (Matt 20:28). In the second case, the soul can refer to the source of feelings and emotions (Matt 26:38, "My soul is very sorrowful"); "the seat and center of life that transcends the earthly" (Jas 1:21). BDAG, ψυχή, 1–3.

15. BDAG, καρδία, 1–2.

These meanings overlap significantly with the Old Testament usage; there is especially continuity between the gospel writers and the prophetic books. The heart is generally the internal part that only God sees, the part connected with inner deliberation.[16] In terms of powers, the heart can think, understand, and remember.[17] There is also the same connection with perception and hardness of heart from the Old Testament.[18] The heart is the source of intentionality, especially connected with doing God's will.[19] It is also the location of emotion such as sorrow or happiness.[20] Like the prophets, New Testament writers assume that when the heart is corrupt, dark, hard, turned from God,[21] it is the source of sinful acts,[22] in spite of the law being inscribed on it.[23] Finally, the heart is also spoken of as the location for true circumcision and the seat of faith or doubt.[24]

So, the heart does not seem to be used as a metaphysical term in opposition to the body. While the heart clearly covers all the relevant aspects of personal agency—thinking, willing, and feeling—there is no clear reason why we should assume the heart is metaphysically dualistic. If the Bible's account of the human person is holistic, and if a primary meaning of the heart is the "center and source of the whole inner life,"[25] then it is unreasonable to suggest that the heart excludes the body's contribution to human agency. In fact, its use as the center and source of physical life suggests a more holistic nuance to the term. For example, Psalm 102:4 (101:5 LXX) reads, "My heart is struck down like grass and has withered; I forget to eat my bread." The heart is also explicitly connected to the lusts and passions of the body in Romans 1:24-37. Therefore, I agree with Welch that the heart is the "moral epicenter of the person,"[26] only correcting that it is not a synonym for the soul, especially with regard to its metaphysical

---

16. Matt 5:28; Acts 5:4; Rom 2:15; 1 Cor 4:5.
17. Matt 13:19; Luke 2:19; Acts 7:23; 8:21-22; 16:14.
18. Matt 19:8; Mark 3:5; Acts 7:51 (Deut 10:16; Exod 32:9); Acts 16:14; Rom 2:5; Eph 4:18.
19. Matt 22:37; Acts 7:23; 8:22; 13:22.
20. John 16:6, 22; Acts 14:17; 21:13.
21. Matt 15:8; 19:8; Mark 3:5; Rom 1:21; 2:5.
22. Matt 12:34; 15:18-19; Mark 7:20-21; Luke 6:45; John 13:2; Acts 5:3; 7:39.
23. Rom 2:15.
24. Mark 11:23; 16:14; Luke 24:25, 38; Rom 2:29; 10:9.
25. BDAG, καρδία, 1b.
26. Welch, "Sinners Learning," 70.

aspect. The heart is a holistic term for the source of our moral orientation, but not strictly a psychological faculty.

Second, emotional voluntarism assumes that the ultimate source of emotion is the heart. While it is true that the heart is ultimate source of our emotion—since the heart is the source of our moral orientation—the heart does not map with Calvin's notion of will. It is, rather, shorthand for human agency. The heart, like the soul and inward person, is the holistic, inward source of agency from which orientation flows. The heart is the principal candidate for both intellectual and volitional censure, involving an unwillingness to see, listen, or understand on the one hand, or disobedience or hypocrisy on the other. So, it is important to resist the strong tendency in American English to associate the word "heart" with emotions as Calvin did.[27] Jonathan Pennington writes, "Unlike in common English parlance, where 'heart' becomes a metaphor for the seat of emotions, *kardia* in biblical usage refers more broadly to 'human life in its totality.'"[28] Likewise, in the New Testament sinful desires and passions are far more frequently associated with the body or flesh.[29]

Third, emotional voluntarism assumes that our emotions reveal our deepest and truest beliefs. This view makes the most sense on the assumption that our emotions come from the heart as the corrupted will. So, internal conflict is a conflict between the corrupt will and the renewed mind, at least according to Calvin's view. And the corrupt will represents something deep, essential, and abiding to human agency. While I do not deny that our minds, intellectual and volitional powers included, are affected by sin, I do not think that the view that our emotions reveal our truest beliefs is warranted by the biblical text.[30]

---

27. The reasons for this correlation are opaque to me. In the ironic words of the webcomic xkcd, "I used to think correlation implied causation. Then I took a statistics class." "Correlation," *xkcd*, accessed December 15, 2017. https://xkcd.com/552/.

28. Jonathan T. Pennington, The Sermon on the Mount and Human Flourishing: A Theological Commentary (Grand Rapids: Baker Academic, 2017), 93.

29. Rom 6:12; 7:7-25; 13:14; Gal 5:16–17; Eph 2:3; 4:22; 1 Thess. 4:4–5; 1 Pet 1:14; 2:11. Even an exception like Matthew 5:28, which simply says lust happens "in his heart," certainly implies physiological involvement. The broader issue is that the language of sinful emotion *originating* in the heart as a metaphysical distinct faculty is absent.

30. Jon Bloom, for example, cites no biblical texts to prove that emotions are "a gauge not a guide." He simply stresses that emotions like delight (Ps 37:4), affection (Rom 12:10), fear (Luke 12:5) anger (Ps 37:8), and joy (Ps 5:11) are important and that they are not the boss

In fact, something like the opposite conclusion seems warranted. Craig Keener highlights the relationship between passions and cognition in *The Mind of the Spirit*. He writes, "[In Romans 1:18–32] Paul argues that humanity irrational distorted God's image through idolatry and that God, in turn, expressed his wrath against this idolatry by handing them over to their own irrational desires."[31] The *ordo cariei* (order of corruption) works something like this: (1) humanity rejected the truth of God for idolatry; (2) in response God darkened their minds; and (3) gave them to the dishonorable passions, which continue to darken them because vice is its own punishment (Rom 1:18–32).[32] By contrast, the *ordo salutis* (simplified) involves (1) righteousness by faith in Jesus, justified freely by his grace through redemption (idolatry corrected, Rom 3:21–31); (2) thereby acquiring the mind of faith, which is itself the beginning of a process of entering into the "reality in Christ and in the Spirit" through cognitive recognition of both a change in status and identity (darkening corrected); and (3) presenting our bodies and members leading to greater and greater sanctification (passions corrected).[33]

If anything, this structure suggests that the corrections of the passions are secondary to the correction of the mind. By inference then, continuing sinful passions in a believer are inconsistent with the believer's actual status, representing the embodiment of former slavery. Sinful emotions, thus, would represent not our deepest and truest beliefs, but would imply ways of embodied being that are inconsistent with our new status in Christ. First Peter 1:14–15 reflects this basic structure, "As obedient children, do not be conformed to the passions of your former ignorance, but as he who

---

(Rom 6:12). Jon Bloom, "Your Emotions Are a Gauge, Not a Guide," *Desiring God*, 3 August 2012, https://www.desiringgod.org/articles/your-emotions-are-a-gauge-not-a-guide.

31. Craig Keener, The Mind of the Spirit: Paul's Approach to Transformed Thinking (Grand Rapids: Baker Academic, 2016), 1.

32. Keener writes, "Ancient hearers who were not Jewish could also understand the concept of false beliefs reaping their own consequences." Keener, *Mind of the Spirit*, 18. Keener develops this progression in Romans 1:18–32 in the first chapter of *Mind of the Spirit*.
This is the inverse of the well-known proverb attributed to Cicero that "virtue is its own reward." Cicero actually writes, "the reward of duty is duty itself" (*offici fructus sit ipsum officium*). Cicero, *De Finibus Bonorum et Malorum*, trans. Harris Rackham, Loeb Classical Library, vol. 17 (Cambridge, MA: Harvard University Press, 1914), II.72.

33. See Keener, *Mind of the Spirit*, 31–54. The only element here that is not clearly expressed in Keener is that presenting our bodies actually participates in the renewal of our passions (Rom 6:19).

called you is holy, you also be holy in all your conduct." I only suggest this reversal tentatively. The real relation between our emotions and our psychological orientation is perhaps quite complex, as is the relationship with our actions. Because of the robustness of the unconscious, it may be the case that emotions usually reveal something deep and important about our orientation that we would not know otherwise. I am merely suggesting that we exercise care, especially in light of embodied habits that arise through experience, like childhood abuse.

BIBLIOGRAPHY

—

A Select Library of Nicene and Post-Nicene Fathers of the Christian Church.
Edited by Philip Schaff and Henry Wace. 28 vols. in 2 series.
1886–1889. Reprinted by Grand Rapids, MI: Eerdmans, 1991.

Abbott, Roger Philip. *Sit on Our Hands, or Stand on Our Feet?: Exploring
a Practical Theology of Major Incident Response for the Evangelical
Catholic Christian Community in the UK.* Eugene, OR: Wipf & Stock,
2013.

Abramowitz, Jonathan S., and Ryan J. Jacoby. "Scrupulosity: A Cognitive-
Behavioral Analysis and Implications for Treatment." *Journal of
Obsessive-Compulsive and Related Disorders* 3 (2014): 140–49.

Adams, Edward. "Calvin's View of Natural Knowledge of God."
International Journal of Systematic Theology 3, no. 3 (November
2001): 280–92.

Adams, Jay. *A Theology of Christian Counseling: More Than Redemption.*
Grand Rapids: Zondervan, 1979.

Adelmann, F. J. *The Quest for the Absolute.* The Hague, Netherlands:
Martinus Nijhoff, 1966.

Ægineta, Paulus. *The Medical Works of Paulus Ægineta, The Greek Physician.*
Translated by Francis Adams. London: J. Welsh, Treuttel, Würtz,
1834.

Alexander, Bruce K., and Curtis P. Shelton. *A History of Psychology in
Western Civilization.* Cambridge: Cambridge University Press,
2014.

Allen, Michael, and Scott Swain. *Reformed Catholicity: The Promise of
Retrieval for Theology and Biblical Interpretation.* Grand Rapids:
Baker Academic, 2015.

Allender, Dan, and Tremper Longman. *The Cry of the Soul: How Our Emotions Reveal Our Deepest Problem about God*. Colorado Springs: NavPress, 1994.

American Psychological Association Dictionary of Psychology. Edited by Gary R. VandenBos. 2nd ed. Washington DC: American Psychological Association, 2015.

Anderson, A. K., and E. A. Phelps. "Is the Human Amygdala Critical for the Subjective Experience of Emotion? Evidence of Intact Dispositional Affect in Patients with Amygdala Lesions." *Journal of Cognitive Neuroscience* 14, no. 5 (2002): 709–20.

Anderson, Neil T. *Freedom in Christ: Small-Group Bible Study*. Ventura, CA: Gospel Light, 2004.

Anderson, Ray S. *On Being Human: Essays in Theological Anthropology*. Grand Rapids: Eerdmans, 1982.

Anselm of Canterbury. *Complete Philosophical and Theological Treatises of Anselm of Canterbury*. Translated by Jasper Hopkins and Herbert Richardson. Minneapolis: Arthur J. Banning, 2000.

Aquinas, Thomas. *Summa Theologiae*. Translated by Alfred J. Freddoso. Updated 10 January 2018. https://www3.nd.edu/~afreddos/summa-translation/TOC.htm.

_____. *The Disputed Questions on Truth*, vol. 3. Translated by Robert William Schmidt. Chicago: Henry Regnery Company, 1952–1954.

Aristotle, *The Complete Works of Aristotle: Revised Oxford Translation*. Edited by Jonathan Barnes. 2 vols. Princeton: Princeton University Press, 1984.

Arnold, Magda B. *Emotion and Personality*. New York: Columbia University Press, 1960.

Audi, Robert. "Realism, Rationality, and Philosophical Method." *Proceedings and Addresses of the American Philosophical Association* 61, no. 1 (1987): 65–74.

Augustine, *City of God*. Translated by Henry Bettenson. New York: Penguin Classics, 2003.

_____. *St. Augustine: The Greatness of the Soul, The Teacher*. Edited by Joseph Colleran. Mahwah, NJ: Paulist Press, 1978.

_____. *A Treatise Concerning Man's Perfection in Righteousness*. In NPNF[1] 5.

_____. *Confessions*. In NPNF[1] 1.

_____. *On the Trinity*. In NPNF[1] 3.

_____. *Of True Religion*. In *Augustine: Early Writings*, edited by
    J. H. S. Burleigh. Library of Christian Classics. Louisville, KY:
    Westminster John Knox Press, 2006.

Austen, Jane. *Pride and Prejudice*. Sweden: Winehouse Classics, 2016.

Backus, Irena D. *Historical Method and Confessional Identity in the Era of
    the Reformation (1378-1615)*. Leiden: Brill, 2003.

Bargh, John A., and Ezequiel Morsella. "The Unconscious Mind."
    Perspectives on Psychological Science 3, no. 1 (January 2008): 73-79.

Barth, Karl. *Church Dogmatics*. The Doctrine of Creation. Vol. III.2. Edited
    by G. W. Bromiley and T. F. Torrance. Translated by H. Knight, et
    al. Edinburgh: T&T Clark, 1960.

Battenhouse, Roy W. "The Doctrine of Man in Calvin and in Renaissance
    Platonism." *Journal of the History of Ideas* 9, no. 4 (October 1948):
    447-71.

Battles, Ford Lewis. *Institutes of the Christian Religion: 1536 Edition*. Grand
    Rapids: Eerdmans, 1975.

_____. "The Sources of Calvin's Seneca Commentary." Pages 38-66 in
    John Calvin. Edited by Basil Hall. Grand Rapids: Eerdmans, 1966.

Bavinck, Herman. *Biblical and Religious Psychology*. Translated by H.
    Hanko. Grand Rapids: Protestant Reformed Theological School,
    1974.

_____. *The Doctrine of God*. Translated by William Hendricksen. Grand
    Rapids: Eerdmans, 1951.

_____. *Foundations of Psychology*. Translated by Jack Vanden Born.
    Master's thesis, Calvin College, 1981. [Herman Bavinck. *Beginselen
    der Psychologie*. 2nd ed. Kampen: J. H. Kok, 1923.]

Baylor, T. Robert. "'With Him in Heavenly Realms': Lombard and Calvin
    on Merit and the Exaltation of Christ." *International Journal of
    Systematic Theology* 17, no. 2 (April 2015): 152-75.

Bechtel, William, and Robert C. Richardson. "Vitalism." Pages 639-42
    in *Routledge Encyclopedia of Philosophy*. Vol. 9. Edited by Edward
    Craig. London: Routledge, 1998.

Belmaker, R. H., and Galila Agram. "Major Depressive Disorder." *New
    England Journal of Medicine* 358, no. 1 (January 2008): 55-68.

Berenz, Erin C., Salpi Kevorkian, Nadia Chowdhury, Danielle M. Dick, Kenneth S. Kendler, and Ananda B. Amstadter. "Posttraumatic Stress Disorder Symptoms, Anxiety Sensitivity, and Alcohol-Use Motives in College Students with a History of Interpersonal Trauma." *Psychology of Addictive Behaviors* 30, no. 7 (2016): 755–63.

Bergland, Christopher. "Joseph LeDoux Reports: Emotions Are 'Higher-Order States.'" *Psychology Today*. 15 February 2017. https://www.psychologytoday.com/us/blog/the-athletes-way/201702/joseph-ledoux-reports-emotions-are-higher-order-states.

Berkhof, Louis. *Systematic Theology*. Carlisle, PA: Banner of Truth, 2005.

Berkouwer, G. C. *Man: The Image of God*. Grand Rapids: Eerdmans, 1962.

Betz, Hans Dieter. *The Sermon on the Mount*. Hermeneia—A Critical and Historical Commentary on the Bible. Minneapolis: Augsburg Fortress, 1995.

Birdsall, J. N. "A Fresh Examination of the Fragment of the Gospel of St. Luke in ms. 0171 and an Attempted Reconstruction with Special Reference to the Recto." Pages 212–27 in *Philologia Sacra: Biblische und patristische Studien für Hermann J. Frede und Walter Thiele zu ihrem siebzigsten Geburtstag*. Edited by Roger Gryson and Vetus Latina. Freiburg: Herder, 1993.

Blocher, Henri. *Original Sin: Illuminating the Riddle*. New Studies in Biblical Theology. Downers Grove, IL: IVP Academic, 2000.

Bloom, Jon. "Lay Aside the Weight of Moodiness," *Desiring God* (blog), August 12, 2016, http://www.desiringgod.org/ articles/lay-aside-the-weight-of-moodiness

_____. "Your Emotions Are a Gauge, Not a Guide," *Desiring God*. 3 August 2012. https://www.desiringgod.org/articles/your-emotions-are-a-gauge-not-a-guide.

Blum, Paul Richard. "The Immortality of the Soul." Pages 211–33 in *The Cambridge Companion to Renaissance Philosophy*. Edited by James Hankins. Cambridge: Cambridge University Press, 2007.

Bögels, Susan, and Vicky Phares. "Fathers' Role in the Etiology, Prevention, and Treatment of Child Anxiety: A Review and New Model." *Clinical Psychology Review* 28 (2008): 539–58.

Boisset, Jean. *Sagesse et Sainteté dans la Pensée de Jean Calvin*. Paris: Presses Universitaires de France, 1959.

Boler, John. "An Image for the Unity of Will in Duns Scotus." *Journal of the History of Philosophy* 32 (1994): 23–44.

————. "Transcending the Natural: Duns Scotus on the Two Selections of the Will." *American Catholic Philosophical Quarterly* 67, no. 1 (1993): 109–26.

Borgman, Brian S. *Feelings and Faith: Cultivating Godly Emotions in the Christian Life.* Wheaton, IL: Crossway, 2009.

Bornheimer, Lindsay A. "Exposure and Response Prevention as an Evidence-Based Treatment for Obsessive-Compulsive Disorder: Considerations for Social Work Practice." *Clinical Social Work Journal* 43 (2015): 38–49.

Bouwsma, William J. *John Calvin: A Sixteenth Century Portrait.* Oxford: Oxford University Press, 1989.

————. "The Quest for the Historical Calvin." *Archiv für Reformationsgeschichte* 77 (1986): 47–57.

Bowerman, Melissa, and Stephen C. Levinson, eds. *Language Acquisition and Conceptual Development.* Language Culture and Cognition. Book 3. Cambridge: Cambridge University Press, 2001.

Boylan, Michael. "Galen: On Blood, Pulse, and the Arteries." *Journal of the History of Biology* 40 (2007): 207–30.

Branick, Vincent. "The Sinful Flesh of the Son of God (Rom 8:3): A Key Image of Pauline Theology." *Catholic Biblical Quarterly* 47 (1985): 246–62.

Breen, Quirinus. *John Calvin: A Study in French Humanism.* Hamden, CT: Archon, 1968.

Bretano, Franz. *Psychology from an Empirical Standpoint.* Abingdon: Routledge, 2015.

Bringsjord, Selmer. *What Robots Can and Can't Be.* Studies in Cognitive Systems. Dordrecht: Springer, 1992.

Brownnut, Michael. "Response to Peter Clarke on 'Determinism, Brain Function and Free Will.'" *Science & Christian Belief* 24, no. 1 (2012): 81–86.

Burghardt, Nesha S., Torfi Sigurdsson, Jack M. Gorman, Bruce S. McEwen, and Joseph E. LeDoux. "Chronic Antidepressant Treatment Impairs the Acquisition of Fear Extinction." *Biological Psychiatry* 73 (2013): 1078–86.

Burk, Denny. "Is Homosexual Orientation Sinful?" *Journal of the Evangelical Theological Society* 58, no. 1 (2015): 95–115.

Burton, Asa. *Essays on Some of the First Principles of Metaphysicks, Ethicks, and Theology*. Portland: Mirror, 1824.

Busch, Lorna Y., Patrick Pössel, and Jeffrey C. Valentine. "Meta-Analyses of Cardiovascular Reactivity to Rumination: A Possible Mechanism Linking Depression and Hostility to Cardiovascular Disease." *Psychological Bulletin* 143, no. 12 (2017): 1378–94.

Butera, Giuseppe. "Thomas Aquinas and Cognitive Therapy: An Exploration of the Promise of Thomistic Psychology." *Philosophy, Psychiatry, & Psychology* 17, no. 4 (December 2010): 347–66.

Byren, Alex. "Intentionality." Pages 405–10 in *Philosophy of Science: An Encyclopedia*. Edited by Sahotra Sarkar and Jessica Pfeifer. New York: Routledge, 2006.

Cahill, L., and J. L. McGaugh. "Mechanisms of Emotional Arousal and Lasting Declarative Memory." *Trends in Neurosciences* 21, no. 7 (1998): 294–99.

Callus, Daniel A. "Origins of the Problem of Unity of Form." *Thomist* 24 (1961): 257–85.

_____. "Two Early Oxford Masters on the Problem of the Plurality of Forms: Adam of Buckfield—Richard Rufus of Cornwall." *Revue neoscholastique de philosophic* 42 (1939): 411–45.

Calvin, Jean. *Calvin's Commentaries*. Translated by John King, et al. 45 vols. Edinburgh: Calvin Translation Society, 1844–56.

Calvin, John. *Bondage and Liberation of the Will*. Edited by A. N. S. Lane. Translated by G. I. Davies. Grand Rapids: Baker Academic, 1996.

_____. *Calvin's Commentaries*. 45 vols. Translated by John King, et al. Edinburgh: Calvin Translation Society, 1844–56.

_____. *Calvin's Commentary on Seneca's* De Clementia. Renaissance Text Series, III. Edited and translated by Ford Lewis Battles and André Malan Hugo. Leiden: Brill, 1969.

_____. *Declaration Povr Maintenir La Vraye Foy que Tiennent tous Chrestians de la Trinité des persones en vn seule Dieu*. Geneve: Jean Crispin, 1554.

_____. *Institutes of the Christian Religion*. Edited by John T. McNeill. Translated by Ford Lewis Battles. 2 vols. Louisville: Westminster John Knox, 2006.

_____. *Institutio Christianae Religionis*. Argentorati: Wendelinum Ribelium, 1543.

_____. *Institutio Totius Christianae Religionis*. Geneva: Ioannis Gerardi, 1550.

_____. *Joannis Calvini opera quae supersunt omnia*. Corpus reformatorum. Edited by Edouard Cunitz, JohannWilhelm Baum, Eduard Wilhelm, and Eugen Reuss. 58 vols. Brunsvigae: C.A. Schwetschke, 1863–1900.

_____. *Johannis Calvin Opera Selecta*. Edited by Peter Barth, Wilhelm Niesel, Dora Scheuner. 5 vols. Munich: Chr. Kaiser, 1926-1952.

_____. *Selected Works of John Calvin: Tracts and Letters*. Edited by Henry Beveridge and Jules Bonnet. Translated by Henry Beveridge. 7 vols. Grand Rapids: Baker Book House, 1983.

Cannon, Walter B. *Bodily Changes in Pain, Hunger, Fear, and Rage: An Account of Recent Researches into the Function of Emotional Excitement*. New York: Appleton, 1927.

_____. *The Wisdom of the Body*. London: Kegan Paul, 1932.

Carruthers, Peter. "Valence and Value." *Philosophy and Phenomenological Research* 9, no. 1 (2017): 51–72.

Carvill, Barbara. "The Calvin Seal: A constant reminder." Excerpts from the Fall 2005 Faculty Conference Address. Calvin University. https://calvin.edu/about/history/calvin-seal.html.

Catechism of the Catholic Church. Mahwah, NJ: Paulist Press, 1994.

Chaplin, William F., Oliver P. John, and Lewis R. Goldberg. "Conceptions of States and Traits: Dimensional Attributes with Ideals as Prototypes." *Journal of Personality and Social Psychology* 54, no. 4 (1988): 541-57.

Charry, Ellen T. *By the Renewing of Your Minds: The Pastoral Function of Christian Doctrine*. Oxford: Oxford University Press, 1999.

_____. *God and the Art of Happiness*. Grand Rapids: Eerdmans, 2010.

Chiarot, Kevin. *The Unassumed is Unhealed: The Humanity of Christ in the Christology of T. F. Torrance*. Eugene, OR: Pickwick, 2013.

Churchland, Patricia Smith. "Can Neurobiology Teach Us Anything
        about Consciousness?" Pages 127–140 in *The Nature of
        Consciousness: Philosophical Debates*. Edited by Ned Block, Owen
        Flanagan, and Güven Güzeldere. Cambridge, MA: MIT Press, 1997.

Cicero. *De Fato, XVIII, in On the Orator: Book 3. On Fate. Stoic Paradoxes.
        Divisions of Oratory*. Translated by Harris Rackham. Loeb Classical
        Library. Vol. 349. Cambridge, MA: Harvard University Press.

_____. *De Finibus Bonorum et Malorum*. Translated by Harris Rackham.
        Loeb Classical Library. Vol. 17. Cambridge, MA: Harvard
        University Press, 1994.

_____. *De Natura Deorum I.16.43-44, in On the Nature of the Gods.
        Academics*. Translated by Harris Rackham. Loeb Classical Library.
        Vol. 268. Cambridge, MA: Harvard University Press, 1933.

_____. *Tusculan Disputations, I.24, in Tusculan Disputations*. Translated
        by John Edward King. Loeb Classical Library. Vol. 141. Cambridge,
        MA: Harvard University Press, 1927.

Clarke, Peter G. H. "Determinism, Brain Function and Free Will." *Science
        and Christian Belief* 22, no. 2 (2010): 133–49.

_____. "Neuroscience and the Soul—A Response to Malcolm Jeeves."
        Science and Christian Belief 21, no. 1 (2009): 61–64.

Clivaz, Clair. "The Angel and the Sweat Like 'Drops of Blood' (Lk 22:43–
        44): $\mathfrak{P}^{69}$ and f^{13}." *Harvard Theological Review* 98, no. 4 (2005): 414–40.

Coakley, Sarah, ed. *Faith Rationality and the Passions*. Malden, MA: Wiley-
        Blackwell, 2012.

Cochran, Elizabeth Agnew. "The Moral Significance of Religious
        Affections: A Reformed Perspective on Emotions and Moral
        Formation." *Studies in Christian Ethics* 28, no. 2 (2015): 150–62.

Cooper, John. *Body, Soul, and Life Everlasting*. 2nd ed. Grand Rapids:
        Eerdmans, 2000.

Corneau, Guy. *Absent Fathers, Lost Sons: The Search for Masculine Identity*.
        C. G. Jung Foundation Books Series. Book 4. Boston: Shambhala,
        1991.

Crivellato, Enrico, and Domenico Ribatti. "Soul, mind, brain: Greek
        philosophy and the birth of neuroscience." *Brain Research Bulletin*
        71 (2007): 327–36.

Dales, Richard C. *The Problem of the Rational Soul in the Thirteenth Century.* Leiden: Brill, 1995.

Damasio, Antonio R. *Descartes' Error: Emotion, Reason, and the Human Brain.* New York: Grosset/Putnam, 1994.

Davis, Stephen. *Risen Indeed: Making Sense of the Resurrection.* Grand Rapids: Eerdmans, 1993.

de Boer, Sander W. *The Science of the Soul: The Commentary Tradition on Aristotle's De anima, c. 1260-1360.* Leuven: Leuven University Press, 2013.

de la Mare, William. *Correctorium fratris Thomae.* Translated by Peter L.P. Simpson. January 2016. http://www.aristotelophile.com/Books/ Translations/DelaMare%20format.pdf.

Dennett, Daniel. "Facing Backwards on the Problem of Consciousness." Pages 33-36 in *Explaining Consciousness: The Hard Problem.* Edited by Jonathan Shear. Cambridge, MA: MIT Press, 1997.

Descartes, René. "Letter to Regius, i. 1642." Pages 148-52 in *Selected Correspondence of Descartes, 1641-1644.* Vol. 3, ed. Trans. Jonathan Bennett (2010-2015), Online: http://www.earlymoderntexts.com/ assets/pdfs/descartes1619_3.pdf.

Des Chene, Dennis. *Life's Form: Late Aristotelian Conceptions of the Soul.* Ithaca, NY: Cornell University Press, 2000.

de Sousa, Ronald. *The Rationality of Emotion.* Cambridge, MA: MIT Press, 1987.

Diagnostic and Statistical Manual of Mental Disorders. 5th ed. Washington DC: American Psychiatric Association, 2013.

Dixon, Thomas. "'Emotion': The History of a Keyword in Crisis." *Emotion Review* 4, no. 4 (October 2012): 338-44.

_____. *From Passions to Emotions: The Creation of a Secular Psychological Category.* Cambridge: Cambridge University Press, 2006.

_____. "Revolting Passions." Pages 298-312 in *Faith, Rationality and the Passions.* Edited by Sarah Coakley. Malden, MA: Blackwell, 2012.

Dobler, Emil. *Falsche Vaterzitate bie Thomas Von Aquin: Gregorius, Bischof von Nyssa oder Nemesius, Bischof von Emesa?* Freiburg: Universitätsverlag Freiburg Schweiz, 2001.

_____. *Indirekte Nemesiuszitate bei Thomas von Aquin: Johannes von Damaskus als Vermittler von Nemesiustexten*. Freiberg: Universitätsverlag Freiburg Schweiz, 2002.

Dodd, C. H. *Gospel and Law*. Cambridge: Cambridge University Press, 1951.

Dretske, Fred. "Misrepresentation." Pages 17–36 in *Belief: Form, Content and Function*. Edited by Radu Bogdan. Oxford: Oxford University Press, 1986.

Drummond, Ian Christopher. "John Duns Scotus on the Passions of the Will." Pages 53–74 in *Emotion and Cognitive Life in Medieval and Early Modern Philosophy*. Edited by Martin Pickavé and Lisa Shapiro. Oxford: Oxford University Press, 2012.

_____. "John Duns Scotus on the Role of the Moral Virtues." PhD diss., University of Toronto, 2016.

Duhem, Pierre. *To Save the Phenomena*. Translated by Edmund Dolan and Chaninah Maschler. Chicago: University of Chicago Press, 1985.

Dutton, Donald G., and Arthur P. Aron. "Some Evidence for Heightened Sexual Attraction Under Conditions of High Anxiety." *Journal of Personality and Social Psychology* 30, no. 4 (1974): 510–17.

Eco, Umberto. *Semiotics and the Philosophy of Language*. Bloomington: Indiana University Press, 1984.

Edwards, Jonathan. *Religious Affections. The Works of Jonathan Edwards*. Edited by Henry Rogers, Sereno Edwards Dwight, and Edward Hickman. Vol. 1. Peabody, MA: Hendrickson, 2004.

Eisen, Jane L., Wayne K. Goodman, Martin B. Keller, Meredith G. Warshaw, Lynne M. DeMarco, Douglas D. Luce, and Steven A. Rasmussen. "Patterns of Remission and Relapse in Obsessive-Compulsive Disorder: A 2-Year Prospective Study." *Journal of Clinical Psychiatry* 60, no. 5 (1999): 346–51.

Ekman, Paul. *Emotions Revealed: Recognizing Faces and Feelings to Improve Communication and Emotional Life*. New York: Owl, 2003.

Elliott, Matthew A. *Faithful Feelings: Rethinking Emotion in the New Testament*. Grand Rapids: Kregel, 2006.

Emory, Margaret. "On Fear, Emotions, and Memory: An Interview with Dr. Joseph LeDoux," *Brain World*. 6 June 2020. http://brainworldmagazine.com/on-fear-emotions-and-memory-rock-starneuroscientist-joseph-ledouxs-new-terms

Erdelyi, Matthew H. *Psychoanalysis: Freud's Cognitive Psychology*. New York: Freeman, 1985.

Erickson, Richard J. "Flesh." Pages 303–306 in *The Dictionary of Paul and his Letters*. Edited by Gerald F. Hawthorne and Ralph P. Martin. Downers Grove, IL: InterVarsity, 1993.

Evans, C. Stephen. "Separable Souls: Dualism, Selfhood, and the Possibility of Life After Death." *Christian Scholar's Review* 34 (2005): 327–40.

Evans, C. Stephen, and Brandon Rickabaugh. "Neuroscience, Spiritual Formation, and Bodily Souls: A Critique of Christian Physicalism." Pages 231–56 in *Christian Physicalism? Philosophical and Theological Criticisms*. Edited by R. Keith Loftin and Joshua R. Farris. Lanham, MD: Lexington, 2017.

_____. "What Does It Mean to Be a Bodily Soul?" *Philosophia Christi* 17, no. 2 (2015): 315–30.

Fedler, Kyle. "Calvin's Burning Heart: Calvin and the Stoics on the Emotions." *Journal of the Society of Christian Ethics* 22 (Fall 2002): 133–62.

Feinstein, J. S., et al., "Fear and panic in humans with bilateral amygdala damage." *Nature Neuroscience* 16 (2013): 270–72.

"Fifth Lateran Council 1512–17 A.D." Papal Encyclicals Online. http://www.papalencyclicals.net/councils/ecum18.htm.

Finney, Charles. *Finney's Systematic Theology: The Complete and Newly Expanded 1878 Edition*. Minneapolis: Bethany House, 1994.

Foa, Edna B., et al. "Treatment of obsessive compulsive disorder by exposure and ritual prevention, clomipramine, and their combination: A randomized, placebo-controlled trial." *American Journal of Psychiatry* 162 (2005): 151–61.

Foa, Edna B., et. al. "Six-month outcomes from a randomized trial augmenting serotonin reuptake inhibitors with exposure and response prevention or risperidone in adults with obsessive-compulsive disorder." *Journal for Clinical Psychiatry* 74, no. 4 (April 2015): 440–46.

Ford, David F. *Self and Salvation: Being Transformed*. Cambridge: Cambridge University Press, 1999.

Foster, John. *The Immaterial Self: A Defense of the Cartesian Dualist Conception of the Mind*. London and New York: Routledge, 1991.

Frey, Jörg. "The Notion of 'Flesh' in 4QInstruction and the Background of Pauline Usage." Pages 197–226 in *Sapiential, Liturgical & Poetical Texts from Qumran. Proceedings of the Third Meeting of the International Organization for Qumran Studies, Published in Memory of Maurice Baillet*. Edited by Daniel K. Falk, F. García Martinez, and Eileen M. Schuller. Leiden: Brill, 2000.

Frijda, Nico H. *The Emotions*. Cambridge: Cambridge University Press, 1986.

Fuchs, Eberhard, and Gabriele Flügge. "Adult Neuroplasticity: More Than 40 Years of Research." *Neural Plasticity* (2014): 1–10.

Galen. *On the Properties of Foodstuffs (De alimentorum facultatibus)*. Translated by Owen Powell. Cambridge: Cambridge University Press, 2003.

Garrett, Brian Jonathan. "What the History of Vitalism Teaches Us About Consciousness and the 'Hard Problem.'" *Philosophy and Phenomenological Research* 72, no. 3 (May 2006): 576–88.

Gazzaniga, Michael S., and Joseph E. LeDoux. *The Integrated Mind*. New York: Plenum, 1978.

Gentner, Dedre, and Susan Goldin-Meadow, eds. *Language in Mind: Advances in the Study of Language and Thought*. Cambridge, MA: MIT Press, 2003.

Gerhardsson, Birger. *The Testing of God's Son (Matthew 4:1–11 & PAR): An Analysis of an Early Christian Midrash*. Translated by John Toy. Lund: Gleerup, 1966. Repr., Eugene, OR: Wipf & Stock, 2009.

Gilbert, Neil W. "The Concept of Will in Early Latin Philosophy." *Journal of the History of Philosophy* 1 (October 1963): 17–36.

Gillman, Florence Morgan. "Another Look at Romans 8:3: In the Likeness of Sinful Flesh.'" *The Catholic Biblical Quarterly* 49 (1987): 597-604.

Gilson, Etienne. "Autour de Pomponazzi: Problematique de l'immortality de l'ame en Italie au debut de XVIC siècle." *Archives d'historie doctrinale et literaire du moyen age* 36 (1961): 163–279.

Gondreau, Paul. *The Passions of Christ's Soul in the Theology of St. Thomas Aquinas*. Scranton, PA: University of Scranton Press, 2009.

————. "The Passions and the Moral Life: Appreciating the Originality of Aquinas." *Thomist* 71 (2007): 419–50.

González-Ayesta, Cruz. "Duns Scotus on the Natural Will." *Vivarium* 50 (2012): 33–52.

————. "Scotus' Interpretation of the Difference Between Voluntas ut Natura and Voluntas ut Voluntas." *Franciscan Studies* 66 (2008): 371–412.

Gordon, Alex. "The Sozzini and Their School." *The Theological Review* 66 (July 1879): 293–322.

Grafman, Jordan. "Conceptualizing functional neuroplasticity." *Journal of Communication Disorders* 33, no. 4 (August 2000): 345–56.

Grane, Leif. *Contra Gabrielem: Luthers Auseinandersetsung mit Gabriel Biel in der Disputatio Contra Scholasticam Theologiam, 1517.* Copenhagen: Gyldenhal, 1962.

A Greek-English Lexicon of the New Testament and Other Early Christian Literature (BDAG). Revised and edited by Frederick William Danker. 3rd ed. Chicago: University of Chicago Press, 2000.

Green, Joel B. *Body, Soul, and Human Life: The Nature of Humanity in the Bible.* Grand Rapids: Baker Academic, 2008.

————. "Eschatology and the Nature of Humans: A Reconsideration of Pertinent Biblical Evidence." *Science and Christian Belief* 14, no. 1 (April 2002): 33–50.

Greenwald, Anthony G. "New Look 3: Unconscious Cognition Reclaimed." *American Psychologist* 47 (June 1992): 766–79.

Greenwald, Anthony G., and Mahzarin R. Banaji. "The Implicit Revolution: Reconceiving the Relation Between Conscious and Unconscious." *American Psychological Association* 72, no. 9 (2017): 861–71.

Grenz, Stanley J. *The Social God and the Relational Self: A Trinitarian Theology of the* Imago Dei. Louisville: Westminster John Knox, 2001.

Griffiths, Paul E. *What Emotions Really Are: The Problem of Psychological Categories.* Chicago: University of Chicago Press, 1997

Grislis, Egil. "Calvin's Use of Cicero in the Institutes I:1–5: A Case Study in Theological Method." *Archiv für Reformationsgeschichts* 62 (1971): 5–37.

Gundry, Robert H. *Sōma in Biblical Theology, with Emphasis on Pauline Anthropology*. Society for New Testament Monograph Series. Vol. 29. Cambridge: Cambridge University Press, 1976.

Gunton, Colin E. *The Promise of Trinitarian Theology*. Edinburgh: T&T Clark, 1991.

Gunton Colin E., and Christoph Schwöbel, eds. *Persons, Divine and Human: King's College Essays in Theological Anthropology*. Edinburgh: T&T Clark, 1991.

Habermas, Gary, and J. P. Moreland. *Beyond Death: Exploring the Evidence for Immortality*. Wheaton, IL: Crossway, 1998.

Haidt, Jonathan. *The Happiness Hypothesis: Finding Modern Truth in Ancient Wisdom*. New York: Basic Books, 2006.

Hall, Basil. "Calvin against the Calvinists." Pages 19–37 in *John Calvin: Courtenay Studies in Reformation Theology*. Edited by G. E. Duffield. Abingdon: Sutton Courtenay, 1966.

Hall, Calvin S., and Gardner Linzey. *Theories of Personality*. 2nd ed. New York: John Wiley, 1970.

Hamilton, Victor P. *The Book of Genesis: Chapters 1–17*. The New International Commentary on the Old Testament. Grand Rapids: Eerdmans, 1990.

Hankinson, Robert. "Partitioning the Soul: Galen on the Anatomy of the Psychic Functions and Mental Illness." Pages 85–106 inn *Partitioning the Soul: Debates from Plato to Leibniz*. Edited by Klaus Corcilius and Dominik Perler. Berlin: De Gruyter, 2014.

Hansen, G. Walter. *The Letter to the Philippians*. Pillar New Testament Commentary. Grand Rapids: Eerdmans, 2009.

Harak, G. Simon. *Virtuous Passions: The Formation of Christian Character*. New York: Paulist Press, 1993.

Harré, Rom, ed. *The Social Construction of Emotions*. New York: Blackwell, 1986.

Harris, David W. "Taxonomizing Speech Acts: Intention & Acts of Meaning Seminar, Week 6." Class notes at Hunter College. New York, NY, March 10, 2016. Posted online: http://danielwharris.com/teaching/ spring16/handouts/Taxonomy.pdf. Accessed January 18, 2017.

Harvey, E. Ruth. *The Inward Wits: Psychological Theory in the Middle Ages and the Renaissance*. Edited by E. H. Gombrich and J. B. Trapp. Warburg Institute Surveys VI. London: Trinity Press, 1975.

Hasker, William. "Nonreductive Physicalism: A Constitutional Response." Pages 88–89 in *In Search of the Soul: Four Views of the Mind-body Problem*. Edited by Joel B. Green and Stuart L. Palmer. Downers Grove, IL: InterVarsity, 2005.

————. "The Case for Emergent Dualism." Pages 61-72 in *The Blackwell Companion to Substance Dualism*. Edited by Jonathan J. Loose, Angus J.L. Menuge, and J.P. Moreland. Hoboken: Wiley, 2018).

Hatfield, Gary. "The Working of the Intellect: Mind and Psychology." *IRCS Technical Reports Series* 90 (1996): 1–36.

Hauerwas, Stanley. *Matthew*. Brazos Theological Commentary on the Bible. Grand Rapids: Baker, 2006.

Hebb, D. O. *The Organization of Behavior: A Neuropsychological Theory*. New York: Wiley, 1949.

Hebrew and Aramaic Lexicon of the Old Testament (HALOT). Edited by Ludwig Koehler, et al. Translated by M. E. J. Richardson, G. J. Jongeling-Vos, and L. J. De Regt. 5 vols. Leiden: Brill, 2000.

Helm, Paul. "Calvin and Calvinism: The Anatomy of a Controversy." *Evangel* 2, no. 10 (1984): 7–10.

————. *Calvin at the Center*. Oxford: Oxford University Press, 2010.

————. *John Calvin's Ideas*. Oxford: Oxford University Press, 2004.

————. "Vermigli, Calvin, and Aristotle's Ethics." *Unio Cum Christo* 3, no. 2 (October 2017): 89–101.

Hembree, E. B., D. S. Riggs, M. J. Kozak, M. E. Franklin, and E. B. Foa. "Long-term efficacy of exposure and ritual prevention therapy and serotonergic medications for obsessive–compulsive disorder." *CNS Spectrums* 8, no. 5 (2003): 363–71.

Herman, Judith Lewis, John Christopher Perry, and Bessel van der Kolk. "Childhood Trauma in Borderline Personality Disorder." *American Journal of Psychiatry* 146, no. 4 (April 1989): 490–95.

Herzog, James M. *Father Hunger: Explorations with Adults and Children*. 3rd ed. New York: Routledge, 2013.

Hippocrates. "The Sacred Disease." Pages 127–82 in *Hippocrates: With an English Translation*. Translated by W. H. S. Jones. Vol 2. Cambridge, MA: Harvard University Press, 1959.

Hirstein, William. *Brain Fiction: Self-Deception and the Riddle of Consciousness*. Cambridge, MA: MIT Press, 2005.

Hirvonen, Vera. *Passions in William Ockham's Philosophical Psychology*. Dordrecht: Kluwer Academic, 2004.

Hodge, Charles. *Commentary on the Epistle to the Romans*. Philadelphia: Grigg and Elliot, 1835. https://books.google.com/books?id=VpMXAAAAYAAJ&dq.

————. *Systematic Theology*. Volume II: Anthropology. Grand Rapids: Eerdmans, 1940.

————. *Systematic Theology*. Volume III: Soteriology. Grand Rapids: Eerdmans, 1940.

Hoekema, Anthony A. *Created in God's Image*. Grand Rapids: Eerdmans, 1986.

Hoitenga, Dewey. *John Calvin and the Will: A Critique and Corrective*. Grand Rapids: Baker, 1997.

Holcombe, Alex O. "Binding Problem." Pages 205–8 in *The Sage Encyclopedia of Perception*. Edited by E. Bruce Goldstein. Thousand Oaks, CA: Sage, 2010.

Holoubek J. E., and A. B. Holoubek. "Blood, sweat, and fear. 'A classification of hematidrosis." *Journal of Medical Chemistry* 27, no. 3–4 (1996): 115–33.

Holziger, H. *Genesis*. Freiburg: J. C. B. Mohr (Paul Siebeck), 1898.

Horton, Michael. *The Christian Faith: A Systematic Theology for Pilgrims on the Way*. Grand Rapids: Zondervan, 2011.

Irwin, T. H. "Splendid Vices? Augustine For and Against Pagan Virtues." *Medieval Philosophy and Theology* 8 (1999): 105–27.

Izard, Carroll E. "Four Systems for Emotion Activation." *Psychological Review* 100, no. 1 (January 1993): 68–90.

Jackson, Stanley W. "Galen—on Mental Disorders." *Journal of the History of the Behavioral Sciences* 5 (1969): 365–84.

Jacoby, Larry L. "A Process-Dissociation Framework for Investigating Unconscious Influences: Freudian Slips, Projective Tests,

Subliminal Perception, and Signal Detection Theory." *Current Directions in Psychological Science* 1, no. 6 (December 1992): 174–79.

James, Susan. *Action and Passion: The Emotions in Seventeenth-Century Philosophy*. Oxford: Clarendon, 1997.

James, William. *The Principles of Psychology*. New York: Henry Holt, 1890.

_____. "What is an Emotion?" *Mind* 9 (1884): 188–205.

Jenson, Robert W. *Systematic Theology*. The Works of God. Vol. 2. Oxford: Oxford University Press, 1999.

Jerajani, H. R., Jaju Bhagyashri, M. M. Phiske, and Nitin Lade, "Hematohidrosis—A Rare Clinical Phenomenon." *Indian Journal of Dermatology* 54, no. 3 (2009): 290–92.

Jewett, Robert. *Paul's Anthropological Terms: A Study of their Use in Context Settings*. Leiden: Brill, 1971.

John, O. P. and S. Srivastava. "The Big-Five Trait Taxonomy: History, Measurement, and Theoretical Perspectives." Pages 102–38 in *Handbook of Personality: Theory and Research*. Edited by L. A. Pervin and O. P. John. Vol. 2. New York: Guilford, 1999.

Johnson, Dru. *Biblical Knowing: A Scriptural Epistemology of Error*. Eugene, OR: Cascade, 2013.

Johnson, Eric L. *God and Soul Care: The Therapeutic Resources of the Christian Faith*. Downers Grove, IL: IVP Academic, 2017.

_____. *Psychology & Christianity: Five Views*. Downers Grove, IL: IVP Academic, 2010.

Johnson, Luke Timothy. *The Gospel of Luke*. Sacra Pagina Series. Vol. 3. Collegeville, MN: Liturgical, 1991.

Jordan, Mark D. "Ideals of *Scientia moralis* and the Invention of the *Summa Theologiae*." Pages 79–97 in *Aquinas's Moral Theory: Essays in Honor of Norman Kretzmann*. Edited by Scott MacDonald and Eleonore Stump. Ithaca, NY: Cornell University Press, 1999.

Josephus. *Jewish Antiquities*. Translated by Louis H. Feldman. Loeb Classical Library. Vol. 8. Cambridge, MA: Harvard University Press, 1965.

Jovanovic, Tanja, Nineequa Q. Blanding, Seth D. Norrholm, Erica Duncan, Bekh Bradley, and Kerry J. Ressler. "Childhood Abuse is Associated with Increased Startle Reactivity in Adulthood." *Depression and Anxiety* 26, no. 11 (2009): 1018–26.

Joyce, James. *Ulysses*. New York: Random House, 1986.

Kahneman, Daniel. *Thinking Fast and Slow*. New York: Farrar, Straus and Giroux, 2011.

Kalinich, Lila J., and Stuart W. Taylor, eds. *The Dead Father: A Psychoanalytic Inquiry*. New York: Routledge, 2009.

Kant, Immanuel. *Critique of Practical Reason*. Translated by Lewis White Beck. 3rd ed. Upper Saddle River, NJ: Prentice-Hall: 1993.

_____. *Critique of Pure Reason*. Translated and edited by Paul Guyer and Allen W. Wood. Cambridge: Cambridge University Press, 1998.

_____. "Grounding for the Metaphysics of Morals." Pages 981–1020 in *Classics of Western Philosophy*. Edited by Steven M. Cahn. 7th ed. Indianapolis: Hackett, 2006.

Kapic, Kelly M. "Anthropology." Pages 165–93 in *Christian Dogmatics: Reformed Theology for the Church Catholic*. Edited by Michael Allen and Scott R. Swain. Grand Rapids: Baker Academic, 2016.

_____. "The Son's Assumption of a Human Nature: A Call for Clarity." *International Journal of Systematic Theology* 3, no. 2 (July 2001): 154–66.

Keener, Craig. *The Mind of the Spirit: Paul's Approach to Transformed Thinking*. Grand Rapids: Baker Academic, 2016.

Kent, Bonnie. "Habits and Virtues (Ia IIae, qq. 49–70)." Pages 116–30 in *The Ethics of Aquinas*. Edited by Alexander Pope. Washington DC: Georgetown University Press, 2002.

_____. *Virtues of the Will: The Transformation of Ethics in the Late Thirteenth Century*. Washington DC: Catholic University of America Press, 1995.

Kessler, Eckhard. "Alexander of Aphrodisias and His Doctrine of the Soul: 1400 Years of Lasting Significance." *Early Science and Medicine* 16 (2011): 1–93.

_____. "The Intellective Soul." Pages 485–534 in *The Cambridge History of Renaissance Philosophy*. Edited by Charles B. Schmitt and Quentin Skinner. Cambridge: Cambridge University Press, 1988.

Kihlstrom, John F. "The Automaticity Juggernaut—or, Are We Autonomous After All?" Pages 155–80 in *Are We Free? Psychology and Free Will*. Edited by J. Baer, J. C. Kaufman, and R. F. Baumeister. New York: Oxford University Press, 2008.

_____. "The Cognitive Unconscious." *Science* 237 (1987): 1445–52.

_____. "The Motivational Unconscious." *Social and Personality Psychology Compass* 13, no. 5 (2019): 1–18.

_____. "The Rediscovery of the Unconscious." Pages 123–29 in *The Mind, The Brain, and Complex Adaptive Systems*. Edited by Harold J. Morowitz and Jerome L. Singer, SFI Studies in the Sciences of Complexity. Vol. 22. Reading, MA: Addison-Wesley, 1995.

Kihlstrom, John F., et al. "The Emotional Unconscious." Pages 30–86 in *Counterpoints: Cognition and Emotion*. Edited by E. Eich et al. New York: Oxford University Press, 2000.

Kim, Alan. "Wilhelm Maximillian Wundt." *Stanford Encyclopedia of Philosophy*. 10 September 2016. https://plato.stanford.edu/entries/wilhelm-wundt/.

Kim, Jaegwon. *Essays in the Metaphysics of Mind*. Oxford: Oxford University Press, 2010.

_____. "Supervenience, Emergence, Realization, Reduction." Pages 556–84 in *Oxford Handbook of Metaphysics*. Edited by Michael J. Loux and Dean W. Zimmerman. Oxford: Oxford University Press, 2010.

King, Peter. "Aquinas on the Emotions." Pages 209–26 in *The Oxford Handbook of Aquinas*. Edited by Brian Davies and Eleonore Stump. Oxford: Oxford University Press, 2011.

_____. "Aquinas on the Passions." Pages 101–32 in *Aquinas's Moral Theory: Essays in Honor of Norman Kretzman*. Edited by Scott McDonald and Eleonore Stump. Ithaca, NY: Cornell University Press, 1999.

_____. "Emotions in Medieval Thought." Pages 167–87 in *The Oxford Handbook on Emotion*. Edited by Peter Goldie. Oxford: Oxford University Press, 2009.

_____. "The Inner Cathedral: Mental Architecture in High Scholasticism." *Vivarium* 46 (2008): 253–74.

_____. "Scotus's Rejection of Anselm: The Two-Wills Theory." Pages 359–78 in *John Duns Scotus 1308-2008: Investigations into His Philosophy*. Edited by L. Honnefelder et al. Münster: Aschendorff, 2011.

Kirsch, Irving. *The Emperor's New Drugs: Exploding the Antidepressant Myth*. London: Bodley Head, 2009.

Kitayama, Shinobu, and Hazel Markus. *Emotion and Culture*. Washington DC: American Psychological Association, 1994.

Klima, Gyula, Fritz Allhoff, and Anand Vaidya, eds. *Medieval Philosophy: Essential Readings with Commentary*. Malden, MA: Blackwell, 2007.

Knuuttila, Simo. *Emotions in Ancient and Medieval Philosophy*. Oxford: Oxford University Press, 2004.

————. *Modalities in Medieval Philosophy*. New York: Routledge, 1993.

Kraal, Anders. "Valla-Style Determinism and the Intellectual Background of Luther's *De servo arbitrio*." *Harvard Theological Review* 108, no. 3 (July 2015): 402–22.

Kraye, Jill. "Pietro Pomponazzi (1462–1525): Secular Aristotelianism in the Renaissance." Pages 92–115in *Philosophers of the* Renaissance. Edited by Paul Richard Blum. Translated by Brian McNeil. Washington DC: Catholic University of America Press, 1999.

Kraye, Jill, and Risto Saarinen, eds. *Moral Philosophy on the Threshold of Modernity*. The New Synthese Historical Library. Vol. 57. Dordrecht: Springer, 2005.

Kretzmann, Norman, and Eleonore Stump, eds. *The Cambridge Companion to Thomas Aquinas*. Cambridge: Cambridge University Press, 1993.

Kugler, Brittany B., Vicky Phares, Alison Salloum, and Eric A. Storch. "The Role of Anxiety Sensitivity in the Relationship Between Posttraumatic Stress Symptoms and Negative Outcomes in Trauma-Exposed Adults." *Anxiety, Stress, and Coping* 29, no. 2 (2016): 187–201.

Kuhn, Karl Allen. *The Heart of Biblical Narrative: Rediscovering Biblical Appeal to the Emotions*. Minneapolis: Fortress, 2009.

Kuhn, Thomas S. *The Structure of Scientific Revolutions*. 3rd ed. Chicago, IL: University of Chicago Press, 1996.

Kusukawa, Sachiko, ed. *Melanchthon: Orations on Philosophy and Education*. Cambridge: Cambridge University Press, 1999.

Laertius, Diogenes. *Lives of Eminent Philosophers*. Translated and edited by R. D. Hicks. Loeb Classical Library. Vol. 2. Cambridge, MA: Harvard University Press, 1995.

Lagerlund, Henrik, and Mikko Yrjönsuuri, eds. *Emotions and Choice from Boethius to Descartes*. Dordrecht: Kluwer Academic, 2002.

Lane, Anthony N. S. "Calvin's Use of the Fathers and the Medievals." *Calvin Theological Journal* 16 (1981): 149–205.

————. *John Calvin: Student of the Church Fathers*. Grand Rapids: Baker, 1999.

Lazarus, Richard. "From Psychological Stress to the Emotions: A History of Changing Outlooks." *Annual Review of Psychology* 44 (1993): 1–21.

Lazarus, Richard S. *Emotion and Adaptation*. New York: Oxford University Press, 1991.

Lazarus, Richard S., and Bernice N. Lazarus. *Passion and Reason: Making Sense of Our Emotions*. Oxford: Oxford University Press, 1996.

LeBouthillier, Daniel M., Matthew G. Fetzner, and Gordon J. Asmundson. "PTSD Symptoms and Anxiety Sensitivity Following Aerobic Exercise." *Mental Health and Physical* 10 (March 2016): 33–39.

LeDoux, Joseph E. *Anxious: Using the Brain to Understand and Treat Fear and Anxiety*. New York: Penguin, 2015.

————. *The Emotional Brain: The Mysterious Underpinnings of Emotional Life*. New York: Simon & Schuster, 1996.

————. "Emotional Colouration of Consciousness: How Feelings Come About." Pages 69–130 in *Frontiers of Consciousness: The Chichele Lectures*. Edited by Lawrence Weiskrantz and Martin Davies. Oxford: Oxford University Press, 2008.

————. "Rethinking the Emotional Brain." *Neuron* 73 (February 2012): 653–76.

LeDoux, Joseph E., and Richard Brown. "A Higher-Order Theory of Emotional Consciousness." *Proceedings of the National Academy of Sciences* 114, no. 10 (January 2017): E2016–25.

Lee, Sukjae. "Scotus on the Will: The Rational Power and the Dual Affections." *Vivarium* 38 (1998): 40–54.

Leget, Carlo. "Moral Theology Upside Down." *Jaarboek Thomas Instituut* 18 (1999): 101–26.

Leibniz, Gottfried. "Primary Truths." In *Philosophical Essays*. Translated by Roger Ariew and Daniel Garber. Indianapolis: Hackett, 1989.

Lewis, C. S. *The Discarded Image*. Cambridge: Cambridge University Press, 2012.

_____. *Surprised by Joy: The Shape of My Early Life*. Orlando: Harcourt, 1955.

_____. "The Weight of Glory." Pp. 25–46 in *The Weight of Glory and Other Addresses*. New York: HarperOne, 2001.

Lewis, Paul Allen. "Rethinking Emotions and the Moral Life in Light of Thomas Aquinas and Jonathan Edwards." PhD diss., Duke University, 1991.

Lewontin, Richard. "The Dream of the Human Genome." *New York Review of Books* 39, no. 10 (28 May 1992): 31–40.

Liddell, Henry George, and Robert Scott. *A Greek-English Lexicon*. Revised by Sir Henry Stuart Jones and Roderick McKenzie. Oxford, Clarendon Press, 1940. Spring 2009. http://perseus.uchicago.edu/Reference/LSJ.html

Locke, John. *An Essay Concerning Human Understanding*. Oxford: Clarendon, 1894.

Lombardo, Nicholas E. *The Logic of Desire: Aquinas on Emotion*. Washington DC: Catholic University of America Press, 2011.

Lombard, Peter. *Libri IV Sententiarum*. Ad Claras Aquas: Typografia Collegii S. Bonaventurae, 1916.

Lottin, Odin. *Psychologie et Morale aux XIIe et XIIIe Siècles*. Tome III. Gembloux: Duculot, 1948–1949.

Luther, Martin. *Bondage of the Will*. Edited by J. I. Packer. Grand Rapids: Baker Academic, 1957.

Lynch, Michael, and Joshua Glasgow. "The Impossibility of Superdupervenience." *Philosophical Studies* 113 (2003): 201–21.

Lyons, William. *Emotion*. Cambridge: Cambridge University Press, 1980.

MacIntyre, Alasdair. *A Short History of Ethics: A History of Moral Philosophy from the Homeric Age to the Twentieth Century*. 2nd ed. Notre Dame: University of Notre Dame Press, 1998.

MacKay, Donald M. *Brains, Machines and Persons*. Grand Rapids: Eerdmans, 1980.

Mahgoub, Osama Mohamed, and Hassan Babiker Abdel-Hafeiz. "Pattern of Obsessive-Compulsive Disorder in Eastern Saudi Arabia." *The British Journal of Psychiatry* 158, no. 6 (June 1991): 840–42.

Manonukul, J., W. Wisuthsarewong, R. Chantorn, A. Vongirad, P. Omeapinyan. "Hematidrosis: A pathologic process or stigmata. A case report with comprehensive histopatholic and immuoperoxidas studies." *American Journal of Dermatopathology* 30, no. 2 (April 2008): 135–39.

Manzoni, T. "The Cerebral Ventricles, the Animal Spirits and the Dawn of Brain Localization of Function." *Archives Italiennes de Biologie* 136 (1998): 103–52.

Mason, Stephen. "Religious Reform and the Pulmonary Transit of the Blood." *History of Science* 41 (2003): 459–71.

Massar, Karlijn, Abraham P. Buunk, and Mark DeChesne. "Jealousy in the blink of an eye: Jealous reactions following subliminal exposure to rival characteristics." *European Journal of Social Psychology* 39 (2009): 768–79.

Mataix-Cols, D., I. M. Marks, J. H. Greist, and L. Baer. "Obsessive-Compulsive Symptom Dimensions as Predictors of Compliance with and Response to Behaviour Therapy: Results from a Controlled Trial." *Psychotherapy and Psychosomatics* 71 (2002): 255–62.

Maté, Gabor. *In the Realm of Hungry Ghosts: Close Encounters with Addiction.* Berkeley, CA: North Atlantic, 2010.

————. *The Stress Disease Connection.* Hoboken, NJ: Wiley, 2011.

Mayr, Ernst. "What is the meaning of 'life'?" Pages 88–101 in *The Nature of Life: Classical and Contemporary Perspectives.* Edited by Mark A. Bedau and Carol E. Cleland. Cambridge: Cambridge University Press, 2010.

McAuley, Edward, Shannon L. Mihalko, and Susan M. Bane. "Acute Exercise and Anxiety Reduction: Does the Environment Matter?" *Journal of Sport & Exercise Psychology* 18 (1996): 408–19.

McClendon, James W., Jr. *Doctrine: Systematic Theology.* Vol. 2. Nashville: Abingdon, 1994.

McDermott, Gerald R. "Jonathan Edwards on the Affections of the Spirit." Pages 279–92 in *The Spirit, The Affections, and the Christian Tradition.* Edited by Dale M. Coulter and Amos Young. Notre Dame: University of Notre Dame Press, 2016.

McDonald, Scott, and Eleonore Stump, eds. *Aquinas's Moral Theory: Essays in Honor of Norman Kretzmann.* Ithaca, NY: Cornell University Press, 1999.

McGaugh, J. L., and M. L. Hertz. *Memory Consolidation*. San Francisco: Albion, 1972.

McGrath, Alister E. "John Calvin and Late Mediaeval Thought: A Study in Late Mediaeval Influences upon Calvin's Theological Development." *Archiv für Reformationsgeschichte* 77 (1986): 58–78.

McIngvale, E., K. Rufino, M. Ehlers, and J. Hart. "An In-Depth Look at the Scrupulosity Dimension of Obsessive-Compulsive Disorder." *Journal of Spirituality in Mental Health*. 19, no. 4 (2017): 295–305.

Melanchthon, Philip. *Loci Communes* in *Melanchthon and Bucer*. Edited by Wilhelm Pauck. Philadelphia: Westminster, 1969.

Merikle, Philip M., Daniel Smilek, and John D. Eastwood. "Perception Without Awareness." *Cognition* 79 (2001): 115–34

Meylan, Edward F. "The Stoic Doctrine of Indifferent Things and the Conception of Christian Liberty in Calvin's *Institutio Religionis Christianae*." *Romantic Review* 8 (1937): 135–45.

Miller, Perry. *The New England Mind: The Seventeenth Century*. Cambridge, MA: Harvard University Press, 1954.

Miner, Robert. *Thomas Aquinas on the Passions: A Study of Summa Theologiae, 1a2ae 22–48*. Cambridge: Cambridge University Press, 2011.

Miu, Andrei C., Mirela I. Bîlc, Ioana Bunea, and Aurora Szentágotai-Tătar. "Childhood Trauma and Sensitivity to Reward and Punishment: Implications for Depressive and Anxiety Symptoms." *Personality and Individual Differences* 119 (2017): 134–40.

Mohler, Ludwig. *Kardinal Bessarion als Theologe, Humanist, und Staatsman: Darstellung*. Darmstadt: Paderborn 1967.

Moncher, Frank J. "A Psychotherapy of Virtue: Reflection on St. Thomas Aquinas' Theology of Moral Virtue." *Journal of Psychology and Christianity* 20, no. 4 (2001): 320–41.

Monfasani, John. "The Averroism of John Argyropoulos and His 'Quaestio utrum intellectus humanus sit perpetuus." *Tatti Studies in the Italian Renaissance* 5 (1993): 157–208.

————. "A tale of two books: Bessarion's *In Calumniatorem Platonis* and Geroge of Trebizond's *Comparatio Philosophorum Platonis et Aristotelis*." *Renaissance Studies*. 22, no. 1 (2007): 1–15.

Moo, Douglas. *The Epistle to the Romans*. The New International
Commentary on the New Testament. Edited by Gordon D. Fee.
Grand Rapids: Eerdmans, 1996.

Moody, Ernest A. "William of Auvergne and His Treatise *De anima*."
Pages 1–110 in *Studies in Medieval Philosophy: Science and Logic*.
Berkeley: University of California Press, 1975.

Mora, George. "Thomas Aquinas and Modern Psychology: A
Reassessment." *Psychoanalytic Review* 64, no. 4 (Winter 1977):
495–530.

Moreland, J. P. "A Critique of and Alternative to Nancey Murphy's
Christian Physicalism." *European Journal for Philosophy of Religion*
8, no. 2 (2016): 107–28.

————. "In Defense of a Thomistic-like Dualism." Pages 102–22 in *The
Blackwell Companion to Substance Dualism*. Edited by Jonathan J.
Loose, Angus J. L. Menuge, and J. P. Moreland. Oxford: Blackwell,
2018.

————. "Tweaking Dallas Willard's Ontology of the Human Person."
Journal of Spiritual Formation & Soul Care 8, no. 2 (2015): 187–202.

Moreland, J. P., and Scott Rae. *Body and Soul: Human Nature and the Crisis
in Ethics*. Downers Grove, IL: InterVarsity, 2000.

Moriarty, Michael. *Disguised Vices: Theories of Virtue in Early Modern
French Thought*. Oxford: Oxford University Press, 2011.

Muller, Richard. "*Fides* and *Cognitio* in Relation to the Problem of
Intellect and Will in the Theology of John Calvin." *Calvin
Theological Journal* 25 (1990): 207–24.

————. *Post-Reformation Reformed Dogmatics: The Rise and Development
of Reformed Orthodoxy, ca. 1520 to ca. 1725*. 4 vols. Grand Rapids:
Baker Academic, 2003.

————. "Scholasticism, Reformation, Orthodoxy, and the Persistence of
Christian Aristotelianism." *Trinity Journal* 19, no. 2 (1998): 81–96.

————. *The Unaccommodated Calvin: Studies in the Foundation of
Theological Tradition*. Edited by David C. Steinmetz. Oxford
Studies in Historical Theology. Oxford: Oxford University Press,
2000.

Murphy, Claudia Eisen. "Aquinas on Our Responsibility for Our
Emotions." *Medieval Philosophy and Theology* 8 (1999): 163–205.

Murphy, Lawrence. "Gabrield Biel as Transmitter of Aquinas to Luther." *Renaissance and Reformation* 19, no. 1 (February 1983): 26–41.

Murphy, Nancey. *Bodies and Souls, or Spirited Bodies?* Cambridge: Cambridge University Press, 2006.

————. "I Cerebrate Myself: Is there a little man inside your brain?" *Books and Culture: A Christian Review* 5, no. 1 (January-February 1999): 24–26.

————. "Non-Reductive Physicalism: Philosophical Issues." Pages 127–148 in *Whatever Happened to the Soul? Scientific and Theological Portraits of Human Nature*. Edited by Warren Brown, Nancey Murphy, and H. Newton Malony. Minneapolis: Fortress, 1998.

————. "Science and Society." Pages 99–131 in *Witness: Systematic Theology*. Edited by James Wm. McClendon Jr. and Nancey Murphy. Vol. 3 Nashville: Abingdon, 2000.

Murray, John. *Epistle to the Romans*. Grand Rapids: Eerdmans, 1997.

Nader, Karim, Glenn E. Schafe, and Joseph LeDoux. "Fear memories require protein synthesis in the amygdala for reconsolidation after retrieval." *Nature* 406 (August 2000): 722–26.

Naidoff, Bruce D. "A Man to Work the Soil: A New Interpretation of Genesis 2–3." *Journal for the Study of the Old Testament* 3, no. 5 (1978): 2–14.

Nardone, Henry F. "St. Thomas Aquinas and the Condemnation of 1277." Diss., Catholic University of America, 1964.

Nietzsche, Friedrich. *Twilight of the Idols*. Translated by Richard Polt. Indianapolis: Hackett, 1997.

Nisbett, Richard E., and Timothy D. Wilson. "Telling more than we can know: Verbal reports on mental processes." *Psychological Review* 84 (1977): 231–59.

Nolan, Paul. *Saint Thomas and the Unconscious Mind*. Washington DC: Catholic University of America Press, 1953.

Nolland, John. "Blessing and Woe." Pages 87–90 in *Dictionary of Jesus and the Gospels*. Edited by Joel B. Green, Jeannine K. Brown, and Nicholas Perin. 2nd ed. Downers Grove, IL: InterVarsity, 2013.Top of Form

Nussbaum, Martha. *Love's Knowledge: Essays on Philosophy and Literature*. Oxford: Oxford University Press, 1990.

_____. *Upheavals of Thought: The Intelligence of Emotions*. Cambridge: Cambridge University Press, 2003.

Oakman, Jonathan, Shannon Gifford, Natasha Chlebowsky. "A Multilevel Analysis of the Interpersonal Behavior of Socially Anxious People." *Journal of Personality* 71, no. 3 (June 2003): 397–434.

Oberman, Heiko A. "Fourteenth-Century Religious Thought: A Premature Profile." *Speculum* 53, no. 1 (January, 1978): 80–93.

_____. *The Harvest of Medieval Theology*. Grand Rapids: Baker Academic, 1983.

_____. "*Initia Calvini*: The Matrix of Calvin's Reformation." *Nederlands Archief voor Kerkgeschiedenis* 72, no. 2 (1992): 113–54.

_____. "Some Notes on the Theology of Nominalism: With Attention to Its Relation to the Renaissance." *The Harvard Theological Review* 53, no. 1 (January 1960): 47–76.

_____. "Via Antiqua and Via Moderna: Late Medieval Prolegomena to Early Reformation Thought." *Journal of the History of Ideas* 48, no. 1 (January-March 1987): 23–40.

Olatunji, Bunmi O., Thomas Armstrong, Qianqian Fan, and Mimi Zhao. "Risk and Resiliency in Posttraumatic Stress Disorder: Distinct Roles of Anxiety and Disgust Sensitivity." *Psychological Trauma* 6, no. 1 (2014): 50–55.

Owsei, Temkin. "On Galen's Pneumatology." *Gesnerus: Swiss Journal of the history of medicine and sciences* 8 (1951): 180–89.

Panksepp, Jaak. *Affective Neuroscience: The Foundations of Human and Animal Emotions*. Oxford: Oxford University Press, 2004.

_____. "The Neuro-Evolutionary Cusp Between Emotions and Cognitions: Implications for Understanding Consciousness and the Emergence of a Unified Mind Science." *Evolution and Cognition* 7, no. 2 (2001): 141–63.

Park, Katharine. "The Organic Soul." Pages 464–84 in *The Cambridge History of Renaissance Philosophy*. Edited by Charles B. Schmitt and Quentin Skinner. Cambridge: Cambridge University Press, 1988.

Park Katharine, and Eckhard Kessler. "The Concept of Psychology." Pages 455–63 in *The Cambridge History of Renaissance Philosophy*. Edited by Charles B. Schmitt, Quentin Skinner, and Eckhard Kessler. Cambridge: Cambridge University Press, 1988.

Partee, Charles. *Calvin and Classical Philosophy*. Edited by Heiko Oberman. Studies in the History of Christian Thought. Leiden: Brill, 1977.

Pascual-Leone, Alvaro, Amir Amedi, Felipe Fregni, and Lotfi B. Merabet. "The Plastic Human Brain Cortex." *Annual Review of Neuroscience* 28, no. 1 (July 2005): 377–401.

Pasnau, Robert. *Metaphysical Themes, 1274–1671*. Oxford: Clarendon, 2011.

————. "Olivi on the Metaphysics of Soul." *Medieval Philosophy and Theology* 6 (1997): 109–32.

————. *Thomas Aquinas on Human Nature*. Cambridge: Cambridge University Press, 2004.

Peacocke, Arthur. "God's Interaction with the World: The Implications of Deterministic 'Chaos' and of Interconnected and Interdependent Complexity." Pages 263–88 in *Chaos and Complexity: Scientific Perspectives on Divine Action*. Edited by Robert J. Russell, Nancey Murphy, and Arthur Peacocke. Vatican City State and Berkeley, CA: Vatican Observatory and Center for Theology and the Natural Sciences, 1995.

Pennington, Jonathan T. *The Sermon on the Mount and Human Flourishing: A Theological Commentary*. Grand Rapids: Baker Academic, 2017.

Perreiah, Alan. "Scotus on Human Emotions." *Franciscan Studies* 56 (1998): 325–45.

Perry, Bruce D. and Maia Szalavitz. *The Boy Who Was Raised as a Dog*. New York: Basic Books, 2017.

Petruzzello, Steven J., Daniel M. Landers, and Walter Salazar. "Exercise and Anxiety Reduction: Examination of Temperature as an Explanation for Affective Change." *Journal of Sport & Exercise Psychology* 15 (1993): 63–76.

Pies, Ronald W. "Psychiatry's New Brain-Mind and the Legend of the 'Chemical Imbalance.'" *Psychiatric Times* (11 July 2011), http://www.psychiatrictimes.com/couch-crisis/psychiatrys-new-brain-mind-and-legend-chemical-imbalance.

Pinckaers, Servais. *Morality: The Catholic View*. Translated by Michael Sherwin. South Bend, IN: St. Augustine's Press, 2001.

————. "Reappropriating Aquinas's Account of the Passions." Pages 273–287 in *The Pinckaers Reader*. Edited by John Berkman and

Craig Steven Titus. Washington DC: Catholic University of America Press, 2005.

_____. *The Sources of Christian Ethics*. Translated by Mary T. Noble. Washington DC: Catholic University of America Press, 1995.

Piper, John. *Desiring God: Meditations of a Christian Hedonist*. Sisters, OR: Multnomah, 1986.

_____. "Hope as the Motivation of Love: 1 Peter 3:9-12." *New Testament Studies* 26, no. 2 (1980): 212-31.

_____. *When I Don't Desire God*. Wheaton, IL: Crossway, 2013.

Plantinga, Alvin. "On Heresy, Mind, and Truth." *Faith and Philosophy* 16, no. 2 (April 1999): 182-93.

_____. *God, Freedom, and Evil*. Grand Rapids: Eerdmans, 1974.

Plato, *Plato: The Collected Dialogues including the Letters*. Edited by Edith Hamilton and Huntington Cairns. Princeton, NJ: Princeton University Press, 1961.

Polanyi, Michael. *Personal Knowledge: Towards a Post-Critical Philosophy*. Chicago: University of Chicago Press, 1974.

_____. *The Tacit Dimension*. Chicago: University of Chicago Press, 1966.

Pope, Alexander, ed. *The Ethics of Aquinas*. Washington DC: Georgetown University Press, 2002.

Pratt, James Bissett. "A Defense of Dualistic Realism." *The Journal of Philosophy, Psychology and Scientific Methods* 14, no. 10 (May 10, 1917): 253-61.

Prendiville, John G. "The Development of the Idea of Habit in the Thought of Saint Augustine." *Traditio: Studies in Ancient and Medieval History, Thought and Religion* 28 (1972): 29-99.

Preus, Anthony. "Intention and Impulse in Aristotle and the Stoics." *Apeiron* 15, no. 1 (1981): 48-58.

Prinz, Jesse. *Gut Reactions: A Perceptual Theory of Emotion*. Oxford: Oxford University Press, 2006.

Raith, Charles, II. *After Merit: John Calvin's Theology of Works and Rewards*. Göttingen: Vanderhoeck & Ruprecht, 2016.

_____. *Aquinas and Calvin on Romans: God's Justification and Our Participation*. Oxford: Oxford University Press, 2014.

Raitt, Jill. "Calvin's Use of Bernard of Clairvaux." *Archive für Reformationsgeschichte* 72 (1981): 98-121.

Ratzinger, Joseph. *Eschatology: Death and Eternal Life.* Edited by A. Nichols. Translated by M. Waldstein. Washington, DC: Catholic University of America, 1988.

Reilly, George. *The Psychology of Saint Albert the Great: Compared with That of Saint Thomas.* Washington DC: Catholic University of America, 1934.

Reno, R. R. *Genesis.* Brazos Theological Commentary on the Bible. Grand Rapids: Brazos, 2010.

Reuter, Karl. *Vom Scholaren bis zum jungen Reformato Studien zum Werdegang Johannes Calvins.* Neukirchen: Neukirchener Verlag, 1981.

Rickabaugh, Brandon L. "A Combination Problem for Emergent Dualism and a Neo-Aristotelian Solution." Paper presented at Dominican Colloquium in Berkeley: Person, Soul and Consciousness, Dominican School of Philosophy and Theology, July 2017.

_____. "Responding to N. T. Wright's Rejection of the Soul." *The Heythrop Journal* (2016): 1–20.

Ricoeur, Paul. *Freedom and Nature: The Voluntary and the Involuntary.* Translated by Erazim V. Kohák. Evanston, IL: Northwestern University Press, 1966.

_____. *Oneself as Another.* Chicago: University of Chicago Press, 1992.

Roberts, Robert C. *Emotion: An Essay in Aid of Moral Psychology.* Cambridge: Cambridge University Press, 2003.

_____. "Emotions and the Fruit of the Spirit." Pages 78–94 in *Psychology and the Christian Faith: An Introductory Reader.* Edited by Stanton L. Jones. Grand Rapids: Baker, 1985.

Robinson, John A. T. *The Body: A Study in Pauline Theology.* Philadelphia: Westminster John Knox, 1952.

Rorty, Amélie Oksenberg. "Aristotle on the Metaphysical Status of the Pathe." *The Review of Metaphysics* 27, no. 3 (March 1984): 521–46.

Rothschild, Clair K. "Holy Sweat: Interpreting Luke's Portrait of Jesus in the Garden." *The Bible Today* 55, no. 3 (2017): 186–92.

Russell, Edward. "Reconsidering Relational Anthropology: A Critical Assessment of John Zizioulas's Theological Anthropology." *International Journal of Systematic Theology* 5, no. 2 (July 2003): 168–86.

Ryle, Gilbert. "Feelings." *The Philosophical Quarterly* 1, no. 3 (April 1951): 193–205.

Saarinen, Risto. *Weakness of Will in Renaissance and Reformation Thought.* Oxford: Oxford University Press, 2011.

Savage, Brandon M., Heidi L. Lujan, Raghavendar R. Thipparthi, and Stephen E. DiCarlo. "Humor, laughter, learning, and health! A brief review." *Advances in Physiology Education* 41 (2017): 341–47.

Schachter, Stanley, and Jerome E. Singer. "Cognitive, Social, and Physiological Determinants of the Emotional State." *Psychological Review* 69, no. 5 (September 1962): 379–99.

Schacter, Daniel L., Daniel T. Gilbert, and Daniel M. Wegner. *Psychology.* 2nd ed. New York: Worth, 2011.

Schäfer, Jürgen. "When They Marry: They Get Wenches." *Shakespeare Quarterly* 22, no. 3 (Summer, 1971): 203–11.

Schreiner, Thomas R. *Romans.* Baker Exegetical Commentary on the New Testament. Edited by Moisés Silva. Grand Rapids: Baker Academic, 1998.

Schulz, Peter. "George Gemistos Plethon (ca. 1360–1454), George of Trebizond (1396–1472), and Cardinal Bessarion (1403–1472): The Controversy between Platonists and Aristotelians in the Fifteenth Century." Pages 23–32 in *Philosophers of the Renaissance.* Edited by Paul Richard Blum. Translated by Brian McNeil. Washington DC: Catholic University of America Press, 1999.

Schwartz, Jeffrey M. *Brain Lock.* New York: ReganBooks, 1996.

———. *The Mind and the Brain: Neuroplasticity and the Power of Mental Force.* New York: ReganBooks, 2002.

———. "A Role for Volition and Attention in the Generation of New Brain Circuitry: Toward A Neurobiology of Mental Force." *Journal of Consciousness Studies* 6, no. 8–9 (1999): 115–42.

———. *You Are Not Your Brain: The 4-Step Solution for Changing Bad Habits, Ending Unhealthy Thinking, and Taking Control of Your Life.* New York: Penguin, 2011.

Schwartz, Jeffrey M., Karron M. Martin, and Lewis R. Baxter. "Neuroimaging and Cognitive-Biobehavioral Self-Treatment for Obsessive Compulsive Disorder: Practical and Philosophical Considerations." Pages 82–101 in *Zwangsstörungen / Obsessive-*

Compulsive Disorders. Edited by Iver Hand, Wayne K. Goodman, and Ulrike Evers. Dupbar Med Communication Series. Berlin: Springer, 1992.

Schwartz, Jeffrey M., Henry P. Stapp, and Mario Beauregard. "Quantum physics in neuroscience and psychology: a neurophysical model of mind-brain interaction." *Philosophical Transactions of the Royal Society B* 360 (2005): 1309–27.

Scotus, John Duns. *Joannis Duns Scoti Opera omnia.* Edited by Luke Wadding. Lyon: Sumptibus Laurentii Durand, 1639.

Selderhuis, Herman J. *Calvin's Theology of the Psalms.* Text and Studies in Reformation and Post-Reformation Thought. Grand Rapids: Baker Academic, 2007.

Senkbeil, Harold. *The Care of Souls: Cultivating a Pastor's Heart.* Bellingham, WA: Lexham Press, 2019.

Sewell, Alida Leni. *Calvin, the Body, and Sexuality.* Amsterdam: VU University Press, 2011.

Sgarbi, Marco. "Benedetto Varchi on the Soul: Vernacular Aristotelianism between Reason and Faith." *Journal of the History of Ideas* 76, no. 1 (January 2015): 1–23.

Sharples, R. W., and P. J. van der Eijk. *Nemesius on the Nature of Man.* Liverpool: Liverpool University Press, 2008.

Shaw, George Bernard. *Pygmalion.* New York: Penguin, 2003.

Shults, F. LeRon. *Reforming Theological Anthropology: After the Philosophical Turn to Relationality.* Grand Rapids: Eerdmans, 2003.

Sibbes, Richard. "The Soul's Conflict with Itself." Pages 119–294 in *Works of Richard Sibbes.* Vol. 1. Edinburgh: Banner of Truth Trust, 1973.

Siemens, David F., Jr. "Neuroscience, Theology, and Unintended Consequences." *Perspectives on Science and Christian Faith.* 57, no. 3 (September 2005): 187–90.

Smith, Chris, Eugenio Frixione, Stanley Finger, and William Clower. *The Animal Spirit Doctrine and the Origins of Neurophysiology.* Oxford: Oxford University Press, 2012.

Smith, James K. A. *Awaiting the King: Reforming Public Theology.* Cultural Liturgies. Vol. 3. Grand Rapids: Baker Academic, 2017.

_____. *Desiring the Kingdom: Worship, Worldview, and Cultural Formation*. Cultural Liturgies. Vol. 1. Grand Rapids: Baker Academic, 2009.

_____. *Imagining the Kingdom: How Worship Works*. Cultural Liturgies. Vol. 2. Grand Rapids: Baker Academic, 2013.

Sobol, Peter. "John Buridan on the Soul and Sensation." Ph.D. dissertation, Indiana University, 1984.

Solomon, Robert. "Emotions, Thoughts and Feelings: What is a 'Cognitive Theory' of the Emotions and Does it Neglect Affectivity." Pages 1–18 in *Royal Institute of Philosophy Supplement*. Edited by A. Hatismoysis. Cambridge: Cambridge University Press, 2003.

_____. *The Passions: The Myth and Nature of Human Emotion*. Notre Dame: University of Notre Dame Press, 1983.

Spina, Frank Anthony. "The 'Ground' for Cain's Rejection (Gen 4): ʾᵃdāmāh in the Context of Gen 1–11." *Zeitschrift für die alttestamentliche Wissenschaft* 104, no. 3 (1992): 319–32.

Stapp, Henry P. "Quantum Interactive Dualism: An Alternative to Materialism." *Zygon* 41, no. 3 (September 2006): 599–616.

Stein, Robert H. *Luke*. The New American Commentary. Vol. 24. Nashville: Broadman, 1992.

Steinbeck, John. *East of Eden*. New York: Penguin Books, 2002.

Steinmetz, David C. "Aquinas for Protestants: What Luther got Wrong." *Christian Century* 122, no. 7 (August 2005): 23–26.

_____. "Calvin as Biblical Interpreter Among the Ancient Philosophers." *Interpretation* 63, no. 2 (2009): 142–53.

Stump, Eleonore. "The Non-Aristotelian Character of Aquinas's Ethics: Aquinas on the Passions." Pages 91–105 in *Faith, Rationality, and the Passions*. Edited by Sarah Coakley. Malden, MA: Wiley-Blackwell, 2012.

_____. "Non-Cartesian Substance Dualism and Materialism Without Reduction." *Faith and Philosophy* 12, no. 4 (October 1995): 505–31.

Stump, James B. "Non-Reductive Physicalism—A Dissenting Voice." *Christian Scholar's Review* 36, no. 1 (Fall 2006): 63–76.

Sui, J., and G. W. Humphreys. "The integrative self: How self-reference integrates perception and memory." *Trends in Cognitive Science* 19, no. 12 (October 2015): 719–28.

Sullivan, John E. *The Image of God: The Doctrine of St. Augustine and Its Influence.* Dubuque, IA: Priory Press, 1963.

Sweeney, Douglas A., and Allen C. Guelzo. *The New England Theology.* Eugene, OR: Wipf & Stock, 2006.

Swinburne, Richard. "Body and Soul." Pages 311–16 in *The Mind-Body Problem: A Guide to the Current Debate.* Edited by R. Warner and T. Szubka. Oxford and Cambridge, MA: Blackwell, 1994.

––––––––. "Dualism Intact." *Faith and Philosophy* 13, no. 1 (January 1996): 68–77.

Sytsma, David S. "The Logic of the Heart: Analyzing the Affections in Early Reformed Orthodoxy." Pages 471–88 in *Church and School in Early Modern Protestantism: Studies in Honor of Richard A. Muller on the Maturation of a Theological Tradition.* Edited by Jordan J. Ballor, David S. Sytsma, and Jason Zuidema. Boston, Brill, 2013.

Taliaferro, Charles. "Animals, Brains, and Spirits." *Faith and Philosophy* 12, no. 4 (October 1995): 567–81.

––––––––. *Consciousness and the Mind of God.* Cambridge: Cambridge University Press, 1994.

Tanner, Norman P., ed. *Decrees of the Ecumenical Councils.* 2 vols. Washington DC: Georgetown University Press, 1990.

Terburg, David, Nicole Hooiveld, Henk Aarts, J. Leon Kenemans, and Jack van Honk. "Eye tracking unconscious face-to-face confrontations: Dominance motives prolong gaze to masked angry faces." *Psychological Science* 22, no. 3 (March 2011): 314–19.

Theological Dictionary of the New Testament. Edited by Gerhard Kittel and Gerhard Friedrich. Grand Rapids: Eerdmans, 1977.

Thiselton, Anthony C. "Flesh." Pages 671–83 in *The New International Dictionary of New Testament Theology.* Edited by Colin Brown. Grand Rapids: Zondervan, 1975.

––––––––. *Interpreting God and the Postmodern Self: On Meaning, Manipulation and Promise.* Edinburgh: T&T Clark, 1995.

Thompson, Curt. *The Soul of Shame: Retelling the Stories We Believe about Ourselves.* Downers Grove, IL: IVP Books, 2015.

Tiedens, Larissa Z., Miguel M. Unzueta, and Maria J. Young. "An Unconscious Desire for Hierarchy? The Motivated Perception of Dominance Complementarity in Task Partners." *Journal of Personality and Social Psychology* 93, no. 3 (2007): 402–14.

Tillyard, Eustace M. *The Elizabethan World Picture*. New York: Vintage, 1959.

Tomkins, Silvan S. "What and where are the primary affects? Some evidence for a theory (with Robert McCarter." Pages 217–62 in *Exploring Affect: The Selected Writings of Silvan S. Tomkins*. Edited by E. Virginia Demos. Cambridge: Maison des Sciences de l'Homme and Cambridge University Press, 1995.

Torrance, T. F. *Calvin's Doctrine of Man*. London: Lutterworth, 1949.

_____. *Reality and Evangelical Theology: The Realism of Christian Revelation*. Downers Grove, IL: InterVarsity, 1999.

Trinkaus, Charles. "The Problem of Free Will in the Renaissance and the Reformation." *Journal of the History of Ideas* 10, no. 1 (January 1949): 51–62.

Trower, Peter, Paul Gilbert, and Georgina Sherling. "Social anxiety, evolution, and self- presentation: An interdisciplinary perspective." Pages 11–45 in *Handbook of Social and Evaluation Anxiety*. Edited by Harold Leitenberg. New York: Plenum, 1990.

Trueman, Carl R. *History and Its Fallacies: Problems Faced in the Writing of History*. Wheaton, IL: Crossway, 2010.

Tuckett, Christopher M. "Luke 22,43–44: The 'Agony' in the Garden and Luke's Gospel." Pages 131–44 in *New Testament Textual Criticism and Exegesis: Festschrift J. Delobel*. Edited by Adelbert Denaux. BETL. Vol. 161. Leuven: Leuven University Press, 2002.

Tulving, Endel. "Episodic Memory and Autonoesis: Uniquely Human?" Pages 3–56 in *The Missing Link in Cognition: Origins of Self-Reflective Consciousness*. Edited by Herbert S. Terrace and Janet Metcalfe. New York: Oxford University Press, 2005.

Turretin, Frances. *Institutes of Elenctic Theology*. Vol. 2. Phillipsberg, NJ: P&R, 1997.

Valenstein, Elliot. *Blaming the Brain: The Truth About Drugs and Mental Health*. New York: Free Press, 1988.

Valla, Lorenzo. "Dialogue on Free Will." Pages 155–84 in *The Renaissance Philosophy of Man*. Edited by Ernst Cassirer, Paul Oskar Kristeller, and John Herman Randall, Jr. Chicago: University of Chicago Press, 1948.

van der Kolk, Bessel. *The Body Keeps the Score: Brain, Mind, and Body in the Healing of Trauma*. New York: Penguin, 2014.

Vanhoozer, Kevin J. *Drama of Doctrine: A Canonical Linguistic Approach to Christian Theology*. Louisville: Westminster John Knox, 2005.

————. "Forming the Performers: How Christians Can Use Canon Sense to Bring Us to Our (Theodramatic) Senses." *Edification: The Transdisciplinary Journal of Christian Psychology* 4, no. 1 (2010): 5–16.

————. *Is There a Meaning in This Text?: The Bible, The Readier, and the Morality of Literary Knowledge*. Grand Rapids: Zondervan, 1998.

————. "Scripture and Theology: On 'Proving' Doctrine Biblically." Pages 141–59 in *The Routledge Companion to the Practice of Christian Theology*. Edited by Mike Higton and Jim Fodor. New York: Routledge, 2015.

————. "From Speech Acts to Scripture Acts: The Covenant of Discourse and the Discourse of the Covenant." Pages 1–49 in *After Pentecost: Language and Biblical Interpretation*. Edited by Craig Bartholomew, Colin J. D. Greene, and Karl Moller. Scripture and Hermeneutics Series. Vol. 2. Grand Rapids: Zondervan, 2001.

————. "Trinitarian Transdisciplinary Hermeneutics: A New Reduction of the Arts (and Sciences) to the Divine Economy." Paper delivered at the meeting of the Transdisciplinary Group, Houston, TX, 22–24 February 2017.

Van Steenberghen, F. *La philosophie au XIIIᵉ siècle*. Louvain-Paris: Éditions Peeters, 1991.

Van Vliet, Jason. *Children of God: The Imago Dei in John Calvin and His Context*. Göttingen: Vanderhoeck & Ruprecht, 2009.

Vermeule, Blakey. "The New Unconscious, A Literary Guided Tour." Pages 463–82 in *The Oxford Handbook of Cognitive Literary Studies*. Edited by Lisa Zunshine. New York: Oxford University Press, 2015.

Viana, Andres G., Eric C. Berenz, Laura J. Dixon, and Flint M. Espil. "Trauma and Deliberate Self-Harm Among Inpatient Adolescents: The Moderating Role of Anxiety Sensitivity." *Psychological Trauma* 9, no. 5 (2017): 509–17.

Vinken, Pierre. *The Shape of the Heart*. New York: Elsevier, 1999.

Vos, Geerhardus. *Reformed Dogmatics*. Translated and edited by Richard
    B. Gaffin, Jr. Vol. 2: Anthropology. Bellingham, WA: Lexham Press,
    2014.

Wang, Zhaoyue, et al. "A Case of Hematidrosis Successfully Treated
    with Propranolol." *American Journal of Dermatopathology* 11, no. 6
    (2010): 440–43.

Ware, Kallistos. "The Humanity of Christ: The Fourth Constantinople
    Lecture." *Journal of Anglican and Eastern Churches Association*
    (1985): 1–11.

Warfield, B. B. "On the Emotional Life of our Lord." Pages 35–90 in
    Biblical and Theological Studies. Edited by B. B. Warfield et al. New
    York: Charles Scribner's Sons, 1922.

Webster, John. "What Makes Theology Theological?" *The Journal of
    Analytic Theology* 3 (2015): 17–28.

Weemse, John. *The Portraiture of the Image of God in Man in His Three
    Estates of Creation, Restauration, Glorification*. 3rd ed. London: John
    Bellamie, 1636.

Weinandy, Thomas. *In the Likeness of Sinful Flesh: An Essay on the
    Humanity of Christ*. New York: T&T Clark, 2006.

Weinberg, Julius. *A Short History of Medieval Philosophy*. Princeton, NJ:
    Princeton University Press, 1964.

Welch, Edward. *Blame It on the Brain*. Phillipsburg, NJ: P&R, 1998.

_____. "Emotions are a Language." *CCEF* (blog). 5 August 2016. https://
    www.ccef.org/resources/blog/emotions-are-a-language.

_____. "Sinners Learning to Act the Miracle." Pages 65–87 in *Acting the
    Miracle: God's Work and Ours in the Mystery of Sanctification*. Edited
    by John Piper and David Mathis. Wheaton, IL: Crossway, 2013.

Wells, David F. *God in the Whirlwind: How the Holy-love of God Reorients
    Our World*. Wheaton, IL: Crossway, 2014.

Wendel, François. *Calvin: Origins and Development of His Religious Thought*.
    Translated by Philip Mairet. New York: Harper & Row, 1950.

Whitaker, Robert. *Anatomy of an Epidemic: Magic Bullets, Psychiatric Drugs,
    and the Astonishing Rise of Mental Illness in America*. New York:
    Broadway, 2010.

Whitaker, Robert, and Lisa Cosgrove. *Psychiatry Under the Influence: Institutional Corruption, Social Injury, and Prescriptions for Reform.* New York: Palgrave McMillan, 2015.

White, Peter A. "Knowing more about what we can tell: 'Introspective access' and causal report accuracy 10 years later." *British Journal of Psychology* 79 (1988): 13–45.

Whitmore, Paul. "A New Mindset for a New Mind." *American Society for Training and Development: T+D* (2009): 60–65.

Wierzbicka, Anna. "Does Language Reflect Culture? Evidence from Australian English." *Language in Society* 15, no. 3 (September 1986): 349–73.

Willard, Dallas. *The Spirit of the Disciplines.* New York: Harper Collins, 1988.

William of Ockham. *Quaestiones in librum secundum sententiarum (Reportatio).* In *Opera philosophica et theologica: Opera theologica,* volume 5. Edited by Gedon Gal and Rega Wood. St. Bonaventure, NY: Franciscan Institute, 1976.

Wilson, Timothy. *Strangers to Ourselves: Discovering the Adaptive Unconscious.* Cambridge, MA: Harvard University Press.

Witherington, Ben, III. *Conflict and Community in Corinth: A Socio-Rhetorical Commentary on I and 2 Corinthians.* Grand Rapids: Eerdmans, 1995.

Wolter, Allan. *Duns Scotus on the Will and Morality.* Washington DC: Catholic University of America Press, 1986.

————., ed. *Philosophical Writings: A Selection.* Indianapolis: Hackett, 1987.

Wolterstorff, Nicholas. *Reason within the Bounds of Religion.* Grand Rapids: Eerdmans, 1984.

Wood, Adam. "The Faculties of the Soul and Some Medieval Mind-Body Problems." *The Thomist* 75 (2011): 585–636.

Wood, Allen. "The Final Form of Kant's Practical Philosophy." Pages 1–22 in *Kant's Metaphysics of Morals: Interpretative Essays.* Edited by Mark Timmons. New York: Cambridge University Press, 2000.

Wright, N. T. *Jesus and the Victory of God.* Christian Origins and the Question of God. Vol. 2. Minneapolis: Fortress, 1996.

_____. "Mind, Spirit, Soul and Body: All for One and One for All
      Reflections on Paul's Anthropology in His Complex Contexts."
      Paper presented to the Society of Christian Philosophers:
      Regional Meeting, Fordham University, 18 March 2011.

_____. *The New Testament and the People of God.* Minneapolis: Fortress,
      1992.

Yabuuchi, Akio. "Hierarchy Politeness: What Brown and Levinson
      Refused to See." *Intellectual Pragmatics* 3, no. 3 (2006): 323–51.

Yandell, Keith. "A Defense of Dualism." *Faith and Philosophy* 12, no. 4
      (October 1995): 548–66.

Yeago, David. "The New Testament and Nicene Dogma: A Contribution to
      the Recovery of Theological Exegesis." *Pro Ecclesia* 3, no. 2 (1994):
      152–64.

Zajonc, Robert. "Feeling and Thinking: Preferences Need No Inferences."
      American Psychologist 35 (1980): 151–75.

Zizioulas, John D. *Being as Communion: Studies in Personhood and the
      Church.* London: Darton, Longman & Todd, 1985.

SUBJECT/AUTHOR INDEX

—

A

affections 19–22, 48, 65, 80n94, 112–14,
    117n89, 138, 144–45, 164, 166,
    169–71, 172, 178–85, 204, 209,
    212, 262n33
angelism 64, 79, 141, 168, 190
anxiety 23–39, 186, 262, 264, 265–68,
    283, 298, 301–6, 314, 323–46,
    347–50
Alexandrism 100–103, 152–57
Aquinas, Thomas 7, 11, 13, 20, 41–91,
    92–93, 96, 107–12, 114–17, 119–
    20, 124, 127–28, 144, 150, 156,
    167, 175, 185, 190–91, 193, 206,
    209–10, 216, 221, 250, 261n31,
    262, 284–84, 293, 297, 314–19
Aristotle 5, 48, 52, 54, 69, 72, 83–87,
    103–5, 132, 135, 144, 152–54, 161,
    164, 172, 189, 313–14, 337
Augustine 20, 64, 65n58, 68n67, 82–83,
    88, 95, 117–19, 120, 148, 160, 171,
    175, 183, 187
Averroism 100–102, 154

B

Bavinck, Herman 8, 205–11, 212n73,
    217n99, 218, 220
Berkhof, Louis 211–12
Berkouwer, G.C. 212–14, 217n99
biblical counseling 36
body
  qualifies agency and emotion 4, 6,
    11, 38, 55–58, 67–75, 80–82, 129,
    141–42, 151n81, 169, 190, 198,
    218, 248–49, 257, 259, 267, 280,
    281, 283, 297–309, 319, 343,
    350–51
  physiology of emotion 37, 51–58,
    297–309
  biblical term (sōma) 252–53, 260–63,
    271–82
Borgman, Brian 29, 30, 32–33
Buridan, John 97–99, 156, 158, 162,
    247n117

C

Calvin, John 11, 14, 93–94, 99, 100,
    104–5, 112, 122–27, 129–96, 208,
    212, 241, 361
chemical imbalance, or
    neurochemicals 34, 37, 262n33,
    293, 298, 301–3, 307–8
Charry, Ellen 16, 252n1
cognitive therapy, and cognitive-
    behavioral therapy 18, 34n42,
    306, 314
confabulation 299–300, 311
consciousness 10, 25, 203nn20–21, 212,
    228–29, 245–36, 248–50, 286–97,
    309–13, 315–16
Cooper, John 15, 224–32, 244, 248
covenant 9, 216–18, 255–59, 279, 281,
    327, 332, 341–42

D

depravity 81, 123, 126, 135, 151, 160, 165,
    168, 172, 177, 181, 240–41, 275,
    283n1
Descartes, René 12, 98–99, 221–22

Des Chene, Dennis 44n7, 104n53,
    153n92, 162
Dixon, Thomas 16, 19–22, 65
Diagnostic and Statistical Manual
    (DSM) 23, 57, 308
drama, theodrama 216, 321
Drummond, Ian 116, 119–22
dualism, see holism, dualistic

E

Edwards, Jonathan 1–2, 11n32, 22n59,
    192, 204
Elliott, Matthew 19, 24n4, 26, 28,
    323–27, 342
emotion
    change or governance 11n34, 13–14,
        24n4, 25n4, 26, 31, 38n52, 38,
        39–40, 48–50, 56, 61–64, 75–82,
        88–91, 142, 151, 179–81, 185–86,
        209, 220n1, 248, 252–53, 256–57,
        281, 307–8, 309–14, 318–19, 322,
        323–27, 345–46, 351–52
    emotional voluntarism 4, 24–30,
        36–39, 210, 220, 323–27, 357–61
    self-understanding 1–4, 24, 290–94,
        298–300, 310–14, 347–50
    sinful emotion 1–2, 23, 32–33, 36n47,
        65n58, 67, 178–79, 191, 181–83,
        323–46, 347, 361–62
eschatology 14, 39, 191, 269, 279–81,
    321, 327, 338, 340–45, 347

F

fear 3n9, 30–31, 71, 74, 136, 182, 195,
    286–88, 291–93, 297–98, 304,
flesh, biblical term (sarx) 118, 142, 218,
    252–53, 259–63, 267–68, 269,
    272–82
free will 108–27, 169–78, 234–36, 238–
    43, 250–51, 295, 301n67, 307
    free choice 83, 107–12, 116–17, 120–22,
        170–75, 191
    determination of the will 61, 75, 79,
        94, 106, 108, 118, 121–27, 171–77,

223, 228–30, 231n44, 234–36,
    238–42, 246–48
Freud, Sigmund 284, 294–95, 309

G

Galen or Galenism 39, 42, 43n5, 45,
    51–58, 70, 81–82, 101, 137,
    142–46, 152, 157, 158n113, 163,
    178, 194, 317
Gethsemane narrative 181–83, 263–68
Gnosticism 68, 151, 267, 271–72, 275,
    277
Gondreau, Paul 13, 66, 69n69, 71–72
Green, Joel 232, 254n6

H

Hatfield, Gary 12, 50n22
habit, habitus 4–5, 11, 38–40, 57–58, 64,
    73, 75, 77, 80–91, 94, 108–10,
    116–17, 119–21, 124, 168, 173,
    178, 188–91, 195, 205, 209–11,
    212, 253, 260–62, 275–82, 297,
    300–303, 314, 321, 336–37, 350,
    351, 353, 355, 363
Haidt, Jonathan 80, 309
heart 2n5–6, 25–29, 36, 39, 53–55, 64,
    70–75, 130n3, 139, 160–69, 176,
    178, 180–81, 195, 203–4, 208–9,
    212, 217n99, 220n1, 261n31, 267,
    324–25, 339, 344, 347, 357–63
Helm, Paul 136n27, 138n37, 161n118, 175,
    176n163, 189, 218n102
Hodge, Charles 190n212, 199, 201–4,
    205, 212
Hoekema, Anthony 199n2, 214–16, 217
homunculus 106, 111–12, 116, 168,
    176–77, 191, 215
Hoitenga, Dewey 167–74, 177n164,
    198n1, 217n100, 241n85
holism, dualistic 6, 14–15, 37n50,
    39–40, 43, 50, 80, 90, 92–100,
    104, 127–28, 141–42, 151n81, 159,
    169, 190–91, 197–98, 200–201,
    210, 216, 217–19, 220–21, 225–28,

230–31, 243–51, 257, 261, 313, 315, 322, 325, 343, 346, 360–61

Holy Spirit 2, 9, 10, 14, 25n5, 33n32, 39, 55n35, 81, 87, 90, 145, 151, 158n113, 173, 179, 181, 195, 253, 258, 261, 276–82, 321, 328n24, 341–45, 346, 351–56

Horton, Michael 216–18

humors 52–57, 58n47, 73–74, 101, 110, 143–46, 150, 318

hylomorphism 43–45, 68, 157, 247

I

imago Dei, image of God 6, 132, 137–42, 153, 159–61, 168, 190, 200–201, 207, 250n129

intellect, see rational powers

intellectualism, see voluntarism and intellectualism

J

James, William 2, 4n15, 284, 293

Johnson, Eric L. 3, 7, 10, 12n34, 268, 350n6, 353n10, 354

K

Kant, Immanuel 12, 129n1, 253n5, 334–42

King, Peter 11, 20, 41, 45, 61n51, 65n58, 80n94, 113n77, 115n79, 117n89

kingdom 39, 139, 171, 181, 270, 280, 322, 327–33, 338–46, 347, 350–51

L

language 236, 239, 250–51, 253, 255–58, 282, 294, 296, 306–9, 309–15, 319–22, 327–43

LeDoux, Joseph 2, 3, 30–35, 286–314, 314–19

Lewis, C.S. 51n24, 66n61, 146n64, 149n73, 320

Lombardo, Nicholas 17, 20–21, 65n58, 68, 80n94

Luther, Martin 93n1, 99, 123, 125–26

M

Melanchthon, Philip 5n16, 126, 140, 143n52, 145, 158, 159n113, 174, 177

memory 30, 35, 46, 54, 61, 155, 160, 209, 237, 246, 286, 289–97, 299, 301–6, 314–18

mental illness 34n41, 36–37, 78, 280, 300–303, 307–8, 318–19

Miner, Robert 44, 76

Moreland, J.P. 7n20, 14–15, 221, 243–51, 263

moral agency 25n5, 29, 62–63, 80–82, 151, 221, 234–42, 246–51, 253, 255–57, 282, 309–14

Muller, Richard 167, 171, 174, 192, 194

Murphy, Nancey 15, 224, 230, 232–43, 245–51

N

neuroplasticity, see plasticity

neuroscience 14, 42, 72, 197, 230, 232–34, 236, 236n73, 243, 245, 247–48, 286–94, 316–19

O

Obsessive Compulsive Disorder (OCD) 23, 31n26, 34n42, 36n46, 78, 301

P

Pasnau, Robert 58n48, 76, 214n80, 247n113

passions 19–22, 39, 41, 58–82, 105–8, 116–23, 127–28, 129–30, 166, 178–83, 195, 269, 272–76, 297, 317, 336–37, 361–62

Pennington, Jonathan 331–33, 338–41, 361

Piper, John 27–28, 326, 335

plasticity 4n15, 11–12, 14, 37–40, 58, 71, 80–82, 90, 104, 122, 168, 178, 190–91, 197, 229n34, 235, 253, 260–62, 275, 278–80, 297, 300–303, 305, 314, 322, 325, 355

Plato 5, 134–36, 155, 157, 159, 179

Platonic Dualism 136, 155, 207–8, 216, 228, 233–34

Polanyi, Michael 8, 9, 296n54

Prinz, Jesse 3n9, 284, 285n6, 286n10, 313n11

psychology
modern psychology 8–9, 18, 21, 284–313
theological psychology 1, 4–7, 8–22, 40, 67, 91, 93, 195–96, 197–98, 205
tiered psychology 4, 6, 14, 37, 43–50, 63, 80–81, 90, 92, 97, 99–100, 127, 142, 151, 168, 186, 199, 204, 210, 216, 250, 281–82, 306, 315–17, 322, 346–47

psychotropic medications 34–35, 302, 347, 351

R

rational powers, will and intellect 20, 39, 43–44, 48–50, 59–68, 72, 75–82, 84–86, 97–98, 100, 105–28, 140–41, 156, 159–78, 185, 188, 190–91, 204–5, 208–10, 212, 215, 218, 241, 315–16, 342, 358–61

Reformed theology 3, 6–7, 14–15, 24n2, 42, 106, 193, 197–219

regeneration 141, 151, 173, 190n212, 195, 212

Roberts, Robert 26, 288n20, 313, 320

S

sanctification 10, 25n5, 40, 89, 189, 190n212, 252–53, 267–68, 274–75, 278–82, 306

Scripture 9–10, 131–37, 155, 164–76, 202, 204, 206, 211, 212, 213, 214, 217–18, 227–28, 230, 244, 321, 328–32, 343

sense appetite or perception 12, 20, 21, 39–40, 45–50, 60–63, 64–65, 68–71, 76–81, 90, 105–6, 114, 117, 119–23, 128, 161–62, 164–65, 168,

177, 185–86, 193, 209, 245, 253, 256, 261n32, 272n64, 286–97, 317, 321–22

Schwartz, Jeffrey 31n26, 38n52, 229n34, 231n44, 301

Scotus, John Duns 97, 112–24, 169–72

soul
immortality of the soul 100–105, 127–28, 131, 138, 151–54, 159, 190
powers, or faculties 5, 11–13, 43–50, 54, 58, 74, 81, 87, 90, 94, 110, 111, 128, 132, 135, 150, 158, 159–69, 175, 177–78, 190–91, 201, 203–4, 209–11, 212, 217–18, 293, 315, 352
nature of the soul 43–45, 94–100, 151–59, 197–98, 201–3, 207–10, 211–12, 213–14, 216–17, 220–51, 253, 261–62, 281, 357–60

speech act theory 255n9, 327–43

spirits, psychic 39, 52–58, 70, 74, 101, 110, 137n32, 143–44, 150, 152, 158n113, 162n119, 163, 297–98, 318

Stoicism 52n26, 64–66, 114–15, 117–19, 134, 138, 176, 183–86, 337, 344

substance 43, 55n35, 56n42, 151–53, 155–57, 159, 201–2, 204, 207, 221–24, 227–31, 247

supervenience 239n83, 239–240

sympathetic nervous system (SNS) 34, 72, 200, 266, 298–99, 348

Sytsma, David 193–94

T

transdisciplinary scholarship 7–10, 198, 206

trauma 24, 301n70, 304–7, 349, 351n7

Turretin, Frances 190, 192

U

unconscious processing 7, 31, 37–38, 250, 284, 291–94, 294–97, 299, 303–9, 309–14, 315–18, 322, 347–49, 363

V

Vanhoozer, Kevin 8, 255, 256n13, 320–21, 327–28, 342
voluntarism and intellectualism 106–12, 167–69, 172–73
virtue 5, 11, 16–17, 20–21, 43, 62, 64–66, 68, 73, 75, 82–92, 94, 105, 115–28, 129, 172, 175, 186–91, 332–41, 343
  and vice 5, 73, 108, 110–12, 178, 318
vitalism 222–23, 249

W

weakness 29n20, 81, 267–70, 278, 352, 353
Welch, Edward 27, 29, 36n48, 357, 360
will, see rational powers Wilson, Timothy 294n42–43, 295, 296n51, 299, 309n97, 310–11, 312
Wood, Adam 94–100
Wundt, Wilhelm 8, 201, 206

SCRIPTURE INDEX

—

OLD TESTAMENT

Genesis

1–3	251
1:26	132, 200
1:28	255
2:7	254
2:8	254
2:9	254
2:15	254
2:16–17	255
2:17	63, 255, 269
2:19	254
2:24	256
3:11	257
3:17	257
3:17–19	279
3:16	258
3:18	353n8
3:19	257, 259
4:10–12	257n19
6:5	28n16, 358, 358n5
8:21	28n16, 358, 358n6
9:4	150
15:15	144
17:17	358n5
18:27	254n8
24:45	358n5
27:41	358n5
34:3	358n8
42:28	28n16, 358, 358n7
50:21	358n8

Exodus

4:14	358n8
7:22	358n5
8:15	358n10
9:14	28n16, 358
9:21	358n9
13	345
15:8	358n3
15:26	259n24
20:12	258
23:19	258
28:29	358n4
32:9	360n18
35:5	358n8
35:21	358n8

Leviticus

19:31	226n20
20:6	226n20

Numbers

16:28	28n16, 358, 358n6
24:13	358n6
32:7–9	358n7

Deuteronomy

4:1	259n24
4:11	358n3
6	345
6:5	166, 359n13
7:12	259n24
10:16	360n18
11:9	258
18:11	226n20
28:65	358n8
29:4	166, 358n5
29:19	358n5
32:6	329n27

Joshua

3:9	259n24
11:20	358n10

Judges

5:9	358n8
5:15	358n5
9:3	358n6
16:25	358n8
18:20	358n8
19:5	358n7
19:22	358n8

1 Samuel

1:13	358n5
2:1	358n8
4:13	358n8
6:6	358n10
10:9	358n12
10:26	358n12
17:32	358n7
25:26	358n8

25:31 .... 28n16, 358
25:37 .... 28n16, 358
28 .... 226n20

2 Samuel

2:16 .... 358n8
7:14 329
7:27 .... 358n7
13:20 .... 358n8
13:33 .... 358n8
14:1 .... 358n8
17:10 .... 358n7
18:14 .... 358n4

1 Kings

3:9 .... 358n5
8:23 .... 359n13
9:3 .... 358n9
10:24 .... 358n5
11:3–7 .... 358n10

2 Kings

9:24 .... 358n4

2 Chronicles

7:14 258

Job

4:19 .... 132, 155, 254n8
10:7–15 147
10:8–9 .... 254n8
10:9 .... 254, 258
13:14 .... 156n100
19:25–27 .... 226n21

Psalm

1:3 .... 281, 352
4:5 345
5:11 .... 361n30
9:1 .... 359n13
9:10 345
13:5 345
16:10 .... 226n21
20:7 .... 37, 345
22:8 345

22:26 .... 28n16, 358
27:8 .... 359n13
28:7 .... 359n13
34:2 144
37:4 .... 361n30
46:1–2 37
49:15 .... 226n21
51:12 .... 53n31
56:3 32
68:5 329
73:26 .... 226n21
89:26 329
90:3 .... 254n8
95:7–9 .... 259n24
102:4 .... 28n16, 360
102:5 .... 60n50
103:4 .... 55n35
103:11–19 258
103:13 329
103:14 .... 254, 254n8, 258
104:15 .... 28n16
104:29 .... 254n8
104:30 258
119:73 .... 254n8, 258
119:109 .... 156n100
139:15 .... 148n67
139:23 .... 53n31
146:4 .... 254n8

Proverbs

18:10 32
23:34 .... 28n16, 358
24:12 .... 53n31
28:13 .... 33n32

Ecclesiastes

12:7 155

Isaiah

1:16–17 339
6:10 .... 358n9
8:19 .... 226n20
14:9–10 226
15:5 .... 358n8
22:19–22 .... 329n26

26:19 226
29:13–14 359
30:1–15 345
30:2–5 37
30:15 37
33:18 .... 358n5
35:4 .... 358n8
38:3 .... 359n13
40:13–14 242
42:6 339
44:18 .... 358n9, 358n10
45:17 341
45:23 341
46:8 .... 358n5
47:10 .... 358n5
49:6 339
51:1 .... 259n24
53 329
54:11–17 341
55:1–2 341
57:15 .... 341, 358n12
58:6–12 341
59:21 341
63:15–16 329
63:17 .... 358n10
64:8 329
65:17–18 341
66:13 330

Jeremiah

3:10 .... 359n13
4:14 .... 359n13
4:18 .... 28n16, 358
5:21–23 .... 358n9, 358n10
8:18 .... 358n8
11:4 .... 259n24
17:1 .... 358n11
17:9 .... 358n11
20:12 .... 359n13
22:1–4 339
24:7 .... 358n12
23:5 258
31:33 .... 276n75, 358n12
32:39 .... 28n16, 358,
358n12

42:14–44:27 345
46:12 .... 358n10
48:36 .... 358n8

Ezekiel

3:7 .... 358n10
11:19 .... 358n12
18:32 166
27:4 .... 28n16, 359
27:25 .... 358n3
36:26 .... 165, 358n12
37 .... 226n21
40:4 .... 358n9

Daniel

12:2 226

Hosea

11:8 .... 358n8

Joel

2:13 180

Amos

2:16 .... 358n7
5:10–13 339

Micah

3:1–10 339

Zechariah

7:12 .... 358n10
14:1–5 265

Malachi

2:2 .... 358n10
2:10 329
4:5–6 .... 358n12

NEW TESTAMENT

Matthew

5:14–16 339
5:20 338
5:28 .... 53n31, 360n16,
361n29
5:48 339
6:2–5 340
6:16 340
6:19–24 328
6:21 338
6:22 145,
6:25 .....156n100, 327, 329
6:25–34 ..... 15, 30, 32, 322,
323–46
6:26 329
6:27 330
6:28 .... 324, 329
6:31 324
6:32 ....329, 332
6:33 ......329–31, 338, 345
6:34 .... 324, 330
7:9–11 30
7:24–26 ....259n24
9:4 .... 53n31
10:28 .....138n36, 227, 281
12:34 .... 360n22
12:34–37 339
13:3–9 351
13:19 ....360n17

15:8 ....360n21
15:18–19 .... 360n22
16:16 342
16:17 ....262n34, 342
16:23 342
16:24–25 342
18:4 341
19:5 .... 262n34
19:8 ....360n18, 360n21
19:23–30 341
22:23–33 244
22:37 .... 166, 201,
360n19
23:1–36 340
23:4 340
23:23 340
23:37 330
26 252
26:1–27:2 263
26:1–46 251
26:2 263
26:6–35 263
26:6–13 263
26:14–16 263
26:17–29 263
26:23 264
26:27–28 264
26:28 279
26:31 264

26:35 264
26:36–46 .... 264, 344
26:37–43 264
26:37 265
26:38 .... 265, 265n44
26:39 265
26:40–41 264
26:41 .... 262n34, 268
26:42 265
26:47–50 265
26:51 265
27 329
27:2 263

Mark

3:5 ....360n18, 360n21
7:20–21 .... 360n22
10:38–40 265
11:23 .... 360n24
12:30 201
12:40 340
16:14 .... 360n24

Luke

1:51 ....28n16, 359
2:19 ....28n16, 359,
360n17
6:45 .... 360n22
10:27 201

12:5.........138n36, 361n30
12:13–21 144
12:20 .... 156n100
16:15 ....28n16, 359
20:37–38...................227
22:39 264
22:44 .... 265, 266
23:42–43 227
24:25 .... 360n24
24:32 ....28n16, 359
24:37 227
24:38 .... 360n24
24:39 ....262n34, 281

John

1:13–14 .... 262n34
3:6..................... 262n34
4:6.......................... 268
5:28–29.....................227
6:51–56 .... 262n34
6:63 .... 262n34
8:15..................... 262n34
13:2.................... 360n22
15:1–11 351
16:6 ....360n20
16:13–15 242
16:22....................360n20
18:10........................ 265
19:5......................353n8
20:22 258

Acts

2:31.................... 262n34
5:3 .... 360n22
5:4 ....360n16
7:23 ...... 360n17, 360n19
7:39 .... 360n22
7:51.....................360n18
8:21–22 ....360n17
8:22 ....360n19
13:22 ....360n19
14:17 .... 360n20
16:14 ....28n16, 359,
      360n17, 360n18
21:13 ....360n20

23:6–9 244
30:35 268

Romans

1:3 .... 262n34
1:16 ....279, 345
1:18–32 .... 189, 276, 362,
      362n32
1:21 ....360n21
1:22 355
1:24–25 281
1:24–37 360
1:26–27 277
2:5 ....360n18, 360n21
2:15 .... 176, 276, 276n75,
      360n16, 360n23
2:18–19 276
2:29 .... 360n24
3–4 270
3:20 .... 262n34
3:21–31 362
4:18....................346, 347
5–12 .... 252, 268, 281
5:1 268
5:1–2....................347
5:2–3.....................345
5:4–5.....................352
5:5 359
5:5–17 270
5:6 .... 259n25, 268,
      270, 278
5:8 ....214, 270
5:9 270
5:10 270
5:11 268
5:12–21.................... 269
5:12–8:27.................. 251
5:13 .... 269n58
5:14................... 269n58
5:15 270
5:16 270
5:17................... 270
5:17–21..................... 271
5:21............ 269, 270, 271
6.........253, 270, 279, 280

6–8................... 280, 322
6–12....................253
6:4........................... 271
6:6.......260, 261, 271, 274,
      275, 279n80
6:6–19............... 271, 274
6:9..........................274
6:11..........................274
6:12 ....272–75, 277, 278,
      361n29, 361/2n30
6:12–13.............. 271, 273
6:13 .... 165n131, 273,
      274, 277
6:13–19....................355
6:14 ....276n74
6:15–17 271
6:16 .... 274, 280
6:17.........................274
6:19 .... 33n32, 274, 275,
      362n33
6:22 274
7................142, 272, 276
7:4–12 271
7:5 ....67, 275, 277
7:5–12 275
7:7–25..........276, 361n29
7:8..........................275
7:13 271
7:14 277
7:18 277
7:19 271
7:23 277
7:23–25.....................281
7:24 .... 279n80
7:24–25.....................277
7:25 269
8 .... 276, 279
8:2.............. 261, 277, 278
8:3 .... 218, 259, 262,
      262n35, 263, 267,
      268, 278
8:3–4 344
8:4..............267, 277, 278
8:5 278
8:6........................... 278

8:7...........................277
8:9............................ 278
8:10 .... 278, 279n80
8:11.....................281, 344
8:12 ....276n74
8:12–14 278
8:13 ....276n74
8:15 279
8:17 279
8:18 279
8:18–25 .... 342, 350
8:19–23 343
8:23 ....279, 281, 327
8:23–25..............344, 356
8:26................. 268, 278
8:27 ....130n3
9:3–8 .... 262n34
11:17–24 351
11:33 242
10:9 .... 360n24
10:10 .... 53n31
12 345
12–15............... 282
12:1–2 .... 280, 280n82,
                        355
12:1–5........................281
12:1–21 251
12:3....................33n32
12:10 ....361n30
12:15 355
13:13–14.....................272
13:14 ...... 262n34, 361n29

1 Corinthians

1:17–2:4.................... 268
1:27...................... 268
1:29 .... 262n34
2:10–11..................... 242
2:11 132
3:5–9 351
4:5 ....360n16
5:5 .... 262n34
6:16 .... 256n12, 262n34
7:28 .... 262n34
10:19–24 146

12 345
12:3...........................355
15 227
15:10 .... 25n5, 279
15:17–19 279
15:39 .... 262n34
15:50 .... 262n34

2 Corinthians

3:18 141
4:10–11......................273
4:11 .... 262n34
4:16 27
5:1–10 244
5:7 355
5:17 342
7:1 .... 132, 138n36,
                        262n34
9:7.................28n16, 359
11:18 .... 262n34
10:2 .... 262n34
12:1–4 227
12:2–4 244
12:7.........262n34, 353n8
12:9 352

Galatians

1:16 .... 262n34
2:3 274
3:1 .... 321n131
3:3 .... 262n34
3:27 345
4:23–29 .... 262n34
5:13–24 .... 262n34
5:16.................. 274, 355
5:16–17............... 279n80,
                        361n29
5:19–20.....................272
5:22–23 351
5:24 .... 274, 279n80
6:2...........................355
6:5...................... 355n18

Ephesians

1:3 352

1:18.........28n16, 166, 352,
                   355, 359
2:3 .... 261, 361n29
2:11–14 .... 262n34
4:13 355
4:16...........................353
4:17–18.....................165
4:17–23......................169
4:18...........................360n18
4:22 ....361n29
4:23 165
4:24 ...... 132, 141, 345, 355
5:19–20.....................272
5:25–29 346
5:31..................... 256n12

Philippians

1:21............................343
1:21–24.....................227
1:22 .... 262n34
1:23................................ 26
1:24 .... 262n34
2:13..........................25n5
2:17.............................343
3:3 .... 262n34
4:6 343
4:6–7 343
4:7 ....327, 344
4:9 352
4:13...........................352

Colossians

1:13 261
1:22 .... 279n80
2:1 .... 262n34
2:5 .... 262n34
2:8...........................353n9
2:11 .... 279n80
2:11–13 .... 262n34
2:11–23.......................281
2:16 ....353n9
2:18 ....353n9
2:19 .... 353, 353n9
2:23 .... 262n34
3:2 81

3:2–3 352
3:5 352
3:10 ...... 132, 141, 345, 355
3:12–17 352

1 Thessalonians

4:4–5 .... 361n29
4:13–18 227

2 Timothy

1:8 345
2:17 137

Hebrews

2:14 .... 262n34, 263
3:15 .... 259n24
4:15 268
5:2 268
10:20 .... 262n34
12:9 132
12:23 132
13:17 .... 138, 138n36

James

1:4 352
1:18 352
4:8 .... 28n16, 359
5:7 352
5:11 352

1 Peter

1:9 .... 132, 133, 155
1:13 132
1:14 .... 361n29
1:22 132
2:11 .... 138n36, 274,
          361n29
2:25 .... 132, 138,
          138n36, 155
3:4 27
3:7 268
3:18 .... 262n34
4:1–2 .... 262n34
6 .... 262n34

2 Peter

2:10 .... 262n34
2:18 ....262n34, 274

1 John

2:16 .... 81, 262, 274
3:20 .... 53n31
4:2 .... 262n34

2 John

7 .... 262n34

Jude

8 .... 262n34
23 .... 262n34

Revelation

2:7 255
6:10 26
17:16 .... 262n34
19:18 .... 262n34
19:21 .... 262n34